## About the Editor

The late Oscar Williams (1900–1964), was himself a distinguished poet. He was the author of five books of poetry, of which *Selected Poems* is one of the most recent, published by October House.

Dylan Thomas has written: "Oscar Williams is without a doubt a very real and important American poet. . . . His powerful imagery and unique personal idiom will add a permanent page to American poetry."

Mr. Williams was the originator and general editor of the "Little Treasury Series," published by Scribner's. His *Little Treasury of Modern Poetry* and his three paperback anthologies, *A Pocket Book of Modern Verse*, *The New Pocket Anthology of American Verse*, and *Immortal Poems of the English Language*, published by Washington Square Press, Inc., are accepted as the present-day classics in their fields and are in wide use in colleges and universities. Robert Lowell has written in *The Sewanee Review:* "Oscar Williams is probably the best anthologist in America."

In 1958, Mr. Williams delivered an official reading of his poems at the Library of Congress and was one of thirty American poets who participated in the Library's Festival of Poetry in 1962. He was the editor for a new series of recordings by poets, of which the first three-record album has been issued by Tale Productions, Colpix, a division of Columbia Pictures Corporation.

# INDEX OF TITLES

Adonais, 527
All the World's a Stage (*As You Like It,*
II, vii), 72
Allegory of the Adolescent and the Adult,
1037
Altarwise by Owl-Light, 1043
An Anatomie of the World, 85
And These Few Precepts (*Hamlet,* I, iii),
74
Auguries of Innocence, 359
The Blessèd Damozel, 729
The Canonization, 104
Captain Carpenter, 983
The Collar, 147
The Convent Threshold, 737
The Darkling Thrush, 787
Death (A Sequence of Poems), 745
Dejection: An Ode, 489
The Deserted Village, 341
Desire, 35
A Dialogue of Self and Soul, 859
Directive, 882
Dover Beach, 711
Elegy Written in a Country Churchyard,
305
Epithalamion, 13
The Eve of St. Agnes, 600
The Extasie, 114
Fern Hill, 1059
The Garden, 211
Greater Love, 997
The Groundhog, 1007
He Jests At Scars (*Romeo and Juliet,* II,
ii), 73
Holy Sonnets, 123
The Hound of Heaven, 811
Hugh Selwyn Mauberley, 911
The Hunting of the Snark, 757
Hymne to God My God, in My Sick-
nesse, 136
I Sing the Body Electric, 699
I Wandered Lonely as a Cloud, 415
Il Penseroso, 186
In Memory of W. B. Yeats, 1013
Kubla Khan: Or, a Vision in a Dream,
435
La Belle Dame sans Merci, 593
L'Allegro, 183
Lament, 1064
The Leaden Echo and the Golden Echo,
804
The Lie, 7
Lines Composed a Few Miles Above
Tintern Abbey, 420
Loving in Truth, 29
The Lunatic, the Lover, and the Poet (*A
Midsummer-Night's Dream,* V, i), 72
Lycidas, 172
A Man's a Man for A' That, 383
Memories of President Lincoln: When
Lilacs Last in the Dooryard Bloom'd,
687
The Mental Traveller, 377
My Last Duchess, 677
Nineteen Hundred and Nineteen, 851

Ode: Intimations of Immortality, 389
Ode on a Grecian Urn, 567
Ode to a Nightingale, 583
Ode to Evening, 323
On Hearing a Symphony of Beethoven,
990
On the Morning of Christ's Nativity, 159
The Phœnix and the Turtle, 39
A Prayer for My Daughter, 839
Rabbi Ben Ezra, 665
The Rape of the Lock, 265
A Refusal to Mourn the Death, by Fire, of
a Child in London, 1055
Remembrance, 683
Resolution and Independence, 428
Richard Cory, 865
The Rime of the Ancient Mariner, 465
Rubáiyát of Omar Khayyám of Nai-
shápúr, 613
Sailing to Byzantium, 831
A Satire Against Mankind, 239
The Scholar-Gipsy, 716
The Second Coming, 846
September 1, 1939, 1022
The Ship of Death, 903
A Shropshire Lad (Selections From), 821
Song, 153
A Song for St. Cecilia's Day, 229
A Song to David, 331
Sonnets (Edna St. Vincent Millay), 989
Sonnets (William Shakespeare), 47
Spenser's Ireland, 935
Stopping by Woods on a Snowy Eve-
ning, 876
Sunday Morning, 889
The Teare, 196
Tears, Idle Tears, 658
They Flee from Me, 1
Three Memorial Sonnets, 1029
To Be, or Not to Be (*Hamlet,* III, i),
74
To Celia, 79
To His Coy Mistress, 201
To the Virgins, to Make Much of Time,
141
To-morrow, and To-morrow, and To-
morrow (*Macbeth,* V, vi), 73
The Transfiguration, 929
The Triumph of Life, 547
Two Choruses from Atalanta in Calydon,
777
Two Tramps in Mud Time, 869
The Two Voices, 641
The Tyger, 373
A Valediction: Forbidding Mourning, 109
The Vanity of Human Wishes, 291
Verses on the Death of Dr. Swift,
D.S.P.D., 249
The Vision of Judgment, 499
The Waste Land, 943
What If a Much of a Which of a Wind,
1003
The World, 224
The Wreck of the Deutschland, 791
The Yachts, 899

# Contents

The Rime of the Ancient Mariner by Samuel Taylor
Coleridge   465
   *Essay by E. M. W. Tillyard*   483
Dejection: An Ode by Samuel Taylor Coleridge   489
   *Essay by Sir Herbert Read*   493
The Vision of Judgment by George Gordon, Lord Byron   499
   *Essay by Peter Quennell*   521
Adonais by Percy Bysshe Shelley   527
   *Essay by Edwin Honig*   540
   *Essay by Carlos Baker*   543
The Triumph of Life by Percy Bysshe Shelley   547
   *Essay by Carlos Baker*   562
Ode on a Grecian Urn by John Keats   567
   *Essay by Kenneth Burke*   569
Ode to a Nightingale by John Keats   583
   *Essay by Cleanth Brooks*   586
La Belle Dame sans Merci by John Keats   593
   *Essay by Robert Graves*   595
The Eve of St. Agnes by John Keats   600
   *Essay by William Stafford*   609
Rubáiyát of Omar Khayyám of Naishápúr by Edward
FitzGerald   613
   *Essay by C. M. Bowra*   625
The Two Voices by Alfred, Lord Tennyson   641
   *Essay by George Barker*   654
Tears, Idle Tears by Alfred, Lord Tennyson   658
   *Essay by Cleanth Brooks*   659
Rabbi Ben Ezra by Robert Browning   665
   *Essay by Roy P. Basler*   673
My Last Duchess by Robert Browning   677
   *Essay by Edwin Honig*   679
Remembrance by Emily Brontë   683
   *Essay by Reed Whittemore*   684
Memories of President Lincoln: When Lilacs Last in the
Dooryard Bloom'd by Walt Whitman   687
   *Essay by Geoffrey Grigson*   696
I Sing the Body Electric by Walt Whitman   699
   *Essay by Mark Strand*   707
Dover Beach by Matthew Arnold   711
   *Essay by James Dickey*   713
The Scholar-Gipsy by Matthew Arnold   716
   *Essay by Arthur Mizener*   722
The Blessèd Damozel by Dante Gabriel Rossetti   729
   *Essay by David Daiches*   733
The Convent Threshold by Christina Rossetti   737
   *Essay by William Stafford*   742
Death (A Sequence of Poems) by Emily Dickinson   745
   *Essay by D. S. Savage*   750
The Hunting of the Snark by Charles L. Dodgson (Lewis
Carroll)   757
   *Essay by Richard Howard*   773

Two Choruses from Atalanta in Calydon by Algernon
   Charles Swinburne    777
     *Essay by Bonamy Dobrée*    782
The Darkling Thrush by Thomas Hardy    787
     *Essay by John Berryman*    788
The Wreck of the Deutschland by Gerard Manley Hopkins    791
     *Essay by James Dickey*    801
The Leaden Echo and the Golden Echo by Gerard Manley
   Hopkins    804
     *Essay by Chad Walsh*    806
The Hound of Heaven by Francis Thompson    811
     *Essay by James Dickey*    817
Selections from A Shropshire Lad by A. E. Housman    821
     *Essay by A. J. M. Smith*    829
Sailing to Byzantium by William Butler Yeats    831
     *Essay by Elder Olson*    833
A Prayer for My Daughter by William Butler Yeats    839
     *Essay by Sarah Youngblood*    842
The Second Coming by William Butler Yeats    846
     *Essay by Richard P. Blackmur*    847
Nineteen Hundred and Nineteen by William Butler Yeats    851
     *Essay by Robin Skelton*    855
A Dialogue of Self and Soul by William Butler Yeats    859
     *Essay by Reed Whittemore*    861
Richard Cory by Edwin Arlington Robinson    865
     *Essay by Mark Strand*    866
Two Tramps in Mud Time by Robert Frost    869
     *Essay by Robert Penn Warren*    871
✓ Stopping by Woods on a Snowy Evening by Robert Frost    876
     *Essay by James Wright*    877
Directive by Robert Frost    882
     *Essay by Philip Booth*    884
✓ Sunday Morning by Wallace Stevens    889
     *Essay by John Crowe Ransom*    893
The Yachts by William Carlos Williams    899
     *Essay by James Dickey*    901
The Ship of Death by D. H. Lawrence    903
     *Essay by Edwin Honig*    908
Hugh Selwyn Mauberley by Ezra Pound    911
     *Essay by William Van O'Connor*    924
The Transfiguration by Edwin Muir    929
     *Essay by Anne Ridler*    931
Spenser's Ireland by Marianne Moore    935
     *Essay by Josephine Miles*    938
The Waste Land by T. S. Eliot    943
     *Essay by Cleanth Brooks*    958
Captain Carpenter by John Crowe Ransom    983
     *Essay by John Berryman*    985
Sonnets by Edna St. Vincent Millay    989
     *Essay by Robert M. Bender*    992

Greater Love by Wilfred Owen                               *997*
   *Essay by Charles Causley*                              *998*
What If a Much of a Which of a Wind by E. E. Cummings *1003*
   *Essay by John Ciardi*                                  *1004*
The Groundhog by Richard Eberhart                         *1007*
   *Essay by Brewster Ghiselin*                            *1010*
In Memory of W. B. Yeats by W. H. Auden                   *1013*
   *Essay by G. S. Fraser*                                 *1017*
September 1, 1939 by W. H. Auden                          *1022*
   *Essay by Mark Schorer*                                 *1025*
Three Memorial Sonnets by George Barker                   *1029*
   *Essay by Martha Fodaski*                               *1032*
Allegory of the Adolescent and the Adult by George
   Barker                                                  *1037*
   *Essay by Robin Skelton*                                *1039*
Altarwise by Owl-Light by Dylan Thomas                    *1043*
   *Essay by William York Tindall*                         *1047*
A Refusal to Mourn the Death, by Fire, of a Child in
   London by Dylan Thomas                                  *1055*
   *Essay by Edwin Honig*                                  *1056*
Fern Hill by Dylan Thomas                                 *1059*
   *Essay by Derek Stanford*                               *1061*
Lament by Dylan Thomas                                    *1064*
   *Essay by Constantine FitzGibbon*                       *1066*

INDEX OF FIRST LINES                                      *1069*
INDEX OF TITLES                                           *1071*

## A NOTE TO THE READER FROM THE PUBLISHER

*Oscar Williams, the editor of this book,*
*died October 12, 1964.*
*At that time, the plan for the anthology was*
*agreed upon and the work of correspondence and editing*
*was well under way. However, since Mr. Williams*
*was not able to see his design through the press,*
*it would be only fair to ascribe any lacks or inconsistencies*
*in the present work to the publisher and house editor*
*who tried to execute the final tasks*
*to the best of their abilities*
*and their understanding of Mr. Williams' total plan.*

# Preface

It is unfortunate that Oscar Williams did not live to see this book published, for it represents the culmination of years of experience on his part as a poet and anthologist. The book was conceived by him as serving a dual purpose. First, to select a small number of English and American poems that could be called true masterpieces, poems that "breathe fire and are filled with heady, intoxicating wine," as he expressed it in a note to me during the early stages of the work. The second purpose of the book was to combine these highly select poems with "gems of the critical art." Each introductory essay was to be by a prominent poet or critic and with few exceptions was to be commissioned especially for the book. In short, Oscar wanted this anthology to be a touchstone of the best poetry in our heritage, as well as an exciting parallel anthology of the best and most important in modern criticism.

Before Oscar's death, the plan for the book was completed as was almost seventy-five percent of the recruitment of essayists. The remaining twenty-five percent had been tentatively assigned or at least discussed between the editor and myself. In no case have I deviated from his plan, except to ask a small number of people to do extra work in order to ensure that the book would be published on schedule. Their names are gratefully enumerated at the end of this Preface.

Oscar planned this book as the representative of no artistic school or faction, but rather as an avid reader of all schools. He always shied away from taking sides in critical controversy and had an enormous capacity for tolerance. Thus, he has included some poems and critics that might seem antithetical to each other. His purpose was not to emphasize their opposition, but rather the inherent excellence of their individual work, by so preserving it "under one roof."

Oscar had promised to write a longish general introduction to the book that would not only lend a unifying force to it but state in positive terms his thinking on the art of poetry.

The lack of this essay is sorely felt. Despite the many conversations we had on that subject, it would be presumptuous of me to try to represent Oscar's final ideas here, and I therefore leave them to silence—or perhaps to the implied argument of this book itself and its innumerable treasures of inclusion.

In a very few instances, there are double essays on a poem. Since over one thousand pieces of correspondence had to be pored over in organizing the book (and the errors were not apparent until very late), I thought it unfair to penalize one or the other essayist by dropping his piece and have therefore included all essays that were delivered and found acceptable. I do this by way of thanks to all writers of the essays, without whose support I could not have completed this book. Moreover, the inherent individuality of these "double" essays are, I am sure, both what Oscar himself would have approved—at least he would have found the choices among them difficult. I therefore leave the choice to the reader.

The words *rhyme* and *rime*, which have the same meaning, are both used in this book; while the former is standard English, some scholars prefer *rime*, which avoids association with *rhythm*. This inconsistency represents the feelings of the essayists themselves. I felt it was better left unregularized. Likewise, the early poems, especially those of the Elizabethans, were not styled completely to one set of rules, this being left to the vagaries of sources where necessary, but, more important, to the choice of each essayist himself. But then, only the fewest of readers will note these deviations.

Special thanks are due the following for their work throughout and even at a very late hour: Walter James Miller, Edwin Honig, James Dickey, Mark Strand, Robert M. Bender, and David R. Slavitt. I want also to express my gratitude to my Assistant Editor, Patricia MacDonald, and Robert J. Palmer, who helped me in the day-to-day work of the vast correspondence, contracts and permissions. Lastly, I could not have seen this book through the press without the assistance of Barbara Huntley, Madelyn Larsen, Barbara Van West, and Robert Hollander.

PHILLIP C. FLAYDERMAN
EDITOR/TRIDENT PRESS

*July 16, 1965*

# SIR THOMAS WYATT
### [1503–1542]

## *They Flee from Me*

They fle from me that sometyme did me seke
With naked fote stalking in my chambre.
I have seen them gentill tame and meke
That nowe are wyld and do not remembre
That sometyme they put thimself in daunger          5
To take bred at my hand; and nowe they raunge
Besely seking with a continuell chaunge.

Thancked be fortune, it hath ben othrewise
Twenty tymes better; but ons in speciall,
In thyn arraye after a pleasaunt gyse,          10
When her lose gowne from her shoulders did fall,
And she me caught in her armes long and small;
Therewithall swetely did me kysse,
And softely saide, *dere hert, howe like you this?*

It was no dreme: I lay brode awaking.          15
But all is torned thorough my gentilnes
Into a straunge fasshion of forsaking;
And I have leve to goo of her goodenes,
And she also to use new fangilnes.
But syns that I so kyndely ame served,          20
I fain would knowe what she hath deserved.

SIR THOMAS WYATT

*From a drawing by Holbein*
*Culver Pictures, Inc.*

---

WYATT

THEY FLEE FROM ME

A great deal of attention has been paid to the metrical procedure, or possibly lack of procedure, of Sir Thomas Wyatt. From the very first, the editor of Tottel's *Miscellany*, in which Wyatt's sonnets, songs and "ballets" were first published fifteen years after the poet's death, revised in the direction of regularity, against the lilt of the speaking, dramatizing voice. Thus what was in manuscript:

> *I have seen them gentill tame and meke*
> *That nowe are wyld and do not remembre*
> *That sometyme they put thimself in daun-*
> *ger . . .*

was "modernized" to

> Once *I have seen them gentle, tame, and meek*
> *That now are wild and do not* once *remem-*
> *ber*
> *That sometimes they* have *put themselves*
> *in danger . . .*

The small changes produce lines regular in meter, but the difference makes it clear that it was in part the irregular patterns of stress that gave the words in the original lines their strong effect of speech. It seems that if Wyatt himself had any thought here of an iambic metrical pattern, he was willing to give it up for the effect of the phrases. Whoever made Tottel's revision was prepared to give up the effect of the phrases for the sake of the regular pattern. Wyatt seems to have been the first poet to use the iambic metrical pattern (however he departed from or reacted against it) in modern English to any extent; his way of using it is hard to define, and no explanation of his practice has ever been generally accepted. From his poetic disciple, Surrey, who said Wyatt had "taught what might be sayd in ryme," to Professor Rollins, who declared him "the pioneer who fumbled in the linguistic difficulties that beset him," the poet's "fashion of making," as he would say, has been praised, jeopardized and dismissed, the adverse party always missing regularity of pattern, the advocates insisting on the true voice of feeling—much as the factions in our own contest of poets today pit "projective" against "metrical" verse, Beat against Academic, free against formal.

It seems to me, though, that in the tendentious efforts to discriminate the degree of Wyatt's consciousness of what he was doing—was he "one of the greatest verse-technicians in the history of the language," or "inferior in harmony of numbers, perspicuity of expression, and facility of phraseology"?—we lose sight of the values that charge his verse, of which the vehicle, of course, is the phrase strong enough to demand the stresses which must accompany it in speech: "It was no dreme: I lay brode awaking." It is as if Sir Thomas Wyatt himself had urged us to look in another place than the cabinet of metrical requirements:

> *Blame not my lute for he must sownde*
> *Of thes or that as liketh me . . .*
> *Tho my songes be sume what strange*
> *And spekes such wordes as toche thy change,*
> *Blame not my lutte.*

There is the point—"such wordes as toche thy change," the verb having the double meaning of "dealing with" and "moving to sympathy." Change, the pathos of mutability, "fallings from us, vanishings"—this is Wyatt's great theme, as it is to be Spenser's and Wordsworth's in centuries to come. Wyatt's life was characterized by terrible political and personal reversals—he was arrested for treason and all his goods confiscated, after having been Henry VIII's ambassador to Spain and France; he separated from his wife, was suspected of an affair with Anne Boleyn ("her that did set our country in a rore"), and returned to his wife as a condition of his restoration to favor. The amatory progress and possibilities of the speaker in his poems is merely a *figura* of the world, another way of expressing the catastrophic revolutions of fortune.

The remarkable quality of Wyatt's response to this universal mutability in existence is his cool-headed, vigilant appraisal of the erotic situation, his refusal to make the lover's "complaint." From Chaucer's "amorous compleint against women unconstant" to Yeats's "mourning the change that has come upon him and his beloved, until he longs for the end of the world," poets have *regretted;* but Wyatt thanks fortune "it hath ben othrewise twenty tymes better." He invokes—surely it is the first time in literature—what we have come to know as the Proustian mechanism: life becomes reality only when we can remember it, and the memory is given to us involuntarily, by our senses; in this case, the epiphanic love scene when the beloved's gown fell from her shoulders and she embraced the lover, speaking those playful, agonizing words, "dere hert, howe like you this?"

The experience, then, was no dream, as Wyatt says, but rather something more like emotion recollected in tranquillity. He is mystified to attach moral qualities or responsibilities to the agent of his overthrow, and indeed in the one hidden metaphor of the poem, seems to imply that the world's way must be accepted resolutely, that being the natural round. This metaphor is punned on doubly in the lady's salutation, "dere hert," for the mysterious figure of the first stanza, as is not often noticed, is that of the deer park. In Renaissance England and subsequently, the nobles kept deer in game preserves, tame on their lands, until they chose to hunt them. The phrase was later applied to the king's "harem," and Norman Mailer, in our own time, has rehabilitated the metaphor in another context. There is, in Wyatt's poem, something entirely natural, inevitable about the does that once "put themselves in danger to take bread at his hand, and now range . . ."; and if there has been "a strange fashion of forsaking," it is after all through the poet's own gentleness that the course of events has "turned." Mutability prevails, but the past "hath been." That is our comfort, and our despair.

SIR WALTER RALEIGH

*The Bettmann Archive*

# SIR WALTER RALEIGH

## [1552–1618]

## *The Lie*

Go, soul, the body's guest,
  Upon a thankless arrant;
Fear not to touch the best;
  The truth shall be thy warrant.
    Go, since I needs must die,          5
    And give the world the lie.

Say to the court, it glows
  And shines like rotten wood;
Say to the church, it shows
  What's good, and doth no good:          10
    If church and court reply,
    Then give them both the lie.

Tell potentates, they live
  Acting by others' action,
Not loved unless they give,               15
  Not strong but by their faction:
    If potentates reply,
    Give potentates the lie.

Tell men of high condition
  That manage the estate,                 20
Their purpose is ambition,
  Their practice only hate:
    And if they once reply,
    Then give them all the lie.

Tell them that brave it most,             25
  They beg for more by spending,
Who, in their greatest cost,
  Seek nothing but commending:
    And if they make reply,
    Then give them all the lie.           30

Tell zeal it wants devotion;
  Tell love it is but lust;

Tell time it is but motion;
    Tell flesh it is but dust:
        And wish them not reply,          35
        For thou must give the lie.

Tell age it daily wasteth;
    Tell honour how it alters;
Tell beauty how she blasteth;
    Tell favour how it falters:          40
        And as they shall reply,
        Give every one the lie.

Tell wit how much it wrangles
    In tickle points of niceness;          45
Tell wisdom she entangles
    Herself in over-wiseness:
        And when they do reply,
        Straight give them both the lie.

Tell physic of her boldness;
    Tell skill it is prevention;          50
Tell charity of coldness;
    Tell law it is contention:
        And as they do reply,
        So give them still the lie.

Tell fortune of her blindness;          55
    Tell nature of decay;
Tell friendship of unkindness;
    Tell justice of delay:
        And if they will reply,
        Then give them all the lie.          60

Tell arts they have no soundness,
    But vary by esteeming;
Tell schools they want profoundness,
    And stand too much on seeming:
        If arts and schools reply,          65
        Give arts and schools the lie.

Tell faith it's fled the city;
    Tell how the country erreth;
Tell, manhood shakes off pity;
    Tell, virtue least preferreth:          70
        And if they do reply,
        Spare not to give the lie.

So when thou hast, as I
　　Commanded thee, done blabbing,
Although to give the lie　　　　75
　　Deserves no less than stabbing,
　　　Stab at thee he that will,
　　　No stab the soul can kill.

*Joseph Bennett*

RALEIGH

THE LIE

"Go, soul, the body's guest!" With this conceit, imperatively delivered, Sir Walter Raleigh launches the poem that gives the lie to the pomp and pretension, the vanity of a worldly Renaissance court. The flesh is separated from the spirit, according to accepted tradition. Learning, religion, art, virtue itself, are seen as part of the practice of falsehood, and here the old values, asserted in the opening conceit, from which the poem departs, triumph over the humanism of a man-seeking, man-centered ideal.

Look, man is but corrupt, the poem says; nevertheless the viewpoint is not medieval. More complex, not centered on the concept of God or of redemption from evil, the attitude censures not sins, not transgressions from the Divine law, but weaknesses, folly and vanity. The poem gives the lie to the ideal of Renaissance man, but the saint is not substituted as the hero. In fact, the poem is devoid of religious content; its negativism toward all the values and accomplishments of a worldly age is directed not toward the exaltation of God and the humbling of human will, but toward a more refined and more sensitive definition of man himself. Hence the poem is an inquiring one, and thus within the ambition of the age; not a redeeming one. No mystery awaits, or is approached. The inquiry is directed toward improvement: how can man *live* better? Not, how can man *die* better. For we have left the medieval cosmos.

The poem examines the tissue of human weaknesses relentlessly, crushing all claims in the manner of a devil's advocate. The world is not being weighed in the balance; it is being indicted without mercy. Granted the revulsion from the world, and noted that this revulsion is not based on religious terms, we can delight in the exquisiteness, the perception, the delicacy of this language, the rhythms and cadences with which the world is stripped of its hypocrisy. We can note the subtlety and cunning with which the recurring couplet is handled at the end of each stanza, so that although the same fact is stated each time, no two statements are alike. This in itself displays the virtuosity of the Renaissance man, showing that Raleigh is not entirely sincere in his repudiation of worldly values. He delights too much in his own wit; he "esteems" his own artfulness too much. The poem has the brilliance and pride of a successful work of art, being not only Raleigh's best, but undoubtedly the best reflective, critical, even satirical lyric of the sixteenth century. It is ironic that its subject is rejection of the world, since its poetic means and accomplishment are so practiced, so artful, so advanced for the time, and so worldly. This is a degree of sophistication of conceit and language that could not have been conceived of in the fifteenth and early sixteenth centuries.

Examine, if you will, the court glowing and shining like rotten wood, an image fully modern in its precision, its pictorial quality, and its demand upon the intelligence and imagination of the reader. An intelligent, even cunning reader is presupposed; one delighting in difficulties of expression, one appreciative of the intricacies of craftsmanship. We are far from the ballad audience, or the one instructed by religious morality. Time is motion, charity is cold; the language, the concepts have kept their vividness over a span of nearly four hundred years because of the wit, the art with which their moral soundness is expressed.

These definitive statements, these full, even scornful rejections, ring across the ages, and we see the objects of their scorn today, in the daily press, in the pull and tug of contemporary political turmoil, financial greed, and manifestations of present-day extravagances of skill and learning. What we call publicity or propaganda, the surrounding of a pathetic competency with all the trappings of glorious achievement, existed in Raleigh's time under the terms of hypocrisy and deceit. The practical men, the managers, practice hate. The politician is rated by his largesse. A public show of public spending is a scheme for greater financial returns; all these people "beg for more by spending."

For all its timeliness, its modernity, "The Lie" recalls not only the delivery of the individual conscience from Christian concepts and the religious terms of sin and redemption, in establishing standards of moral conduct, but also the basic truths about human nature and human endeavor with which the ancients wrestled. Man is seen here as existing in society, are not isolated; hence to his fellows in this community he owes certain obligations, expects certain recompenses for his effort, his loyalty, or his faith.

But faith is fled, honor is altered; it is not original sin which corrupts the soul of man in society, it is not falling from Grace; it is some defect in man's vanity that causes him to seek only himself, while existing in society. That is, to create a tyrannous, superb isolation of power and pretence while in the midst of his fellows. The eremitic ideal of perfection through solitude, of isolated contemplation, a medieval concept, is here not even considered, not even rejected. Instead man creates a corrupt community in which to sell his soul: to barter it for pretence; in a word, for the approbation and wonderment of the ignorant and the debased; the mob who follow the world's values.

And here we return to the point of departure: "Go, soul, the body's guest." We are still close enough to the medieval mind that soul and body are seen as separate. Hence the soul, detached and invulnerable, released from temptations that are fleshly and prideful, can stab without being stabbed. This Platonic concept provides the basic structure of idea, the unifying mechanism, the device of the poem. Upon it is dressed and impaled all the wit and wisdom, the worldly craft and guileful success of Renaissance man. "The Lie," transitional, subtle, Platonic, moralistic, defying, prideful, departing from a concealed base of Christian morality, is one of the greatest poems of the Renaissance, and one of the greatest poems of all time, forever modern, forever pagan, forever deriving from the concealed God of traditional religion who had become unfashionable in the intellectual terms of Raleigh's time. It is as much as we can do to assimilate the truths of Raleigh's poem to the contingencies of our own age; human nature, forever unchanging, takes the stab of "The Lie" today as in the sixteenth century and in the sixth century before Christ.

# EDMUND SPENSER

[1552–1599]

## *Epithalamion*

Ye learnèd sisters, which have oftentimes
Beene to me ayding, others to adorne,
Whom ye thought worthy of your gracefull rymes,
That even the greatest did not greatly scorne
To heare theyr names sung in your simple layes,     5
But joyèd in theyr praise;
And when ye list your owne mishaps to mourne,
Which death, or love, or fortunes wreck did rayse,
Your string could soone to sadder tenor turne,
And teach the woods and waters to lament             10
Your dolefull dreriment:
Now lay those sorrowfull complaints aside;
And, having all your heads with girlands crownd,
Helpe me mine owne loves prayses to resound;
Ne let the same of any be envide:                    15
So Orpheus did for his owne bride!
So I unto my selfe alone will sing;
The woods shall to me answer, and my Eccho ring.

Early, before the worlds light-giving lampe
His golden beame upon the hils doth spred,           20
Having disperst the nights unchearefull dampe,
Doe ye awake; and, with fresh lusty-hed,
Go to the bowre of my belovèd love,
My truest turtle dove;
Bid her awake; for Hymen is awake,                   25
And long since ready forth his maske to move,
With his bright Tead that flames with many a flake,
And many a bachelor to waite on him,
In theyr fresh garments trim.
Bid her awake therefore, and soone her dight,        30
For lo! the wishèd day is come at last,
That shall, for all the paynes and sorrowes past,
Pay to her usury of long delight:

*13*

EDMUND SPENSER

*The Bettmann Archive*

And, whylest she doth her dight,
Doe ye to her of joy and solace sing,                                    35
That all the woods may answer, and your eccho ring.

Bring with you all the Nymphes that you can heare
Both of the rivers and the forrests greene,
And of the sea that neighbours to her neare:
Al with gay girlands goodly wel beseene.                                 40
And let them also with them bring in hand
Another gay girland
For my fayre love, of lillyes and of roses,
Bound truelove wize, with a blew silke riband.
And let them make great store of bridale poses,                         45
And let them eeke bring store of other flowers,
To deck the bridale bowers.
And let the ground whereas her foot shall tread,
For feare the stones her tender foot should wrong,
Be strewed with fragrant flowers all along,                             50
And diapred lyke the discolored mead.
Which done, doe at her chamber dore awayt,
For she will waken strayt;
The whiles doe ye this song unto her sing,
The woods shall to you answer, and your Eccho ring.                     55

Ye Nymphes of Mulla, which with carefull heed
The silver scaly trouts doe tend full well,
And greedy pikes which use therein to feed;
.(Those trouts and pikes all others doo excell;)
And ye likewise, which keepe the rushy lake,                           60
Where none doo fishes take;
Bynd up the locks the which hang scatterd light,
And in his waters, which your mirror make,
Behold your faces as the christall bright,
That when you come whereas my love doth lie,                           65
No blemish she may spie.
And eke, ye lightfoot mayds, which keepe the deere,
That on the hoary mountayne used to towre;
And the wylde wolves, which seeke them to devoure,
With your steele darts doo chace from comming neer;                    70
Be also present heere,
To helpe to decke her, and to help to sing,
That all the woods may answer, and your eccho ring.

Wake now, my love, awake! for it is time;
The Rosy Morne long since left Tithones bed,                           75
All ready to her silver coche to clyme;

And Phœbus gins to shew his glorious hed.
Hark! how the cheerefull birds do chaunt theyr laies
And carroll of Loves praise.
The merry Larke hir mattins sings aloft;                    80
The Thrush replyes; the Mavis descant playes;
The Ouzell shrills; the Ruddock warbles soft;
So goodly all agree, with sweet consent,
To this dayes merriment.
Ah! my deere love, why doe ye sleepe thus long?            85
When meeter were that ye should now awake,
T' awayt the comming of your joyous make,
And hearken to the birds love-learnèd song,
The deawy leaves among!
Nor they of joy and pleasance to you sing,                 90
That all the woods them answer, and theyr eccho ring.

My love is now awake out of her dreames,
And her fayre eyes, like stars that dimmèd were
With darksome cloud, now shew theyr goodly beams
More bright then Hesperus his head doth rere.             95
Come now, ye damzels, daughters of delight,
Helpe quickly her to dight:
But first come ye fayre houres, which were begot
In Joves sweet paradice of Day and Night;
Which doe the seasons of the yeare allot,                100
And al, that ever in this world is fayre,
Doe make and still repayre:
And ye three handmayds of the Cyprian Queene,
The which doe still adorne her beauties pride,
Helpe to addorne my beautifullest bride:                 105
And, as ye her array, still throw betweene
Some graces to be seene;
And, as ye use to Venus, to her sing,
The whiles the woods shal answer, and your eccho ring.

Now is my love all ready forth to come:                  110
Let all the virgins therefore well awayt:
And ye fresh boyes, that tend upon her groome,
Prepare your selves; for he is comming strayt.
Set all your things in seemely good aray,
Fit for so joyfull day:                                   115
The joyfulst day that ever sunne did see.
Faire Sun! shew forth thy favourable ray,
And let thy lifull heat not fervent be,
For feare of burning her sunshyny face,
Her beauty to disgrace.                                   120

O fayrest Phœbus! father of the Muse!
If ever I did honour thee aright,
Or sing the thing that mote thy mind delight,
Doe not thy servants simple boone refuse;
But let this day, let this one day, be myne;    125
Let all the rest be thine.
Then I thy soverayne prayses loud wil sing,
That all the woods shal answer, and theyr eccho ring.

Harke! how the Minstrils gin to shrill aloud
Their merry Musick that resounds from far,    130
The pipe, the tabor, and the trembling Croud,
That well agree withouten breach or jar.
But, most of all, the Damzels doe delite
When they their tymbrels smyte,
And thereunto doe daunce and carrol sweet,    135
That all the sences they doe ravish quite;
The whyles the boyes run up and downe the street,
Crying aloud with strong confusèd noyce,
As if it were one voyce,
Hymen, iö Hymen, Hymen, they do shout;    140
That even to the heavens theyr shouting shrill
Doth reach, and all the firmament doth fill;
To which the people standing all about,
As in approvance, doe thereto applaud,
And loud advaunce her laud;    145
And evermore they Hymen, Hymen sing,
That al the woods them answer, and theyr eccho ring.

Loe! where she comes along with portly pace,
Lyke Phœbe, from her chamber of the East,
Arysing forth to run her mighty race,    150
Clad all in white, that seemes a virgin best.
So well it her beseemes, that ye would weene
Some angell she had beene.
Her long loose yellow locks lyke golden wyre,
Sprinckled with perle, and perling flowres atweene,    155
Doe lyke a golden mantle her attyre;
And, being crownèd with a girland greene,
Seeme lyke some mayden Queene.
Her modest eyes, abashèd to behold
So many gazers as on her do stare,    160
Upon the lowly ground affixèd are;
Ne dare lift up her countenance too bold,
But blush to heare her prayses sung so loud,
So farre from being proud.

Nathlesse doe ye still loud her prayses sing,     165
That all the woods may answer, and your eccho ring.

Tell me, ye merchants daughters, did ye see
So fayre a creature in your towne before;
So sweet, so lovely, and so mild as she,
Adorned with beautyes grace and vertues store?     170
Her goodly eyes lyke Saphyres shining bright,
Her forehead yvory white,
Her cheekes lyke apples which the sun hath rudded,
Her lips lyke cherryes charming men to byte,
Her brest like to a bowle of creame uncrudded,     175
Her paps lyke lyllies budded,
Her snowie necke lyke to a marble towre;
And all her body like a pallace fayre,
Ascending up, with many a stately stayre,
To honors seat and chastities sweet bowre.     180
Why stand ye still ye virgins in amaze,
Upon her so to gaze,
While ye forget your former lay to sing,
To which the woods did answer, and your eccho ring?

But if ye saw that which no eyes can see,     185
The inward beauty of her lively spright,
Garnisht with heavenly guifts of high degree,
Much more then would ye wonder at that sight,
And stand astonisht lyke to those which red
Medusaes mazeful hed.     190
There dwels sweet love, and constant chastity,
Unspotted fayth, and comely womanhood,
Regard of honour, and mild modesty;
There vertue raynes as Queene in royal throne,
And giveth lawes alone,     195
The which the base affections doe obay,
And yeeld theyr services unto her will;
Ne thought of thing uncomely ever may
Thereto approach to tempt her mind to ill.
Had ye once seene these her celestial threasures,     200
And unrevealèd pleasures,
Then would ye wonder, and her prayses sing,
That al the woods should answer, and your echo ring.

Open the temple gates unto my love,
Open them wide that she may enter in,     205
And all the postes adorne as doth behove,
And all the pillours deck with girlands trim,

For to receyve this Saynt with honour dew,
That commeth in to you.
With trembling steps, and humble reverence,                    210
She commeth in, before th' Almighties view;
Of her ye virgins learne obedience,
When so ye come into those holy places,
To humble your proud faces:
Bring her up to th' high altar, that she may                    215
The sacred ceremonies there partake,
The which do endlesse matrimony make;
And let the roring Organs loudly play
The praises of the Lord in lively notes;
The whiles, with hollow throates,                              220
The Choristers the joyous Antheme sing,
That al the woods may answere, and their eccho ring.

Behold, whiles she before the altar stands,
Hearing the holy priest that to her speakes,
And blesseth her with his two happy hands,                     225
How the red roses flush up in her cheekes,
And the pure snow, with goodly vermill stayne
Like crimsin dyde in grayne:
That even th' Angels, which continually
About the sacred Altare doe remaine,                           230
Forget their service and about her fly,
Ofte peeping in her face, that seems more fayre,
The more they on it stare.
But her sad eyes, still fastened on the ground.
Are governèd with goodly modesty,                              235
That suffers not one looke to glaunce awry,
Which may let in a little thought unsownd.
Why blush ye, love, to give to me your hand,
The pledge of all our band!
Sing, ye sweet Angels, Alleluya sing,                          240
That all the woods may answere, and your eccho ring.

Now al is done: bring home the bride againe;
Bring home the triumph of our victory:
Bring home with you the glory of her gaine;
With joyance bring her and with jollity.                        245
Never had man more joyfull day then this,
Whom heaven would heape with blis,
Make feast therefore now all this live-long day;
This day for ever to me holy is.
Poure out the wine without restraint or stay,                   250

Poure not by cups, but by the belly full,
Poure out to all that wull,
And sprinkle all the postes and wals with wine,
That they may sweat, and drunken be withall.
Crowne ye God Bacchus with a coronall,                    255
And Hymen also crowne with wreathes of vine;
And let the Graces daunce unto the rest,
For they can doo it best:
The whiles the maydens doe theyr carroll sing,
To which the woods shall answer, and theyr eccho ring.    260

Ring ye the bels, ye yong men of the towne,
And leave your wonted labors for this day:
This day is holy; doe ye write it downe,
That ye for ever it remember may.
This day the sunne is in his chiefest hight,              265
With Barnaby the bright,
From whence declining daily by degrees,
He somewhat loseth of his heat and light,
When once the Crab behind his back he sees.
But for this time it ill ordainèd was,                    270
To chose the longest day on all the yeare,
And shortest night, when longest fitter weare:
Yet never day so long, but late would passe.
Ring ye the bels, to make it weare away,
And bonefiers make all day;                               275
And daunce about them, and about them sing,
That all the woods may answer, and your eccho ring.

Ah! when will this long weary day have end,
And lende me leave to come unto my love?
How slowly do the houres theyr numbers spend!             280
How slowly does sad Time his feathers move!
Hast thee, O fayrest Planet, to thy home,
Within the Westerne fome:
Thy tyrèd steedes long since have need of rest.
Long though it be, at last I see it gloome,               285
And the bright evening-star with golden creast
Appeare out of the East.
Fayre childe of beauty! glorious lampe of love!
That all the host of heaven in ranks doost lead,
And guydest lovers through the nights sad dread,          290
How chearefully thou lookest from above,
And seemest to laugh atweene thy twinkling light,
As joying in the sight

Of these glad many, which for joy doe sing,
That all the woods them answer, and their echo ring! 295

Now ceasse, ye damsels, your delights fore-past;
Enough it is that all the day was youres:
Now day is doen, and night is nighing fast,
Now bring the Bryde into the brydall boures.
The night is come, now soon her disaray, 300
And in her bed her lay;
Lay her in lillies and in violets,
And silken courteins over her display,
And odourd sheetes, and Arras coverlets.
Behold how goodly my faire love does ly, 305
In proud humility!
Like unto Maia, when as Jove her took
In Tempe, lying on the flowry gras,
Twixt sleepe and wake, after she weary was,
With bathing in the Acidalian brooke. 310
Now it is night, ye damsels may be gon,
And leave my love alone,
And leave likewise your former lay to sing:
The woods no more shall answere, nor your echo ring.

Now welcome, night! thou night so long expected, 315
That long daies labour doest at last defray,
And all my cares, which cruell Love collected
Hast sumd in one, and cancellèd for aye:
Spread thy broad wing over my love and me,
That no man may us see; 320
And in thy sable mantle us enwrap,
From feare of perill and foule horror free.
Let no false treason seeke us to entrap,
Nor any dread disquiet once annoy
The safety of our joy; 325
But let the night be calme, and quietsome,
Without tempestuous storms or sad afray:
Lyke as when Jove with fayre Alcmena lay,
When he begot the great Tirynthian groome:
Or lyke as when he with thy selfe did lie 330
And begot Majesty.
And let the mayds and yong men cease to sing;
Ne let the woods them answer nor thyr eccho ring.

Let no lamenting cryes, nor dolefull teares,
Be heard all night within, nor yet without: 335
Ne let false whispers, breeding hidden feares,

Breake gentle sleepe with misconceivèd dout.
Let no deluding dreames, nor dreadfull sights,
Make sudden sad affrights;
Ne let house-fyres, nor lightnings helpelesse harmes,    340
Ne let the Pouke, nor other evill sprights,
Ne let mischivous witches with theyr charmes,
Ne let hob Goblins, names whose sence we see not,
Fray us with things that be not:
Let not the shriech Oule nor the Storke be heard,    345
Nor the night Raven, that still deadly yels;
Nor damnèd ghosts, cald up with mighty spels,
Nor griesly vultures, make us once affeard:
Ne let th' unpleasant Quyre of Frogs still croking
Make us to wish theyr choking.    350
Let none of these theyr drery accents sing;
Ne let the woods them answer, nor theyr eccho ring.

But let stil Silence trew night-watches keepe,
That sacred Peace may in assurance rayne,
And tymely Sleep, when it is tyme to sleepe,    355
May poure his limbs forth on your pleasant playne;
The whiles an hundred little wingèd loves,
Like divers-fethered doves,
Shall fly and flutter round about your bed,
And in the secret darke, that none reproves,    360
Their prety stealthes shal worke, and snares shal spread
To filch away sweet snatches of delight,
Conceald through covert night.
Ye sonnes of Venus, play your sports at will!
For greedy pleasure, carelesse of your toyes,    365
Thinks more upon her paradise of joyes,
Then what ye do, albe it good or ill.
All night therefore attend your merry play,
For it will soone be day:
Now none doth hinder you, that say or sing;    370
Ne will the woods now answer, nor your Eccho ring.

Who is the same, which at my window peepes?
Or whose is that faire face that shines so bright?
Is it not Cinthia, she that never sleepes,
But walkes about high heaven al the night?    375
O! fayrest goddesse, do thou not envy
My love with me to spy:
For thou likewise didst love, though now unthought,
And for a fleece of wooll, which privily

The Latmian shepherd once unto thee brought, 380
His pleasures with thee wrought.
Therefore to us be favorable now;
And sith of wemens labours thou hast charge,
And generation goodly dost enlarge,
Encline thy will t'effect our wishfull vow, 385
And the chast wombe informe with timely seed
That may our comfort breed:
Till which we cease our hopefull hap to sing;
Ne let the woods us answere, nor our Eccho ring.

And thou, great Juno! which with awful might 390
The lawes of wedlock still dost patronize;
And the religion of the faith first plight
With sacred rites hast taught to solemnize;
And eeke for comfort often callèd art
Of women in their smart; 395
Eternally bind thou this lovely band,
And all thy blessings unto us impart.
And thou, glad Genius! in whose gentle hand
The bridale bowre and geniall bed remaine,
Without blemish or staine; 400
And the sweet pleasures of theyr loves delight
With secret ayde doest succour and supply,
Till they bring forth the fruitfull progeny;
Send us the timely fruit of this same night.
And thou, fayre Hebe! and thou, Hymen free! 405
Grant that it may so be.
Til which we cease your further prayse to sing;
Ne any woods shall answer, nor your Eccho ring.

And ye high heavens, the temple of the gods,
In which a thousand torches flaming bright 410
Doe burne, that to us wretched earthly clods
In dreadful darknesse lend desirèd light
And all ye powers which in the same remayne,
More then we men can fayne!
Poure out your blessing on us plentiously, 415
And happy influence upon us raine,
That we may raise a large posterity,
Which from the earth, which they may long possesse
With lasting happinesse,
Up to your haughty pallaces may mount, 420
And, for the guerdon of theyr glorious merit,
May heavenly tabernacles there inherit,

Of blessèd Saints for to increase the count.
So let us rest, sweet love, in hope of this,
And cease till then our tymely joyes to sing: 425
The woods no more us answer, nor our eccho ring!

*Song! made in lieu of many ornaments,*
*With which my love should duly have been dect,*
*Which cutting off through hasty accidents,*
*Ye would not stay your dew time to expect,* 430
*But promist both to recompens;*
*Be unto her a goodly ornament,*
*And for short time an endlesse moniment.*

*Walter James Miller*

SPENSER
EPITHALAMION

Edmund Spenser's masterpiece, "Epithalamion" is also our master key to understanding his genius and techniques. In this wedding ode, he manages by means of shifting emphases and moods to transform a conventional ritual into an exciting story. And by means of that word magic known best to him and rarely approximated by anyone else, he renders simple English into superb music.

The wedding he celebrates is his own: he was married to Elizabeth Boyle on June 11, 1594, "the joyfulst day that ever sunne did see." As he tells us in his envoy, or postscript, he offered this song to his bride in lieu of wedding gifts that had not arrived on time. But Spenser had already commemorated every phase of their eighteen-month courtship in his series of eighty-eight sonnets, "Amoretti." Gifts or no gifts, he was hardly the man to let the consummation go unrecorded.

Surely part of the pleasure of the occasion for him was the chance to explore the form of the epithalamion, the hymn that the ancients sang as the bride was led to her chamber (*epithalamion* means, in Greek, "for the bedroom"). Following tradition, then, he opens his hymn by invoking the muses ("learned sisters"), invites the local nymphs and virgins to admire his beloved, rejoices at her homecoming, describes the wedding feast and the making of the marriage bed. His framework is classical, but his setting is British. Calling on the nymphs, for example, gives him a chance to quickly survey the countryside and the wildlife, as these guardians of trout, pike, and deer come in from stream and hill.

The continuous excitement of the poem, it seems to me, is generated by the groom's oscillating from joy to anxiety, from restlessness to surrender, from the realistic to the idealistic and the mythic.

For much of the way, his uneasiness seems to be a matter of simple humility—the whole situation is too good to be true, he still cannot believe his good luck, he "knocks wood" as he asks the fates to let this day be perfect. Aside from this understandable superstitiousness, there are hints of real cause for anxiety. "Cruell Love" has made the courtship a difficult one for Spenser; the bride has also suffered "paynes and sorrowes" during their romance. No wonder he frets when she oversleeps. And one grim line suggests perhaps the darkest threat of all: "Let no false treason seeke us to entrap." As an English official in oppressed Ireland, Spenser could not revel with abandonment even on his wedding night. (Only a few years after this prophetic line was published, Spenser and his family barely escaped with their lives as their castle was burned down by Irish nationalists.)

Tension is built up too by the poet's conflicting needs to speed the total day to its climax yet to slow it down for enjoyment of its separate moments. Chafing at how the hours drag on, he regrets now the folly of having set the wedding for what, in the Elizabethan calendar, is the longest day of the year. Yet he pauses perfectly poised to notice that the choristers in their ecstasy sing with "hollow throates," that the shouts of boys in the street blend into "one voyce," that wine ought to be poured "by the belly full."

Now the realistic so dominates him that he wants the nymphs to comb their hair and wash their faces. Later he is seized by the ecstasy of idealization—in four successive stanzas, Elizabeth is angel, goddess, saint. This particular conflict, at least, is resolved in what is the artistic crisis of the poem. Spenser does not accept a sharp Christian dichotomy between the flesh and the spirit; rather he sees the physical and the spiritual as coexisting on a Platonic continuum. Hence his description of his bride mounts from sensuous appreciation of each detail of her body to a total enjoyment of her physique as an expression of spiritual glamour.

The excitement is further intensified by the poet's shifting point of view, his flexible perspective. First he describes the bride's preparations, not from direct observation of course but from distant imagination as the narrator; then he is with the throngs appraising her beauty; suddenly, breathtakingly, we realize he is holding her hand, he is with her at the altar. Separated again, he once more feeds on imagination and knowledge of custom; then suddenly he too is on the nuptial couch.

And here Spenser gives us interesting examples of the function of mythology. To describe the look on the bride's face as her lover enters her chamber, Spenser modestly escapes into the legend of Maia and Jove. To suggest the pleasures on the Spenserian marriage bed, he thinks how Jove lay with Alcmena, how Endymion came to Cynthia. Mythology gives the poet archetypal analogies for free associations, for indirect expression of the unbearably direct experience.

Mythology also of course provides Spenser with most of his running metaphors, and, to the modern reader at least, his reliance on some twenty-odd references to classical myths constitutes his greatest weakness. His master simile, though, is based on everyday experience:

> *And all her body like a pallace fayre,*
> *Ascending up, with many a stately stayre*

Here, at a crucial moment, Spenser uses a bold conceit, one that even Freudian critics could approve of as coming directly from fundamental symbolism of the deepest emotions.

But Spenser differs from most poets in this respect: he is concerned not so much with stunning metaphors and purple passages as with total effect. For that reason, perhaps, he brings his craftsmanship to bear mainly on his music. He writes poetry the way a good singer sings—with purity of tone, perfect divisions and enunciation to make separate words stand out. His voice is easily and smoothly regulated— as a singing master would say, his voice is "on the breath."

In the simplest lines, we find, if we look hard enough, for it rarely obtrudes, the most deliberate artistry born of long practice. One masterful trick is his great range of vowel sounds within a single line. Notice that in saying aloud:

> *Helpe to addorne my beautifullest bride*

or

> *With joyance bring her and with jollity*

we are mouthing an unusually large number of different sounds for such a short number of syllables. We are forced to speak with mouth wide open, to put our voice-producing apparatus through full exercise of its repertory.

This love of variety in tones enables Spenser to make greater capital than other poets can of similarity in sounds.

When he shifts over to emphasize the same consonant, as the *f* in:

*From feare of perrill and foule horror free*

or to emphasize the same vowel sound, *or:*

*And let the roring Organs loudly play*
*The praises of the Lord in lively notes;*

. . .

*The Choristers the joyous Antheme sing*

he achieves greater intensity because of the greater contrast.

Not the least of the technical tricks behind the success of "Epithalamion" is Spenser's design of a special stanza form. Each of the twenty-three stanzas is eighteen or nineteen lines long; about fourteen of the lines are in iambic pentameter, like:

*That all the sences they doe ravish quite*

He achieves bright contrasts to this basic five-foot line by using unexpected short lines, scattered trimeters like:

*My truest turtle dove*

and then a suddenly relaxing long line, an alexandrine, at the end:

*That all the woods may answer, and your eccho ring*

These variations prevent monotony in rhythm and in the distance between rhymes.

The six-foot concluding line is a refrain, but one so ingeniously varied that it comes less as a repetition and more as a surprise. The variations are used now to get up momentum; now for dramatic effect, as when the virgins in their amazement forget to sing; and now to slow down the action, as when the groom wants quiet in the bridal suite.

These, surely, are a few of the reasons why "Epithalamion" is considered one of the greatest poems in English and why Spenser is considered to be a "poet's poet."

# SIR PHILIP SIDNEY

[1554–1586]

## Loving in Truth

Loving in truth, and fain in verse my love to show,
  That she, dear she, might take some pleasure of my pain,
Pleasure might cause her read, reading might make her
    know,
  Knowledge might pity win, and pity grace obtain,
I sought fit words to paint the blackest face of woe;     5
  Studying inventions fine, her wits to entertain,
Oft turning others' leaves to see if thence would flow
  Some fresh and fruitful showers upon my sun-burned
    brain.
But words came halting forth, wanting Invention's stay;
  Invention, Nature's child, fled step-dame Study's blows,  10
And others' feet still seemed but strangers in my way.
  Thus, great with child to speak, and helpless in my throes,
    Biting my truant pen, beating myself for spite,
    "Fool," said my Muse to me, "look in thy heart and
    write."

SIR PHILIP SIDNEY

*The Bettmann Archive*

# Earle Birney

## SIDNEY
### LOVING IN TRUTH

"Loving in Truth" is the introduction to a series of sonnets titled "Astrophel and Stella." The last line, which gives the whole composition its meaning, is generally held to be Sidney's plain assertion that the sonnets will flow from genuine love, the experience of passion, and not from books.

There is no doubt, of course, that young Sir Philip Sidney wrote "Astrophel and Stella," to a flesh and blood woman, whose identity has never been disputed. The "dear she" is Penelope Devereux, his aunt's ward, whom the poet had met six years before, in 1575, when he was twenty-one and she thirteen. Between that time and the writing of the poem the two had certainly seen something of each other. Her father, the Earl of Essex, recently deceased, had indeed expressed on his deathbed the hope that Sidney would wed her, and a marriage contract may even have been drawn up. But old Essex died virtually bankrupt and without influence (his wife was said to have been hated by Queen Elizabeth), and young Penelope found herself, with a dowry of only two hundred pounds, married off against her will to a certain Lord Rich (on whose pat name Sidney puns in a later sonnet). There is evidence that the marriage was unhappy and that, shortly after Sidney's tragic death at Zutphen, she became the mistress of Sir Thomas Blount. As for Sidney, soon after the marriage he retired from court and busied himself in writing "Astrophel and Stella," in which he carefully identifies Penelope as the star, his Stella, and himself as Astrophel, the star-lover. He did not, it is true, publish the poems—they appeared shortly after his death—but their printing was by the open consent of Sidney's sister, the Countess of Pembroke. And it has been argued that Sidney had withheld them from anything but private circulation only because they revealed too much of a very real passion for Penelope, including even a hint, in one sonnet, that their love had been consummated.

Biographical arguments, however, are seldom reliable

enough to prove passion in a poet. The very openness with
which both Penelope and her family, even though she was
freshly married to Lord Rich, accepted her identification as
Stella, might be taken as an argument that Sidney's original
readers regarded his sonnets as merely the conventional
compliments of a courtier. Certainly Sidney himself does not
seem to have done anything to protest his love for Penelope
*before* her marriage, or to prevail on her family or his to
make him the bridegroom. The sonnets were written after
the event, at a time when Sidney was making plans for his
own wedding to a fourteen-year-old daughter of his friend
Walsingham. About all this the sonnets are discreetly silent,
nor does Sidney even hint that relatives are at the same time
seeking to arrange a betrothal between him and Penelope's
own sister! It is even possible that Sidney never knew
Penelope more than casually, that she was to him simply a
young cousin whom he encountered occasionally at court,
and that he chose her for his Stella only because she was
safely married off, though still young, beautiful and nobly
born—an excellent love symbol for a poet who wants to try
his hand at sonnets and to say things about love. A strong
hint that this was indeed Sidney's attitude is dropped in his
later "Defence of Poesy," where he writes that he never desired to be considered a poet even though in his younger
years, "overmastered by some thoughts, I yielded an inky
tribute." It is thought and not feeling, the mind, not the heart,
which he remembers dominating him.

What then are we to make of this sonnet? "Loving in
truth" Sidney says he was—but at once he couples that
protestation with a literary incentive, the displaying of his
love in verse, a motive which is at once linked with a series of
others: the entertainment of the lady through melodious
words which in turn may persuade her that he woos her, that
wooing is a state to be pitied, and pity, once awakened, may
lead to the granting of love. There is nothing in all this chain
of arguments that had not already been said in the sonnets of
Wyatt and Surrey a generation earlier, or in the ballades of
Chaucer two hundred years before, or by dozens of French
and Italian poets even earlier. Whatever the truth of the
loving, the statement of it is an act of literary imitation, a
rhetorically correct *gradatio*. Yet the poem survives the
conventionality of its opening by proceeding, after the fourth
line, at first to confess, and then to repudiate, the stereotypes
it is employing. The poet went looking for words, he tells us,
and studied "inventions" or rhetorical devices, "oft turning

others' leaves"—and that very phrase suggests that Sidney had been turning the pages of the French love poet Du Bellay, where this image is put to like use. But his brain will not respond to such stimuli: it has been parched, sunburned in the heat of love; the words that come out contain concrete verbal "inventions" but lack the perception and imagination of genuine abstract "Invention," of the creativity that is born of being natural and avoiding the overstudious, the "academic." The feet of others tread what should be his private path. (Yet even in saying this Sidney continues his strict twelve-syllable-line metrics modelled on De Baïf, and borrows a stock pun on metrical feet which Spenser had recently made in reference to Chaucer!) And so, laboring with his brain child, with the great subject of his love, but unable to struggle through the pains of parturition to birth, at last inspiration comes, his Muse speaks:

*"Fool," said my Muse to me, "look in thy heart and write."*

And yet . . . and yet . . . is it as simple as that? Does Sidney indeed mean by "heart" what we generally take him to mean: that the best poetry comes from a faithful recording of our emotions? Surely what is the center of his preoccupations in this poem is Stella; it is her image he is telling himself to gaze at, for she is the source of all his poetical invention. The sonnets that follow this in the "Astrophel" sequence all corroborate this interpretation. Sidney, throughout the sequence, is interested in phrasing principles for the writing of love poetry, but the basic principle is always, for him, the cavalier one: the wooing and worship of the lady. Hold her image at the center (he calls it "heart"; it could as justly be called "mind" for the purpose of this poem) and the poem will flow easily and truly from that source like "fresh and fruitful showers," for it will describe her, celebrate her beauty and its power, memorialize the source of loveliness and freshness. The language, however, will not turn out to be very different from that of other love poets—nor the ideas, as comparison of the words and images in the remaining sonnets of "Astrophel and Stella" with those of Ronsard, Du Bellay, and Petrarch, will quickly reveal. Cupid sends his darts from Stella's eyes; her eyebrows are his bows; desire combats reason; and true beauty, virtue is. The "heart" into which Sidney looked was a complex one; some of the blood that fed it flowed down from Ovid and some from Dante, and the beat was often that of the Pleiades rather than of Nature's Pump.

And for all that, this opening sonnet of "Astrophel and Stella" remains a poem we never forget, a work of unwavering art, whatever its artfulness, a poem that leaps to the triumphant climax of its last line, where the sudden eloquent simplicity of Chaucer is born again and sent down the years for Shakespeare's use, and all men's pleasure.

## Desire

Thou blind man's mark, thou fool's self-chosen snare,
   Fond fancy's scum, and dregs of scattered thought;
Band of all evils, cradle of causeless care;
   Thou web of will, whose end is never wrought;
Desire, desire! I have too dearly bought,       5
   With price of mangled mind, thy worthless ware;
Too long, too long, asleep thou hast me brought,
   Who should my mind to higher things prepare.
But yet in vain thou hast my ruin sought;
   In vain thou madest me to vain things aspire;    10
   In vain thou kindlest all thy smoky fire;
For virtue hath this better lesson taught,
    Within myself to seek my only hire,
    Desiring nought but how to kill desire.

*Walter James Miller*

SIDNEY

DESIRE

How to keep the passions under control—how to maintain one's poise when caught in a romantic hurricane—is a problem older than Plato and newer than psychoanalysis. Until men refashion themselves as brains on wheels, they will cherish Sidney's sonnet on desire as a neat expression of this sweet predicament.

Sidney achieves his main effect, it seems to me, by a subtle contrast between intellectual progress and emotional undertow. Ostensibly the speaker in the poem, bitter over the way his lust has blinded and degraded him, moves decisively toward the strong conviction that now he will seek his equilibrium in himself, now he desires only to kill desire.

But meanwhile another, simpler play on that key word has escaped him. Coming to the point where he must put aside scornful epithets and name his enemy directly, the speaker does not simply address her as "Desire!"

Rather he lingers voluptuously over the name: "Desire, desire!" This ambivalent cry, softening his contempt, echoes down to the last line. We sense that for all his protests, the speaker is much too involved, he has had only a lover's quarrel with desire.

What appears to be an effortless statement of man's disequilibrium is actually a product of Sidney's careful balance between talent and craftsmanship. As evidence of his talent, note how he reaches us immediately with the ironical figure "blind man's mark." Whether a man expresses it by stretching a bowstring, pegging the ball to second, or making a smooth landing, he regards marksmanship as central to his ego. It hurts to think that in responding to lust, he is likely to hit the target not through coordination of his powers but out of blindness. The point is driven home in a series of equally apt and startling images—"fancy's scum," "mangled mind"—expressing the speaker's self-contempt for his self-derangement.

Technically, the poem is intricately worked, yet it doesn't show; we have to analyze it to see it. Sidney casts his speaker's trembling resoluteness into sonnet form because this fourteen-line pattern, calling for a break in thought after the eighth (or twelfth) line, is suitable for expressing conflict or reversal; thus the speaker uses the first eight lines, or the octave, to describe desire's victories, and the last six, the sestet, to predict virtue's comeback. Now most English poets, including Shakespeare, allow themselves up to seven different rhymes in the sonnet, and Sidney himself usually needs five; but here he is able to do a very tight job with three. His internal music he achieves partly through his usual successions of round vowel sounds, partly through a close interweaving of consonant rhymes: *w*orthless *w*are, *w*eb of *w*ill, *c*radle of *c*auseless *c*are. Yet neither eleven such initial rhymes nor frequent repetition of three end rhymes draws attention to technique as such. A real Renaissance virtuoso, Sidney does not accent his virtuosity.

Distinguished as a poem in its own right, "Desire" is also important for its place in literary history. Note that I have referred to the "I" in this sonnet not as Sidney but as "the speaker" because the poet does not offer this as a personal lyric. Rather it is one of almost eighty lovely poems interspersed throughout his prose-romance *Arcadia*, most of them supposedly written or spoken or sung by the characters. In these works, which constitute Sidney's apprenticeship, he experimented with metrical patterns—*terza rima*, double sestina, *ottava rima*, variations of the sonnet—in an effort to find the most appropriate forms for modern English, just about to come into its own as a literary tongue.

As a result of these experiments, Sidney developed the strong, natural style in which he composed his "Astrophel and Stella," the sonnet sequence that, circulating in manuscript, touched off the sonneteering craze in England. (In that cycle, Sidney comes to accept his conflict over desire as part of man's condition:

> *It is true that eyes are formed to serve*
> *The inward light, and that the heavenly part*
> *Ought to be king . . .*
>
> *True, and yet true that I must Stella love.*)

Although thousands of sonnets were published thereafter during the Elizabethan period, Sidney's were surpassed only by Shakespeare's and otherwise equaled only by Spenser's.

WILLIAM SHAKESPEARE

*Alleged portrait of Shakespeare,
attributed to Burbage*

*The Bettmann Archive*

# WILLIAM SHAKESPEARE
## [1564–1616]

### *The Phœnix and the Turtle*

Let the bird of loudest lay,
On the sole Arabian tree,
Herald sad and trumpet be,
To whose sound chaste wings obey.

But thou shrieking harbinger,     5
Foul precurrer of the fiend,
Augur of the fever's end,
To this troop come thou not near!

From this session interdict
Every fowl of tyrant wing,     10
Save the eagle, feath'red king;
Keep the obsequy so strict!

Let the priest in surplice white,
That defunctive music can,
Be the death-divining swan,     15
Lest the requiem lack his right.

And thou treble-dated crow,
That thy sable gender mak'st
With the breath thou giv'st and tak'st,
'Mongst our mourners shalt thou go.     20

Here the anthem doth commence:
Love and Constancy is dead;
Phœnix and the turtle fled
In a mutual flame from hence.

So they lov'd as love in twain     25
Had the essence but in one;
Two distincts, division none:
Number there in love was slain.

Hearts remote, yet not asunder;
Distance, and no space was seen     30
'Twixt this turtle and his queen:
But in them it were a wonder.

So between them love did shine,
That the turtle saw his right
Flaming in the phœnix' sight;                    35
Either was the other's mine.

Property was thus appalled,
That the self was not the same;
Single nature's double name
Neither two nor one was called.                  40

Reason, in itself confounded,
Saw division grow together,
To themselves yet either neither;
Simple were so well compounded

That it cried, "How true a twain                 45
Seemeth this concordant one!
Love hath reason, Reason none,
If what parts can so remain."

Whereupon it made this threne
To the phœnix and the dove,                      50
Co-supremes and stars of love,
As chorus to their tragic scene.


### THRENOS

Beauty, Truth, and Rarity,
Grace in all simplicity,
Here enclos'd, in cinders lie.                   55

Death is now the phœnix' nest;
And the turtle's loyal breast
To eternity doth rest,

Leaving no posterity:
'Twas not their infirmity,                       60
It was married chastity.

Truth may seem, but cannot be;
Beauty brag, but 'tis not she;
Truth and Beauty buried be.

To this urn let those repair                     65
That are either true or fair;
For these dead birds sigh a prayer.

# William Empson

## SHAKESPEARE
## THE PHOENIX AND THE TURTLE

This exquisite but baffling poem is the only one written by Shakespeare for publication with other poets on a common theme, and his only consistent use of the metaphysical style; it appeared at the end of *Love's Martyr*, an allegory by Robert Chester beside other verses by Marston, Chapman, Jonson, and "Ignoto." The publication (dedicated to Sir John Salusbury, 1601, unlicensed) came out at the height of the War of the Theatres, when the contributors were quarrelling, and just after the execution of Essex, when it was very dangerous to excite the suspicions of the Queen.

A modern reader of the poem needs to form some idea of what the point was at the time. The edition by Carleton Brown of *Poems by Sir John Salusbury and Robert Chester* (1914) for the Early English Text Society is a mine of information and entertainment about these characters, and its argument has never been refuted. One should also read *The Mutual Flame* (1955) by Professor Wilson Knight; his survey of the background of the thought is very fine, but I think it essential to realize that all the poems are concerned to praise Sir John Salusbury and his wife. He would not have been at all pleased if they had done any of the many other things which critics have suggested.

A line of Jonson's poetry in *Love's Martyr* had been quoted a year earlier in *England's Parnassus* (1600), and this helps to show that the contributions of the playwrights had been made before middle 1599, before Jonson quarrelled with Marston. Hence the reason Shakespeare sounds sad in this poem is not that he has just begun his tragic period; probably, when he wrote it to praise the Welsh Sir John, he was also making Henry V say:

> *Though it appear a little out of fashion*
> *There is much care and valour in this Welshman.*

Shakespeare was a connoisseur of the absurd near-Tudors who were frequent at Elizabeth's court, and would certainly have run his eye over this impressive specimen.

Sir John, the squire of Lleweny in north Denbighshire, had married in 1586 at the age of twenty an illegitimate but recognized daughter of the King of Man (or Earl of Derby). His crest was a white lion, and he was sometimes called "The Lion" or "The Strong." He was a determined Church of England man, and often quarrelled with supporters of the Essex faction. In 1595, Salusbury came to London as law student and squire of the body to the Queen; in 1597 he printed some love poems at the end of "Sinetes Passion" by Robert Parry, who calls him "The Patron"; they spell out acrostically the names of three adored ladies. In June 1601, he was knighted by the Queen herself, and in October he was standing for Parliament in Denbighshire. This was his brief period of triumph, and clearly he rushed the book into print to celebrate it. After the Queen's death he could no longer get official employment, because James preferred Scotsmen. He died in 1612, and his surviving son bought one of James' new baronetcies in 1619, so at least the old lion had not ruined the estate. He would have been a very useful patron for the young Jonson, who probably coaxed the other play-wrights into putting on a show; and I am sure that Jonson would think shame of trying to make fun of him in public.

Chester, the author of *Love's Martyr* was probably the resident chaplain at the big house of Lleweny, anyway a dependent who wrote an allegory to praise the family. A poem at the wedding had already called the lady a royal bird, and the squire though prone to duels was what a later age called "a martyr to the fair," very attentive to ladies, so it seemed all right to make him love's martyr, the turtle to her phoenix.

In the allegory, the phoenix complains to Nature about her difficulties (the status of a half-royal bastard might be hard to fix), and Nature gives her an irrelevant world tour; at last they meet the phoenix, and Nature with-draws. The phoenix asks whether the turtle has been chaste, and on being reassured explains that for her to pro-duce issue requires burning alive; both birds at once col-lect twigs, so there is no interval for "married chastity." The phoenix wants to spare the turtle, but the turtle insists on burning with it; most fortunately, because otherwise "Love had been murdered in the infancy;/Without these two no love at all can be." (Shakespeare, on the other hand, says that since the deaths of the two birds, true love cannot be found; he, too, treats them as its magical causes.) An eyewitness account of the burning, by a pelican, concludes Chester's poem; some extra verses, a good deal freer in their moral tone, were probably composed by the turtle.

To praise a grand marriage by calling it a martyrdom is radically absurd, all the more so if probable, and poor Chester became uneasily aware of this in the years while he was turning out the patriotic encyclopedia section (the main myth was probably composed to celebrate the birth of a daughter, a year after the marriage; she would be fourteen in 1601, and Marston's contribution is in praise of her). When Chester briefed Jonson, explaining the theme, which was to be treated by as many poets as he could collect, Chester would be driven to be definite, and he evidently said that the hidden meaning was "married chastity." (He must have been brought to London for the negotiation, as the squire could not have said this about himself.) At any rate, the main poem added by Jonson puzzles about married chastity, in a very plain-man way; it seems a new idea to him. Modern critics often assume that Shakespeare, when he said the phoenix had no posterity because of married chastity, was deliberately stepping out of line to express his personal distaste for reproduction; but he and Jonson would not both use the idea unless it had been set.

Jonson sternly tells Vice that such a thing is possible, and then considers what it can be:

> Turtles *can chastely die.*
> *And yet (in this to express ourself more clear)*
> *We do not number here*
> *Such spirits as are only continent*
> *Because* Lust's *means are spent;*
> *Or those, who doubt the common mouth of* Fame,
> *And for their* Place, *or* Name,
> *Cannot so safely sin: Their* Chastity
> *Is mere* Necessity.
> *Nor mean we those, whom* Vows *and* Conscience
> *Have filed with* Abstinence . . .

It is clear at least that he is not writing about the Queen. He seems to be describing a husband who spares his wife the act of sex so as not to offend her delicacy; to make sure it is from this motive only, the poet excludes the case of a pious vow. But he keeps saying that to demand the act would be a "sin," which he would not really believe. I suppose the young

dramatist was keen to grasp all the current modes of aspiration, however sickly or alien to his personal taste; thus he is
not a hypocrite so far as he is speaking "in character"; but
still, critics need not keep telling us to admire the stern
morality of the poem.

Shakespeare later made the good man Posthumus, astonished at losing his bet on the near-frigidity of his wife, say:

> *Me of my lawful pleasure she restrain'd*
> *And pray'd me oft forbearance; did it with*
> *A pudency so rosy the sweet view on't*
> *Might well have warmed old Saturn . . .*
>
> Cymbeline, II, v

He takes for granted that the effect would be to make the
husband's demand more pressing. Shakespeare, as well as
Jonson, reflects that one could not respect married chastity if
a husband used it to hide impotence; the thought does not
convey a spontaneous sympathy for it; also, I don't expect
they would say this if they were secretly thinking about
homosexuality. When the poem says:

> *So between them love did shine,*
> *That the turtle saw his right*
> *Flaming in the phoenix' sight;*
> *Either was the other's mine.*

Wilson Knight quotes a gloss: "The turtle saw his justification for existence in the appreciation with which the phoenix
regarded him"; but I think the basic idea is again the marital
right of the husband, even though the next line promotes the
woman to equal status, as in the "Extasie" of Donne. I should
expect married chastity to be morally very low, giving the
couple much opportunity and craving to torment one another; but, if it meant spacing out the childbirths, that was a
much neglected piece of charity—it would have saved the
life, for example, of Ann Donne. However, we need not
accuse Salusbury of married chastity in any form, not even
faithfulness. His marriage produced four children in the first
four years and six in the next ten (no twins); and one of his
bastards had been baptised in the parish church in 1597. No
wonder Jonson argued.

Shakespeare does not discuss the idea, but uses it for
dramatic effect; his poem needs to be regarded as part of a
sequence. He expresses the despair felt by the spectators of
the burning (Reason is here the voice of the chaster birds)
before the trick works and a new phoenix rises from the

ashes. Then Marston has to bounce in and contradict
Shakespeare, though his first line is a hurried compliment:

> *O twas a moving Epicidium!*
> *Can Fire? Can Time? Can blackest Fate consume*
> *So rare creation? No, tis thwart to sense;*
> *Corruption quakes to touch such excellence.*
>
> *. . .*
>
> *Let me stand numbed with wonder; never came*
> *So strong amazement on astonished eye*
> *As this, this measureless pure Rarity.*

It is splendid rhetoric; Marston could do this when imagining
an adequate subject for verse, though not when faced with a
real one. So far from ignoring his colleagues here, Shakespeare remembered the passage for the end of *The Winter's
Tale.*

Wilson Knight showed that the phoenix commonly symbolizes a love denied bodily consummation, since that would
be adulterous or homosexual or politically disruptive, and the
love is driven to more spiritual courses. Hence, he thought,
the poem is probably about the squire's love for his wife's
sister. This would avoid the absurdity of praising his marriage as a martyrdom, but here we are in a turbulent area,
which made C. S. Lewis call Spenser the first poet who dared
say it is convenient to love one's own wife (poor Chester was
running Spenser close for the priority). Salusbury, in bringing out the poem to celebrate his knighthood, wanted to
increase the glory of his house, which would descend to his
son and heir; poems about adultery might be printable but
were trivial. But I think the argument has a secondary truth;
what keeps the absurd poem of Chester sweet is his love for
his master. This kind of love was avowable and usually
untormented, but Chester in presenting himself as the gazing
pelican claims a share in the honors of sacrifice; her young
ones feed their "hungry fancies" on her breasts. He has been
underrated, I think; as long as he is praising his dear Lion he
has any amount of limpid depth. And why should not his
apparent absurdity express something profound? If anything
seems wrong with his theme, he says as he lumbers towards
the end, the fault must be in the treatment:

> *tis lameness of the mind*
> *That had no better skill; yet let it pass,*
> *For burdenous loads are set upon an Ass.*

This is the royal generosity of the Shakespearean clown, and Shakespeare was quite right to salute it.

We know that Chapman thought the whole affair funny, though in a grave pedantic manner, because he headed his piece (which praised the traditional knight who had learned his virtues from serving his lady) "Peristeros, or the male Turtle." He has had to invent a masculine form for the word, since the Greeks considered all doves female; the creatures themselves do not know which sex they are, but try out the alternatives. A female phoenix had been invented by the Renaissance to gratify a taste for Amazons (till then its solitary sex had been "known to God alone"), but it seems that a turtle wearing the trousers was a real novelty, not only to a classicist. The Lion, as his poet remarks, was safe from ridicule even when presented as a turtle. The Latin *tur tur* would give the cooing of the pets of Venus, in the minds of the poets, a deeper note of sultry desire; to make them into symbols of married chastity thus put an extra strain upon the gravity of the reader—it had been the charm of the silly creatures that no frustration attended their single-minded passions.

Shakespeare's poem is a wide valley brimful of an unspecified sorrow, but one should also feel, before hearing any explanation, the gaiety inherent in its effects of sound. As the anthem of the birds reaches its severest exultation their tweeting modulates into the arch babytalk of a dandling nurse; as we soar heavenward between the "co-supremes," we pass mysteriously near the cow that jumped over the moon:

> *To themselves yet either neither;*
> *Simple were so well compounded.*

# *Sonnets*

### I

From fairest creatures we desire increase,
That thereby beauty's rose might never die,
But as the riper should by time decease,
His tender heir might bear his memory:
But thou, contracted to thine own bright eyes,     5
Feed'st thy light's flame with self-substantial fuel,
Making a famine where abundance lies,
Thyself thy foe, to thy sweet self too cruel.
Thou that art now the world's fresh ornament
And only herald to the gaudy spring,               10
Within thine own bud buriest thy content
And, tender churl, mak'st waste in niggarding.
  Pity the world, or else this glutton be,
    To eat the world's due, by the grave and thee.


### 3

Look in thy glass, and tell the face thou viewest
Now is the time that face should form another;
Whose fresh repair if now thou not renewest,
Thou dost beguile the world, unbless some mother.
For where is she so fair whose unear'd womb         5
Disdains the tillage of thy husbandry?
Or who is he so fond will be the tomb
Of his self-love, to stop posterity?
Thou art thy mother's glass, and she in thee
Calls back the lovely April of her prime;           10
So thou through windows of thine age shalt see,
Despite of wrinkles, this thy golden time.
  But if thou live rememb'red not to be,
    Die single, and thine image dies with thee.

## 6

Then let not winter's ragged hand deface
In thee thy summer ere thou be distill'd:
Make sweet some vial; treasure thou some place
With beauty's treasure, ere it be self-kill'd.
That use is not forbidden usury                          5
Which happies those that pay the willing loan;
That's for thyself to breed another thee,
Or ten times happier, be it ten for one.
Ten times thyself were happier than thou art,
If ten of thine ten times refigur'd thee.               10
Then what could death do, if thou shouldst depart,
Leaving thee living in posterity?
   Be not self-will'd, for thou art much too fair
   To be death's conquest and make worms thine heir.

## 9

Is it for fear to wet a widow's eye
That thou consum'st thyself in single life?
Ah! if thou issueless shalt hap to die,
The world will wail thee like a makeless wife;
The world will be thy widow and still weep              5
That thou no form of thee hast left behind,
When every private widow well may keep
By children's eyes her husband's shape in mind.
Look, what an unthrift in the world doth spend
Shifts but his place, for still the world enjoys it;    10
But beauty's waste hath in the world an end,
And kept unus'd, the user so destroys it.
   No love toward others in that bosom sits
   That on himself such murd'rous shame commits.

## 10

For shame! deny that thou bear'st love to any,
Who for thyself art so unprovident.
Grant, if thou wilt, thou art belov'd of many,
But that thou none lov'st is most evident;
For thou art so possess'd with murd'rous hate           5
That 'gainst thyself thou stick'st not to conspire,
Seeking that beauteous roof to ruinate
Which to repair should be thy chief desire.
O, change thy thought, that I may change my mind!
Shall hate be fairer lodg'd than gentle love?          10

Be, as thy presence is, gracious and kind,
Or to thyself at least kind-hearted prove:
Make thee another self for love of me,
That beauty still may live in thine or thee.

12

When I do count the clock that tells the time,
And see the brave day sunk in hideous night;
When I behold the violet past prime,
And sable curls [all] silver'd o'er with white;
When lofty trees I see barren of leaves                5
Which erst from heat did canopy the herd,
And summer's green all girded up in sheaves
Borne on the bier with white and bristly beard;
Then of thy beauty do I question make
That thou among the wastes of time must go,            10
Since sweets and beauties do themselves forsake
And die as fast as they see others grow;
  And nothing 'gainst Time's scythe can make defence
  Save breed, to brave him when he takes thee hence.

14

Not from the stars do I my judgement pluck,
And yet methinks I have astronomy;
But not to tell of good or evil luck,
Of plagues, of dearths, or seasons' quality;
Nor can I fortune to brief minutes tell,               5
'Pointing to each his thunder, rain, and wind,
Or say with princes if it shall go well,
By oft predict that I in heaven find:
But from thine eyes my knowledge I derive,
And, constant stars, in them I read such art           10
As "Truth and beauty shall together thrive,
If from thyself to store thou wouldst convert;"
  Or else of thee this I prognosticate:
  "Thy end is truth's and beauty's doom and date."

15

When I consider everything that grows
Holds in perfection but a little moment,
That this huge stage presenteth nought but shows
Whereon the stars in secret influence comment;
When I perceive that men as plants increase,           5
Cheered and check'd even by the self-same sky,

Vaunt in their youthful sap, at height decrease,
And wear their brave state out of memory;
Then the conceit of this inconstant stay
Sets you most rich in youth before my sight,          10
Where wasteful Time debateth with Decay
To change your day of youth to sullied night;
  And all in war with Time for love of you,
  As he takes from you, I engraft you new.


## 18

Shall I compare thee to a summer's day?
Thou art more lovely and more temperate:
Rough winds do shake the darling buds of May,
And summer's lease hath all too short a date;
Sometime too hot the eye of heaven shines,          5
And often is his gold complexion dimm'd;
And every fair from fair sometime declines,
By chance or nature's changing course untrimm'd:
But thy eternal summer shall not fade
Nor lose possession of that fair thou ow'st;          10
Nor shall Death brag thou wand'rest in his shade,
When in eternal lines to time thou grow'st;
  So long as men can breathe or eyes can see,
  So long lives this, and this gives life to thee.


## 20

A woman's face with Nature's own hand painted
Hast thou, the master-mistress of my passion;
A woman's gentle heart, but not acquainted
With shifting change, as is false women's fashion;
An eye more bright than theirs, less false in rolling,          5
Gilding the object whereupon it gazeth;
A man in hue all hues in his controlling,
Which steals men's eyes and women's souls amazeth.
And for a woman wert thou first created;
Till Nature, as she wrought thee, fell a-doting,          10
And by addition me of thee defeated
By adding one thing to my purpose nothing.
  But since she prick'd thee out for women's pleasure,
  Mine be thy love, and thy love's use their treasure.


## 29

When, in disgrace with Fortune and men's eyes,
I all alone beweep my outcast state,

And trouble deaf heaven with my bootless cries,
And look upon myself and curse my fate,
Wishing me like to one more rich in hope,                    5
Featur'd like him, like him with friends possess'd,
Desiring this man's art, and that man's scope,
With what I most enjoy contented least;
Yet in these thoughts myself almost despising,
Haply I think on thee; and then my state,                    10
Like to the lark at break of day arising
From sullen earth, sings hymns at heaven's gate;
   For thy sweet love rememb'red such wealth brings
   That then I scorn to change my state with kings.


### 30

When to the sessions of sweet silent thought
I summon up remembrance of things past,
I sigh the lack of many a thing I sought,
And with old woes new wail my dear time's waste.
Then can I drown an eye, unus'd to flow,                    5
For precious friends hid in death's dateless night,
And weep afresh love's long since cancell'd woe,
And moan th' expense of many a vanish'd sight.
Then can I grieve at grievances foregone,
And heavily from woe to woe tell o'er                    10
The sad account of fore-bemoaned moan,
Which I new pay as if not paid before.
   But if the while I think on thee, dear friend,
   All losses are restor'd and sorrow's end.


### 53

What is your substance, whereof are you made,
That millions of strange shadows on you tend?
Since every one hath, every one, one shade,
And you, but one, can every shadow lend.
Describe Adonis, and the counterfeit                    5
Is poorly imitated after you;
On Helen's cheek all art of beauty set,
And you in Grecian tires are painted new.
Speak of the spring and foison of the year:
The one doth shadow of your beauty show,                    10
The other as your bounty doth appear;
And you in every blessed shape we know.
   In all external grace you have some part,
   But you like none, none you, for constant heart.

## 55

Not marble nor the gilded monuments
Of princes shall outlive this pow'rful rhyme;
But you shall shine more bright in these contents
Than unswept stone besmear'd with sluttish time.
When wasteful war shall statues overturn,                    5
And broils root out the work of masonry,
Nor Mars his sword nor war's quick fire shall burn
The living record of your memory.
'Gainst death and all-oblivious enmity
Shall you pace forth; your praise shall still find room       10
Even in the eyes of all posterity
That wear this world out to the ending doom.
   So, till the Judgement that yourself arise,
   You live in this, and dwell in lovers' eyes.

## 65

Since brass, nor stone, nor earth, nor boundless sea,
But sad mortality o'er-sways their power,
How with this rage shall beauty hold a plea,
Whose action is no stronger than a flower?
O, how shall summer's honey breath hold out                  5
Against the wreckful siege of batt'ring days,
When rocks impregnable are not so stout,
Nor gates of steel so strong, but Time decays?
O fearful meditation! Where, alack,
Shall Time's best jewel from Time's chest lie hid?           10
Or what strong hand can hold his swift foot back?
Or who his spoil [of] beauty can forbid?
   O, none, unless this miracle have might,
   That in black ink my love may still shine bright.

## 73

That time of year thou mayst in me behold
When yellow leaves, or none, or few, do hang
Upon those boughs which shake against the cold,
Bare [ruin'd] choirs where late the sweet birds sang.
In me thou see'st the twilight of such day                   5
As after sunset fadeth in the west,
Which by and by black night doth take away,
Death's second self, that seals up all in rest.
In me thou see'st the glowing of such fire
That on the ashes of his youth doth lie,                     10

As the death-bed whereon it must expire,
Consum'd with that which it was nourish'd by.
  This thou perceiv'st, which makes thy love more strong,
  To love that well which thou must leave ere long.

### 87

Farewell! thou art too dear for my possessing,
And like enough thou know'st thy estimate.
The charter of thy worth gives thee releasing;
My bonds in thee are all determinate.
For how do I hold thee but by thy granting,      5
And for that riches where is my deserving?
The cause of this fair gift in me is wanting,
And so my patent back again is swerving.
Thyself thou gav'st, thy own worth then not knowing,
Or me, to whom thou gav'st it, else mistaking;     10
So thy great gift, upon misprision growing,
Comes home again, on better judgement making.
  Thus have I had thee as a dream doth flatter—
  In sleep a king, but waking no such matter.

### 93

So shall I live, supposing thou art true,
Like a deceived husband; so love's face
May still seem love to me, though alter'd new—
Thy looks with me, thy heart in other place.
For there can live no hatred in thine eye;     5
Therefore in that I cannot know thy change.
In many's looks the false heart's history
Is writ in moods and frowns and wrinkles strange;
But heaven in thy creation did decree
That in thy face sweet love should ever dwell;     10
Whate'er thy thoughts or thy heart's workings be,
Thy looks should nothing thence but sweetness tell.
  How like Eve's apple doth thy beauty grow,
  If thy sweet virtue answer not thy show!

### 94

They that have pow'r to hurt and will do none,
That do not do the thing they most do show,
Who, moving others, are themselves as stone,
Unmoved, cold, and to temptation slow,
They rightly do inherit heaven's graces     5
And husband nature's riches from expense;

They are the lords and owners of their faces,
Others but stewards of their excellence.
The summer's flow'r is to the summer sweet
Though to itself it only live and die,                    10
But if that flow'r with base infection meet,
The basest weed outbraves his dignity:
    For sweetest things turn sourest by their deeds;
    Lilies that fester smell far worse than weeds.


### 95

How sweet and lovely dost thou make the shame
Which, like a canker in the fragrant rose,
Doth spot the beauty of thy budding name!
O, in what sweets dost thou thy sins enclose!
That tongue that tells the story of thy days,            5
Making lascivious comments on thy sport,
Cannot dispraise but in a kind of praise;
Naming thy name blesses an ill report.
O, what a mansion have those vices got
Which for their habitation chose out thee,               10
Where beauty's veil doth cover every blot
And all things turns to fair that eyes can see!
    Take heed, dear heart, of this large privilege;
    The hardest knife ill-us'd doth lose his edge.


### 106

When in the chronicle of wasted time
I see descriptions of the fairest wights,
And beauty making beautiful old rhyme
In praise of ladies dead and lovely knights;
Then, in the blazon of sweet beauty's best,              5
Of hand, of foot, of lip, of eye, of brow,
I see their antique pen would have express'd
Even such a beauty as you master now.
So all their praises are but prophecies
Of this our time, all you prefiguring;                   10
And, for they look'd but with divining eyes,
They had not [skill] enough your worth to sing:
    For we, which now behold these present days,
    Have eyes to wonder, but lack tongues to praise.


### 107

Not mine own fears, nor the prophetic soul
Of the wide world, dreaming on things to come,

Can yet the lease of my true love control,
Suppos'd as forfeit to a confin'd doom.
The mortal moon hath her eclipse endur'd, 5
And the sad augurs mock their own presage;
Incertainties now crown themselves assur'd,
And peace proclaims olives of endless age.
Now with the drops of this most balmy time
My love looks fresh, and Death to me subscribes, 10
Since, spite of him, I'll live in this poor rhyme,
While he insults o'er dull and speechless tribes:
 And thou in this shalt find thy monument,
 When tyrants' crests and tombs of brass are spent.

### 116

Let me not to the marriage of true minds
Admit impediments. Love is not love
Which alters when it alteration finds,
Or bends with the remover to remove.
O, no! it is an ever-fixed mark 5
That looks on tempests and is never shaken;
It is the star to every wand'ring bark,
Whose worth's unknown, although his height be taken.
Love's not Time's fool, though rosy lips and cheeks
Within his bending sickle's compass come; 10
Love alters not with his brief hours and weeks,
But bears it out even to the edge of doom.
 If this be error and upon me proved,
 I never writ, nor no man ever loved.

### 129

Th' expense of spirit in a waste of shame
Is lust in action; and till action, lust
Is perjur'd, murd'rous, bloody, full of blame,
Savage, extreme, rude, cruel, not to trust;
Enjoy'd no sooner but despised straight, 5
Past reason hunted, and no sooner had
Past reason hated, as a swallow'd bait
On purpose laid to make the taker mad;
[Mad] in pursuit and in possession so;
Had, having, and in quest to have, extreme; 10
A bliss in proof, and [prov'd, a] very woe;
Before, a joy propos'd; behind, a dream.
 All this the world well knows; yet none knows well
 To shun the heaven that leads men to this hell.

### 146

Poor soul, the centre of my sinful earth,
Fool'd by these rebel powers that thee array!
Why dost thou pine within and suffer dearth,
Painting thy outward walls so costly gay?
Why so large cost, having so short a lease,    5
Dost thou upon thy fading mansion spend?
Shall worms, inheritors of this excess,
Eat up thy charge?  Is this thy body's end?
Then, soul, live thou upon thy servant's loss,
And let that pine to aggravate thy store;    10
Buy terms divine in selling hours of dross:
Within be fed, without be rich no more.
   So shalt thou feed on Death that feeds on men,
   And Death once dead, there's no more dying then.

## Robert Gorham Davis

### SHAKESPEARE
### SONNETS

If the word "wrong" is permissible where literary pleasures are concerned, then we must agree that it is easy to be fascinated by Shakespeare's sonnets for the wrong reasons. Sometimes these keep us from appreciating the sonnets for the right ones.

The wrong reasons are encouraged by the mystery of the man who wrote the poems. Shakespeare, after all, by general consensus is the greatest poet who ever lived, and his life was not so very remote from us in time. When he was at the height of his powers, English settlement had already begun in North America. Some of his plays had command performances at one of the most brilliant and literate courts that ever existed in the West. Yet of the man himself, who sat at a table in some room or other, year after year, writing the speeches of Lear, Falstaff, Katherine, Cleopatra, speaking magically in all those different voices—of the man himself, the creator.of so much, we know virtually nothing.

Socrates, St. Paul, Ovid, Augustine, Abelard, Dante and Montaigne speak to us freely across the ages in their own voices, articulating their deepest and most personal concerns. Shakespeare, the supremely eloquent, keeps silent about such matters, and the silence baffles and frustrates us. We live in a period in which we cannot rest until the utmost intimacies are laid bare. All we have of Shakespeare are a few legal documents, some doubtful legends, and the frank, obviously heartfelt tribute of Ben Jonson, a fellow genius. This tribute alone is enough to take care of the Baconians, to assure us that Shakespeare was indeed Shakespeare and wrote Shakespeare's plays. But any biography which runs to more than three pages has to be concocted from surmises and inferences, usually of the wilder kind. We know as little about Shakespeare as about Aeschylus and Sophocles, though they lived two thousand years before him.

Can one find the man himself in the characters of his

plays? No, he is too complete a dramatist for that. Each character is superbly formed at once to meet and transcend the requirements of the particular theme and plot and situation. Shakespeare is neither any one character, or all together. The range of types is too great. They are not, like Hemingway's heroes, the enlarged and sentimentalized portrait of their maker. They represent the extremes of human possibility as a Renaissance man, well read in a few classics, conceived them. It is tempting, of course, to find Shakespeare in Hamlet, yet this is purely wishful. Both are enigmatic. Both play ironically with words. But most cultivated Elizabethans played with words. Shakespeare simply was better at it than anybody else. He retired in prosperity to the best house in Stratford and applied for a family coat of arms. Whatever unknown inner torment he suffered, he was no Danish prince contending with a murderous, usurping uncle. At least not any more than he was a Moorish general or a Welsh private soldier—or Bottom or Ariel or Caliban.

This leaves us only the sonnets to puzzle over, which are not dramatic, but lyric. According to theory, the pure dramatist projects himself so completely into the imagined world of the play, subordinates himself so completely to its requirements, that no trace of his private personality remains. In the lyric, on the other hand, the poet is supposed to take the world into himself, dominate it, color it with his own personality and moods.

In the sonnets Shakespeare actually says "I." He is not telling sad stories of the death of kings but—it would seem— talking of his own experiences in his own proper voice. No wonder these poems have been seized on with desperate eagerness and forced to provide keys to the puzzle of his life and character, as if they were in the same class as Plato's Seventh Letter about his experiences with the Tyrant of Syracuse, or Ovid's verse epistles from bitter exile near the Black Sea. Historical documents are combed to find the names and real histories of the handsome youth, the dark lady, the rival poet. The sonnets were probably not printed in an order established by Shakespeare himself, so there is the fun of rearranging them to bring out more clearly the presumed life story hidden in them.

But if we respond to the poems fully for what they really are, we learn that the promise of autobiographical revelation is a distracting mirage. Here are characters, too, just as in the plays—the character of the poet, the poet's beautiful friend, the rival poet, the mistress. But with no defined plot, no *mise en scène*, no named places and people, the characters remain far more generalized and ideal than in the plays. The poet is representing kinds of being, modes of being, provided him by a well-established literary tradition coming from earlier classic times through Provence and Italy, and already practiced in England by a host of accomplished sonneteers. Shakespeare accepted the tradition as given and felt no need to introduce into it the peculiarities of his personal history, whatever they may have been. Here is a totally different world from that of the *Great and Small Testaments* of François Villon. Born a century and a third earlier, Villon is much more modern by our standards with his bitter specificity, his highly realistic catalogues of object, places, events and historical personages.

The impersonality of Shakespeare's poetic attitude is evident in the several poems offering immortality to his friend. This does not in the least mean that the character and deeds of the friend will be made known as Thucydides made Alcibiades known; or Plutarch, Antony. The lines give life, but only by memorializing what is universal in the experience of love and friendship, not what is peculiar and private. The beauty of the friend becomes beauty itself, symbolized as eternal summer. Preserved in unchanging words, it never fades so long as man can read. But the "thee" given continual life by the words does not—and should not—appear to the reader as some unique individual with a name, parents, a certain color of hair, certain gestures, a university career, his body later buried in a still existing and identifiable grave. Nor are there existential moments, as in the poems of Donne, when we are made conscious of the grotesque mingling of elements in immediately lived experience. When Shakespeare speaks of his own—or rather the poet's—dissatisfactions, doubts and regrets, or when he cites, always in very general terms, changes wrought by time and history, it is simply to affirm emphatically by contrast the permanence of ideal beauty reflected over and over again in the passing temporal beauties of the real world.

Shakespeare is close to Platonism. As in the *Symposium* or *Timaeus* or *Protagoras*, a beautiful youth is important because he calls forth the pure experience of beauty itself. This can be captured in words, for words symbolize concepts, ideas, essences, and if they are beautiful words, beautifully arranged, they heighten our capacity for contemplating the ideas of beauty carried in the words. Since the "thee" or "you" can be any person evoking love and the sense of beauty, he is more appropriately described by metaphors, names of flowers, for instance, than by his own name and distinctive modes of behavior. For the same reasons, Shakespeare is content to mention those flowers which most traditionally symbolize beauty—roses and lilies, for instance. Sometimes he merely says "flower." In the plays he is much more specific, as in Perdita's speech in *The Winter's Tale* (IV, iv) about pale primroses and bold oxlips and daffodils "that come before the swallow dares."

In the sonnets intensity is achieved not by specification but hyperbole. For Shakespeare, though, it is not false hyperbole. For him the *idea* of beauty is always superior to any particular temporal embodiment of it. In number six, when he wants to celebrate the beauty of the human body, he boldly makes his friend exceed the two traditional exemplars of physical loveliness, Adonis and Helen. It does not matter that Adonis is masculine and Helen feminine. Ideal beauty knows no differentiation by sex. Such Platonism explains why, in the sonnets, a male beloved is addressed in terms which seem more suited to a woman. Shakespeare was no homosexual, however, though the homosexuals have often claimed him as one of their own. He rules out this possibility in a witty, brutally specific word play in the sonnet beginning, "A woman's face. . . ."

That beauty as such is more important than the identity of its particular embodiment is also expressed in the frequent sonnets urging the beautiful young man to marry. Beauty's rose never dies so long as new roses spring up. Age finds its golden time renewed in children and grandchildren.

But if the sonnets are impersonal and treat traditional generalized images, what gives them their distinction, makes them so beloved? As contrasted with the plays, where event and truth, history and imagination, the particular and the general, marvelously combine, the power and beauty of the sonnets are almost purely verbal. This is different from saying that they are *merely* verbal. The rhymes, assonances, repetitions and other musical effects of all kinds are designed to demonstrate and reinforce the idea of beauty carried conceptually by the words.

Sometimes assonances and internal rhyme are foremost, as in the third sonnet:

*For where is she so fair whose uneared womb*

Here the easy musical rhyme of *where* and *fair* leads us
through assonance to the bold, almost catachrestical figure of
the "uneared womb" that "disdains the tillage of thy husbandry." Through the punning play on "husbandry," the
ears of corn or grain are identified with the child brought forth
from a womb. Conventional metaphors never become dead
metaphors for Shakespeare; to keep both the literal and
figurative meanings alive for us he often brings them together
with an intentional effect of shock.

Sometimes Shakespeare plays with the different grammatical or lexical forms of a word:

> *And beauty making beautiful old rhyme*

or

> *Which alters when it alteration find*

or

> *And death, once dead, there's no more dying then*

Sometimes he extends sequences of monosyllables, as in

> *Of hand, of foot, of lip, of eye, of brow*

or

> *Since brass, nor stone, nor earth, nor boundless sea*

Here the introduction of the dissyllabic adjective "boundless"
provides a dramatic pause at the same time that it intensifies
the imaginative expansion of vision.

The sonnets, even some of the best known of them, are by
no means perfect. Many were probably written early, experi-
mentally, while Shakespeare was learning his craft, and were
published without his consent or editorial assistance. They
have faults that go naturally with their virtues. Word plays
and metaphoric elaboration are often too ingenious, or sustained longer than their intrinsic suggestiveness warrants, as
in the use of a commercial vocabulary in numbers nine and
fifteen, or the changes rung on *shade* and *shadow* in number
six. Sometimes the syntax becomes too charged and involuted
for lyric grace, as in numbers ten and fourteen.

In Shakespeare's chosen form of the sonnet, the final
rhymed couplet is a problem. Often these two rhyme-linked
lines fail to provide an organic climax or completion for what
has gone before. The couplet tends to detach itself as a
self-sufficient observation or aphorism. In number nine, for
instance, the final couplet introduces a quite different comparison from the one so carefully sustained in the twelve preced-

ing lines. The conclusion often makes us uncomfortably conscious of the necessities of rhyme, especially since Shakespeare is sometimes lazy and ends a sonnet with an inadequate final word that happens to rhyme, instead of recasting lines thirteen and fourteen until both end with words which not only rhyme but are strong and right in meaning. In sonnet number twelve, tombs of brass have to be "spent" for no good reason except that "spent" rhymes with "monument" in the much firmer preceding line.

But since we know Shakespeare only as an artist, these flaws in early work make him more human, more approachable. We watch his love of words and of the manipulation of words develop into the love of ideas and of ideal beauty expressed through words. And without going further biographically than the poems themselves warrant, we can see being laid here the basis of a philosophy of life which carried him through the anguish of the great tragedies into the relative tranquillity of his final dramatic and poetic phase. The traditional expression of the persistence of beauty, truth, and love becomes more than traditional, becomes a genuine matter of conviction that stood the test of the profoundest dramatic exploration of evil and suffering. By the evidence of the sonnets and plays together, the sweetness and strength of character celebrated by Ben Jonson were not qualities merely given Shakespeare by luck and temperament, but achieved and maintained through concordant disciplines in art and thought and life.

# William Empson

## SHAKESPEARE
## THEY THAT HAVE POW'R TO HURT
## AND WILL DO NONE

It is agreed that "They that have pow'r to hurt and will do none" is a piece of grave irony, but there the matter is generally left; you can work through all the notes in the variorum without finding out whether flower, lily, "owner," and person addressed are alike or opposed. One would like to say that the poem has all possible such meanings, digested into some order, and then try to show how this is done, but the mere number of possible interpretations is amusingly too great. Taking the simplest view (that any two may be alike in some one property), any one of the four either is or is not and either should or should not be like each of the others, yields 4,096 possible movements of thought, with other possibilities. The niggler is routed here; one has honestly to consider what seems important.

"The best people are indifferent to temptation and detached from the world; nor is this state selfish, because they do good by unconscious influence, like the flower. You must be like them; you are quite like them already. But even the best people must be continually on their guard, because they become the worst, just as the pure and detached lily smells worst, once they fall from their perfection." ("One's prejudice against them is only one's consciousness of this fact"— the hint of irony in the poem might be covered by this.) It is a coherent enough Confucian sentiment, and there is no very clear hint of irony in the words. No doubt *as stone* goes intentionally too far for sympathy, and there is a suggestive gap in the argument between octet and sestet, but one would not feel this if it were Shakespeare's only surviving work.

There is no reason why the subtlety of the irony in so complex a material must be capable of being pegged out into verbal explanations. The vague and generalized language of the descriptions, which might be talking about so many sorts of people as well as feeling so many things about them, somehow makes a unity like a crossroads, which analysis does not deal with by exploring down the roads; makes a solid flute on which you can play a multitude of tunes, whose solidity no list of all possible tunes would go far to explain. The balance of feeling is both very complex and very fertile; experiences are recorded, and metaphors invented, in the sonnets, which he went on "applying" as a dramatist, taking particular cases of them as if they were wide generalizations, for the rest of his life. One can't expect, in writing about such a process, to say anything very tidy and complete.

But one does not start interpreting out of the void, even though the poem, once partly interpreted, seems to stand on its own. If this were Shakespeare's only surviving work it would still be clear, supposing one knew about the other Elizabethans, that it involves somehow their feelings about the Machiavellian, the wicked plotter who is exciting and civilized and in some way right about life; which seems an important though rather secret element in the romance that Shakespeare extracted from his patron. In any case one has only to look at the sonnets before and after it to be sure that it has some kind of irony. The one before is full of fear and horror at the hypocrisy he is so soon to recommend; and yet it is already somehow cuddled, as if in fascination or out of a refusal to admit that it was there.

So the "summer's flow'r" may be its appleblossom. His virtue is still sweet, whether he has any or not; the clash of fact with platonic idealism is too fearful to be faced directly. In the sonnet after, with a blank and exhausted humility, it has been faced; there remains for the expression of his love, in the least flaunting of poetry, the voice of caution.

*How sweet and lovely dost thou make the shame*

. . .

*Take heed, dear heart, of this large privilege*

The praise of hypocrisy is in a crucial and precarious condition of balance between these two states of mind.

The root of the ambivalence, I think, is that W. H., to whom the sonnets are addressed, is loved as an *arriviste*, for an impudent worldliness that Shakespeare finds shocking and delightful. The reasons why he treated his poet badly are the same as the reasons why he was fascinating, which gives its immediate point to the profound ambivalence about the selfishness of the flower. Perhaps he is like the cold person in his hardness and worldly judgment, not in his sensuality and generosity of occasional impulse; like the flower in its beauty, vulnerability, tendency to excite thoughts about the shortness of life, self-centeredness and power in spite of it to give pleasure, not in its innocence and fertility; but the irony may make any of these change over. Both owner and flower seem self-centered and inscrutable, and the cold person is at least like the lily in that it is symbolically chaste, but the summer's flower, unlike the lily, seems to stand for the full life of instinct. It is not certain that the owner is liable to fester as the lily is—Angelo did, but W. H. is usually urged to acquire the virtues of Angelo. Clearly there is a jump from octet to sestet; the flower is not like the owner in its solitude and its incapacity to hurt or simulate; it might be because of this that it is of a summer only and may fester; yet we seem chiefly meant to hold W. H. in mind and take them as parallel.

They may *show*, while hiding the alternative, for the first couplet, the power to hurt or the determination not to hurt, cruelty or mercy; for the second, the strength due to chastity or to sensual experience; for either, a reckless or cautious will, and the desire for love or for control—all whether they are stealers of hearts or of public power. They are a very widespread group; we are only sure at the end that some kind of hypocrisy has been advised and threatened.

> *They rightly do inherit heaven's graces*
> *And husband nature's riches from expense;*

Either "inherit, they alone, by right" or "inherit what all men inherit and use it rightly"; these correspond to the opposed views of W. H. as aristocrat and vulgar careerist. There is a similar range of idea, half hidden by the pretence of easy filling of the form, in the pun on *graces* and shift to *riches*. "Heaven's graces" may be prevenient grace (strength from God to do well); or personal graces that seem to imply heavenly virtues (the charm by which you deceive people); or merely God's gracious gift of *nature's riches*, which again may be the personal graces, or the strength and taste that make him capable either of "upholding his house" or of taking his pleasure, or merely the actual wealth of which he is an *owner*. Clearly this gives plenty of room for irony in the statement that the cold people, with their fine claims, do well all round; it also conveys "I am seeing you as a whole; I am seeing these things as necessary rather than as your fault."

> *They are the lords and owners of their faces,*
> *Others, but stewards of their excellence.*

It may be their beauty they put to their own uses, high or low, or they may just have poker-faces; this gives the same range of statement. Others may be stewards of their own excellence (in contrast with *faces*—"though they are enslaved they may be better and less superficial than the cold people") or of the cold people's excellence (with a suggestion of "Their Excellencies"); the less plausible sense is insisted on by the comma after *others*. This repeats the doubt about how far the cold people are really excellent, and there may be a hint of a doubt about how far the individual is isolated, which anticipates the metaphor of the flower. And "stewards of their own excellence" may be like "stewards of the buttery" or like "stewards of a certain lord"; either "the good things they have do good to others, not to them" (they are too generous; I cannot ask you to aim so high in virtue, because I desire your welfare, not other people's, and indeed because you wouldn't do it anyway) or "they are under the power of their own impulses, which are good things so long as they are not in power" (they are deceived; acts caused by weakness are not really generous at all). Yet this may be the condition of the flower and the condition for fullness of life; you cannot know beforehand what life will bring you if you open yourself to it, and certainly the flower does not; it is because they are unnatural and unlike flowers that the cold people rule nature, and the cost may be too great. Or the flower and the cold person may be two unlike examples of the limitation necessary to success, one experienced in its own nature, the other in the world; both, the irony would imply, are in fact *stewards*.

A Christian parable is at work in both octet and sestet; in the octet, that of the talents. You will not be forgiven for hoarding your talents; some sort of success is demanded; you must at least use your powers to the full even if for your own squalid purpose. The pain and wit and solemnity of *rightly*, its air of summing up a long argument, depend on the fact that these metaphors have been used to recommend things to W. H. before.

> *Natures bequest gives nothing but doth lend,*
> *And being frank she lends to those are free:*
>
> *Who lets so fair a house fall to decay,*
> *Which husbandry in honour might uphold,*

Rightly to be free with yourself, in the first simple paradox, was the best saving of yourself (you should put your money into marriage and a son); it is too late now to advise that, or to say it without being sure to be understood wrongly (this is 94; the first sonnet about his taking Shakespeare's mistress is 40); the advice to be generous as natural has become the richer but more contorted advice to be like the flower. Rightly to husband nature's riches, earlier in the sequence, was to accept the fact that one is only steward of them;

> *Thou that art now the world's fresh ornament*
> *And only herald to the gaudy spring,*
> *Within thine own bud buriest thy content,*
> *And, tender churl, mak'st waste in niggarding.*

the flower was wrong to live to itself alone, and would become a tattered weed (2) whether it met with infection or not.

Though indeed *husbandry* is still recommended; it is not the change of opinion that has so much effect, but the use of the same metaphors with a shift of feeling in them. The legal metaphors (debts to nature and so forth) used for the loving complaint that the man's chastity was selfish are still used when he becomes selfish in his debauchery; Shakespeare's own notation here seems to teach him; the more curiously because the metaphors were used so flatly in the earliest sonnets (1, 2, 4, 6, then 13; not again till now), only formally urging marriage, and perhaps written to order. It is like using a mathematical identity which implies a proof about a particular curve and then finding that it has a quite new meaning if you take the old constants as variables. It is these metaphors that have grown, till they involve relations between a man's powers and their use, his nature and his will, the individual and the society, which could be applied afterwards to all human circumstances.

> *The summer's flower is to the summer sweet,*
> *Though to itself, it only live and die*

The use of *the* summer's flower about a human being is enough to put it at us that the flower will die by the end of summer, that the man's life is not much longer, and that the pleasures of the creature therefore cannot be despised for what they are. *Sweet to the summer* (said of the flower), since the summer is omnipresent and in a way Nature herself, may mean "sweet to God" (said of the man); or may mean "adding to the general sweetness; sweet to everybody that comes across it in its time." It may do good to others, though not by effort, or may simply be a good end in itself (or combining these, may only be able to do good by concentrating on itself as an end); a preparatory evasion of the central issue about egotism.

Either "though it lives only for itself" or "though, in its own opinion, so far as it can see, it does no more than live and die." In the first it is a rose, extravagant and doing good because the public likes to see it flaunting; in the second a violet, humble and doing good in private through an odor of sanctity. It is the less plausible sense which is insisted on in editions that place a comma after *itself*. Or you may well say that the flower is neither, but the final lily; the whole passage is hinting at the lilies of the field like whom Solomon was not arrayed.

This parable itself combines what the poem so ingeniously keeps on combining; the personal power of beauty and the political power of wisdom; so as to imply that the political power has in itself a sort of beauty and the personal beauty, however hollow it may be, a sort of moral grandeur through power. But in England "consider the lilies of the field," were we not at once told of their glory, would suggest lilies-of-the-valley; that name indeed occurs in the "Song of Solomon," in surprising correspondence to the obviously grandiose Rose of Sharon. Shakespeare, I think, had done what the inventor of the name must have done, had read into the random flower-names of the Bible the same rich clash of suggestion—an implied mutual comparison that elevates both parties—as he makes here between the garden flower and the wild flower. The first sense (the rose) gives the root idea—"a brilliant aristocrat like you gives great pleasure by living as he likes; for such a person the issue of selfishness does not arise"; this makes W. H. a Renaissance Magnificent Man, combining all the virtues with a manysidedness like that of these phrases about him. The unlikeness of the cold people and the flowers, if you accept them as like, then implies "man is not placed like flowers and though he had best imitate them may be misled in doing so; the Machiavellian is much more really like the flower than the Swain is." And yet there is a suggestion in the comparison to the flower (since only beauty is demanded of it—sonnet 54 made an odd and impermanent attempt at quelling this doubt by equating truth with scent) that W. H. has only power to keep up an air of reconciling in himself the inconsistent virtues, or even of being a Machiavellian about the matter, and that it is this that puts him in danger like the flower. Or however genuine he may be, he is pathetic; such a man is all too "natural"; there is no need to prop up our ideas about him with an aristocratic "artificial" flower. So this class-centered praise is then careful half to hide itself by adding the second sense and the humble flower, and this leads it to a generalization: "all men do most good to others by fulfilling their own natures." Full as they are of Christian echoes, the sonnets are concerned with an idea strong enough to be balanced against Christianity: they state the opposite to the idea of self-sacrifice.

But the machinery of the statement is peculiar; its clash of admiration and contempt seems dependent on a clash of feeling about the classes. One might connect it with that curious trick of pastoral that for extreme courtly flattery—perhaps to give self-respect to both poet and patron, to show that the poet is not ignorantly easy to impress, nor the patron to flatter—writes about the poorest people; and with those jazz songs that give an intense effect of luxury and silk underwear by pretending to be about slaves naked in the fields. To those who care chiefly about biography, this trick must seem monstrously tantalizing: Wilde built the paradox of his essay on it, and it is true that Shakespeare might have set the whole thing to work from the other end about a highly trained mudlark brought in to act his princesses. But it is the very queerness of the trick that makes it so often useful in building models of the human mind; and yet the power, no less than the universality, of this poem depends on generalizing the trick so completely as to seem independent of it.

> *But if that flow'r with base infection meet,*
> *The basest weed outbraves his dignity:*
> *For sweetest things turn sourest by their deeds;*
> *Lilies that fester smell far worse than weeds.*

It is not clear how the metaphor from "meet" acts; it may be like "meet with disaster"—"if it catches infection, which would be bad luck," or like meeting someone in the street, as most men do safely—"*any* contact with infection is fatal to so peculiarly placed a creature." The first applies to the natural and unprotected flower, the second to the lily that has the hubris and fate of greatness. They are not of course firmly separated, but *lilies* are separated from the *flower* by a colon and an intervening generalization, whereas the flower is only separated from the cold people (not all of whom need be lilies) by a colon; certainly the flower as well as the lily is in danger, but this does not make them identical and equal to W. H. The neighboring sonnets continually say that his deeds can do nothing to destroy his sweetness, and this seems to make the terrible last line point at him somewhat less directly. One may indeed take it as "Though so debauched, you keep your looks. Only mean people who never give themselves heartily to anything can do that. But the best hypocrite is found out in the end, and shown as the worst." But Shakespeare may also be congratulating W. H. on an imperfection which acts as a preservative; he is a son of the world and can protect himself, like the cold people, or a spontaneous and therefore fresh sinner, like the flower; he may safely stain, as heaven's sun, the kisser of carrion, staineth. At any rate it is not of virginity, at this stage, that he can be accused. The smell of a big lily is so lush and insolent, suggests so powerfully both incense and pampered flesh—the traditional metaphor about it is so perfect—that its festering can only be that due to the hubris of spirituality; it is ironically generous to apply it to the careerist to whom hypocrisy is recommended; and yet in the fact that we seem meant to apply it to him there is a glance backwards, as if to justify him, at the ambition involved in even the most genuine attempt on heaven. You may say that Shakespeare dragged in the last line as a quotation from *Edward III* that doesn't quite fit; it is also possible that (as often happens to poets, who tend to make in their lives a situation they have already written about) he did not till now see the full width of its application.

In a sense the total effect is an evasion of Shakespeare's problem; it gives him a way of praising W. H. in spite of anything. In the flower the oppositions are transcended; it is because it is self-concentrated that it has so much to give and because it is undesigning that it is more grandiose in beauty than Solomon. But it is held in mind chiefly for comfort; none of the people suggested to us are able to imitate it very successfully; nor if they could would they be safe. Yet if W. H. has festered, that at least makes him a lily, and at least not a stone; if he is not a lily, he is in the less danger of festering.

I must try to sum up the effect of so complex an irony, half by trying to follow it through a gradation. "I am praising to you the contemptible things you admire, you little plotter; this is how the others try to betray you through flattery; yet it is your little generosity, though it show only as lewdness, which will betray you; for it is wise to be cold, both because you are too inflammable and because I have been so much hurt by you who are heartless; yet I can the better forgive you through that argument from our common isolation; I must praise to you your very faults, especially your selfish-

ness, because you can now be safe only by cultivating them
further; yet this is the most dangerous of necessities; people
are greedy for your fall as for that of any of the great;
indeed no one can rise above common life, as you have done
so fully, without in the same degree sinking below it; you
have made this advice real to me, because I cannot despise it
for your sake; I am only sure that you are valuable and in
danger."

# Speeches from the Plays

### THE LUNATIC, THE LOVER, AND THE POET

The lunatic, the lover, and the poet
Are of imagination all compact.
One sees more devils than vast hell can hold;
That is, the madman. The lover, all as frantic,
Sees Helen's beauty in a brow of Egypt.      5
The poet's eye, in a fine frenzy rolling,
Doth glance from heaven to earth, from earth to heaven;
And as imagination bodies forth
The forms of things unknown, the poet's pen
Turns them to shapes and gives to airy nothing      10
A local habitation and a name.

*A Midsummer-Night's Dream*, V, i

### ALL THE WORLD'S A STAGE

               All the world's a stage,
And all the men and women merely players.
They have their exits and their entrances,
And one man in his time plays many parts,
His acts being seven ages. At first the infant,      5
Mewling and puking in the nurse's arms.
Then the whining school-boy, with his satchel
And shining morning face, creeping like snail
Unwillingly to school. And then the lover,
Sighing like furnace, with a woeful ballad      10
Made to his mistress' eyebrow. Then a soldier,
Full of strange oaths, and bearded like the pard,
Jealous in honour, sudden, and quick in quarrel,
Seeking the bubble reputation
Even in the cannon's mouth. And then the justice,      15
In fair round belly with good capon lin'd,
With eyes severe and beard of formal cut,
Full of wise saws and modern instances;
And so he plays his part. The sixth age shifts
Into the lean and slipper'd pantaloon,      20
With spectacles on nose and pouch on side,

His youthful hose, well sav'd, a world too wide
For his shrunk shank; and his big manly voice,
Turning again toward childish treble, pipes
And whistles in his sound. Last scene of all,     25
That ends this strange eventful history,
Is second childishness and mere oblivion,
Sans teeth, sans eyes, sans taste, sans every thing.

*As You Like It*, II, vii


## HE JESTS AT SCARS

He jests at scars that never felt a wound.
But, soft! what light through yonder window breaks?
It is the east, and Juliet is the sun.
Arise, fair sun, and kill the envious moon,
Who is already sick and pale with grief     5
That thou, her maid, art far more fair than she.
Be not her maid, since she is envious;
Her vestal livery is but sick and green,
And none but fools do wear it; cast it off.
It is my lady, O, it is my love!     10
O, that she knew she were!
She speaks, yet she says nothing; what of that?
Her eye discourses; I will answer it.—
I am too bold, 'tis not to me she speaks.
Two of the fairest stars in all the heaven,     15
Having some business, [do] entreat her eyes
To twinkle in their spheres till they return.
What if her eyes were there, they in her head?
The brightness of her cheek would shame those stars,
As daylight doth a lamp; her eyes in heaven     20
Would through the airy region stream so bright
That birds would sing and think it were not night.
See, how she leans her cheek upon her hand!
O, that I were a glove upon that hand,
That I might touch that cheek!     25

*Romeo and Juliet*, II, ii


## TO-MORROW, AND TO-MORROW, AND TO-MORROW

To-morrow, and to-morrow, and to-morrow
Creeps in this petty pace from day to day
To the last syllable of recorded time;

And all our yesterdays have lighted fools
The way to dusty death. Out, out, brief candle!                    5
Life's but a walking shadow, a poor player
That struts and frets his hour upon the stage
And then is heard no more. It is a tale
Told by an idiot, full of sound and fury,
Signifying nothing.                                               10

*Macbeth*, V, vi


### AND THESE FEW PRECEPTS

And these few precepts in thy memory
See thou character. Give thy thoughts no tongue,
Nor any unproportion'd thought his act.
Be thou familiar, but by no means vulgar.
The friends thou hast, and their adoption tried,                  5
Grapple them to thy soul with hoops of steel;
But do not dull thy palm with entertainment
Of each [new]-hatch'd, unfledg'd comrade. Beware
Of entrance to a quarrel; but being in,
Bear 't that the opposed may beware of thee.                     10
Give every man thine ear, but few thy voice;
Take each man's censure, but reserve thy judgement.
Costly thy habit as thy purse can buy,
But not express'd in fancy; rich, not gaudy;
For the apparel oft proclaims the man,                           15
And they in France of the best rank and station
Are most select and generous in that.
Neither a borrower nor a lender be;
For loan oft loses both itself and friend,
And borrowing dulls the edge of husbandry.                       20
This above all: to thine own self be true,
And it must follow, as the night the day,
Thou canst not then be false to any man.
Farewell; my blessing season this in thee!

*Hamlet*, I, iii


### TO BE, OR NOT TO BE

To be, or not to be: that is the question.
Whether 'tis nobler in the mind to suffer
The slings and arrows of outrageous fortune,
Or to take arms against a sea of troubles,

And by opposing end them. To die; to sleep;                    5
No more; and by a sleep to say we end
The heart-ache and the thousand natural shocks
That flesh is heir to. 'Tis a consummation
Devoutly to be wish'd. To die; to sleep;—
To sleep? Perchance to dream! Ay, there's the rub;                    10
For in that sleep of death what dreams may come,
When we have shuffl'd off this mortal coil,
Must give us pause. There's the respect
That makes calamity of so long life:
For who would bear the whips and scorns of time,                    15
The oppressor's wrong, the [proud] man's contumely,
The pangs of dispriz'd love, the law's delay,
The insolence of office, and the spurns
That patient merit of the unworthy takes,
When he himself might his quietus make                    20
With a bare bodkin? Who would fardels bear,
To grunt and sweat under a weary life,
But that the dread of something after death,
The undiscover'd country from whose bourn
No traveller returns, puzzles the will                    25
And makes us rather bear those ills we have
Than fly to others that we know not of?
Thus conscience does make cowards of us all;
And thus the native hue of resolution
Is sicklied o'er with the pale cast of thought,                    30
And enterprises of great pith and moment
With this regard their currents turn [awry],
And lose the name of action.

*Hamlet*, III, i

# Walter James Miller

## SPEECHES FROM SHAKESPEARE'S PLAYS

About one hundred speeches in Shakespeare's plays can be enjoyed as separate poems; as a matter of fact, some of them are among the most widely known, quoted, and recited poems in world literature. The six we discuss here demonstrate the Bard's versatility in making memorable poetry out of almost any type of utterance. Essentially, the first three are statements of concepts, intellectual observations, while the others are lyric expressions of deep emotional states. They demonstrate too Shakespeare's easy mastery in word music, metaphor, sustained rhetoric, and—with few exceptions—his success in blending technique into overall effect.

"To thine own self be true" offers a package of precepts for personal success. Seven pat rules in practical matters, culminating in one grand generalization, are delivered in rapid-fire order. Each one is made memorable by the use of balance, antithesis, or contrast. Swift continuity is achieved through the metric regularity—most of the lines are "end-stopped" and adhere closely to the basic pattern of iambic pentameter:

*Give every man thine ear but few thy voice*

Subordinating figures of speech to speed, Shakespeare uses here only the simplest metaphors, involving easy concepts: hoops, night and day, and the cutting edge of a knife—the last perfectly appropriate for husbandry.

This speech by Polonius to his son illustrates one of the Bard's outstanding gifts—his ability to compress popular wisdom into proverbial statements. At least five of the neat formulations in this passage are in common use in writing and speaking today.

"All the world's a stage" combines two popular Renaissance ideas—we are all actors in the theater of life, and a man grows through seven stages of development—that are best known to us today through Shakespeare's expression of them. For this speaker (the "melancholy" Jaques), the poet uses a looser verse form—many of the lines contain extra syllables—and he can relax into more complex and sensuous imagery. Note the artistic selection of vital details—the aging man's "shrunk shank" and the soldier "full of strange oaths" —and the two magnificent and commonly quoted metaphors: the lover sighing like a furnace; the superb contrast between the floating, fragile bubble of glory and the solid cannon's blasting finality.

"The lunatic, the lover, and the poet" is a compact expression of the kinship between unique perspective, romance, and art. For the modern reader, it is marred only by the Elizabethan chauvinism in the smug idea that an African cannot be so beautiful as Helen of Troy; in such matters Shakespeare (or at least the speaker, Theseus) was a child of his day. But in other matters, like understanding the way art concretizes the imaginary—

> *. . . the poet's pen*
> *. . . gives to airy nothing*
> *A local habitation and a name*

—Shakespeare is an adult for all time.

The other passages illustrate Shakespeare's genius in recreating archetypal human situations; such powerful poetry has made Romeo, Hamlet, and Macbeth, the speakers in these last three selections, characters in world mythology.

The opening line, "He jests at scars that never felt a wound," is itself a permanent part of our proverbial lore, a pithy description of the critic whose knowledge of what he criticizes comes from observation not participation. It is also, we should note in these days of homage to Simone de Beauvoir, a good example of how men regard courtship as a species of warfare. The rest of the speech, in which Romeo contemplates his beloved from a distance, is a classic expression of the excesses of romantic wonderment and yearning. In a series of extravagant conceits, Juliet becomes the main source of the world's light. These flights of abstract celestial imagery suddenly culminate in a picture of direct physical contact, and the contrast is delicious.

"To be or not to be" is perhaps the most famous phrase in poetry, quoted freely in seventy-five languages to express that point in despair at which man contemplates suicide. In the second line, the phrase takes on a contrapuntal significance—to be active or passive?—with activity itself ironically recognized as a form of self-destruction. In graceful rhetoric —graceful although, as pedants fail to note, he ends two sentences with prepositions—Hamlet philosophizes toward the twin conclusions that the only reason to go on living is that death may be even worse a nightmare, and that such power to reason ("conscience" here means "consciousness") makes man puzzled, stymied, and passive. The metaphors are utterly functional, never drawing attention to themselves. The sweet sad music is achieved largely in successions of tuneful vowels; the movement begins in a loose blank verse (the first four lines each contain an extra syllable) that tightens when appropriate into a tense, emphatic iambic:

*For who would bear the whips and scorns of time*

. . .

*When he himself might his quietus make*

"To-morrow, and to-morrow, and to-morrow" sums up life's futility for the man who plays life against itself. The raving Macbeth wanders from image to image, each perfectly free-associated to the others, each making life as he has known it one or two removes from reality: a shadow, a play, an idiot's tale. The musical texture of the passage is so intricate as to defy belief, so invisible is it to ordinary scrutiny. In nine lines, there are four alliterations (*petty pace, dusty death*, etc.), eight assonant *ay* rhymes (*pace, player, stage,* etc.), and seventeen uses of the *s* sound, including the tight cross-stitchings of *s* and *f* in "struts and frets" and "Full of sound and fury, / Signifying nothing."

With such consummate artistry in every passage, it's plain to see why most lovers of poetry—including this writer—find it easier to quote Shakespeare than to explain him. Shakespeare, who would have agreed with Gertrude Stein that "a rose is a rose is a rose," would have preferred it that way.

# BEN JONSON
## [1573–1637]

### *To Celia*

Drink to me only with thine eyes,
 And I will pledge with mine;
Or leave a kiss but in the cup
 And I'll not look for wine.
The thirst that from the soul doth rise          5
 Doth ask a drink divine;
But might I of Jove's nectar sup,
 I would not change for thine.

I sent thee late a rosy wreath,
 Not so much honouring thee          10
As giving it a hope that there
 It could not wither'd be;
But thou thereon didst only breathe
 And sent'st it back to me;
Since when it grows, and smells, I swear,          15
 Not of itself but thee!

BEN JONSON

*The Bettmann Archive*

# Earle Birney

## JONSON
## TO CELIA

For the last two hundred years at least, Ben Jonson's "Drink
to me only with thine eyes" has been one of the best known
and most loved lyrics in the English language. So wedded are
words and music that it is difficult to pronounce its opening
line without beginning, within one's head at least, to sing it.
In this sense, it is one of our most authentic lyrics. It has
become, in fact, a sort of modern folk song, for its opening
quatrain, if not the whole poem, has entered into the common
Anglo-Saxon inheritance. It is sung by thousands today who
would not be able to guess who wrote the words. As for the
music, not even the specialist can tell us anything definite
about its origins. Jonson may never have heard his poem sung
at all, and certainly not to the tune we know, which was not
attached to it until the mid-eighteenth century. Since then
the music has attracted many arrangers, including even
Mozart, but the credit for the basic melody, which in its
precision and slow grace and suavity so perfectly matches the
words of Ben Jonson, can be given only to some unknown
composer of "ayres" from Tudor days.

So fresh still are these words, yet so typically "Renaissance" in their separate simplicity and the subtle elegance of
their total effect, that it is always a shock to the young
literary scholar to learn that Jonson composed them not in a
burst of spontaneous creativity but by fitting together, almost
word by word, his own translations of several prose passages
in four separate love letters written in classical Greek by an
obscure Athenian philosopher, Philostratus (A.D. circa 170–
245). "Drink to me with thine eyes only," wrote Philostratus,
"or, if thou wilt, putting the cup to thy lips, fill it with kisses
and so bestow it upon me." Parallels as close, from the same
"Epistles," have been found for every line of Jonson's poem,
including the adroit compliment paid to the lady after she has
sent back his garland of roses (the "rosy wreath").

Neither the discovery of Jonson's indebtedness, however,

nor even the fact that the poet himself never disclosed it, should shock us. Jonson's age did not share our notions of property rights in literature; and, in any case, Philostratus' work was, as we would say, "in the public domain." A poet today might conceivably work as close as this to an ancient source. Our concept of literary honesty, of course, would prompt him to attach some acknowledgment of his source. That Jonson did not do so cannot, however, be easily ascribed to dishonesty. He published this poem in the first folio collection of his work, in 1616. By that time his reputation was firmly established; and it was based, then as now, primarily on his achievements as a dramatist, in which he was acknowledged to be second only to his recently deceased friend, William Shakespeare. In masque writing he had no equal, and he was generally regarded, in the days of the first two Stuart kings, as England's most brilliant satirist and most learned wit and conversationalist. He had neither need nor motive to increase his literary stature with other men's buskins, and the small number of songs he wrote suggests that he was not ambitious to rival Herrick or other lyricists. Apart from a few songs with which he adorned his masques and some of his plays, his lyrics seem to have been composed largely for his own amusement. The educated upper class, who would be virtually the only readers of his "Forest" (the section, in his first collection, where he assembles his lyrics), were themselves sufficiently versed in Greek and Roman literature to assume that Jonson's poems, so obviously combining the virtues of verbal simplicity with very artful form, were indeed products of classical models—especially since Jonson's other work showed him to be steeped in the classics, and indeed a translator, on occasion, of Latin poets. For the great Ben to have called attention, in print, to his little song's debt to Philostratus would have been regarded as a piece of pedantry at least, if not of supererogation.

And what should be said now, of Philostratus? A sophist who wrote, among other things, a series of picturesque sketchès of his fellow philosophers, and a series of satiric-erotic "Alexandrine" letters—but his only really living work is contained within the sixteen lines of Ben Jonson's song "To Celia."

That Jonson could have fashioned it by a feat of translator's mosaic is remarkable enough, but the true achievement is something much more. It is to have created, out of careful bookishness and conscious labor, a poem that quite transcends the "academic," and achieves not only a glistening and

melodic unity all its own, but a charm that seems still rose-
fresh, and heady as wine. It is a charm that springs from a
peculiarly civilized gaiety, and is not remote from humor or
even, at moments, from self-parody. The poem's success, in
this mode, raises it far above the ordinary run of Jonson's
lyrics (which indeed smell of the night lamp) and places it
rather with the very best moments in his dramatic works,
where classical learning, intellectual ingenuity, and dexterous
wit suddenly fuse and are transmuted into clear and lovely
lyricism.

The clarity, of course, as with any poem written three and
a half centuries ago, is in danger of being lost by the changes
in the language. The twentieth century reader may need to
remind himself that love "pledges," like toasts, were made by
touching the lips to the wine cup and "supping"; and he may
not know that the Elizabethans could use the word "change"
where we must say, for fear of ambiguity, "accept in exchange."

These are negligible hurdles, and they trouble few. "The
most beautiful love song in our language" a recent compiler
of songs for schools calls it. And yet, if it is, the achievement
flies in the face of the belief, still widely held, that the purest
songs well up spontaneously and almost without effort, in
men, as it would seem to (but only seem) in birds. For the
evidence is plain not only that Jonson's poem was ingeniously
constructed out of Philostratus' prose but that it was subsequently reworked and polished till scarcely a phrase remained unaltered from its first draft. How carefully Jonson
sought to perfect the rhythm and to create the illusion of
spontaneity may be gleaned by noting some of the changes.
*Only*, in the first line, was an alteration from "Celia"; *I'll not
look for wine* was *I'll expect no wine; doth rise* was originally *proceed*. *Sip* becomes *sup; sent to thee, sent thee late.
To honour* becomes *honouring;* and *like itself* to *of itself*. By
such infinite small pains and calculations, such a poem is
brought to the full flowering of its music and its meaning.

It is possible, of course, still to prefer the sort of song that
is incontrovertibly spontaneous—that is, if one can be sure of
having found an example—lyrics more ingenuous than ingenious, and written out of real passion for a real woman.
Jonson did indeed remark that Celia was an anagram for
Alice, and he may well have written and presented the poem,
devotedly, to a flesh and blood woman—but only, perforce,
after he had made his preliminary pastiche from the Greek.
Certainly for Swinburne none of Jonson's songs, not even

this, for all their "vigour of thought, purity of phrase, condensed and polished rhetoric, refined and appropriate eloquence, studious and serious felicity of expression and fortunate elaboration of verse" ever quite touched "the goal of lyric triumph" that Herrick reached. Swinburne may well have been right, but in the still far-ranging world where "Drink to me only" is still sung, in concert hall or radio booth or by campfire—and where Herrick's songs, and Swinburne's alas, are not—it might be difficult to find someone to agree.

# JOHN DONNE

## [1573–1631]

### An Anatomie of the World

#### THE FIRST ANNIVERSARY

The entrie into the worke.

When that rich Soule which to her heaven is
    gone,
Whom all do celebrate, who know they have
    one,
(For who is sure he hath a Soule, unlesse
It see, and judge, and follow worthinesse,
And by Deedes praise it? hee who doth
    not this,    5
May lodge an In-mate soule, but 'tis not his.)
When that Queene ended here her progresse
    time,
And, as t'her standing house to heaven did
    climbe,
Where loath to make the Saints attend her long,
She's now a part both of the Quire,
    and Song,    10
This World, in that great earthquake lan-
    guished;
For in a common bath of teares it bled,
Which drew the strongest vitall spirits out:
But succour'd then with a perplexed doubt,
Whether the world did lose, or gaine
    in this,    15
(Because since now no other way there is,
But goodnesse, to see her, whom all would see,
All must endeavour to be good as shee,)
This great consumption to a fever turn'd,
And so the world had fits; it joy'd,
    it mourn'd;    20
And, as men thinke, that Agues physick are,
And th'Ague being spent, give over care,
So thou sicke World, mistak'st thy selfe to bee
Well, when alas, thou'rt in a Lethargie.

Her death did wound and tame thee then,
and then                                      25
Thou might'st have better spar'd the Sunne, or
Man.
That wound was deep, but 'tis more misery,
That thou hast lost thy sense and memory.
'Twas heavy then to heare thy voyce of mone,
But this is worse, that thou art speechlesse
growne.                                       30
Thou hast forgot thy name, thou hadst; thou
wast
Nothing but shee, and her thou hast o'rpast.
For as a child kept from the Font, untill
A prince, expected long, come to fulfill
The ceremonies, thou unnam'd had'st laid,     35
Had not her comming, thee her Palace made:
Her name defin'd thee, gave thee forme, and
frame,
And thou forgett'st to celebrate thy name.
Some moneths she hath beene dead (but being
dead,
Measures of times are all determined)         40
But long she'ath beene away, long, long, yet none
Offers to tell us who it is that's gone.
But as in states doubtfull of future heires,
When sicknesse without remedie empares
The present Prince, they're loth it should
be said,                                      45
The Prince doth languish, or the Prince is dead:
So mankinde feeling now a generall thaw,
A strong example gone, equall to law,
The Cyment which did faithfully compact,
And glue all vertues, now resolv'd,
and slack'd,                                  50
Thought it some blasphemy to say sh'was dead,
Or that our weaknesse was discovered
In that confession; therefore spoke no more
Than tongues, the Soule being gone, the losse
deplore.
But though it be too late to succour thee,    55
Sicke World, yea, dead, yea putrified, since shee
Thy'intrinsique balme, and thy preservative
Can never be renew'd, thou never live,
I (since no man can make thee live) will try,
What wee may gaine by thy Anatomy.            60

JOHN DONNE

*The Bettmann Archive*

Her death hath taught us dearely, that thou art
Corrupt and mortall in thy purest part.
Let no man say, the world it selfe being dead,
'Tis labour lost to have discovered
The worlds infirmities, since there is none    65
Alive to study this dissection;

What life
the world
hath stil

For there's a kinde of World remaining still,
Though shee which did inanimate and fill
The world, be gone, yet in this last long night,
Her Ghost doth walke; that is, a glimmering
    light,    70
A faint weake love of vertue, and of good,
Reflects from her, on them which understood
Her worth; and though she have shut in all day,
The twilight of her memory doth stay;
Which, from the carcasse of the old world,
    free,    75
Creates a new world, and new creatures bee
Produc'd: the matter and the stuffe of this,
Her vertue, and the forme our practice is:
And though to be thus elemented, arme
These creatures, from home-borne intrinsique
    harme,    80
(For all assum'd unto this dignitie,
So many weedlesse Paradises bee,
Which of themselves produce no venemous
    sinne,
Except some forraine Serpent bring it in)
Yet, because outward stormes the strongest
    breake,    85
And strength it selfe by confidence growes
    weake,

The sick-
nesses
of the
World.

This new world may be safer, being told
For with due temper men doe then forgoe,
The dangers and diseases of the old:
Or covet things, when they their true worth
    know.    90

Impossi-
bility of
health.

There is no health; Physitians say that wee,
At best, enjoy but a neutralitie.
And can there bee worse sicknesse, than to know
That we are never well, nor can be so?
Wee are borne ruinous: poore mothers
    cry,    95
That children come not right, nor orderly;

Except they headlong come and fall upon
An ominous precipitation.
How witty's ruine! how importunate
Upon mankinde! it labour'd to frustrate    100
Even Gods purpose; and made woman, sent
For mans reliefe, cause of his languishment.
They were to good ends, and they are so still,
But accessory, and principall in ill;
For that first marriage was our funerall:    105
One woman at one blow, then kill'd us all,
And singly, one by one, they kill us now.
We doe delightfully our selves allow
To that consumption; and profusely blinde,
We kill our selves to propagate our kinde.    110
And yet we do not that; we are not men:
There is not now that mankinde, which was
    then,
When as, the Sunne and man did seeme to strive,
(Joynt tenants of the world) who should survive;
When, Stagge, and Raven, and the long-liv'd
    tree,    115
Compar'd with man, dy'd in minoritie;
When, if a slow pac'd starre had stolne away
From the observers marking, he might stay
Two or three hundred yeares to see't againe,
And then make up his observation
    plaine;    120
When, as the age was long, the sise was great;
Mans growth confess'd, and recompenc'd the
    meat;
So spacious and large, that every Soule
Did a faire Kingdome, and large Realme
    controule:
And when the very stature, thus erect,    125
Did that soule a good way towards heaven direct.
Where is this mankinde now? who lives to age,
Fit to be made *Methusalem* his page?
Alas, we scarce live long enough to try
Whether a true made clocke run right,
    or lie.    130
Old Grandsires talke of yesterday with sorrow,
And for our children wee reserve to morrow.
So short is life, that every peasant strives,
In a torne house, or field, to have three lives.

*Shortnesse of life.*

And as in lasting, so in length is man　　135
Contracted to an inch, who was a spanne;
For had a man at first in forrests stray'd,
Or shipwrack'd in the Sea, one would have
　　laid
A wager, that an Elephant, or Whale,
That met him, would not hastily assaile　　140
A thing so equall to him: now alas,
The Fairies, and the Pigmies well may passe
As credible; mankinde decayes so soone,
We'are scarce our Fathers shadowes cast at
　　noone:
Onely death addes t'our length: nor are wee
　　growne　　　　　　　　　　　　　　145
In stature to be men, till we are none.
But this were light, did our lesse volume hold
All the old Text; or had wee chang'd to gold
Their silver; or dispos'd into lesse glasse
Spirits of vertue, which then scatter'd was.　150
But 'tis not so: w'are not retir'd, but dampt;
And as our bodies, so our mindes are crampt:
'Tis shrinking, not close weaving that hath thus,
In minde, and body both bedwarfed us.
Wee seeme ambitious, Gods whole worke
　　t'undoe;　　　　　　　　　　　　　155
Of nothing hee made us, and we strive too,
To bring our selves to nothing backe; and wee
Doe what wee can, to do't so soone as hee.
With new diseases on our selves we warre,
And with new Physicke, a worse Engin
　　farre.　　　　　　　　　　　　　　160
Thus man, this worlds Vice-Emperour, in whom
All faculties, all graces are at home;
And if in other creatures they appeare,
They're but mans Ministers, and Legats
　　there,
To worke on their rebellions, and reduce　165
Them to Civility, and to mans use:
This man, whom God did wooe, and loth
　　t'attend
Till man came up, did downe to man descend,
This man, so great, that all that is, is his,
Oh what a trifle, and poore thing he is!　　170
If man were any thing, he's nothing now:

Helpe, or at least some time to wast, allow
T'his other wants, yet when he did depart
With her whom we lament, hee lost his heart.
She, of whom th'Ancients seem'd
    to prophesie,                                    175
When they call'd vertues by the name of *shee;*
Shee in whom vertue was so much refin'd,
That for Allay unto so pure a minde
Shee tooke the weaker Sex; shee that could drive
The poysonous tincture, and the staine
    of *Eve,*                                       180
Out of her thoughts, and deeds; and purifie
All, by a true religious Alchymie;
Shee, shee is dead; shee's dead: when thou
    knowest this,
Thou knowest how poore a trifling thing man is.
And learn'st thus much by our
    Anatomie,                                       185
The heart being perish'd, no part can be free.
And that except thou feed (not banquet) on
The supernaturall food, Religion,
Thy better Growth growes withered, and scant;
Be more than man, or thou'rt lesse than
    an Ant.                                         190
Then, as mankinde, so is the worlds whole
    frame
Quite out of joynt, almost created lame:
For, before God had made up all the rest,
Corruption entred, and deprav'd the best:
It seis'd the Angels, and then first of all        195
The world did in her cradle take a fall,
And turn'd her braines, and tooke a generall
    maime,
Wronging each joynt of th'universall frame,
The noblest part, man, felt it first; and then
Both beasts and plants, curst in the curse
    of man.                                         200

**Decay of nature in other parts.**
So did the world from the first houre decay,
That evening was beginning of the day,
And now the Springs and Sommers which we
    see,
Like sonnes of women after fiftie bee.
And new Philosophy calls all in doubt,             205
The Element of fire is quite put out;

The Sun is lost, and th'earth, and no mans wit
Can well direct him where to looke for it.
And freely men confesse that this world's spent,
When in the Planets, and the Firmament   210
They seeke so many new; then see that this
Is crumbled out againe to his Atomies.
'Tis all in peeces, all cohaerence gone;
All just supply, and all Relation:
Prince, Subject, Father, Sonne, are things
     forgot,                                215
For every man alone thinkes he hath got
To be a Phœnix, and that then can bee
None of that kinde, of which he is, but hee.
This is the worlds condition now, and now
She that should all parts to reunion bow,   220
She that had all Magnetique force alone,
To draw, and fasten sundred parts in one;
She whom wise nature had invented then
When she observ'd that every sort of men
Did in their voyage in this worlds Sea
     stray,                                 225
And needed a new compasse for their way:
She that was best, and first originall
Of all faire copies, and the generall
Steward to Fate; she whose rich eyes, and breast
Guilt the West Indies, and perfum'd the
     East;                                  230
Whose having breath'd in this world, did bestow
Spice on those Iles, and bad them still smell so,
And that rich Indie which doth gold interre,
Is but as single money, coyn'd from her:
She to whom this world must it selfe refer,   235
As Suburbs, or the Microcosme of her,
Shee, shee is dead; shee's dead: when thou
     knowst this,
Thou knowst how lame a cripple this world is.
And learn'st thus much by our Anatomy,
That this worlds generall sickenesse
     doth not lie                           240
In any humour, or one certaine part;
But as thou sawest it rotten at the heart,
Thou seest a Hectique feaver hath got hold
Of the whole substance, not to be contrould,
And that thou hast but one way, not t'admit   245
The worlds infection, to be none of it.

For the worlds subtilst immateriall parts
Feele this consuming wound, and ages darts.
For the worlds beauty is decai'd, or gone,
Beauty, that's colour, and proportion.     250
We thinke the heavens enjoy their Sphericall,
Their round proportion embracing all.
But yet their various and perplexed course,
Observ'd in divers ages, doth enforce
Men to finde out so many Eccentrique
    parts,     255
Such divers downe-right lines, such overthwarts,
As disproportion that pure forme: It teares
The Firmament in eight and forty sheires,
And in these Constellations then arise
New starres, and old doe vanish from
    our eyes:     260
As though heav'n suffered earthquakes, peace or
    war,
When new Towers rise, and old demolish't are.
They have impal'd within a Zodiake
The free-borne Sun, and keepe twelve Signes
    awake
To watch his steps; the Goat and Crab
    controule,     265
And fright him backe, who else to either Pole
(Did not these Tropiques fetter him) might
    runne:
For his course is not round; nor can the
    Sunne
Perfit a Circle, or maintaine his way
One inch direct; but where he rose
    to-day     270
He comes no more, but with a couzening line,
Steales by that point, and so is Serpentine:
And seeming weary with his reeling thus,
He means to sleepe, being now falne nearer us.
So, of the Starres which boast that they
    doe runne     275
In Circle still, none ends where he begun.
All their proportion's lame, it sinkes, it swels.
For of Meridians, and Parallels,
Man hath weav'd out a net, and this net throwne
Upon the Heavens, and now they are
    his owne.     280
Loth to goe up the hill, or labour thus

To goe to heaven, we make heaven come
    to us.
We spur, we reine the starres, and in their race
They're diversly content t'obey our pace.
But keepes the earth her round proportion
    still?                                             285
Doth not a Tenarif, or higher Hill
Rise so high like a Rocke, that one might thinke
The floating Moone would shipwrack there, and
    sinke?
Seas are so deepe, that Whales being strooke
    to day,
Perchance to morrow, scarse at
    middle way                                        290
Of their wish'd journies end, the bottome, die.
And men, to sound depths, so much line untie,
As one might justly thinke, that there would rise
At end thereof, one of th'Antipodies:
If under all, a Vault infernall bee,                         295
(Which sure is spacious, except that we
Invent another torment, that there must
Millions into a straight hot roome be thrust)
Then solidnesse, and roundnesse have no
    place.
Are these but warts, and pock-holes
    in the face                                       300
Of th'earth? Thinke so: but yet confesse, in this
The worlds proportion disfigured is;

**Disorder**
**in the**
**world.**

That those two legges whereon it doth rely,
Reward and punishment are bent awry.
And, Oh, it can no more be questioned,              305
That beauties best, proportion, is dead,
Since even griefe it selfe, which now alone
Is left us, is without proportion.
Shee by whose lines proportion should bee
Examin'd, measure of all Symmetree,                 310
Whom had that Ancient seen, who thought
    soules made
Of Harmony, he would at next have said
That Harmony was shee, and thence infer,
That soules were but Resultances from her,
And did from her into our bodies goe,               315
As to our eyes, the formes from objects flow:
Shee, who if those great Doctors truly said
That the Arke to mans proportions was made,

Had been a type for that, as that might be
A type of her in this, that contrary          320
Both Elements, and Passions liv'd at peace
In her, who caus'd all Civill war to cease.
Shee, after whom, what forme soe'r we see,
Is discord, and rude incongruitie;
Shee, shee is dead, shee's dead; when thou
    knowst this,                               325
Thou knowst how ugly a monster this
    world is:
And learn'st thus much by our Anatomie,
That here is nothing to enamour thee:
And that, not only faults in inward parts,
Corruptions in our braines, or in our
    hearts,                                     330
Poysoning the fountaines, whence our actions
    spring,
Endanger us: but that if every thing
Be not done fitly'and in proportion,
To satisfie wise, and good lookers on,
(Since most men be such as most thinke
    they bee)                                  335
They're lothsome too, by this Deformitee.
For good, and well, must in our actions meete;
Wicked is not much worse than indiscreet.
But beauties other second Element,
Colour, and lustre now, is as neere spent.    340
And had the world his just proportion,
Were it a ring still, yet the stone is gone.
As a compassionate Turcoyse which doth tell
By looking pale, the wearer is not well,
As gold falls sicke being stung
    with Mercury,                             345
All the worlds parts of such complexion bee.
When nature was most busie, the first weeke,
Swadling the new born earth, God seem'd to like
That she should sport her selfe sometimes,
    and play,
To mingle, and vary colours every day:        350
And then, as though shee could not make inow,
Himselfe his various Rainbow did allow.
Sight is the noblest sense of any one,
Yet sight hath only colour to feed on,
And colour is decai'd: summers robe
    growes                                      355

Duskie, and like an oft dyed garment showes.
Our blushing red, which us'd in cheekes to spred,
Is inward sunke, and only our soules are red.
Perchance the world might have recovered,
If she whom we lament had not beene
        dead:                                                360
But shee, in whom all white, and red, and blew
(Beauties ingredients) voluntary grew,
As in an unvext Paradise; from whom
Did all things verdure, and their lustre come,
Whose composition was miraculous,                            365
Being all colour, all Diaphanous,
(For Ayre, and Fire but thick grosse bodies
        were,
And liveliest stones but drowsie, and pale to her,)
Shee, shee, is dead; shee's dead: when thou
        know'st this,
Thou knowst how wan a Ghost this
        our world is:                                        370

Weak-
nesse in
the want
of corre-
spond-
ence of
heaven
and
earth.

And learn'st thus much by our Anatomie,
That it should more affright, than pleasure thee.
And that, since all faire colour then did sinke,
'Tis now but wicked vanitie, to thinke
To colour vicious deeds with
        good pretence,                                       375
Or with bought colors to illude mens sense.
Nor in ought more this worlds decay appeares,
Than that her influence the heav'n forbeares,
Or that the Elements doe not feele this,
The father, or the mother barren is.                         380
The cloudes conceive not raine, or doe not
        powre,
In the due birth time, downe the balmy showre;
Th'Ayre doth not motherly sit on the earth,
To hatch her seasons, and give all things birth;
Spring-times were common cradles, but are
        tombes;                                               385
And false-conceptions fill the generall wombes;
Th'Ayre showes such Meteors, as none can see,
Not only what they meane, but what they bee;
Earth such new wormes, as would have
        troubled much
Th'Ægyptian *Mages* to have made
        more such.                                            390
What Artist now dares boast that he can bring

Heaven hither, or constellate any thing,
So as the influence of those starres may bee
Imprison'd in an Hearbe, or Charme, or Tree,
And doe by touch, all which those stars could
    doe?                                                   395
The art is lost, and correspondence too.
For heaven gives little, and the earth takes
    lesse,
And man least knowes their trade and purposes.
If this commerce twixt heaven and earth were not
Embarr'd, and all this traffique
    quite forgot,                                            400
She for whose losse we have lamented thus,
Would worke more fully, and pow'rfully on us:
Since herbes, and roots, by dying lose not all,
But they, yea Ashes too, are medicinall,
Death could not quench her vertue so,
    but that                                               405
It would be (if not follow'd) wondred at:
And all the world would be one dying Swan,
To sing her funerall praise, and vanish then.
But as some Serpents poyson hurteth not,
Except it be from the live Serpent shot,                     410
So doth her vertue need her here, to fit
That unto us; shee working more than it.
But shee, in whom to such maturity
Vertue was growne, past growth, that it must die;
She, from whose influence all Impressions
    came,                                                  415
But, by Receivers impotencies, lame,
Who, though she could not transubstantiate
All states to gold, yet guilded every state,
So that some Princes have some temperance;
Some Counsellors some purpose
    to advance                                            420
The common profit; and some people have
Some stay, no more than Kings should give, to
    crave,
Some women have some taciturnity,
Some nunneries some graines of chastitie.
She that did thus much, and much more
    could doe,                                             425
But that our age was Iron, and rustie too,
Shee, shee is dead; shee's dead; when thou
    knowst this

Thou knowst how drie a Cinder this world is
And learn'st thus much by our Anatomy,
That 'tis in vaine to dew, or mollifie          430
It with thy teares, or sweat, or blood: nothing
Is worth our travaile, griefe, or perishing,
But those rich joyes, which did possesse her
    heart,
Of which she's now partaker, and a part.
But as in cutting up a man that's dead,          435
The body will not last out, to have read
On every part, and therefore men direct
Their speech to parts, that are of most effect;
So the worlds carcasse would not last, if I
Were punctuall in this Anatomy;          440
Nor smels it well to hearers, if one tell
Them their disease, who faine would think
    they're well.
Here therefore be the end: And, blessed maid,
Of whom is meant what ever hath been said,
Or shall be spoken well by any tongue,          445
Whose name refines course lines, and makes
    prose song,
Accept this tribute, and his first yeares rent,
Who till his darke short tapers end be spent,
As oft as thy feast sees this widowed earth,
Will yearely celebrate thy second birth,          450
That is, thy death; for though the soule of man
Begot when man is made, 'tis borne but then
When man doth die; our body's as the wombe,
And, as a Midwife, death directs it home.
And you her creatures, whom she workes
    upon,          455
And have your last, and best concoction
From her example, and her vertue, if you
In reverence to her, do thinke it due,
That no one should her praises thus rehearse,
As matter fit for Chronicle, not verse;          460
Vouchsafe to call to minde that God did make
At last, and lasting'st peece, a song. He spake
To *Moses* to deliver unto all,
That song, because hee knew they would let
    fall
The Law, the Prophets, and the History,          465
But keepe the song still in their memory:

Conclu-
sion.

Such an opinion (in due measure) made
Me this great Office boldly to invade:
Nor could incomprehensibleness deterre
Mee from thus trying to emprison her,      470
Which when I saw that a strict grave could doe,
I saw not why verse might not do so too.
Verse hath a middle nature: heaven keepes
      Soules,
The Grave keepes bodies, Verse the Fame en-
      roules.

*Robert M. Bender*

DONNE

THE FIRST ANNIVERSARY

The only two poems Donne himself took care to publish during his own lifetime were the two "Anniversaries," written to commemorate the death of Elizabeth Drury, the only daughter of Sir Robert Drury, a very wealthy and influential man in Donne's day. Sir Robert had placed great hopes in his daughter, and her death at the age of fifteen was no doubt a cause of momentous grief. Donne never knew the girl; it is even doubtful that he ever saw her. He apparently began "The First Anniversary" with the thought of attracting Sir Robert's attention, and perhaps eventually his patronage. It is true that in 1611, the year in which the poem was first published, one year after Elizabeth's death, Donne went with his family to live in the household of Sir Robert and continued on there for a number of years.

These facts would seem to tell us a great deal about Donne's magnificent poem; in fact, they merely tell us why he began to write it. That it is an occasional piece is manifest, but it is nonetheless true that Donne became so involved with his subject that the poem as we have it is much more than the mere commemoration of an individual death. Donne's original title for the poem gives us a clue to its content: "An Anatomie of the World: Wherein, by occasion of the untimely death of Mistris Elizabeth Drury the frailty and the decay of this whole world is represented." The death of Elizabeth Drury was nothing less than the occasion for Donne's extended meditation upon the state of the world; the poem itself is nothing less than an expression of Donne's response to the continuing human condition.

There has probably been no age in which intelligent men could look about and truly say, all is well. Donne's age gave less cause for optimism, less cause for a feeling of well-being, than many. Shakespeare has Hamlet observe that "the time is out of joint." Donne tells us that "as mankinde, so is the worlds whole frame / Quite out of joynt": it is much the same thing. King James was by no means the awe-inspiring, order-provoking monarch that Queen Elizabeth had been. Religious controversy, between Catholics and Protestants, was creating turmoil and dissent in England as well as on the continent. The "new science" and the "new philosophy," which raised the hopes of so many great thinkers, were raising more questions than they answered, creating more doubts than they resolved. It did not require the death of a prominent man's fifteen-year-old daughter to set a man of Donne's intellect, not to mention temperament, thinking about the "frailty and the decay of this whole world," but the death apparently did give Donne an opportunity to make a poem of his meditations.

"The First Anniversary" is a systematic dissection, an "anatomy," of the ills of the world, and implicitly of man, for man and the world are the same in Donne's conception. The ailments manifest in the world are also present in man, for man is a microcosm, a little world, in which all the effects of the great world are mirrored. Metaphorically the world is thus spoken of as an individual. So Donne describes the illness that ensued at the death of Elizabeth Drury:

> *This World, in that great earthquake languished;*
> *For in a common bath of teares it bled,*
> *Which drew the strongest vitall spirits out*

The world falls to a "consumption," then to a "fever," and finally remains in a "lethargie." But this is merely a description of the sickness—the symptoms, as it were. The dissection goes much deeper.

Penetrating through the surface of things, Donne observes that "there is no health." At best, men and the world "enjoy but a neutralitie." Men continually frustrate their own well-being and God's purposes. Women, sent "for mans reliefe," bring him more woe: "That first marriage was our funerall." And it remains ever so:

> *One woman at one blow, then kill'd us all,*
> *And singly, one by one, they kill us now.*

Once, in biblical times, giants of long life, men are now shrunken in both stature and longevity, "contracted to an inch." And to make matters worse, instead of concentrating what meager supply of virtue there is in his shrunken frame, man merely expands his propensity for evil.

And so it goes. The decay and disorder in man is reflected in "this whole world." Spring and summer are no longer so glorious as they once were. Beauty—proportion and color—is gone. Correspondence between heaven and earth is lacking. The new science, having proved astrology false, has produced nothing to stand in its place; so Donne laments:

> *What Artist now dares boast that he can bring*
> *Heaven hither, or constellate any thing,*
> *So as the influence of those starres may bee*
> *Imprison'd in an Hearbe, or Charme, or Tree,*
> *And doe by touch, all which those stars could doe?*
> *The art is lost, and correspondence too.*

The observations Donne makes in his "anatomy," and his arguments too, are not new. Men had been making such observations at least since medieval times. And though there is also an important classical tradition of commentary upon the world's decay, this poem reveals the strong medieval affinities in Donne's character. In one sense, "The First Anniversary" is really a compendious history of mankind, beginning with the golden age, here associated with the creation and biblical times, and ending with fallen modern times. In this sense, it is the history of man's unsuccessful struggle with evil, his inability to control his own nature or direct his own course. But as magnificent as the description of the world's decay is in this poem, what is even more striking is the resolution with which Donne accepts it.

Five times in this long poem Donne uses a refrain which is eventually to embody his conclusion. Its music as verse is magnificent; the first instance is:

> *Shee, shee is dead; shee's dead; when thou knowest this,*
> *Thou knowest how poore a trifling thing man is.*

And the music becomes finer with each development. But it is not the music, finally, but the sense that strikes us most. And progressively we see the world as less and less an evil. Donne speaks of it as a lame cripple, an ugly monster, a ghost, and finally merely as a dry cinder. But the end is not despair, for the anatomy has a lesson:

> *Shee, shee is dead; shee's dead; when thou knowst this*
> *Thou knowst how drie a Cinder this world is.*
> *And learn'st thus much by our Anatomy,*
> *That 'tis in vaine to dew, or mollifie*
> *It with thy teares, or sweat, or blood: nothing*
> *Is worth our travaile, griefe, or perishing,*
> *But those rich joyes, which did possesse her heart,*
> *Of which she's now partaker, and a part.*

Of course this resolution is Christian; it speaks of a better world hereafter, and Elizabeth's death is rightly seen by Donne as her "second birth." But the resolution is not so specifically Christian as to deny the reader his own belief in a better reality. Always in this poem we have the contrast between what should be and what is, a contrast between Donne's idealization of Elizabeth Drury and the world as it appears. Metaphorically, Donne places Elizabeth at a time in history before man's fall; all that comes after her is therefore naturally decayed. Such a view leads to a contempt for worldly things and a continual longing for the serene calm of the other world, here embodied in the spirit of Elizabeth. It is the longing that gives the poem its fine meditative quality.

Taken as a lament for a single private person, "The First Anniversary" is, of course, inflated. Ben Jonson, Donne's friend and rival, even criticized the poem for being profane and blasphemous in its excessive praise of Elizabeth Drury. Such criticism, however, misses Donne's point. He has made Elizabeth the universal of goodness and virtue; as such, he is not praising an individual when he praises her but rather the qualities she represents. And after all, the religious feeling of the poem is tempered by Donne's cynicism, sometimes classical, sometimes medieval, and by his magnificent wit, as strong here as in any of his early rakish poems. In the end, it is misleading to think of Donne's view as pessimistic. "The First Anniversary," despite its criticism of the world, or perhaps really because of it, is an expression of man's continuing faith in man and in the prospect of a better world.

# The Canonization

For Godsake hold your tongue, and let me love,
  Or chide my palsie, or my gout,
My five gray haires, or ruin'd fortune flout,
    With wealth your state, your minde with Arts improve
      Take you a course, get you a place,      5
      Observe his honour, or his grace,
Or the Kings reall, or his stamped face
  Contemplate, what you will, approve,
  So you will let me love.

Alas, alas, who's injur'd by my love?         10
  What merchants ships have my sighs drown'd?
Who saies my teares have overflow'd his ground?
    When did my colds a forward spring remove?
      When did the heats which my veines fill
      Adde one more to the plaguie Bill?      15
Soldiers finde warres, and Lawyers finde out still
  Litigious men, which quarrels move,
  Though she and I do love.

Call us what you will, wee are made such by love;
  Call her one, mee another flye,       20
We'are Tapers too, and at our owne cost die,
    And wee in us finde the'Eagle and the Dove.
      The Phœnix ridle hath more wit
      By us, we two being one, are it.
So to one neutrall thing both sexes fit,      25
  Wee dye and rise the same, and prove
  Mysterious by this love.

Wee can dye by it, if not live by love,
  And if unfit for tombes and hearse
Our legend bee, it will be fit for verse;      30
    And if no peece of Chronicle wee prove,
      We'll build in sonnets pretty roomes;
      As well a well wrought urne becomes

The greatest ashes, as halfe-acre tombes,
And by these hymnes, all shall approve                                    35
Us *Canoniz'd* for Love:

And thus invoke us; You whom reverend love
Made one anothers hermitage;
You, to whom love was peace, that now is rage;
Who did the whole worlds soule contract, and drove       40
Into the glasses of your eyes
(So made such mirrors, and such spies,
That they did all to you epitomize,)
Countries, Townes, Courts: Beg from above
A patterne of your love!                                                       45

*Edwin Honig*

---

DONNE
THE CANONIZATION

This is one of Donne's most intellectually agile pieces in *Songs and Sonnets,* his collection of youthful poems. "The Canonization" is sometimes held up as a prime example of the poet's bold, heretical way of fusing together sacred and profane ideas. The excitement of the poem surely has something to do with Donne's ironic juggling of this taboo. But there were other poets, less gifted and more sensational, who did as well with the same taboo. Donne is not sensationalizing here—he is not being naughty for the sake of being naughty. Writing a poem about love, he is caught up by the need to celebrate and eternalize some form of it. To do this he must make of the common human experience, not the relative or even passingly ludicrous thing it is often taken for, but something glorious, absolute. From being the merely harassed and gossiped-about pair in the first stanza, the lovers are transformed to the martyred and even sanctified state of lying dead in their tomb, the subject of popular adoration and heavenly intercession, in the last stanza.

Going along with this metamorphosis, there is a strange double-take in the end. For there we recognize that from the point of view of time, we are still in the present, listening to the blissful conclusion of a speech that started only a moment ago by berating an envious adversary. He whom the speaker first directed by oath to be silent ("For Godsake hold your tongue, and let me love") is shown in the last lines to be invoking the speaker and his beloved as saints, martyred by his envy, to "Beg from above / A patterne of your love!"

If it is not wholly an imprecation against the envious and against worldly disbelief, the poem is a charm, depending upon the imaginative power and art of words (poetry and prayer) to preserve love from attack and to convert disbelief into belief, gossip and malice into adoration. We are asked to watch the slanderous eavesdropper and spy of the first stanza being reduced (or elevated) to the posture of a prayerful worshipper in the end. In effect, something like a phyiscal conversion has been accomplished: the poet's verbal judo has thrown his silenced antagonist from a stance of overbearing intrusion to a position of supine mercy-begging—if not on his back literally, then on his knees.

The charm seems to work, but by what means? Some of these have been mentioned: by a fusion of secular and divine ideas; by the tone of imprecation made to serve a charm-creating interest; by the illusion of having interrupted a speech with a monologue in which the speaker seeks to crush his opponent with the sanctity of love. Looked at more closely, these effects seem to be part of a singularly flexible, many-sided argument in poetic form. And what is called the argument is increasingly impressive because all its persuasive logical and rhetorical points, though carefully calculated, seem to be presented by a passionate voice, spontaneously.

The argument is built up from the beginning to conform with the symmetrical nine-line arrangement of the five stanzas. It is modulated to make use of the linear and even cesural units in each stanza so as to frame the rhetoric of invocation, abjuration, periodicity, antithesis, and oxymoron. Each stanza takes up a different burden of proof. Finally, we admire the poet's art as we would that of a speaker who is given just so many minutes to present his case and who fulfills the limitation exactly. When this is done five times in succession, the effect is not only increased fivefold but infinitely, since this is a poem, not a piece of debate merely.

In the first stanza the speaker presents his own disadvantaged situation through images of infirmity equated with the world's mind- and wealth-improving pursuits. But when we come on "the King's reall, or his stamped face / Contemplate," the pun momentarily stops us. Then we are aware that the language has deepened with emblematic force as well as with the implied gloss on the scriptural "render unto Caesar" pronouncement. The arrestments of language are exploited in the second stanza, where the case is reinforced by rhetorical questions; and rhetorical questions in Donne usually signify conceits and hyperboles, further deepeners of theme.

So, in the third stanza, follow hyperboles no longer based as before on the imagery of nature and social intercourse, but on paradoxes and emblematic figures of spiritual things. In the fourth stanza, where the theme has been driven deeper and secured, there is a new turn. Previously the speaker was pleading for peace and freedom; now he suggests, half-ironically, that these can be found only in death and poetry. This

turn brings to the surface the speaker's restless desire, persistently underlying the argument from the beginning, for
martyrdom and the justification of earthly love in heaven.
The concluding stanza exploits ecstatically the implications of
such a solution in the imagined apotheosis of the lovers.

Thus the canonization idea, introduced so suddenly, it
seems, in the last stanza, has actually been in the offing from
the first. And shocking though it may seem, appearing so
near the end of the poem, Donne fits it in by making it part
of his argument: an enumeration of the conditions and
reasons for the lovers' being canonized in all their pure,
spiritual prowess.

The surprise and effectiveness of this last turn almost
obscure the fact that the poet has also created a double reversal in the end. The first reversal, mentioned above, is the
subject's and object's exchange of places: the speaker is no
longer begging the antagonist to hold his tongue but is now
being beseeched by the antagonist to intercede for him in
heaven. Also, the antagonist, whose slanderous tongue the
speaker silenced at the start of the poem, now has soft,
prayerful words thrust into his astounded mouth. This is the
speaker's revenge. It is also the note that seals off the poem so
beautifully and conclusively as a charm.

## A Valediction: Forbidding Mourning

As virtuous men passe mildly away,
    And whisper to their soules, to goe,
Whilst some of their sad friends doe say,
    The breath goes now, and some say, no:

So let us melt, and make no noise,        5
    No teare-floods, nor sigh-tempests move,
T'were prophanation of our joyes
    To tell the layetie our love.

Moving of th'earth brings harmes and feares,
    Men reckon what it did and meant,      10
But trepidation of the spheares,
    Though greater farre, is innocent.

Dull sublunary lovers love
    (Whose soule is sense) cannot admit
Absence, because it doth remove        15
    Those things which elemented it.

But we by a love, so much refin'd,
    That our selves know not what it is,
Inter-assured of the mind,
    Care lesse, eyes, lips, and hands to misse.    20

Our two soules therefore, which are one,
    Though I must goe, endure not yet
A breach, but an expansion,
    Like gold to ayery thinnesse beate.

If they be two, they are two so        25
    As stiffe twin compasses are two,
Thy soule the fixt foot, makes no show
    To move, but doth, if the'other doe.

And though it in the center sit,
    Yet when the other far doth rome,      30

It leanes, and hearkens after it,
   And growes erect, as that comes home.

Such wilt thou be to mee, who must
   Like th'other foot, obliquely runne;
Thy firmnes drawes my circle just,         35
   And makes me end, where I begunne.

# I. A. Richards

## DONNE
### A VALEDICTION: FORBIDDING MOURNING

Walton's *Life of Donne* says that this poem was given by Donne to Anne More, his wife, when he left for France with Sir Thomas Drury in 1611. It seems likely that it makes references to two others of Donne's "Valedictions" as well as to "The Extasie." One of these, "Of Weeping," is filled with "teare-floods" and "sigh-tempests" (line 6); the other, "Of the Booke," can tell us who "the layetie" (line 8) are.
"Of Weeping," lines 17, 18:

> *Till thy teares mixt with mine doe overflow*
> *This world, by waters sent from thee, my heaven*
>   *dissolved so.*

lines 24, 25:

> *Since thou and I sigh one anothers breath,*
> *Who e'r sighes most, is cruellest, and hastes the*
>   *others death.*

"Of the Booke," line 22:

> *Wee for loves clergie only'are instruments*

i.e., only for those "by love refin'd" ("The Extasie," line 21), "whom loves subliming fire invades" ("Of the Booke," line 13), will our example, collected from our letters, serve as instruments, means of instruction. The laity will make nothing of it all.

Comparison of parting with death was a favorite device with Donne. The lovers are too securely united for protestations and commotion to be in place. Moreover it would be "prophanation" (line 7), bringing the unworthy into the shrine, if they were to talk about their love to others than the happy few who know.

Verse three: earthquakes seem portents; but motions of the outer spheres, their to and fro oscillation as of a balance (a theory proposed about 950 and still current astronomy in Donne's time) had never been thought to do anyone any hurt. So parting which brings about only such movement in their love need not be dreaded.

Verse four: a foolish, stupid, imperceptive sort of love, subject as are all things beneath the moon to ebb and flow, a love in which the senses attempt to rule, cannot permit, cannot put up with, separation; because that takes away the very elements (in sense and appetite) that make such love up.

Verse five: but we, in whom our love, being so much restored to its true nature as to be to us an incomprehensible, we who are made safe each by the other and guaranteed mutual understanding and possession, suffer less from not being able to see and touch one another. See "The Extasie," lines 21, 30, 55, and my commentary. The two poems thus confirm one the other.

Verse six: "not yet": the phrase here carries no suggestion that there will ever be any break between them. The meaning of "yet" is, here, "nonetheless, still, as before."

Verses seven and eight: the derivation of the word *compass* has to do with stepping together. As the outer leg moves, the central must too—attentively inclining as though listening, and becoming upright again when the outer approaches as though in ease and content and happy expectation.

Verse nine: there has been discussion as to whether the image here is of the completion of a circle or of the closing of the compass when its task is done. Each seems equally relevant. Circles are emblematic of perfection. In Plato's *Timaeus*, well known to Donne, the Creator gave the world, as the fairest and most perfect of intelligible beings, the form of a globe. Moreover, the circle is the emblem of the soul's proper course.

> When reason is hovering around the sensible world and when the circle of the diverse, also moving truly, imparts the intimations of sense to the whole soul, then arise opinions and beliefs sure and certain. But when reason is concerned with the rational, and the circle of the same, moving smoothly, declares it, then intelligence and knowledge are necessarily achieved.

The two final lines of the poem, accordingly, are saying that it is her steadfastness which makes the courses of his soul be as they should be and makes him in the end return whence he came.

In my beginning is my end

as in "East Coker." The dissatisfaction that some have felt at the repetition of *makes*—which led the editor of the Nonesuch Donne to print *drawes* (found in one MS) instead, and may be why Walton has

>    *And me to end where I begunne*

—springs perhaps from insufficient comprehension of this depth of meaning. The repetition of the creative word here rightly echoes that return. So does the renewal, in *runne* and *begunne*, of the opening rime, *one*, in verse six, and the echo in the thought of the last line of the thought of the first.

## The Extasie

Where, like a pillow on a bed,
    A Pregnant banke swel'd up, to rest
The violets reclining head,
    Sat we two, one anothers best.
Our hands were firmely cimented          5
    With a fast balme, which thence did spring,
Our eye-beames twisted, and did thred
    Our eyes, upon one double string;
So to'entergraft our hands, as yet
    Was all the meanes to make us one,        10
And pictures in our eyes to get
    Was all our propagation.
As 'twixt two equall Armies, Fate
    Suspends uncertaine victorie,
Our soules, (which to advance their state,     15
    Were gone out,) hung 'twixt her, and mee.
And whil'st our soules negotiate there,
    Wee like sepulchrall statues lay;
All day, the same our postures were,
    And wee said nothing, all the day.       20
If any, so by love refin'd,
    That he soules language understood,
And by good love were growen all minde,
    Within convenient distance stood,
He (though he knew not which soul spake,    25
    Because both meant, both spake the same)
Might thence a new concoction take,
    And part farre purer than he came.
This Extasie doth unperplex
    (We said) and tell us what we love,     30
Wee see by this, it was not sexe,
    Wee see, we saw not what did move:
But as all severall soules containe
    Mixture of things, they know not what,

Love, these mixt soules, doth mixe againe,                    35
    And makes both one, each this and that.
A single violet transplant,
    The strength, the colour, and the size,
(All which before was poore, and scant,)
    Redoubles still, and multiplies.                    40
When love, with one another so
    Interinanimates two soules,
That abler soule, which thence doth flow,
    Defects of lonelinesse controules.
Wee then, who are this new soule, know,                    45
    Of what we are compos'd, and made,
For, th'Atomies of which we grow,
    Are soules, whom no change can invade.
But O alas, so long, so farre
    Our bodies why doe wee forbeare?                    50
They are ours, though they are not wee, Wee are
    The intelligences, they the spheares.
We owe them thankes, because they thus,
    Did us, to us, at first convay,
Yeelded their forces, sense, to us,                    55
    Nor are drosse to us, but allay.
On man heavens influence workes not so,
    But that it first imprints the ayre,
Soe soule into the soule may flow,
    Though it to body first repaire.                    60
As our blood labours to beget
    Spirits, as like soules as it can,
Because such fingers need to knit
    That subtile knot, which makes us man:
So must pure lovers soules descend                    65
    T'affections, and to faculties,
Which sense may reach and apprehend,
    Else a great Prince in prison lies.
To'our bodies turne wee then, that so
    Weake men on love reveal'd may looke;                    70
Loves mysteries in soules doe grow,
    But yet the body is his booke.
And if some lover, such as wee,
    Have heard this dialogue of one,
Let him still marke us, he shall see                    75
    Small change, when we'are to bodies gone.

# I. A. Richards

---

### DONNE
### THE EXTASIE

This poem has been interpreted in very different ways and praised and blamed for surprisingly different reasons. Here, for example, are four equally opposed readings of four highly qualified authorities.

> The author evidently intends to offer, in poetic guise, an intellectual definition of the ecstatic state of two souls, which emerge from their bodies and blend so completely that they become one. The Greek term *ekstasis*, "going forth," is literally paraphrased in line 14: "Our soules (which to advance their state, were *gone out*,)," a line which must be contrasted with the final one: "Small change, when we'are *to bodies gone*"; i.e., when we return to unecstatic normal life. In view of the interpretation I have just suggested for Donne's poem, it is hardly necessary to state that I am utterly opposed to the opinion offered by the late Professor Legouis . . . who . . . sees in our poem a "sophistical" and "insidious" plea for physical consummation.
>
> Now, in order to justify such a carnal interpretation, Legouis has interpreted line 50 ("Our bodies why doe wee forbeare?") as if *forbear* meant, not "endure, tolerate," as I have understood it, but "restrain, control" ("*pourquoi s'abstiennent nos corps si longtemps?*"). Furthermore, in the last line: "Small change, when we'are to bodies gone," which I have explained as referring to the inevitable return from ecstasy to everyday life, he evidently sees an allusion to physical love. Before such Gallic worldly wisdom, such familiarity with the age-old stratagems of a resourceful seducer (of a Valmont in *Les Liaisons Dangereuses*), how naive my own earnest remarks may appear!

Leo Spitzer, *A Method of Interpreting Literature*, pp. 8–20

With Mr. Spitzer's opinions we may compare:

I trace in his poetry three levels of sentiment. On the lowest level (lowest, that is, in order of complexity), we have the celebration of simple appetite, as in "Elegy XIX". . . . On the highest level, we have the poems of ostentatiously virtuous love, "The Undertaking," "A Valediction: Forbidding Mourning," and "The Extasie." You may deny, as perhaps some do, that the romantic conception of "pure" passion has any meaning; but certainly, if there is such a thing, it is not like this. It does not prove itself pure by talking about purity. It does not keep on drawing distinctions between spirit and flesh to the detriment of the latter and then explaining why the flesh is, after all, to be used.

This is what Donne does, and the result is singularly unpleasant. The more he labours the deeper "dun is in the mire," and it is quite arguable that "The Extasie" is a much nastier poem than the nineteenth "Elegie." What any sensible woman would make of such a wooing, it is difficult to imagine—or would be difficult if we forgot the amazing protective faculty which each sex possesses of not listening to the other.

C. S. Lewis, *Seventeenth Century Studies*, pp. 95–96

After which we may do well to consider what sort of a wooing "this dialogue of one" may be and what, in fact, a sensible woman does make of it.

On what grounds does Mr. Lewis object to Donne "drawing distinctions between spirit and flesh to the detriment of the latter"? What else could he do? Could a man of his time and of his religion have thought of the flesh either as equal to or as indistinguishable from the spirit? . . . Donne, in "The Extasie," is attempting (by his usual means of employing a series of analogies) to explain that the union of spirit with spirit expresses itself in the flesh, just as the soul lives in the body and, in this world, cannot exist without it.

Joan Bennett, *Seventeenth Century Studies*, pp. 95–96

Let us now, so warned, give the poem as close a reading as we can.

Lines 1–4: The scenery, this mixture of bedroom and out-of-doors is puzzling: the metaphorical meanings of "pregnant" are somewhat hidden by "swel'd up." The bank is covered with violets, and the lovers, who are in line 38 somehow like a violet (but lines 38–42 may be an interpolation), are later to rest their reclining heads all day, lines 18–19. In line 4 they are sitting and are "we two, one anothers best": each is not only the one that the other likes best, but the one that is *best* for the other. The rest of the poem is about this *best* in the deepest possible sense.

Lines 5–6: They are handfast, with both hands. There is the strongest suggestion of betrothal. The "balme" is balm of Gilead, warmth, comfort, shelter, given and returned; "which thence did spring": the handclasp is the source of the balm.

Lines 7–8 make many readers blink. These two pairs of eyes are gazing into one another so close together that each pair sees, and is seen by, the other as only one single eye—an emblem of the unity the poem is to contemplate.

Lines 9–12: "as yet" is clear warning; further "meanes" and further "propagation" are to come. About ten years earlier (1603) Shakespeare had written:

> . . . *nor doth the eye itself,*
> *That most pure spirit of sense, behold itself,*
> *Not going from itself; but eye to eye oppos'd*
> *Salutes each other with the other's form;*
> *For speculation turns not to itself*
> *Till it hath travell'd and is mirror'd there*
> *Where it may see itself.*
>
> *Troilus and Cressida*, III, *iii*

Lines 13–16: What is this sudden and surprising military metaphor doing here? With it we are swept off into the atmosphere of high politics, almost of Zeus poising Greek and Trojan destinies in his golden balance. And it is "to advance their state" (as on a Field of the Cloth of Gold) that the "soules . . . were gone out." Perhaps this only asserts the sovereign rank of these souls that are, through this negotiation, becoming so united. They are too equal for there to be any question of a victory for one over the other. Something far more interesting is hanging in the balance, and the poem is to tell us what this is.

Lines 17–20: What a change from the lively eye-to-eye posture of lines 7–8. They are like Knight and Lady on their tomb—while the Extasie continues. It began as soon as they were "gone out." So motionless are their bodies that "wee said nothing all the day."

Lines 21–28: Poems often pause to tell the Reader what is happening—as here; "so by love refin'd": the poem is an account of this refining. The root meaning of "fine," here, is end and aim; what is refined is made again as it should be.

Refining is especially the process of separating metal from ore and the poem is going on to talk of "dross" and "allay" (alloy). "Soules language": as distinguished from what tongues can say. Though their bodies say nothing, the soules talk together on and on. What they jointly say is reported in the poem which is simply, from line 29 on, this report. "And by good love were growen all minde": the report is going to explain, very precisely, that "growen all minde" does not mean exclusion or disregard of the body, but body's development to become mind. "Concoction": a ripening or making ready by heat, as in cooking; "farre purer": the poem exists to clarify what this means.

Lines 29–32: "doth unperplex": what has been tangled is unravelled; "and tell us what we love": the greatest and hardest of all questions is answered by this extasie. "We see by this it was not sexe": the Oxford Dictionary gives this as the earliest occurrence of *sex* in this, its most frequent modern use. The line could be the introduction of this meaning for it. What a career it has had! "We see we saw not": we now see that formerly we did not see. "What did move": taken together with "what we love," this phrase is the key to the poem. Two passages, one from Plato, one from Aristotle, help with it.

> Socrates is speaking: When it comes to the good, everyone wants the thing itself and what only seems good isn't good enough for anyone. . . . This then, the good, is what every soul is looking for, and for this every soul does all that it does, feeling in some way what it is, but troubled and uncertain and unable to see clearly enough.
>
> —*Republic* VI, 506E

It is then the Idea of the Good that is really, in and behind all we do and what each soul is seeking.

> There is a mover which moves without being moved, being eternal. . . . And the object of thought and the object of desire move in this way; they move without being moved.
>
> —*Metaphysics*, 1072a

Since this Extasie can "tell us what we love," it thereby can make us see "what did move."

Another quotation—equally well known to Donne—will help us here:

> Thoun hast made us unto Thyself, and our hearts are
> restless till they find their rest in Thee.
>
> —(St. Augustine, *Confessions*, I, i, i)

That this great traditional meaning is present here much
else in Donne's writing will confirm. When Anne More, his
wife, died in 1617, he wrote "Holy Sonnet XVII" (page 129).

Donne's meeting with Anne More, 1598, and their marriage, 1601 (which cost him a year in the Fleet Prison),
changed him profoundly. It is not strange that he should have
put his knowledge of this change into his poetry. Compare
the "Holy Sonnet XVII's" "and my good is dead" with "one
another's best" in line 4 of "The Extasie", and the sonnet's "so
streams do show their head" with "tell us what we love" in
line 30.

Lines 33–44: "Several soules": separate souls; "they know
not what": when they become one soul they do know just
that; "interinanimates": like two logs each of which makes
the other burn; "defects of loneliness": chief of which is
ignorance—of what we are.

Lines 49–52: Here comes the turning point of the poem,
and the place from which the chief differences as to what it is
doing derive. The key-word is "forbeare"; some—as we have
seen—want to take this as "endure, put up with." Push this
and we would get: "Why don't we commit suicide?" Others
take "forbeare," as "refrain, abstain from using and enjoying."
The reader has to choose in accord with his understanding of
the rest of the poem. "The intelligences . . . the spheres":
Ptolemaic cosmology; each of the nine concentric spheres has
its angelic intelligence which governs it. So these two souls
have one common sphere, which they jointly govern: their
bodies.

Lines 53–56: "Did us, to us, at first convay": it was their
bodies that enabled them to see and talk with one another
before they had such fuller knowledge of one another as they
now have. "Yeelded their forces, sense, to us": surrendered
their sensory powers, appetites, etc., became *ours* (line 51).
"Nor are drosse to us, but allay": not scum from smelting or
impurity to be separated, but something to temper or abate;
also, an alloy, as nickel, etc., which can make steel stronger
and sharper than mere iron.

Lines 57–60: Medieval physics, meteorology, and astrology.

Lines 61–64: Medieval physiology. The animal spirits produced by the blood were thought necessary to tie body and
soul together.

Lines 65–68: The climax or summit of the poem. "T'affec-tions, and to faculties": we might say, to emotions (passions) and to the will, that is, to feelings and to resolves. "Which sense may reach and apprehend." Is it the affections and faculties that can control sense, as a policeman apprehends a burglar? Or is it sense that manages to attain to and under-stand what the affections and faculties would teach it? By whichever way (or both), the intelligence (line 52) governs sense only through the affections and faculties. The doctrine is Plato's in *The Republic* (435, 587): the courageous ele-ment, the spirited, is the necessary executive if the governing mind is to maintain its due control over the appetites and desires. The soul can only rule the senses through what descriptive psychology calls the sentiments. "Else a great Prince in prison lies": How we understand this will really be a reflection, a gathering together of our understanding of the rest of the poem. We should not forget that the prime duty of a great prince is to govern, to restore and preserve order. Who have imprisoned him and how are relevant questions. The prison house is Plato's image (515, 517).

Lines 69–72: "To our bodies turn we then" (compare lines 49–50 and line 76). The two who all day "like sepulchrall statues lay" are now to make love: the visible, sensory symbol of the invisible mystery contemplated in the extasie. The souls which "to advance their state" were "gone out" are now returning to write and read that transcription that is the body.

Lines 73–76: "And if some lover such as we." Compare lines 20–26. Any such lover would be "so by love refin'd / That he soules language understood, / And by good lover were growen all minde." Is it then unreasonable to conclude that the subject, the aim and end of the poem is to record what that good love and the good that it loves must be? Coleridge, who described Donne's poetry so admirably:

*With Donne, whose muse on dromedary trots,*
*Wreathe iron pokers into true-love knots;*
*Rhyme's sturdy cripple, fancy's maze and clue,*
*Wit's forge and fire-blast, meaning's press and screw,*

can best sum up:

Nothing is wanted but the eye, which is the light of this house, the light which is the eye of this soul. This *seeing* light, this *enlightening* eye, is Reflection. It is more, indeed, than is ordinarily meant by that word;

but it is what a *Christian* ought to mean by it, and to know too, whence it first came, and still continues to come—of what light even this light is *but* a reflection.

—*Aids to Reflection*, Aphorism IX

So streams do show their heads.

# Holy Sonnets

## I

Thou hast made me, And shall thy worke decay?
Repaire me now, for now mine end doth haste,
I runne to death, and death meets me as fast,
And all my pleasures are like yesterday;
I dare not move my dimme eyes any way,          5
Despaire behind, and death before doth cast
Such terrour, and my feeble flesh doth waste
By sinne in it, which it t'wards hell doth weigh;
Onely thou art above, and when towards thee
By thy leave I can looke, I rise againe;          10
But our old subtle foe so tempteth me,
That not one houre my selfe I can sustaine;
Thy Grace may wing me to prevent his art,
And thou like Adamant draw mine iron heart.

## II

As due by many titles I resigne
My selfe to thee, O God, first I was made
By thee, and for thee, and when I was decay'd
Thy blood bought that, the which before was thine;
I am thy sonne, made with thy selfe to shine,          5
Thy servant, whose paines thou hast still repaid,
Thy sheepe, thine Image, and, till I betray'd
My selfe, a temple of thy Spirit divine;
Why doth the devill then usurpe on mee?
Why doth he steale, nay ravish that's thy right?          10
Except thou rise and for thine owne worke fight,
Oh I shall soone despaire, when I doe see
That thou lov'st mankind well, yet wilt'not chuse me,
And Satan hates mee, yet is loth to lose mee.

## III

O might those sighes and teares returne againe
Into my breast and eyes, which I have spent,

That I might in this holy discontent
Mourne with some fruit, as I have mourn'd in vaine;
In mine Idolatry what showres of raine                    5
Mine eyes did waste? what griefs my heart did rent?
That sufferance was my sinne; now I repent;
'Cause I did suffer I must suffer paine.
Th'hydroptique drunkard, and night-scouting thiefe,
The itchy Lecher, and selfe tickling proud                10
Have the remembrance of past joyes, for reliefe
Of comming ills. To (poore) me is allow'd
No ease; for, long, yet vehement griefe hath beene
Th'effect and cause, the punishment and sinne.


#### IV

Oh my blacke Soule! now thou art summoned
By sicknesse, deaths herald, and champion;
Thou art like a pilgrim, which abroad hath done
Treason, and durst not turne to whence hee is fled,
Or like a thiefe, which till deaths doome be read,        5
Wisheth himselfe delivered from prison;
But damn'd and hal'd to execution,
Wisheth that still he might be imprisoned.
Yet grace, if thou repent, thou canst not lacke;
But who shall give thee that grace to beginne?            10
Oh make thy selfe with holy mourning blacke,
And red with blushing, as thou art with sinne;
Or wash thee in Christs blood, which hath this might
That being red, it dyes red soules to white.


#### V

I am a little world made cunningly
Of Elements, and an Angelike spright,
But black sinne hath betraid to endlesse night
My worlds both parts, and (oh) both parts must die.
You which beyond that heaven which was most high          5
Have found new sphears, and of new lands can write,
Powre new seas in mine eyes, that so I might
Drowne my world with my weeping earnestly,
Or wash it if it must be drown'd no more:
But oh it must be burnt! alas the fire                    10
Of lust and envie have burnt it heretofore,
And made it fouler; Let their flames retire,
And burne me ô Lord, with a fiery zeale
Of thee and thy house, which doth in eating heale.

## VI

This is my playes last scene, here heavens appoint
My pilgrimages last mile; and my race
Idly, yet quickly runne, hath this last pace,
My spans last inch, my minutes latest point,
And gluttonous death, will instantly unjoynt          5
My body, and soule, and I shall sleepe a space,
But my ever-waking part shall see that face,
Whose feare already shakes my every joynt:
Then, as my soule, to'heaven her first seate, takes flight,
And earth-borne body, in the earth shall dwell,       10
So, fall my sinnes, that all may have their right,
To where they'are bred, and would presse me, to hell.
Impute me righteous, thus purg'd of evill,
For thus I leave the world, the flesh, the devill.

## VII

At the round earths imagin'd corners, blow
Your trumpets, Angells, and arise, arise
From death, you numberlesse infinities
Of soules, and to your scattred bodies goe,
All whom the flood did, and fire shall o'erthrow,     5
All whom warre, dearth, age, agues, tyrannies,
Despaire, law, chance, hath slaine, and you whose eyes,
Shall behold God, and never tast deaths woe.
But let them sleepe, Lord, and mee mourne a space,
For, if above all these, my sinnes abound,            10
'Tis late to aske abundance of thy grace,
When wee are there; here on this lowly ground,
Teach mee how to repent; for that's as good
As if thou'hadst seal'd my pardon, with thy blood.

## VIII

If faithfull soules be alike glorifi'd
As Angels, then my fathers soul doth see,
And adds this even to full felicitie,
That valiantly I hels wide mouth o'rstride:
But if our mindes to these soules be descry'd         5
By circumstances, and by signes that be
Apparent in us, not immediately,
How shall my mindes white truth by them be try'd?
They see idolatrous lovers weepe and mourne,
And vile blasphemous Conjurers to call               10
On Jesus name, and Pharisaicall

Dissemblers feigne devotion. Then turne
O pensive soule, to God, for he knowes best
Thy true griefe, for he put it in my breast.

### IX

If poysonous mineralls, and if that tree,
Whose fruit threw death on else immortall us,
If lecherous goats, if serpents envious
Cannot be damn'd; Alas; why should I bee?
Why should intent or reason, borne in mee,                 5
Make sinnes, else equall, in mee more heinous?
And mercy being easie, and glorious
To God; in his sterne wrath, why threatens hee?
But who am I, that dare dispute with thee
O God? Oh! of thine onely worthy blood,                   10
And my teares, make a heavenly Lethean flood,
And drowne in it my sinnes blacke memorie;
That thou remember them, some claime as debt,
I thinke it mercy, if thou wilt forget.

### X

Death be not proud, though some have called thee
Mighty and dreadfull, for, thou art not soe,
For, those, whom thou think'st, thou dost overthrow,
Die not, poore death, nor yet canst thou kill mee.
From rest and sleepe, which but thy pictures bee,          5
Much pleasure, then from thee, much more must flow,
And soonest our best men with thee doe goe,
Rest of their bones, and soules deliverie.
Thou art slave to Fate, Chance, kings, and desperate men,
And dost with poyson, warre, and sicknesse dwell,         10
And poppie, or charmes can make us sleepe as well,
And better than thy stroake; why swell'st thou then?
One short sleepe past, wee wake eternally,
And death shall be no more; death, thou shalt die.

### XI

Spit in my face you Jewes, and pierce my side,
Buffet, and scoffe, scourge, and crucifie mee,
For I have sinn'd, and sinn'd, and onely hee,
Who could do no iniquitie, hath dyed:
But by my death can not be satisfied                      5
My sinnes, which passe the Jewes impiety:

They kill'd once an inglorious man, but I
Crucifie him daily, being now glorified.
Oh let mee then, his strange love still admire:
Kings pardon, but he bore our punishment.          10
And *Jacob* came cloth'd in vile harsh attire
But to supplant, and with gainfull intent:
God cloth'd himselfe in vile mans flesh, that so
Hee might be weake enough to suffer woe.

### XII

Why are wee by all creatures waited on?
Why doe the prodigall elements supply
Life and food to mee, being more pure than I,
Simple, and further from corruption?
Why brook'st thou, ignorant horse, subjection?      5
Why dost thou bull, and bore so seelily
Dissemble weaknesse, and by'one mans stroke die,
Whose whole kinde, you might swallow and feed upon?
Weaker I am, woe is mee, and worse than you,
You have not sinn'd, nor need be timorous.          10
But wonder at a greater wonder, for to us
Created nature doth these things subdue,
But their Creator, whom sin, nor nature tyed,
For us, his Creatures, and his foes, hath dyed.

### XIII

What if this present were the worlds last night?
Marke in my heart, O Soule, where thou dost dwell,
The picture of Christ crucified, and tell
Whether that countenance can thee affright,
Teares in his eyes quench the amazing light,        5
Blood fills his frownes, which from his pierc'd head fell.
And can that tongue adjudge thee unto hell,
Which pray'd forgiveness for his foes fierce spight?
No, no; but as in my idolatrie
I said to all my profane mistresses,                10
Beauty, of pitty, foulnesse onely is
A signe of rigour: so I say to thee,
To wicked spirits are horrid shapes assign'd,
This beauteous forme assures a pitious minde.

### XIV

Batter my heart, three person'd God; for, you
As yet but knocke, breathe, shine, and seeke to mend;

That I may rise, and stand, o'erthrow mee,'and bend
Your force, to breake, blowe, burn and make me new.
I, like an usurpt towne, to'another due,                    5
Labour to'admit you, but Oh, to no end,
Reason your viceroy in mee, mee should defend,
But is captiv'd, and proves weake or untrue.
Yet dearely'I love you,'and would be loved faine,
But am betroth'd unto your enemie:                          10
Divorce mee,'untie, or breake that knot againe,
Take mee to you, imprison mee, for I
Except you'enthrall mee, never shall be free,
Nor ever chast, except you ravish mee.


### XV

Wilt thou love God, as he thee? then digest,
My Soule, this wholsome meditation,
How God the Spirit, by Angels waited on
In heaven, doth make his Temple in thy brest.
The Father having begot a Sonne most blest,                5
And still begetting, (for he ne'r begonne)
Hath deign'd to chuse thee by adoption,
Coheire to'his glory,'and Sabbaths endlesse rest;
And as a robb'd man, which by search doth finde
His stolne stuffe sold, must lose or buy'it againe:        10
The Sonne of glory came downe, and was slaine,
Us whom he'had made, and Satan stolne, to unbinde.
'Twas much, that man was made like God before,
But, that God should be made like man, much more.


### XVI

Father, part of his double interest
Unto thy kingdome, thy Sonne gives to mee,
His joynture in the knottie Trinitie
Hee keepes, and gives to me his deaths conquest.
This Lambe, whose death, with life the world hath blest,   5
Was from the worlds beginning slaine, and he
Hath made two Wills, which with the Legacie
Of his and thy kingdome, doe thy Sonnes invest.
Yet such are thy laws, that men argue yet
Whether a man those statutes can fulfill;                  10
None doth; but all-healing grace and spirit
Revive againe what law and letter kill.
Thy lawes abridgement, and thy last command
Is all but love; Oh let this last Will stand!

### XVII

Since she whom I lov'd hath payd her last debt
To Nature, and to hers, and my good is dead,
And her Soule early into heaven ravished,
Wholly on heavenly things my mind is sett.
Here the admyring her my mind did whett          5
To seeke thee God; so streames do shew their head;
But though I have found thee, and thou my thirst hast fed,
A holy thirsty dropsy melts mee yett.
But why should I begg more Love, when as thou
Dost wooe my soule for hers; offring all thine:          10
And dost not only feare least I allow
My Love to Saints and Angels things divine,
But in thy tender jealosy dost doubt
Least the World, Fleshe, yea Devill putt thee out.

### XVIII

Show me deare Christ, thy Spouse, so bright and clear.
What! is it She, which on the other shore
Goes richly painted? or which rob'd and tore
Laments and mournes in Germany and here?
Sleepes she a thousand, then peepes up one yeare?          5
Is she selfe truth and errs? now new, now outwore?
Doth she, and did she, and shall she evermore
On one, on seaven, or on no hill appeare?
Dwells she with us, or like adventuring knights
First travaile we to seeke and then make Love?          10
Betray kind husband thy spouse to our sights,
And let myne amorous soule court thy mild Dove,
Who is most trew, and pleasing to thee, then
When she'is embrac'd and open to most men.

### XIX

Oh, to vex me, contraryes meet in one:
Inconstancy unnaturally hath begott
A constant habit; that when I would not
I change in vowes, and in devotione.
As humorous is my contritione          5
As my prophane Love, and as soone forgott:
As ridlingly distemper'd, cold and hott,
As praying, as mute; as infinite, as none.
I durst not view heaven yesterday; and to day
In prayers, and flattering speaches I court God:          10

To morrow I quake with true feare of his rod.
So my devout fitts come and go away
Like a fantastique Ague: save that here
Those are my best dayes, when I shake with feare.

# A. Alvarez

## DONNE
## HOLY SONNETS

I suspect that Donne did not much like the sonnet as a literary form. There are, after all, none at all in the *Songs and Sonnets*, despite the title. Elsewhere in his collected poems there are half a dozen verse letters to young friends-about-town, all sonnets, all early, and all—with one possible exception—worthless. To produce his best work Donne needed a form much freer than that of the sonnet, a form with subtler rhythms and a less defined rhyme-scheme that could move with the movement of his sensibility, contain and echo the twists of his logic. Even when he used rhymed couplets, in the "Elegies" and "Satyres," he handled the meter with such freedom and treated the rhymes so off-handedly that his natural speaking voice was enriched by the ghost of that strictest of molds; it became a kind of echo chamber enhancing his natural resonance and individuality.

This genius for using every metrical form as though it had never been used by anyone before, as though he had just invented it, casually and specially for the occasion, deserted Donne when he first turned seriously to sonnets in about 1607. That self-contained and intertwined series, "La Corona," is, for him, startlingly unstartling and staid. It reads as though he had adopted the mode as a deliberate act of self-discipline, a means of chastening his Muse as he was gradually chastening his life and ambitions in his long decision to enter the church. The *Holy Sonnets* are later—though the bulk came only a couple of years after "La Corona" if Miss Helen Gardner is right in her dating, and on these scholarly matters she usually is. Certainly, they are an altogether more individual achievement than "La Corona," but an achievement almost in the teeth of the sonnet form. They have none of the usual neatness or charm or grace that the Elizabethans had made seem obligatory. He merely used the inherent tightness of the sonnet to reflect both personal tensions and the highly organized, compressed thinking that, with Donne, always went with emotional disturbance.

This taut complexity of tone defines the kind of poems the *Holy Sonnets* are. They have nothing to do with the certainties of faith. On the contrary, they are about the lack of faith, about guilt, hesitation, uncertainty and spiritual failure; about, in short, the obstructions to revelation rather than about revelation itself. I have written elsewhere[1] that unlike George Herbert, Donne was continually arguing out his position with God in such a way as to make you believe that there was a good deal to be said on both sides. So the sonnets are inner debates, the outcome of which is never wholly certain. And they are carried out with a good deal of intricate theological argument.

The result is a distinct and unresolved clash between the private, the spiritual and the worldly. The best of them have that unforced and utterly individual note that was part of Donne's unique contribution to English poetry. They also have that other part of his contribution: the wholly unacademic effortlessness of intellectual reference. Donne's intellectualism, I mean, was very much that of a man of the world; his wide and intense learning was counterbalanced by an equally wide and intense sophistication. The clash, then, is in the way Donne used this worldly, sophisticated tone to cope with those moments at which personal anxiety and theology intersect. His gift is to make worldliness seem spiritual and faith a matter of sense and sensibility.

> *And thou like Adamant draw mine iron heart . . .*
> *Nor ever chast, except you ravish mee . . .*

The writing is so convinced, the rhythm moves so subtly and individually, that you scarcely notice that, as figures of speech, these lines are two of the most extreme and "conceited" in the series. The point—if it needs making again—is that in Donne's maturest work the conceit was in no way self-conscious, eye-catching or knock-you-down. It was, instead, an indication of the intellectual command and range of experience he brought to bear on his poems. It was a sign that he was not restricting his responses for the sake of propriety or of any false concept of purity of poetical tone. His triumph is that he makes it seem utterly natural to talk of the love of God and of religious conflict in terms of science and sex.

So his assurance is the product of great sophistication—intellectual and emotional as well as poetic. Consider, for example:

> *At the round earths imagin'd corners*

[1] *The School of Donne.* New York, Pantheon, 1961.

Even at the beginning of one of the most powerful and, in every sense, rousing of all his sonnets, he does not relax his intellectual precision for rhetorical effect. Note, I mean, that "imagin'd." According to the notes, Donne had in mind a passage from Revelations: "I saw four angels standing at the four corners of the earth." But Donne the seventeenth century intellectual, with his "hydroptique, immoderate desire of humane learning and languages" cannot accept St. John's inaccuracy: the earth is round, it has no corners. Precision above all things.

With this precision goes an intricate, personal theological questioning. In a way, the great dramatic outburst—"At the round earths imagin'd corners," "Death be not proud," "Batter my heart"—are not typical of the overall tone of the *Holy Sonnets*. The note is generally more pausing, inturned and probing: "Thou hast made me, And shall thy work decay?", "As due by many titles I resigne," "I am a little world made cunningly," "If faithfull soules," "If poysonous mineralls," "Why are wee by all creatures waited on?", "Oh, to vex me, contraryes meet in one"; and so on. The questions, premises, suppositions and imagined situations are teased out in detail, with great exactness and shows of logic.

This is not, I think, always an advantage. Within the confines of the sonnet Donne's habitual logical compression sometimes jams up, so that, for example, when he plagiarizes himself, the religious verse sounds less convinced and convincing than the secular:

*You which beyond that heaven which was most high*
*Have found new sphears, and of new lands can write,*
*Powre new seas in mine eyes, that so I might*
*Drowne my world with my weeping earnestly,*
*Or wash it, if it must be drown'd no more:*
*But oh it must be burnt!*

That is one of his favorite images, which he had worked out often and better before: in "The Good-Morrow," "A Valediction: Of Weeping" and "A Nocturnall Upon S. Lucies Day." Compared with those three poems, the holy sonnet seems thinner, less urgent, more stilted, and shriller.

The occasions of the *Holy Sonnets* are, of course, rather more formal and circumscribed than those of the *Songs and Sonnets*. Indeed, the latest academic theory—which I don't believe—is that the poems are formal to the extent of being deliberate exercises in Ignatian meditation. Be that as it may, Donne certainly seems to have used them as a showcase for

himself in the role of learned and devout theologian. In other
words, they often read like a dry run for the sermons. And in
some ways, the sonnets and the sermons are alike. We remember both for those marvellous outbursts when Donne,
that tense, supremely intelligent and sensitive, and curiously
modern intellectual, pulls out every trick of passionate rhetoric he can muster in order, finally, to convince himself of
the truth of what he is saying. Yet in the sermons these are
only isolated passages in long, scrupulous theological analyses.
Even "Death's Duell," that last and most extraordinary performance, which inspired one listener to comment that
Donne had "preach't his own Funeral Sermon," is meticu-
lously argued and detailed despite its intensity, eloquence
and infinitely dramatic situation.

The *Holy Sonnets* record some of the private, internal
conflicts which lay behind the grander public occasions of his
preaching. Yet the poems, too, are most successful when
most dramatic. Their drama however is less of situation than
of language. It was a question of endowing a staid form with
a certain intensity of action. Donne did so by using a technique he had discovered most triumphantly in an early poem,
"Elegie XVI":

> . . . *I saw him I,*
> *Assail'd, fight, taken, stabb'd, bleed, fall, and die.*

The best of the *Holy Sonnets* are informed by the same
battering speed and attack:

> *All whom the flood did, and fire shall o'erthrow,*
> *All whom warre, dearth, age, agues, tyrannies,*
> *Despaire, law, chance, hath slaine . . .*
>
> · · ·
>
> *Thou art slave to Fate, Chance, kings, and desperate*
>    *men,*
> *And dost with poyson, warre, and sicknesse dwell,*
> *And poppie, or charmes can make us sleepe as well,*
> *And better then thy stroake . . .*
>
> · · ·
>
> *Batter my heart, three person'd God; for, you*
> *As yet but knocke, breathe, shine, and seeke to mend;*
> *That I may rise, and stand, o'erthrow mee,'and bend*
> *Your force, to breake, blowe, burn and make me*
>    *new . . .*

It is a technical solution to a kind of behavioral problem. Part of Donne's perennial power came from his awareness of himself and of the figure he was cutting at the instant of writing. But this awareness depended, naturally, on the presence of an audience, whether it was one girl or a whole fashionable churchful. In contrast, the *Holy Sonnets* were debates with himself and with God, whose presence and reactions, even if they could possibly be presumed, certainly couldn't be predicted. So Donne created the drama and the audience by assault. He reversed the situation of his love poems, writing as though he himself were the recipient of the aggressive masculinity and seductive quickness of response that was always, whatever the circumstances, his peculiar *forte*. In his "Elegie," Thomas Carew wrote of Donne:

> . . . *the flame*
> *Of thy brave Soule, that shot such heat and light,*
> *As burnt our earth, and made our darknesse bright,*
> *Committed holy Rapes upon our Will* . . .

By some curious technical sleight of style Donne, in his *Holy Sonnets,* seems to be both the lover and the loved.

The problem, then, was how a highly sophisticated, worldly man whose poetic force relied to a large extent on his awareness of himself acting *in* the world, wrote poetry of inner, spiritual debate without abandoning his natural strength and vitality. The answer was only partly in the usual metaphysical solution—relentlessly worldly figures of speech —and only partly in Donne's adoption of his later scholastic role of the intricate theologian and preacher. The main solution was in creating drama out of the form and language themselves. It was the drama of language in continual, fruitful conflict with the stubborn and restrictive shape of the conventional sonnet.

## Hymne to God My God, in My Sicknesse

Since I am coming to that Holy roome,
  Where, with thy Quire of Saints for evermore,
I shall be made thy Musique; As I come
  I tune the Instrument here at the dore,
  And what I must doe then, thinke here before.          5

Whilst my Physitians by their love are growne
  Cosmographers, and I their Mapp, who lie
Flat on this bed, that by them may be showne
  That this is my South-west discoverie
  *Per fretum febris*, by these streights to die,          10

I joy, that in these straits, I see my West;
  For, though theire currants yeeld returne to none,
What shall my West hurt me? As West and East
  In all flatt Maps (and I am one) are one,
  So death doth touch the Resurrection.          15

Is the Pacifique Sea my home? Or are
  The Easterne riches? Is *Jerusalem?*
*Anyan,* and *Magellan,* and *Gibraltare,*
  All streights, and none but streights, are wayes to them,
  Whether where *Japhet* dwelt, or *Cham,* or *Sem.*          20

We thinke that *Paradise* and *Calvarie,*
  *Christs* Crosse, and *Adams* tree, stood in one place;
Looke Lord, and finde both *Adams* met in me;
  As the first *Adams* sweat surrounds my face,
  May the last *Adams* blood my soule embrace.          25

So, in his purple wrapp'd receive mee Lord,
  By these his thornes give me his other Crowne;
And as to others soules I preach'd thy word,
  Be this my Text, my Sermon to mine owne,
  Therefore that he may raise the Lord throws down.          30

*Louis L. Martz*

---

DONNE
HYMNE TO GOD MY GOD, IN MY SICKNESSE

This poem represents an epitome of the art of religious meditation, as practiced throughout Europe and England during the seventeenth century. The opening stanza recalls the deliberate mode of preparation that preceded every period of formal meditation, according to the devout instructions of the time. The end and aim of the "spiritual exercise," as in the Jesuit practice of meditation, was clearly foreseen, and the process of the meditation fully planned and set forth in articulated stages. Thus Donne, lying on what he thinks will be his deathbed, prepares a hymn of praise to God, prefiguring the hymns he believes he will be singing in the afterlife of peace which he has strenuously sought throughout a varied and turbulent lifetime. The poem was probably written during Donne's nearly fatal illness in 1623, when he had just passed his fiftieth year, although Izaak Walton may be right in dating the poem at the time of Donne's last illness in 1631. In any case, the poem sums up the poetical and meditative disciplines of a lifetime, bringing all of Donne's Renaissance experience to focus upon this moment of the soul's passage:

> *As I come*
> *I tune the Instrument here at the dore,*
> *And what I must doe then, thinke here before.*

The emphasis falls upon the deliberate act of *thinking*, that quality of "passionate ratiocination" that Grierson long ago saw as one of the distinctive qualities of the "metaphysical" style in poetry. It was a mode of poetry widely practiced in the Europe and England of Donne's era, a mode that found its essential inspiration in the discovery of analogies between the outer world of nature, the macrocosm, and the little world of man, the microcosm. This highly intellectual style in poetry coincided easily and inevitably with the contemporary art of religious meditation, which likewise worked through such analogies, or "similitudes," as they were called. The most famous aspect of the Jesuit method of meditation was its emphasis upon beginning the process with what was called the "composition of place"—which might evoke before the eyes of the imagination some scene from the life of Christ or a saint, or might develop some imaginative comparison, designed to give a concrete setting for the meditative action. One can see from this hymn how the metaphysical style and the meditative method have here combined to assist Donne in the creation of one of his greatest poems. For the whole poem depends upon a precisely developed analogy between the outer world and the inner world, an analogy which Donne uses as the opening "composition" for his meditation on death. His physicians, charting the course of his disease, have become the geographers of his body; spread out flat upon his bed, he has become a map on which the doctors are charting forth a "South-west discoverie" such as Magellan made. But the "streights" through which this passage will be made are the straits, the difficulties and pains, of death: *Per fretum febris*, "through the straits of fever." *Fretum* is a rich word here, for it means in Latin both a strait of water, and, by transference, any condition of raging, swelling, violence, or heat. The witty play on words in itself shows a remarkable equanimity, that striking ability of Donne (and kindred poets, such as George Herbert or Andrew Marvell) to view his own situation from a distance, to hold his own body and soul off at arm's length and study his situation in objective detail, as the art of meditation encouraged one to do.

So Donne foresees his westward passage, toward sundown, but as he questions himself, he finds joy in the prospect, for he knows that a flat map is only an illusory diagram: at the far edge, West becomes East, sundown becomes sunrise. The word Orient indeed derives from the Latin verb meaning "to arise"; and in the old religious tradition that Donne cites in his sermons, another name for Christ was Oriens, the rising sun (son). "So death doth touch the Resurrection."

Donne's meditative questioning in stanzas three and four indicates a process of analysis bent upon understanding the goal of his passage, and indeed the very questions imply the goal, for the "Pacifique Sea," the "Easterne riches," and Jerusalem are all symbols of the "Holy roome" that Donne is now approaching:

> *Is the Pacifique Sea my home? Or are*
> *The Easterne riches? Is* Jerusalem?
> Anyan, *and* Magellan, *and* Gibraltare,
> *All streights, and none but streights, are wayes to them,*
> *Whether where* Japhet *dwelt, or* Cham, *or* Sem.

The compressed phrasing here contains a mine of implications. The traveller to the peaceful ocean, or to the wealth of the Orient, or to that holy city whose name means "Vision of Peace," may move through the "Straits of Anyan" (supposed by old geographers to separate Asia and America), or the Straits of Magellan, or the Straits of Gibraltar. But however he goes, the voyage is full of pain and difficulty. And this is true whatever regions of the earth he may sail from or sail between: "Whether where *Japhet* dwelt, or *Cham*, or *Sem*." In thus describing these regions Donne is indicating the ancient division of the world into the inheritance given to the three sons of Noah: Europe (Japheth), Africa (Ham), and Asia (Shem). In so doing he reminds us of the antiquity, the universality, and the inevitability of those straits that face every man who seeks his ultimate home.

In the geography of Donne's present moment there is only one goal, the heavenly Paradise made possible by Calvary, redemption by the sacrifice of Christ. In the macrocosm this singleness of aim is shown by the fact that the Paradise of Eden (usually set in Mesopotamia) and Calvary have both been located in the same region of the earth, the Near East. In the same way Adam and Christ now meet in the sick man on his bed. The sweat of his fever fulfills the curse laid upon the first Adam ("In the sweat of thy face shalt thou eat bread"), but the blood of Christ (the second and last of God's special creations in the form of man) will, the speaker hopes, redeem his soul. He prays that, as his funeral shroud, he may be wrapped in the blood of Christ, a royal garment of purple, and that thus he may be granted the Crown of Glory in Heaven. So the poem ends with a recapitulation of the central paradox: death is the passage to life, West and East are one, flatness leads to rising: "Therefore that he may raise the Lord throws down."

The closing prayer reminds us that the entire poem, after the manner of meditation in Donne's era, has been spoken in the presence of God, who is addressed confidently in the opening lines:

> *Since I am comming to that Holy roome,*
> *Where, with thy Quire of Saints for evermore,*
> *I shall be made thy Musique*

That presence is never forgotten in the poem, for what follows is a testimony of faith presented as a hymn of gratitude to the Creator. Thus, after his prologue, the speaker begins his meditation by presenting the vivid images that dramatize his present condition; and as these images develop, the dying man turns to question himself, making sure that he understands the import of these straits in which he finds himself. The meaning found, he turns in a final "colloquy" to God, ending his meditation in the traditional way, with a prayer in conversation with the Lord. So we have here, clearly revealed in miniature, all the essential components of a full religious meditation, as described in countless handbooks of Donne's day, and especially in the Jesuit exercises: Preparation, Composition, Discourse (in the old sense of analytic reasoning), and Colloquy; or to use other terms of the time, Memory, Understanding, and Will, the three powers of the Soul which are unified in the process of meditation, forming an interior trinity that represents an image, though defaced, of the greater Trinity.

Donne's poem thus becomes the full and perfect tuning of that "instrument" that was John Donne himself: his lifelong practice of poetry, his profound studies in theology, his vital interest in the Renaissance world of voyaging, his brilliant sermons now filling ten volumes, his lifelong habits of introspective meditation—all these are drawn together, driven to a focus by the power of Donne's self-dramatizing intellect. If one wonders to find such wit and ingenuity manifested even at the moment of death, the answer is clear: here is the instrument that God has made, and at the last moment, it is proper that the unique timbre and tone of the instrument should be revealed in all its subtle intensity.

# ROBERT HERRICK
## [1591–1674]

### *To the Virgins, to Make Much of Time*

Gather ye Rose-buds while ye may,
    Old Time is still a flying:
And this same flower that smiles to day,
    To morrow will be dying.

The glorious Lamp of Heaven, the Sun,       5
    The higher he's a getting,
The sooner will his Race be run,
    And nearer he's to Setting.

That Age is best, which is the first,
    When Youth and Blood are warmer;     10
But being spent, the worse, and worst
    Times, still succeed the former.

Then be not coy, but use your time;
    And while ye may, goe marry:
For having lost but once your prime,
    You may for ever tarry.     15

ROBERT HERRICK

*From a rare print by Marshall,*
*prefixed to his "Hesperides"*

**The Bettmann Archive**

## Anthony Ostroff

---

### HERRICK
### TO THE VIRGINS, TO MAKE MUCH OF TIME

Our interest in Herrick, for so long called "the sweetest songster of the cavaliers" (how the appellation cloys today!), must, in part, surprise us. The cavaliers, with their drawing-room verse in the age of Donne, full of precious Corinnas, Electras, Antheas, in London dreaming up their Greek and Roman pastorals almost a score of centuries too late—how can we give our attention to them so removed from their own realities, thus that much more from ours? Perhaps their meadows and maidens are the very stuff that dreams are made on—archetypal idylls we're as ready to read in verse by day as compose, ourselves, in sleep, by night.

But no, this won't quite do. Save for Herrick, and maybe his Master Ben, we don't much read the cavaliers except in class. (Allow an exception or two for Suckling, Lovelace, Waller, even Rochester and Anonymous, who still may take our fancy fleetingly—once or twice.) Is it then the quality of song, the felicitous flow of verse like music—*to* music, indeed, much of the time—that captures us? There's artistry enough in Herrick, surely, to win us on this ground alone. A perfect craftsman at his minor craft (if we take it to be minor). Still, there must be substance for the form to go around, and what does Herrick give us that we care for? Doubtless, above all, an attitude: a Yea to life. That's the important thing. And it begins with love. Thus Herrick's central subject: woman. No, it's more than that—it's how we think on her.

> *A sweet disorder in the dresse*
> *Kindles in cloathes a wantonnesse*

he begins one of his poems. Two lines and already she's there, the one we desire, beneath that careless garb. Or is it our desire we really see? Desire and appreciation—they're the figure of our thought that Herrick fathers forth so well. Take his Julia. Is she less than ours?

> *When as in silks my* Julia *goes,*
> *Then, then (me thinks) how sweetly flowes*
> *That liquefaction of her clothes.*
>
> *Next, when I cast mine eyes and see*
> *That brave Vibration each way free;*
> *O how that glittering taketh me!*

How stunningly right, "that brave vibration each way free"! Whether coming or going, by breasts or by buttocks, she has us. Herrick has us, in his praise. Julia is immanent by fashion's shrewd, rhetorical device made poetry: those clothes that *seem* to be the subject, yet but "become" it as do jewels or perfume a woman's mystery. (The poem's title is "Upon Julia's Clothes.") There's the marvelous progression of the rhyme, for instance: *goes, flows, clothes*—how consummately *clothes* becomes a coda in these variations on a theme! Music and meaning married—as again, in more strictly semantic fashion, in *see, free, me.* The whole spun out as on stringed instruments: the *l*s of *silks* and *Julia*, the *n*s that intervene, the liquid theme returned in *sweetly flows* and *clothes.* And so, by similar art to the end with that brilliant pizzicatto of the *t*s: *that glittering taketh me.* Not only this. The diction: *liquefaction, brave vibration, glittering*—dazzling words, in their places. Herrick is too little acknowledged as the master of diction that he is. Perhaps the mastery seems to be in too small a cause, especially in that century of thunder and lightning—Milton and Donne and the rest. But how wondrously well Herrick's meaning, word by word, is also musical. He is a melodist. And if music is the food of love. . . .

Thus to the poem before us, a poem *everybody* knows. Is it one of Herrick's best? It's his most popular. What makes it so? "To the Virgins, to Make Much of Time." How all too quaint, the *serious* mind will cry out. There's none of the gorgeous working of, say, Marvell's "To His Coy Mistress," on a similar theme—nor even does it compare to Herrick's own "Corinna's Gone A-Maying."

"Old Time is still a flying . . . To morrow will be dying." The thesis from which the poem argues is set at once, yet the chilling message doesn't hurt us much. We hardly hear "Time's winged chariot hurrying near," our eye is not cast out to "deserts of vast eternity," as in Marvell's splendid poem. But what do we want of a poem? Ah, there's the rub that maybe makes us keep this one: it's *practical!* Useful poetry. There's little enough in any language, but this one works. How many lovers through history have used it in their early years when courtship and seduction are so apt to be complex? (Youngsters all believe in immortality; no use to try to make death real to them.) "To the virgins," indeed. It's not so plural, really, when we come to practical affairs. (Consider that move from "ye" to "You" at the end.)

What? But it's not a poem of seduction? He says "While ye may, go *marry*"? True enough, the point is there, and—dreary truth!—"having lost but once your prime, / You may forever tarry." We cannot overlook it. Yet this is but as Hollywood: anything's allowed if but the fornicators marry in the end. No, no, it's not marriage Mr. Herrick wants for his virgins. (Is it?)

Not that Herrick felt he had to hide himself in what he wrote. In "To Anthea, Who May Command Him Any Thing," playing the Elizabethan pun on *die* that stands for the climax and end of the act of love as well as of life, he's plain enough. The poem ends:

> *Thou art my life, my love, my heart,*
> *The very eyes of me:*
> *And hast command of every part,*
> *To live and die for thee.*

The sexual part looms large enough in that! But maybe in his parish in Devon, where we think he wrote the poem that we now approach, he had to tell his virgins, "marry," though "merry" was what he meant. No matter to us. The poem, either way, is a delight, and we must go both ways.

But all this shirks the task of a proper introduction. Yet, one thing the poem doesn't ask, for all its darkening, and perfectly structured argument: sobriety. And what it doesn't need are program notes. Still, a note or two:

"Gather ye Rose-buds while ye may"—the author's warmth and delicacy appear at once (need attention be called to this?). "Old Time is still a flying"—the sense of familiarity, even affection, mark out a pleasantry to ease us against the harshness of the ultimate meaning. It is this graciousness of Herrick's that almost always wins us to him all the way. Then: "This same flower that smiles to day"—how it's animated by its smile! The abstract fact we know comes next—"To morrow [it] will be dying"—but the life and charm today are what captivate us here. So the lament is gentle in its effect.

Stanza two: Still the ominous message isn't desperate; there still is time; the sun's ascending yet. And even though we know its application's dark, the basic figure doesn't freeze us: the sun spans the heavens, sinks—then rises again. (Do we need a footnote to remind us of an age in which night was *night*, with no buttons to push for light?) Life's not over in a day—until it's done. And yet the chilling note *is* there. "The sooner will his race be run"—the speed with which the span is spanned makes for urgency at last: that "race" that will be run is us. We're children of the sun—best in the beginning, "when youth and blood are warmer." The harshest moment follows this, in stanza three, with the poem's only repetition—or semirepetition: *worse . . . worst* make a mean crescendo.

Thus the poem does sneak up on us. But after all, in the end it's not so dread an announcement of old age and death (though they lurk near), nor statement of the lonely plight of bachelors and old maids. True, one must admit a nice—and cruel—irony in that use of "tarry" at the close: not dalliance, emptiness. And yet the poem's not an awesome proclamation of the road to doom we all are travelling; the terms are too abstract and too traditional to strike true terror. Terror's not the intention. Instead: an invitation to life. Here, for all its deadline argument, is the poem's first and best impact. The warning with which the poem begins, the warning with which it ends, the evidence in between, bidding us take heed—all become a single, affirmative command. The secret is: the poem's negatives are never prohibitions. Here is its beauty for our time, when simple affirmations are so rare. Herrick's was no more easy age than ours in most respects, and yet it stepped outside itself and sang, at times. If the songs solved little, they were yet relief, and so they are today. Life's short, and hell is all around, but while we're here there's pleasure to be had. There is, O Ladies, love! Can we resist the charm that brevity gives to life? It's that charm, more than the brevity, that Herrick makes us see.

Then no more words about this poem. Let us make much of time, not omitting poetry. As Herrick has it, "Live merrily and trust to good verses."

## *The Collar*

I struck the board, and cry'd, "No more;
    I will abroad."
What, shall I ever sigh and pine?
My lines and life are free; free as the road,
    Loose as the winde, as large as store.        5
        Shall I be still in suit?
Have I no harvest but a thorn
To let me bloud, and not restore
What I have lost with cordiall fruit?
        Sure there was wine                        10
Before my sighs did drie it: there was corn
    Before my tears did drown it;
    Is the yeare onely lost to me?
    Have I no bayes to crown it,
No flowers, no garlands gay? all blasted,       15
        All wasted?
    Not so, my heart; but there is fruit,
        And thou hast hands.
Recover all thy sigh-blown age
On double pleasures; leave thy cold dispute      20
Of what is fit and not; forsake thy cage,
        Thy rope of sands,
Which pettie thoughts have made; and made to thee
    Good cable, to enforce and draw,
        And be thy law,                            25
While thou didst wink and wouldst not see.
        Away! take heed;
        I will abroad.
Call in thy death's-head there, tie up thy fears;
        He that forbears                           30
    To suit and serve his need
        Deserves his load.
But as I rav'd and grew more fierce and wilde
        At every word,
    Methought I heard one calling, "Childe";      35
        And I reply'd, "My Lord."

GEORGE HERBERT

*The Bettmann Archive*

*Dudley Fitts*

---

HERBERT
THE COLLAR

"The Collar" is a miniature drama of revolt against moral authority, a brief violence stilled by a single word almost before it has got well under way. A collar is a leash, a yoke. A man's conscience is like a leash: it will not always let him do what he thinks he would like to do. God yokes us, and we are told that his yoke is easy, but the poem intends for the moment not to find it so. An occupation, or profession, can be a "collar" too: the ministry, for example—and George Herbert was an Anglican priest; indeed, by a kind of metonymy that should not be read into this poem, since it would not have obtained in Herbert's day, we distinguish the priesthood by a special kind of collar. And finally, a man's memories are a leash. What he was, or what he once dreamed that he might be, is all too likely to interfere with conduct at times of self-pity or other weakness. An imaginative man, like any normal dog, has his moments of hating the leash and wishing that he could slip it. "The Collar" represents such a moment.

As often happens in Herbert's work, the image proposed by the title is developed only by implication in the poem itself. Thus the collar, which we may take as representing any of the kinds of control that I have mentioned, is dropped in favor of such parallel symbols as "cage" (line 21), "rope of sands" (line 22), "cable" (line 24), and "deaths head" (line 29). All of these images carry the idea of bugbears long and needlessly submitted to and now, in a sudden revulsion of feeling, to be cast off and denied. The rebel is impetuous; he seems young, and certainly he is sorry for himself. The texture of his speech is dense with physical materials in contrast: fruit, bays, flowers, wine, against thorns, sand, bonds. At the very beginning he "strikes the board," that is to say the table where he is sitting at dinner: the rejection, in a way, of the very sustenance that his heated imagination would desire. And at the last, one word brings him to order.

A limiting way of reading the poem is to take it autobiographically, as the record of a mood arising from George Herbert's personal predicament as a man torn between the world and the spirit. He was born to high station; he was ambitious for worldly honors, and his ambitions were confirmed while he was still a very young man by a series of brilliant university appointments and the favor of powerful friends and patrons, including his king. Everything pointed in the direction of a spectacular career in diplomacy or perhaps in the royal court. On the other hand, his health was always poor; he was devoted to, but obviously dominated by, his mother, who was one of the truly extraordinary women of her time; and the religious strain that strikes one even in his youthful letters and his early Greek and Latin poems became increasingly powerful as a series of physical and social disappointments urged him towards taking holy orders, which he did less than three years before his premature death. Read in this light, the poem would be an expression of religious negation, of a very human reluctance to say goodbye to the glitter and promise of the secular world and assume the life of an obscure country priest. It is not a mistake to read "The Collar" in this way: elsewhere, in the first of his poems called "Affliction," he glosses it himself:

> *Whereas my birth and spirit rather took*
> > *The way that takes the town;*
> *Thou didst betray me to a lingring book,*
> > *And wrapt me in a gown . . .*
>
> *Yet, for I threatned oft the siege to raise,*
> > *Not simpring all mine age,*
> *Thou often didst with Academick praise*
> > *Melt and dissolve my rage.*
> *I took the sweetned pill, till I came where*
> *I could not go away, nor persevere.*

The "sweetned pill" here seems to be his university honors, but the tone would be the same for the honors of priesthood. Actuality, compared to the sweet glitter of the past, is bitterness; a yoke is bitter.

Such a reading is possible, certainly, but it is not entirely satisfactory. It would be better to regard the poem without reference to court, university, or orders. The predicament is general: every one of us has known the collar and has longed to slip it. If we were passionate enough, and metrists sufficiently accomplished, we might write the first thirty-two lines of "The Collar"; so far, it is a superbly adolescent outburst. It is in the last four lines, however—indeed, in the last five words—that we watch the transformation into superb poetry.

This transformation has been prefigured throughout. The rebel's tone is brave enough, even frantic; but there has never been any real doubt about the outcome. The word *childe* has been in control from the beginning, and the ranter knows it.

The control, further, is delicately and insistently indicated by the management of meter and rime. George Herbert's technical range is very large, thanks to his absorption in the instrumental and vocal music of his time. His book employs more than one hundred stanza forms, many of them extremely complicated; but in "The Collar" he abandons the stanza entirely and composes in a relatively free rhapsodic manner. "Relatively": because we note a firm control of meter in spite of the irregularity of line length. Tetrameters are yoked (that word again!) with dimeters, trimeters with pentameters; but the beat is pervasive, unfailing, reinforced again and again by the strong rimes that bind the unequal lines together and keep the whole rhapsody in order. That is to say, the poem is, formally, what it is "about." Here is a kind of kinetic onomatopoeia, the sonal effects of rhythm and rime used to reduce and govern the would-be chaos of the speaker's outburst. It is this discreet ordering of the utterance, as much as anything, that accounts for the poem's impact.

THOMAS CAREW

*From the portrait by Van Dyke*

*The Bettmann Archive*

# THOMAS CAREW

## [1595–1639?]

### *Song*

Ask me no more where Jove bestows,
When June is past, the fading rose;
For in your beauty's orient deep
These flowers, as in their causes, sleep.

Ask me no more whither do stray          5
The golden atoms of the day;
For in pure love heaven did prepare
Those powers to enrich your hair.

Ask me no more whither doth haste
The nightingale, when May is past;      10
For in your sweet dividing throat
She winters and keeps warm her note.

Ask me no more where those stars 'light
That downwards fall in dead of night;
For in your eyes they sit, and there      15
Fixèd become as in their sphere.

Ask me no more if east or west
The Phœnix builds her spicy nest;
For unto you at last she flies,
And in your fragrant bosom dies.         20

# Mark Van Doren

CAREW

SONG

In the five stanzas of this formal song a lover pays five compliments to his lady. She is not named; nor does the song itself have any name except this noncommittal one that begins, casually enough, with the indefinite article: "A Song" —as if any lover, anywhere or at any time, might be understood to have seized a musical instrument of some sort and, looking into his lady's eyes, strummed it five times as he sang five answers to five questions which she or someone else has asked. It is not necessarily she who has put the questions. Perhaps she is perfectly silent, smiling as she listens; or she may not be here at all; she may indeed not exist, though we should prefer to think she does. The questions may well be the lover's own, which he has invented for the sake of their answers. They are rhetorical; they assist statement.

The five statements to which they lead are all, if one pleases, extravagant. Where does Jove, the king of the universe, send roses when they fade? Into your beauty, where they sleep. What is the destination, if any, of the sunlight's particles? Your hair, which they were created to adorn. Where does the nightingale fly when she stops singing? Into your throat, where she continues to sing until another season returns. Where do falling stars go? Into your eyes, as into the place for which they were intended. Where does the phoenix, that fabulous Arabian bird which lives forever by alternately burning itself and rising newborn from the ashes, build its nest upon which this act of immortality may be accomplished? In your bosom, of course.

Doubtless it is the extravagance of the compliments at which the lady smiles. Yet she is pleased, for she knows that her lover is trying to be absolute in the expression of his love. The things he says are true for him because he loves her without qualification. If to an indifferent person they would sound exaggerated or fantastic, he trusts her not to find them so; he counts on her to understand, as of course he understands, that overstatement is adoration's natural language. Only too much love is love enough; or rather, only too strong a statement is strong at all. The exact truth about her, supposing it could be put into words, would be inadequate to his purpose, which is to suggest that this after all is the exact truth—for him, anyway. He too smiles as he sings, watching his lady's eyes for signs that she measures the playful force with which he overstates his case. Absolute eloquence is the minimum effect at which he aims. All or nothing, as with any lover in the world, is the motto of his words and music.

But whereas he is like any other lover in his feeling he is different in his art. He is formal to what might seem a fault if we did not become aware of the resources he is using. We might let the matter go with conventional terms, or hum some current song; he explores nature, science, and myth in search of symbols that will carry his meaning. And he composes his poem with the utmost care for its structure, metrically and otherwise. The five stanzas are highly regular in their rhythm, and each of them strictly honors a pattern of syntax as well as a pattern of rhyme. Each first line begins with *ask me no more*, and each third line with *for*. The punctuation almost never varies. The rhyme scheme is the couplet scheme; and yet it is proper that the poem should appear as stanzas, as quatrains, for each set of four lines, with its asking and its answering couplet, is complete in itself, bringing the poem to a pause from which it will start again.

When it starts again, will it be any farther along? Is the poem aiming to be more than a series of statements—five, as it happens, and this is the number of the fingers on the hand that strokes the instrument whence the music comes—strung as stationary beads are strung, one after another on the string? Or is there movement in the whole? Does the poem climb? Does it reach a conclusion? Does it have a climax?

A progression appears if we consider the successive stanzas in terms of the activity, or the amount of activity, each describes. The first stanza, for example, contains no activity at all. Nothing could be quieter than the act, if it is an act, of sleeping in one's cause as the oak sleeps in the acorn or the rose in its seed, its root, waiting patiently to become itself. If this is an act, it must be done in a deep place out of time's reach; for cause itself is not a temporal thing. The place, indeed, is as deep as the lady's beauty, which is an *orient* deep. A famous word, sufficient in itself to have created Carew's reputation. For it suggests many things: the East, the brilliant spaces out of which suns rise, radiance itself, and the more general idea of source or origin—wells or fountains out of which come forth again whatever things have descended into them, or life which can be where death once was. Yet the tangible activity is nil. All is potentiality, and the sweet promise of more in place of less. Nor is the promise lightly stated: Jove is the agent of its fulfilment, and his name alliterates powerfully, decisively, with *June*.

The second stanza, breaking the trance of the first, sets things in motion, but small things, and indeed the smallest we can conceive. Atoms of light are finer than even the motes we watch dancing in a sunbeam; yet those motes will do for an image, particularly if we think of them as golden, as gold dust floating. The irregular accents we hear in the word *whither* are in the interest of what now is to be achieved: our sense of irreducible, indivisible, and all but invisible particles of matter set free—"whither do stray"—to wander where they will. Their will, in fact, is to wander toward that place of which their creator was thinking when he ground them up so light and fine. They are to settle upon my lady's already golden hair, where they will be noticed only as perfection is noticed, gracing what once seemed, yet only seemed, to be sufficiently beautiful without it.

The third stanza follows a larger creature to its destination. The nightingale, which sounds as well as is seen—where is its song continued after music's season closes? For such a singer cannot really cease; something must keep her voice warm and sweet, ready to be heard again. And here the poet runs a risk. For his answer, which is that the bird flies into his lady's throat and remains there, could be grotesque or painful if he did not know how to manage the reader's responses. He manages them, among other ways too mysterious to understand, by the word *dividing* and by the alliteration of *winters* with *warm*. *Dividing* is a musical term of Carew's century, the seventeenth, and refers to the art of descant, or singing in harmony, or performing in parts. It is a technical term for the miracle by which the many divisions of a song melt finally into one sweet thing, the song itself. The lady's throat, like the whole body of the nightingale, is where music may be said to live, singing for its own pleasure, making sound or no sound as it chooses; wintering, or waiting, in the warmth of its own notes until it chooses to sing so that all may hear. The lady is speaking or singing now; the nightingale will sing in May; but both are the same in idea, and it is in fact idea that entertains us here, not fact, not feathers, not vocal cords, not flesh in any form, nor even any audible sound. Again it is

the promise of sound, the certainty that music remains possible, which reassures us after the disappearance of the
nightingale. She has not disappeared after all, any more than
the flowers of Jove can be said to have died, or the atoms of
day to have wandered nowhere.

The fourth stanza reaches far into the universe—a dark
universe, too, for now it is the dead of night—and sees the
most startling of all movements. Stars fall. And where? Into
my lady's eyes, where the quietest of verbs is found for what
they do. They *sit*, fixed as proper stars are fixed, in the
spheres which an old astronomy assumed were there to
contain them. These spheres made music, too, grander than
that of the nightingale; but the poem, though it lets us think
of this, says nothing further about it. Our attention is on the
lady's eyes, which are bright not merely as stars are bright in
the conventional comparison, but happy in their brightness
because they are the home to which celestial wanderers
have come. Once more the image of motion has given way to
the image of rest; the moving object has plunged into the
medium best fitted to receive it and henceforth to display it.

In the final stanza the mythical phoenix, more potent to our
imagination than even the brightest star, plunges also to her
rest. But it is not the rest of death. It is a rest after which
action will commence again as life recommences in new
birth. Nor does it matter where this happens. East or west is
immaterial now; we remember *orient* in the third line of the
poem, but we are far away from even the remotest east, as
we are far away from any west. The phoenix, searching for
that spicy place where she can seem to die and yet not die,
speeds unerringly to my lady's fragrant bosom, whence she
will spring into future flight that contrasts with the quiet
power, stated itself so noiselessly in stanza one, exerted by the
causes of things. The poem returns to its beginning; draws a
circle back through the world of atoms, birds, and stars; and
enters, so to speak, itself.

The lady, meanwhile, has not moved, nor has the rhythm
of the song abandoned its stateliness, its all but monotonous
march of heavy and light syllables, its iambic walk which
only in the fifth, seventh, ninth, twelfth, and sixteenth lines
shifts momentarily into trochaic. Nor has the singer for one
instant relaxed the formality of his smile. He has never
become personal. He has kept his mind among metaphysical
things, letting science and philosophy do his work of praise.
But it was not praise either; it was compliment, which is
more intimate and fanciful a thing. The lady never deserved

this much. Or did she? The music says she did, and so does the gravity which still lingers in the lover's face. She deserved all that words can say when words refer to the greatest and highest things in the world: immortal things, whose home she is. *Dies* is the last word of the poem, yet death is the last thing it suggests. If any love can last forever, this love will. If any poem can, then this one must.

# JOHN MILTON
[1608–1674]

## *On the Morning of Christ's Nativity*

This is the Month, and this the happy morn
Wherein the Son of Heav'n's eternal King,
Of wedded Maid, and Virgin Mother born,
Our great redemption from above did bring;
For so the holy sages once did sing,     5
   That he our deadly forfeit should release,
And with his Father work us a perpetual peace.

That glorious Form, that Light unsufferable,
And that far-beaming blaze of Majesty,
Wherewith he wont at Heav'n's high Council-Table,     10
To sit the midst of Trinal Unity,
He laid aside; and here with us to be,
   Forsook the Courts of everlasting Day,
And chose with us a darksome House of mortal Clay.

Say Heav'nly Muse, shall not thy sacred vein     15
Afford a present to the Infant God?
Hast thou no verse, no hymn, or solemn strain,
To welcome him to this his new abode,
Now while the Heav'n by the Sun's team untrod,
   Hath took no print of the approaching light,     20
And all the spangled host keep watch in squadrons bright?

See how from far upon the Eastern road
The Star-led Wizards haste with odours sweet:
O run, prevent them with thy humble ode,
And lay it lowly at his blessed feet;     25
Have thou the honour first, thy Lord to greet,
   And join thy voice unto the Angel Quire,
From out his secret Altar toucht with hallow'd fire.

### THE HYMN

**I**

It was the Winter wild,
While the Heav'n-born child,                                    30
   All meanly wrapt in the rude manager lies;
Nature in awe to him
Had doff't her gaudy trim,
   With her great Master so to sympathize:
It was no season then for her                                  35
To wanton with the Sun, her lusty Paramour.

**II**

Only with speeches fair
She woos the gentle Air
   To hide her guilty front with innocent Snow,
And on her naked shame,                                        40
Pollute with sinful blame,
   The Saintly Veil of Maiden white to throw,
Confounded, that her Maker's eyes
Should look so near upon her foul deformities.

**III**

But he her fears to cease,                                     45
Sent down the meek-ey'd Peace;
   She crown'd with Olive green, came softly sliding
Down through the turning sphere,
His ready Harbinger,
   With Turtle wing the amorous clouds dividing,       50
And waving wide her myrtle wand,
She strikes a universal Peace through Sea and Land.

**IV**

No War, or Battle's sound
Was heard the World around,
   The idle spear and shield were high up hung;       55
The hooked Chariot stood
Unstain'd with hostile blood;
   The Trumpet spake not to the armed throng,
And Kings sat still with awful eye,
As if they surely knew their sovran Lord was by.              60

**V**

But peaceful was the night
Wherein the Prince of light

JOHN MILTON

*The Bettmann Archive*

His reign of peace upon the earth began:
The Winds, with wonder whist,
Smoothly the waters kiss't,                                        65
    Whispering new joys to the mild Ocean,
Who now hath quite forgot to rave,
While Birds of Calm sit brooding on the charmed wave.


### VI

The Stars with deep amaze
Stand fixt in steadfast gaze,                                      70
    Bending one way their precious influence,
And will not take their flight,
For all the morning light,
    Or *Lucifer* that often warn'd them thence;
But in their glimmering Orbs did glow,                            75
Until their Lord himself bespake, and bid them go.


### VII

And though the shady gloom
Had given day her room,
    The Sun himself withheld his wonted speed,
And hid his head for shame,                                        80
As his inferior flame,
    The new enlight'n'd world no more should need;
He saw a greater Sun appear
Than his bright Throne, or burning Axletree could bear.


### VIII

The Shepherds on the Lawn,                                         85
Or ere the point of dawn,
    Sat simply chatting in a rustic row;
Full little thought they than,
That the mighty *Pan*
    Was kindly come to live with them below;                      90
Perhaps their loves, or else their sheep,
Was all that did their silly thoughts so busy keep.


### IX

When such music sweet
Their hearts and ears did greet,
    As never was by mortal finger strook,                         95
Divinely-warbled voice
Answering the stringed noise,

As all their souls in blissful rapture took:
The Air such pleasure loth to lose,
With thousand echoes still prolongs each heav'nly close.    100

### X

Nature that heard such sound
Beneath the hollow round
   Of *Cynthia's* seat, the Airy region thrilling,
Now was almost won
To think her part was done,                          105
   And that her reign had here its last fulfilling;
She knew such harmony alone
Could hold all Heav'n and Earth in happier union.

### XI

At last surrounds their sight
A Globe of circular light,                           110
   That with long beams the shame-fac't night array'd,
The helmed Cherubim
And sworded Seraphim
   Are seen in glittering ranks with wings display'd,
Harping in loud and solemn quire,                    115
With unexpressive notes to Heav'n's new-born Heir.

### XII

Such Music (as 'tis said)
Before was never made,
   But when of old the sons of morning sung,
While the Creator Great                              120
His constellations set,
   And the well-balanc't world on hinges hung,
And cast the dark foundations deep,
And bid the welt'ring waves their oozy channel keep.

### XIII

Ring out ye Crystal spheres,                         125
Once bless our human ears,
   (If ye have power to touch our senses so)
And let your silver chime
Move in melodious time;
   And let the Bass of Heav'n's deep Organ blow;    130
And with your ninefold harmony
Make up full consort to th' Angelic symphony.

### XIV

For if such holy Song
Enwrap our fancy long,
　Time will run back, and fetch the age of gold,　　　135
And speckl'd vanity
Will sicken soon and die,
　And leprous sin will melt from earthly mould,
And Hell itself will pass away,
And leave her dolorous mansions to the peering day.　　140

### XV

Yea, Truth and Justice then
Will down return to men,
　Th'enamel'd *Arras* of the Rain-bow wearing,
And Mercy set between,
Thron'd in Celestial sheen,　　　145
　With radiant feet the tissued clouds down steering,
And Heav'n as at some festival,
Will open wide the Gates of her high Palace Hall.

### XVI

But wisest Fate says no,
This must not yet be so,　　　150
　The Babe lies yet in smiling Infancy,
That on the bitter cross
Must redeem our loss;
　So both himself and us to glorify:
Yet first to those ychain'd in sleep,　　　155
The wakeful trump of doom must thunder through the deep,

### XVII

With such a horrid clang
As on mount *Sinai* rang
　While the red fire, and smould'ring clouds out brake:
The aged Earth aghast　　　160
With terror of that blast,
　Shall from the surface to the centre shake,
When at the world's last session,
The dreadful Judge in middle Air shall spread his throne.

### XVIII

And then at last our bliss　　　165
Full and perfect is,

But now begins; for from this happy day
Th'old Dragon under ground,
In straiter limits bound,
    Not half so far casts his usurped sway,       170
And wrath to see his Kingdom fail,
Swinges the scaly Horror of his folded tail.

### XIX

The Oracles are dumb,
No voice or hideous hum
    Runs through the arched roof in words deceiving.    175
*Apollo* from his shrine
Can no more divine,
    With hollow shriek the steep of *Delphos* leaving.
No nightly trance, or breathed spell,
Inspires the pale-ey'd Priest from the prophetic cell.    180

### XX

The lonely mountains o'er,
And the resounding shore,
    A voice of weeping heard, and loud lament;
From haunted spring and dale
Edg'd with poplar pale,    185
    The parting Genius is with sighing sent;
With flow'r-inwov'n tresses torn
The Nymphs in twilight shade of tangled thickets mourn.

### XXI

In consecrated Earth,
And on the holy Hearth,    190
    The *Lars*, and *Lemures* moan with midnight plaint;
In Urns and Altars round,
A drear and dying sound
    Affrights the *Flamens* at their service quaint;
And the chill Marble seems to sweat,    195
While each peculiar power forgoes his wonted seat.

### XXII

*Peor* and *Baalim*
Forsake their Temples dim,
    With that twice-batter'd god of *Palestine*,
And mooned *Ashtaroth*,    200
Heav'n's Queen and Mother both,

Now sits not girt with Tapers' holy shine,
The Libyc *Hammon* shrinks his horn,
In vain the *Tyrian* Maids their wounded *Thammuz* mourn.

### XXIII

And Sullen *Moloch*, fled,                                205
Hath left in shadows dread
   His burning Idol all of blackest hue;
In vain with Cymbals' ring
They call the grisly king,
   In dismal dance about the furnace blue;              210
The bruitish gods of *Nile* as fast,
*Isis* and *Orus*, and the Dog *Anubis* haste.

### XXIV

Nor is *Osiris* seen
In *Memphian* Grove or Green,
   Trampling the unshow'r'd Grass with lowings loud:    215
Nor can he be at rest
Within his sacred chest,
   Naught but profoundest Hell can be his shroud:
In vain with Timbrel'd Anthems dark
The sable-stoled Sorcerers bear his worshipt Ark.       220

### XXV

He feels from *Juda's* Land
The dreaded Infant's hand,
   The rays of *Bethlehem* blind his dusky eyn;
Nor all the gods beside,
Longer dare abide,                                      225
   Nor *Typhon* huge ending in snaky twine:
Our Babe, to show his Godhead true,
Can in his swaddling bands control the damned crew.

### XXVI

So when the Sun in bed,
Curtain'd with cloudy red,                              230
   Pillows his chin upon an Orient wave,
The flocking shadows pale
Troop to th'infernal jail;
   Each fetter'd Ghost slips to his several grave,
And the yellow-skirted *Fays*                           235
Fly after the Night-steeds, leaving their Moon-lov'd maze.

## XXVII

But see! the Virgin blest,
Hath laid her Babe to rest.
   Time is our tedious Song should here have ending;
Heav'n's youngest teemed Star      240
Hath fixt her polisht Car,
   Her sleeping Lord with Handmaid Lamp attending:
And all about the Courtly Stable,
Bright-harness'd Angels sit in order serviceable.

# Jackson Mathews

---

## MILTON
### ON THE MORNING OF CHRIST'S NATIVITY

It seems suitable in an anthology of poems to try reading the Nativity Ode as if for the first time. Milton's poems have been studied so much, and most of them require so much learning to be fully read, that there may be some point in beginning for once with all the innocence we can.

Particularly when it is a poem so close to song as this. Not all of his early poems were written under the sign of music. That ineradicable pair so favored by the textbook makers, "L'Allegro" and "Il Penseroso," from which most of us suffered our first knowledge of this poet, are something closer to exercises on the metronome. The Nativity Ode was his first great inspired piece, and music had something to do with inspiring it.

Reading a poem is not like listening to music, but it may be a good idea to hear out the "musical" part of a poem before going on to the other performances, of imagery and sense. Two or three hearings before thinking too much about what is said, feeling one's way into the formal arrangements—the rhyming, the varying measures, the effects of the two stanza forms—this would be a good start, with Milton's Ode.

In the induction the movement seems to suspend us about midway between thinking and singing. In each stanza we begin moving toward a close in the fifth line, where the "unexpected" couplet is modulated by an echo from the previous alternate rhyme. In the closing couplet, our attention is lifted and sustained by a delay—the last line being lengthened by one beat.

The hymn is in a different measure. Here the movement is both faster and slower, lighter, more lyrical yet more thoughtful than in the induction. Metrically, the poem's riskiest element is the feminine rhyming in *ing;* and the young poet's handling of it is a sign of his mastery, as his daring to use it at all is probably a sign of his youth. The spacing of these *ing* rhymes seems just about perfectly managed. Falling as they do in stanzas three, ten, nineteen and twenty-seven—at the not-quite-regular intervals of seven, nine, and eight stanzas—their impact on the reader may be somewhat as follows. Stanza three: "Wonderful! Let's have more of this right away." Stanza ten: "That was a long wait, but worth it. Maybe they will come oftener now." Stanza nineteen: "An even longer wait. I see I am not to be pampered." Stanza twenty-seven: "Good, good."

For his meter in the ode Milton may have learned a good deal from Spenser's "Prothalamion," but the stanzas of the hymn are his own invention. There seems to be nothing else quite like them in English poetry.

The young man of twenty-one who wrote this poem was already incredibly learned. He had grown up in London where at school all day, and with a tutor at home until midnight, he had studied Latin, Greek, Hebrew, Italian, and French—which meant, as languages were then taught, that he had not only learned to read but to speak most of these languages and to write poems and letters in them. It was not considered necessary to study English. By the end of grammar school, he had read at least the following Latin and Greek authors in the original: Cato, Aesop, Terence, Ovid, Caesar, Sallust, Virgil, Cicero, Martial, Hesiod, Theocritus, Horace, Homer, Isocrates, Euripides, and Juvenal, and the Greek Testament. He had certainly read a great deal besides in Italian and English, and could write Latin poems in the manner of Ovid and Horace. When he came to write the Nativity Ode, he had written far more poems in Latin and Italian than in English.

No wonder that when young Milton went on to Cambridge he began to turn with joy and relief to writing in his own language. He tells us this in a poem, "At a Vacation Exercise in the Colledge, part Latin, part English." The English part begins "Hail native Language," and goes on to beg "her" forgiveness for his neglect, promising high devotion in the future.

Music, too, had made a deep impression on his mind. He had learned it from his father, who composed madrigals and sacred songs that were published in the same collections with Morley, Byrd, and Dowland. A friend of the family tells us that the son too was an accomplished organist and singer: "He had a delicate tuneable Voice and had good skill: his father instructed him: he had an Organ in his house: he played on that most."

For a poet like Milton, the experience of music was bound to bring with it the *idea* of music, both as an intellectual instrument and as a formative source of figure and movement in his imagination. In his early days at Cambridge, for one of the Latin speeches he was required to write and deliver, he took as his subject "The Music of the Spheres," arguing from Pythagoras and Plato that each of the planetary spheres sounds a note as it revolves, and all together they make a harmony which for man is the sign of the divine order of the universe; and that only those who are pure in body and mind can hear that music. Chastity was a moral imperative. These three then—chastity, music, and divine order in the world— came together in the young poet's mind, and were to appear again and again in his early poems. They are fundamental to the Nativity Ode.

This beautiful poem came to him, he tells us, very early on Christmas morning of 1629, in his room at Christ's College where he was staying on for the holidays. He seems to have finished writing it in a fairly short time.

This was certainly one of the extraordinary moments of his life. He gave an uncommonly full account of it to his closest boyhood friend, in a letter in Latin elegiacs written at about the same time. In that letter, the teasing gaiety that was usual with him in writing to his friend suddenly turned into a note of strong personal resolve to become worthy of the poet's mission. His friend the elegiac poet, inspired by love, wine, and high living, was the heroic poet but must be a man of ascetic discipline like Pythagoras, eating little, drinking only water; his youth must be chaste, his character without a stain; for the bard is sacred to the gods, he is their priest.

At the end of the letter all indirection was dropped, and Milton spoke with such fine simplicity about the Nativity Ode, which he had just been writing. Here, in translation, is what he said:

> But if you would like to know what I am doing . . . I am singing the heavenly birth of the King of Peace; the happy age promised in the sacred books; the crying of the infant God in a stable under a shabby roof, who with his Father rules the realms above; the star-bearing

sky, and the angels singing in the heavens; and the gods suddenly stricken in their shrines.

I made this poem as a gift for Christ on His birthday; the first light of Christmas dawn brought it to me. It is composed in my native tongue, and is for you also; you will be my judge when I recite it to you.

Milton had great affection for his Ode. He always put it at the head of his collected poems.

## *Lycidas*

In this Monody the Author bewails a learned Friend, unfortunately drown'd in his Passage from *Chester* on the *Irish* Seas, 1637. And by occasion foretells the ruin of our corrupted Clergy then in their height.

Yet once more, O ye Laurels, and once more
Ye Myrtles brown, with Ivy never sere,
I come to pluck your Berries harsh and crude,
And with forc'd fingers rude,
Shatter your leaves before the mellowing year.               5
Bitter constraint, and sad occasion dear,
Compels me to disturb your season due:
For *Lycidas* is dead, dead ere his prime,
Young *Lycidas*, and hath not left his peer:
Who would not sing for *Lycidas?* he knew               10
Himself to sing, and build the lofty rhyme.
He must not float upon his wat'ry bier
Unwept, and welter to the parching wind,
Without the meed of some melodious tear.
  Begin then, Sisters of the sacred well,               15
That from beneath the seat of *Jove* doth spring,
Begin, and somewhat loudly sweep the string.
Hence with denial vain, and coy excuse,
So may some gentle Muse
With lucky words favour my destin'd Urn,               20
And as he passes turn,
And bid fair peace be to my sable shroud.
For we were nurst upon the self-same hill,
Fed the same flock, by fountain, shade, and rill.
  Together both, ere the high Lawns appear'd               25
Under the opening eye-lids of the morn,
We drove afield, and both together heard
What time the Gray-fly winds her sultry horn,
Batt'ning our flocks with the fresh dews of night,
Oft till the Star that rose, at Ev'ning, bright               30

Toward Heav'n's descent had slop'd his westering wheel.
Meanwhile the Rural ditties were not mute,
Temper'd to th'Oaten Flute:
Rough *Satyrs* danc'd, and *Fauns* with clov'n heel,
From the glad sound would not be absent long, 35
And old *Damaetas* lov'd to hear our song.
   But O the heavy change, now thou art gone,
Now thou art gone, and never must return!
Thee Shepherd, thee the Woods, and desert Caves,
With wild Thyme and the gadding Vine o'ergrown, 40
And all their echoes mourn.
The Willows and the Hazel Copses green
Shall now no more be seen,
Fanning their joyous Leaves to thy soft lays.
As killing as the Canker to the Rose, 45
Or Taint-worm to the weanling Herds that graze,
Or Frost to Flowers, that their gay wardrobe wear,
When first the White-thorn blows,
Such, *Lycidas*, thy loss to Shepherd's ear.
   Where were ye Nymphs when the remorseless deep 50
Clos'd o'er the head of your lov'd *Lycidas?*
For neither were ye playing on the steep,
Where your old *Bards*, the famous *Druids*, lie,
Nor on the shaggy top of *Mona* high,
Nor yet where *Deva* spreads her wizard stream: 55
Ay me, I fondly dream!
Had ye been there—for what could that have done?
What could the Muse herself that *Orpheus* bore,
The Muse herself, for her enchanting son
Whom Universal nature did lament, 60
When by the rout that made the hideous roar,
His gory visage down the stream was sent,
Down the swift *Hebrus* to the *Lesbian* shore?
   Alas! What boots it with uncessant care
To tend the homely slighted Shepherd's trade, 65
And strictly meditate the thankless Muse?
Were it not better done as others use,
To sport with *Amaryllis* in the shade,
Or with the tangles of *Neaera's* hair?
*Fame* is the spur that the clear spirit doth raise 70
(That last infirmity of Noble mind)
To scorn delights, and live laborious days;
But the fair Guerdon when we hope to find,
And think to burst out into sudden blaze,

Comes the blind *Fury* with th'abhorred shears,                    75
And slits the thin-spun life. But not the praise,
*Phoebus* repli'd, and touch'd my trembling ears;
*Fame* is no plant that grows on mortal soil,
Nor in the glistering foil
Set off to th'world, nor in broad rumour lies,                    80
But lives and spreads aloft by those pure eyes
And perfect witness of all judging *Jove;*
As he pronounces lastly on each deed,
Of so much fame in Heav'n expect thy meed.

  O Fountain *Arethuse,* and thou honour'd flood,                    85
Smooth-sliding *Mincius,* crown'd with vocal reeds,
That strain I heard was of a higher mood:
But now my Oat proceeds,
And listens to the Herald of the Sea
That came in *Neptune's* plea.                    90
He ask'd the Waves, and ask'd the Felon winds,
What hard mishap hath doom'd this gentle swain?
And question'd every gust of rugged wings
That blows from off each beaked Promontory.
They knew not of his story,                    95
And sage *Hippotades* their answer brings,
That not a blast was from his dungeon stray'd,
The Air was calm, and on the level brine,
Sleek *Panope* with all her sisters play'd.
It was that fatal and perfidious Bark                    100
Built in th'eclipse, and rigg'd with curses dark,
That sunk so low that sacred head of thine.

  Next *Camus,* reverend Sire, went footing slow,
His Mantle hairy, and his Bonnet sedge,
Inwrought with figures dim, and on the edge                    105
Like to that sanguine flower inscrib'd with woe.
Ah! Who hath reft (quoth he) my dearest pledge?
Last came, and last did go,
The Pilot of the *Galilean* lake.
Two massy Keys he bore of metals twain,                    110
(The Golden opes, the Iron shuts amain).
He shook his Mitred locks, and stern bespake:
How well could I have spar'd for thee, young swain,
Enough of such as for their bellies' sake,
Creep and intrude and climb into the fold?                    115
Of other care they little reck'ning make,
Than how to scramble at the shearers' feast,
And shove away the worthy bidden guest.
Blind mouths! that scarce themselves know how to hold

A Sheep-hook, or have learn'd aught else the least          120
That to the faithful Herdman's art belongs!
What recks it them? What need they? They are sped;
And when they list, their lean and flashy songs
Grate on their scrannel Pipes of wretched straw.
The hungry Sheep look up, and are not fed,          125
But swoln with wind, and the rank mist they draw,
Rot inwardly, and foul contagion spread:
Besides what the grim Wolf with privy paw
Daily devours apace, and nothing said;
But that two-handed engine at the door          130
Stands ready to smite once, and smite no more.
  Return *Alpheus*, the dread voice is past,
That shrunk thy streams; Return *Sicilian* Muse,
And call the Vales, and bid them hither cast
Their Bells and Flowrets of a thousand hues.          135
Ye valleys low where the mild whispers use
Of shades and wanton winds and gushing brooks,
On whose fresh lap the swart Star sparely looks,
Throw hither all your quaint enamell'd eyes,
That on the green turf suck the honied showers,          140
And purple all the ground with vernal flowers.
Bring the rathe Primrose that forsaken dies,
The tufted Crow-toe, and pale Jessamine,
The white Pink, and the Pansy freakt with jet,
The glowing Violet,          145
The Musk-rose, and the well attir'd Woodbine,
With Cowslips wan that hang the pensive head,
And every flower that sad embroidery wears:
Bid *Amaranthus* all his beauty shed,
And Daffadillies fill their cups with tears,          150
To strew the Laureate Hearse where *Lycid* lies.
For so to interpose a little ease,
Let our frail thoughts dally with false surmise.
Ay me! Whilst thee the shores, and sounding Seas
Wash far away, where'er thy bones are hurl'd,          155
Whether beyond the stormy *Hebrides*,
Where thou perhaps under the whelming tide
Visit'st the bottom of the monstrous world;
Or whether thou to our moist vows denied,
Sleep'st by the fable of *Bellerus* old,          160
Where the great vision of the guarded Mount
Looks toward *Namancos* and *Bayona's* hold;
Look homeward Angel now, and melt with ruth:
And, O ye *Dolphins*, waft the hapless youth.

Weep no more, woeful Shepherds weep no more,   165
For *Lycidas* your sorrow is not dead,
Sunk though he be beneath the wat'ry floor,
So sinks the day-star in the Ocean bed,
And yet anon repairs his drooping head,
And tricks his beams, and with new spangled Ore,   170
Flames in the forehead of the morning sky:
So *Lycidas*, sunk low, but mounted high,
Through the dear might of him that walk'd the waves,
Where other groves, and other streams along,
With *Nectar* pure his oozy Locks he laves,   175
And hears the unexpressive nuptial Song,
In the blest Kingdoms meek of joy and love.
There entertain him all the Saints above,
In solemn troops, and sweet Societies
That sing, and singing in their glory move,   180
And wipe the tears for ever from his eyes.
Now *Lycidas* the Shepherds weep no more;
Henceforth thou art the Genius of the shore,
In thy large recompense, and shalt be good
To all that wander in that perilous flood.   185
     Thus sang the uncouth Swain to th'Oaks and rills,
While the still morn went out with Sandals gray.
He touch't the tender stops of various Quills,
With eager thought warbling his *Doric* lay:
And now the Sun had stretch't out all the hills,   190
And now was dropt into the Western bay;
At last he rose, and twitch't his Mantle blue:
Tomorrow to fresh Woods, and Pastures new.

*Richard P. Adams*

## MILTON
## LYCIDAS

It has been made increasingly evident by critics in recent years that the drowning of Edward King was the occasion, rather than the subject, of "Lycidas." Milton's concern was generally with the life, death, and resurrection of the dedicated poet, and specifically with his own situation at the time. From this premise it follows that there are no digressions in the poem, and that the form and traditions of pastoral elegy are entirely appropriate to its intentions.

Every serious poet must at some time come to an emotional realization of the length of art and the shortness of life. He, more than most men, desires immortality, which he tries to achieve in his works, to leave, as Milton said, "something so written to aftertimes, as they should not willingly let it die." It is an appalling thought that he may die himself before his work is done, and this thought may be most sharply imposed upon him by the death of a friend or acquaintance who is also a poet of some worth or promise. Such an event is likely to be felt an impelling occasion to find some way of reconciling the desire for immortality with the certainty of death. Many poets, from Moschus or (whoever wrote the "Lament for Bion") to Matthew Arnold, have used for this purpose the conventions of pastoral elegy as established by Theocritus in his "Lament for Daphnis." They have made additions and modifications, but the continuity of the traditional form remains unbroken. Milton chose it because he considered it an appropriate vehicle for the expression of his feelings. The result renders any apology absurd.

The conventions of pastoral elegy were appropriate because they had been hammered out over the centuries by poets concerned, as Milton was, with the problem and the mystery of death. In the cultural medium of their origin, the Hellenistic world of the third century B.C., the most popular solutions of the problem of death were expressed in the rituals of various fertility cults. It is therefore not surprising to find that Adonis appeared in the Fifteenth and Thirtieth Idylls of Theocritus, and that Bion's pastoral elegy was a "Lament for Adonis." Similarly, in the "Lament for Bion," a long list of mourners was capped by the statement that "Cypris loves thee far more than the kiss wherewith she kissed the dying Adonis." Analogies between the conventions of fertility ritual and those of pastoral elegy are numerous and obvious, and some of them at least were clearly seen by Milton, who used them to reinforce the imagery of "Lycidas." He also used appropriate Christian materials and some references to medieval history and legend where they matched his pattern.

The result is a remarkably tight amalgam of death-and-rebirth imagery, drawn from a more than catholic variety of sources. It is far from being merely eclectic, however. Each individual image and reference has its immediate purpose and its relevancy to the form of the whole.

The emotional pattern of the poem consists of a twofold movement. First it goes, from the announcement of the friend's death, downward through various expressions of sorrow to despair; then comfort is offered, and the sequence reverses itself, until the conclusion is reached in heavenly joy. It is the conventional pattern of pastoral elegy, at least from the time of Virgil, and it is at the same time the pattern of Milton's feeling about death at the time he wrote "Lycidas." There is no mystery or contradiction in the facts that "Lycidas" is one of the most richly traditional and conventional of all pastoral elegies, and that it is at the same time one of the most intensely personal in its expression of the poet's emotion. The two things do not conflict; they work together and reinforce each other. This effect can be demonstrated by an examination of individual images in relation to the overall pattern.

The opening invocation exposes a vein of death-and-rebirth imagery concerned with various forms of vegetation. The laurel, the myrtle, and the ivy are evergreens. Besides being emblems of poetry, they are symbols of immortality generally, in contrast to deciduous plants. All of them have been held sacred to fertility gods and demigods. Adonis, in one version of his myth, was born out of a myrtle tree. The laurel was supposed to have been a sweetheart of Apollo transformed into a tree to escape his pursuit. The ivy was sacred to Dionysus.

The transformation by some diety of a mortal into a plant or flower was a favorite symbol of immortality in the classi-

cal myths. It is recalled in Milton's reference to "that sanguine flower inscrib'd with woe" (line 106); that is, the
hyacinth, which sprang from the blood of a young prince of
Amyclae beloved and accidentally killed by Apollo, just as
the rose (line 45) was said to have sprung from the blood of
Adonis and the violet (line 145) from that of Attis, the fertility demigod of Phrygia. The amaranth ("Amaranthus," line
149) was also a symbol of immortality; its Greek root, coined
for the purpose, meant "unfading." In *Paradise Lost* Milton
spoke of it as

> *Immortal Amarant, a Flow'r which once*
> *In Paradise, fast by the Tree of Life*
> *Began to bloom . . .* [III, 354–56]

These specific references are of course in addition to the
general applications of the annual cycle of blighted and reviving vegetation. The ritual observances in the fertility cults
were designed partly to assist in the completion of the cycle,
the revival of the demigod being accompanied by a sympathetic revival of fertility in plants and animals. In this connection the pathetic fallacy, one of the most persistent of the
conventions of pastoral elegy, is no fallacy at all but a perfectly logical aspect of the ritual. In pastoral elegy, however,
the application is often reversed, as it is in "Lycidas," so that
flowers, and vegetation generally, symbolize the promise of
rebirth for the poet's friend as well as the mourning for his
death.

The fact that King died by drowning perhaps fortuitously
but nonetheless effectively opened up to Milton a much
larger range of death-and-rebirth imagery, which he exploited with his usual thoroughness. No less than fifty lines,
out of a total of 193, are concerned with water in one way or
another. Water was of course a prime symbol of fertility in
all the ancient cults, for reasons that Milton seems to recognize in connection with his flowers, which grow near "gushing brooks" (line 137) and which "suck the honied showers"
(line 140). By the same association, the two friends had gone
out "by fountain, shade, and rill" (line 24), "Batt'ning our
flocks with the fresh dews of night" (line 29). He himself
sang "to th'Oaks and rills" (line 186). Several references involving water are specifically to themes of death and rebirth,
one of the most definite being the legend of Alpheus and
Arethusa (lines 132–33), to which Milton had referred in
"Arcades":

> *Divine* Alpheus, *who by secret sluice,*
> *Stole under Seas to meet his* Arethuse. . . . [30–31]

The nymph herself, transformed into a fountain, is a symbol
of immortality in much the same sense as the rose, the violet,
and the hyacinth. Milton's personification in "Lycidas" of
Cambridge University as the River Cam ("Comus," line 103)
is in harmony, and St. Peter as "The Pilot of the *Galilean* lake"
(line 109) is nearly related. This reference emphasizes the
pattern of death and rebirth in two specific connections, the
story of Peter's walk on the water, beginning to sink and
being raised by Christ, and the fact that he was the keeper of
the keys. The first item is reserved, while the second is developed immediately:

> *Two massy Keys he bore of metals twain,*
> (*The Golden opes, the Iron shuts amain*) [110–11]

Milton goes to some length to show that water, the principle of life, is not responsible for the death of Lycidas.
Triton ("the Herald of the Sea," line 89) testifies that the
winds were at home and that the Nereids ("Sleek *Panope*
with all her sisters," line 99) were attending to their duty as
protectresses of ships and sailors. The blame is put finally on
the manmade ship that, in defiance of the powers of nature,
had been "Built in th'eclipse, and rigg'd with curses dark"
(line 101).

For some reason the descent into water which is often a
feature of death-and-rebirth cycles is, if not often, at least
sometimes associated with the dragon-fight theme, especially
in North European mythology. Beowulf's fight with Gren-
del's mother in the cave under the mere is perhaps the most
familiar example. Milton did not know *Beowulf*, but he
paralleled the incident in "Lycidas":

> *Where thou perhaps under the whelming tide*
> *Visit'st the bottom of the monstrous world;*
> *Or whether thou to our moist vows denied,*
> *Sleep'st by the fable of* Bellerus *old,*
> *Where the great vision of the guarded Mount*
> *Looks toward* Namancos *and* Bayona's *hold* [157–63]

The parallel is complete if the word "monstrous" is interpreted to mean "full of monsters." There is no uncertainty
about the references to Corineus, the slayer of Gogmagog,
and to St. Michael, the dragon fighter par excellence of
Christian tradition. The appeal to the dolphins to "waft the
hapless youth" (line 164) follows naturally. It may refer to

the story of Palaemon, whose body was carried ashore by dolphins, or to that of Arion, who was saved by them from drowning, or both. Ovid told a somewhat similar story of Bacchus, to which Milton referred in "Comus" (lines 48–49).

The descent into and re-emergence from water is specifically related by Milton to the setting and rising of the sun as a symbol of death and rebirth. (For the present interpretation it makes little difference whether the term "day-star" is taken to mean the sun itself or whether, as seems likely, it refers to Hesperus and Lucifer [Jerram, p. 85]. If the day-star is not the sun, it accompanies the sun in its death-and-rebirth journey under the ocean.)

> *Weep no more, woeful Shepherds weep no more,*
> *For* Lycidas *your sorrow is not dead,*
> *Sunk though he be beneath the wat'ry floar,*
> *So sinks the day-star in the Ocean bed,*
> *And yet anon repairs his drooping head,*
> *And tricks his beams, and with new spangled Ore,*
> *Flames in the forehead of the morning sky:*
> *So* Lycidas, *sunk low, but mounted high,*
> *Through the dear might of him that walk'd the waves*
> [165–73]

Besides respecifying and reinforcing the reference to St. Peter's adventure (line 109) this passage coordinates two accounts of the sun's journey from rising to setting. The first of these represents in parallel the life of the two friends at Cambridge (lines 25–31), and the second represents the life of the surviving poet:

> *Thus sang the uncouth Swain to th' Oaks and rills,*
> *While the still morn went out with Sandals gray.*
> *He touch't the tender stops of various Quills,*
> *With eager thought warbling his* Doric *lay:*
> *And now the Sun had stretch't out all the hills,*
> *And now was dropt into the Western Bay;*
> *At last he rose, and twich't his Mantle blew:*
> *Tomorrow to fresh Woods, and Pastures new.*
> [186–93]

These passages render in a very striking way the pattern of life, death, and rebirth with which the poem as a whole is concerned.

The last quotation recalls the fact that Milton was expressing his own feelings in "Lycidas," and not any abstract or general or public sorrow. The personal note established in the first five lines is maintained throughout. It is struck again in the passage where he puts himself in the dead man's place (lines 19–22), hoping that "some gentle Muse" will turn aside to confer on him the immortality which he is giving King. He deliberately takes to himself here the emotional experience of death and, at least by implication, of rebirth.

The nadir of the movement from life through death to resurrection follows logically by way of the reference to Orpheus, in which death is presented as final. The reference expands in at least three directions, two of which are exploited. Orpheus's descent into the underworld and not-quite-successful effort to rescue Eurydice is the most obvious, and perhaps for that reason the one that Milton neglects. The death of Orpheus at the hands of the Bacchanals, his dismemberment, and the journey of his head to Lesbos are the things that occupy Milton's attention first. The parallels between this event and the deaths of Adonis, Attis, Osiris, and other fertility demigods have been pointed out by modern scholars. The facts that he was a singer, i.e., a poet, that he died a violent death, that his head was thrown into the water, and that his mother Calliope, the muse of epic poetry, mourned his death, made him sufficiently adaptable to the general pattern of pastoral elegy and to Milton's treatment. The third direction gives Milton, in the "digression" on fame, most scope for the expression of his personal feelings, both of despair and of hope. Identifying himself with Orpheus as before with King, he asks what is the use of casting his pearls before the swine by whom the god is killed, to whom he has paid his respects in "Comus" and whom he is about to attack in the passage on the corrupt clergy. Then Phoebus, the patron of Orpheus, representing Milton's patron Christ, promises him his final reward in Heaven.

Such are the means by which Milton in "Lycidas" interrelated elements from the fertility cults, the tradition of pastoral elegy, the Christian religion, and his own past with the purpose and most richly the effect of rendering his present emotion. Such, by the same token, is the meaning of the phrase "With eager thought," and such again is the promise of "fresh Woods, and Pastures new."

## L'Allegro

Hence loathed Melancholy
   Of *Cerberus* and blackest midnight born,
In *Stygian* Cave forlorn
   'Mongst horrid shapes, and shrieks, and sights unholy,
Find out some uncouth cell,        5
   Where brooding darkness spreads his jealous wings,
And the night-Raven sings;
   There under *Ebon* shades, and low-brow'd Rocks,
As ragged as thy Locks,
   In dark *Cimmerian* desert ever dwell.      10
But come thou Goddess fair and free,
In Heav'n yclep'd *Euphrosyne*,
And by men, heart-easing Mirth,
Whom lovely *Venus* at a birth
With two sister Graces more       15
To Ivy-crowned *Bacchus* bore;
Or whether (as some Sager sing)
The frolic Wind that breathes the Spring,
*Zephyr* with *Aurora* playing,
As he met her once a-Maying,      20
There on Beds of Violets blue,
And fresh-blown Roses washt in dew,
Fill'd her with thee a daughter fair,
So buxom, blithe, and debonair.
Haste thee nymph, and bring with thee     25
Jest and youthful Jollity,
Quips and Cranks, and wanton Wiles,
Nods, and Becks, and Wreathed Smiles,
Such as hang on *Hebe's* cheek,
And love to live in dimple sleek;     30
Sport that wrinkled Care derides,
And Laughter holding both his sides.
Come, and trip it as ye go
On the light fantastic toe,

And in thy right hand lead with thee,                         35
The Mountain Nymph, sweet Liberty;
And if I give thee honour due,
Mirth, admit me of thy crew
To live with her, and live with thee,
In unreproved pleasures free;                                 40
To hear the Lark begin his flight,
And singing startle the dull night,
From his watch-tow'r in the skies,
Till the dappled dawn doth rise;
Then to come in spite of sorrow,                              45
And at my window bid good morrow,
Through the Sweet-Briar, or the Vine,
Or the twisted Eglantine;
While the Cock with lively din,
Scatters the rear of darkness thin,                           50
And to the stack, or the Barn door,
Stoutly struts his Dames before;
Oft list'ning how the Hounds and horn
Cheerly rouse the slumb'ring morn,
From the side of some Hoar Hill,                              55
Through the high wood echoing shrill;
Some time walking not unseen
By Hedge-row Elms, on Hillocks green,
Right against the Eastern gate,
Where the great Sun begins his state,                         60
Rob'd in flames, and Amber light,
The clouds in thousand Liveries dight;
While the Plowman near at hand,
Whistles o'er the Furrow'd Land,
And the Milkmaid singeth blithe,                              65
And the Mower whets his scythe,
And every Shepherd tells his tale
Under the Hawthorn in the dale.
Straight mine eye hath caught new pleasures
Whilst the Lantskip round it measures,                        70
Russet Lawns and Fallows Gray,
Where the nibbling flocks do stray;
Mountains on whose barren breast
The labouring clouds do often rest;
Meadows trim with Daisies pied,                               75
Shallow Brooks, and Rivers wide.
Towers and Battlements it sees
Bosom'd high in tufted Trees,
Where perhaps some beauty lies,

The Cynosure of neighbouring eyes.                        80
Hard by, a Cottage chimney smokes,
From betwixt two aged Oaks,
Where *Corydon* and *Thyrsis* met,
Are at their savoury dinner set
Of Herbs, and other Country Messes,                       85
Which the neat-handed *Phyllis* dresses;
And then in haste her Bow'r she leaves,
With *Thestylis* to bind the Sheaves;
Or if the earlier season lead
To the tann'd Haycock in the Mead.                        90
Sometimes with secure delight
The up-land Hamlets will invite,
When the merry Bells ring round,
And the jocund rebecks sound
To many a youth, and many a maid,                         95
Dancing in the Chequer'd shade;
And young and old come forth to play
On a Sunshine Holiday,
Till the live-long day-light fail;
Then to the Spicy Nut-brown Ale,                         100
With stories told of many a feat,
How *Faery Mab* the junkets eat;
She was pincht and pull'd, she said,
And he, by Friar's Lanthorn led,
Tells how the drudging *Goblin* sweat                    105
To earn his Cream-bowl duly set,
When in one night, ere glimpse of morn,
His shadowy Flail hath thresh'd the Corn
That ten day-labourers could not end;
Then lies him down the Lubber Fiend,                     110
And, stretch'd out all the Chimney's length,
Basks at the fire his hairy strength;
And Crop-full out of doors he flings,
Ere the first Cock his Matin rings.
Thus done the Tales, to bed they creep,                  115
By whispering Winds soon lull'd asleep.
Tow'red Cities please us then,
And the busy hum of men,
Where throngs of Knights and Barons bold,
In weeds of Peace high triumphs hold,                    120
With store of Ladies, whose bright eyes
Rain influence, and judge the prize
Of Wit, or Arms, while both contend
To win her Grace, whom all commend.

There let *Hymen* oft appear                                    125
In Saffron robe, with Taper clear,
And pomp, and feast, and revelry,
With mask, and antique Pageantry—
Such sights as youthful Poets dream
On Summer eves by haunted stream.                               130
Then to the well-trod stage anon,
If *Jonson's* learned Sock be on,
Or sweetest *Shakespeare*, fancy's child,
Warble his native Wood-notes wild.
And ever against eating Cares,                                  135
Lap me in soft *Lydian* Airs,
Married to immortal verse,
Such as the meeting soul may pierce
In notes, with many a winding bout
Of linked sweetness long drawn out,                             140
With wanton heed, and giddy cunning,
The melting voice through mazes running;
Untwisting all the chains that tie
The hidden soul of harmony;
That *Orpheus'* self may heave his head                         145
From golden slumber on a bed
Of heapt *Elysian* flow'rs, and hear
Such strains as would have won the ear
Of *Pluto*, to have quite set free
His half-regain'd *Eurydice*.                                   150
These delights if thou canst give,
Mirth, with thee I mean to live.

## *Il Penseroso*

Hence vain deluding joys,
   The brood of folly without father bred,
How little you bested,
   Or fill the fixed mind with all your toys;
Dwell in some idle brain,                                       5
   And fancies fond with gaudy shapes possess,
As thick and numberless
   As the gay motes that people the Sun-Beams,

Or likest hovering dreams,
   The fickle Pensioners of *Morpheus'* train.     10
But hail thou Goddess, sage and holy,
Hail divinest Melancholy,
Whose Saintly visage is too bright
To hit the Sense of human sight;
And therefore to our weaker view,     15
O'erlaid with black, staid Wisdom's hue.
Black, but such as in esteem,
Prince *Memnon's* sister might beseem,
Or that Starr'd *Ethiop* Queen that strove
To set her beauty's praise above     20
The Sea Nymphs, and their powers offended.
Yet thou art higher far descended;
Thee bright-hair'd *Vesta* long of yore,
To solitary *Saturn* bore;
His daughter she (in *Saturn's* reign,     25
Such mixture was not held a stain).
Oft in glimmering Bow'rs and glades
He met her, and in secret shades
Of woody *Ida's* inmost grove,
While yet there was no fear of *Jove*.     30
Come pensive Nun, devout and pure,
Sober, steadfast, and demure,
All in a robe of darkest grain,
Flowing with majestic train,
And sable stole of *Cypress* Lawn,     35
Over thy decent shoulders drawn.
Come, but keep thy wonted state,
With ev'n step, and musing gait,
And looks commercing with the skies,
Thy rapt soul sitting in thine eyes:     40
Theré held in holy passion still,
Forget thyself to Marble, till
With a sad Leaden downward cast,
Thou fix them on the earth as fast.
And join with thee calm Peace and Quiet,     45
Spare Fast, that oft with gods diet,
And hears the Muses in a ring
Aye round about *Jove's* Altar sing.
And add to these retired Leisure,
That in trim Gardens takes his pleasure;     50
But first, and chiefest, with thee bring
Him that yon soars on golden wing,
Guiding the fiery-wheeled throne,

The Cherub Contemplation;
And the mute Silence hist along,                         55
'Less *Philomel* will deign a Song,
In her sweetest, saddest plight,
Smoothing the rugged brow of night.
While *Cynthia* checks her Dragon yoke,
Gently o'er th' accustom'd Oak;                          60
Sweet Bird that shunn'st the noise of folly,
Most musical, most melancholy!
Thee Chantress oft the Woods among,
I woo to hear thy even-Song;
And missing thee, I walk unseen                          65
On the dry smooth-shaven Green,
To behold the wand'ring Moon,
Riding near her highest noon,
Like one that had been led astray
Through the Heav'n's wide pathless way;                  70
And oft, as if her head she bow'd,
Stooping through a fleecy cloud.
Oft on a Plat of rising ground,
I hear the far-off *Curfew* sound,
Over some wide-water'd shore,                            75
Swinging slow with sullen roar;
Or if the Air will not permit,
Some still removed place will fit,
Where glowing Embers through the room
Teach light to counterfeit a gloom,                      80
Far from all resort of mirth,
Save the Cricket on the hearth,
Or the Bellman's drowsy charm,
To bless the doors from nightly harm:
Or let my Lamp at midnight hour,                         85
Be seen in some high lonely Tow'r,
Where I may oft out-watch the *Bear*,
With thrice great *Hermes*, or unsphere
The spirit of *Plato* to unfold
What Worlds, or what vast Regions hold                   90
The immortal mind that hath forsook
Her mansion in this fleshly nook:
And of those *Dæmons* that are found
In fire, air, flood, or under ground,
Whose power hath a true consent                          95
With Planet, or with Element.
Sometime let Gorgeous Tragedy
In Scepter'd Pall come sweeping by,

Presenting *Thebes*, or *Pelop's* line,
Or the tale of *Troy* divine, 100
Or what (though rare) of later age,
Ennobled hath the Buskin'd stage.
But, O sad Virgin, that thy power
Might raise *Musaeus* from his bower,
Or bid the soul of *Orpheus* sing 105
Such notes as, warbled to the string,
Drew iron tears down *Pluto's* cheek,
And made Hell grant what Love did seek.
Or call up him that left half told
The story of *Cambuscan* bold, 110
Of *Camball*, and of *Algarsife*,
And who had *Canace* to wife,
That own'd the virtuous Ring and Glass,
And of the wond'rous Horse of Brass,
On which the *Tartar* King did ride; 115
And if aught else great Bards beside
In sage and solemn tunes have sung,
Of Tourneys and of Trophies hung,
Of Forests, and inchantments drear,
Where more is meant than meets the ear. 120
Thus night oft see me in thy pale career,
Till civil-suited Morn appear,
Not trickt and frounc't as she was wont
With the Attic Boy to hunt,
But Kerchieft in a comely Cloud, 125
While rocking Winds are Piping loud,
Or usher'd with a shower still,
When the gust hath blown his fill,
Ending on the rustling Leaves,
With minute drops from off the Eaves. 130
And when the Sun begins to fling
His flaring beams, me Goddess bring
To arched walks of twilight groves,
And shadows brown that *Sylvan* loves
Of Pine or monumental Oak, 135
Where the rude Axe with heaved stroke
Was never heard the Nymphs to daunt,
Or fright them from their hallow'd haunt.
There in close covert by some Brook,
Where no profaner eye may look, 140
Hide me from Day's garish eye,
While the Bee with Honied thigh,
That at her flow'ry work doth sing,

And the Waters murmuring
With such consort as they keep,                    145
Entice the dewy-feather'd Sleep;
And let some strange mysterious dream
Wave at his Wings in Airy stream,
Of lively portraiture display'd,
Softly on my eye-lids laid.                        150
And as I wake, sweet music breathe
Above, about, or underneath,
Sent by some spirit to mortals good,
Or th'unseen Genius of the Wood.
But let my due feet never fail                     155
To walk the studious Cloister's pale,
And love the high embowed Roof,
With antic Pillars massy proof,
And storied Windows richly dight,
Casting a dim religious light.                     160
There let the pealing Organ blow
To the full voic'd Quire below,
In Service high and Anthems clear,
As may with sweetness, through mine ear,
Dissolve me into extasies,                         165
And bring all Heav'n before mine eyes.
And may at last my weary age
Find out the peaceful hermitage,
The Hairy Gown and Mossy Cell,
Where I may sit and rightly spell                  170
Of every Star that Heav'n doth shew,
And every Herb that sips the dew;
Till old experience do attain
To something like Prophetic strain.
These pleasures *Melancholy* give,                 175
And I with thee will choose to live.

*Richard Wilbur*

---

## MILTON
### L'ALLEGRO AND IL PENSEROSO

These companion poems have been much and well discussed, but until such recent studies as D.C. Allen's they have generally been denied any complexity or weight. It is not hard to see why that has happened. "L'Allegro" and "Il Penseroso" do not have such conspicuous verbal wit as characterizes some other works of Milton's youth; elegant logic, bold word play, and virtuoso similes are lacking, and therefore it has been easy to take the poems for simple and charming exercises. They have been thought to consist mainly of brief, pleasant and generalized evocations of the preferred experiences of the Cheerful or Enjoying Man, on the one hand, and the Thoughtful Man on the other.

But these are witty poems; and their wit, which is the index of their seriousness, must initially be found in the implications of their structure. One may see at first glance that the two poems develop in a similar manner: "L'Allegro" begins with a dismissal of Melancholy and then, having summoned Mirth and Liberty and their train, proceeds to consider the ways in which a cheerful man might divert himself from dawn until late at night; "Il Penseroso" begins with a dismissal of "vain, deluding joys" and then, having summoned Melancholy, Contemplation, and their train, proceeds to consider what might—between evening and morning—content the thoughtful man. Perceiving such broad resemblances in structure, the reader will perhaps feel challenged to decide what these poems are to each other: are they to be contrasted in their subjects, or compared, or treated as complementary, or seen as indifferently parallel?

An initial clue is to be found in the fact that the Melancholy dismissed at the opening of "L'Allegro" is not the serenely pondering kind described in the neighboring poem, but a condition of social and mental alienation; moreover, the redundancy of the passage, which in ten lines offers us *blackest, Stygian, darkness, raven, ebon,* and *dark,* implies a tone of deadpan jocularity. The corresponding lines of "Il Penseroso," though suitably less extravagant, resemble the dismissal passage of "L'Allegro" in that they are directed not against the moderate enjoyments of Milton's cheerful man, but against empty foolishness. The poems, in short, pretend to attack each other but do not, and their initial relationship is one of sham debate. The implication of this might be that *allegro* and *penseroso* are not mutually exclusive, not necessarily at war, and may in fact be the comfortably alternating moods of a single personality.

This last possibility is strengthened by Milton's refusal, in the invocation of "L'Allegro," to settle for the traditional parentage of Euphrosyne. Bacchus and Venus would beget a sensual and appetitive Mirth, and Milton is not after that sort of cheerfulness; he therefore contrives a sager myth of his own, in which Euphrosyne is begotten by Zephyr (the West Wind) and Aurora (the Dawn) on the freshest of spring mornings. The resultant goddess, who will preside over the pleasures of the first poem, is a chaste and delicate spirit, not deeply incompatible with her rival Melancholy, whose descent from Saturn and Vesta argues purity and contemplative solitude. Judging by their invocations, then, the companion poems celebrate two dispositions that, whatever their differences, agree in respect of chastity, and indicate, by their exclusion of sensuality, that they belong not to men generally but to a particular kind of man.

As the two poems proceed to catalogue the gratifications of the cheerful man and the thoughtful man, the impression that these are alternative aspects of one personality is continually strengthened. Both men are walkers; both have literary sensibilities; both are fond of the drama, and of music, and make reference to Orpheus. Less obviously, and more importantly, the two are approached to one another by their common qualities of detachment, leisureliness, and freedom from "care." The cheerful man is at no time imagined as a participant in anything; he enjoys all serenely at a distance, as spectator or auditor, and the closest he comes to gregariousness is in his willingness to be "not unseen" in his country rambles, or to join the (unmentioned) audience of a comedy or concert. Nor does the cheerful man's world oppose itself by garish brightness to the dim milieux of the other poem; "L'Allegro's" morning sun may be "rob'd in flames," but for the most part the poem's shade and quiet color suggest no quarrel with "Il Penseroso," but a measure of affinity.

There are also, needless to say, salient differences between the two poems, which the similarities serve to emphasize: the towers and stars of one poem are significantly *not* the towers and stars of the other, and so on. But these differences are more readily understood once one has arrived—prompted again by the structure—at the logic of each poem's list of pleasures. "L'Allegro's" list, because it begins at daybreak and proceeds horologically, may seem at first to represent "a day in the life of a cheerful man," but one soon apprehends (through its hesitation between possibilities) that it is really a series of tentative envisionings by such a man, in which he considers what—depending on the hour and the season—it would "oft" or "some time" suit him to see or hear. The enumeration of pleasures progresses from dawn until some indefinite hour of the night, but this is not its only progression: we move also from country peasants and their frolics to city aristocrats and sophisticated entertainments; from naive and everyday sense-experience to refined and exquisite sense-experience. The details of this development cannot be traced here, but the idea, once grasped, is easily applied. It is easy to see how, beginning with perceptions or visions of plants, animals, and rustics, the cheerful man contemplates a sensuous world progressively transformed and spiritualized by fancy, by convention, by manners, by ceremony, and by art. The poem climbs a ladder of aesthetic experience, which begins with bird song and ends with the ecstatic intricacies of Lydian music. What is implied, as we soon come to see, is a way of life: the way of life of an aesthete or artist, whose whole activity is the distillation of beauty from the raw materials of everyday existence.

If we now turn to "Il Penseroso," and to the characterization of Melancholy, we are at once aware of a decided contrast. Whereas Mirth was a spirit devoted to sense data, to enjoyable perceptions of the eye and ear, Melancholy is clothed in an invisible, transcendental light, and is associated from the first with the supersensuous. As a child of the Golden Age, when heaven and earth were at one, she sponsors a kind of contemplation that continually refers what is "below" to what is "above," and seeks to redeem and transmute the leaden actualities of our fallen world. The thoughtful man's pleasures, like those of his alter ego, are presented in an ascending scale of value. First comes the sort of sense experience that might suit his solitary mood, and prompt his kind of spiritual musing: the nightingale puts him in mind of a chantress at vespers, and the watchman seems to intone a blessing. Second, we have his pursuit, through science, philosophy, or art, of the hidden truths of this world and the next; third, his arrival by way of such knowledge at an intimate communion with divine harmonies in nature; and finally, his attainment through worship to ecstatic glimpses of heaven. The reader should notice how the account of the morning, and of the morning walk, is full of words—beginning with *kerchieft, piping, usher'd,* and *arched*—that remind one of a church service, the effect being that the natural world, thus suggestively "hallowed," becomes a figurative narthex to the literal church which follows. As this example shows, Milton's twin poems do, after all, contain verbal wit; but the word play does not really stand forth, or disclose its serious drift, until the reader has begun to make out the intention of the structure.

"Il Penseroso" closes with the hope that "old experience" will "attain / To something like Prophetic strain," and this may persuade the reader that the companion poems are sequentially related—that they propose a kind of ideal biography, in which a sensitive, temperate man devotes his youth to aesthetic pleasure, and his riper years to the still higher joys of philosophy and religion. This is certainly a part of the truth: "L'Allegro" does indeed stress youth, and "Il Penseroso" age; taken as a sequence, the poems call for the refinement and final transcendence of sense experience, and the progressive liberation of the soul through a hierarchy of disciplines. But of course, the relationship of the poems is not merely sequential, it is also rotary: the close of "Il Penseroso" leads back to the opening of "L'Allegro," where "peaceful hermitage" and "mossy cell" ("Il Penseroso," lines 168–69) are dismissed as "Stygian" and "uncouth." The implication of this perpetual *da capo* is that the single speaker of these companion poems hopes to alternate, throughout his life's pilgrimage, between the complementary moods and pleasures that they represent—that at any stage of life he will wish himself both *allegro* and *penseroso,* in seasonable proportions. The reading of Plato must not wait, after all, for middle age; a sunshine holiday is, Milton declares, for young and old alike; a life should have aspiring direction, but also a humane fullness and variety.

Like "Lycidas," which finds a Christian consolation within a pastoral elegy, the companion poems exceed the promise of their convention, although they do so more covertly. These delightful poems, with their short measures and prompt rhymes, may seem at first to do no more than define two dispositions and catalogue their ideal pursuits. Yet as one answers the questions that their structure proposes, one discovers a program for the encompassing of a range of experience, the precise evaluation of its diverse pleasures, and its gradual transmutation toward the knowledge and praise of God. This short essay can offer only a most general statement of Milton's implicit thought; as for the particular relationships within and between the poems, which are of an inexhaustible intricacy and relevance, I leave their study to the fortunate reader. He will find evidence that John Milton was from the beginning, in large patterns and in least details, a master of significant structure and the greatest verse architect in our literature.

# RICHARD CRASHAW
## [1613–1649]

## *The Teare*

What bright soft thing is this?
Sweet *Mary* thy faire Eyes expence?
　　A moist sparke it is,
　　A watry Diamond; from whence
The very Terme, I think, was found　　　　5
The water of a *Diamond*.

　　O 'tis not a Teare,
　　'Tis a starre about to drop
　　　From thine eye its spheare;
　　　The Sunne will stoope and take it up.　10
Proud will his sister be to weare
This thine eyes Iewell in her Eare.

　　O 'tis a Teare,
　　Too true a Teare; for no sad eyne,
　　　How sad so e're　　　　　　　　15
　　Raine so true a Teare as thine;
Each Drop leaving a place so deare,
Weeps for it selfe, is its owne Teare.

　　Such a Pearle as this is,
　　(Slipt from *Aurora's* dewy Brest)　　20
　　　The Rose buds sweet lip kisses;
　　And such the Rose its selfe when vext
With ungentle flames, does shed,
Sweating in too warme a Bed.

　　Such the Maiden Gemme　　　　25
　　By the wanton Spring put on,
　　　Peeps from her Parent stemme,
　　And blushes on the manly Sun:
This watry Blossome of thy Eyne
Ripe, will make the richer Wine.　　30

　　Faire Drop, why quak'st thou so?
　　'Cause thou streight must lay thy Head
　　　In the Dust? ô no;

The Dust shall never bee thy Bed:
A pillow for thee will I bring,                    35
Stuft with Downe of Angels wing.

    Thus carryed up on high,
    (For to Heaven thou must goe)
    Sweetly shalt thou lye,
    And in soft slumbers bath thy woe;          40
Till the singing Orbes awake thee,
And one of their bright *Chorus* make thee.

    There thy selfe shalt bee
    An eye, but not a weeping one,
    Yet I doubt of thee,                          45
    Whither th'hadst rather there have shone
An eye of Heaven; or still shine here
In th'Heaven of *Mary's* eye, a *Teare*.

*Dudley Fitts*

## CRASHAW
### THE TEARE

The first two poems in Crashaw's *Steps to the Temple* (1646), "The Weeper" and "The Teare," are concerned with "Mary called Magdalene, out of whom went seven devils" (*Luke* 8:2). By ancient tradition, though on no biblical evidence, she is identified with the repentant "woman in the city, which was a sinner" (*Luke* 7:37) who washed Jesus' feet with her tears, wiped them with her hair, and anointed them with an unguent that she had brought in an alabaster box. "The Weeper" is the longer and more intricately wrought of the two poems, and certain of its baroque roulades of diction—for example,

> *Upwards thou dost weepe,*
> *Heavens bosome drinks the gentle streame.*
> *Where th' milky rivers meet,*
> *Thine Crawles above and is the Creame*

—have given it an uncomfortable kind of notoriety. It is followed immediately by "The Teare," and L.C. Martin, the editor of the definitive text of Crashaw, suggests that this smaller poem may represent material left over from the longer. Clearly there is a close similarity of diction and tone, and in the edition of 1648 the fifth stanza of "The Teare" actually turns up in "The Weeper." Nevertheless the shorter lyric is a poem in its own right. It is less extravagant, less mannered, than "The Weeper," and it may be that it carries greater conviction, that it is on the whole a more reasonable expression of religious experience.

"Reasonable," one says, as though reason in mystical poetry were a *desideratum*. Crashaw is above all an ecstatic, and his mind works by a logic that achieves its solutions and discoveries by forcing metaphors, tropes in general, to the very limits of sense, beyond which lies madness. Moreover, he is in love with ceremony and decoration. Here is no simplicity, either of feeling or of expression. The anecdote in Luke is

strange, but it is first of all homely: we think, Yes, she acted
so, and He replied so, and it is as though we had been there
in the Pharisee's house. The poet will have none of this.
Characteristically he seizes upon a material detail, the Magdalene's weeping, and makes a series of symbolic prolifera-
tions of it. Weeping is tears; tears are water; let us take one
drop of this water—which, since it is the water of repentance,
is holy water—and turn it into a poem. The method turns
upon comparisons, conventionally enough; what is unusual,
what is baroque and disturbing, is the unexpectedness of these
comparisons. The tear is a moist spark; a watery diamond; a
meteor; a tear indeed, but such a tear as the world had hardly
seen before. Weight, texture, color, motion—all are caught
up and concentrated in this drop of water, which for all its
tininess seems to expand as if it were to engulf the poet's
thought. So much ingenuity has gone into the working out
of these conceits, so much delight in the elaboration of image
and idea, that we tend to forget the beauty of the original
scene in our response to this coruscation of art; and from
one point of view, that may serve as a warning derogation of
the baroque in religious expression.

To take only one example: in stanza five, the tear is
compared to an unripe grape that blushes into maturity
under the influence of the sun. A drop of water is round, and
so is a grape; very well. But *blushes*, together with the associations set up by *maiden*, *wanton*, and *manly*, bring in a new
comparison, a sexual one: the bride blushes in the presence of
her groom. Thirdly, when the grape has blushed ripe, one
can make wine of it. Wine is a liquid; a wine drop is round,
like a drop of water; the Magdalene's tears are like wine. But
how? In that they are suffused with the color of modesty
(the blood of guilt?), and so are transformed. And finally the
idea of transformation may recall to us the first miracle that
Jesus wrought, the changing of water into wine at the marriage feast in Cana. Mary Magdalene was a woman of the
streets, a sinner, in her unredeemed state quite alien to the
clean mysteries of marriage; but now she is changed by the
Lord's presence, and the water of her tears becomes precious
and saving, akin to the wine of the Eucharist. So much, and
more, can be divined here; the danger lies in the act of
divination itself, in letting ingenuity (which is a response to
décor) take over the stage to the exclusion of anything else.

Mystical contemplation has its own modes, and they need
not correspond to those of reasoned discourse. Ecstasy knows
no rules at all. In such poems as "The Teare" there is an

attempt to impose formal order—here, the order of hyper-
bolic metaphor—upon material that either resists form or
flees from it. When the intractable is made tractable (lines
17–18, 31–33), it can acquire a moving power; when it eludes
control (lines 5–6, with their quibble upon "water of a
*Diamond*"; line 12, where the tear becomes an ear-ornament
for the moon), there is danger of frigidity, even of silliness.
"The Teare" is flawed, perhaps, though it does not, as "The
Weeper" does, become silly. The flaws, if they are flaws, are
the inevitable blemishes of the baroque in any form of art: a
sinning by excess, a temporary plunging beyond control.

# ANDREW MARVELL

## [1621–1678]

### *To His Coy Mistress*

Had we but World enough, and Time,
This coyness Lady were no crime.
We would sit down, and think which way
To walk, and pass our long Loves Day.
Thou by the *Indian Ganges* side                    5
Should'st rubies find: I by the Tide
Of *Humber* would complain. I would
Love you ten years before the Flood:
And you should if you please refuse
Till the Conversion of the *Jews*.                  10
My vegetable Love should grow
Vaster than Empires, and more slow.
An hundred years should go to praise
Thine Eyes, and on thy Forehead Gaze.
Two hundred to adore each Breast:                   15
But thirty thousand to the rest;
·An Age at least to every part,
And the last Age should show your Heart.
For Lady you deserve this State;
Nor would I love at lower rate.                     20
    But at my back I alwaies hear
Time's wingèd Charriot hurrying near:
And yonder all before us lye
Desarts of vast eternity.
Thy Beauty shall no more be found,                  25
Nor, in thy marble Vault, shall sound
My ecchoing Song: then Worms shall try
That long preserv'd Virginity:
And your quaint Honour turn to dust,
And into ashes all my Lust.                         30
The Grave's a fine and private place,
But none I think do there embrace.
    Now therefore, while the youthful hew
Sits on thy skin like morning dew,

And while thy willing Soul transpires                    35
At every pore with instant Fires,
Now let us sport us while we may,
And now, like am'rous birds of prey,
Rather at once our Time devour
Than languish in his slow-chapt pow'r.                   40
Let us roll all our Strength, and all
Our sweetness, up into one Ball:
And tear our Pleasures with rough strife
Thus, though we cannot make our Sun
Thorough the Iron gates of Life.                         45
Stand still, yet we will make him run.

ANDREW MARVELL

*Culver Pictures, Inc.*

# J. V. Cunningham

---

MARVELL

TO HIS COY MISTRESS

The poetic is often thought to be at the opposite pole from the logical, yet there are poems of note that seem to be logical, poems in which the subject and structure of the poem is conceived and expressed syllogistically. Anyone at all acquainted with modern criticism and the poems that are currently in fashion will think in this connection of Marvell's "To His Coy Mistress." The apparent structure of that poem is an argumentative syllogism, explicitly stated, "Had we but World enough, and Time," the poet says,

*This coyness Lady were no crime*

. . .

*But at my back I alwaies hear*
*Time's winged Charriot hurrying near*

. . .

*Now therefore,*

. . .

*. . . let us sport us while we may*

If we had all the space and time in the world, we could delay consummation. But we do not. Therefore. The structure is formal. The poet offers to the lady a practical syllogism, and if she assents to it, the appropriate consequence, he hopes, will follow.

The logical nature of the argument here has been generally recognized, though often with a certain timidity. Mr. Eliot hazards: "the three strophes of Marvell's poem have something like a syllogistic relation to each other."[1] And in a recent scholarly work we read: "The dialectic of the poem lies not only or chiefly in the formal demonstration explicit in its three stanzas, but in all the contrasts evoked by its images and in the play between the immediately sensed and

[1] T. S. Eliot, *Selected Essays*. New York, 1950. This and subsequent quotations are from pp. 253–55.

the intellectually apprehended" (*Seventeenth Century Verse and Prose*, New York, 1951). That is, the logic is recognized, but minimized, and our attention is quickly distracted to something more reputable in a poem, the images or the characteristic tension of metaphysical poetry. For Mr. Eliot the more important element in this case is a principle of order common in modern poetry and often employed in his own poems. He points out that the theme of Marvell's poem is "one of the great traditional commonplaces of European literature . . . the theme of . . . 'Gather ye rose-buds,' of 'Go, lovely rose.' "Where the wit of Marvell," he continues, "renews the theme is in the variety and order of the images." The dominant principle of order in the poem, then, is an implicit one rather than the explicit principle of the syllogism, and implicit in the succession of images.

Mr. Eliot explains the implicit principle of order in this fashion:

> In the first of the three paragraphs Marvell plays with a fancy that begins by pleasing and leads to astonishment. . . . We notice the high speed, the succession of concentrated images, each magnifying the original fancy. When this process has been carried to the end and summed up, the poem turns suddenly with that surprise which has been one of the most important means of poetic effect since Homer:
>
> > *But at my back I alwaies hear*
> > *Time's wingèd Charriot hurrying near:*
> > *And yonder all before us lye*
> > *Desarts of vast eternity.*
>
> A whole civilization resides in these lines:
>
> > *Pallida Mors aequo pulsat pede pauperum tabernas*
> > *Regumque turres . . .*
>
> A modern poet, had he reached the height, would very likely have closed on this moral reflection.

What is meant by this last observation becomes clear a little later, where it is said that the wit of the poem "forms the crescendo and diminuendo of a scale of great imaginative power." The structure of the poem, then, is this: it consists of a succession of images increasing in imaginative power to the sudden turn and surprise of the image of time, and then decreasing to the conclusion. But is there any sudden turn and surprise in the image of time? and does the poem consist of a succession of images?

This talk of images is a little odd, since there seem to be relatively few in the poem if one means by "image" what people usually do—a descriptive phrase that invites the reader to project a sensory construction. The looming imminence of Time's winged chariot is, no doubt, an image, though not a full-blown one, since there is nothing in the phrasing that properly invites any elaboration of sensory detail. But when Mr. Eliot refers to "successive images" and cites "my *vegetable* love," with *vegetable* italicized, and "Till the conversion of the Jews," one suspects that he is provoking images where they do not textually exist. There is about as much of an image in "Till the conversion of the Jews" as there would be in "till the cows come home," and it would be a psychiatrically sensitive reader who would immediately visualize the lowing herd winding slowly o'er the lea. But "my *vegetable* love" will make the point. I have no doubt that Mr. Eliot and subsequent readers do find an image here. They envisage some monstrous and expanding cabbage, but they do so in ignorance. *Vegetable* is no vegetable but an abstract and philosophical term, known as such to the educated man of Marvell's day. Its context is the doctrine of the three souls: the rational, which in man subsumes the other two; the sensitive, which men and animals have in common and which is the principle of motion and perception; and, finally, the lowest of the three, the vegetable soul, which is the only one that plants possess and which is the principle of generation and corruption, of augmentation and decay. Marvell says, then, my love, denied the exercise of sense but possessing the power of augmentation, will increase "Vaster than empires." It is an intellectual image, and hence no image at all but a conceit. For if one calls any sort of particularity or detail in a poem an "image," the use of the wrong word will invite the reader to misconstrue his experience in terms of images, to invent sensory constructions and to project them on the poem.

A conceit is not an image. It is a piece of wit. It is, in the tradition in which Marvell was writing, among other possibilities, the discovery of a proposition referring to one field of experience in terms of an intellectual structure derived from another field, and often enough a field of learning, as is the case in "my vegetable love." This tradition, though it goes back to the poetry of John Donne, and years before that, was current in Marvell's day. The fashionable poetry at the time

he was writing this poem, the poetry comparable to that of
Eliot or of Auden in the last two decades, was the poetry of
John Cleveland, and the fashionable manner was generally
known as "Clevelandizing." It consisted in the invention of a
series of witty hyperbolical conceits, sometimes interspersed
with images, and containing a certain amount of roughage in
the form of conventional erotic statements:

> *Thy Beauty shall no more be found,*
> *Nor, in thy marble Vault, shall sound*
> *My ecchoing Song . . .*

It was commonly expressed in the octosyllabic couplet.
Cleveland, for example, writes "Upon Phillis Walking in a
Morning before Sun-rising":

> *The trees, (like yeomen of the guard,*
> *Serving more for pomp than ward) . . .*

The comparison here does not invite visualization. It would
be inappropriate to summon up the colors and serried ranks
of the guard. The comparison is made solely with respect to
the idea: the trees, like the guard, serve more for pomp than
ward. Again:

> *The flowers, called out of their beds,*
> *Start and raise up their drowsy heads,*
> *And he that for their color seeks*
> *May find it vaulting to her cheeks,*
> *Where roses mix,—no civil war*
> *Between her York and Lancaster.*

One does not here picture in panorama the Wars of the
Roses. One sees rather the aptness and the wit of York and
Lancaster, the white rose and the red, reconciled in her
cheeks, or one rejects it as forced and far-fetched. This is a
matter of taste.

But if the poem is not a succession of images, does it
exhibit that other principle that Mr. Eliot ascribes to it—the
turn and surprise he finds in the abrupt introduction of
Time's chariot, which form a sort of fulcrum on which the
poem turns? Subsequent critics have certainly felt that it has.
In *Reading Poems* (ed. W. Thomas and S. G. Brown), we
read:

> The poem begins as a conventional love poem in which
> the lover tries to persuade his mistress to give in to his
> entreaties. But with the introduction of the image of
> the chariot in line 21, the poet becomes obsessed by the

terrible onrush of time, and the love theme becomes scarcely more than an illustration of the effect which time has upon human life.

And the leading scholar in the field, Douglas Bush, a man who is generally quite unhappy with Mr. Eliot's criticism, nevertheless says:

> the poet sees the whole world of space and time as the setting for two lovers. But wit cannot sustain the pretence that youth and beauty and love are immortal, and with a quick change of tone—like Catullus' *nobis cum semel occidit brevis lux* or Horace's *sed Timor et Minae* —the theme of time and death is developed with serious and soaring directness.

These, I believe, are not so much accounts of the poem as accounts of Mr. Eliot's reading of the poem. Let us question the fact. Does the idea of time and death come as any surprise in this context? The poem began, "Had we but world enough and time." That is, it began with an explicit condition contrary to fact, which, by all grammatical rules, amounts to the assertion that we do not have world enough and time. There is no surprise whatever when the proposition is explicitly made in line 21. It would rather have been surprising if it had not been made. Indeed, the only question we have in this respect, after we have read the first line, is: How many couplets will the poet expend on the ornamental reiteration of the initial proposition before he comes to the expected *but?* The only turn in the poem is the turn which the structure of the syllogism had led us to await.

Mr. Eliot compares the turn and surprise which he finds in this poem to a similar turn in an ode of Horace, and the scholars seem to corroborate the comparison. This is the fourth ode of the first book:

> *solvitur acris hiems grata vice veris et Favoni,*
> *trahuntque siccas machinae carinas.*

The poem begins with a picture of spring and proceeds by a succession of images, images of the external world and mythological images:

> Sharp winter relaxes with the welcome change to spring and the west wind, and the cables haul the dry keels of ships. The herd no longer takes pleasure in its stalls or the farmer in his fire, and the pastures no

longer whiten with hoar frost. Cytherean Venus leads
her dancers beneath the overhanging moon, and the
beautiful graces and nymphs strike the ground with
alternate foot, while blazing Vulcan visits the grim
forges of the Cyclops. Now is the time to wind your
bright hair with green myrtle or with the flowers that
the thawed earth yields. Now is the time to sacrifice to
Faunus in the shadowed woods, whether it be a lamb he
asks or a kid:

> *pallida mors aequo pulsat pede pauperum tabernas
> regumque turres.*

Pallid death with indifferent foot strikes the poor man's
hut and the palaces of kings. Now, fortunate Sestius, the
brief sum of life forbids our opening a long account
with hope. Night will soon hem you in, and the fabled
ghosts, and Pluto's meager house.

Death occurs in this poem with that suddenness and lack of
preparation with which it sometimes occurs in life. The
structure of the poem is an imitation of the structure of such
experiences in life. And as we often draw a generalization
from such experiences, so Horace, on the sudden realization
of the abruptness and impartiality of death, reflects:

*Vitae summa brevis spem nos vetat incohare longam*
[The brief sum of life forbids our opening a long ac-
count·with hope].

But the proposition is subsequent to the experience; it does
not rule and direct the poem from the outset. And the experience in Horace *is* surprising and furnishes the fulcrum on
which the poem turns. It has, in fact, the characteristics that
are ascribed to Marvell's poem but that Marvell's poem does
not have. The two are two distinct kinds of poetry, located
in distinct and almost antithetical traditions; both are valuable
and valid methods, but one is not to be construed in terms of
the other.

In brief, the general structure of Marvell's poem is syllogistic, and it is located in the Renaissance tradition of formal
logic and of rhetoric. The structure exists in its own right
and as a kind of expandable filing system. It is a way of
disposing of, of making a place for, elements of a different
order: in this case, Clevelandizing conceits and erotic propositions in the tradition of Jonson and Herrick. These reiterate
the propositions of the syllogism. They do not develop the

syllogism, and they are not required by the syllogism; they are free and extra. There could be more or less of them, since there is nothing in the structure that determines the number of interpolated couplets. It is a matter of tact and a matter of the appetite of the writer and the reader.

## The Garden

How vainly men themselves amaze
To win the Palm, the Oke, or Bayes;
And their uncesant Labours see
Crown'd from some single Herb or Tree,
Whose short and narrow vergèd Shade      5
Does prudently their Toyles upbraid;
While all Flow'rs and all Trees do close
To weave the Garlands of repose.

Fair quiet, have I found thee here,
And Innocence thy Sister dear!      10
Mistaken long, I sought you then
In busy Companies of Men.
Your sacred Plants, if here below,
Only among the Plants will grow.
Society is all but rude,      15
To this delicious Solitude.

No white nor red was ever seen
So am'rous as this lovely green.
Fond Lovers, cruel as their Flame,
Cut in these Trees their Mistress name.      20
Little, Alas, they know, or heed,
How far these Beauties Hers exceed!
Fair Trees! where s'eer your barkes I wound,
No Name shall but your own be found.

When we have run our Passions heat,      25
Love hither makes his best retreat.
The *Gods*, that mortal Beauty chase,
Still in a tree did end their race.
*Apollo* hunted *Daphne* so,
Only that She might Laurel grow.      30
And *Pan* did after *Syrinx* speed,
Not as a Nymph, but for a Reed.

What wondrous Life in this I lead!
Ripe Apples drop about my head;
The Luscious Clusters of the Vine                    35
Upon my Mouth do crush their Wine;
The Nectaren, and curious Peach,
Into my hands themselves do reach;
Stumbling on Melons, as I pass,
Insnar'd with Flow'rs, I fall on Grass.              40

Mean while the Mind, from pleasure less,
Withdraws into its happiness;
The Mind, that Ocean where each kind
Does streight its own resemblance find;
Yet it creates, transcending these,                  45
Far other Worlds, and other Seas;
Annihilating all that's made
To a green Thought in a green Shade.

Here at the Fountains sliding foot,
Or at some Fruit-trees mossy root,                   50
Casting the Bodies Vest aside,
My Soul into the boughs does glide:
There like a Bird it sits, and sings,
Then whets, and combs its silver Wings,
And, till prepared for longer flight,                55
Waves in its plumes the various light.

Such was that happy Garden-state,
While Man there walk'd without a Mate:
After a Place so pure, and sweet,
What other help could yet be meet!                   60
But 'twas beyond a Mortal's share
To wander solitary there:
Two Paradises 'twere in one
To live in Paradise alone.

How well the skillful Gardner drew                   65
Of flow'rs and herbes this Dial new;
Where from above the milder Sun
Does through a fragrant Zodiack run;
And as it works, th' industrious Bee
Computes its time as well as we.                     70
How could such sweet and wholsome Hours
Be reckon'd but with herbs and flow'rs!

# William Empson

## MARVELL
## THE GARDEN

The chief point of the poem is to contrast and reconcile conscious and unconscious states, intuitive and intellectual modes of apprehension; and yet that distinction is never made, perhaps could not have been made; his thought is implied by his metaphors. There is something very Far-Eastern about this; I was set to work on the poem by Dr. Richards' discussion of a philosophical argument in his book on Mencius. The Oxford edition notes bring out a crucial double meaning (so that this is not my own fancy) in the most analytical statement of the poem, about the mind—

> *Annihilating all that's made*
> *To a green Thought in a green Shade.*

"Either 'reducing the whole material world to nothing material, *i.e.* to a green thought.' or 'considering the material world as of no value compared to a green thought'"; either contemplating everything or shutting everything out. This combines the idea of the conscious mind, including everything because understanding it, and that of the unconscious animal nature, including everything because in harmony with it. Evidently the object of such a fundamental contradiction (seen in the etymology: turning all *ad nihil, to* nothing, and *to* a thought) is to deny its reality; the point is not that these two are essentially different but that they must cease to be different so far as either is to be known. So far as he has achieved his state of ecstasy he combines them, he is "neither conscious nor not conscious," like the seventh Buddhist state of enlightenment. This gives its point, I think, to the other ambiguity, clear from the context, as to whether the *all* considered was *made* in the mind of the author or the Creator; to so peculiarly "creative" a knower there is little difference between the two. Here as usual with "profound" remarks the strength of the thing is to combine unusually intellectual with unusually primitive ideas; thought about the conditions of knowledge with a magical idea that the adept controls the external world by thought.

The vehemence of the couplet, and this hint of physical power in thought itself (in the same way as the next line gives it color), may hint at an idea that one would like to feel was present, as otherwise it is the only main idea about nature that the poem leaves out; that of the "Hymn to David" and "The Ancient Mariner," the Orpheus idea, that by delight in nature when terrible man gains strength to control it. This grand theme too has a root in magic; it is an important version of the idea of the man powerful because he has included everything in himself; the idea is still strong, one would think, among the mountain climbers and often the scientists, and deserves a few examples here. I call it the idea of the "Hymn to David," though being hidden behind the religious one it is nowhere overtly stated, except perhaps in the line

> *Praise above all, for praise prevails.*

David is a case of Orpheuslike behavior because his music restrained the madness of Saul.

> *His furious foes no more maligned*
> *When he such melody divined,*
> *And sense and soul detained;*

By *divining*—intuiting—the harmony behind the universe he "makes it divine," rather as to discover a law of nature is to "give nature laws," and this restrains the madman who embodies the unruled forces of nature from killing him. The main argument of the verses describing nature (or nature as described by David) is that the violence of Nature is an expression of her adoration of God, and therefore that the man of prayer who also adores God delights in it and can control it.

> *Strong the gier eagle on his sail*
> *Strong against tide, th' enormous whale*
> *Emerges, as he goes.*

> *But stronger still, in earth or air*
> *Or in the sea, the man of prayer,*
> *And far beneath the tide.*

The feeling is chiefly carried by the sound; long Latin words are packed into the short lines against a short one-syllable rhyming word full of consonants; it is like dancing in heavy skirts; he juggles with the whole cumbrous complexity of the

world. The "Mariner" makes a more conscious and direct use
of the theme, but in some degree runs away from it at the
end. The reason it was a magical crime for a sailor to kill the
albatross is that the albatross both occurs among terrible
scenes of nature and symbolizes man's power to extract life
from them, so ought doubly to be delighted in. So long as the
mariner is horrified by the creatures of the calm he is their
slave; he is set free to act, in the supreme verses of the poem,
as soon as he delights in them. The final moral is

> *He prayeth best, that loveth best*
> *All things both great and small.*

But that copybook maxim is fine only if you can hold it
firmly together with such verses as this, which Coleridge
later omitted:

> *The very deeps did rot; oh Christ*
> *That such a thing could be;*
> *Yea, slimy things did crawl with legs*
> *Upon the slimy sea.*

And it was these creatures, as he insisted in the margin by
giving the same name to both, that the mariner blessed
unaware when he discovered their beauty. This is what
Coleridge meant by alternately saying that the poem has too
much of the moral and too little; knowing what the conventional phrases of modern Christianity ought to mean, he
thought he could shift to a conventional moral that needs to
be based upon the real one. Byron's nature poetry gives more
obvious examples of the theme; he likes to compare a storm
on the Jura or what not to a woman whom, we are to feel,
only Byron could dominate. Poe was startled and liberated by
it into a symbol of its own achievement; the sailor in "The
Maelstrom" is so horrified as to be frozen, through a trick of
neurosis, into idle curiosity, and this becomes a scientific
interest in the portent which shows him the way to escape
from it.

Nature when terrible is no theme of Marvell's, and he gets
this note of triumph rather from using nature when peaceful
to control the world of man.

> *How safe, methinks, and strong, behind*
> *These Trees have I encamp'd my Mind;*
> *Where Beauty, aiming at the Heart,*
> *Bends in some Tree its useless Dart;*
> *And where the World no certain Shot*

> *Can make, or me it toucheth not.*
> *But I on it securely play,*
> *And gall its Horsemen all the Day.*

The masculine energy of the last couplet is balanced immediately by an acceptance of nature more masochist than passive, in which he becomes Christ with both the nails and the thorns ("Appleton House," lxxvi.).

> *Bind me ye* Woodbines *in your 'twines,*
> *Curle me about ye gadding* Vines,
> *And Oh so close your Circles lace,*
> *That I may never leave this Place:*
> *But, lest your Fetters prove too weak,*
> *Ere I your Silken Bondage break,*
> *Do you,* O Brambles, *chain me too,*
> *And courteous* Briars *nail me through.*

He does not deify himself more actively, and in any case the theme of "The Garden" is a repose.

> *How vainly men themselves amaze*
> *To win the Palm, the Oke, or Bayes;*
> *And their uncessant Labours see*
> *Crown'd from some single Herb or Tree,*
> *Whose short and narrow vergèd Shade*
> *Does prudently their Toyles upbraid;*
> *While all Flow'rs and all Trees do close*
> *To weave the Garlands of repose.*

This first verse comes nearest to stating what seems the essential distinction, between powers inherent and powers worked out in practice, being a general and feeling one could be; in this ideal case, so the wit of the thing claims, the power to have been a general is already satisfied in the garden. "Unemployment" is too painful and normal even in the fullest life for such a theme to be trivial. But self-knowledge is possible in such a state so far as the unruly impulses are digested, ordered, made transparent; not by their being known, at the time, as unruly. Consciousness no longer makes an important distinction; the impulses, since they must be balanced already, neither need it to put them right nor are put wrong by the way it forces across their boundaries. They let themselves be known because they are not altered by being known, because their principle of indeterminacy no longer acts. This idea is important for all the versions of pastoral, for the pastoral figure is always ready to be the critic; he not only includes everything but may in some unexpected way know it.

Another range of his knowledge might be mentioned here. I am not sure what arrangement of flower-beds is described in the last verse, but it seems clear that the sun goes through the "zodiac" of flowers in one day, and that the bees too, in going from one bed to another, reminding us of the labors of the first verse, pass all summer in a day. They compute their time as well as we in that though their lives are shorter they too contract all experience into it, and this makes the poet watch over large periods of time as well as space. So far as he becomes Nature, he becomes permanent. It is a graceful finale to the all-in-one theme, but not, I think, very important; the crisis of the poem is in the middle.

Once you accept the Oxford edition's note you may as well apply it to the whole verse.

> *Mean while the Mind, from pleasure less,*
> *Withdraws into its happiness;*
> *The Mind, that Ocean where each kind*
> *Does streight its own resemblance find;*
> *Yet it creates, transcending these,*
> *Far other Worlds, and other Seas,*
> *Annihilating . . .*

"From pleasure less." Either "from the lessening of pleasure"—"we are quiet in the country, but our dullness gives a sober and self-knowing happiness, more intellectual than that of the overstimulated pleasures of the town"; or "made less by this pleasure"—"The pleasures of the country give a repose and intellectual release which make me less intellectual, make my mind less worrying and introspective." This is the same puzzle as to the consciousness of the thought; the ambiguity gives two meanings to pleasure, corresponding to his Puritan ambivalence about it, and to the opposition between pleasure and happiness. "Happiness," again, names a conscious state, and yet involves the idea of things falling right, happening so, not being ordered by an anxiety of the conscious reason. (So that as a rule it is a weak word; it is by seeming to look at it hard and bring out its implications that the verse here makes it act as a strong one.)

The same doubt gives all their grandeur to the next lines. The sea if calm reflects everything near it; the mind as knower is a conscious mirror. Somewhere in the sea are sea lions and seahorses and everything else, though they are different from land ones; the unconsciousness is unplumbed and pathless, and there is no instinct so strange among the beasts that it lacks its fantastic echo in the mind. In the first version thoughts are shadows, in the second (like the green thought) they are as solid as what they image; and yet they still correspond to something in the outer world, so that the poet's intuition is comparable to pure knowledge. This metaphor may reflect back so that "withdraws" means the tide going down; the "mind" is "less" now, but will return, and it is now that one can see the rock-pools. On the Freudian view of an ocean, *withdraws* would make this repose in nature a return to the womb; anyway it may mean either "withdraws into self-contemplation" or "withdraws altogether, into its mysterious processes of digestion." "Streight" may mean "packed together," in the microcosm, or "at once"; the beasts see their reflection (perhaps the root idea of the metaphor) as soon as they look for it; the calm of nature gives the poet an immediate self-knowledge. But we have already had two entrancingly witty verses about the sublimation of sexual desire into a taste for nature (I should not say that this theme was the main emotional drive behind the poem, but it takes up a large part of its overt thought), and the *kinds* look for their *resemblance*, in practice, out of a desire for *creation;* in the mind, at this fertile time for the poet, they can *find* it "at once," being "packed together." The transition from the beast and its reflection to the two pairing beasts implies a transition from the correspondences of thought with fact to those of thought with thought, to find which is to be creative; there is necessarily here a suggestion of rising from one "level" of thought to another; and in the next couplet not only does the mind transcend the world it mirrors, but a sea, to which it is parallel, transcends both land and sea too, which implies self-consciousness and all the antinomies of philosophy. Whether or not you give "transcendent" the technical sense "predicable of all categories" makes no great difference; in including everything in itself the mind includes as a detail itself and all its inclusions. And it is true that the sea reflects the other worlds of the stars; Donne's metaphor of the globe is in the background. Yet even here the double meaning is not lost; all land beasts have their sea beasts, but the sea also has the kraken; in the depths as well as the transcendence of the mind are things stranger than all the kinds of the world.

Miss M.C. Bradbrook has pointed out to me that the next verse, while less triumphant, gives the process a more firmly religious interpretation.

*Here at the Fountains sliding foot,*
*Or by some Fruit-trees mossy root,*
*Casting the Bodies Vest aside,*
*My Soul into the boughs does glide:*
*There like a Bird it sits, and sings,*
*Then whets, and combs its silver Wings,*
*And, till prepared for longer flight,*
*Waves in its plumes the various Light.*

The bird is the dove of the Holy Spirit and carries a suggestion of the rainbow of the covenant. By becoming inherent in everything, he becomes a soul not pantheist but clearly above and apart from the world even while still living in it. Yet the paradoxes are still firmly maintained here, and the soul is as solid as the green thought. The next verse returns naturally and still with exultation to the jokes in favor of solitude against women.

*Green* takes on great weight here, as Miss Sackville West pointed out, because it has been a pet word of Marvell's before. To list the uses before the satires may seem an affection of pedantry, but shows how often the word was used; and they are pleasant things to look up. In the Oxford text: pages 12, line 23; 17, line 18; 25, line 11; 27, line 4; 38, line 3; 45, line 3; 46, line 25; 48, line 18; 49, line 48; 70, line 376; 71, line 390; 74, line 510; 122, line 2. Less rich uses: 15, line 18; 21, line 44; 30, line 55; 42, line 14; 69, line 339; 74, lines 484, 496; 78, line 628; 85, line 82; 89, line 94; 108, line 196. It is connected here with grass, buds, children, an as yet virginal prospect of sexuality, and the peasant stock from which the great families emerge. The "unfathomable" grass makes the soil fertile and shows it to be so; it is the humble, permanent, undeveloped nature, which sustains everything, and to which everything must return. No doubt D.H. Lawrence was right when he spoke up for "Leaves of Grass" against Whitman and said they felt themselves to be very aristocratic, but that too is eminently a pastoral fancy. Children are connected with this both as buds, and because of their contact with nature (as in Wordsworth), and unique fitness for heaven (as in the Gospels).

*The tawny mowers enter next,*
*Who seem like Israelites to be,*
*Walking on foot through a green sea*

connects greenness with oceans and gives it a magical security;

> *And in the greenness of the grass*
> *Did see my hopes as in a glass*

connects greenness with mirrors and the partial knowledge of the mind. The complex of ideas he concentrates into this passage, in fact, had been worked out already, and in a context that shows how firmly these ideas about Nature were connected with direct pastoral. The poem indeed comes immediately after a pastoral series about the mower of grass.

> *I am the Mower Damon, known*
> *Through all the Meadows I have mown;*
> *On me the Morn her dew distills*
> *Before her darling Daffodils.*

In these meadows he feels he has left his mark on a great territory, if not on everything, and as a typical figure he has mown all the meadows of the world; in either case nature gives him regal and magical honours, and I suppose he is not only the ruler but the executioner of the daffodils—the Clown as Death.

> *Only for him no Cure is found,*
> *Whom Juliana's Eyes do wound.*
> *'Tis death alone that this must do:*
> *For Death thou art a Mower too.*

He provides indeed more conscious and comic mixtures of heroic and pastoral:

> *every Mower's wholesome heat*
> *Smelled like an Alexander's sweat.*

It is his grand attack on gardens that introduces both the connection through wit between the love of woman and of nature, which is handled so firmly in "The Garden":

> *No white nor red was ever seen*
> *So am'rous as this lovely green.*

and the belief that the fruitful attitude toward nature is the passive one:

> *His [the gardener's] green Seraglio has its Eunuchs too;*
> *Lest any Tyrant him outdoe.*
> *And in the Cherry he does Nature vex,*
> *To procreate without a Sex.*
> *'Tis all enforced; the Fountain and the Grot;*
> *While the sweet Fields do lye forgot;*
> *Where willing Nature does to all dispence*

> *A wild and fragrant Innocence:*
> *And* Fauns *and* Faryes *do the Meadows till,*
> *More by their presence than their skill.*

It is Marvell himself who tills the Garden by these magical and contemplative powers.

Grass indeed comes to be taken for granted as the symbol of pastoral humility:

> *Unhappy Birds! what does it boot*
> *To build below the Grasses' Root;*
> *When Lowness is unsafe as Hight,*
> *And Chance o'ertakes what scapeth Spight?*

It is a humility of Nature from which she is still higher than man, so that the grasshoppers preach to him from their pinnacles:

> *And now to the Abyss I pass*
> *Of that unfathomable Grass,*
> *Where men like Grashoppers appear,*
> *But Grashoppers are Gyants there;*
> *They, in there squeking Laugh, contemn*
> *Us as we walk more low than them:*
> *And, from the Precipices tall*
> *Of the green spire's, to us do call.*

It seems also to be an obscure merit of grass that it produces "hay," which was the name of a country dance, so that the humility is gaiety.

> *With this the golden fleece I shear*
> *Of all these Closes ev'ry Year,*
> *And though in Wool more poor than they,*
> *Yet I am richer far in Hay.*

To nineteenth century taste the only really poetical verse of the poem is the central fifth of the nine; I have been discussing the sixth, whose dramatic position is an illustration of its very penetrating theory. The first four are a crescendo of wit, on the themes "success or failure is not important, only the repose that follows the exercise of one's powers" and "women, I am pleased to say, are no longer interesting to me, because nature is more beautiful." One effect of the wit is to admit, and so make charming, the impertinence of the second of these, which indeed the first puts in its place; it is only for a time, and after effort among human beings, that he can enjoy solitude. The value of these moments made it fitting to pretend they were eternal; and yet the lightness of his expression of their sense of power is more intelligent, and so more convincing, than Wordsworth's solemnity on the same theme, because it does not forget the opposing forces.

> *When we have run our Passions heat,*
> *Love hither makes his best retreat.*
> *The* Gods, *that mortal Beauty chase,*
> *Still in a Tree did end their race.*
> Apollo *hunted* Daphne *so,*
> *Only that She might Laurel grow,*
> *And* Pan *did after* Syrinx *speed,*
> *Not as a Nymph, but for a Reed.*

The energy and delight of the conceit has been sharpened or keyed up here till it seems to burst and transform itself; it dissolves in the next verse into the style of Keats. So his observation of the garden might mount to an ecstasy which disregarded it; he seems in this next verse to imitate the process he has described, to enjoy in a receptive state the exhilaration which an exercise of wit has achieved. But striking as the change of style is, it is unfair to empty the verse of thought and treat it as random description; what happens is that he steps back from overt classical conceits to a rich and intuitive use of Christian imagery. When people treat it as the one good "bit" of the poem one does not know whether they have recognized that the alpha and omega of the verse are the apple and the fall.

> *What wondrous Life in this I lead!*
> *Ripe Apples drop about my head;*
> *The Luscious Clusters of the Vine*
> *Upon my Mouth do crush their Wine;*
> *The Nectaren, and curious Peach,*
> *Into my hands themselves do reach;*
> *Stumbling on Melons, as I pass,*
> *Insnar'd with Flow'rs, I fall on Grass.*

*Melon*, again, is the Greek for apple; "all flesh is *grass*," and its own "flowers" here are the snakes in it that stopped Eurydice. Mere grapes are at once the primitive and the innocent wine; the *nectar* of Eden, and yet the blood of sacrifice. "Curious" could mean "rich and strange" (nature), "improved by care" (art) or "inquisitive" (feeling toward me, since Nature is a mirror, as I do towards her). All these eatable beauties give themselves so as to lose themselves, like a lover, with a forceful generosity; like a lover they *ensnare* him. It is the triumph of the attempt to impose a sexual interest upon nature; there need be no more Puritanism in this use of sacrificial ideas than is already inherent in the praise of solitude; and it is because his repose in the orchard hints at such a variety of emotions that he is contemplating *all that's made*. Sensibility here repeats what wit said in the verse before; he tosses into the fantastic treasure chest of the poem's thought all the pathos and dignity that Milton was to feel in his more celebrated garden; and it is while this is going on, we are told in the next verse, that the mind performs its ambiguous and memorable withdrawal. For each of the three central verses he gives a twist to the screw of the microscope and is living in another world.

# HENRY VAUGHAN

[1622–1695]

## The World

I Saw Eternity the other night
Like a great *Ring* of pure and endless light,
    All calm, as it was bright,
And round beneath it, Time in hours, days, years
    Driv'n by the spheres         5
Like a vast shadow mov'd, In which the world
    And all her train were hurl'd;
The doting Lover in his queintest strain
    Did their Complain,
Neer him, his Lute, his fancy, and his flights,     10
    Wits sour delights,
With gloves, and knots the silly snares of pleasure
    Yet his dear Treasure
All scatter'd lay, while he his eys did pour
    Upon a flowr.         15

The darksome States-man hung with weights and woe
Like a thick midnight-fog mov'd there so slow
    He did nor stay, nor go;
Condemning thoughts (like sad Ecclipses) scowl
    Upon his soul,         20
And Clouds of crying witnesses without
    Pursued him with one shout.
Yet dig'd the Mole, and lest his ways be found
    Workt under ground,
Where he did Clutch his prey, but one did see     25
    That policie,
Churches and altars fed him, Perjuries
    Were gnats and flies,
It rain'd about him bloud and tears, but he
    Drank them as free.         30

The fearfull miser on a heap of rust
Sate pining all his life there, did scarce trust
    His own hands with the dust,

Yet would not place one peece above, but lives
    In feare of theeves.              35
Thousands there were as frantick as himself
    And hug'd each one his pelf,
The down-right Epicure plac'd heav'n in sense
    And scornd pretence
While others slipt into a wide Excesse     40
    Said little lesse;
The weaker sort slight, triviall wares Inslave
    Who think them brave,
And poor, despised truth sate Counting by
    Their victory.           45

Yet some, who all this while did weep and sing,
And sing, and weep, soar'd up into the *Ring*,
    But most would use no wing.
O fools (said I,) thus to prefer dark night
    Before true light.           50
To live in grots, and caves, and hate the day
    Because it shews the way,
The way which from this dead and dark abode
    Leads up to God,
A way where you might tread the Sun, and be     55
    More bright than he.
But as I did their madnes so discusse
    One whisper'd thus,
*This Ring the Bride-groome did for none provide*
    *But for his bride.*           60

# R. A. Durr

## VAUGHAN
## THE WORLD

Perhaps the chief prerequisite to an enlarged regard of
Henry Vaughan's poetry is the realization that his language is
symbolical: flower, bird, sun, storm, fountain, stream, and
grove compose a unique and marvelous country of the mind
at the same time that they celebrate the truth and beauty of
the natural creation. For a genuine symbol, as Coleridge
taught, "partakes of the reality which it renders intelligible."
Reality, for Vaughan, is God, and the creation, witnessed
with an awakened consciousness, partakes of Him and renders Him intelligible. "For the invisible things of him from
the creation of the world are clearly seen, being understood
by the things that are made . . ." (*Romans* 1:20). As
Vaughan states, "All things here show him heaven . . .";
man's true business is to "observe God in his works." Thus,
the seed's growth to flower and fruit is a parable of the
maturation in man of his Divine Original to love and its
consequence of good works and peace of mind; difficult
journeys over land and sea symbolize the *via dolorosa*, the
road of trials, which the pilgrim soul must travel toward the
New Jerusalem of spiritual life; and the courtship and marriage of lovers is an *allegoria* of the true relation between
God and creation, spirit (*pneuma*) and soul (*psyche*), eternity and time. These are Vaughan's major metaphors; his
poetry orients to them. And each serves to embody his single
theme: regeneration.

For there are two "worlds" in Vaughan's view, the illusory
and the real, or, in terms explicit in the poem itself, the
temporal and the eternal. His poetic work is about the
growth, or passage, from the one to the other and, hence,
ultimately the union of the two. It is hard to be exact in
delineating these two worlds, however. The usual designa-
tions, "natural" and "manmade," are only roughly approxi-
mate and liable to a common confusion. For flower and sun,
grass and star, can as readily be part of the "manmade world"

as trinkets and titles, toys and riches, which can, in turn—perhaps not so readily—be understood as "natural." Things in themselves are indifferent; everything depends upon the mind of man. The fellow in the street, looking at the sun, sees a bright object about the size and shape of a guinea, but Blake saw a choir of heavenly angels singing hallelujah. To most men in Vaughan's day, stones were negligible, inanimate objects, very low on the scale of being, but to the poet stones though dumb are deep in admiration. For Whitman, "a leaf of grass is no less than the journeywork of the stars."

The world of Vaughan's contempt and prophetic ire is *maya,* illusion: literally, man's abstract measurements, or categories, *natura naturata,* nature fixed and dead. All things are seen through the glass of conventional preconception, darkly, and not in the light of direct revelation as fluent interrelationships, *natura naturans.* Men, merely wards, are bound by the arbitrary mandates of, perversely, their own misapprehensions codified; and so they have been disinherited of the wonder and mystery of life, their birthright, the free gift of God. Time, precisely, occupies the tyrants' throne, casting a pall upon the land. For while His name is *Now,* His essence all *Act* (in the language of Thomas Traherne), time bids us look before and after, anticipate and regret, so that in taking anxious thought we wobble and miss the mark of the Eternal Now, our only actual life. It is in this sense, in missing the mark, in being mistaken, that the illusory world is sinful and not of the Father.

Once a man has been graced with a glimpse of reality—the other night, say—the shadow world of his habitual dreaming, so seeming-bright, becomes appalling to his reawakened visionary powers (reawakened, because as children we lived in eternity's sunrise). As though a magic lantern of deceit had hitherto afforded him his only light, he sees now by the white radiance of eternity that the world of the fretful ego of insatiable demand "did onley paint and lie." Its pleasures are hallucinatory; its fruits, for which the worldlings pay the price of true life ("A quickness, which my God hath kist"), turn bitter in their mouths. Lover-by-rote, States-man, miser, Epicure, and dotard of bourgeois beatitudes dwell in Plato's cave, mistaking shape for forms, gall for manna, inanity for wealth, satiety for satisfaction, and enthrallment for enhancement. They starve at a plenteous board, consuming gilt-edged menus for the mind—a universal madness.

Only the disaffected, the disillusioned, weep and—apparent paradox—sing; but those who mourn and know they are unfulfilled, seeking sustenance, are blessed: they soar, they are changed, in the twinkling of an eye, unto eternity. But why *do* the rest stay below? Why *will* they whirl in the darkly turning sphere of time? Vaughan's answer seems stern, almost Calvinistic: they are not engaged, they are not chosen. But this is poetry, not doctrine, and its final note is neither harsh nor condemnatory. Vaughan has raged, not without cause and justice, against the perennial insanities of men. But the still, small voice, the whisper, comes from beyond his range of knowledge, though it speaks in his imagery, and tells him: Never mind, it is all right, this is the way it is. And so the poet ends his poem, *sub specie aeternitatis.*

# JOHN DRYDEN

[1631–1700]

## A Song for St. Cecilia's Day

From Harmony, from heav'nly Harmony  
   This universal Frame began:  
   When Nature underneath a heap  
     Of jarring Atomes lay,  
   And cou'd not heave her Head,         5  
The tuneful Voice was heard from high:  
   Arise, ye more than dead.  
Then cold and hot and moist and dry  
In order to their Stations leap,  
     And MUSICK's pow'r obey.         10  
From Harmony, from heavenly Harmony  
   This universal Frame began:  
   From Harmony to Harmony  
Through all the Compass of the Notes it ran,  
The Diapason closing full in Man.         15  

What passion cannot MUSICK raise and quell?  
     When *Jubal* struck the corded Shell,  
   His listening Brethren stood around,  
   And, wond'ring, on their Faces fell  
   To worship that Celestial Sound.        20  
Less than a God they thought there could not dwell  
    Within the hollow of that Shell  
    That spoke so sweetly, and so well.  
What passion cannot MUSICK raise and quell?  

   The TRUMPETs loud Clangor         25  
     Excites us to Arms  
   With shrill Notes of Anger  
     And mortal Alarms.  
   The double double double beat  
     Of the thund'ring DRUM        30  
Cryes, heark the Foes come;  
Charge, Charge, 'tis too late to retreat.

The soft complaining FLUTE
In dying Notes discovers
The Woes of hopeless Lovers,                            35
Whose Dirge is whispered by the warbling LUTE.

Sharp VIOLINS proclaim
Their jealous Pangs and Desperation,
Fury, frantick Indignation,
Depth of Pains and height of Passion,                  40
For the fair, disdainful Dame.

But O! what Art can teach
What human Voice can reach
The sacred ORGANS praise?
Notes inspiring holy Love,                             45
Notes that wing their heav'nly Ways
To mend the Choires above.

*Orpheus* cou'd lead the savage race,
And Trees unrooted left their place,
Sequacious of the Lyre;                                50
But bright CECILIA rais'd the wonder high'r:
When to her Organ vocal Breath was given,
An Angel heard, and straight appear'd,
Mistaking Earth for Heav'n.

GRAND CHORUS

*As from the Pow'r of Sacred Lays*                     55
*The Spheres began to move,*
*And sung the great Creator's Praise*
*To all the bless'd above;*
*So, when the last and dreadful Hour*
*This crumbling Pageant shall devour,*                 60
*The* TRUMPET *shall be heard on high,*
*The dead shall live, the living die,*
*And* MUSICK *shall untune the Sky.*

JOHN DRYDEN

*The Bettmann Archive*

# David Daiches

## DRYDEN
### A SONG FOR ST. CECILIA'S DAY

The title of this poem proclaims its formal and ceremonial nature. Saint Cecilia, the early Christian martyr who developed into the patroness of music, was commemorated on her festival day (November 22nd) by musical performances; during the last twenty years of the seventeenth century the Musical Society of London celebrated the day with a concert and a religious service, the former including an ode, written for the occasion, set to music. This poem is one of two such odes that Dryden wrote. The occasion as well as the title thus indicate that the poem is a public praise of music. In form it is an ode—an "irregular ode" as Dryden and his contemporaries understood the term. This meant that the poet was free to vary the stanza form, metrical scheme and rhyme scheme to suit the needs of the shifting feeling in individual passages. This kind of poem was thus quite different from any of the other poetic genres recognized at this time: there was no prescribed form or basic pattern, and the appropriateness with which the poet varied line length and stanza shape was the criterion on which the success of the poem was estimated.

The poem is thus public and celebratory, rhetorical rather than lyrical in feeling, and at the same time an almost exhibitionist piece of virtuosity. An ode of this kind is bound in some degree to be a sort of glorious showing off. We sense the poet's exultation in his own skill, as we are aware of the pride in their uniforms and bearing displayed by those taking part in some gorgeous traditional pageantry. Indeed, the poem makes the point that the whole universe is a "pageant" (i.e., stage) which was created by music in the first place and which will be dissolved by the music of the last trump:

> So, when the last and dreadful Hour
> This crumbling Pageant shall devour,
> The TRUMPET shall be heard on high,
> The dead shall live, the living die,
> And MUSICK shall untune the Sky.

These concluding lines of the poem round out the concept that the pageant of human history takes place between the Creation and the Last Judgment, each of which crucial occasions being bound up with music. It is within the brackets of this thought, as it were, that the poem moves.

The poem opens with a great declaratory statement:

> *From Harmony, from Heav'nly Harmony*
> *This universal Frame began.*

The repetition of the word *harmony*, which is accompanied the second time by the emphatic, glorifying adjective *heav'nly*, gives more than the effect of emphasis: *heav'nly*, coming as it does before the repetition of *harmony*, provides a note of both qualification and expansion. Not any old harmony—*heav'nly* harmony, the greatest, most universal kind. Dryden is both telling us what kind of harmony this is—heavenly harmony—and informing us of the fact that harmony is something heavenly; the adjective both limits and describes, both qualifies and expands. And when followed by the grand generalizing line

> *This universal Frame began*

the initial statement is rounded off to achieve an opening of robust assertion. "Universal Frame" is deliberately abstract, suggesting the total pattern of the universe. It is important for Dryden's purpose that the order should be as it is here: first harmony, then the universal frame. Word order, in determining the distribution of emphasis, is of the highest importance in this kind of rhetorical poetry. The last five lines of the first stanza could, for example, be put in a more obviously logical order:

> *This universal Frame began*
> *From Harmony, which closed in Man.*

And how tame that would be!

After the grand statement of the opening two lines, the poet goes on to explain in more detail what he means. It was the harmonizing power of music, summoned by the Creator, that first brought the "jarring Atomes" together to achieve order out of chaos and so produce the created universe. The language here is very carefully chosen:

> *When Nature underneath a heap*
> *Of jarring Atomes lay,*
> *And cou'd not heave her Head,*

> *The tuneful Voice was heard from high:*
> *Arise, ye more than dead.*

*Heap* and *jarring* suggest disorder, and *heave* suggests an
activity slow and laborious. *Tuneful* contrasts with *jarring,* as
the *leap* (in line 9) contrasts with *heave:*

> *Then cold and hot and moist and dry*
> *In order to their Stations leap,*
> *And* MUSICK's *pow'r obey.*

*Cold, hot, moist,* and *dry* are of course the four elements of
medieval and Renaissance physics and psychology (deriving
originally from the Greek philosopher Epicurus, who
thought of the universe as composed of these four warring
elements). The spontaneity and agility of *leap* contrasts not
only with the slow, laboring *heave:* it both contrasts and
combines with *obey.* The elements "In order to their Stations
leap, / And MUSICK's pow'r obey," thus behaving freely and
spontaneously and at the same time behaving in obedience to
a higher power. They are both free and subordinated. To
leap in order and in obedience is to find true freedom in
service as well as to find true order in spontaneity. This
fundamental and profound paradox is suggested by the vocabulary, not elaborated, and then the stanza comes to a close
with a recapitulation of the opening assertion and the further
statement of the culminating position of Man in the creation:

> *Through all the Compass of the Notes it ran,*
> *The Diapason closing full in Man.*

The entire range of notes in the scale are sounded and Man—
the summit of the Creation, the top of the scale that runs
from inanimate Nature up to Man, the "Great Chain of
Being"—brings the music to a close. (One meaning of the
word *close,* and a common one in the seventeenth century,
was "the conclusion of a musical phrase, theme, or movement"—O.E.D.) We move from Nature in line 3 to Man at
the conclusion of the stanza. The concluding two lines are
both full iambic pentameters, the only two in this stanza,
forming a pentameter couplet that gives gravity, poise and
completion to the stanza as a whole. The underlying idea of
this opening stanza is the Platonic and Pythagorean one of
the harmony of the spheres and the relation between music
and order.

The first stanza having concluded triumphantly with
"Man," the second takes up the passions of which man is

capable. There are only two rhymes in these nine lines, and this helps to give the effect of order being imposed on disorder, as music controls the passions. Again the variation in line-length follows the curve of the meaning and the emotion. The reference to the biblical Jubal ("he was the father of all such as handle the harp and pipe"—*Genesis* 4:21) provides the archetypal touch. Jubal was the first musician, according to the Bible, and Dryden imagines him with his harp made from a tortoise shell ("corded Shell") performing a primeval ceremony of public worship through the elemental force of primitive music. The line

> *When* Jubal *struck the corded Shell*

deftly combines the elemental with the stylized, while the succeeding line

> *His listening Brethren stood around*

suggests harmony transferred from a pattern of sound into brotherly love.

The third stanza provides a sudden and complete shift in rhythm, an obvious—perhaps even too obviously rhetorical—attempt to imitate in the sound and rhythm of words the martial notes of trumpet and drum and the thundering of marching feet. The metrical scheme changes four times in this short stanza: the first four lines have one pattern, basically dactyllic; then comes the thumping beat of the fourth and fifth lines; the sixth line has a rhythm all its own; and the seventh · begins with two isolated strong beats ("Charge, Charge") before returning to the dactyllic beat heard earlier. The passion of unrequited love is the theme of the fourth stanza, rendered in an appropriate cadence and an appropriate diction. The stylization of language here ("the soft complaining FLUTE") almost suggests that this kind of lovers' melancholy is itself, if not a literary affectation, at least a highly conventional mood. One might almost call the language of these four lines extravagantly literary. "Dying Notes," "hopeless Lovers," "warbling LUTE," all suggest that the poet is deliberately imitating art rather than life, or perhaps rather that he is (with just a hint of irony?) indicating that in our moods of love, life imitates art rather than vice versa.

The "sharp VIOLINS" of the fifth stanza (and the tone of the newly introduced violin was "sharp" as compared with the duller tone of the older viol) introduce the more violent love emotions of jealousy, rage and despair, and here again the rhythmic pattern is appropriate and the language suitably strong, heightened by alliteration (*fury, frantick; pains, passion*), while the three "feminine" rhymes bunched up together in the middle of the stanza increase the effect of fierce feeling. Only in the last line of this stanza, with the expression "the fair, disdainful Dame," do we perhaps get a suggestion that the lady, at least, is playing a conventional part in this affair. The terms "fair" and "disdainful," especially when used together, do seem to suggest deliberate conventionality of language.

Any thought of playing a conventional part is immediately banished with the contrasting exclamation "But O!" with which the sixth stanza opens. The organ, instrument of divine worship, is presented in language of primal simplicity ("holy Love," "heav'nly Ways"), including a high proportion of one-syllable words (twenty-four out of thirty in the stanza, with all the words in both the first and the last lines monosyllables except for the very last word, *above*).

Human passion and the effect on it of music having been illustrated with reference to worship, martial courage, unhappy love, jealous rage, and religious feeling (religion thus opens and closes the sequence), Dryden in stanza seven now turns to classical mythology to provide an inclusive summing up and then to the Christian example of Saint Cecilia to show the superiority of Christian musical power over pagan. Orpheus was the great classical examplar of control through music: he could control both Man and Nature:

> Orpheus *cou'd lead the savage race,*
> *And Trees unrooted left their Place,*
> *Sequacious of the Lyre.*

Both the "savage race" and "trees" are part of undisciplined nature, yet in following Orpheus' lyre they could be both tamed and formed into an order, a pattern. Nowhere is Dryden's skill in achieving a whole area of suggested meaning merely by choice of diction more evident than in that line

> *Sequacious of the Lyre.*

This deliberately stylized expression (*sequacious of* for *following*) suggests the formality imposed on the "savage race" and the "trees unrooted" by the power of music. We think of the stylization of movement found in the dance, the ballet. But Cecilia does more than Orpheus; in a fine conceit,

Dryden tells that her playing on the organ led an angel to mistake earth for heaven.

The concluding "Grand Chorus" moves into a steadier iambic beat than we have yet heard in the poem, suggesting a series of major chords sounding with high confidence in a grand culminating statement. The steady movement of the final five lines is remarkably impressive, and the paradox of music, which originally made possible the Creation, finally *un*tuning the sky is bold and effective. The fact that the last three lines have the same rhyme produces a striking effect of cumulation as the poem comes to its rousing conclusion:

> *The* TRUMPET *shall be heard on high,*
> *The dead shall live, the living die,*
> *And* MUSICK *shall untune the Sky.*

JOHN WILMOT, EARL OF ROCHESTER

*Culver Pictures, Inc.*

# JOHN WILMOT,
# EARL OF ROCHESTER
## [1647–1680]

## A Satire Against Mankind

Were I (who to my cost already am
One of those strange prodigious Creatures *Man*.)
A Spirit free, to choose for my own share,
What Case of Flesh, and Blood, I pleas'd to weare,
I'd be a *Dog*, a *Monkey*, or a *Bear*.                    5
Or any thing but that vain *Animal*,
Who is so proud of being rational.
The senses are too gross, and he'll contrive
A Sixth, to contradict the other Five;
And before certain instinct, will preferr             10
*Reason*, which Fifty times for one does err.
*Reason*, an *Ignis fatuus*, in the *Mind*,
Which leaving light of Nature, sense behind;
Pathless and dang'rous wandring ways it takes,
Through errors, Fenny-*Boggs*, and Thorny *Brakes;*      15
Whilst the misguided follower, climbs with pain,
*Mountains* of Whimseys, heap'd in his own *Brain:*
Stumbling from thought to thought, falls head-long down,
Into doubts boundless Sea, where like to drown,
Books bear him up awhile, and makes him try,             20
To swim with Bladders of *Philosophy;*
In hopes still t'oretake the'escaping light,
The *Vapour* dances in his dazl[ed] sight,
Till spent, it leaves him to eternal Night.
Then Old Age, and experience, hand in hand,             25
Lead him to death, and make him understand,
After a search so painful, and so long,
That all his Life he has been in the wrong;
Hudled in dirt, the reas'ning *Engine* lyes,
Who was so proud, so witty, and so wise.                30
*Pride* drew him in, as *Cheats*, their *Bubbles*, catch,
And makes him venture, to be made a *Wre[t]ch*.
His wisdom did his happiness destroy,

Aiming to know [t]hat *World* he shou'd enjoy;
And *Wit*, was his vain frivolous pretence,                    35
Of pleasing others, at his own expence.
For *Witts* are treated just like common *Whores*,
First they're enjoy'd, and then kickt out of *Doores:*
The pleasure past, a threatning doubt remains,
That frights th'enjoyer, with succeeding pains:               40
*Women* and *Men* of *Wit*, are dang'rous Tools,
And ever fatal to admiring *Fools*.
Pleasure allures, and when the *Fopps* escape,
'Tis not that they're belov'd, but fortunate,
And therefore what they fear, at least they hate.            45
    But now methinks some formal Band, and Beard,
Takes me to task, come on Sir I'm prepar'd.
    *Then by your favour, any thing that's writ*
*Against this gibeing jingling knack call'd* Wit,
*Likes me abundantly, but you take care,*                     50
*Upon this point, not to be too severe.*
*Perhaps my* Muse, *were fitter for this part,*
*For I profess, I can be very smart*
*On* Wit, *which I abhor with all my heart:*
*I long to lash it in some sharp Essay,*                      55
*But your grand indiscretion bids me stay,*
*And turns my Tide of Ink another way.*
*What rage ferments in your degen'rate mind,*
*To make you rail at Reason, and Mankind?*
*Blest glorious* Man! *to whom alone kind* Heav'n,            60
*An everlasting* Soul *has freely giv'n;*
*Whom his great* Maker *took such care to make,*
*That from himself he did the* Image *take;*
*And this fair frame, in shining* Reason *drest,*
*To dignifie his* Nature, *above* Beast.                      65
Reason, *by whose aspiring influence,*
*We take a flight beyond material sense,*
*Dive into* Mysteries, *then soaring pierce,*
*The flaming limits of the* Universe.
*Search* Heav'n *and* Hell, *find out what's acted there,*    70
*And give the* World *true grounds of hope and fear.*
    Hold mighty Man, I cry, all this we know,
From the Pathetique Pen of *Ingello;*
From *P[atrick's] Pilgrim,* S[ibbs'] [soliloquies],
And 'tis this very reason I despise.                          75
This supernatural gift, that makes a *Myte,*
Think he is the Image of the Infinite:
Comparing his short life, void of all rest,

To the *Eternal*, and the ever blest.
This busie, puzling, stirrer up of doubt, 80
That frames deep *Mysteries*, then finds 'em out;
Filling with Frantick Crowds of thinking *Fools*,
Those Reverend *Bedlams*, *Colledges*, and *Schools*
Borne on whose Wings, each heavy *Sot* can pierce,
The limits of the boundless Universe. 85
So charming Oyntments, make an Old *Witch* flie,
And bear a Crippled Carcass through the Skie.
'Tis this exalted Pow'r, whose bus'ness lies,
In *Nonsense*, and impossibilities.
This made a Whimsical *Philosopher*, 90
Before the spacious *World*, his *Tub* prefer,
And we have modern *Cloysterd Coxcombs*, who
Retire to think, cause they have naught to do.
But thoughts, are giv'n for Actions government,
Where Action ceases, thoughts impertinent: 95
Our *Sphere* of Action, is lifes happiness,
And he who thinks Beyond, thinks like an *Ass*.
Thus, whilst 'gainst false reas'ning I inveigh,
I own right *Reason*, which I wou'd obey:
That *Reason* that distinguishes by sense, 100
And gives us *Rules*, of good, and ill from thence:
That bounds desires, with a reforming Will,
To keep 'em more in vigour, not to kill.
Your *Reason* hinders, mine helps t'enjoy,
Renewing Appetites, yours wou'd destroy. 105
My Reason is my *Friend*, yours is a *Cheat*,
Hunger call's out, my Reason bids me eat;
Perversely yours, your Appetite does mock,
This asks for Food, that answers what's a Clock?
This plain distinction Sir your doubt secures, 110
'Tis not true Reason I despise but yours.
Thus I think Reason righted, but for *Man*,
I'le nere recant defend him if you can.
For all his Pride, and his Philosophy,
'Tis evident, *Beasts* are in their degree, 115
As wise at least, and better far than he.
Those *Creatures*, are the wisest who attain,
By surest means, the ends at which they aim.
If therefore *Jowler*, finds, and Kills his *Hares*,
Better than *M[eres]*, supplyes Committee Chairs; 120
Though one's a *States-man*, th'other but a *Hound*,
*Jowler*, in Justice, wou'd be wiser found.
You see how far *Mans* wisedom here extends,

Look next, if humane Nature makes amends;
Whose Principles, most gen'rous are, and just,                    125
And to whose *Moralls*, you wou'd sooner trust.
Be Judge your self, I'le bring it to the test,
Which is the basest *Creature Man*, or *Beast?*
*Birds*, feed on *Birds, Beasts*, on each other prey,
But Savage *Man* alone, does *Man*, betray:                       130
Prest by necessity, they Kill for Food,
*Man*, undoes *Man*, to do himself no good.
With Teeth, and Claws by Nature arm'd they hunt,
Natures allowances, to supply their want.
But *Man*, with smiles, embraces, Friendships, praise,            135
Unhumanely his Fellows life betrays;
With voluntary pains, works his distress,
Not through necessity, but wantonness.
For hunger, or for Love, they fight, or tear,
Whilst wretched *Man*, is still in Arms for fear;                 140
For fear he armes, and is of Armes afraid,
By fear, to fear, successively betray'd
Base fear, the source whence his best passion[s] came,
His boasted Honor, and his dear bought Fame.
That lust of Pow'r, to which he's such a *Slave*,                 145
And for the which alone he dares be brave:
To which his various Projects are design'd,
Which makes him gen'rous, affable, and kind.
For which he takes such pains to be thought wise,
And screws his actions, in a forc'd disguise:                     150
Leading a tedious life in Misery,
Under laborious, mean *Hypocrisie*.
Look to the bottom, of his vast design,
Wherein *Mans* Wisdom, Pow'r, and Glory joyn;
The good he acts, the ill he does endure,                         155
'Tis all for fear, to make himself secure.
Meerly for safety, after Fame we thirst,
For all Men, wou'd be *Cowards* if they durst.
And honesty's against all common sense,
*Men* must be *Knaves*, 'tis in their own defence.                160
*Mankind's* dishonest, if you think it fair,
Amongst known *Cheats*, to play upon the square,
You'le be undone . . .
Nor can weak truth, your reputation save,
The *Knaves*, will all agree to call you *Knave*.                 165
Wrong'd shall he live, insulted o're, opprest,
Who dares be less a *Villain*, than the rest.
Thus Sir you see what humane Nature craves,

Most Men are *Cowards*, all Men shou'd be *Knaves:*
The diff'rence lyes (as far as I can see)                    170
Not in the thing it self, but the degree;
And all the subject matter of debate,
Is only who's a *Knave*, of the first *Rate?*
   All this with indignation have I hurl'd,
At the pretending part of the proud World,                   175
Who swolne with selfish vanity, devise,
False freedomes, holy Cheats, and formal Lyes
Over their fellow *Slaves* to tyrannize.
   But if in *Court*, so just a Man there be,
(In *Court*, a just Man, yet unknown to me.)                 180
Who does his needful flattery direct,
Not to oppress, and ruine, but protect;
Since flattery, which way so ever laid,
Is still a Tax on that unhappy Trade.
If so upright a *States-Man*, you can find,                   185
Whose passions bend to his unbyass'd Mind;
Who does his Arts, and *Policies* apply,
To raise his *Country*, not his *Family;*
Nor while his Pride, own'd Avarice withstands,
Receives Aureal Bribes, from *Friends* corrupted hands.      190
   Is there a *Church-Man* who on *God* relyes?
Whose Life, his Faith, and Doctrine Justifies?
Not one blown up, with vain Prelatique Pride,
Who for reproof of Sins, does *Man* deride:
Whose envious heart with his obstrep'rous sawcy Elo-
   quence,                                            195
Dares chide at *Kings*, and raile at Men of sense.
Who from his Pulpit, vents more peevish Lyes,
More bitter railings, scandals, Calumnies,
Than at a Gossipping, are thrown about,
When the good *Wives*, get drunk, and then fall out.         200
None of that sensual *Tribe*, whose Tallents lye,
In Avarice, *Pride*, *Sloth*, and *Gluttony*.
Who hunt good Livings, but abhor good Lives,
Whose Lust exalted, to that height arrives
They act *Adultery* with their own *Wives*.                  205
And e're a score of Years compleated be,
Can from the lofty *Pulpit* proudly see,
Half a large *Parish*, their own *Progeny*.
   Nor doating B—— who wou'd be ador'd,
For domineering at the *Councel Board;*                      210
A greater *Fop*, in business at Fourscore,
Fonder of serious *Toyes*, affected more,

Than the gay glitt'ring *Fool*, at Twenty proves,
With all his noise, his tawdrey Cloths, and Loves.
    But a meek humble Man, of modest sense,        215
Who Preaching peace, does practice continence;
Whose pious life's a proof he does believe,
Misterious truths, which no *Man* can conceive.
If upon *Earth* there dwell such *God-like Men*,
I'le here recant my *Paradox* to them.       220
Adore those *Shrines* of *Virtue*, *Homage* pay,
And with the *Rabble World*, their *Laws* obey.
If such there are, yet grant me this at least,
*Man* differs more from *Man*, than *Man* from *Beast*.

*Robert M. Bender*

---

WILMOT
A SATIRE AGAINST MANKIND

"A Satire Against Mankind" is unmatched in English literature for the unrelenting savagery of its attack. Even at the start we are struck by the corrosive grimness of Rochester's satire. Neither Dryden nor Pope, not even Swift, have written anything quite so filled with despair as Rochester's vision, at the beginning of the poem, of aged, dying man:

> *Then Old Age, and experience, hand in hand,*
> *Lead him to death, and make him understand,*
> *After a search so painful, and so long,*
> *That all his Life he has been in the wrong;*
> *Hudled in dirt, the reas'ning Engine lyes,*
> *Who was so proud, so witty, and so wise.*

Taken merely as direct statement this is startling, but it is the very refinement of the poetry, in contrast to the directness of the statement, that makes the attack so savage. Through careful alternation Rochester couples just those qualities that make man's life seem so despicable. Old age, a natural cause, and experience, accumulated so slowly, lead most certainly to death, so uncertainly to understanding. And, of course, the understanding is only the realization that everything has been wrong. The search is not only painful, it is long. Thomas Hobbes, Rochester's contemporary, in his analysis of the human condition, writes of the life of man being "nasty and brutish, but short." Rochester would even deny this redeeming brevity. The rhyme of long and wrong further emphasizes the futility of man's struggle and the weakness of his understanding. And finally, the image of a human body, really devoid of anything human, merely an "Engine," "hudled in dirt," contrasted with man's foremost qualities, his pride, his wit, and his wisdom, placed in just the right order, strikes a note of truth so penetrating that, having hardly begun, we are immediately caught up in Rochester's satire.

Rochester himself never knew old age; he merely observed it in others. Of the conditions of human existence he had more certain knowledge. In his short life he made himself known as a poet of real genius—and as a libertine of untold notoriety. A favorite of King Charles II, Rochester was frequently banished for his excesses, and almost as frequently pardoned. Within his own lifetime he saw more scandalous acts attached to his name than any one man could have committed in twice the years he lived. He no doubt saw much at court to criticize, and his ample wit gave him a fine perspective of his material. Some of his love lyrics are superb in their frankness, but his real masterpiece is "A Satire Against Mankind."

The poem's greatness lies in Rochester's technique and in the way he goes about his attack upon mankind. Instead of lashing out directly at man's lesser qualities, the brutishness that makes him a kin to the rest of the inhabitants of the animal world, Rochester chooses to condemn man's most prized ability, the one thing that so separates him from the rest of God's creation, his reason. Ironically enough, Rochester praises the animals for the very qualities that should be present in man, and his final condemnation is of man's subversion of his animal nature, his refusal to follow his senses, "the light of nature," and his foolish dependence upon his own faulty reason.

From the very start Rochester aligns himself with the animals against man; he violently disavows his own species and owns he would rather be "a *Dog*, a *Monkey*, or a *Bear*," animals all familiar for their sometimes almost human ways. The first section of the poem moves swiftly and without interruption. Having condemned man for the folly of his reason, he shows that Pride is really a kind of charlatan that entices man to his own destruction. As for wit, it gets a man nowhere:

> *For* Witts *are treated just like common* Whores,
> *First they're enjoy'd, and then kickt out of* Doores.

Without ever making it his primary concern, Rochester is thus able to slyly condemn much of the sordidness of man's relations with man, and woman too.

Here Rochester breaks off his attack, or at least seems to. He introduces a member of "some formal Band"—no doubt a scholar, and a wit—whom he imagines might object to his attack upon mankind. Instead of talking sense, though, the bearded fellow shows himself to be the worst of wits (not only is the poor fellow's appeal to his muse fatuous, but his remarks are full of the most trite expressions of the day—"gibeing jingling knack," "Tide of Ink") and leads us directly to Rochester's attack on reason. This is reason, or at least what passes as such, says Rochester, and so he has made his point even before he comes to it.

Just as Rochester's straw man has defended man's reason and his wit, Rochester himself tells us what true reason is:

> *That* Reason *that distinguishes by sense,*
> *And gives us* Rules, *of good, and ill from thence:*
> *That bounds desires, with a reforming Will,*
> *To keep 'em more in vigour, not to kill.*

The reason he would have us accept is not the one that stems from man's pride, but that stems from an observation of nature. Put in this way "reason" becomes acceptable, but Rochester has been playing slyly with us again. He is now ready to accept "right reason," but that still leaves man undefended.

Having disposed of reason, Rochester is now free for a more direct attack on man, and all his misguided actions so frequently justified by "reason." In contrast to the animals, man's actions are seen to stem not from need, but from hypocrisy. Animals "Kill for Food"; "*Man*, undoes *Man*, to do himself no good." Animals merely prey upon one another, men are only too capable of betrayal. And in the end, Rochester summons up judgments against which there can be no defence. Men act from fear, he tells us, and concludes that they would all "be *Cowards* if they durst." There is no reply to such criticism. At best we can answer, "Oh, yes, men do dare to be cowards," but then we have condemned man even more severely. Given the choice as to whether men are better cowards or knaves, we hardly know what to answer. And once more we are caught when Rochester concludes that the only genuine controversy among men is as to who is the best knave.

Not content to attack mankind so generally, Rochester turns to our finest professions: law, politics, and religion. In an age as corrupt as his, he did not need to look far for examples. Oppression by the law, avarice in politics, lechery among the clergy are the familiar subjects of satire.

The finest stroke of all, however, is saved for last. Having so disposed of man, his reason, and his cherished institutions, Rochester allows that there well may be, somewhere, a "meek humble Man," a genuinely good man motivated by good will.

Such a man would no doubt be criticized by all of Rochester's opponents—the very notion is incredible. Yet Rochester allows that such a man may exist, but concludes that if he does, this

Man *differs more from* Man, *than* Man *from* Beast.

The end is hopelessness. Rochester is more scathing in his satire than we are apt to like or appreciate. And it may be commented that his judgment is not the final word, nor an acceptable view of man; but it is difficult to find a more determined and unrelenting attack, so filled with true wit, upon mankind.

## Verses on the Death of Dr. Swift, D.S.P.D.

*Occasioned by reading a maxim in Rochefoucault*
*"Dans l'adversité de nos meilleurs amis nous trouvons*
*quelquechose, qui ne nous deplaist pas."*

As Rochefoucault his maxims drew
From nature, I believe 'em true;
They argue no corrupted mind
In him; the fault is in mankind.

    This maxim more than all the rest         5
Is thought too base for human breast;
"In all distresses of our friends
We first consult our private ends,
While nature kindly bent to ease us,
Points out some circumstance to please us."    10

    If this perhaps your patience move
Let reason and experience prove.

    We all behold with envious eyes,
Our equal raised above our size;
Who would not at a crowded show,          15
Stand high himself, keep others low?
I love my friend as well as you,
But would not have him stop my view;
Then let him have the higher post;
I ask but for an inch at most.           20

    If in a battle you should find,
One, whom you love of all mankind,
Had some heroic action done,
A champion killed, or trophy won;
Rather than thus be over-topt,         25
Would you not wish his laurels cropt?

    Dear honest Ned is in the gout,
Lies rackt with pain, and you without:

How patiently you hear him groan!
How glad the case is not your own!     30

What poet would not grieve to see,
His brethren write as well as he?
But rather than they should excel,
He'd wish his rivals all in Hell.

Her end when emulation misses,     35
She turns to envy, stings and hisses:
The strongest friendship yields to pride,
Unless the odds be on our side.

Vain human kind! Fantastic race!
Thy various follies, who can trace?     40
Self-love, ambition, envy, pride,
Their empire in our hearts divide:
Give others riches, power, and station,
'Tis all on me an usurpation.
I have no title to aspire;     45
Yet, when you sink, I seem the higher.
In Pope, I cannot read a line,
But with a sigh, I wish it mine:
When he can in one couplet fix
More sense than I can do in six:     50
It gives me such a jealous fit,
I cry, pox take him, and his wit.

Why must I be outdone by Gay,
In my own hum'rous biting way?

Arbuthnot is no more my friend,     55
Who dares to irony pretend;
Which I was born to introduce,
Refin'd it first, and shew'd its use.

St. John, as well as Pultney knows,
That I had some repute for prose;     60
And till they drove me out of date,
Could maul a Minister of State:
If they have mortified my pride,
And made me throw my pen aside;
If with such talents Heav'n hath blest 'em     65
Have I not reason to detest 'em?

To all my foes, dear Fortune, send
Thy gifts, but never to my friend:
I tamely can endure the first,
But, this with envy makes me burst.     70

JONATHAN SWIFT

*Painting by Jervas*
*National Portrait Gallery*
*The Bettmann Archive*

Thus much may serve by way of proem,
Proceed we therefore to our poem.

The time is not remote, when I
Must by the course of nature die:
When I foresee my special friends,                    75
Will try to find their private ends:
Tho' it is hardly understood,
Which way my death can do them good:
Yet, thus methinks, I hear 'em speak:
See, how the Dean begins to break:                    80
Poor gentleman, he droops apace,
You plainly find it in his face:
That old vertigo in his head,
Will never leave him, till he's dead:
Besides, his memory decays,                           85
He recollects not what he says;
He cannot call his friends to mind;
Forgets the place where last he din'd:
Plies you with stories o'er and o'er,
He told them fifty times before.                      90
How does he fancy we can sit,
To hear his out-of-fashion'd wit?
But he takes up with younger folks,
Who for his wine will bear his jokes:
Faith, he must make his stories shorter,              95
Or change his comrades once a quarter:
In half the time, he talks them round;
There must another set be found.

For poetry, he's past his prime,
He takes an hour to find a rhyme:                     100
His fire is out, his wit decay'd,
His fancy sunk, his muse a jade.
I'd have him throw away his pen;
But there's no talking to some men.

And, then their tenderness appears,                   105
By adding largely to my years:
"He's older than he would be reckon'd,
And well remembers Charles the Second.

"He hardly drinks a pint of wine;
And that, I doubt, is no good sign.                   110
His stomach too begins to fail:
Last year we thought him strong and hale;

But now, he's quite another thing;
I wish he may hold out till Spring."

Then hug themselves, and reason thus;      115
"It is not yet so bad with us."

In such a case they talk in tropes,
And, by their fears express their hopes:
Some great misfortune to portend,
No enemy can match a friend;      120
With all the kindness they profess,
The merit of a lucky guess,
(When daily howd'y's come of course,
And servants answer; *Worse and worse*)
Would please 'em better than to tell,      125
That, God be prais'd, the Dean is well.
Then he who prophecy'd the best,
Approves his foresight to the rest:
"You know, I always fear'd the worst,
And often told you so at first:"      130
He'd rather choose that I should die,
Than his prediction prove a lie.
Not one foretells I shall recover;
But, all agree, to give me over.

Yet should some neighbour feel a pain,      135
Just in the parts, where I complain;
How many a message would he send?
What hearty prayers that I should mend?
Enquire what regimen I kept;
What gave me ease, and how I slept?      140
And more lament, when I was dead,
Than all the sniv'llers round my bed.

My good companions, never fear,
For though you may mistake a year;
Though your prognostics run too fast,      145
They must be verified at last.

Behold the fatal day arrive!
"How is the Dean? He's just alive.
Now the departing prayer is read:
He hardly breathes. The Dean is dead."      150
Before the passing-bell begun,
The news thro' half the town has run.
"O, may we all for death prepare!
What has he left? And who's his heir?

I know no more than what the news is,                    155
'Tis all bequeath'd to public uses.
To public use! A perfect whim!
What had the public done for him!
Mere envy, avarice, and pride!
He gave it all:—But first he died.                       160
And had the Dean, in all the nation,
No worthy friend, no poor relation?
So ready to do strangers good,
Forgetting his own flesh and blood?"

Now Grub-Street wits are all employ'd;                   165
With elegies, the town is cloy'd:
Some paragraph in ev'ry paper,
To curse the Dean, or bless the Drapier.

The doctors tender of their fame,
Wisely on me lay all the blame:                          170
"We must confess his case was nice;
But he would never take advice:
Had he been rul'd, for aught appears,
He might have liv'd these twenty years:
For when we open'd him we found,                         175
That all his vital parts were sound."

From Dublin soon to London spread,
'Tis told at Court, the Dean is dead.

Kind Lady Suffolk in the spleen,
Runs laughing up to tell the Queen.                      180
The Queen, so gracious, mild, and good,
Cries, "Is he gone? 'Tis time he should.
He's dead you say; why let him rot;
I'm glad the medals were forgot.
I promised them, I own; but when?                        185
I only was the Princess then;
But now as Consort of the King,
You know 'tis quite a different thing."

Now, Chartres at Sir Robert's levee
Tells, with a sneer, the tidings heavy:                  190
"Why, is he dead without his shoes?"
(Cries Bob) "I'm sorry for the news;
Oh, were the wretch but living still,
And in his place my good friend Will;
Or, had a mitre on his head                              195
Provided Bolingbroke were dead."

Now Curl his shop from rubbish drains,
Three genuine tomes of Swift's Remains.
And then to make them pass the glibber,
Revised by Tibbalds, Moore, and Cibber.          200
He'll treat me as he does my betters.
Publish my will, my life, my letters.
Revive the libels born to die;
Which Pope must bear, as well as I.

Here shift the scene, to represent               205
How those I love, my death lament.
Poor Pope will grieve a month; and Gay
A week; and Arbuthnot a day.

St. John himself will scarce forbear,
To bite his pen, and drop a tear.                210
The rest will give a shrug and cry,
I'm sorry; but we all must die.
Indifference clad in wisdom's guise,
All fortitude of mind supplies:
For how can stony bowels melt,                   215
In those who never pity felt;
When *we* are lash'd, *they* kiss the rod;
Resigning to the will of God.

The fools, my juniors by a year,
Are tortur'd with suspense and fear.             220
Who wisely thought my age a screen,
When death approach'd, to stand between:
The screen remov'd, their hearts are trembling,
They mourn for me without dissembling.

My female friends, whose tender hearts           225
Have better learn'd to act their parts.
Receive the News in doleful dumps,
"The Dean is dead, (and what is trumps?)
Then Lord have mercy on his soul.
(Ladies I'll venture for the vole.)              230
Six Deans they say must bear the pall.
(I wish I knew what king to call.)
Madam, your husband will attend
The funeral of so good a friend.
No Madam, 'tis a shocking sight,                 235
And he's engag'd to-morrow night!
My Lady Club would take it ill,
If he should fail her at Quadrille.
He lov'd the Dean. (I lead a heart.)

But dearest friends, they say, must part.          240
His time was come, he ran his race;
We hope he's in a better place."

Why do we grieve that friends should die?
No loss more easy to supply.
One year is past; a different scene;                245
No further mention of the Dean;
Who now, alas, no more is mist,
Than if he never did exist.
Where's now this fav'rite of Apollo?
Departed; and his works must follow:               250
Must undergo the common fate;
His kind of wit is out of date.
Some country squire to Lintot goes,
Enquires for Swift in verse and prose:
Says Lintot, "I have heard the name:               255
He died a year ago." The same.
He searcheth all his shop in vain;
"Sir you may find them in Duck-lane:
I sent them with a load of books,
Last Monday to the pastry-cooks.                   260
To fancy they cou'd live a year!
I find you're but a stranger here.
The Dean was famous in his time;
And had a kind of knack at rhyme:
His way of writing now is past;                    265
The town hath got a better taste:
I keep no antiquated stuff;
But, spick and span I have enough.
Pray, do but give me leave to shew 'em;
Here's Colley Cibber's Birth-day Poem.             270
This Ode you never yet have seen,
By Stephen Duck, upon the Queen.
Then, here's a Letter finely penn'd
Against the Craftsman and his friend;
It clearly shows that all reflection               275
On ministers, is disaffection.
Next, here's Sir Robert's Vindication,
And Mr. Henly's last Oration:
The hawkers have not got 'em yet,
Your Honour please to buy a set?                   280

    "Here's Wolston's Tracts, the twelfth edition:
'Tis read by ev'ry politician:

The Country Members, when in town,
To all their Boroughs send them down:
You never met a thing so smart;                285
The courtiers have them all by heart;
Those Maids of Honour (who can read)
Are taught to use them for their Creed.
The Rev'rend author's good intention,
Hath been rewarded with a pension:             290
He doth an honour to his gown,
By bravely running priest-craft down:
He shews, as sure as God's in *Glo'ster*,
That Jesus was a grand imposter:
That all his miracles were cheats,             295
Perform'd as jugglers do their feats:
The Church had never such a writer:
A shame, he hath not got a mitre!"

Suppose me dead; and then suppose
A club assembled at the Rose;                  300
Where from discourse of this and that,
I grow the subject of their chat:
And, while they toss my name about,
With favour some, and some without;
One quite indiff'rent in the cause,            305
My character impartial draws:

"The Dean, if we believe report,
Was never ill received at Court:
As for his works in verse and prose,
I own my self no judge of those:               310
Nor, can I tell what critics thought 'em:
But, this I know, all people bought 'em;
As with a moral view design'd
To cure the vices of mankind:
His vein, ironically grave,                    315
Expos'd the fool, and lash'd the knave:
To steal a hint was never known,
But what he writ was all his own.

"He never thought an honour done him,
Because a Duke was proud to own him;           320
Would rather slip aside, and choose
To talk with wits in dirty shoes:
Despis'd the fools with stars and garters,
So often seen caressing Chartres:
He never courted men in station,               325

Nor persons had in admiration:
Of no man's greatness was afraid,
Because he sought for no man's aid.

"Though trusted long in great affairs,
He gave himself no haughty airs:       330
Without regarding private ends,
Spent all his credit for his friends:
And only chose the wise and good;
No flatt'rers; no allies in blood;
But succour'd virtue in distress,       335
And seldom fail'd of good success;
As numbers in their hearts must own,
Who, but for him, had been unknown.

"With Princes kept a due decorum,
But never stood in awe before 'em:       340
He follow'd David's lesson just,
In Princes never put thy trust.
And, would you make him truly sour;
Provoke him with a slave in power:
The Irish Senate, if you named,       345
With what impatience he declaimed!
Fair LIBERTY was all his cry;
For her he stood prepar'd to die;
For her he boldly stood alone;
For her he oft expos'd his own.       350
Two Kingdoms, just as faction led,
Had set a price upon his head;
But, not a traitor could be found,
To sell him for six hundred pound.

"Had he but spar'd his tongue and pen,       355
He might have rose like other men:
But, power was never in his thought;
And, wealth he valu'd not a groat:
Ingratitude he often found,
And pitied those who meant the wound:       360
But, kept the tenor of his mind,
To merit well of human kind:
Nor made a sacrifice of those
Who still were true, to please his foes.
He labour'd many a fruitless hour       365
To reconcile his friends in power;
Saw mischief by a faction brewing,
While they pursu'd each others' ruin.

But, finding vain was all his care,
He left the Court in mere despair.                      370

"And, oh! how short are human schemes!
Here ended all our golden dreams.
What St. John's skill in State affairs,
What Ormond's valour, Oxford's cares,
To save their sinking country lent,                     375
Was all destroy'd by one event.
Too soon that precious life was ended,
On which alone, our weal depended.
When up a dangerous faction starts,
With wrath and vengeance in their hearts:               380
By solemn League and Cov'nant bound,
To ruin, slaughter, and confound;
To turn religion to a fable,
And make the government a Babel:

"Pervert the law, disgrace the gown,                    385
Corrupt the senate, rob the crown;
To sacrifice old England's glory,
And make her infamous in story.
When such a tempest shook the land,
How could unguarded virtue stand?                       390

"With horror, grief, despair the Dean
Beheld the dire destructive scene:
His friends in exile, or the Tower,
Himself within the frown of Power;
Pursued by base envenom'd pens,                         395
Far to the land of slaves and fens;
A servilè race in folly nurs'd,
Who truckle most, when treated worst.

"By innocence and resolution,
He bore continual persecution;                          400
While numbers to preferment rose;
Whose merits were, to be his foes.
When, ev'n his own familiar friends
Intent upon their private ends;
Like renegadoes now he feels,                           405
Against him lifting up their heels.

"The Dean did by his pen defeat
An infamous destructive cheat.
Taught fools their int'rest how to know;
And gave them arms to ward the blow.                    410
Envy hath own'd it was his doing,

To save that helpless land from ruin,
While they who at the steerage stood,
And reapt the profit, sought his blood.

"To save them from their evil fate,          415
In him was held a crime of state.
A wicked monster on the bench,
Whose fury blood could never quench;
As vile and profligate a villain,
As modern Scroggs, or old Tressilian;        420
Who long all justice had discarded,
Nor fear'd he GOD, nor man regarded;
Vow'd on the Dean his rage to vent,
And make him of his zeal repent;
But Heav'n his innocence defends,            425
The grateful people stand his friends;
Not strains of law, nor Judges' frown,
Nor topics brought to please the Crown,
Nor witness hir'd, nor jury pick'd,
Prevail to bring him in convict.             430

"In exile with a steady heart,
He spent his Life's declining part;
Where, folly, pride, and faction sway,
Remote from St. John, Pope, and Gay.

"His friendship there to few confin'd,       435
Were always of the middling kind:
No fools of rank, a mungril breed,
Who fain would pass for lords indeed:
Where titles give no right or power,
And peerage is a wither'd flower,            440
He would have held it a disgrace,
If such a wretch had known his face.
On rural squires, that kingdom's bane,
He vented oft his wrath in vain:
Biennial squires, to market brought;         445
Who sell their souls and votes for naught;
The nation stript go joyful back,
To rob the Church, their tenants rack,
Go snacks with thieves and rapparees,
And, keep the peace, to pick up fees:        450
In every job to have a share,
A jail or barrack to repair;
And turn the tax for public roads
Commodious to their own abodes.

"Perhaps I may allow, the Dean     455
Had too much satire in his vein:
And seem'd determin'd not to starve it,
Because no age could more deserve it.
Yet, malice never was his aim;
He lash'd the vice but spar'd the name.     460
No individual could resent,
Where thousands equally were meant.
His satire points at no defect,
But what all mortals may correct;
For he abhorr'd that senseless tribe,     465
Who call it humour when they jibe:
He spar'd a hump or crooked nose,
Whose owners set not up for beaux.
True genuine dulness moved his pity,
Unless it offer'd to be witty.     470
Those, who their ignorance confess'd,
He ne'er offended with a jest;
But laugh'd to hear an idiot quote,
A verse from Horace, learn'd by rote.

"He knew an hundred pleasant stories,     475
With all the turns of Whigs and Tories:
Was cheerful to his dying day,
And friends would let him have his way.

"He gave the little wealth he had,
To build a house for fools and mad:     480
And shew'd by one satyric touch,
No nation wanted it so much:
That Kingdom he hath left his debtor,
I wish it soon may have a better."

# Jacques Barzun

---

## SWIFT
### VERSES ON THE DEATH OF DR. SWIFT, D.S.P.D.

What happens to personality after death has always engaged the feelings of men and spurred their imagination, especially men in whom personality is intense. Dante made a supernatural epic out of this emotion, and Swift wrote three (actually four) satirical poems. The best of these, entitled "On the Death of Dr. Swift," has been shown to consist of two poems, one long and one short, composed during 1731 and 1732. These were joined by Pope into the famous one here under review, after its two elements had been separately published in 1733 and 1739.

The theme common to both is ostensibly the maxim by La Rochefoucauld that Swift quotes as epigraph. But one notices immediately that, in Swift's rendering, the object of the satire is not the impurity of our affections; it is rather the idea of our "private ends"—a phrase that recurs like a leitmotiv through the five hundred lines. "Private ends" are the opposite not merely of the public good, but of generosity, selflessness, decency, magnanimity—in a word, detachment from the petty wants and mean pleasures that cluster around the miserable self.

It is this contrast that we find exhibited with great verve in the first 280 lines of the poem. Here the root of human folly and evil is shown to be the itch to compare, envy, and surpass—the pecking order of barnyard fowl translated into the forms and ranks that society assigns or denies. In the course of establishing his own part in that struggle, Swift introduces subtle compliments to his literary friends Pope, Arbuthnot, and Gay, as well as to his political friends, Bolingbroke (St. John) and Pultney. Now this fusion of politics and art, characteristic of the times, is essential to an understanding of the poem. If we forget either, we are bound to think the form and substance incoherent (as some critics have done), and to wish that Swift did not range from satire to self-praise. The integrity of the poem lies in Swift's representation of himself as a man who was simultaneously patriot, moralist, and literary genius.

As patriot, that is, as a man who used his talents to defend liberty in two kingdoms, giving up honors and rewards—private ends—in order to speak out, and at times risking violence in order to serve as a symbol of resistance, Swift does not hesitate to set forth the justification of his political career. In so doing he falls under his own condemnation of self-centering pride; that is inevitable. And he even misstates the truth, for it is not true that he always attacked the fault and never the person: in this very poem he names names—poets, publishers, prime ministers—and attacks living persons, this again being consonant with the manners of the times.

But as moralist, Swift earns pardon for this mixture of strength and weakness by the irony of his self-knowledge and self-condemnation. He declares his envy, knows that he is hated for misanthropy, sees how readily his works of genius appear malicious and "exaggerated." The question is, whose standard is just? All he finds is moral anarchy. How perfect for his purpose is the bequest of his property to support a public madhouse, on the pretext that no nation ever was more in need of one! And how pluperfect the astonished rejoinder—"public use! . . . What had the public done for him?" The sudden solicitude of that public for some unknown member of the Dean's family who should inherit from him is a stroke of genius that fittingly brings about the first great climax of the poem in the words "He gave it all—but first he died."

What is hard for some readers to grasp in Swift (and this, not merely in the present poem but throughout his work) is that the violence, the apparent hatred of all men and of himself, expresses an outraged tenderness. To call this indignation at the vices of mankind, as Swift himself did in his epitaph, is to explain only half: in that same epitaph, the "savage indignation" *lacerates his heart*. And in our poem too, contemplating his own death and the pleasure tempered by mild regret that it will afford his acquaintance, he lacerates his heart by belittling the affection he craves, and also by seeing why men and women cannot act otherwise than they do. The old serve as a screen to protect the living from the thought of death, and it is ultimately the fear of death, the hatred of death, that moves the self in its ridiculous or despicable antics. Swift is undoubtedly wrong when he professes never to have lashed a fault that reason could not correct. On the contrary, what lashed *him* into a clear-eyed frenzy over human actions was the sense of human impotence to make them noble and kind. One must remember the motto of his youth, "Sweetness and light," and remember that it was a gloomy young man, virtually an orphan, and reared in circumstances galling to his conscious genius, who coined that phrase to express the joint aspirations of his nature and his reason.

In the end, the only sense of power he could take comfort in was that of art. And here again he succumbs in this poem to the temptation of pride. He is proud of being an original author, a moral author, a selling author; just as he is proud of never having used his genius to support snobbery, oppression, or his own preferment.

The poem is thus in its very candor a demonstration of what it most wishes to assert—the error and inconsistency of mankind, even of the most conscious and gifted of mankind. The motions of Swift's spirit self-portrayed are as varied and incompatible as the points of view he adopts to make his case. It is the totality that, as in life, survives the analysis that would destroy; it is the orchestration of satire, humor, pride, aggression, pity, wit, and passion that makes a great poem out of two fragments, a maxim, and half a dozen visions—all etched in words as simple and neatly fixed as their designer was complex and sublimely restless.

# ALEXANDER POPE
## [1688-1744]

## The Rape of the Lock

*Nolueram, Belinda, tuos violare capillos,*
*Sed juvat hoc precibus me tribuisse tuis.*
MARTIAL

### CANTO I

What dire Offence from am'rous Causes springs,
What mighty Contests rise from trivial Things,
I sing—This Verse to *Caryll*, Muse! is due;
This, ev'n *Belinda* may vouchsafe to view:
Slight is the Subject, but not so the Praise,     5
If She inspire, and He approve my Lays.
  Say what strange Motive, Goddess! cou'd compel
A well-bred *Lord* t'assault a gentle *Belle?*
Oh say what stranger Cause, yet unexplor'd,
Cou'd make a gentle *Belle* reject a *Lord?*     10
In Tasks so bold, can Little Men engage,
And in soft Bosoms dwells such mighty Rage?
  *Sol* thro' white Curtains shot a tim'rous Ray,
And op'd those Eyes that must eclipse the Day;
Now Lapdogs give themselves the rowzing Shake,     15
And sleepless Lovers, just at Twelve, awake:
Thrice rung the Bell, the Slipper knock'd the Ground,
And the press'd Watch return'd a silver Sound.
*Belinda* still her downy Pillow prest,
Her Guardian *Sylph* prolong'd the balmy Rest.     20
'Twas he had summon'd to her silent Bed
The Morning-Dream that hover'd o'er her Head.
A Youth more glitt'ring than a *Birth-night Beau,*
(That ev'n in Slumber caus'd her Cheek to glow)
Seem'd to her Ear his winning Lips to lay,     25
And thus in Whispers said, or seem'd to say.
  Fairest of Mortals, thou distinguish'd Care
Of thousand bright Inhabitants of Air!
If e'er one Vision touch'd thy infant Thought,

Of all the Nurse and all the Priest have taught,    30
Of airy Elves by Moonlight Shadows seen,
The silver Token, and the circled Green,
Or Virgins visited by Angel-Pow'rs,
With Golden Crowns and Wreaths of heavn'ly Flow'rs,
Hear and believe! thy own Importance know,    35
Nor bound thy narrow Views to Things below.
Some secret Truths from Learned Pride conceal'd,
To Maids alone and Children are reveal'd:
What tho' no Credit doubting Wits may give?
The Fair and Innocent shall still believe.    40
Know then, unnumber'd Spirits round thee fly,
The light *Militia* of the lower Sky;
These, tho' unseen, are ever on the Wing,
Hang o'er the *Box*, and hover round the *Ring*.
Think what an Equipage thou hast in Air,    45
And view with scorn *Two Pages* and a *Chair*.
As now your own, our Beings were of old,
And once inclos'd in Woman's beauteous Mold;
Thence, by a soft Transition, we repair
From earthly Vehicles to these of Air.    50
Think not, when Woman's transient Breath is fled,
That all her Vanities at once are dead:
Succeeding Vanities she still regards,
And tho' she plays no more, o'erlooks the Cards.
Her Joy in gilded Chariots, when alive,    55
And Love of *Ombre*, after Death survive.
For when the Fair in all their Pride expire,
To their first Elements their Souls retire:
The Sprights of fiery Termagants in Flame
Mount up, and take a *Salamander*'s Name.    60
Soft yielding Minds to Water glide away,
And sip with *Nymphs*, their Elemental Tea.
The graver Prude sinks downward to a *Gnome*,
In search of Mischief still on Earth to roam.
The light Coquettes in *Sylphs* aloft repair,    65
And sport and flutter in the Fields of Air.
   Know farther yet; Whoever fair and chaste
Rejects Mankind, is by some *Sylph* embrac'd:
For Spirits, freed from mortal Laws, with ease
Assume what Sexes and what Shapes they please.    70
What guards the Purity of melting Maids,
In Courtly Balls, and Midnight Masquerades,
Safe from the treach'rous Friend, the daring Spark,

ALEXANDER POPE

*The Bettmann Archive*

The Glance by Day, the Whisper in the Dark;
When kind Occasion prompts their warm Desires,                    75
When Musick soften, and when Dancing fires?
'Tis but their *Sylph*, the wise Celestials know,
Tho '*Honour* is the Word with Men below.

    Some Nymphs there are, too conscious of their Face,
For Life predestin'd to the *Gnomes*' Embrace.                    80
These swell their Prospects and exalt their Pride,
When Offers are disdain'd, and Love deny'd.
Then gay Ideas crowd the vacant Brain;
While Peers and Dukes, and all their sweeping Train,
And Garters, Stars and Coronets appear,                          85
And in soft Sounds, *Your Grace* salutes their Ear.
'Tis these that early taint the Female Soul,
Instruct the Eyes of young *Coquettes* to roll,
Teach Infant-Cheeks a bidden Blush to know,
And little Hearts to flutter at a *Beau*.                        90

    Oft when the World imagine Women stray,
The *Sylphs* thro' mystick Mazes guide their Way,
Thro' all the giddy Circle they pursue,
And old Impertinence expel by new.
What tender Maid but must a Victim fall                          95
To one Man's Treat, but for another's Ball?
When *Florio* speaks, what Virgin could withstand,
If gentle *Damon* did not squeeze her Hand?
With varying Vanities, from ev'ry Part,
They shift the moving Toyshop of their Heart;                    100
Where Wigs with Wigs, with Sword-knots Sword-knots
    strive,
Beaus banish Beaus, and Coaches Coaches drive.
This erring Mortals Levity may call,
Oh blind to Truth! the *Sylphs* contrive it all,

    Of these am I, who thy Protection claim,                  105
A watchful Sprite, and *Ariel* is my Name.
Late, as I rang'd the Crystal Wilds of Air,
In the clear Mirror of thy ruling *Star*
I saw, alas! some dread Event impend,
Ere to the Main this Morning Sun descend.                        110
But Heav'n reveals not what, or how, or where:
Warn'd by thy *Sylph*, oh Pious Maid beware!
This to disclose is all thy Guardian can.
Beware of all, but most beware of man!

    He said; when *Shock*, who thought she slept too long,    115
Leapt up, and wak'd his Mistress with his Tongue.

'Twas then *Belinda!* if Report say true,
Thy Eyes first open'd on a *Billet-doux;*
*Wounds, Charms,* and *Ardors,* were no sooner read,
But all the Vision vanish'd from thy Head.          120
    And now, unveil'd, the *Toilet* stands display'd,
Each Silver Vase in mystic Order laid.
First, rob'd in White, the Nymph intent adores
With Head uncover'd, the *Cosmetic* Pow'rs.
A heav'nly Image in the Glass appears,          125
To that she bends, to that her Eyes she rears;
Th'inferior Priestess, at her Altar's side,
Trembling, begins the sacred Rites of Pride.
Unnumber'd Treasures ope at once, and here
The various Off'rings of the World appear;          130
From each she nicely culls with curious Toil,
And decks the Goddess with the glitt'ring Spoil.
This Casket *India's* glowing Gems unlocks,
And all *Arabia* breathes from yonder Box.
The Tortoise here and Elephant unite,          135
Transform'd to *Combs,* the speckled and the white.
Here Files of Pins extend their shining Rows,
Puffs, Powders, Patches, Bibles, Billet-doux.
Now awful Beauty puts on all its Arms;
The Fair each moment rises in her Charms,          140
Repairs her Smiles, awakens ev'ry Grace,
And calls forth all the Wonders of her Face;
Sees by Degrees a purer Blush arise,
And keener Lightnings quicken in her Eyes.
The busy *Sylphs* surround their darling Care;          145
These set the Head, and those divide the Hair,
Some fold the Sleeve, whilst others plait the Gown;
And *Betty's* prais'd for Labours not her own.

CANTO II

Not with more Glories, in th' Etherial Plain,
The Sun first rises o'er the purpled Main,
Than issuing forth, the Rival of his Beams
Lanch'd on the Bosom of the Silver *Thames.*
Fair Nymphs, and well-drest Youths around her shone,          5
But ev'ry Eye was fix'd on her alone.
On her white Breast a sparkling *Cross* she wore,
Which *Jews* might kiss, and Infidels adore.
Her lively Looks a sprightly Mind disclose,
Quick as her Eyes, and as unfix'd as those:          10

Favours to none, to all she Smiles extends,
Oft she rejects, but never once offends.
Bright as the Sun, her Eyes the Gazers strike,
And, like the Sun, they shine on all alike.
Yet graceful Ease, and Sweetness void of Pride,          15
Might hide her Faults, if *Belles* had Faults to hide:
If to her share some Female Errors fall,
Look on her Face, and you'll forget 'em all.
　This Nymph, to the Destruction of Mankind,
Nourish'd two Locks, which graceful hung behind          20
In equal Curls, and well conspir'd to deck
With shining Ringlets the smooth Iv'ry Neck.
Love in these Labyrinths his Slaves detains,
And mighty Hearts are held in slender Chains.
With hairy Sprindges we the Birds betray,          25
Slight Lines of Hair surprize the Finny Prey,
Fair Tresses Man's Imperial Race insnare,
And Beauty draws us with a single Hair.
　Th' Adventrous *Baron* the bright Locks admir'd,
He saw, he wish'd, and to the Prize aspir'd:          30
Resolv'd to win, he meditates the way,
By Force to ravish, or by Fraud betray;
For when Success a Lover's Toil attends,
Few ask, if Fraud or Force attain'd his Ends.
　For this, ere *Phœbus* rose, he had implor'd          35
Propitious Heav'n, and ev'ry Pow'r ador'd,
But chiefly *Love*—to *Love* an Altar built,
Of twelve vast *French* Romances, neatly gilt.
There lay three Garters, half a Pair of Gloves;
And all the Trophies of his former Loves.          40
With tender *Billet-doux* he lights the Pyre,
And breathes three am'rous Sighs to raise the Fire.
Then prostrate falls, and begs with ardent Eyes
Soon to obtain, and long possess the Prize:
The Pow'rs gave Ear, and granted half his Pray'r,          45
The rest, the Winds dispers'd in empty Air.
　But now secure the painted Vessel glides,
The Sun-beams trembling on the floating Tydes,
While melting Musick steals upon the Sky,
And soften'd Sounds along the Waters die.          50
Smooth flow the Waves, the Zephyrs gently play,
*Belinda* smil'd, and all the World was gay.
All but the *Sylph*—With careful Thoughts opprest,
Th'impending Woe sate heavy on his Breast.

He summons straight his Denizens of Air;                      55
The lucid Squadrons round the Sails repair:
Soft o'er the Shrouds Aerial Whispers breathe,
That seem'd but *Zephyrs* to the Train beneath.
Some to the Sun their Insect-Wings unfold,
Waft on the Breeze, or sink in Clouds of Gold.                60
Transparent Forms, too fine for mortal Sight,
Their fluid Bodies half dissolv'd in Light.
Loose to the Wind their airy Garments flew,
Thin glitt'ring Textures of the filmy Dew;
Dipt in the richest Tincture of the Skies,                    65
Where Light disports in ever-mingling Dies,
While ev'ry Beam now transient Colours flings,
Colours that change whene'er they wave their Wings.
Amid the Circle, on the gilded Mast,
Superior by the Head, was *Ariel* plac'd;                     70
His Purple Pinions opening to the Sun,
He rais'd his Azure Wand, and thus begun.
    Ye *Sylphs* and *Sylphids*, to your Chief give Ear,
*Fays, Fairies, Genii, Elves*, and *Dæmons* hear!
Ye know the Spheres and various Tasks assign'd,              75
By Laws Eternal, to th' Aerial Kind.
Some in the Fields of purest *Æther* play,
And bask and whiten in the Blaze of Day.
Some guide the Course of wandring Orbs on high,
Or roll the Planets thro' the boundless Sky.                 80
Some less refin'd, beneath the Moon's pale Light
Pursue the Stars that shoot athwart the Night,
Or suck the Mists in grosser Air below,
Or dip their Pinions in the painted Bow,
Or brew fierce Tempests on the wintry Main,                  85
Or o'er the Glebe distill the kindly Rain.
Others on Earth o'er human Race preside,
Watch all their Ways, and all their Actions guide:
Of these the Chief the Care of Nations own,
And guard with Arms Divine the *British Throne*.             90
    Our humbler Province is to tend the Fair,
Not a less pleasing, tho' less glorious Care.
To save the Powder from too rude a Gale,
Nor let th' imprison'd Essences exhale,
To draw fresh Colours from the vernal Flow'rs,              95
To steal from Rainbows ere they drop in Show'rs
A brighter Wash; to curl their waving Hairs,
Assist their Blushes, and inspire their Airs;

Nay oft, in Dreams, Invention we bestow,
To change a *Flounce*, or add a *Furbelo*.                           100
    This Day, black Omens threat the brightest Fair
That e'er deserv'd a watchful Spirit's Care;
Some dire Disaster, or by Force, or Slight,
But what, or where, the Fates have wrapt in Night.
Whether the Nymph shall break *Diana*'s Law,                         105
Or some frail *China* Jar receive a Flaw,
Or stain her Honour, or her new Brocade,
Forget her Pray'rs, or miss a Masquerade,
Or lose her Heart, or Necklace, at a Ball;
Or whether Heav'n has doom'd that *Shock* must fall.                 110
Haste then ye Spirits! to your Charge repair;
The flutt'ring Fan be *Zephyretta*'s Care;
The Drops to thee, *Brillante*, we consign;
And, *Momentilla*, let the Watch be thine;
Do thou, *Crispissa*, tend her fav'rite Lock;                        115
*Ariel* himself shall be the Guard of *Shock*.
    To Fifty chosen *Sylphs*, of special Note,
We trust th' important Charge, the *Petticoat*:
Oft have we known that sev'nfold Fence to fail,
Tho' stiff with Hoops, and arm'd with Ribs of Whale.                 120
Form a strong Line about the Silver Bound,
And guard the wide Circumference around.
    Whatever Spirit, careless of his Charge,
His Post neglects, or leaves the Fair at large,
Shall feel sharp Vengeance soon o'ertake his Sins,                   125
Be stopt in *Vials*, or transfixt with *Pins*;
Or plung'd in Lakes of bitter *Washes* lie,
Or wedg'd whole Ages in a *Bodkin*'s Eye:
*Gums* and *Pomatums* shall his Flight restrain,
While clog'd he beats his silken Wings in vain;                      130
Or Alom-*Stypticks* with contracting Power
Shrink his thin Essence like a rivell'd Flower.
Or as *Ixion* fix'd, the Wretch shall feel
The giddy Motion of the whirling Mill,
In Fumes of burning Chocolate shall glow,                            135
And tremble at the Sea that froaths below!
    He spoke; the Spirits from the Sails descend;
Some, Orb in Orb, around the Nymph extend,
Some thrid the mazy Ringlets of her Hair,
Some hang upon the Pendants of her Ear;                              140
With beating Hearts the dire Event they wait,
Anxious, and trembling for the Birth of Fate.

## CANTO III

Close by those Meads for ever crown'd with Flow'rs,
Where *Thames* with Pride surveys his rising Tow'rs,
There stands a Structure of Majestick Frame,
Which from the neighb'ring *Hampton* takes its Name.
Here *Britain*'s Statesmen oft the Fall foredoom      5
Of Foreign Tyrants, and of Nymphs at home;
Here Thou, Great *Anna!* whom three Realms obey,
Dost sometimes Counsel take—and sometimes *Tea*.
   Hither the Heroes and the Nymphs resort,
To taste awhile the Pleasures of a Court;      10
In various Talk th' instructive hours they past,
Who gave the *Ball*, or paid the *Visit* last:
One speaks the Glory of the *British Queen*,
And one describes a charming *Indian Screen;*
A third interprets Motions, Looks, and Eyes;      15
At ev'ry Word a Reputation dies.
*Snuff*, or the *Fan*, supply each Pause of Chat,
With singing, laughing, ogling, and all that.
   Mean while declining from the Noon of Day,
The Sun obliquely shoots his burning Ray;      20
The hungry Judges soon the Sentence sign,
And Wretches hang that Jury-men may Dine;
The Merchant from th' *Exchange* returns in Peace,
And the long Labours of the *Toilette* cease—
*Belinda* now, whom Thirst of Fame invites,      25
Burns to. encounter two adventrous Knights,
At *Ombre* singly to decide their Doom;
And swells her Breast with Conquests yet to come.
Strait the three Bands prepare in Arms to join,
Each Band the number of the Sacred Nine.      30
Soon as she spreads her Hand, th' Aerial Guard
Descend, and sit on each important Card:
First *Ariel* perch'd upon a *Matadore*,
Then each, according to the Rank they bore;
For *Sylphs*, yet mindful of their ancient Race,      35
Are, as when Women, wondrous fond of Place.
   Behold, four *Kings* in Majesty rever'd,
With hoary Whiskers and a forky Beard;
And four fair *Queens* whose hands sustain a Flow'r,
Th' expressive Emblem of their softer Pow'r;      40
Four *Knaves* in Garbs succinct, a trusty Band,
Caps on their heads, and Halberds in their hand;
And Particolour'd Troops, a shining Train,

Draw forth to Combat on the Velvet Plain.
The skilful Nymph reviews her Force with Care;     45
*Let Spades be Trumps!* she said, and Trumps they were.
Now move to War her Sable *Matadores*,
In Show like Leaders of the swarthy *Moors*.
*Spadillio* first, unconquerable Lord!
Led off two captive Trumps, and swept the Board.     50
As many more *Manillio* forc'd to yield,
And march'd a Victor from the verdant Field.
Him *Basto* follow'd, but his Fate more hard
Gain'd but one Trump and one *Plebeian* Card.
With his broad Sabre next, a Chief in Years,     55
The hoary Majesty of *Spades* appears;
Puts forth one manly Leg, to sight reveal'd;
The rest his many-colour'd Robe conceal'd.
The Rebel-*Knave*, who dares his Prince engage,
Proves the just Victim of his Royal Rage.     60
Ev'n mighty *Pam* that Kings and Queens o'erthrew,
And mow'd down Armies in the Fights of *Lu*,
Sad Chance of War! now, destitute of Aid,
Falls undistinguish'd by the Victor *Spade!*
Thus far both Armies to *Belinda* yield;     65
Now to the *Baron* Fate inclines the Field.
His warlike *Amazon* her Host invades,
Th' Imperial Consort of the Crown of *Spades*.
The *Club*'s black Tyrant first her Victim dy'd,
Spite of his haughty Mien, and barb'rous Pride:     70
What boots the Regal Circle on his Head,
His Giant Limbs in State unwieldy spread?
That long behind he trails his pompous Robe,
And of all Monarchs only grasps the Globe?
The *Baron* now his *Diamonds* pours apace;     75
Th' embroider'd *King* who shows but half his Face,
And his refulgent *Queen*, with Pow'rs combin'd,
Of broken Troops an easie Conquest find.
*Clubs, Diamonds, Hearts*, in wild Disorder seen,
With Throngs promiscuous strow the level Green.     80
Thus when dispers'd a routed Army runs,
Of *Asia*'s Troops, and *Africk*'s Sable Sons,
With like Confusion different Nations fly,
Of various Habit and of various Dye,
The pierc'd Battalions dis-united fall,     85
In Heaps on Heaps; one Fate o'erwhelms them all.
The *Knave of Diamonds* tries his wily Arts,

And wins (oh shameful Chance!) the *Queen of Hearts.*
At this, the Blood the Virgin's Cheek forsook,
A livid Paleness spreads o'er all her Look;          90
She sees, and trembles at th' approaching Ill,
Just in the Jaws of Ruin, and *Codille.*
And now, (as oft in some distemper'd State)
On one nice *Trick* depends the gen'ral Fate.
An *Ace* of Hearts steps forth: The *King* unseen          95
Lurk'd in her Hand, and mourn'd his captive *Queen.*
He springs to Vengeance with an eager pace,
And falls like Thunder on the prostrate *Ace.*
The Nymph exulting fills with Shouts the Sky,
The Walls, the Woods, and long Canals reply.          100
    Oh thoughtless Mortals! ever blind to Fate,
Too soon dejected, and too soon elate!
Sudden these Honours shall be snatch'd away,
And curs'd for ever this Victorious Day.
    For lo! the Board with Cups and Spoons is crown'd,          105
The Berries crackle, and the Mill turns round.
On shining Altars of *Japan* they raise
The silver Lamp; the fiery Spirits blaze.
From silver Spouts the grateful Liquors glide,
While *China*'s Earth receives the smoking Tyde.          110
At once they gratify their Scent and Taste,
And frequent Cups prolong the rich Repast.
Strait hover round the Fair her Airy Band;
Some, as she sip'd, the fuming Liquor fann'd,
Some o'er her Lap their careful Plumes display'd,          115
Trembling, and conscious of the rich Brocade.
*Coffee,* (which makes the Politician wise,
And see thro' all things with his half-shut Eyes)
Sent up in Vapours to the *Baron*'s Brain
New Stratagems, the radiant Lock to gain.          120
Ah cease rash Youth! desist ere 'tis too late,
Fear the just Gods, and think of *Scylla*'s Fate!
Chang'd to a Bird, and sent to flit in Air,
She dearly pays for *Nisus*' injur'd Hair!
    But when to Mischief Mortals bend their Will,          125
How soon they find fit Instruments of Ill!
Just then, *Clarissa* drew with tempting Grace
A two-edg'd Weapon from her shining Case;
So Ladies in Romance assist their Knight,
Present the Spear, and arm him for the Fight.          130
He takes the Gift with rev'rence, and extends
The little Engine on his Fingers' Ends,

This just behind *Belinda*'s Neck he spread,
As o'er the fragrant Steams she bends her Head:
Swift to the Lock a thousand Sprights repair, 135
A thousand Wings, by turns, blow back the Hair,
And thrice they twitch'd the Diamond in her Ear,
Thrice she look'd back, and thrice the Foe drew near.
Just in that instant, anxious *Ariel* sought
The close Recesses of the Virgin's Thought; 140
As on the Nosegay in her Breast reclin'd,
He watch'd th' Ideas rising in her Mind,
Sudden he view'd, in spite of all her Art,
An Earthly Lover lurking at her Heart.
Amaz'd, confus'd, he found his Pow'r expir'd, 145
Resign'd to Fate, and with a Sigh retir'd.
    The Peer now spreads the glitt'ring *Forfex* wide,
T'inclose the Lock; now joins it, to divide.
Ev'n then, before the fatal Engine clos'd,
A wretched *Sylph* too fondly interpos'd; 150
Fate urg'd the Sheers, and cut the *Sylph* in twain,
(But Airy Substance soon unites again)
The meeting Points the sacred Hair dissever
From the fair Head, for ever and for ever!
    Then flash'd the living Lightning from her Eyes, 155
And Screams of Horror rend th' affrighted Skies.
Not louder Shrieks to pitying Heav'n are cast,
When Husbands or when Lap-dogs breathe their last,
Or when rich *China* Vessels, fal'n from high,
In glittring Dust and painted Fragments lie! 160
    Let Wreaths of Triumph now my Temples twine,
(The Victor cry'd) the glorious Prize is mine!
While Fish in Streams, or Birds delight in Air,
Or in a Coach and Six the *British* Fair,
As long as *Atalantis* shall be read, 165
Or the small Pillow grace a Lady's Bed,
While *Visits* shall be paid on solemn Days,
When numerous Wax-lights in bright Order blaze,
While Nymphs take Treats, or Assignations give,
So long my Honour, Name, and Praise shall live! 170
    What Time wou'd spare, from Steel receives its date,
And Monuments, like Men, submit to Fate!
Steel cou'd the Labour of the Gods destroy,
And strike to Dust th' Imperial Tow'rs of *Troy;*
Steel cou'd the Works of mortal Pride confound, 175
And hew Triumphal Arches to the Ground.

What Wonder then, fair Nymph! thy Hairs shou'd feel
The conqu'ring Force of unresisted Steel?

CANTO IV

But anxious Cares the pensive Nymph opprest,
And secret Passions labour'd in her Breast.
Not youthful Kings in Battel seiz'd alive,
Not scornful Virgins who their Charms survive,
Not ardent Lovers robb'd of all their Bliss,     5
Not ancient Ladies when refus'd a Kiss,
Not Tyrants fierce that unrepenting die,
Not *Cynthia* when her *Manteau's* pinn'd awry,
E'er felt such Rage, Resentment and Despair,
As Thou, sad Virgin! for thy ravish'd Hair.     10
    For, that sad moment, when the *Sylphs* withdrew,
And *Ariel* weeping from *Belinda* flew,
*Umbriel*, a dusky melancholy Spright,
As ever sully'd the fair face of Light,
Down to the Central Earth, his proper Scene,     15
Repair'd to search the gloomy Cave of *Spleen*.
    Swift on his sooty Pinions flitts the *Gnome*,
And in a Vapour reach'd the dismal Dome.
No cheerful Breeze this sullen Region knows,
The dreaded *East* is all the Wind that blows.     20
Here, in a Grotto, sheltred close from Air,
And screen'd in Shades from Day's detested Glare,
She sighs for ever on her pensive Bed,
*Pain* at her Side, and *Megrim* at her Head.
    Two Handmaids wait the Throne: Alike in Place,     25
But diff'ring far in Figure and in Face.
Here stood *Ill-nature* like an *ancient Maid*,
Her wrinkled Form in *Black* and *White* array'd;
With store of Pray'rs, for Mornings, Nights, and Noons,
Her Hand is fill'd; her Bosom with Lampoons.     30
    There *Affectation* with a sickly Mien
Shows in her Cheek the Roses of Eighteen,
Practis'd to Lisp, and hang the Head aside,
Faints into Airs, and languishes with Pride;
On the rich Quilt sinks with becoming Woe,     35
Wrapt in a Gown, for Sickness, and for Show.
The Fair-ones feel such Maladies as these,
When each new Night-Dress gives a new Disease.
    A constant *Vapour* o'er the Palace flies;
Strange Phantoms rising as the Mists arise;     40

Dreadful, as Hermit's Dreams in haunted Shades,
Or bright as Visions of expiring Maids.
Now glaring Fiends, and Snakes on rolling Spires,
Pale Spectres, gaping Tombs, and Purple Fires:
Now Lakes of liquid Gold, *Elysian* Scenes, 45
And Crystal Domes, and Angels in Machines.
    Unnumber'd Throngs on ev'ry side are seen
Of Bodies chang'd to various Forms by *Spleen*.
Here living *Teapots* stand, one Arm held out,
One bent; the Handle this, and that the Spout: 50
A Pipkin there like *Homer*'s *Tripod* walks;
Here sighs a Jar, and there a Goose-pye talks;
Men prove with Child, as pow'rful Fancy works,
And Maids turn'd Bottels, call aloud for Corks.
    Safe past the *Gnome* thro' this fantastick Band, 55
A Branch of healing *Spleenwort* in his hand.
Then thus addrest the Pow'r—Hail wayward Queen!
Who rule the Sex to Fifty from Fifteen,
Parent of Vapours and of Female Wit,
Who give th' *Hysteric* or *Poetic* Fit, 60
On various Tempers act by various ways,
Make some take Physick, others scribble Plays;
Who cause the Proud their Visits to delay,
And send the Godly in a Pett, to pray.
A Nymph there is, that all thy Pow'r disdains, 65
And thousands more in equal Mirth maintains.
But oh! if e'er thy *Gnome* could spoil a Grace,
Or raise a Pimple on a beauteous Face,
Like Citron-Waters Matrons' Cheeks inflame,
Or change Complexions at a losing Game; 70
If e'er with airy Horns I planted Heads,
Or rumpled Petticoats, or tumbled Beds,
Or caus'd Suspicion when no Soul was rude,
Or discompos'd the Head-dress of a Prude,
Or e'er to costive Lap-Dog gave Disease, 75
Which not the Tears of brightest Eyes could ease:
Hear me, and touch *Belinda* with Chagrin;
That single Act gives half the World the Spleen.
    The Goddess with a discontented Air
Seems to reject him, tho' she grants his Pray'r. 80
A wondrous Bag with both her Hands she binds,
Like that where once *Ulysses* held the Winds;
There she collects the Force of Female Lungs,
Sighs, Sobs, and Passions, and the War of Tongues.

A Vial next she fills with fainting Fears,⁢ 85
Soft Sorrows, melting Griefs, and flowing Tears.
The *Gnome* rejoicing bears her Gifts away,
Spreads his black Wings, and slowly mounts to Day.
Sunk in *Thalestris'* Arms the Nymph he found,
Her Eyes dejected and her Hair unbound. 90
Full o'er their Heads the swelling Bag he rent,
And all the Furies issued at the Vent.
*Belinda* burns with more than mortal Ire,
And fierce *Thalestris* fans the rising Fire.
O wretched Maid! she spread her Hands, and cry'd, 95
(While *Hampton*'s Ecchos, wretched Maid! reply'd)
Was it for this you took such constant Care
The *Bodkin, Comb*, and *Essence* to prepare;
For this your Locks in Paper-Durance bound,
For this with tort'ring Irons wreath'd around? 100
For this with Fillets strain'd your tender Head,
And bravely bore the double Loads of Lead?
Gods! shall the Ravisher display your Hair,
While the Fops envy, and the Ladies stare!
*Honour* forbid! at whose unrival'd Shrine 105
Ease, Pleasure, Virtue, All, our Sex resign.
Methinks already I your Tears survey,
Already hear the horrid things they say,
Already see you a degraded Toast,
And all your Honour in a whisper lost! 110
How shall I, then, your helpless Fame defend?
'Twill then be Infamy to seem your Friend!
And shall this Prize, th' inestimable Prize,
Expos'd thro' Crystal to the gazing Eyes,
And heighten'd by the Diamond's circling Rays, 115
On that Rapacious Hand for ever blaze?
Sooner shall Grass in *Hide*-Park *Circus* grow,
And Wits take Lodgings in the Sound of *Bow;*
Sooner let Earth, Air, Sea, to *Chaos* fall,
Men, Monkies, Lap-dogs, Parrots, perish all! 120
She said; then raging to *Sir Plume* repairs,
And bids her *Beau* demand the precious Hairs:
(*Sir Plume*, of *Amber Snuff-box* justly vain,
And the nice Conduct of a *clouded Cane*)
With earnest Eyes, and round unthinking Face, 125
He first the Snuff-box open'd, then the Case,
And thus broke out—"My Lord, why, what the Devil?
Z—ds! damn the Lock! 'fore Gad, you must be civil!
Plague on't! 'tis past a Jest—nay prithee, Pox!

Give her the Hair"—he spoke, and rapp'd his Box.                    130
It grieves me much (reply'd the Peer again)
Who speaks so well shou'd ever speak in vain.
But by this Lock, this sacred Lock I swear,
(Which never more shall join its parted Hair,
Which never more its Honours shall renew,                           135
Clipt from the lovely Head where late it grew)
That while my Nostrils draw the vital Air,
This Hand, which won it, shall for ever wear.
He spoke, and speaking, in proud Triumph spread
The long-contended Honours of her Head.                             140
   But *Umbriel*, hateful *Gnome!* forbears not so;
He breaks the Vial whence the Sorrows flow.
Then see! the *Nymph* in beauteous Grief appears,
Her Eyes half-languishing, half-drown'd in Tears;
On her heav'd Bosom hung her drooping Head,                         145
Which, with a Sigh, she rais'd; and thus she said.
   For ever curs'd be this detested Day,
Which snatch'd my best, my fav'rite Curl away!
Happy, ah ten times happy, had I been,
If *Hampton-Court* these Eyes had never seen!                       150
Yet am not I the first mistaken Maid,
By Love of *Courts* to num'rous Ills betray'd.
Oh had I rather un-admir'd remain'd
In some lone Isle, or distant *Northern* Land;
Where the gilt *Chariot* never marks the Way,                       155
Where none learn *Ombre*, none e'er taste *Bohea!*
There kept my Charms conceal'd from mortal Eye,
Like Roses that in Desarts bloom and die.
What mov'd my Mind with youthful Lords to rome?
O had I stay'd, and said my Pray'rs at home!                        160
'Twas this, the Morning *Omens* seem'd to tell;
Thrice from my trembling hand the *Patch-box* fell;
The tott'ring *China* shook without a Wind,
Nay, *Poll* sate mute, and *Shock* was most Unkind!
A *Sylph* too warn'd me of the Threats of Fate,                     165
In mystic Visions, now believ'd too late!
See the poor Remnants of these slighted Hairs!
My hands shall rend what ev'n thy Rapine spares:
These, in two sable Ringlets taught to break,
Once gave new Beauties to the snowie Neck.                          170
The Sister-Lock now sits uncouth, alone,
And in its Fellow's Fate foresees its own;
Uncurl'd it hangs, the fatal Sheers demands;
And tempts once more thy sacrilegious Hands.

Oh hadst thou, Cruel! been content to seize 175
Hairs less in sight, or any Hairs but these!

### CANTO V

She said: the pitying Audience melt in Tears,
But *Fate* and *Jove* had stopp'd the *Baron*'s Ears.
In vain *Thalestris* with Reproach assails,
For who can move when fair *Belinda* fails?
Not half so fixt the *Trojan* cou'd remain, 5
While *Anna* begg'd and *Dido* rag'd in vain.
Then grave *Clarissa* graceful wav'd her Fan;
Silence ensu'd, and thus the Nymph began.
 Say, why are Beauties prais'd and honour'd most,
The wise Man's Passion, and the vain Man's Toast? 10
Why deck'd with all that Land and Sea Afford,
Why Angels call'd, and Angel-like ador'd?
Why round our Coaches crowd the white-glov'd Beaus,
Why bows the Side-box from its inmost Rows?
How vain are all these Glories, all our Pains, 15
Unless good Sense preserve what Beauty gains:
That Men may say, when we the Front-box grace,
Behold the first in Virtue, as in Face!
Oh! if to dance all Night, and dress all Day,
Charm'd the Small-pox, or chas'd old Age away; 20
Who would not scorn what Huswife's Cares produce,
Or who would learn one earthly Thing of Use?
To patch, nay ogle, might become a Saint,
Nor could it sure be such a Sin to paint.
But since, alas! frail Beauty must decay, 25
Curl'd or uncurl'd, since Locks will turn to grey,
Since painted, or not painted, all shall fade,
And she who scorns a Man, must die a Maid;
What then remains, but well our Pow'r to use,
And keep good Humour still whate'er we lose? 30
And trust me, Dear! good Humour can prevail,
When Airs, and Flights, and Screams, and Scolding fail.
Beauties in vain their pretty Eyes may roll;
Charms strike the Sight, but Merit wins the Soul.
 So spoke the Dame, but no Applause ensu'd; 35
*Belinda* frown'd, *Thalesris* call'd her Prude.
To Arms, to Arms! the fierce Virago cries,
And swift as Lightning to the Combate flies.
All side in Parties, and begin th' Attack;
Fans clap, Silks russle, and tough Whalebones crack; 40

Heroes' and Heroins' Shouts confus'dly rise,
And base, and treble Voices strike the Skies.
No common Weapons in their Hands are found,
Like Gods they fight, nor dread a mortal Wound.
　　So when bold *Homer* makes the Gods engage,    45
And heav'nly Breasts with human Passions rage;
'Gainst *Pallas, Mars; Latona, Hermes* arms;
And all *Olympus* rings with loud Alarms.
*Jove*'s Thunder roars, Heav'n trembles all around;
Blue *Neptune* storms, the bellowing Deeps resound;    50
*Earth* shakes her nodding Tow'rs, the Ground gives way;
And the pale Ghosts start at the Flash of Day!
　　Triumphant *Umbriel* on a Sconce's Height
Clapt his glad Wings, and sate to view the Fight:
Propt on their Bodkin Spears, the Sprights survey    55
The growing Combat, or assist the Fray,
　　While thro' the Press enrag'd *Thalestris* flies,
And scatters Deaths around from both her Eyes,
A *Beau* and *Witling* perish'd in the Throng,
One dy'd in *Metaphor*, and one in *Song*.    60
*O cruel Nymph! a living Death I bear,*
Cry'd *Dapperwit*, and sunk beside his Chair.
A mournful Glance Sir *Fopling* upwards cast,
*Those Eyes are made so killing*—was his last:
Thus on *Meander*'s flow'ry Margin lies    65
Th' expiring Swan, and as he sings he dies.
　　When bold Sir *Plume* had drawn *Clarissa* down,
*Chloe* stept in, and kill'd him with a Frown;
She smil'd to see the doughty Hero slain,
But at her Smile, the Beau reviv'd again.    70
　　Now *Jove* suspends his golden Scales in Air,
Weighs the Men's Wits against the Lady's Hair;
The doubtful Beam long nods from side to side;
At length the Wits mount up, the Hairs subside.
　　See fierce *Belinda* on the *Baron* flies,    75
With more than usual Lightning in her Eyes;
Nor fear'd the Chief th' unequal Fight to try,
Who sought no more than on his Foe to die.
But this bold Lord, with manly Strength indu'd,
She with one Finger and a Thumb subdu'd:    80
Just where the Breath of Life his Nostrils drew,
A Charge of *Snuff* the wily Virgin threw;
The *Gnomes* direct, to ev'ry Atome just,
The pungent Grains of titillating Dust.

Sudden, with starting Tears each Eye o'erflows,    85
And the high Dome re-ecchoes to his Nose.
Now meet thy Fate, incens'd *Belinda* cry'd,
And drew a deadly *Bodkin* from her Side.
(The same, his ancient Personage to deck,
Her great great Grandsire wore about his Neck    90
In three *Seal-Rings;* which after, melted down,
Form'd a vast *Buckle* for his Widow's Gown:
Her infant Grandame's *Whistle* next it grew,
The *Bells* she gingled, and the *Whistle* blew;
Then in a *Bodkin* grac'd her Mother's Hairs,    95
Which long she wore, and now *Belinda* wears.)
Boast not my Fall (he cry'd) insulting Foe!
Thou by some other shalt be laid as low.
Nor think, to die dejects my lofty Mind;
All that I dread, is leaving you behind!    100
Rather than so, ah let me still survive,
And burn in *Cupid*'s Flames,—but burn alive.
*Restore the Lock!* she cries; and all around
*Restore the Lock!* the vaulted Roofs rebound.
Not fierce *Othello* in so loud a Strain    105
Roar'd for the Handkerchief that caus'd his Pain.
But see how oft Ambitious Aims are cross'd,
And Chiefs contend 'till all the Prize is lost!
The Lock, obtain'd with Guilt, and kept with Pain,
In ev'ry place is sought, but sought in vain:    110
With such a Prize no Mortal must be blest,
So Heav'n decrees! with Heav'n who can contest?
Some thought it mounted to the Lunar Sphere,
Since all things lost on Earth, are treasur'd there.
There Heroes' Wits are kept in pondrous Vases,    115
And Beaus' in *Snuff-boxes* and *Tweezer-Cases.*
There broken Vows, and Death-bed Alms are found,
And Lovers' Hearts with Ends of Riband bound;
The Courtier's Promises, and Sick Man's Pray'rs,
The Smiles of Harlots, and the Tears of Heirs,    120
Cages for Gnats, and Chains to Yoak a Flea;
Dry'd Butterflies, and Tomes of Casuistry.
But trust the Muse—she saw it upward rise,
Tho' mark'd by none but quick Poetic Eyes:
(So *Rome*'s great Founder to the Heav'ns withdrew,    125
To *Proculus* alone confess'd in view.)
A sudden Star, it shot thro' liquid Air,
And drew behind a radiant *Trail of Hair.*

Not *Berenice*'s Locks first rose so bright,
The Heav'ns bespangling with dishevel'd Light.     130
The *Sylphs* behold it kindling as it flies,
And pleas'd pursue its Progress thro' the Skies.
    This the *Beau-monde* shall from the *Mall* survey,
And hail with Musick its propitious Ray.
This, the blest Lover shall for *Venus* take,     135
And send up Vows from *Rosamonda*'s Lake.
This *Partridge* soon shall view in cloudless Skies,
When next he looks thro' *Galilæo*'s Eyes;
And hence th' Egregious Wizard shall foredoom
The Fate of *Louis*, and the Fall of *Rome*.     140
    Then cease, bright Nymph! to mourn thy ravish'd Hair
Which adds new Glory to the shining Sphere!
Not all the Tresses that fair Head can boast
Shall draw such Envy as the Lock you lost.
For, after all the Murders of your Eye,     145
When, after Millions slain, your self shall die;
When those fair Suns shall sett, as sett they must,
And all those Tresses shall be laid in Dust;
*This Lock*, the Muse shall consecrate to Fame,
And mid'st the Stars inscribe *Belinda*'s Name!     150

# A. J. M. Smith

---

POPE

## THE RAPE OF THE LOCK

When, some time in 1711, Robert, seventh Lord Petre, the youthful scion of a prominent Roman Catholic family of well-to-do landowners, snipped a lovelock from the head of Miss Arabella Fermor, he caused an angry little tempest that threatened to break up a long-standing family friendship. A mutual friend of the Fermors and the Petres, a certain Mr. John Caryll, suggested to another member of their circle, the brilliant new poet Alexander Pope, that he should "write a poem to make a jest of it, and laugh them together again." Pope found the task congenial, and he set to work at once on the poem that, as it turned out, was to bring him universal fame and to make the name of Arabella Fermor immortal. Her transfigured lock shines forever as one of the brightest constellations in the poetic firmament.

An early version of the poem was published anonymously in 1712 in a popular miscellany of contemporary verse. It consisted of only two cantos and was without its most striking and original feature, the wholly delightful fairy element of the sylphs and gnomes. Against the advice of Addison, who said the poem was perfect as it stood, Pope expanded his piece to five cantos, introduced his miniature angels and tiny demons, which he had been reading about in a vast French romance based on the teachings of the Rosicrucians, and in March 1714 published it over his own name as *The Rape of the Locke: An Heroi-Comical Poem*. What was originally little more than a graceful and elegant *jeu d'esprit* had become a poem the like of which does not exist in any language. For a comparable union of wit and beauty we have to go to the other arts, to the *Marriage of Figaro* of Mozart or the canvases of Watteau.

"It is made of gauze and silver spangles," said Hazlitt. "The most glittering appearance is given to everything, to paste, pomatum, billet-doux, and patches. Airs, languid airs, breathe around. . . . No pains are spared, no profusion of ornament, no splendour of poetic diction, to set off the meanest things.

The balance between the concealed irony and the assumed gravity is as nicely trimmed as the balance of power in Europe. The little is made great, and the great little. You hardly know whether to laugh or weep. . . . It is the perfection of the mock-heroic."

The mock heroic was one of the most frequently used satirical devices of the seventeenth and eighteenth centuries, the age of Boileau, Dryden, Swift, and Pope, and because the "heroic poem," as the epic was called then, was taken seriously, the mock heroic was taken seriously too. Dryden, in the dedication to his translation of Virgil's "Aeneid," called the epic poem "the greatest work which the soul of man is able to perform." In the mock heroic, the trivial, the ordinary, the minute, and the mean are elevated to the ironically sublime: a bodkin becomes a spear, a game of cards a battle, and a girl making up her face at her dressing table a devotee at the shrine of Venus. More than this, the form and the traditional episodic structure of the classical epic is followed religiously. In *The Rape of the Lock* there are the opening invocation, the statement of theme, and the dedication, just as in Homer, Virgil, and Milton. There are descriptions of social rites presented as religious rites—Belinda before her mirror, the Baron's sacrifice upon an altar of love-romances and erotica, the almost ritualistic drinking of coffee, and the speeches that precede and follow every significant action. Among these are some that make an essential part of the classical epic—the roll call of heroes, the description of weapons, the battle or the duel, and the descent into the underworld. Pope's "battles," which are skirmishes in the universal battle of the sexes, are a game of omber (to the eighteenth century what bridge is to us) and a drawing-room brouhaha; his descent into the underworld is the visit of a gnome to the Cave of Spleen in the fourth canto.

This scene is particularly remarkable. It is filled with parodies and allusions. Homer, Virgil, Spenser, and Milton are all touched upon. But the greatest triumph of the episode is the skillful way in which the poet "points a moral to adorn his tale"—another essential responsibility of the writer of the serious epic. This scene is also full of medical and scientific lore, and Pope succeeds in leveling a thoroughly rational and sensible attack on the fashionable diseases of melancholia and hypochondria, which, in a passage of Swiftian intensity that carries us from a lady's darkened sickroom to the corridors of bedlam, are shown to be preludes to madness itself unless corrected by good humor and good sense. Good humor and good sense are remedies for the affectations of society in general, and for such distortions of value as have brought about the unnecessary fuss over Lord Petre's "crime"—this is the practical "lesson," which half seriously and half ironically the poem was expected to teach. The moral function of the classical epic is concentrated in Clarissa's speech in the fifth canto.

This not only imitates an essential feature of the serious epic—to inculcate a moral—but it is a mock-heroic parody of the speech of Sarpedon to Glaucus in the twelfth book of the *Iliad*. The speech is fruitless, of course, and the folly and willfulness of Belinda and the Baron and their partisans make the poem a necessity to laugh them back to reason.

The poem is able to accomplish so much because, among other things, it is a triumph of style. Whoever reading *The Rape of the Lock* right through could ever think the heroic couplet monotonous, or the "artificial poetic diction of the eighteenth century" anything but a delightful foil to the rougher, tougher, coarser lingo of everyday usage! Such lines as these, which describe the dragonfly-like sylphs as they disport themselves around the masts of Belinda's "painted vessel" on the waters of the Thames, are as sensuous and melodious as anything in Keats:

> *Some to the Sun their Insect-Wings unfold,*
> *Waft on the Breeze, or sink in Clouds of Gold.*
> *Transparent Forms, too fine for mortal Sight,*
> *Their fluid bodies half dissolv'd in Light.*
> *Loose to the Wind their airy Garments flew,*
> *Thin glitt'ring Textures of the filmy Dew;*
> *Dipt in the richest Tincture of the Skies,*
> *Where Light disports in ever-mingling Dies*
>
> [II: 59–62]

At other times the diction is as common and familiar and the style as "low" as in Defoe or Swift. The angry spluttering of Sir Plume protesting the cutting of the lock is conveyed in these thoroughly naturalistic lines:

> *He first the Snuff-box open'd, then the Case,*
> *And thus broke out—"My Lord, why, what the Devil?*
> *Z—ds! damn the Lock! fore Gad, you must be civil!*
> *Plague on't! 'tis past a Jest—nay prithee, Pox!*
> *Give her the Hair"—he spoke, and rapp'd his Box*
>
> [II: 126–30]

In spite of its realism, this passage, and others like it, is mock heroic in its mingling of the grand and the absurd, or rather its confusion of the trivial and the heroic. In the minds of the beaux and belles the trivial *is* the heroic, and it is this reversal of values that provokes the laughter and contempt that Pope's satire pours out upon affectation and foolishness. For the most part the satire is an unstressed and well-mannered irony that makes it doubly effective in the social milieu in which it lives and has its being. The vanity of women and the arrogance of men, the triviality and irresponsibility, the selfishness and yet the charm, the confusion of values in which the significant and the ephemeral are almost indistinguishable are all shown up—but always delicately and with a finesse that gives Pope's pointed barbs their penetrating power.

Under the glittering surface, however, there are depths, and once in a while, though for a brief moment only, Pope takes a quick glance into "the accepted hells beneath."

> *Mean while declining from the Noon of Day,*
> *The Sun obliquely shoots his burning Ray;*
> *The hungry Judges soon the Sentence sign,*
> *And Wretches hang that Jury-men may Dine*
>
> [III: 19–22]

The intensity and depth of the poem really lie, however, in its treatment of sex. The "Rape" of the title is symbolic of a real rape, and the sylphs are crystallizations of the idea, properly, of Honor, and, mistakenly, of Reputation. Ambiguity, suggestion, and innuendo are used to make it quite clear that the war of the sexes is a real war, as devastating and important as that provoked by the rape of Helen. There is a pregnant ambiguity in the famous lines praising the beauty of Belinda:

> *On her white Breast a sparkling Cross she wore,*
> *Which Jews might kiss, and Infidels adore*
>
> [II: 7–8]

where it is not clear whether it is the cross or the breast which is affirmed to be kissable and adorable. The innuendo in Belinda's expostulation to the Baron:

> *Oh hadst thou, Cruel! been content to seize*
> *Hairs less in sight, or any Hairs but these!*
>
> [IV: 175–76]

is another indication of depths below depths and a sign that in the mock heroic, "fair and foul are close of kin"—in the words of a modern poet who, it has not been sufficiently realized, has an affinity with Pope in his skillful fusion of high and low styles and the heroic and the comic.

One word may be added as postscript about the real life of the personages involved. The poem seems to have succeeded, eventually, in its purpose of healing the breach between the Fermors and the Petres. Arabella was pleased, as she might well have been, and not a little vain, it is said, of her distinction. Only Sir Plume (a certain Sir George Browne) was angry—as well he might have been too, for he alone was made ridiculous. It would be pleasant to be able to record that everything ended happily with the marriage of the hero and the heroine, but that was not to be. Lord Petre married a younger and richer heiress than Belinda before the poem was published, and less than a year later, before the longer version of the poem appeared, he was dead of smallpox at the age of twenty-three. Arabella married a gentleman of Berkshire in 1714 or 1715. She became the mother of six children and died, probably at the age of forty-seven, in March of 1737 or 1738, about eleven months after her husband. Her immortality is assured:

> This Lock, *the Muse shall consecrate to Fame,*
> *And mid'st the Stars inscribe* Belinda's *Name!*
>
> [V:149–150]

SAMUEL JOHNSON

*The Bettmann Archive*

# SAMUEL JOHNSON

## [1709–1784]

## *The Vanity of Human Wishes*

### THE TENTH SATIRE OF JUVENAL IMITATED

Let observation with extensive view,
Survey mankind, from China to Peru;
Remark each anxious toil, each eager strife,
And watch the busy scenes of crouded life;
Then say how hope and fear, desire and hate,     5
O'erspread with snares the clouded maze of fate,
Where wav'ring man, betray'd by vent'rous pride,
To tread the dreary paths without a guide,
As treach'rous phantoms in the mist delude,
Shuns fancied ills, or chases airy good;     10
How rarely reason guides the stubborn choice,
Rules the bold hand, or prompts the suppliant voice;
How nations sink, by darling schemes oppress'd,
When vengeance listens to the fool's request.
Fate wings with ev'ry wish th' afflictive dart,     15
Each gift of nature, and each grace of art,
With fatal heat impetuous courage glows,
With fatal sweetness elocution flows,
Impeachment stops the speaker's pow'rful breath,
And restless fire precipitates on death.     20
But scarce observ'd, the knowing and the bold
Fall in the gen'ral massacre of gold;
Wide-wasting pest! that rages unconfin'd,
And crouds with crimes the records of mankind;
For gold his sword the hireling ruffian draws,     25
For gold the hireling judge distorts the laws;
Wealth heap'd on wealth, nor truth nor safety buys,
The dangers gather as the treasures rise.
Let hist'ry tell where rival kings command,
And dubious title shakes the madded land,     30
When statutes glean the refuse of the sword,
How much more safe the vassal than the lord;

Low skulks the hind beneath the rage of pow'r,
And leaves the wealthy traytor in the Tow'r,
Untouch'd his cottage, and his slumbers sound,                    35
Tho' confiscation's vulturs hover round.
The needy traveller, serene and gay,
Walks the wild heath, and sings his toil away.
Does envy seize thee? crush th' upbraiding joy,
Increase his riches and his peace destroy;                        40
Now fears in dire vicissitude invade,
The rustling brake alarms, and quiv'ring shade,
Nor light nor darkness bring his pain relief,
One shews the plunder, and one hides the thief.
Yet still one gen'ral cry the skies assails,                      45
And gain and grandeur load the tainted gales;
Few know the toiling statesman's fear or care,
Th' insidious rival and the gaping heir.
Once more, Democritus, arise on earth,
With chearful wisdom and instructive mirth,                       50
See motley life in modern trappings dress'd,
And feed with varied fools th' eternal jest:
Thou who couldst laugh where want enchain'd caprice,
Toil crush'd conceit, and man was of a piece;
Where wealth unlov'd without a mourner dy'd,                      55
And scarce a sycophant was fed by pride;
Where ne'er was known the form of mock debate,
Or seen a new-made mayor's unwieldy state;
Where change of fav'rites made no change of laws,
And senates heard before they judg'd a cause;                     60
How wouldst thou shake at Britain's modish tribe,
Dart the quick taunt, and edge the piercing gibe?
Attentive truth and nature to descry,
And pierce each scene with philosophic eye.
To thee were solemn toys or empty shew,                          65
The robes of pleasure and the veils of woe:
All aid the farce, and all thy mirth maintain,
Whose joys are causeless, or whose griefs are vain.
Such was the scorn that fill'd the sage's mind,
Renew'd at ev'ry glance on humankind;                            70
How just that scorn ere yet thy voice declare,
Search every state, and canvass ev'ry pray'r.
Unnumber'd suppliants croud Preferment's gate,
Athirst for wealth, and burning to be great;
Delusive Fortune hears th' incessant call,                       75

They mount, they shine, evaporate, and fall.
On ev'ry stage the foes of peace attend,
Hate dogs their flight, and insult mocks their end.
Love ends with hope, the sinking statesman's door
Pours in the morning worshiper no more;                                    80
For growing names the weekly scribbler lies,
To growing wealth the dedicator flies,
From every room descends the painted face,
That hung the bright Palladium of the place,
And smoak'd in kitchens, or in auctions sold,                              85
To better features yields the frame of gold;
For now no more we trace in ev'ry line
Heroic worth, benevolence divine:
The form distorted justifies the fall,
And detestation rids th' indignant wall.                                   90
   But will not Britain hear the last appeal,
Sign her foes doom, on guard her fav'rites zeal?
Through Freedom's sons no more remonstrance rings,
Degrading nobles and controuling kings;
Our supple tribes repress their patriot throats,                           95
And ask no questions but the price of votes;
With weekly libels and septennial ale,
Their wish is full to riot and to rail.
   In full-blown dignity, see Wolsey stand,
Law in his voice, and fortune in his hand:                                 100
To him the church, the realm, their pow'rs consign,
Thro' him the rays of regal bounty shine,
Turn'd by his nod the stream of honour flows,
His smile alone security bestows:
Still to new heights his restless wishes tow'r,                            105
Claim leads to claim, and pow'r advances pow'r;
Till conquest unresisted ceas'd to please,
And rights submitted, left him none to seize.
At length his sov'reign frowns—the train of state
Mark the keen glance, and watch the sign to hate.                          110
Where-e'er he turns he meets a stranger's eye,
His suppliants scorn him, and his followers fly;
At once is lost the pride of aweful state,
The golden canopy, the glitt'ring plate,
The regal palace, the luxurious board,                                     115
The liv'ried army, and the menial lord.
With age, with cares, with maladies oppress'd,
He seeks the refuge of monastic rest.
Grief aids disease, remember'd folly stings,
And his last sighs reproach the faith of kings.                            120

Speak thou, whose thoughts at humble peace repine,
Shall Wolsey's wealth, with Wolsey's end be thine?
Or liv'st thou now, with safer pride content,
The wisest justice on the banks of Trent?
For why did Wolsey near the steeps of fate,                    125
On weak foundations raise th' enormous weight?
Why but to sink beneath misfortune's blow,
With louder ruin to the gulphs below?
What gave great Villiers to th' assassin's knife,
And fixed disease on Harley's closing life?                    130
What murder'd Wentworth, and what exil'd Hyde,
By kings protected, and to kings ally'd?
What but their wish indulg'd in courts to shine,
And pow'r too great to keep, or to resign?
When first the college rolls receive his name,                 135
The young enthusiast quits his ease for fame;
Through all his veins the fever of renown
Burns from the strong contagion of the gown;
O'er Bodley's dome his future labours spread,
And* Bacon's mansion trembles o'er his head.                   140
Are these thy views? proceed, illustrious youth,
And virtue guard thee to the throne of Truth!
Yet should thy soul indulge the gen'rous heat,
Till captive Science yields her last retreat;
Should Reason guide thee with her brightest ray,              145
And pour on misty Doubt resistless day;
Should no false Kindness lure to loose delight,
Nor Praise relax, nor Difficulty fright;
Should tempting Novelty thy cell refrain,
And Sloth effuse her opiate fumes in vain;                     150
Should Beauty blunt on fops her fatal dart,
Nor claim the triumph of a letter'd heart;
Should no Disease thy torpid veins invade,
Nor Melancholy's phantoms haunt thy shade;
Yet hope not life from grief or danger free,                  155
Nor think the doom of man revers'd for thee:
Deign on the passing world to turn thine eyes,
And pause awhile from letters, to be wise;
There mark what ills the scholar's life assail,
Toil, envy, want, the patron, and the jail.                   160
See nations slowly wise, and meanly just,
To buried merit raise the tardy bust.

* There is a tradition, that the study of friar Bacon, built on an
arch over the bridge, will fall, when a man greater than Bacon shall
pass under it.

If dreams yet flatter, once again attend,
Hear Lydiat's life, and Galileo's end.

Nor deem, when learning her last prize bestows,     165
The glitt'ring eminence exempt from foes;
See when the vulgar 'scape, despis'd or aw'd,
Rebellion's vengeful talons seize on Laud,
From meaner minds, tho' smaller fines content,
The plunder'd palace or sequester'd rent;     170
Mark'd out by dangerous parts he meets the shock,
And fatal Learning leads him to the block:
Around his tomb let Art and Genius weep,
But hear his death, ye blockheads, hear and sleep.

The festal blazes, the triumphal show,     175
The ravish'd standard, and the captive foe,
The senate's thanks, the gazette's pompous tale,
With force resistless o'er the brave prevail.
Such bribes the rapid Greek o'er Asia whirl'd,
For such the steady Romans shook the world;     180
For such in distant lands the Britons shine,
And stain with blood the Danube or the Rhine;
This pow'r has praise, that virtue scarce can warm,
Till fame supplies the universal charm.

Yet Reason frowns on War's unequal game,     185
Where wasted nations raise a single name,
And mortgag'd states their grandsires wreaths regret,
From age to age in everlasting debt;
Wreaths which at last the dear-bought right convey
To rust on medals, or on stones decay.     190

On what foundation stands the warrior's pride,
How just his hopes let Swedish Charles decide;
A frame of adamant, a soul of fire,
No dangers fright him, and no labours tire;
O'er love, o'er fear, extends his wide domain,     195
Unconquer'd lord of pleasure and of pain;
No joys to him pacific scepters yield,
War sounds the trump, he rushes to the field;
Behold surrounding kings their pow'r combine,
And one capitulate, and one resign;     200
Peace courts his hand, but spreads her charms in vain;
"Think nothing gain'd," he cries, "till nought remain,
"On Moscow's walls till Gothic standards fly,
"And all be mine beneath the polar sky."
The march begins in military state,     205
And nations on his eye suspended wait;
Stern Famine guards the solitary coast,

And Winter barricades the realms of Frost;
He comes, not want and cold his course delay;—
Hide, blushing Glory, hide Pultowa's day:      210
The vanquish'd hero leaves his broken bands,
And shews his miseries in distant lands;
Condemn'd a needy supplicant to wait,
While ladies interpose, and slaves debate.
But did not Chance at length her error mend?      215
Did no subverted empire mark his end?
Did rival monarchs give the fatal wound?
Or hostile millions press him to the ground?
His fall was destin'd to a barren strand,
A petty fortress, and a dubious hand;      220
He left the name, at which the world grew pale,
To point a moral, or adorn a tale.
    All times their scenes of pompous woes afford,
From Persia's tyrant to Bavaria's lord.
In gay hostility, and barb'rous pride,      225
With half mankind embattled at his side,
Great Xerxes comes to seize the certain prey,
And starves exhausted regions in his way;
Attendant Flatt'ry counts his myriads o'er,
Till counted myriads sooth his pride no more;      230
Fresh praise is try'd till madness fires his mind,
The waves he lashes, and enchains the wind;
New pow'rs are claim'd, new pow'rs are still bestow'd,
Till rude resistance lops the spreading god;
The daring Greeks deride the martial show,      235
And heap their vallies with the gaudy foe;
Th' insulted sea with humbler thoughts he gains,
A single skiff to speed his flight remains;
Th' incumber'd oar scarce leaves the dreaded coast
Through purple billows and a floating host.      240
    The bold Bavarian, in a luckless hour,
Tries the dread summits of Cesarean pow'r,
With unexpected legions bursts away,
And sees defenceless realms receive his sway;
Short sway! Austria spreads her mournful charms,      245
The queen, the beauty, sets the world in arms;
From hill to hill the beacons rousing blaze
Spreads wide the hope of plunder and of praise;
The fierce Croatian, and the wild Hussar,
And all the sons of ravage croud the war;      250
The baffled prince in honour's flatt'ring bloom
Of hasty greatness finds the fatal doom,

His foes derision, and his subjects blame,
And steals to death from anguish and from shame.
Enlarge my life with multitude of days,                    255
In health, in sickness, thus the suppliant prays;
Hides from himself his state, and shuns to know,
That life protracted is protracted woe.
Time hovers o'er, impatient to destroy,
And shuts up all the passages of joy:                      260
In vain their gifts the bounteous seasons pour,
The fruit autumnal, and the vernal flow'r,
With listless eyes the dotard views the store,
He views, and wonders that they please no more;
Now pall the tasteless meats, and joyless wines,           265
And Luxury with sighs her slave resigns.
Approach, ye minstrels, try the soothing strain,
Diffuse the tuneful lenitives of pain:
No sounds alas would touch th' impervious ear,
Though dancing mountains witness'd Orpheus near;           270
Nor lute nor lyre his feeble pow'rs attend,
Nor sweeter musick of a virtuous friend,
But everlasting dictates croud his tongue,
Perversely grave, or positively wrong.
The still returning tale, and ling'ring jest,              275
Perplex the fawning niece and pamper'd guest,
While growing hopes scarce awe the gath'ring sneer,
And scarce a legacy can bribe to hear;
The watchful guests still hint the last offence,
The daughter's petulance, the son's expence,              280
Improve his heady rage with treach'rous skill,
And mould his passions till they make his will.
  Unnumber'd maladies his joints invade,
Lay siege to life and press the dire blockade;
But unextinguish'd Avarice still remains,                  285
And dreaded losses aggravate his pains;
He turns, with anxious heart and cripled hands,
His bonds of debt, and mortgages of lands;
Or views his coffers with suspicious eyes,
Unlocks his gold, and counts it till he dies.             290
  But grant, the virtues of a temp'rate prime
Bless with an age exempt from scorn or crime;
An age that melts with unperceiv'd decay,
And glides in modest Innocence away;
Whose peaceful day Benevolence endears,                    295
Whose night congratulating Conscience cheers;
The gen'ral fav'rite as the gen'ral friend:

Such age there is, and who shall wish its end?
  Yet ev'n on this her load Misfortune flings,
To press the weary minutes flagging wings:                    300
New sorrow rises as the day returns,
A sister sickens, or a daughter mourns.
Now kindred Merit fills the sable bier,
Now lacerated Friendship claims a tear.
Year chases year, decay pursues decay,                        305
Still drops some joy from with'ring life away;
New forms arise, and diff'rent views engage,
Superfluous lags the vet'ran on the stage,
Till pitying Nature signs the last release,
And bids afflicted worth retire to peace.                     310
  But few there are whom hours like these await,
Who set unclouded in the gulphs of fate.
From Lydia's monarch should the search descend,
By Solon caution'd to regard his end,
In life's last scene what prodigies surprise,                 315
Fears of the brave, and follies of the wise?
From Marlb'rough's eyes the streams of dotage flow,
And Swift expires a driv'ler and a show.
  The teeming mother, anxious for her race,
Begs for each birth the fortune of a face:                    320
Yet Vane could tell what ills from beauty spring;
And Sedley curs'd the form that pleas'd a king.
Ye nymphs of rosy lips and radiant eyes,
Whom Pleasure keeps too busy to be wise,
Whom Joys with soft varieties invite,                         325
By day the frolick, and the dance by night,
Who frown with vanity, who smile with art,
And ask the latest fashion of the heart,
What care, what rules your heedless charms shall save,
Each nymph your rival, and each youth your slave?             330
Against your fame with fondness hate combines,
The rival batters, and the lover mines.
With distant voice neglected Virtue calls,
Less heard and less, the faint remonstrance falls;
Tir'd with contempt, she quits the slipp'ry reign,            335
And Pride and Prudence take her seat in vain.
In croud at once, where none the pass defend,
The harmless Freedom, and the private Friend.
The guardians yield, by force superior ply'd;
By Int'rest, Prudence; and by Flatt'ry, Pride.                340
Now beauty falls betray'd, despis'd, distress'd,

And hissing Infamy proclaims the rest.
Where then shall Hope and Fear their objects find?
Must dull Suspence corrupt the stagnant mind?
Must helpless man, in ignorance sedate,                   345
Roll darkling down the torrent of his fate?
Must no dislike alarm, no wishes rise,
No cries attempt the mercies of the skies?
Enquirer, cease, petitions yet remain,
Which heav'n may hear, nor deem religion vain.            350
Still raise for good the supplicating voice,
But leave to heav'n the measure and the choice,
Safe in his pow'r, whose eyes discern afar
The secret ambush of a specious pray'r.
Implore his aid, in his decisions rest,                   355
Secure whate'er he gives, he gives the best.
Yet when the sense of sacred presence fires,
And strong devotion to the skies aspires,
Pour forth thy fervours for a healthful mind,
Obedient passions, and a will resign'd;                   360
For love, which scarce collective man can fill;
For patience sov'reign o'er transmuted ill;
For faith, that panting for a happier seat,
Counts death kind Nature's signal of retreat:
These goods for man the laws of heav'n ordain,            365
These goods he grants, who grants the pow'r to gain;
With these celestial wisdom calms the mind,
And makes the happiness she does not find.

# Donald Davie

## JOHNSON
### THE VANITY OF HUMAN WISHES

"To have the virtues of good prose is the first and minimum requirement of great poetry." This was the disconcerting opinion of T.S. Eliot after he had pondered two long poems by the young Dr. Johnson, *London* (1738) and *The Vanity of Human Wishes* (1749). What Eliot says is true, but not at all clear. For there is more than one sort of good prose. One sort of good prose that has little or nothing to do with Johnson's poetry is the prose of some great novelists, the French prose of Stendhal or Flaubert, the English prose of Henry James, wonderfully exact and particular in rendering the uniqueness of persons and of milieux. Johnson is not much interested in uniqueness; he wants to generalize. He cares less for how people differ than for what they have in common. Both interests are legitimate, but the one is more the novelist's, the other more the moralist's. Johnson's poetry has the virtues not of good novelist's prose, but of the sort of prose he wrote himself. And Johnson wrote prose as a moralist. But what is more to the point is to remember that he compiled a great dictionary. For we often think, and sometimes we find it said, that the dictionary is always and everywhere the poet's enemy; that the dictionary tries to imprison a word inside a definition, whereas the poet is always rescuing the word from this prison cage, extending its meaning so that it escapes its own definition. The truth seems to be that this liberation of the word is indeed, at some times, a true and honorable task for the poet. But Johnson undertook just the opposite task, the forcing of words back into the dictionary definitions they were escaping from. Johnson is one of those poets who undertake to serve the language, and all of us who use it, by shredding away the looseness of usage, sharpening the tools that words are, giving them once again the cutting edge of a sharply defined meaning. The words he is concerned with are more the moralist's words than the novelist's, but the dictionary maker's exactness—his awareness of the precise dictionary-meaning of every word he uses—is the glory of Johnson's verse as of his prose.

As Ezra Pound put it, "The merits of the lexicographer are there in *The Vanity of Human Wishes*, the fine weighing and placing of the epithet." Yes, and not epithets only, but all parts of speech:

> *Let observation with extensive view,*
> *Survey mankind, from China to Peru*

This, the first couplet of the poem, is far from the best. But it is better than was thought by the man who objected that all it said was, "Let observation with extensive observation observe. . . ." *We* may use words so loosely that for us "observation" and "view" and "survey" all amount to the same thing; Johnson did not. And observation was for him a very important matter, as anyone can see from what he wrote about Shakespeare. According to Johnson, it is by nothing more occult than observation that the poet discovers the truths that he tells in his poems; his first duty is to keep his eyes open, and his wits about him, and his sympathies quick, as he moves about the world. This is what Pound meant when he said of Johnson's poetry that it is "verse for the man of fifty, who has a right to metrical pleasures perhaps as much as his juniors." This sounds grudging, and certainly fifty is putting it rather high, but what Pound means is that the longer you have knocked about the world, and the more you have seen of the world, the more you will be struck by the sheer truthfulness of what Johnson says; and this must be so, in view of the importance Johnson gave to "observation." The particular couplet that Pound had in mind (lines 161–62) is a famous one:

> *See nations slowly wise, and meanly just,*
> *To buried merit raise the tardy bust.*

The commentators say that what Johnson had particularly in mind here is the case of the poet Samuel Butler (1618–1620), author of "Hudibras," who was given £300 by Charles II, with the promise of more. The promise was never kept and Butler, who died in poverty, was buried at a friend's expense, though a monument ("the tardy bust") was raised to him after his death. But no one needs this reference; all we need is to have knocked about the world long enough to know how seldom fame comes to the right man until too late.

This is a thing that everyone knows after a fashion, but equally it is a thing that every man has to learn anew for himself. And this is typical of the truths that Johnson tells. He does not think that observation will at all often discover truths previously undreamt of; what it does is to make us feel vividly and with assurance truths to which we have always given languid assent. Johnson seldom says anything that is not a commonplace, but he says it with a pungency and passion that show he has experienced it afresh for himself (the passion shows itself most in the succinctness). This is why this poem, like the earlier "London," is an imitation (in the strict sense that eighteenth century critics gave to that term) of a satire by Juvenal: by showing how all that Juvenal said of Roman society is true of the English society that Johnson knew, Johnson aims to show that the truths he is enunciating are *permanent* truths, which is to say, commonplaces.

However, if some truths are permanent, not every age acknowledges them to be so; what is accepted as commonplace for centuries may suddenly be challenged. Pound challenged the central commonplace of Johnson's poem when, after praising it, he suddenly decided, "Yet taking it by and large the poem is buncombe. Human wishes are not vain in the least." Are they not? All the Christian centuries thought they were, not just because Scripture said so, but because experience corroborated what Scripture said. When Pound turned mutinous about it, he was a non-Christian or post-Christian reader refusing a Christian commonplace. For "The Vanity of Human Wishes" is a profoundly Christian document, like everything else that Johnson wrote.

One does not have to be Christian, however, to wonder if Pound has not changed his mind through the salutary disillusionment he has suffered since he wrote that thirty years ago. And one does not have to be Christian to appreciate Johnson's poem, for other religions besides Christianity have held that human wishes are vain—after all, the Book of Ecclesiastes is in the Old Testament, not the New. On the other hand, Johnson, as a Christian, had hopes (though in his case they were shaky ones) of another world than this; and so Johnson's pessimism about this world, though it is real enough, is not the counsel of despair it may seem to the irreligious.

Though we need not know about the author of "Hudibras" to take the force of "buried merit" and "tardy bust," on the other hand there are lines 219–220, which conclude a magisterially succinct narrative of the career of Charles XII of Sweden:

> *His fall was destin'd to a barren strand,*
> *A petty fortress, and a dubious hand*

This shows the weighing of the epithet in all its glory, but we realize this only if we know that the conqueror who had ravaged half Europe was killed on his own doorstep, at Fredricshall in Norway, and quite probably not by the enemy but by one of his own soldiers. Another example of the emptiness of military and imperial glory can be appreciated only if we know the outline of the War of the Austrian Succession, which was concluded in the very year Johnson published his daringly topical verses about it. "Bavaria's lord" (line 224) or "the bold Bavarian" (line 241) was the Elector of Bavaria who in 1740, when the Austrian Empire passed to Maria Theresa, claimed the imperial throne (line 242), and with the help of the French occupied Vienna (line 244). He was elected Emperor. But Maria Theresa ("fair Austria," line 245) appealed to her Hungarian subjects ("the wild Hussar," line 249). The Elector's death in 1745, while the conflict was still undecided, was hastened by the strain of insecurity (lines 251–55).

Thus not all of the poem is plain sailing for the modern reader. How could it be? Johnson's humility as a poet forces him to the discipline of observation: it is his conviction that significance is not *made* by the poem, out of words or out of the poet's soul, but is *found* by the poem in the realities that the poet explores—and this means that we have to hold the poem up against the realities it offers to deal with. Johnson felt nothing of that arrogance, so exciting and splendid sometimes as we find it in other poets, which sets out to make of a poem a self-sufficient world answering to no laws but those of its own form. Johnson's poem, though it has much formal and rigorous splendor, leans unashamedly on the common and public world of experience; to take the force of it we need less to be wise about poetry than to be wise and experienced about things very remote from poetry, about how the world goes.

THOMAS GRAY

*The Bettmann Archive*

# THOMAS GRAY
## [1716–1771]

## *Elegy Written in a Country Churchyard*

The Curfew tolls the knell of parting day,
   The lowing herd wind slowly o'er the lea,
The plowman homeward plods his weary way,
   And leaves the world to darkness and to me.

Now fades the glimmering landscape on the sight,     5
   And all the air a solemn stillness holds,
Save where the beetle wheels his droning flight,
   And drowsy tinklings lull the distant folds;

Save that from yonder ivy-mantled tow'r
   The moping owl does to the moon complain     10
Of such as, wand'ring near her secret bow'r,
   Molest her ancient solitary reign.

Beneath those rugged elms, that yew-tree's shade,
   Where heaves the turf in many a mould'ring heap,
Each in his narrow cell for ever laid,     15
   The rude Forefathers of the hamlet sleep.

The breezy call of incense-breathing Morn,
   The swallow twitt'ring from the straw-built shed,
The cock's shrill clarion, or the echoing horn,
   No more shall rouse them from their lowly bed.     20

For them no more the blazing hearth shall burn,
   Or busy housewife ply her evening care:
No children run to lisp their sire's return,
   Or climb his knees the envied kiss to share.

Oft did the harvest to their sickle yield,     25
   Their furrow oft the stubborn glebe has broke:
How jocund did they drive their team afield!
   How bow'd the woods beneath their sturdy stroke!

Let not Ambition mock their useful toil,
   Their homely joys, and destiny obscure;     30
Nor Grandeur hear with a disdainful smile
   The short and simple annals of the poor.

The boast of heraldry, the pomp of pow'r,
  And all that beauty, all that wealth e'er gave,
Awaits alike th' inevitable hour: 35
  The paths of glory lead but to the grave.

Nor you, ye Proud, impute to These the fault,
  If Memory o'er their Tomb no Trophies raise,
Where through the long-drawn aisle and fretted vault
  The pealing anthem swells the note of praise. 40

Can storied urn or animated bust
  Back to its mansion call the fleeting breath?
Can Honour's voice provoke the silent dust,
  Or Flatt'ry soothe the dull cold ear of death?

Perhaps in this neglected spot is laid 45
  Some heart once pregnant with celestial fire;
Hands, that the rod of empire might have sway'd,
  Or waked to ecstasy the living lyre.

But Knowledge to their eyes her ample page
  Rich with the spoils of time did ne'er unroll; 50
Chill Penury repress'd their noble rage,
  And froze the genial current of the soul.

Full many a gem of purest ray serene
  The dark unfathom'd caves of ocean bear:
Full many a flower is born to blush unseen, 55
  And waste its sweetness on the desert air.

Some village Hampden that with dauntless breast
  The little tyrant of his fields withstood,
Some mute inglorious Milton, here may rest,
  Some Cromwell guiltless of his country's blood. 60

Th' applause of list'ning senates to command,
  The threats of pain and ruin to despise,
To scatter plenty o'er a smiling land,
  And read their history in a nation's eyes,

Their lot forbade: nor circumscribed alone 65
  Their growing virtues, but their crimes confined;
Forbade to wade through slaughter to a throne,
  And shut the gates of mercy on mankind;

The struggling pangs of conscious truth to hide, 70
  To quench the blushes of ingenuous shame,
Or heap the shrine of Luxury and Pride
  With incense kindled at the Muse's flame.

Far from the madding crowd's ignoble strife
   Their sober wishes never learn'd to stray;        75
Along the cool sequester'd vale of life
   They kept the noiseless tenor of their way.

Yet ev'n these bones from insult to protect
   Some frail memorial still erected nigh,
With uncouth rhymes and shapeless sculpture deck'd,        80
   Implores the passing tribute of a sigh.

Their name, their years, spelt by th' unletter'd muse,
   The place of fame and elegy supply:
And many a holy text around she strews,
   That teach the rustic moralist to die.        85

For who, to dumb Forgetfulness a prey,
   This pleasing anxious being e'er resign'd,
Left the warm precincts of the cheerful day,
   Nor cast one longing ling'ring look behind?

On some fond breast the parting soul relies,        90
   Some pious drops the closing eye requires;
E'en from the tomb the voice of Nature cries,
   E'en in our Ashes live their wonted Fires.

For thee, who, mindful of th' unhonour'd dead,
   Dost in these lines their artless tale relate;        95
If chance, by lonely contemplation led,
   Some kindred spirit shall inquire thy fate,

Haply some hoary-headed Swain may say,
   "Oft have we seen him at the peep of dawn
Brushing with hasty steps the dews away        100
   To meet the sun upon the upland lawn.

"There at the foot of yonder nodding beech
   That wreathes its old fantastic roots so high,
His listless length at noontide would he stretch,
   And pore upon the brook that babbles by.        105

"Hard by yon wood, now smiling as in scorn,
   Mutt'ring his wayward fancies he would rove,
Now drooping, woeful wan, like one forlorn,
   Or crazed with care, or cross'd in hopeless love.

"One morn I miss'd him on the custom'd hill,        110
   Along the heath and near his fav'rite tree;
Another came, nor yet beside the rill,
   Nor up the lawn, nor at the wood was he;

"The next with dirges due in sad array
  Slow through the church-way path we saw him borne,   115
Approach and read (for thou canst read) the lay
  Graved on the stone beneath yon aged thorn."


### THE EPITAPH

*Here rests his head upon the lap of Earth*
  *A Youth to Fortune and to Fame unknown*         120
*Fair Science frown'd not on his humble birth,*
  *And Melancholy mark'd him for her own.*

*Large was his bounty, and his soul sincere,*
  *Heav'n did a recompense as largely send:*
*He gave to Mis'ry all he had, a tear,*           125
  *He gain'd from Heav'n ('twas all he wish'd) a friend.*

*No farther seek his merits to disclose,*
  *Or draw his frailties from their dread abode,*
*(There they alike in trembling hope repose,)*
  *The bosom of his Father and his God.*          130

*Cleanth Brooks*

---

GRAY

ELEGY WRITTEN IN A COUNTRY CHURCHYARD

For readers who insist that great poetry can make use of
"simple eloquence"—a straightforward treatment of "poetic"
material, free from any of the glozings of rhetoric—"Elegy
Written in a Country Churchyard" must seem the classical
instance. And by the same token, the "Elegy" would appear
to be the most difficult poem to subsume under the standard
theory of poetic structure.

In Gray's poem, the imagery does seem to be intrinsically
poetic; the theme, true; the "statement," free from ambiguity,
and free from irony. Indeed, I.A. Richards is able to use the
first stanza of the "Elegy" as an example of what he says "we
are apt to regard as the normal standard case" where "the
prose-sense appears to be the source of the rest of our
response," in contrast to that type of poetic structure (which
Richards illustrates by Blake's "Memory, hither come") in
which the "prose-sense" has little or nothing to do with the
reader's response.

It is noteworthy, however, that Richards writes "appears to
be the source," for we can conceive of the prose-sense as the
*exclusive* source of the poetic effect only as a limiting case. In
no actual poem is the reader's response determined solely by
the prose-sense. Still, what the "Elegy" "says" as poetry does
seem so close to what the prose-sense manages to say that the
reader is tempted to think of the prose-sense as the poetic
content, a content which in this poem is transmitted, essentially unqualified, to the reader by means of the poetic form,
which, in this case, merely supplies a discreet decoration to
the content.

There are a number of evidences, however, which ought to
put us on our guard against accepting so simple an account of
the relation of form to content, even in this poem. For
example, there are the Milton references with which the
poem, as has frequently been pointed out, is suffused. The
rude forefathers of the village not only have in their com-

pany "mute inglorious Miltons." They are conceived of as young Miltonic swains: "How jocund did they drive their team afield"—just as, "Under the opening eye-lids of the morn," Lycidas and his companion "drove a field." Or consider the famous "Full many a gem" stanza. I suspect that the gem which "the dark unfathom'd caves of ocean bear" and the flower "born to blush unseen" derive ultimately from the great speech of Comus with its "unsought diamonds" from "the Deep" and, ten lines down, its "neglected rose" that "withers on the stalk"—though Gray himself may well have been unconscious of the Miltonic echo.

Some of the echoes Gray was plainly conscious of, as his specification of some of them in his notes would indicate; and many of them are from Milton, though many others are not. One of the non-Miltonic echoes which seems clearly resonant to me but which Gray does not mention (and of which perhaps he was not conscious) is that of the "Dying Emperor Hadrian to his Soul." In Prior's translation it runs:

> Poor little, pretty, flutt'ring Thing,
>     Must We no longer live together?
> And dost Thou preene thy trembling Wing,
>     To take the Flight Thou know'st not whither?
> Thy humorous Vein, thy pleasing Folly
>     Lyes all neglected, all forgot:
> And pensive, wav'ring, melancholy,
>     Thou dread'st and hop'st Thou know'st not what.

One may compare:

> For who, to dumb Forgetfulness a prey,
>     This pleasing anxious being e'er resigned,
> Left the warm precincts of the chearful day,
>     Nor cast one longing ling'ring look behind.

The "Elegy" is thus—like "The Waste Land"—a tissue of allusions and half-allusions. If the materials of which it is composed are "poetic," they have been made poetic by other poets. The point is not, surely, that as we read the "Elegy" we are to be fully conscious of all the references. But the audience for which Gray wrote and which gave its admiration to the poem was aware of many of them. We had therefore better not discount the effect of such allusions on an appreciation of the poem, even though it may be difficult to assess the particular function of each of them in detail. (How important they are may be judged by the response to the poem made by an audience which is *really* completely unaware of them: our public school system, it may be said, is rapidly providing such an audience for the purposes of making such a test.)

Yet, let me repeat, the precise modifications made by these allusions are difficult to assess and more difficult to prove. A better way to get at the alleged simplicity and directness of the "Elegy" is through an examination of its use of the conventional. Why is the poem rich and meaningful instead of merely trite and "conventional"? Do the conventional "materials" remain conventional, or are they somehow rendered dramatic and moving? And if they are rendered dramatic, how is this accomplished?

One can touch upon this question at an obvious level by considering the personifications. There are many of them in the "Elegy." Do they weigh the poem down beneath a clutter of lifeless eighteenth-century ornament, or do they come alive as convincing metaphors which carry the poem on the tide of their energy? Some of them, it must be confessed— "Let not Ambition mock their useful toil"—seem vulnerable to Coleridge's charge that they have acquired little more of the persóna than can be accorded by a capital letter.

The personifications, I think, can, as a matter of fact, be justified. But they cannot be justified in the conventional account. They are certainly not vivid and fresh metaphors. The personifications indeed furnish perhaps the sharpest instance of the general problem which the conventional accounts of the poem fail to solve. Such accounts of the poem cannot explain why the "large and general truths" of this poem, when expressed quite as clearly in other poems, and decorated there with materials out of the same poetic wardrobe, fail as the "Elegy" does not fail. On this point indeed the success of past criticism has not been so notable as to preclude another sort of account.

In the first place, it may be of interest to note that very little description is lavished upon the churchyard itself. There is stanza four, of course: "Beneath those rugged elms, etc." There are also, later in the poem, passing allusions to the "short and simple annals of the poor," to "this neglected spot," to the "frail memorial" with its "uncouth rhymes"— but these later references tend to be general, not specific. What the attention is focused on, even in the first stanzas, is not the graveyard itself, but what can be seen by a man standing in the graveyard: "the lowing herd wind slowly o'er the lea," the fading landscape, the ivy-mantled tower from which the owl hoots.

Even the dead, when the poet refers to them specifically, are described in terms of what they were—the village (in the churchyard of which they lie) as it was when the men were alive. It is primarily a village at dawn ("The breezy call of incense-breathing Morn") or a village at noon ("Oft did the harvest to their sickle yield"), not the night-shrouded village on which the speaker now looks out. And the one reference in this passage to the village at evening is to the village of the past when the "blazing hearth" burned for the return of the men who are now dead.

These points are perhaps too obvious to seem worth making. But there must be no mistake as to what is going on: the poem is not a simple mood piece, centered on the description of the churchyard itself. Certainly, the poem does not derive its vitality from either a "realistic" or a "poetic" description of the churchyard as such. (This is not to say that the "graveyard imagery" is not typical of the century, or that it does not have its importance. It *is* to say that the "graveyard imagery" does not, by its mere presence, convert the "Elegy" into a poem.)

Indeed, one can go further. The churchyard is described for the most part, not directly, but by contrast with its opposite: the great abbey church. And there are actually more references to the details of the abbey church as a burial place than to the details of the country churchyard itself.

This becomes plain when we see that the personifications are actually the allegoric figures, beloved by the eighteenth century, which clutter a great abbey church such as that at Bath or at Westminster. It is true that Gray does not restrict himself to the sculptured figures of Memory, Honor, Knowledge; and it is true that he calls some of them by their less flattering names: Ambition, Grandeur, Flattery, Luxury, Pride. But we recognize them clearly enough, even so. They wear the glazed "disdainful smile" of eighteenth-century mortuary sculpture. They take up the conventional attitudes of such sculpture: one leans to soothe the ear—one unrolls the lettered scroll. They are to be met with

*Where through the long-drawn aisle and fretted vault*
*The pealing anthem swells the note of praise.*

The marks of their identification seem plain enough. Even so, some readers may hesitate to accept it. Was Gray actually conscious of such a purpose? Is not such a device too witty, too ingenious for a poet of Gray's sensibility? But this is, if not to beg the question, at least to ask the question badly: for the self-consciousness of the artist is not necessarily involved. The appeal is to be made to the poem itself.

The rural graveyard in its simplicity calls up for the speaker memories of another kind of burial-place, one in which heraldry visibly makes its boast, and one filled with "storied urn" and "animated bust." "Honour," at least, it must be granted, is treated as one of the personifications on an allegorical monument:

> *Can storied urn or animated bust*
> *Back to its mansion call the fleeting breath?*
> *Can Honour's voice provoke the silent dust . . .*

But whether we treat the personifications as sculptures, or as terms used in the grandiloquent epitaphs, or merely as the poet's own projections of the pomp implied by the ornate burial-place—in any case, they are used ironically. That is to say, they are contrasted with the humble graves of the country churchyard, and they are meant, in contrast, to seem empty, flat, and lifeless. For "Honour" to possess more vitality as a metaphor would run counter to the intention of the poem. We can put the matter in this way: the more richly and dramatically realized "Honour" becomes, the more plausible it would be to feel that Honour could "provoke the silent dust." Conversely, the more fully dead, the more flatly abstract "Flatt'ry" is, the more absurdly ironical becomes its attempt to "soothe the dull cold ear of death." (There is, of course, here a further level of irony: "Flatt'ry" attempts what it cannot perform; but further, it is witless in its attempt to do what has already been done: the ear has been fully "soothed" already.)

Once we see that the purpose of the poem demands that the personifications be used ironically, one is allowed to see some of the supporting ironical devices. They are rich, and some of them are intricate. For example, the speaker asks "Ambition" not to mock the rustics' "homely joys." "Homely" would mean primarily "concerned with the home" —the children running to "lisp their sire's return"—with which the speaker has dealt in an earlier stanza. But "homely" probably still had the meanings (still preserved in America though it has died out in England) of "plain," unadorned. (Milton used it in this sense, and Shakespeare clearly employs it.)

"Grandeur" is not to smile at the "short and simple annals of the poor." Properly speaking, of course, the poor do not have "annals." Kingdoms have annals, and so do kings, but the peasantry does not. The choice of the term is ironical, and yet the "short and simple" records of the poor are their "annals"—the important records for them.

A more important and brilliant example of such irony occurs in the eleventh stanza. An "animated" bust would presumably be one into which the breath of life had been breathed—a speaking likeness, endowed by the chisel of the sculptor with the soul itself. But the most "animated" bust (*anima* = breath, soul) cannot call the fleeting *anima* of the dead man back to its "mansion." And the mansion receives its qualification in the next line: it is no more than silent dust.

Mr. William Empson has commented on the function of the images in the famous fourteenth stanza:

> What this means, as the context makes clear, is that eighteenth-century England had no scholarship system or *carrière ouverte aux talents*. This is stated as pathetic, but the reader is put into a mood in which one would not try to alter it. (It is true that Gray's society, unlike a possible machine society, was necessarily based on manual labor, but it might have used a man of special ability wherever he was born.) By comparing the social arrangement to Nature he makes it seem inevitable, which it was not, and gives it a dignity which was undeserved. Furthermore, a gem does not mind being in a cave and a flower prefers not to be picked; we feel that the man is like the flower, as short-lived, natural, and valuable, and this tricks us into feeling that he is better off without opportunities. The sexual suggestion of *blush* brings in the Christian idea that virginity is good in itself, and so that any renunciation is good; this may trick us into feeling it is lucky for the poor man that society keeps him unspotted from the World. The tone of melancholy claims that the poet understands the considerations opposed to aristocracy, though he judges against them; the truism of the reflections in the churchyard, the universality and impersonality this gives to the style, claim as if by comparison that we ought to accept the injustice of society as we do the inevitability of death.

As a counterpoise to the conventional view that sees in the gem-flower comparison only "decoration," this is excellent. But Empson, in his anxiety to establish the "latent political ideas," has extended the implications a little further than the total context of the whole poem warrants.

For the present it will be better to consider the further development the metaphors receive in the next stanza. The arrangement of the three instances is more subtle than it may at first glance seem. The "prose-sense," of course, is clear enough: a village Hampden is a Hampden *in petto;* a mute Milton, a man with the potentialities of a Milton without Milton's achievement; and the Cromwell of the case, one who had the potentialities of a Cromwell but who did not realize Cromwell's crimes. But the stanza suggests much more, and qualifies the prose-sense greatly. As we have already remarked, the three names really form a very cunningly contrived scale. We easily accept the "village Hampden," for his case is proved, and the comparison involved is a rather obvious one. He protests against tyranny, and thus is a petty Hampden, a "village" Hampden. We accept it the more readily because the implication that the village-Hampden might have, had fate placed him on a larger stage, been Hampden himself, is not pressed. But our acceptance of this case carries over to the next where it may help to secure conviction for the claim that the "mute inglorious Milton" might possibly have achieved Milton's glory had "Chill Penury" not "repress'd" his "noble rage"—though here there is no achievement—merely potential achievement, to be accepted on faith. The Cromwell example is, of course, the boldest item and makes most demand upon our acceptance. Here not even potentiality is stressed, but rather the negative virtues, the freedom from the Cromwellian crimes. We are asked to accept the fact that the guiltless Cromwell might have realized the virtues *because* the nonrealization of the crimes is proved.

The last line goes on to suggest the essentially ironical observation that there can be no *real* Cromwell without blood-guilt. This last point is very pertinent to the argument the following stanzas make: that the village Hampdens and Cromwells, had not "their lot forbade," might well have indulged in the worst of "heroic" crimes—waded through slaughter to a throne—or, that the mute inglorious Miltons might have committed the worst of artistic sins—might have heaped

> . . . *the shrine of Luxury and Pride*
> *With incense kindled at the Muse's flame.*

It is true, of course, that the speaker does not insist that this would have been the inevitable course that they must have taken had not their "lot forbade." The speaker has admitted

that they possessed "growing virtues" to be "circumscribed"
as well as "crimes" to be "confined." Yet the implied judgment is severely realistic: many of the "rude Forefathers"
would have ended in cruelty and empty vanity had they
"learn'd to stray" into the "paths of glory." The paths of
glory lead but to the grave, but so does the path along which
the "plowman homeward plods his weary way." The graves
are different, as we have seen. But both are graves—the fact
of death cannot be glossed over—this is the matter on which
Gray's irony exerts its force: not on the sentimental matter
which would try to make of the plowman's "narrow cell"
something less than a grave.

One last point before we leave this subject of what the
"rude Forefathers" might have become. The poet says that
"Their sober wishes never *learn'd* to stray." This constitutes
a careful inversion of the usual terms. One expects straying
to be "natural," not something to be learned. One "learns" to
*refrain* from straying. Knowledge has therefore conferred a
favor, whatever her intentions, in refusing to unroll "to their
eyes her ample page." For what Knowledge has to give is
associated with madness, not sobriety. The rustics' wishes
need no sobering discipline—they are already sober; "knowledge" would drive them into ignoble competition with the
rest of the "madding crowd." The description of the page of
Knowledge as "Rich with the spoils of time" is not literary
decoration. It is appropriate and it distinguishes Knowledge
as most men know it from the Science which we shall meet
with at the close of the poem.

Yet we misread the poem if we conclude that Gray is here
merely anxious to insist for the villagers, as for the Eton
schoolboys, that where "Ignorance is bliss / 'Tis folly to be
wise." He has not overly insisted upon their joys. The portrayal of them has been realistic, not sentimental. And it has
been impossible for them to be wise: it has not been a matter
of volition at all: "Their lot forbade. . . ." We shall not
come to an instance of choice until we come to the case that
concludes the poem.

But if the poem thus far has ended to contrast the country
churchyard and the abbey tombs, with the twentieth stanza
the two are drawn together once more. The contrast gives
perspective to the rustic churchyard, but the comparison is
used fairly. The abbey burial ground is, in its turn, humanized by the churchyard. Even the extravagances on
which the poet has looked sardonically are rooted finally in
something so deep that it can be found in the country

churchyard too: the churchyard has its memorials, though "frail," its rhymes, though "uncouth," and its sculpture, though "shapeless." If the passage carries on the contrast between the sumptuous magnificence of the ornate tombs and those other tombs of "this neglected" spot, and thus adds to the pathos of the rustic graves, it tends to account for the ornate tombs by making them, after all, the expression of a basic human impulse. The "Proud," thus, partake of the pathos in a queer, ironical fashion. For their attempts to hold on to "the warm precincts of the cheerful day"—attempts which the speaker has shown to be ineffectual—appear the more desperate in proportion as their luxury exceeds the simple tomb.

The Miltonic inversion of the twenty-second stanza supports the effect very nicely. "For who, to dumb Forgetfulness a prey," etc., can mean: for what man, having forgotten himself completely, ever left the cheerful day without casting back a look of regret. Actually most of us will read it as meaning: for what man ever resigned this being as a prey to oblivion without casting back one look of regret. But, on reflection, the two meanings tend to coalesce. To forget one's human nature sufficiently to be able cheerfully to leave the "warm precincts of the cheerful day" makes a demand as heroic as that of cheerfully resigning oneself to being forgotten by other men. In either case, one becomes the prey to "dumb Forgetfulness." The general commentary on death (which ends with line 92) has thus brought the proud and the humble together in a common humanity. The impulse to hold on to life—to strive against the encompassing oblivion—is to be found under the "yew-tree's shade" as well as beneath the "fretted vault." If the one has been treated with more pathos, the other with more irony, still neither can be effectual, and both in their anguish of attempt are finally deeply human.

The poet, it seems to me, carries very fairly here between both groups. To press, with Empson, the poet's complacency in seeming to accept the fate of the humble is to ignore these elements in the poem. Thomas Gray, as a man, may or may not have been guilty of such complacency. But we are not dealing with Gray's political ideas. We are dealing with what the "Elegy" "says"—something that is not quite the same thing.

Any doubt as to this last point should be dissipated by a consideration of the resolution of the poem. For what is the *speaker's* choice? After all, if the rude Forefathers of the village could not choose, since Knowledge did not unroll her ample page to them, *he* at least can choose. "Fair Science frown'd not on his humble birth." He *need* not be buried in the churchyard in which he actually wishes to be buried.

But before one goes on to examine the significance of his choice, it is well to begin with the first lines of the "resolution." With line 93 the speaker comes to apply the situation to himself. He should, therefore, be saying

> *For* me, *who, mindful of th' unhonour'd Dead*
> Do *in these lines their artless tale relate;*
> *If chance, by lonely contemplation led,*
> *Some kindred Spirit shall inquire* my *fate,* etc.

(In the first stanza the speaker was willing to say *me:* "And leaves the world to darkness and to me.") Dramatically, what has happened is that the meditation has gone on so fervently that in talking to himself, the speaker has lost his identity as an ego. The commentary that has been going on, though it has begun as that of the solitary observer, has become more general, more external. It would be a nice point to determine precisely *who* does speak this twenty-fourth stanza: the spirit of the place, the Muse, Melancholy, one side of the speaker's own nature? Presumably, the speaker is a part of the observer's own nature; but in any case, the observer is willing to be addressed in the second person: he is willing to see himself as he shall be, merely one with the others in the country churchyard.

We have said that this last section of the poem is to be considered the resolution of the poem: first, we have had the case of those who could not choose, the "rude Forefathers of the hamlet"; next, the Proud, who chose, but chose in vanity; lastly, there is the present case, the man who is able to choose, and chooses the "neglected spot" after all. But though his choice is a kind of vindication of the lot forced upon the rustics—a point which Empson's discussion of the poet's attitude fails to take into account—still, it will not do to insist upon the speaker's conscious choice lest it seem too smugly heroic; or to make his identification with the rustics too easy, lest it seem unrealistic. It is better that the "I" to be buried should treat that self as passive, as he does. Moreover, stanza twenty-four grows out of the preceding stanza: it is human for the parting soul to wish for an understanding friend:

> *E'en from the tomb the voice of Nature cries,*
> *E'en in our Ashes live their wonted Fires.*

The speaker does not attempt to sustain an inhumanly heroic role. He too yearns for "Some kindred Spirit" who shall inquire his fate; and he provides an epitaph to be read by that unknown friend. Furthermore, he sees clearly that his motives in keeping himself in obscurity—in confining himself to "the cool sequester'd vale of life"—will hardly be understood by the unlettered companions who accompany him through the vale. Their "sober wishes never learn'd" the vanity of straying from it; his, sobered by wisdom, have learned the folly of straying from it. They, saved by ignorance, cannot comprehend his saving knowledge. It is a nice touch, therefore, which has the observer envisage with complete realism the account of him which the "hoary-headed Swain" would necessarily give to the inquirer. To the Swain, he will be a creature pathetically inexplicable, and perhaps crazy:

> *Now drooping, woeful wan, like one forlorn,*
> *Or crazed with care, or crossed in hopeless love.*

It is significant that the hoary-headed Swain cannot read the epitaph, which might explain the observer's conduct and his choice. But even if he could read the epitaph, it is evident that he still could not understand it, for the implication is that only a "kindred Spirit" could understand. In its way, then, his own epitaph will be more lonely than the other epitaphs about it—those on which the name and years "spelt by th' unletter'd muse, / The place of fame and elegy supply."

And what of the epitaph itself? Does it furnish a proper climax for the poem? Or is it, after all, trite, flat, with an eighteenth-century tameness? Landor regarded it as a tin kettle tied to the tail of an otherwise noble poem; and certainly the epitaph has come in for very little praise ever since the poem was published. But before one undertakes to defend the epitaph as poetry, it is better to make sure first that we understand it—in itself, and in its relation to the rest of the poem.

To take up the first question (for the silence of the commentators here warns us that the explication had better not be taken for granted): what does the epitaph say in itself? In the first place, it implies the choice of which we have spoken in its very first line. His head will be laid upon the "lap of Earth"—the grave will be in the churchyard, not within the church. And the lines that follow have to do with the choice further: he will be unknown, but not because his "lot forbade." Fair Science did *not* frown upon his humble birth, as she has upon the humble birth of his companions in the churchyard. Why does the poet not go on to write: "But Melancholy . . ."? This would be an easier reading: that is, he had the knowledge requisite for entering into the competition for fame, but he was incapacitated by Melancholy. But the poet's choice of the conjunction "and" compels the richer reading: Melancholy is something more than a disease which rendered him unfit for the "madding crowd's ignoble strife." It is associated with "Fair Science," which in turn is differentiated by the association from the earlier "Knowledge" with which we might have been tempted to identify it. Melancholy becomes thus, in association with Science, a kind of wisdom which allows him to see through the vanities that delude the Proud.

"Large was his bounty. . . ." How? Because, like the widow's mite, what he gave to Misery represented his all. How did Heaven render him as largely prosperous? Because Heaven gave him everything that he could possibly wish. Are the oppositions here merely pertly ironical? If we take the epitaph in isolation, perhaps they are. But the ironies of this stanza have the whole of the poem behind them. This epitaph, which the speaker contemplates as one to which the kindred Spirit may be directed by the hoary-headed Swain, is to be read in the light of the commentary already made upon those that recite the short and simple annals of the poor, and those others that are dictated by "the pomp of pow'r." This epitaph commemorates one of the literally poor ("all he had, a tear") but it claims to be the epitaph of a man who was rich—in his bounty to the miserable, and in the possessions Heaven has showered upon him. (If, again, the paradox seem too easy, too brittle, we must in fairness take the stanza in terms of the context already established: there, it has certainly been implied that a true friend is the rarest of things. The trophies Memory raises over the tombs of the proud admit Flattery to their company.)

And now for the last stanza: is it modesty that requests the reader to seek no farther "his merits to disclose"? Two of the "merits" have already been disclosed. Have these two been chosen because they are modest and ordinary, or because they are in reality superlatively rare? If we are alive to the context, we can use both these answers: generosity to the poor and the proofs of Heaven's favor (in accomplishment, in achievement) are the common matter of epitaphs. In this sense, the speaker's imagined epitaph is thus typical and conventional. Yet these "merits" are more often boasted of rather than exemplified.

But there is a better reason still for the choice: the merits disclosed are those that have special reference to the opinion of the world: what Heaven bestowed, and what the recipient himself bestowed to the needy. Thus far the imagined epitaph complies with the demands of the world; for the rest, his other "merits" and his frailties—these have another reference. Knowledge of them is already possessed by the only Being who can judge them and thus the only Being to whom they are pertinent.

Even so, the reader may not be altogether convinced, as I am not altogether convinced, that the epitaph with which the poem closes is adequate. But surely its intended function is clear, and it is a necessary function if the poem is to have a structure and is not to be considered merely a loose collection of poetic passages.

Moreover, it ought to be equally clear that the epitaph is not to be judged in isolation. It is part of a context, and a very rich context. We have to read it in terms of the conditions for a certain dramatic propriety that the context sets up. Among those conditions are these: it must be a recognizable epitaph, even a humble epitaph, modest in what it says, and modest, perhaps even as an example of art. For it is the epitaph, after all, of a "Youth to Fortune and to Fame unknown." It must be closely related to the evening meditation in the churchyard, for it is an outgrowth of that meditation.

But what, then, of the "kindred Spirit" who may some day read it? How is he, coming upon the epitaph, and reading it, naked of the context of the whole meditation—what is he to be expected to make of it? It is all very well to treat the poem as a dramatic structure, but if we do, then will the epitaph for the "kindred Spirit" incorporate within itself enough of a qualifying context? Or will it not seem to him rather flat and bare? But the poet has evidently taken this question into account. The "kindred Spirit" must presumably know something of the youth, though "to Fortune and to Fame unknown," if he is to be able to inquire about his fate at all. He will come to the epitaph possessed by a proper mood, led to this spot by "lonely contemplation." And the fact that he is a "kindred Spirit" will supply for him much of the context which the poet has elaborately built up for us in the poem itself. Indeed, the poet has prepared us, the readers, to be the "kindred Spirit" if we wish. The poet has been too good a poet, in his practice at least, for him to rely here upon the "prose-sense" of the epitaph as such. Whatever its merit (or lack of merit) as a poem in its own right, it is not the "Elegy Written in a Country Churchyard," nor is the reader brought to it in isolation as the "kindred Spirit" may be, nor is Gray merely identical with the youth in the poem who is "to Fortune and to Fame unknown."

In the poem, as we have seen, the epitaph is set over against the "shapeless sculpture" of the churchyard and also over against the "storied urn" of the abbey church. We have tried to see what its relation to each is. But when we come to Gray himself, it is the whole "Elegy" that is *his* storied urn—it is the poem itself, the "lines" in which he relates the "artless tale" of the villagers—all the lines of the poem, the whole poem, taken as a poetic structure. As for the urn that stands beside the "animated bust," its stories are supposed to be the material proper to art, and surely, as the speaker of the poem envisages the storied urn, they have been treated artfully—in all the senses of that ambiguous word. By contrast, the "tale" the speaker of the poem undertakes to relate is admittedly "artless." It is conventionally regarded as matter that cannot be turned into art. It is artless in this sense because the men whose tale it is were themselves artless—too innocent, too simple to have a significant story. Their story is merely a tale; it is no more properly a set of "annals" than the tale of Donne's lovers is properly a "chronicle."

But is Gray's telling of the "artless tale" really artless? The tale is simple enough, to be sure; but is the telling simple: is the structure of the poem simple? Not, most of us will agree, in the sense that it lacks art—not in the sense that it is either a casual collection of poetic "materials" or in the sense that it is the "artless" rendition of a set of poetic truths. The "Elegy" has a structure, which we neglect at our peril if we mean to pass judgment on it as a poem, or even if we are merely to point to it as a poem. It is a "storied urn," after all, and, many of us will conclude that, like Donne's, it is a "well wrought urne," superior to the half-acre tombs of the Proud.

# WILLIAM COLLINS
[1721–1759]

## Ode to Evening

If aught of oaten stop, or pastoral song,
May hope, chaste Eve, to soothe thy modest ear,
 Like thy own solemn springs,
 Thy springs and dying gales;

O nymph reserved, while now the bright-hair'd sun  5
Sits in yon western tent, whose cloudy skirts,
 With brede ethereal wove,
 O'erhang his wavy bed:

Now air is hush'd save where the weak-eyed bat
With short shrill shriek flits by on leathern wing,  10
 Or where the beetle winds
 His small but sullen horn,

As oft he rises, 'midst the twilight path
Against the pilgrim borne in heedless hum:
 Now teach me, maid composed,  15
 To breathe some soften'd strain,

Whose numbers, stealing through thy darkening vale,
May not unseemly with its stillness suit,
 As, musing slow, I hail
 Thy genial loved return!  20

For when thy folding-star arising shows
His paly circlet, at his warning lamp
 The fragrant hours, and elves
 Who slept in buds the day,

And many a nymph who wreathes her brows with sedge,  25
And sheds the freshening dew, and, lovelier still,
 The pensive pleasures sweet,
 Prepare thy shadowy car:

Then lead, calm votaress, where some sheety lake
Cheers the lone heath, or some time-hallow'd pile,  30

Or upland fallows grey
Reflect its last cool gleam.

Or if chill blustering winds, or driving rain,
Prevent my willing feet, be mine the hut
    That from the mountain's side          35
    Views wilds and swelling floods,

And hamlets brown, and dim-discover'd spires,
And hears their simple bell, and marks o'er all
    Thy dewy fingers draw
    The gradual dusky veil.          40

While Spring shall pour his show'rs, as oft he wont,
And bathe thy breathing tresses, meekest Eve!
    While Summer loves to sport
    Beneath thy lingering light;

While sallow Autumn fills thy lap with leaves,      45
Or Winter, yelling through the troublous air,
    Affrights thy shrinking train,
    And rudely rends thy robes:

So long, regardful of thy quiet rule,
Shall Fancy, Friendship, Science, rose-lipp'd Health    50
    Thy gentlest influence own,
    And hymn thy favourite name!

WILLIAM COLLINS

*At the age of 14*
*The Bettmann Archive*

# David Daiches

COLLINS

ODE TO EVENING

The form of this unrhymed lyric was suggested by Milton's attempt to give some idea in English of a classical Latin verse-form in his rendering of the fifth ode of the first book of Horace's "Odes." Milton's translation begins:

> *What slender Youth bedew'd with liquid odours*
> *Courts thee on Roses in some pleasant Cave,*
> *Pyrrha for whom bind'st thou*
> *In wreaths thy golden Hair,*
> *Plain in thy neatness;* . . .

Collins' poem is quite different in subject and in tone, but like Milton's it attempts to achieve the effect of rhyme without actually employing rhyme. The regular alternation between two lines with five metrical feet and two lines with three produces an almost hypnotic effect, which is part of the quiet evening feeling the poet is trying to capture. The variation in vowel sounds is also deliberately contrived: the poem ought to be read aloud and the vowels listened to.

The regular placing throughout the poem of words suggesting quiet and a sense of almost reverential calm helps to establish the tone—"chaste," "soothe," "solemn," "reserved," "hush'd," "soften'd," "pensive," "calm," and many others. The "oaten stop or pastoral song" to which the poet refers at the beginning suggests the traditional classical pastoral mode: he offers this pastoral meditation as a tribute to the special kind of reflective mood which he associates with evening. It is interesting that the opening sentence is not at once completed. "*If* aught of oaten stop . . . may hope . . . to soothe thy modest ear"—*then*, one expects to find, perhaps pastoral effort may do so. But the poet gets carried into his mood-creating description of the evening before he has had time to finish this thought: evening takes control, as it were, and the poet succumbs to it.

The poem has an extraordinary *flow*, which leads on in its

winding way sometimes at the expense of syntactical clarity. There is a delicate formality about the language. This formality is indicated at the beginning by the personification of evening ("chaste Eve"; Collins originally had "O pensive Eve," then altered it), who is addressed with a kind of shy courtliness. Eve's ear is "modest": the poet must be gentle and—in the best sense of the word—conventional in his language. The diction of the poem is in the tradition of poetic diction that the eighteenth century developed from Joshua Sylvester's translation of Du Bartas and George Sandys' translation of Ovid in the seventeenth century. Thus "gale" had in eighteenth century poetry the very specific meaning of "gentle breeze" and it is in this sense that Collins uses the word in line 4. The two lines

*Like thy own solemn springs,*
*Thy springs and dying gales*

also illustrate a use of repetition which is bound up with the continuous flow already referred to. First the springs stand by themselves as "solemn springs," then they appear, this time without any adjective, in association with "dying gales." The progression, noun-with-adjective, noun alone, new-noun-with-new-adjective produces a curious winding motion; that motion is emphasized, too, by the devices Collins uses to draw out the poem—if not into a single sentence then at least into something that, when read aloud, sounds very like it. "*While now* the bright-hair'd sun . . . yon western tent, *whose cloudy skirts* . . . air is hush'd *save where* the weak-eyed bat . . . *or where* . . ." and so the flow goes on. At first sight, "now teach me" in line 15 seems to be the opening of a new sentence; but careful rereading suggests that this is the lost balancing clause we looked for earlier in vain as the counterpart of the opening "if." The sense thus would be: "If any pastoral poem may please you, chaste Eve, now, while the evening sights and sounds rise before me, teach me to compose an appropriate poem." So line 15 does not mark a new beginning, but continues the flow, which is maintained with such binding words and constructions as "*whose* numbers . . . *as*, musing slow, I hail . . . *for when* . . . *who* slept in buds . . . *then* lead . . . *or if* . . . *while* Spring . . . *or* Winter . . *so* long . . . shall. . . ."

Personification is not confined to the evening. "The bright-hair'd sun / Sits in yon western tent" and "The pensive pleasures sweet / Prepare thy shadowy car." This lies somewhere between personification and mythology, suggesting a

half-commitment to classical myth which gives just that air
of shyness, or tentative moves towards an acceptable poem
("If aught of oaten stop . . . may hope, chaste Eve, to soothe
thy modest ear") that represents the stance of the poet from
the beginning. As the poet builds up his impressions of
evening mood, "musing slow," the images with the drowsy
effect of the repeated use of disyllabic adjective followed by
monosyllabic noun ("weak-eyed bat," "leathern wing," "twilight path," "heedless hum," "soften'd strain," "darkening
vale," "sheety lake," etc.) steadily create the suggestion of
human feeling responding to natural objects. There is a
careful placing of the poet with respect to the different mood-
producing objects, which sometimes he approaches ("Then
lead, calm votaress . . .") and sometimes sees from a distance
("dim-discover'd spires"). The original scene suggests a summer evening, but in the latter part of the poem the poet
builds up brief suggestions of the different way evening looks
in different seasons, again with that half-mythologizing,
which is reminiscent of the second stanza of Keats's "To
Autumn":

> *While sallow Autumn fills thy lap with leaves;*
> *Or Winter, yelling through the troublous air,*
> *Affrights thy shrinking train.*

In the end, human feeling responding to natural objects links
the two worlds of man and of nature securely together, so
that "Fancy, Friendship, Science [a word that had a much
wider meaning in the eighteenth century than it now has],
rose-lipp'd Health" own the influence of the evening scene
and join in celebrating it.

The poem depends heavily on its adjectives. In addition to
the special kind of adjectives preceding monosyllabic nouns
already mentioned, there are mood-producing adjectives such
as "*last cool* gleam," "*dewy* fingers," "*dusky* veil," "*lingering*
light." And there are carefully devised, set descriptions of
appropriate evening-objects, reminiscent sometimes of Gray's
"Elegy" and sometimes of Keats's "Autumn," such as:

> *Now air is hush'd save where the weak-ey'd bat,*
> *With short shrill shriek flits by on leathern wing,*
> *Or where the beetle winds*
> *His small but sullen horn,*

> *As oft he rises, 'midst the twilight path*
> *Against the pilgrim borne in heedless hum.*

This reminds us of Gray's:

> *Now fades the glimmering landscape on the sight,*
> *And all the air a solemn stillness holds,*
> *Save where the beetle wheels his droning flight,*
> *And drowsy tinklings lull the distant folds,*

also of Keats's

> *Then in a wailful choir the small gnats mourn*
> *Among the river sallows, borne aloft*
> *Or sinking as the light wind lives or dies.*

Notice also the effective way in which Collins suggests the utter stillness of the evening broken by the bat's screams: "with short shrill shriek flits by" is a succession of cutting monosyllables which cut into the hush of the poem as the bat's cry cuts into the hush of the evening.

This is one of the few really successful English poems written in a wholly formal meter yet without rhyme. In this respect it is comparable to the otherwise very different poem of the Elizabethan Thomas Campion, "Rose-Cheek'd Laura," which was also written to provide an English rhymeless equivalent of a Latin classical meter.

CHRISTOPHER SMART

*Pembroke Library, Cambridge*

# CHRISTOPHER SMART

[1722–1771]

## A Song to David

O thou, that sit'st upon a throne,
With harp of high majestic tone,
    To praise the King of kings:
And voice of heav'n-ascending swell,
Which, while its deeper notes excel,        5
    Clear, as a clarion, rings:

To bless each valley, grove and coast,
And charm the cherubs to the post
    Of gratitude in throngs;
To keep the days on Zion's mount,        10
And send the year to his account,
    With dances and with songs:

O Servant of God's holiest charge,
The minister of praise at large,
    Which thou may'st now receive;        15
From thy blest mansion hail and hear,
From topmost eminence appear
    To this the wreath I weave.

Great, valiant, pious, good, and clean,
Sublime, contemplative, serene,        20
    Strong, constant, pleasant, wise!
Bright effluence of exceeding grace;
Best man!—the swiftness and the race,
    The peril, and the prize!

Great—from the lustre of his crown,        25
From Samuel's horn, and God's renown,
    Which is the people's voice;
For all the host, from rear to van,
Applauded and embrac'd the man—
    The man of God's own choice.        30

Valiant—the word, and up he rose—
The fight—he triumph'd o'er the foes,

Whom God's just laws abhor;
And arm'd in gallant faith he took
Against the boaster, from the brook,      35
    The weapons of the war.

Pious—magnificent and grand;
'Twas he the famous temple plann'd:
    (The seraph in his soul)
Foremost to give the Lord his dues,      40
Foremost to bless the welcome news,
    And foremost to condole.

Good—from Jehudah's genuine vein,
From God's best nature good in grain,
    His aspect and his heart;      45
To pity, to forgive, to save,
Witness En-gedi's conscious cave,
    And Shimei's blunted dart.

Clean—if perpetual prayer be pure,
And love, which could itself inure      50
    To fasting and to fear—
Clean in his gestures, hands, and feet,
To smite the lyre, the dance complete,
    To play the sword and spear.

Sublime—invention ever young,      55
Of vast conception, tow'ring tongue,
    To God th' eternal theme;
Notes from yon exaltations caught,
Unrivall'd royalty of thought,
    O'er meaner strains supreme.      60

Contemplative—on God to fix
His musings, and above the six
    The sabbath-day he blest;
'Twas then his thoughts self-conquest prun'd,
To bless and bear the rest.
    And heavenly melancholy tun'd,      65

Serene—to sow the seeds of peace,
Rememb'ring, when he watch'd the fleece,
    How sweetly Kidron purl'd—
And plant perpetual paradise
To further knowledge, silence vice,      70
    When God had calm'd the world.

Strong—in the Lord, who could defy
Satan, and all his powers that lie

In sempiternal night;                                    75
And hell, and horror, and despair
Were as the lion and the bear
 To his undaunted might.

Constant—in love to God THE TRUTH,
Age, manhood, infancy, and youth—    80
 To Jonathan his friend
Constant, beyond the verge of death;
And Ziba, and Mephibosheth,
 His endless fame attend.

Pleasant—and various as the year;    85
Man, soul, and angel, without peer,
 Priest, champion, sage and boy;
In armour, or in ephod clad,
His pomp, his piety was glad;
 Majestic was his joy.    90

Wise—in recovery from his fall,
Whence rose his eminence o'er all,
 Of all the most revil'd;
The light of Israel in his ways,
Wise are his precepts, prayer and praise,    95
 And counsel to his child.

  *  *  *  *

For ADORATION all the ranks
Of angels yield eternal thanks,
 And DAVID in the midst;
With God's good poor, which, last and least    100
In man's esteem, thou to thy feast,
 O blessed bridegroom, bidst.

For ADORATION seasons change,
And order, truth, and beauty range,
 Adjust, attract, and fill:    105
The grass the polyanthus cheques;
And polish'd porphyry reflects,
 By the descending rill.

Rich almonds colour to the prime
For ADORATION; tendrils climb,    110
 And fruit-trees pledge their gems;
And Ivis with her gorgeous vest
Builds for her eggs her cunning nest,
 And bell-flowers bow their stems.

With vinous syrup cedars spout;                          115
From rocks pure honey gushing out,
  For ADORATION springs:
All scenes of painting crowd the map
Of nature; to the mermaid's pap
  The scaled infant clings.                              120

The spotted ounce and playsome cubs
Run rustling 'mongst the flow'ring shrubs,
  And lizards feed the moss;
For ADORATION beasts embark,
While waves upholding halcyon's ark                      125
  No longer roar and toss.

While Israel sits beneath his fig,
With coral root and amber sprig
  The wean'd advent'rer sports;
Where to the palm the jasmin cleaves,                    130
For ADORATION 'among the leaves
  The gale his peace reports.

Increasing days their reign exalt,
Nor in the pink and mottled vault
  Th' opposing spirits tilt;                             135
And, by the coasting reader spy'd,
The silverlings and crusions glide
  For ADORATION gilt.

For ADORATION rip'ning canes
And cocoa's purest milk detains                          140
  The western pilgrim's staff;
Where rain in clasping boughs inclos'd,
And vines with oranges dispos'd,
  Embower the social laugh.

Now labour his reward receives,                          145
For ADORATION counts his sheaves
  To peace, her bounteous prince;
The nectarine his strong tint imbibes,
And apples of ten thousand tribes,
  And quick peculiar quince.                             150

The wealthy crops of whit'ning rice
'Mongst thyine woods and groves of spice,
  For ADORATION grow;
And, marshall'd in the fenced land,
The peaches and pomegranates stand,                      155
  Where wild carnations blow.

The laurels with the winter strive;
The crocus burnishes alive
   Upon the snow-clad earth.
For ADORATION myrtles stay
To keep the garden from dismay,
   And bless the sight from dearth.

The pheasant shews his pompous neck;
And ermine, jealous of a speck,
   With fear eludes offence:
The sable, with his glossy pride,
For ADORATION is descried,
   Where frosts the wave condense.

The cheerful holly, pensive yew,
And holy thorn, their trim renew;
   The squirrel hoards his nuts:
All creatures batten o'er their stores,
And careful nature all her doors,
   For ADORATION shuts.

For ADORATION, DAVID's Psalms
Lift up the heart to deeds of alms;
   And he, who kneels and chants,
Prevails his passions to control,
Finds meat and med'cine to the soul,
   Which for translation pants.

For ADORATION, beyond match,
The scholar bulfinch aims to catch
   The soft flue's iv'ry touch;
And, careless on the hazel spray,
The daring redbreast keeps at bay
   The damsel's greedy touch.

For ADORATION, in the skies,
The Lord's philosopher espies
   The Dog, the Ram, and Rose;
The planet's ring, Orion's sword;
Nor is his greatness less ador'd
   In the vile worm that glows.

For ADORATION on the strings
The western breezes work their wings,
   The captive ear to soothe.—
Hark! 'tis a voice—how still, and small—
That makes the cataracts to fall,
   Or bids the sea be smooth.

For ADORATION, incense comes
From bezoar, and Arabian gums;        200
   And from the civet's furr:
But as for pray'r, or ere it faints,
Far better is the breath of saints
   Than galbanum and myrrh.

For ADORATION, from the down        205
Of dam'sins to th' anana's crown,
   God sends to tempt the taste;
And while the luscious zest invites,
The sense, that in the scene delights,
   Commands desire be chaste.        210

For ADORATION, all the paths
Of grace are open, all the baths
   Of purity refresh;
And all the rays of glory beam
To deck the man of God's esteem,        215
   Who triumphs o'er the flesh.

For ADORATION, in the dome
Of Christ the sparrows find an home;
   And on his olives perch:
The swallow also dwells with thee,        220
O man of God's humility,
   Within his Saviour's CHURCH.

Sweet is the dew that falls betimes,
And drops upon the leafy limes;
   Sweet Hermon's fragrant air:        225
Sweet is the lily's silver bell,
And sweet the wakeful tapers smell
   That watch for early pray'r.

Sweet the young nurse with love intense,
Which smiles o'er sleeping innocence;        230
   Sweet when the lost arrive:
Sweet the musician's ardour beats,
While his vague mind's in quest of sweets,
   The choicest flow'rs to hive.

Sweeter in all the strains of love,        235
The language of thy turtle dove,
   Pair'd to thy swelling chord;
Sweeter with ev'ry grace endu'd,
The glory of thy gratitude,
   Respir'd unto the Lord.        240

Strong is the horse upon his speed;
Strong in pursuit the rapid glede,
    Which makes at once his game;
Strong the tall ostrich on the ground;
Strong through the turbulent profound          245
    Shoots xiphias to his aim.

Strong is the lion—like a coal
His eyeball—like a bastion's mole
    His chest against the foes:
Strong the gier-eagle on his sail,          250
Strong against tide, th' enormous whale
    Emerges, as he goes.

But stronger still, in earth and air,
And in the sea, the man of pray'r:
    And far beneath the tide;          255
And in the seat to faith assign'd,
Where ask is have, where seek is find,
    Where knock is open wide.

Beauteous the fleet before the gale;
Beauteous the multitudes in mail,          260
    Rank'd arms and crested heads:
Beauteous the garden's umbrage mild,
Walk, water, meditated wild,
    And all the bloomy beds.

Beauteous the moon full on the lawn;          265
And beauteous, when the veil's withdrawn,
    The virgin to her spouse:
Beauteous the temple deck'd and fill'd,
When to the heav'n of heav'ns they build
    Their heart-directed vows.          270

Beauteous, yea beauteous more than these,
The shepherd king upon his knees,
    For his momentous trust;
With wish of infinite conceit,
For man, beast, mute, the small and great,          275
    And prostrate dust to dust.

Precious the bounteous widow's mite:
And precious, for extreme delight,
    The largess from the churl:
Precious the ruby's blushing blaze,          280
And alba's blest imperial rays,
    And pure cerulean pearl.

Precious the penitential tear;
And precious is the sigh sincere,
    Acceptable to God:                          285
And precious are the winning flow'rs,
In gladsome Israel's feast of bow'rs,
    Bound on the hallow'd sod.

More precious that diviner part
Of David, ev'n the Lord's own heart,            290
    Great, beautiful, and new:
In all things where it was intent,
In all extremes, in each event,
    Proof-answ'ring true to true.

Glorious the sun in mid career;                 295
Glorious th' assembled fires appear;
    Glorious the comet's train:
Glorious the trumpet and alarm;
Glorious th' almighty stretch'd-out arm;
    Glorious th' enraptur'd main:               300

Glorious the northern lights astream;
Glorious the song, when God's the theme:
    Glorious the thunder's roar:
Glorious hosanna from the den;
Glorious the catholic amen;                     305
    Glorious the martyr's gore:

Glorious—more glorious is the crown
Of Him, that brought salvation down
    By meekness, call'd thy Son;
Thou that stupendous truth believ'd,            310
And now the matchless deed's achiev'd,
    DETERMIN'D, DAR'D, and DONE.

# James Dickey

---

### SMART

#### A SONG TO DAVID

How shall we deal with the mad in their perfect disguises?
From the beginning we have suspected them of magic and
have wanted what they have, the revelations. But how may
we come by these and still retain our own sanity? What must
*we* do in order to connect safely with the insane at their clairvoyant and dangerous levels? One may have heard "A Song
to David" referred to, for example, as "the great mad song of
Smart," and may perhaps also have heard in a twentieth century dream that verses of it were inscribed on the walls of
eighteenth century Bedlam. What happens, then, when one
goes into the poem, clutching sanity like an amulet but with
the mind apprehensively and avidly trembling for the lightning of another man's self-destructive revelations?

At first there is simple disappointment. There seems little
magic to it, little madness. There is only the rhyme scheme
A-A-B-C-C-B with all but the three-beat B lines regular
four-beat English tetrameter, surely the strictest and unlike-
liest of corsets for the dancing of biblical frenzy that one has
heard the poem is. At first one may be reminded of another
poet's—Robert Lowell's—reference to madness, to "its hackneyed speech, its homicidal eye," and may reflect that,
though the hackneyed speech is pretty much in evidence here,
the flash of true madness, the homicidal angel-seeing eye, is
not. And yet, and yet. . . .

It is a poem about the musician David, whom Smart sees as
a kind of Old Testament Orpheus. And, as one imagines was
true of the Orphic song, the effect of the poem is really in the
rapt continuation rather than in the first notes. Slowly begun,
the ecstasy and wildness grow, the weird and wonderful and
yet natural-seeming comparisons pile tirelessly on each other,
the tempo keeps pushing up and up, the certitude increases,
the poem rises from plateau to plateau of affirmation, and the
control over the stanza is as complete at the end as it was at
the unpromising beginning. It may very well be that "A Song
to David" *is* the ultimate mad song, combining reason and un-

reason, inspiration and the strictest of forms, wedding the impossible and the mundane, the visionary and the prosaic in hard-headed English raised to the unlikely altitude of prophecy. Yet, odd as it is, it is not the *practicality* of Smart's obsessed, obsessive vision that we keep holding our breaths over, but rather what seems at every moment to be showing through the form: the possibility that this poem, so obviously and historically and certifiably mad, may indeed, could we but grasp it whole, give us what we have always wanted from the insane: the life-extending, life-deepening insight, the ultimate symbolic sanity.

The poem is made of genius-flashes full of the concealing-cunning of the lunatic: madness dictating the pious, predictable rhymes to which, because of genius, something unpredictable has happened. It is this wild freshness, the fanatical shrewdness, the God's-idiot mysterious confidence and clearness of it, that makes it the marvellous poem it is. Note, for instance, the peculiar and superb use of the Greek alphabet as a system which includes anything and everything there is, subsumed in the days of the week, the days of God's creation of the world, and so on. Look at the unforgettable phrases that Smart seems able to throw in anywhere without traducing his meters or his meaning: phrases like "look upward to the past," and "the Lord is just and glad." Long as it is, the poem is filled with marvels, and they seem to engender each other as effortlessly as the stanzas fulfill their rhymes. It is one of the most joyous and inventive prayers ever prayed, one of the most individual and mysterious, and probably one of the most Godlike. One hopes fervently that Dr. Johnson sensed something or all of this when he said "I'd as lief pray with Kit Smart as with any man"; a prayer with Kit Smart is likely to lift you straight off the floor, or off the London pavements where he frequently knelt.

Smart is a more commonsensical or madder Blake. "A Song to David" is "a glorious hosannah from the den," a wild, well-ordered rereading of part of the Bible as though it were a pagan sun-myth, and it leaves us with an uneasy and exalted feeling: that there is nothing in any poetry to match the madman who rhymes; that poetic forms, for so long worn threadbare by the empty rehearsal of their mere conventions, are renewable only under such perilous conditions; that it takes this, madness, but that once the thing is shown—determined, dared, and done—then both strict poetic forms and the language that uses them have a new chance, a new breathing-space under heaven.

# OLIVER GOLDSMITH

[1728–1774]

## *The Deserted Village*

Sweet Auburn! loveliest village of the plain,
Where health and plenty cheer'd the labouring swain,
Where smiling spring its earliest visit paid,
And parting summer's lingering blooms delay'd:
Dear lovely bowers of innocence and ease, 5
Seats of my youth, when every sport could please,
How often have I loiter'd o'er thy green,
Where humble happiness endear'd each scene;
How often have I paus'd on every charm,
The shelter'd cot, the cultivated farm, 10
The never-failing brook, the busy mill,
The decent church that topp'd the neighbouring hill,
The hawthorn bush, with seats beneath the shade,
For talking age and whisp'ring lovers made;
How often have I bless'd the coming day, 15
When toil remitting lent its turn to play,
And all the village train, from labour free,
Led up their sports beneath the spreading tree;
While many a pastime circled in the shade,
The young contending as the old survey'd; 20
And many a gambol frolick'd o'er the ground,
And sleights of art and feats of strength went round;
And still as each repeated pleasure tir'd,
Succeeding sports the mirthful band inspir'd;
The dancing pair that simply sought renown, 25
By holding out to tire each other down;
The swain mistrustless of his smutted face,
While secret laughter titter'd round the place;
The bashful virgin's side-long looks of love,
The matron's glance that would those looks reprove: 30
These were thy charms, sweet village; sports like these,
With sweet succession, taught e'en toil to please;
These round thy bowers their cheerful influence shed,
These were thy charms—But all these charms are fled.

Sweet smiling village, loveliest of the lawn,    35
Thy sports are fled, and all thy charms withdrawn;
Amidst thy bowers the tyrant's hand is seen,
And desolation saddens all thy green:
One only master grasps the whole domain,
And half a tillage stints thy smiling plain:    40
No more thy glassy brook reflects the day,
But chok'd with sedges, works its weedy way.
Along thy glades, a solitary guest,
The hollow-sounding bittern guards its nest;
Amidst thy desert walks the lapwing flies,    45
And tires their echoes with unvaried cries.
Sunk are thy bowers in shapeless ruin all,
And the long grass o'ertops the mould'ring wall;
And trembling, shrinking from the spoiler's hand,
Far, far away, thy children leave the land.    50

Ill fares the land, to hast'ning ills a prey,
Where wealth accumulates, and men decay:
Princes and lords may flourish, or may fade;
A breath can make them, as a breath has made;
But a bold peasantry, their country's pride,    55
When once destroy'd, can never be supplied.

A time there was, ere England's griefs began,
When every rood of ground maintain'd its man;
For him light labour spread her wholesome store,
Just gave what life requir'd, but gave no more:    60
His best companions, innocence and health;
And his best riches, ignorance of wealth.

But times are alter'd; trade's unfeeling train
Usurp the land and dispossess the swain;
Along the lawn, where scatter'd hamlets rose.    65
Unwieldy wealth, and cumbrous pomp repose;
And every want to opulence allied,
And every pang that folly pays to pride.
Those gentle hours that plenty bade to bloom,
Those calm desires that ask'd but little room,    70
Those healthful sports that grac'd the peaceful scene,
Liv'd in each look, and brighten'd all the green;
These, far departing, seek a kinder shore,
And rural mirth and manners are no more.

Sweet AUBURN! parent of the blissful hour,    75
Thy glades forlorn confess the tyrant's power.
Here as I take my solitary rounds,

OLIVER GOLDSMITH

*From the painting by*
*Sir Joshua Reynolds*

**The Bettmann Archive**

Amidst thy tangling walks, and ruin'd grounds,
And, many a year elaps'd, return to view
Where once the cottage stood, the hawthorn grew,                    80
Remembrance wakes with all her busy train,
Swells at my breast, and turns the past to pain.

In all my wand'rings round this world of care,
In all my griefs—and GOD has given my share—
I still had hopes my latest hours to crown,                    85
Amidst these humble bowers to lay me down;
To husband out life's taper at the close,
And keep the flame from wasting by repose.
I still had hopes, for pride attends us still,
Amidst the swains to show my book-learn'd skill,                    90
Around my fire an evening group to draw,
And tell of all I felt, and all I saw;
And, as a hare, whom hounds and horns pursue,
Pants to the place from whence at first she flew,
I still had hopes, my long vexations pass'd,                    95
Here to return—and die at home at last.

O blest retirement, friend to life's decline,
Retreats from care, that never must be mine,
How happy he who crowns in shades like these,
A youth of labour with an age of ease;                    100
Who quits a world where strong temptations try
And, since 'tis hard to combat, learns to fly!
For him no wretches, born to work and weep,
Explore the mine, or tempt the dangerous deep;
No surly porter stands in guilty state                    105
To spurn imploring famine from the gate;
But on he moves to meet his latter end,
Angels around befriending Virtue's friend;
Bends to the grave with unperceiv'd decay,
While Resignation gently slopes the way;                    110
And, all his prospects bright'ning to the last,
His Heaven commences ere the world be pass'd!

Sweet was the sound, when oft at evening's close
Up yonder hill the village murmur rose;
There, as I pass'd with careless steps and slow,                    115
The mingling notes came soften'd from below,
The swain responsive as the milk-maid sung,
The sober herd that low'd to meet their young;
The noisy geese that gabbled o'er the pool,
The playful children just let loose from school;                    120

The watchdog's voice that bay'd the whisp'ring wind,
And the loud laugh that spoke the vacant mind;
These all in sweet confusion sought the shade,
And fill'd each pause the nightingale had made.
But now the sounds of population fail,                                125
No cheerful murmurs fluctuate in the gale,
No busy steps the grass-grown foot-way tread,
For all the bloomy flush of life is fled.
All but yon widow'd, solitary thing
That feebly bends beside the plashy spring;                           130
She, wretched matron, forc'd, in age, for bread,
To strip the brook with mantling cresses spread,
To pick her wintry faggot from the thorn,
To seek her nightly shed, and weep till morn;
She only left of all the harmless train,                             135
The sad historian of the pensive plain.

Near yonder copse, where once the garden smil'd,
And still where many a garden flower grows wild;
There, where a few torn shrubs the place disclose,
The village preacher's modest mansion rose.                          140
A man he was to all the country dear,
And passing rich with forty pounds a year;
Remote from towns he ran his godly race,
Nor e'er had chang'd, nor wished to change his place;
Unpractis'd he to fawn, or seek for power,                           145
By doctrines fashion'd to the varying hour;
Far other aims his heart had learned to prize,
More skill'd to raise the wretched than to rise.
His house was known to all the vagrant train,
He chid their wand'rings, but reliev'd their pain;                   150
The long-remember'd beggar was his guest,
Whose beard descending swept his aged breast;
The ruin'd spendthrift, now no longer proud,
Claim'd kindred there, and had his claims allow'd;
The broken soldier, kindly bade to stay,                             155
Sat by his fire, and talk'd the night away;
Wept o'er his wounds, or tales of sorrow done,
Shoulder'd his crutch, and show'd how fields were won.
Pleas'd with his guests, the good man learn'd to glow,
And quite forgot their vices in their woe;                           160
Careless their merits, or their faults to scan,
His pity gave ere charity began.

Thus to relieve the wretched was his pride,
And e'en his failings lean'd to Virtue's side;

But in his duty prompt at every call,     165
He watch'd and wept, he pray'd and felt, for all.
And, as a bird each fond endearment tries
To tempt its new-fledg'd offspring to the skies,
He tried each art, reprov'd each dull delay,
Allur'd to brighter worlds, and led the way.     170

Beside the bed where parting life was laid,
And sorrow, guilt, and pain, by turns dismay'd,
The reverend champion stood. At his control,
Despair and anguish fled the struggling soul;
Comfort came down the trembling wretch to raise,     175
And his last falt'ring accents whisper'd praise.

At church, with meek and unaffected grace,
His looks adorn'd the venerable place;
Truth from his lips prevail'd with double sway,
And fools, who came to scoff, remain'd to pray.     180
The service pass'd, around the pious man,
With steady zeal, each honest rustic ran;
Even children follow'd with endearing wile,
And pluck'd his gown, to share the good man's smile.
His ready smile a parent's warmth express'd,     185
Their welfare pleas'd him, and their cares distress'd;
To them his heart, his love, his griefs were given,
But all his serious thoughts had rest in Heaven.
As some tall cliff, that lifts its awful form,
Swells from the vale, and midway leaves the storm,     190
Though round its breast the rolling clouds are spread,
Eternal sunshine settles on its head.

Beside yon straggling fence that skirts the way,
With blossom'd furze unprofitably gay,
There, in his noisy mansion, skill'd to rule,     195
The village master taught his little school;
A man severe he was, and stern to view;
I knew him well, and every truant knew;
Well had the boding tremblers learn'd to trace
The day's disasters in his morning face;     200
Full well they laugh'd, with counterfeited glee,
At all his jokes, for many a joke had he;
Full well the busy whisper, circling round,
Convey'd the dismal tidings when he frown'd;
Yet he was kind; or if severe in aught,     205
The love he bore to learning was in fault;
The village all declar'd how much he knew;

'Twas certain he could write, and cypher too;
Lands he could measure, terms and tides presage,
And e'en the story ran that he could gauge.     210
In arguing too, the parson own'd his skill,
For e'en though vanquish'd, he could argue still;
While words of learned length and thund'ring sound
Amazed the gazing rustics rang'd around,
And still they gaz'd, and still the wonder grew,     215
That one small head could carry all he knew.

But past is all his fame. The very spot
Where many a time he triumph'd, is forgot.
Near yonder thorn, that lifts its head on high,
Where once the sign-post caught the passing eye,     220
Low lies that house where nut-brown draughts inspir'd,
Where grey-beard mirth and smiling toil retir'd,
Where village statesmen talk'd with looks profound,
And news much older than their ale went round.
Imagination fondly stoops to trace     225
The parlour splendours of that festive place;
The white-wash'd wall, the nicely sanded floor,
The varnish'd clock that click'd behind the door;
The chest contriv'd a double debt to pay,
A bed by night, a chest of drawers by day;     230
The pictures plac'd for ornament and use,
The twelve good rules, the royal game of goose;
The hearth, except when winter chill'd the day,
With aspen boughs, and flowers, and fennel gay;
While broken tea-cups, wisely kept for show,     235
Rang'd o'er the chimney, glisten'd in a row.

Vain, transitory splendours! Could not all
Reprieve the tottering mansion from its fall!
Obscure it sinks, nor shall it more impart
An hour's importance to the poor man's heart;     240
Thither no more the peasant shall repair
To sweet oblivion of his daily care;
No more the farmer's news, the barber's tale,
No more the wood-man's ballad shall prevail;
No more the smith his dusky brow shall clear,     245
Relax his pond'rous strength, and lean to hear;
The host himself no longer shall be found
Careful to see the mantling bliss go round;
Nor the coy maid, half willing to be press'd,
Shall kiss the cup to pass it to the rest.     250

Yes! let the rich deride, the proud disdain,
These simple blessings of the lowly train;
To me more dear, congenial to my heart,
One native charm, than all the gloss of art;
Spontaneous joys, where Nature has its play,    255
The soul adopts, and owns their first-born sway;
Lightly they frolic o'er the vacant mind,
Unenvied, unmolested, unconfin'd:
But the long pomp, the midnight masquerade,
With all the freaks of wanton wealth array'd,    260
In these, ere triflers half their wish obtain,
The toiling pleasure sickens into pain;
And, e'en while fashion's brightest arts decoy,
The heart distrusting asks, if this be joy.

Ye friends to truth, ye statesmen, who survey    265
The rich man's joys increase, the poor's decay,
'Tis yours to judge, how wide the limits stand
Between a splendid and a happy land.
Proud swells the tide with loads of freighted ore,
And shouting Folly hails them from her shore;    270
Hoards, e'en beyond the miser's wish abound,
And rich men flock from all the world around.
Yet count our gains. This wealth is but a name
That leaves our useful products still the same.
Not so the loss. The man of wealth and pride    275
Takes up a space that many poor supplied;
Space for his lake, his park's extended bounds,
Space for his horses, equipage, and hounds;
The robe that wraps his limbs in silken sloth
Has robb'd the neighbouring fields of half their growth,    280
His seat, where solitary sports are seen,
Indignant spurns the cottage from the green;
Around the world each needful product flies,
For all the luxuries the world supplies:
While thus the land adorn'd for pleasure, all    285
In barren splendour feebly waits the fall.

As some fair female unadorn'd and plain,
Secure to please while youth confirms her reign,
Slights every borrow'd charm that dress supplies,
Nor shares with art the triumph of her eyes:    290
But when those charms are pass'd, for charms are frail,
When time advances, and when lovers fail,
She then shines forth, solicitous to bless,
In all the glaring impotence of dress.

Thus fares the land, by luxury betray'd,　　295
In nature's simplest charms at first array'd;
But verging to decline, its splendours rise,
Its vistas strike, its palaces surprise;
While scourg'd by famine from the smiling land,
The mournful peasant leads his humble band;　　300
And while he sinks, without one arm to save,
The country blooms—a garden, and a grave.

Where then, ah! where, shall poverty reside,
To 'scape the pressure of contiguous pride?
If to some common's fenceless limits stray'd,　　305
He drives his flock to pick the scanty blade,
Those fenceless fields the sons of wealth divide,
And e'en the bare-worn common is denied.

If to the city sped—What waits him there?
To see profusion that he must not share;　　310
To see ten thousand baneful arts combin'd
To pamper luxury, and thin mankind;
To see those joys the sons of pleasure know
Extorted from his fellow creature's woe.
Here, while the courtier glitters in brocade,　　315
There the pale artist plies the sickly trade;
Here, while the proud their long-drawn pomps display,
There the black gibbet glooms beside the way.
The dome where Pleasure holds her midnight reign
Here, richly deck'd, admits the gorgeous train;　　320
Tumultuous grandeur crowds the blazing square,
The rattling chariots clash, the torches glare.
Sure scenes like these no troubles e'er annoy!
Sure these denote one universal joy!
Are these thy serious thoughts?—Ah, turn thine eyes　　325
Where the poor houseless shiv'ring female lies.
She once, perhaps, in village plenty bless'd,
Has wept at tales of innocence distress'd;
Her modest looks the cottage might adorn,
Sweet as the primrose peeps beneath the thorn;　　330
Now lost to all; her friends, her virtue fled,
Near her betrayer's door she lays her head,
And, pinch'd with cold, and shrinking from the shower,
With heavy heart deplores that luckless hour,
When idly first, ambitious of the town,　　335
She left her wheel and robes of country brown.

Do thine, sweet AUBURN, thine, the loveliest train,
Do thy fair tribes participate her pain?

E'en now, perhaps, by cold and hunger led,
At proud men's doors they ask a little bread!        340

   Ah, no. To distant climes, a dreary scene,
Where half the convex world intrudes between,
Through torrid tracts with fainting steps they go,
Where wild Altama murmurs to their woe.
Far different there from all that charm'd before,        345
The various terrors of that horrid shore;
Those blazing suns that dart a downward ray,
And fiercely shed intolerable day;
Those matted woods where birds forget to sing,
But silent bats in drowsy clusters cling;        350
Those pois'nous fields with rank luxuriance crown'd,
Where the dark scorpion gathers death around;
Where at each step the stranger fears to wake
The rattling terrors of the vengeful snake;
Where crouching tigers wait their hapless prey,        355
And savage men more murd'rous still than they;
While oft in whirls the mad tornado flies,
Mingling the ravag'd landscape with the skies.
Far different these from every former scene,
The cooling brook, the grassy-vested green,        360
The breezy covert of the warbling grove,
That only shelter'd thefts of harmless love.

   Good heaven! what sorrows gloom'd that parting day,
That call'd them from their native walks away;
When the poor exiles, every pleasure pass'd,        365
Hung round their bowers, and fondly look'd their last,
And took a long farewell, and wish'd in vain
For seats like these beyond the western main;
And shudd'ring still to face the distant deep,
Return'd and wept, and still return'd to weep.        370
The good old sire, the first prepar'd to go
To new-found worlds, and wept for others' woe;
But for himself, in conscious virtue brave,
He only wish'd for worlds beyond the grave.
His lovely daughter, lovelier in her tears,        375
The fond companion of his helpless years,
Silent went next, neglectful of her charms,
And left a lover's for a father's arms.
With louder plaints the mother spoke her woes,
And bless'd the cot where every pleasure rose        380
And kiss'd her thoughtless babes with many a tear,
And clasp'd them close, in sorrow doubly dear;

Whilst her fond husband strove to lend relief
In all the silent manliness of grief.

O Luxury! thou curs'd by Heaven's decree,          385
How ill exchang'd are things like these for thee!
How do thy potions, with insidious joy
Diffuse their pleasures only to destroy!
Kingdoms, by thee, to sickly greatness grown,
Boast of a florid vigour not their own;          390
At every draught more large and large they grow,
A bloated mass of rank unwieldy woe;
Till sapp'd their strength, and every part unsound,
Down, down they sink, and spread a ruin round.

E'en now the devastation is begun,          395
And half the business of destruction done;
E'en now, methinks, as pond'ring here I stand,
I see the rural virtues leave the land:
Down where yon anchoring vessel spreads the sail,
That idly waiting flaps with ev'ry gale,          400
Downward they move, a melancholy band,
Pass from the shore, and darken all the strand.
Contented toil, and hospitable care,
And kind connubial tenderness, are there;
And piety, with wishes plac'd above,          405
And steady loyalty, and faithful love.
And thou, sweet Poetry, thou loveliest maid,
Still first to fly where sensual joys invade;
Unfit in these degenerate times of shame,
To catch the heart, or strike for honest fame;          410
Dear charming nymph, neglected and decried,
My shame in crowds, my solitary pride;
Thou source of all my bliss, and all my woe,
That found'st me poor at first, and keep'st me so;
Thou guide by which the nobler arts excel,          415
Thou nurse of every virtue, fare thee well!
Farewell, and Oh! where'er thy voice be tried,
On Torno's cliffs, or Pambamarca's side,
Whether where equinoctial fervours glow,
Or winter wraps the polar world in snow,          420
Still let thy voice, prevailing over time,
Redress the rigours of th' inclement clime;
Aid slighted truth; with thy persuasive strain
Teach erring man to spurn the rage of gain;
Teach him, that states of native strength possess'd,          425

Though very poor, may still be very bless'd;
That trade's proud empire hastes to swift decay,
As ocean sweeps the labour'd mole away;
While self-dependent power can time defy,
As rocks resist the billows and the sky.                    430

# Charles Tomlinson

## GOLDSMITH
## THE DESERTED VILLAGE

A critical exercise, commonly set for students, is to have them compare "The Deserted Village" (1770) with "The Village" by Crabbe (1783). They are supposed, by way of this comparison, to find Goldsmith guilty of idealizing Auburn, while Crabbe is the unremitting and therefore admirable realist. As dull people will always find dull reasons for demoting excellent poetry, it seems worthwhile urging the student not to take the comparison too seriously. Crabbe, with his thorough-going, though somewhat heavy-handed realism, has a different end in view from Goldsmith's. Both, however, are unanimous in pointing out genuine social evils in village life. Indeed, Goldsmith, in his dedicatory letter to Sir Joshua Reynolds, insists "I have taken all possible pains, in my country excursions, for these four or five years past, to be certain of what I allege; . . . all my views and inquiries have led me to believe those miseries real, which I here attempt to display." On the other side of the picture, if Goldsmith prefers to recall "the charms" of Auburn rather than the birth of every idiot or illegitimate child, there is a propriety in this, for the village no longer exists and he is concerned with recording those qualities that made its existence worthwhile. Furthermore, Auburn stands for the idea of a village, one that embodies—and the style of weighty generalization brings the notion alive—certain traditional and indispensable human virtues, a moderate way of living as against "unwieldy wealth, and cumbrous pomp" and "every want to opulence allied."

Auburn derives, to some extent, from the Irish village of Lissoy where Goldsmith lived as a child. But its fate is generalized to comprehend that of English villages he had seen. It is deserted because, in extending his private domain, its owner had turned the peasantry out of their houses. Thus:

*The robe that wraps his limbs in silken sloth*
*Has robb'd the neighbouring fields of half their growth*

[279–80]

The metaphorical force of this has something of the boldness of a later poet, William Blake, whose "Echoing Green,"
for all its differences, owes a debt to Goldsmith's own green
where all the generations, "the young contending as the old
survey'd," are united beneath "the spreading tree." The
detailed background behind such evictions as those of Lissoy
can be read in Kenneth Maclean's *The Agrarian Age*. And
yet to explain "The Deserted Village" simply in terms of its
economic and social theme, to drown the poem in a discussion about the relative merits of small holdings and large
ones, is to miss its deeper meaning. The decay of the village
society, which Goldsmith laments, supplies, rather, an image
of the frailty of all human society and of most human hopes.
It is this that gives the poem its almost Johnsonian sense of
"the vanity of human wishes": every character in it is
threatened and every vista points towards further miseries.
Appropriately enough, Johnson wrote the last four lines, and
from him Goldsmith clearly learned a certain massiveness of
effect, as in:

> *Ill fares the land, to hast'ning ills a prey,*
> *Where wealth accumulates, and men decay*
>
> [51-52]

Here, the latinate antithesis of the second line is given
urgency by that rapid metamorphosis of the adverb, *ill*, into
the plural noun, *ills*. The all-over tone of Goldsmith's poem
is, however, much lighter than Johnson's, the "melting sentiment," as Eliot has put it, "just saved by the precision of [the]
language." (*Poetry in the Eighteenth Century*) Half a century later, such a triumph of tone would become impossible and Goldsmith's genuine tenderness degenerated into
the parlor ballads of Tom Moore.

Suzanne Langer (*Feeling and Form*) draws attention to
the way Goldsmith's description of the village green (lines
9-24) is poetically articulated by its recurrence to the idea of
a dance ("lent its turn," "circled," "frolick'd o'er the
ground," "went round," "repeated," "succeeding"). She goes
on to complain that the poem weakens as it loses this kind of
musical coherence and its compactness is sacrificed for "moralizing" and "weak literal appeal." However, her image for
poetry (i.e., the symbolist one of its being "like music") does
not take us very far with a poem of this kind, where there is
so much direct statement and the poet means what he says.
The form is not that of the shorter symbolist or post-sym-
bolist poem that Mrs. Langer (and perhaps the modern

reader in general) would like it to be, but much closer to the logical layout of an essay (Goldsmith was, of course, a fluent essayist). There is room within such a poetic form for passages of varying intensity such as the symbolist-aesthetic scarcely permits. The form of the essay is heightened, as Donald Davie shows (*The Late Augustans*) by those "emotional reverberations of words whose logical connection is slight." The reverberations mostly reinforce that frailty we have already mentioned, and rural life, Davie comments, is associated with "the life of a flower, the bloom on the skin of fruit, trembling and shrinking and flying, murmurs on the wind, a guttering candle, a hunted hare."

"The Deserted Village" is also a poem based on many literary precedents: its author knew this, and wished his readers to know it. One of the pleasures of poetry for the eighteenth century was that of recognition. The feeling that what the great literature of the past had set its stamp on was of lasting human interest, permeated this pleasure. Thus for Johnson it was not "individual" emotions that mattered, but representative ones, "images which find a mirror in every mind, and . . . sentiments to which every bosom returns an echo." (*Life of Gray*) Johnson finds these in Gray's "Elegy," and they are there also in the precedents of "The Deserted Village." Its standards are such as have been rehearsed by countless classical authors and Biblical texts. It partakes of the shared morality of what has been called the English country house poem, a genre practiced by Jonson, Carew, Herrick, Marvell and Pope, and within which what has beauty is also useful—has memorable beauty, perhaps, *because* it is useful, like Goldsmith's "busy mill," "never-failing brook," "cultivated farm," "decent church." Classical literature from Homer onwards had had its place for types of ideal virtue, and here once more Goldsmith is following precedent—his parson and schoolmaster "ideal" certainly, but recognizably human, not cloyingly virtuous. The way in which Goldsmith brings before us his portraits of types is deliberately "literary," done in the manner of previous authors. Far from covering his tracks, he quotes, in lines 141–42, directly from one of the most famous of poetic galleries—Chaucer's "Prologue":

> *A man he was to all the country dear,*
> *And passing rich with forty pounds a year*

Whittier, in "Snow-Bound," displays a similar awareness of writing within a portrait genre.

Precedent shows itself again in two memorable images—
that in which Goldsmith compares the parson to "some tall
cliff" with clouds at its base but its top in sunshine (lines
189–92), and another where the state becomes, so to speak,
the body politic (lines 389–94). The first of these images has
many sources in Latin literature and French, and Young had
used it in his "Night Thoughts." Shakespeare, to give only
one example, plays many variations on the second. Goldsmith
is also consciously variating on a traditional notion and his
achievement in doing so is to be measured by the force of his
language:

> *Kingdoms, by thee [luxury], to sickly greatness grown,*
> *Boast of a florid vigour not their own* [389–390]

"Florid" as applied to "vigour" is perfect, and so is the
expression of the gigantism of growth and overthrow in the
lines that come next.

This exactness of language is something the reader can
discover for himself; and its continual and various deftness is
what makes "The Deserted Village" a superior poem to the
one-key "Village" of Crabbe. Consider the verb, "works,"
and how it describes in line 42 the effort and motion of an
obstructed brook that

> . . . *chok'd with sedges, works its weedy way*

—an obstruction caught also by the alliteration. There are the
parentheses where an undercurrent of feeling is quietly
acknowledged in passing:

> *In all my griefs—and* GOD *has given my share* [84]

> *I still had hopes, for pride attends us still* [89]

There is the felicity of Goldsmith's description of village
sounds mingling together—in lines 123–24, children, geese,
watchdog, and laughing peasant:

> *These all in sweet confusion sought the shade,*
> *And fill'd each pause the nightingale had made*

There is the strength of

> *More skill'd to raise the wretched than to rise* [148]

in the lines on the parson and, in line 162,

> *His pity gave ere charity began*

There is the schoolmaster, followed by the circumlocution
that stands for his pupils (lines 199–200):

> *Well had the boding tremblers learn'd to trace*
> *The day's disasters in his morning face*

Merely to list these things grows tiresome for the reader and the critic must content himself with a single further example—lines 287–302. In these lines there is the stock image of the old beauty trying to recapture her charms—and it is, again, by means of the language that Goldsmith "makes it new"—

> *In all the glaring impotence of dress.*

He uses her progress from "nature's simplest charms" to decline as a parallel to that of the land "by luxury betrayed." The climax of the passage has great force:

> *But verging to decline, its splendours rise,*
> *Its vistas strike, its palaces surprise;*
> *While scourg'd by famine from the smiling land,*
> *The mournful peasant leads his humble band*

Davie supplies an excellent note on this, in which he draws attention to the fact that the second line uses "the vocabulary of the landscape gardener—his 'striking vistas' and 'surprise views'— . . . with bitter irony." Again, as Davie remarks, Goldsmith renovates another stock adjective in "smiling land" by endowing it with "a new tragic implication: the land smiles heartlessly on the wretched."

"The Deserted Village" is an excellent example of the "middle-weight" poem, less trenchant than Johnson's "Vanity," and yet secure in the possession of its Augustan standards—moral directness, elegance, and lucidity. Goldsmith's range has been well summarized in the Latin epitaph that Johnson wrote for the tablet beneath his bust in Westminster Abbey: "A powerful yet gentle master."

The following points, not already glossed, may be of use to the reader:

Line 232: "The twelve good rules, the royal game of goose." The rules (which included "Urge no healths," "Profane no divine ordinances," "Touch no state matters") accompanied an engraving of Charles I's execution on an old broadside. The game of goose was played on a board with dice.

Line 316: "artist" here equals artisan, artisan contrarily often being used in the sense of artist.

Line 344: the "wild Altama" is the River Altamaha in Georgia.

Line 418: "On Torno's cliffs, or Pambamarca's side." The Tornea is a river in the extreme north of Sweden, Pambamarca a mountain in South America, near Quito.

# WILLIAM BLAKE
[1757-1827]

## Auguries of Innocence

To see a World in a Grain of Sand
And a Heaven in a Wild Flower,
Hold Infinity in the palm of your hand
And Eternity in an hour.

A Robin Red breast in a Cage                          5
Puts all Heaven in a Rage.
A dove house fill'd with doves & Pigeons
Shudders Hell thro' all its regions.
A dog starv'd at his Master's Gate
Predicts the ruin of the State.                       10
A Horse misus'd upon the Road
Calls to Heaven for Human blood.
Each outcry of the hunted Hare
A fibre from the Brain does tear.
A Skylark wounded in the wing,                        15
A Cherubim does cease to sing.
The Game Cock clip'd & arm'd for fight
Does the Rising Sun affright.
Every Wolf's & Lion's howl
Raises from Hell a Human Soul.                        20
The wild deer, wand'ring here & there,
Keeps the Human Soul from Care.
The Lamb misus'd breeds Public strife
And yet forgives the Butcher's Knife.
The Bat that flits at close of Eve                    25
Has left the Brain that won't Believe.
The Owl that calls upon the Night
Speaks the Unbeliever's fright.
He who shall hurt the little Wren
Shall never be belov'd by Men.                        30
He who the Ox to wrath has mov'd
Shall never be by Woman lov'd.
The wanton Boy that kills the Fly
Shall feel the Spider's enmity.

He who torments the Chafer's sprite                    35
Weaves a Bower in endless Night.
The Caterpiller on the Leaf
Repeats to thee thy Mother's grief.
Kill not the Moth nor Butterfly,
For the Last Judgment draweth nigh.                    40
He who shall train the Horse to War
Shall never pass the Polar Bar.
The Beggar's Dog & Widow's Cat,
Feed them & thou wilt grow fat.
The Gnat that sings his Summer's song                  45
Poison gets from Slander's tongue.
The poison of the Snake & Newt
Is the sweat of Envy's Foot.
The Poison of the Honey Bee
Is the Artist's Jealousy.                              50
The Prince's Robes & Beggar's Rags
Are Toadstools on the Miser's Bags.
A truth that's told with bad intent
Beats all the Lies you can invent.
It is right it should be so;                           55
Man was made for Joy & Woe;
And when this we rightly know
Thro' the World we safely go,
Joy & Woe are woven fine,
A Clothing for the Soul divine;                        60
Under every grief & pine
Runs a joy with silken twine.
The Babe is more than swadling Bands;
Throughout all these Human Lands
Tools were made, & Born were hands,                    65
Every Farmer Understands.
Every Tear from Every Eye
Becomes a Babe in Eternity;
This is caught by Females bright
And return'd to its own delight.                       70
The Bleat, the Bark, Bellow & Roar
Are Waves that Beat on Heaven's Shore.
The Babe that weeps the Rod beneath
Writes Revenge in realms of death.
The Beggar's Rags, fluttering in Air,                  75
Does to Rags the Heavens tear.
The Soldier, arm'd with Sword & Gun,
Palsied strikes the Summer's Sun.
The poor Man's Farthing is worth more

WILLIAM BLAKE

*Self-portrait*

*The Bettmann Archive*

Than all the Gold on Afric's Shore.      80
One Mite wrung from the Labrer's hands
Shall buy & sell the Miser's Lands:
Or, if protected from on high,
Does the whole Nation sell & buy.
He who mocks the Infant's Faith      85
Shall be mock'd in Age & Death.
He who shall teach the Child to Doubt
The rotting Grave shall ne'er get out.
He who respects the Infant's faith
Triumphs over Hell & Death.      90
The Child's Toys & the Old Man's Reasons
Are the Fruits of the Two seasons.
The Questioner, who sits so sly,
Shall never know how to Reply.
He who replies to words of Doubt      95
Doth put the Light of Knowledge out.
The Strongest Poison ever known
Came from Caesar's Laurel Crown.
Nought can deform the Human Race
Like to the Armour's iron brace.      100
When Gold & Gems adorn the Plow
To peaceful Arts shall Envy Bow.
A Riddle or the Cricket's Cry
Is to Doubt a fit Reply.
The Emmet's Inch & Eagle's Mile      105
Make Lame Philosophy to smile.
He who Doubts from what he sees
Will ne'er Believe, do what you Please.
If the Sun & Moon should doubt,
They'd immediately Go out.      110
To be in a Passion you Good may do,
But no Good if a Passion is in you.
The Whore & Gambler, by the State
Licenc'd, build that Nation's Fate.
The Harlot's cry from Street to Street      115
Shall weave old England's winding Sheet.
The Winner's Shout, the Loser's Curse,
Dance before dead England's Hearse.
Every Night & every Morn
Some to Misery are Born.      120
Every Morn & every Night
Some are Born to sweet delight.
Some are Born to sweet delight,
Some are Born to Endless Night.

We are led to Believe a Lie     125
When we see not Thro' the Eye
Which was Born in a Night to perish in a Night
When the Soul Slept in Beams of Light.
God Appears & God is Light
To those poor Souls who dwell in Night,     130
But does a Human Form Display
To those who Dwell in Realms of day.

# Kathleen Raine

---

## BLAKE
### AUGURIES OF INNOCENCE

"Auguries of Innocence" exists only as a fair copy in the so-called Pickering manuscript, which was made, it is supposed, about 1803. It may be presumed, in the absence of positive evidence, that the Pickering manuscript was written after 1800, after the early Prophetic Books and *Songs of Innocence and Experience,* but before "Milton" and "Jerusalem"; in any case, at a time when Blake had reached his poetic maturity and, through his long and wide studies in the literature of the Perennial Philosophy available to him (the learning of the imagination), his spiritual maturity also. The form of the poem is simple, its substance profound and complex.

The form is, indeed, that of an English oral tradition of weather-saws and proverbs; and there is one, which comes very close to Blake's theme, that he must in some form have known:

> *Hunt a robin or a wren*
> *Never prosper boy or man*

This couplet does not express a sentimental humanitarianism in our remote ancestors, but is, most likely, associated with the sacred or magical character of wren and robin, pre-Christian in origin. But Blake's thought is as remote from the first as it is from this archaic taboo.

Blake had meditated long on the contrasting states that he names *innocence* and *experience;* they remain as a recurring theme in the later Prophetic Books, as they are of the early "Songs," which take their titles from the two states. It is important to understand at the outset that *innocence* was, for Blake, the original consciousness of life; *experience* a state of lesser knowledge. Locke, against whom so much of Blake's eloquent argument is directed, had based his theories (essentially those of modern behaviorism) on the supposition that a newborn child is a *tabula rasa* for experience to write upon, and that all knowledge comes from without, through the senses. To Blake this view was anathema; he held the view, traditional in the Platonic, vedantic Christian, and all other metaphysical traditions, that the soul is a pre-existent form, a living spirit that "descends" into the material world, assuming a body as a "garment"—a term Blake borrowed from the neo-Platonists whose works he had read in Thomas Taylor's translations. The soul upon entering this world of "experience," or generation, exchanges its waking state of knowledge for the "deadly sleep" or "death" (Blake again uses both these Platonic terms continually) of forgetfulness; only through recollection (anamnesis in Plato's sense), and not through experience gained through the senses and stored in memory, can the forgetful soul return to its radical perfection. There is no question of Blake at any time using the word *innocence* in the sense of inexperience; or *experience* as a state of knowledge of any kind: it is, on the contrary, a state of forgetfulness and illusion, of spiritual death. The title page of "Songs of Experience" shows weepers mourning the dead—the souls who have, according to the Platonic symbolism Blake adopted, fallen or "died" from an eternal to a temporal state or "world." Each of the poems in "Songs of Experience" describes some aspect or "state" of error.

Blake explicitly denies—indeed most eloquently combats—Locke's view that we "learn from experience" or that "error or experiment" are the means by which we discover truth. "Error is Created. Truth is Eternal." His "Auguries of Innocence," therefore, represent aspects of "what Eternally Exists, Really and unchangeably," beneath the illusory surface of events that man in his state of spiritual torpor calls reality. The four lines that preface the poem, and continue, like the sun, to give out light, however often we may return to them without their ever becoming less radiant, contain the quintessence of Blake's wisdom.

For Blake, infinity and eternity were, as in Plato's *Timaeus* and the *Hermetica* (sources for his thought on time and space), nonspatial and nontemporal. The central error of the materialist philosophy that he combated—from Descartes and Bacon to Locke and Newton—was, as Blake saw it, an illusory view of the space-time world. Already in the eighteenth century, and especially in Protestant countries, the religious view of the natural universe differed little from that of positivist science; "nature" was regarded as a solid and substantial reality, to which heaven and hell were, so to say, annexes, themselves increasingly conceived in spatio-temporal terms. Blake followed the traditional metaphysics, which he

discovered through the Protestant mystic Boehme, through
Swedenborg, Plato, Taylor's works and translations of
Plotinus and other neo-Platonists, through Berkeley's "im-
materialist" philosophy, and even from the vedic hymns
translated by Sir William Jones; the sources of such knowledge were not far to seek for a discerning mind even in the
year 1800. Blake held that mind is not in space, but space is in
mind, the primary stuff of the universe. This eternal mind
lives all lives, of sand or wild flower, little winged fly, spider,
emmet, moth, lamb or wolf or man. Such poets as Young,
whose "Night Thoughts" Blake had illustrated, had fallen
under the melancholy spell of the vast spaces of the Newtonian night sky; and to such Blake had addressed his poem
"The Fly," which reminds us that omnipresent mind is no
less present in the smallest than in the largest manifestation of
being. Newton had written that the Pantocrator was to be
adored because of his vastness; but Blake loved the mystery
of the Incarnation of the Logos as "a little weeping babe"
entering this world in every birth, *multum in parvule*. His
own preference for images of the minute—wild thyme, fly,
worm, lark, grain of sand—is related to what Boehme calls in
his writings (and Blake borrows the phrase) the "opening of
the centers of the birth of life"; the manifestation of the
spatial from the nonspatial, a constantly repeated miracle.
Every being is such a "center," which "opens" into its own
space-time, its own universe; somewhat as Whitehead was
later to imagine it. Blake was also familiar with Taylor's
edition of Proclus' commentaries on Euclid, and the derivation of plane from line, line from point; as of all series of
numbers from unity. Spatial vastness did not impress a mind
trained in a mode of thought that makes Locke's seem naive.

   Blake invariably used the term heaven to describe the
"within" of every living creature. So indeed it is defined in
the Gospel, "The Kingdom of Heaven is within you"; but,
while deist Protestantism was becoming increasingly colored
by Cartesian and Newtonian notions of space, this meaning
was lost sight of, to be renewed in the writings of Swedenborg, who developed the theme at great length and with
much imaginative insight in such works as *Heaven and
Hell* and the *Divine Love and Wisdom of the Angels*.
The "heavens" and "hells" of Swedenborg are the inner
worlds of consciousness of which the bodily form is the
"correspondence," or as Boehme and the alchemists term it,
the "signature." This mode of thought, recently reappearing
in the writings of Teilhard de Chardin, is, one may say,

traditionally orthodox; positivism is a fallacy whose reign is perhaps almost at an end even in the field of material science in which it took its origin. Blake was, from its foundation, a member of the London Swedenborgian society, and his works are saturated with Swedenborgian terms and images, none the less after his rejection of some aspects of Swedenborg's thought (at a time when he was discovering more reputable formulations of tradition) in *The Marriage of Heaven and Hell.* Swedenborg, a scientist in training, was himself fascinated by the strange beings of insects, bees, bats, spiders, and the like, the stranger and more remote modes of consciousness these represent; and in this Blake seems to have followed him. Both were fascinated by such lives not as a naturalist interested in morphology might be, but in amazement at the strangeness of the "ideas" in the divine Logos; "My mind is not as thy mind, nor my thoughts as thy thoughts." It is not surprising that a poet, early fascinated by such creatures as the insects of the "winepress" of Los, alien and myriadfold manifestations of the Logos, should have chosen the Book of Job, God's revelation to man of his inexhaustible strangeness, transcending reason, as the theme of his twenty-two famous engravings.

As in natural creation, so in man, the variety and mystery of innate life is inexhaustible. In "Visions of the Daughters of Albion," one of Blake's themes is education; and to the Lockean view that a child's mind must be trained and conditioned ("One law for lion and Ox is oppression") he opposes the argument that the creatures are, as Berkeley puts it, "spirits of different orders and capacities." The material vehicle of life, of "eye, ear, mouth or skin," is much the same in all, a mere handful of dust, which dissolves into chaos in the absence of the informing soul.

> *With what sense is it that the chicken shuns the ravenous hawk?*
> *With what sense does the tame pigeon measure out the expanse?*
> *With what sense does the bee form cells? have not the mouse & frog*
> *Eyes and ears and sense of touch? yet are their habitations*
> *And their pursuits as different as their forms and as their joys.*
> *Ask the wild ass why he refuses burdens, and the meek camel*

*Why he loves man: is it because of eye, ear, mouth or skin,*
*Or breathing nostrils? No, for these the wolf and tyger have.*
*Ask the blind worm the secrets of the grave, and why her spires*
*Love to curl round the bones of death; and ask the rav'nous snake*
*Where she gets poison, & the wing'd eagle why he loves the sun;*
*And then tell me the thoughts of man, that have been hid of old.*

The hidden thoughts of man, unknown to reason, are the innate ideas of the Imagination. Because of man's centrality in the created world (in Christian terms, the Logos became incarnate in man in a central sense not realized in the animal creation) man may enter in some measure into the "mind" of nature. The catalogue of creatures in "Auguries of Innocence" is to be understood as a variety of states of being—ideas—embodied in lamb, spider, or cockchafer, which also have their correspondence in ourselves; since the mind expressed in nature is innate also in ourselves. Since all the multitude of ideas embodied in manifested nature exist together in the one and indivisible mind ("Jesus the Imagination," as Blake says, or—using Swedenborg's term—"the Divine Humanity") we cannot with impunity damage or destroy any part of the cosmos without affecting not only other parts but also ourselves; for "all things are comprehended in their Eternal Forms in the divine body of the Saviour, the True Vine of Eternity, the Human Imagination . . . around him were seen the Images of Existences according to a certain order suited to my Imaginative Eye." The Last Judgment is the tearing aside of the curtain of oblivion that prevents us from realizing not only the inner reality and life of the world, but the coexistence of all life within this living unity.

Every birth is a manifestation of the divine Imagination; but the Questioner (line 93) is the human selfhood (we should now say *ego*), which owes its existence to sense impressions, retained by memory and ordered by the *ratio* (the *ratio* is essentially a mechanism for the comparison, in quantitative terms, of sense data; an instrument, as it were, of the temporal body itself). In this sense alone Locke's view is, in the natural world, realized. This process is "experience" and its agent, the figure of the fallen *ratio*, plays a central part in Blake's mythology as Urizen, or "Satan the Selfhood." The world, as it appears to this "fallen" mind, is the true metaphysical hell. "Milton" is the work in which Blake most fully developed the contrast between the selfhood and the divine humanity; Satan's kingdom, the temporal world of the *ratio*, and the eternal kingdom of the Imagination. Milton, "the inspired man," type of the poet, wars against the kingdom cut off from the divine influx, "casting Off" the selfhood by invocation of and attention to the imagination. The *self* of the temporal world Blake with exactness calls a "false body," an accretion:

> *The Negation is the Spectre, the Reasoning Power in Man:*
> *This is a false Body, in Incrustation over my Immortal Spirit, a Selfhood which must be put off & annihilated alway.*
>
> *To cleanse the Face of my Spirit by Self-examination,*
> *To bathe in the Waters of Life, to wash off the Not Human,*
> *I come in Self-annihiliation & the grandeur of Inspiration,*
> *To cast off Rational Demonstration by Faith in the Saviour,*
> *To cast off Bacon, Locke & Newton from Albion's covering,*
> *To take off his filthy garments & clothe him with Imagination,*
> *To cast off Bacon, Locke & Newton from Albion's*

Experience is the world of "the false body," Satan's kingdom cut off from the kingdom of heaven within; and Imagination is called "the Saviour" because it alone can release humanity from the prisons of "experience" into which souls descend. Such is the essence of the philosophy that underlies the deceptive simplicity of "Auguries of Innocence."

Like all Blake's writings, this poem is interwoven with traditional themes; the learning of imagination and intuitive insights. Such questions, for example, as the relativity of space are endlessly argued by Locke and Berkeley; and from the burning preoccupations of the century following Newton comes

> *The Emmet's Inch & Eagle's Mile*

Many pages of Berkeley's philosophy are summed up in

> If the Sun & Moon should doubt,
> They'd immediately Go out

—"their *esse* is *percipi*" in Berkeley's phrase; and perhaps Yeats was thinking of Blake as well as of Berkeley when he wrote of

> . . . God-appointed Berkeley that proved all things a
>     dream,
> That this pragmatical preposterous pig of a world, its
>     farrow that so solid seem,
> Must vanish on the instant if the mind but change its
>     theme.

When in a letter Blake wrote "To me This World is all One continued Vision of Fancy or Imagination" he was not expressing some vague enthusiasm but stating his metaphysical standpoint:

> I know that This World Is a World of Imagination & Vision. I see Every thing I paint In This World, but Every body does not see alike. To the Eyes of the Miser a Guinea is more beautiful than the Sun, & a bag worn with the use of Money has more beautiful proportions than a Vine filled with Grapes. The tree which moves some to tears of joy is in the Eyes of others only a green thing that stands in the way. Some See Nature all Ridicule & Deformity, & by these I shall not regulate my proportions; & Some Scarce see Nature at all. But to the Eyes of the Man of Imagination, Nature is Imagination itself. As a man is, So he Sees. As the Eye is formed, such are its Powers.

The image of seeing with, "not thro' the Eye" occurs in other contexts throughout Blake's writings, of which the best known is the conclusion of his account of his composition on the "Vision of the Last Judgment": "I question not my Corporeal or Vegetative Eye any more than I would Question a Window concerning a Sight. I look thro' it & not with it." Yet this image, the very essence of Blake's thought, has a long history; it is of the essence likewise of the perennial wisdom of which Blake, a traditional thinker in a society that had as a whole lapsed from tradition, was an orthodox, as he was also an inspired, prophet. We find almost the same words in Swedenborg, whose heterodoxy (in his own world) likewise represented a partial return toward traditional metaphysics:

. . . how sensually, that is, how much from the bodily senses and the darkness thereof they think in spiritual things who say that Nature is from herself; they think from the eye, and cannot think from the Understanding; thought from the Eye shuts the Understanding, but Thought from the Understanding, opens the Eye.

and behind Swedenborg, Plato:

It appears to me, Socrates, that it is more proper to consider the eyes and ears as things through which, rather than as things by which, we perceive.

Paracelsus, whom Blake himself names as one of his chief masters, called the senses "coffers in which the senses are generated"; and a passage in the *Hermetica* points out that though the senses are many, there is only one undivided consciousness which expresess itself through all. So we find continually: behind Blake's apparent simplicity extend long vistas of knowledge, in many fields; his aphorisms sum up, in unforgettable form, a wealth of traditional wisdom that in him receives a new verification and life.

With four such lines the poem opens, and so it closes:

> *God Appears & God is Light*
> *To those poor Souls who dwell in Night,*
> *But does a Human Form Display*
> *To those who Dwell in Realms of day.*

This reversal of what might be expected must have puzzled many readers of the poem; ought not a naïve anthropomorphism to give way, with greater knowledge and vision, to a more impersonal metaphysical insight, such as we find in the Indian religions and in the Platonic philosophy? In Hinduism, for example, a popular polytheism resolves itself, at a higher level, into a nonhuman and even atheist perspective. But Blake's Christianity is not less profound than these: rather his standpoint is different. His great theme is the Logos, "Jesus the Imagination," the Second Person of the Christian Trinity. He had understood that the human mind can encompass nothing beyond that Logos; and that the central mystery of the Incarnation is the realization of the Divine Imagination in man; his Jesus is the eternal Christ, born with every human birth. For Swedenborg, too, the centrality of the "Divine Humanity" was a leading doctrine of the New Church and realization of the New Age, which began, so he said, "in the heavens" in 1757, the year of Blake's birth. According to Swedenborg, God seen "afar off" appears to the angels like the sun to which their faces are continually turned; "and the heat thence proceeding, in its essence, is love, and the light thence proceeding, in its essence, is wisdom." All, like the Little Black Boy of Blake's poem, experience the heat and light of the divine source; but only those who have learned "To lean in joy upon our father's knee" have realized that the higher, qualitative truth, love and wisdom—the divine counterpart of these natural attributes—lie beyond the quantitative "heat" and "light" of the sun of life. Swedenborg's Heavenly Man is a composite vision of the innumerable multitudes of souls within the mystical Body; and for Blake, every man is "a Divine Member of the Divine Jesus." Thus, Blake has not lessened the idea of God, but extended the idea of man to a consciousness that at once fills, contains, and is, his universe:

*God becomes as we are, that we may be as he is.*

## The Tyger

Tyger! Tyger! burning bright
In the forests of the night,
What immortal hand or eye
Could frame thy fearful symmetry?

In what distant deeps or skies          5
Burnt the fire of thine eyes?
On what wings dare he aspire?
What the hand dare seize the fire?

And what shoulder, & what art,
Could twist the sinews of thy heart?    10
And when thy heart began to beat,
What dread hand? & what dread feet?

What the hammer? what the chain?
In what furnace was thy brain?
What the anvil? what dread grasp        15
Dare its deadly terrors clasp?

When the stars threw down their spears,
And water'd heaven with their tears,
Did he smile his work to see?
Did he who made the Lamb make thee?     20

Tyger, Tyger! burning bright
In the forests of the night,
What immortal hand or eye,
Dare frame thy fearful symmetry?

# Roy P. Basler

---

BLAKE

THE TYGER

Consider the image presented in the first stanza of "The Tyger," and the question asked. What is the simplest communication made by the image? Terror in the beholder, power to harm in the image. Beyond this there is communication of something not wholly of this world. Tigers do not burn, though the color of the tiger may suggest fire; jungle forests may be so dark as to suggest night, but could not be with strict rational logic called "forests of the night." What we have in the image is of the mind, surely, but not wholly of the rational, conscious mind. It is something of a dream image, conveying terror before a symbol of power to harm, and, like all dream images, made of the stuff known to the conscious mind but given in a fusion of non sequiturs (fire-tiger-forest-night) that have, nevertheless, linking associations and analogies: tigers roam the forests, and darkness and fire (light) are archetypal opposites in any language or experience. The communication of fear before power to harm lies in what the poet and reader see as a mental image.

Continuing with the question asked in the first stanza, we find a query that supposes that the image has been created, "framed" by a hand, instructed by an eye, even as a painter paints a picture, and that the creator is perhaps immortal (not of this world) and the image awe-inspiring in symmetry (perfection). But the query is not a statement, please note. As a question, it asks, rather than answers, "Whence came this image?" We shall keep this in mind to apply to the questions asked in following stanzas, for the poet is not necessarily positing anything beyond the images.

The questions that continue in the rest of the poem re-iterate and elaborate the question of the first stanza, the elaboration suggesting the possibility of an other-worldly or non-natural creator. Not until the next-to-last stanza, however, is there any specific, undebatable reference to deity. There, in an allusion to the unsuccessful revolt of the angels that provides *Paradise Lost* with its antecedent action, the question is put: Did God smile at the victorious conclusion of the war in heaven and then create something more terrible than Satan's pride? The allusion to the lamb provides an obvious contrast with the tiger, but also introduces a possible clue to allegory, since the lamb is the traditional symbol of peace and Christlike spirit. Biblical reference to the lion and the lamb as symbols of extremes in nature comes to mind at once, and the reader may leap to an interpretation of the tiger as the antichrist, except that such an interpretation would be anticlimactic when the poet employs "dare" to replace "could" in repeating the first stanza as the poem's conclusion.

There would be little daring involved for a supreme God who has smiled at the victorious conclusion of one struggle if he created nothing more terrible than the satanic power he had already vanquished. Surely, the tiger does not represent Satan, but something more terrible, whether or not created by God. But perhaps the question is not meant by the poet to imply an affirmative answer, and we may do well to reconsider.

Upon reflection, the tiger may not represent the supernatural at all, but something within the soul of man. Blake's poetry testifies abundantly to the fact that he was most appalled by the infinite extremes of the human psyche, love-hate, trust-fear. Psychologically, this symbolism has little that can be objected to. It provides a satisfactory symbolic climax in the poem's conclusion to match the dramatic climax of the rhetorical questions reached in the reference to deity in the next-to-last stanza, and what is more significant, provides a powerful meaning—one that turns on the new word "dare," which replaces the "could" used in the first stanza. The question at last is: Would an immortal deity dare create on earth something more fearful than the power he had thrown out of heaven? The question is left to the reader for answer.

This seems to me the most satisfactory reading of the poem. The traditional interpretation that the tiger symbolizes the wrath of God does not make sense to me now and did not when I first read the poem years ago, although I had then no alternative. It fails to make sense, not because the tiger is inapropos as a symbol of divine wrath, but because the dramatic framework includes deity as a possible creator of the tiger, not as the tiger itself. The poet's inclusive question is: What creator can be conceived capable of perpetrating man's scope for fear and hate?

The psychological implications of the poem are satisfying whether one answers the poet's question with God as creator, or with life-force as creator. From a Freudian point of view, the psyche encompasses the extremes symbolized in tiger and lamb no less than does the mythology that Blake created in his poetry. The orthodox Christian mythology does not encompass both extremes in deity, but does in man. The relegation of Satan to a secondary power, permitted to pursue evil by an absolute God who is thus responsible for the continuation of what He could at any moment terminate, is an anomaly which theology has rationalized but has never made wholly acceptable to human intelligence.

Hence Blake's question in this poem, like his questions in other poems, was meant in the eighteenth century to challenge orthodox theology and at the same time the too-simply rational deism that was in intellectual favor at the time. Both deism and orthodox Christianity failed Blake, apparently, because they divorced the dual aspects of the soul on a supernatural plane, and deism failed even further by its impossible attempt to dismiss the darker aspect from this world by insisting that since a reasonable deity created it, "whatever is, is right." Blake understood in his fashion, no less than Freud, the duality ruling the realm of the psyche.

## The Mental Traveller

I travel'd thro' a Land of Men,
A Land of Men & Women too,
And heard & saw such dreadful things
As cold Earth wanderers never knew.

For there the Babe is born in joy          5
That was begotten in dire woe;
Just as we Reap in joy the fruit
Which we in bitter tears did sow.

And if the Babe is born a Boy
He's given to a Woman Old,              10
Who nails him down upon a rock,
Catches his shrieks in cups of gold.

She binds iron thorns around his head,
She pierces both his hands & feet,
She cuts his heart out at his side        15
To make it feel both cold & heat.

Her fingers number every Nerve,
Just as a Miser counts his gold;
She lives upon his shrieks & cries,
And she grows young as he grows old.      20

Till he becomes a bleeding youth,
And she becomes a Virgin bright;
Then he rends up his Manacles
And binds her down for his delight.

He plants himself in all her Nerves,      25
Just as a Husbandman his mould;
And she becomes his dwelling place
And Garden fruitful seventy fold.

An aged Shadow, soon he fades,
Wand'ring round an Earthly Cot,           30
Full filled all with gems & gold
Which he by industry had got.

377

And these are the gems of the Human Soul,
The rubies & pearls of a lovesick eye,
The countless gold of the akeing heart,                    35
The martyr's groan & the lover's sigh.

They are his meat, they are his drink;
He feeds the Beggar & the Poor
And the wayfaring Traveller:
For ever open is his door.                                 40

His grief is their eternal joy;
They make the roofs & walls to ring;
Till from the fire on the hearth
A little Female Babe does spring.

And she is all of solid fire                               45
And gems & gold, that none his hand
Dares stretch to touch her Baby form,
Or wrap her in his swaddling-band.

But She comes to the Man she loves,
If young or old, or rich or poor;                          50
They soon drive out the aged Host,
A Beggar at another's door.

He wanders weeping far away,
Untill some other take him in;
Oft blind & age-bent, sore distrest,                       55
Untill he can a Maiden win.

And to allay his freezing Age
The Poor Man takes her in his arms;
The Cottage fades before his sight,
The Garden & its lovely Charms.                            60

The Guests are scatter'd thro' the land,
For the Eye altering alters all;
The Senses roll themselves in fear,
And the flat Earth becomes a Ball;

The stars, sun, Moon, all shrink away,                     65
A desart vast without a bound,
And nothing left to eat or drink,
And a dark desart all around.

The honey of her Infant lips,
The bread & wine of her sweet smile,                       70
The wild game of her roving Eye,
Does him to Infancy beguile;

For as he eats & drinks he grows
Younger & younger every day;
And on the desart wild they both          75
Wander in terror & dismay.

Like the wild Stag she flees away,
Her fear plants many a thicket wild;
While he pursues her night & day,
By various arts of Love beguil'd,          80

By various arts of Love & Hate,
Till the wide desart planted o'er
With Labyrinths of wayward Love,
Where roam the Lion, Wolf & Boar,

Till he becomes a wayward Babe,          85
And she a weeping Woman Old.
Then many a Lover wanders here;
The Sun & Stars are nearer roll'd.

The trees bring forth sweet Extacy
To all who in the desert roam;          90
Till many a City there is Built;
And many a pleasant Shepherd's home.

But when they find the frowning Babe,
Terror strikes thro' the region wide:
They cry "The Babe! the Babe is Born!"          95
And flee away on Every side.

For who dare touch the frowning form,
His arm is wither'd to its root;
Lions, Boars, Wolves, all howling flee,
And every Tree does shed its fruit.          100

And none can touch that frowning form,
Except it be a Woman Old;
She nails him down upon the Rock,
And all is done as I have told.

# Northrop Frye

## BLAKE
## THE MENTAL TRAVELLER

In Blake's poem, "The Mental Traveller," we have a vision of
the cycle of human life from birth to death to rebirth. The
two characters of the poem are a male and a female figure
moving in opposite directions, one growing old as the other
grows young and vice versa. The cyclical relation between
them runs through four cardinal points: a son-mother phase,
a husband-wife phase, a father-daughter phase, and a fourth
phase of what Blake calls spectre and emanation, terms corresponding roughly to Shelley's alastor and epipsyche. None
of these phases is quite true: the mother is only a nurse, the
wife merely "bound down" for the male's delight, the daughter a changeling, and the emanation does not "emanate," but
remains elusive. The male figure represents humanity, and
therefore includes women—the "female will" in Blake becomes associated with women only when women dramatize
or mimic the above relations in human life, as they do in the
courtly-love convention. The female figure represents the
natural environment, which man partially but never wholly
subdues. The controlling symbolism of the poem, as the four
phases suggest, is lunar.

To the extent that the encyclopedic form concerns itself
with the cycle of human life, an ambivalent female archetype
appears in it, sometimes benevolent, sometimes sinister, but
usually presiding over and confirming the cyclical movement.
One pole of her is represented by an Isis figure, a Penelope or
Solveig, who is the fixed point on which the action ends. The
goddess who frequently begins and ends the cyclical action is
closely related. This figure is Athene in the "Odyssey" and
Venus in the "Aeneid"; in Elizabethan literature, for political
reasons, usually some variant of Diana, like the Faerie Queen
in Spenser. The alma Venus who suffuses Lucretius' great
vision of life balanced in the order of nature is another
version. Beatrice in Dante presides over not a cycle but a
sacramental spiral leading up to deity, as does, in a far less

concrete way, the Ewig-Weibliche of Faust. At the opposite pole is a figure—Calypso or Circe in Homer, Dido in Virgil, Cleopatra in Shakespeare, Duessa in Spenser, sometimes a "terrible mother" but often sympathetically treated—who represents the opposite direction from the heroic quest. Eve in Milton, who spirals man downward into the Fall, is the contrasting figure to Beatrice.

In the ironic age there are naturally a good many visions of a cycle of experience, often presided over by a female figure with lunar and femme-fatale affiliations. Yeats's "Vision," which Yeats was quite right in associating with "The Mental Traveller," is based on this symbolism, and more recently Mr. Robert Graves's "The White Goddess" has expounded it with even greater learning and ingenuity. In Eliot's *Waste Land*, the figure in the background is less "the lady of situations" than the androgynous Tiresias, and although there is a fire sermon and a thunder sermon, both with apocalyptic overtones, the natural cycle of water, the Thames flowing into the sea and returning through death in the spring rains, is the containing form of the poem. In Joyce's *Ulysses* a female figure at once maternal, marital, and meretricious, a Penelope who embraces all her suitors, merges in her sleep with the drowsy spinning earth, constantly affirming but never forming, and taking the whole book with her.

ROBERT BURNS

*The Bettmann Archive*

# ROBERT BURNS
## [1759–1796]

## *A Man's a Man for A' That*

Is there for honest poverty
    That hangs his head, an' a' that;
The coward slave—we pass him by,
    We dare be poor for a' that!
For a' that, an' a' that,                                   5
    Our toils obscure an' a' that,
The rank is but the guinea's stamp,
    The man's the gowd for a' that.

What though on hamely fare we dine,
    Wear hoddin grey, an' a' that?                      10
Gie fools their silks, and knaves their wine,
    A man's a man for a' that.
For a' that, an' a' that,
    Their tinsel show an' a' that,
The honest man, tho' e'er sae poor,                        15
    Is king o' men for a' that.

Ye see yon birkie ca'd a lord,
    Wha struts, an' stares, an' a' that;
Tho' hundreds worship at his word,
    He's but a coof for a' that,                         20
For a' that, an' a' that,
    His ribband, star, an' a' that,
The man o' independent mind
    He looks an' laughs at a' that.

A prince can mak a belted knight,                          25
    A marquis, duke, an' a' that;
But an honest man's aboon his might,
    Gude faith, he maunna fa' that!
For a' that, an' a' that,
    Their dignities an' a' that,                         30
The pith o' sense, an' pride o' worth,
    Are higher rank than a' that.

Then let us pray that come it may,
  (As come it will for a' that,)
That Sense and Worth, o'er a' the earth, 35
  Shall bear the gree, an' a' that.
For a' that, an' a' that,
  It's coming yet for a' that,
That man to man, the world o'er,
  Shall brithers be for a' that. 40

*Paul Goodman*

BURNS

A MAN'S A MAN FOR A' THAT

For us at present to understand this poem of Burns written
during the French Revolution, it is useful to contrast it with
Bert Brecht's play, *A Man's a Man*, written during our century. Without doubt Brecht was aware of the line, "A
man's a man for a' that," and his play is a sardonic comment
on it.

Brecht's point is just the opposite of Burns' indignation and
pride. It is that a man can be drained of his worth and pith of
sense, and entirely warped and remolded by brainwashing,
regimenting, bribing, and terrorizing, until he fits the needs
of the state powers that manipulate him; and then, *after* he
has been artifically remade, he blatantly boasts, "A man's a
man!" In Brecht's play, a simple Irish laborer who starts out
to buy a fish in the market is molded into a soldier of British
imperialism. In our generation, poets talk about the con-
formism induced by technology, bureaucracy, schooling,
mass-communications, and so forth. Brecht is sarcastic and
disapproving, but he thinks that there is no residue of humanity that can withstand shaping by the powers that be. But
one might ask whether his own anger is not such a residue of
humanity.

Burns, however, wrote in the climate of the eighteenth
century Enlightenment—e.g., Rousseau or Kant—that held
that there is an underlying human nature shared by all mankind; there is common sense, common human feeling, and a
human virtue and justice that are "aboon the might" of
princes. This nature has been corrupted by the wars, follies,
money, and exploitation of kings, courtiers, and the rich, but
the task of revolution is to bring about the day that all men
will be brothers and esteem what is worth esteeming. This
day "is coming yet, for a' that."

Burns said of this ballad, "The piece is not really poetry,"
probably referring to its didactic and even sloganeering style,
unlike the fantasy, sentiment, or dramatic story-telling of

"real" poetry, in his view. But it is poetry, nevertheless, if only because of the lively passion of its contempt and pride that breathes in the sharp epithets and is beautifully conveyed by the impatience of the persistent "for a' that and a' that" like a strong gesture of a hand sweeping trivialities aside. And there *is* a dramatic story: Burns is telling them off. The poem was written not long before his death at an early age after a life that indeed exemplified honesty and independent mind and was sorely hurt by grinding poverty. (I am ashamed that we paid him two pounds for the book of songs that I learned in childhood and still sing.)

Whether or not it is a poem, this poem—for it is a poem—used to be immensely admired and often quoted by poor, hard-working people. I have frequently heard it from old winos who were once militant in the labor movement, typically in the I.W.W., the most militant wing of the labor movement. In their old age and personal defeat, the words of Burns still gave them dignity and a little fire. Such men, too, had a character peculiar to many poems of Burns: a considerable intellectuality couched in the vernacular of the street. In the best poems of Burns, the light peppering of Scotch words in a strictly English syntax expresses just this combination: high culture and popular voice. It is interesting to compare Burns with Wordsworth, who also wrote in the public speech: Burns's culture is far more neo-classical than Wordsworth's, yet he is more immediately concerned with common people than Wordsworth, who is more philosophical.

But I must make one more comparison, to put this poem in its proper context. The refrain "for a' that and a' that" appears prominently in an earlier poem of Burns, the cantata, "The Jolly Beggars." And here the theme is "I like the jades, for a' that" and that "inclination" should determine behavior. The moral seems to be libertine and careless, and quite different from the virtuous indignation of honest poverty, independent mind, and pith of sense. Yet it is clear from the body of Burns's poems that he did not think there was a contradiction at all: he felt that spontaneous pleasure, poetry, and sexuality *were* virtues, and that, contrary to the usual belief, Scotch puritanism and being "unco guid" were wicked and doomed the strait-laced to the devil. (But when Tam o'Shanter is drunk and lecherous, the Devil gets only the end of his horse's tail.) That is, in a more earthy and less rapturous way, he is in agreement with Blake writing at the same time, and he is saying something not much different from the highly philosophical "Ode" of Schiller, that it is joy that binds all mankind together.

Thus, whether it is said merrily in 1785 or impatiently in 1795, "for a' that and a' that" means the same thing: let us dismiss status, money, false morality, and false religion, and get back to fundamentals:

*The deities that I adore*
*are Social Peace and Plenty;*
*I'm better pleased to make one more*
*than be the death of twenty.*

WILLIAM WORDSWORTH

*Painting by Henry William Pickersgill*
*National Portrait Gallery*
*The Bettmann Archive*

# WILLIAM WORDSWORTH

[1770–1850]

## Ode

### INTIMATIONS OF IMMORTALITY FROM
### RECOLLECTIONS OF EARLY CHILDHOOD

*"The Child is father of the Man;*
*And I could wish my days to be*
*Bound each to each by natural piety."*

There was a time when meadow, grove, and stream,
The earth, and every common sight,
    To me did seem
    Apparelled in celestial light,
The glory and the freshness of a dream.      5
It is not now as it hath been of yore;—
    Turn wheresoe'er I may,
    By night or day,
The things which I have seen I now can see no more.

    The Rainbow comes and goes,      10
    And lovely is the Rose,
    The Moon doth with delight
Look round her when the heavens are bare,
    Waters on a starry night
    Are beautiful and fair;      15
  The sunshine is a glorious birth;
  But yet I know, where'er I go,
That there hath past away a glory from the earth.

Now, while the birds thus sing a joyous song,
    And while the young lambs bound      20
    As to the tabor's sound,
To me alone there came a thought of grief:
A timely utterance gave that thought relief,
    And I again am strong:
The cataracts blow their trumpets from the steep;      25
No more shall grief of mine the season wrong;
I hear the Echoes through the mountains throng,

The Winds come to me from the fields of sleep,
     And all the earth is gay;
          Land and sea                                    30
     Give themselves up to jollity,
          And with the heart of May
     Doth every beast keep holiday;—
          Thou Child of Joy,
Shout round me, let me hear thy shouts, thou happy
     Shepherd-Boy!                                        35

Ye blessèd Creatures, I have heard the call
     Ye to each other make; I see
The heavens laugh with you in your jubilee;
     My heart is at your festival,
     My head hath its coronal,                            40
The fulness of your bliss, I feel—I feel it all.
     Oh evil day! if I were sullen
     While Earth herself is adorning,
          This sweet May-morning,
     And the children are culling                         45
          On every side,
     In a thousand valleys far and wide,
     Fresh flowers, while the sun shines warm,
And the Babe leaps up on his mother's arm:
     I hear, I hear, with joy I hear!                     50
     —But there's a Tree, of many, one,
A single Field which I have looked upon,
Both of them speak of something that is gone:
     The Pansy at my feet
     Doth the same tale repeat:                           55
Whither is fled the visionary gleam?
Where is it now, the glory and the dream?

Our birth is but a sleep and a forgetting:
The Soul that rises with us, our life's Star,
     Hath had elsewhere its setting,                      60
          And cometh from afar:
     Not in entire forgetfulness,
     And not in utter nakedness,
But trailing clouds of glory do we come
          From God, who is our home:                      65
Heaven lies about us in our infancy!
Shades of the prison-house begin to close
     Upon the growing Boy,
But he beholds the light, and whence it flows,
     He sees it in his joy;                               70

The Youth, who daily farther from the east
   Must travel, still is Nature's priest,
   And by the vision splendid
   Is on his way attended;
At length the Man perceives it die away,      75
And fade into the light of common day.

Earth fills her lap with pleasures of her own;
Yearnings she hath in her own natural kind,
And, even with something of a mother's mind,
   And no unworthy aim,      80
   The homely nurse doth all she can
To make her Foster-child, her inmate Man,
   Forget the glories he hath known,
And that imperial palace whence he came.

Behold the Child among his new-born blisses,      85
A six years' darling of a pigmy size!
See, where 'mid work of his own hand he lies,
Fretted by sallies of his mother's kisses,
With light upon him from his father's eyes!
See, at his feet, some little plan or chart,      90
Some fragment from his dream of human life,
Shaped by himself with newly-learned art;
   A wedding or a festival,
   A mourning or a funeral;
     And this hath now his heart,      95
   And unto this he frames his song:
     Then will he fit his tongue
To dialogues of business, love, or strife;
   But it will not be long
   Ere this be thrown aside,      100
   And with new joy and pride
The little Actor cons another part;
Filling from time to time his "humorous stage"
With all the Persons, down to palsied Age,
That Life brings with her in her equipage;      105
   As if his whole vocation
   Were endless imitation.

Thou, whose exterior semblance doth belie
   Thy soul's immensity;
Thou best philosopher, who yet dost keep      110
Thy heritage, thou eye among the blind,
That, deaf and silent, read'st the Eternal Deep,
Haunted forever by the Eternal Mind,—

Mighty prophet! seer blest!
On whom those truths do rest, 115
Which we are toiling all our lives to find,
In darkness lost, the darkness of the grave;
Thou, over whom thy Immortality
Broods like the Day, a master o'er a slave,
A Presence which is not to be put by; 120
Thou little Child, yet glorious in the might
Of heaven-born freedom on thy being's height,
Why with such earnest pains dost thou provoke
The years to bring the inevitable yoke,
Thus blindly with thy blessedness at strife? 125
Full soon thy Soul shall have her earthly freight,
And custom lie upon thee with a weight,
Heavy as frost, and deep almost as life!

O joy! that in our embers
Is something that doth live, 130
That nature yet remembers
What was so fugitive!
The thought of our past years in me doth breed
Perpetual benediction: not indeed
For that which is most worthy to be blest; 135
Delight and liberty, the simple creed
Of childhood, whether busy or at rest,
With new-fledged hope still fluttering in his breast:—
Not for these I raise
The song of thanks and praise; 140
But for those obstinate questionings
Of sense and outward things,
Fallings from us, vanishings;
Blank misgivings of a Creature
Moving about in worlds not realized, 145
High instincts before which our mortal nature
Did tremble like a guilty thing surprised:
But for those first affections,
Those shadowy recollections,
Which, be they what they may, 150
Are yet the fountain-light of all our day,
Are yet a master-light of all our seeing;
Uphold us, cherish, and have power to make
Our noisy years seem moments in the being
Of the Eternal Silence: truths that wake, 155
To perish never:

Which neither listlessness, nor mad endeavor,
   Nor man nor boy,
Nor all that is at enmity with joy,
Can utterly abolish or destroy!      160
   Hence in a season of calm weather
   Though inland far we be,
Our souls have sight of that immortal sea
   Which brought us hither,
   Can in a moment travel thither,      165
And see the children sport upon the shore,
And hear the mighty waters rolling evermore.

Then sing, ye Birds, sing, sing a joyous song!
   And let the young lambs bound
   As to the tabor's sound!      170
We in thought will join your throng,
   Ye that pipe and ye that play,
   Ye that through your hearts today
   Feel the gladness of the May!
What though the radiance which was once so bright      175
Be now forever taken from my sight,
   Though nothing can bring back the hour
Of splendor in the grass, of glory in the flower;
   We will grieve not, rather find
   Strength in what remains behind;      180
   In the primal sympathy
   Which having been must ever be;
   In the soothing thoughts that spring
   Out of human suffering;
   In the faith that looks through death,      185
In years that bring the philosophic mind.

And O, ye Fountains, Meadows, Hills, and Groves,
Forebode not any severing of our loves!
Yet in my heart of hearts I feel your might;
I only have relinquished one delight      190
To live beneath your more habitual sway.
I love the Brooks which down their channels fret,
Even more than when I tripped lightly as they;
The innocent brightness of a new-born Day
   Is lovely yet;      195
The Clouds that gather round the setting sun
Do take a sober coloring from an eye
That hath kept watch o'er man's mortality;

Another race hath been, and other palms are won.
Thanks to the human heart by which we live,                    200
Thanks to its tenderness, its joys, and fears,
To me the meanest flower that blows can give
Thoughts that do often lie too deep for tears.

## Lionel Trilling

### WORDSWORTH
### ODE: INTIMATIONS OF IMMORTALITY
### FROM RECOLLECTIONS OF EARLY CHILDHOOD

Criticism, we know, must always be concerned with the poem itself. But a poem does not always exist only in itself: sometimes it has a very lively existence in its false or partial appearances. These simulacra of the actual poem must be taken into account by criticism; and sometimes, in its effort to come at the poem as it really is, criticism does well to allow the simulacra to dictate at least its opening moves. In speaking about Wordsworth's "Ode: Intimations of Immortality from Recollections of Early Childhood," I should like to begin by considering an interpretation of the poem which is commonly made. According to this interpretation—I choose for its brevity Dean Sperry's statement of a view which is held by many other admirable critics—the "Ode" is "Wordsworth's conscious farewell to his art, a dirge sung over his departing powers."

How did this interpretation—erroneous, as I believe—come into being? The "Ode" may indeed be quoted to substantiate it, but I do not think it has been drawn directly from the poem itself. To be sure, the "Ode" is not wholly perspicuous. Wordsworth himself seems to have thought it difficult, for in the Fenwick notes he speaks of the need for competence and attention in the reader. The difficulty does not lie in the diction, which is simple, or even in the syntax, which is sometimes obscure, but rather in certain contradictory statements that the poem makes, and in the ambiguity of some of its crucial words. Yet the erroneous interpretation I am dealing with does not arise from any intrinsic difficulty of the poem itself but rather from certain extraneous and unexpressed assumptions that some of its readers make about the nature of the mind.

Nowadays it is not difficult for us to understand that such tacit assumptions about the mental processes are likely to lie hidden beneath what we say about poetry. Usually, despite

our general awareness of their existence, it requires great
effort to bring these assumptions explicitly into consciousness. But in speaking of Wordsworth, one of the commonest
of our unexpressed ideas comes so close to the surface of our
thought that it needs only to be grasped and named. I refer to
the belief that poetry is made by means of a particular poetic
faculty, a faculty which may be isolated and defined.

It is this belief, based wholly upon assumption, which
underlies all the speculations of the critics who attempt to
provide us with explanations of Wordsworth's poetic decline
by attributing it to one or another of the events of his life. In
effect any such explanation is a way of *defining* Wordsworth's poetic faculty: what the biographical critics are
telling us is that Wordsworth wrote great poetry by means
of a faculty that depended on his relations with Annette
Vallon, or by means of a faculty that operated only so long
as he admired the French Revolution, or by means of a
faculty that flourished by virtue of a particular pitch of
youthful sense-perception or by virtue of a certain attitude
toward Jeffrey's criticism or by virtue of a certain relation
with Coleridge.

Now no one can reasonably object to the idea of mental
determination in general, and I certainly do not intend to
make out that poetry is an unconditioned activity. Still, this
particular notion of mental determination that implies that
Wordsworth's genius failed when it was deprived of some
single emotional circumstance is so much too simple and so
much too mechanical that I think we must inevitably reject
it. Certainly what we know of poetry does not allow us to
refer the making of it to any single faculty. Nothing less than
the whole mind, the whole man, will suffice for its origin.
And such was Wordsworth's own view of the matter.

There is another unsubstantiated assumption at work in the
common biographical interpretation of the "Ode." This is the
belief that a natural and inevitable warfare exists between the
poetic faculty and the faculty by which we conceive or
comprehend general ideas. Wordsworth himself did not
believe in this antagonism—indeed, he held an almost contrary view—but Coleridge thought that philosophy had en-
croached upon and destroyed his own powers, and the critics
who speculate on Wordsworth's artistic fate seem to prefer
Coleridge's psychology to Wordsworth's own. Observing in
the "Ode" a contrast drawn between something called "the
visionary gleam" and something called "the philosophic

mind," they leap to the conclusion that the "Ode" is Wordsworth's conscious farewell to his art, a dirge sung over departing powers.

I am so far from agreeing with this conclusion that I believe the "Ode" is not only not a dirge sung over departing powers but actually a dedication to new powers. Wordsworth did not, to be sure, realize his hopes for these new powers, but that is quite another matter.

As with many poems, it is hard to understand any part of the "Ode" until we first understand the whole of it. I will therefore say at once what I think the poem is chiefly about. It is a poem about growing; some say it is a poem about growing old, but I believe it is about growing up. It is incidentally a poem about optics and then, inevitably, about epistemology; it is concerned with ways of seeing and then with ways of knowing. Ultimately it is concerned with ways of acting, for, as usual with Wordsworth, knowledge implies liberty and power. In only a limited sense is the "Ode" a poem about immortality.

Both formally and in the history of its composition the poem is divided into two main parts. The first part, consisting of four stanzas, states an optical phenomenon and asks a question about it. The second part, consisting of seven stanzas, answers that question and is itself divided into two parts, of which the first is despairing, the second hopeful. Some time separates the composition of the question from that of·the answer; the evidence most recently adduced by Professor de Selincourt seems to indicate that the interval was two years.

The question which the first part asks is this:

> *Whither is fled the visionary gleam?*
> *Where is it now, the glory and the dream?*

All the first part leads to this question, but although it moves in only one direction it takes its way through more than one mood. There are at least three moods before the climax of the question is reached.

The first stanza makes a relatively simple statement. "There was a time" when all common things seemed clothed in "celestial light," when they had "the glory and the freshness of a dream." In a poem ostensibly about immortality we ought perhaps to pause over the word "celestial," but the present elaborate title was not given to the poem until much later, and conceivably at the time of the writing of the first part the idea of immortality was not in Wordsworth's mind at all. Celestial light probably means only something different from ordinary, earthly, scientific light; it is a light of the mind, shining even in darkness—"by night or day"—and it is perhaps similar to the light which is praised in the invocation to the third book of *Paradise Lost.*

The second stanza goes on to develop this first mood, speaking of the ordinary, physical kind of vision and suggesting further the meaning of "celestial." We must remark that in this stanza Wordsworth is so far from observing a diminution of his physical senses that he explicitly affirms their strength. He is at pains to tell us how vividly he sees the rainbow, the rose, the moon, the stars, the water and the sunshine. I emphasize this because some of those who find the "Ode" a dirge over the poetic power maintain that the poetic power failed with the failure of Wordsworth's senses. It is true that Wordsworth, who lived to be eighty, was said in middle life to look much older than his years. Still, thirty-two, his age at the time of writing the first part of the "Ode," is an extravagantly early age for a dramatic failure of the senses. We might observe here, as others have observed elsewhere, that Wordsworth never did have the special and perhaps modern sensibility of his sister or of Coleridge, who were so aware of exquisite particularities. His finest passages are moral, emotional, subjective; whatever visual intensity they have comes from his response to the object, not from his close observation of it.

And in the second stanza Wordsworth not only confirms his senses but he also confirms his ability to perceive beauty. He tells us how he responds to the loveliness of the rose and of the stars reflected in the water. He can deal, in the way of Fancy, with the delight of the moon when there are no competing stars in the sky. He can see in Nature certain moral propensities. He speaks of the sunshine as a "glorious birth." But here he pauses to draw distinctions from that fascinating word *glory:* despite his perception of the sunshine as a glorious birth, he knows "that there hath past away a glory from the earth."

Now, with the third stanza, the poem begins to complicate itself. It is *while* Wordsworth is aware of the "optical" change in himself, the loss of the "glory," that there comes to him "a thought of grief." I emphasize the word *while* to suggest that we must understand that for some time he had been conscious of the "optical" change *without* feeling grief. The grief, then, would seem to be coincidental with but not necessarily caused by the change. And the grief is not of long duration, for we learn that

> *A timely utterance gave that thought relief,*
> *And I again am strong.*

It would be not only interesting but also useful to know what that "timely utterance" was, and I shall hazard a guess; but first I should like to follow the development of the "Ode" a little further, pausing only to remark that the reference to the timely utterance seems to imply that, although the grief is not of long duration, still we are not dealing with the internal experiences of a moment, or of a morning's walk, but of a time sufficient to allow for development and change of mood; that is, the dramatic time of the poem is not exactly equivalent to the emotional time.

The fourth stanza goes on to tell us that the poet, after gaining relief from the timely utterance, whatever that was, felt himself quite in harmony with the joy of Nature in spring. The tone of this stanza is ecstatic, and in a way that some readers find strained and unpleasant and even of doubtful sincerity. Twice there is a halting repetition of words to express a kind of painful intensity of response: "I feel—I feel it all," and "I hear, I hear, with joy I hear!" Wordsworth sees, hears, feels—and with that "joy" that both he and Coleridge felt to be so necessary to the poet. But despite the response, despite the joy, the ecstasy changes to sadness in a wonderful modulation which quite justifies the antecedent shrillness of affirmation:

> *—But there's a Tree, of many, one,*
> *A single Field which I have looked upon.*
> *Both of them speak of something that is gone:*
> *The Pansy at my feet*
> *Doth the same tale repeat:*
> *And what they utter is the terrible question:*
> *Whither is fled the visionary gleam?*
> *Where is it now, the glory and the dream?*

Now, the interpretation that makes the "Ode" a dirge over departing powers and a conscious farewell to art takes it for granted that the visionary gleam, the glory, and the dream, are Wordsworth's names for the power by which he made poetry. This interpretation gives to the "Ode" a place in

Wordsworth's life exactly analogous to the place that "Dejection: An Ode" has in Coleridge's life. It is well known how
intimately the two poems are connected; the circumstances
of their composition make them symbiotic. Coleridge in his
poem most certainly does say that his poetic powers are gone
or going; he is very explicit, and the language he uses is very
close to Wordsworth's own. He tells us that upon "the
inanimate cold world" there must issue from the soul "a light,
a glory, a fair luminous cloud," and that this glory *is* joy,
which he himself no longer possesses. But Coleridge's poem,
although it responds to the first part of Wordsworth's, is not
a recapitulation of it. On the contrary, Coleridge is precisely
contrasting his situation with Wordsworth's. As Professor de
Selincourt says in his comments on the first version of
"Dejection," this contrast "was the root idea" of Coleridge's
ode (*Wordsworthian and Other Studies*). In April of 1802,
Wordsworth was a month away from his marriage to Mary
Hutchinson, on the point of establishing his life in a felicity
and order which became his genius, while Coleridge was at
the nadir of despair over his own unhappy marriage and his
hopeless love for Sara, the sister of Wordsworth's fiancée.
And the difference between the situations of the two friends
stands in Coleridge's mind for the difference in the states of
health of their respective poetic powers.

Coleridge explicitly ascribes the decay of his poetic power
to his unhappiness, which worked him harm in two ways—
by forcing him to escape from the life of emotion to find
refuge in intellectual abstraction and by destroying the joy
which, issuing as "a light, a glory, a fair luminous cloud," so
irradiated the world as to make it a fit object of the shaping
power of imagination. But Wordsworth tells us something
quite different about himself. He tells us that he has strength,
that he has joy, but still he has not the glory. In short, we
have no reason to assume that, when he asks the question at
the end of the fourth stanza, he means, "Where has my
creative power gone?" Wordsworth tells us how he made
poetry; he says he made it out of the experience of his senses
as worked upon by his contemplative intellect, but he nowhere tells us that he made poetry out of visionary gleams,
out of glories, or out of dreams.

To be sure, he writes very often about gleams. The word
*gleam* is a favorite one with him, and a glance at the Lane
Cooper concordance will confirm our impression that
Wordsworth, whenever he has a moment of insight or

happiness, talks about it in the language of light. His great poems are about moments of enlightenment, in which the metaphoric and the literal meaning of the word are at one— he uses *glory* in the abstract modern sense, but always with an awareness of the old, concrete, iconographic sense of a visible nimbus. In *The Varieties of Religious Experience,* William James speaks of the "hallucinatory or pseudo-hallucinatory luminous phenomena, *photisms,* to use the term of the psychologists," the "floods of light and glory," that characterize so many moments of revelation. James mentions one person who, experiencing the light, was uncertain of its externality.

But this momentary and special light is the subject matter of Wordsworth's poetry, not the power of making it. The moments are moments of understanding, but he does not say that they make writing poetry any easier. Indeed, in lines 59–131 of the first book of *The Prelude,* he expressly says that the moments of clarity are by no means always matched by poetic creativity.

As for dreams and poetry, there is some doubt about the meaning that Wordsworth gave to the word "dream" used as a metaphor. In "Expostulation and Reply" he seems to say that dreaming—"dream my time away"—is a good thing, but he is ironically using his interlocutor's depreciatory word, and he really does not mean "dream" at all. In the Peele Castle verses, which have so close a connection with the "Immortality Ode," he speaks of the "Poet's dream" and makes it synonymous with "gleam," with "the light that never was, on sea or land," and with the "consecration." But the beauty of the famous lines often makes us forget to connect them with what follows, for Wordsworth says that gleam, light, consecration, and dream would have made an "illusion," or, in the 1807 version, a "delusion." Professor Beatty reminds us that in the 1820 version Wordsworth destroyed the beauty of the lines in order to make his intention quite clear. He wrote:

> . . . *and add a gleam*
> *Of lustre known to neither sea nor land,*
> *But borrowed from the youthful Poet's Dream.*

That is, according to the terms of Wordsworth's conception of the three ages of man, the youthful Poet was, as he had a right to be, in the service of Fancy and therefore saw the sea as calm. But Wordsworth himself can now no longer see in the way of Fancy; he has, he says, "submitted to a new control." This seems to be at once a loss and a gain. The loss: "A power is gone, which nothing can restore." The gain: "A deep distress hath humanized my Soul"; this is gain because happiness without "humanization" "is to be pitied, for 'tis surely blind"; to be "housed in a dream" is to be "at distance from the kind" (i.e., mankind). In the "Letter to Mathetes" he speaks of the Fancy as "dreaming"; and the Fancy is, we know, a lower form of intellect in Wordsworth's hierarchy, and peculiar to youth.

But although, as we see, Wordsworth uses the word "dream" to mean illusion, we must remember that he thought illusions might be very useful. They often led him to proper attitudes and allowed him to deal successfully with reality. In *The Prelude* he tells us how his reading of fiction made him able to look at the disfigured face of the drowned man without too much horror; how a kind of superstitious conviction of his own powers was useful to him; how, indeed, many of the most critical moments of his boyhood education were moments of significant illusion; and in *The Excursion* he is quite explicit about the salutary effects of superstition. But he was interested in dreams not for their own sake but for the sake of reality. Dreams may *perhaps* be associated with poetry, but reality *certainly* is; and reality for Wordsworth comes fullest with Imagination, the faculty of maturity. The loss of the "dream" may be painful, but it does not necessarily mean the end of poetry.

And now for a moment I should like to turn back to the "timely utterance," because I think an understanding of it will help get rid of the idea that Wordsworth was saying farewell to poetry. Professor Garrod believes that this "utterance" was "My heart leaps up when I behold," which was written the day before the "Ode" was begun. Certainly this poem is most intimately related to the "Ode"—its theme, the legacy left by the child to the man, is a dominant theme of the "Ode," and Wordsworth used its last lines as the "Ode's" epigraph. But I should like to suggest that the "utterance" was something else. In line 43, Wordsworth says, "Oh evil day! if I were sullen," and the word "sullen" leaps out at us as a striking and carefully chosen word. Now there is one poem in which Wordsworth says that he was sullen; it is "Resolution and Independence."

We know that Wordsworth was working on the first part

of the "Ode" on the 27th of March, the day after the composition of the rainbow poem. On the 17th of June he added a little to the "Ode," but what he added we do not know. Between these two dates Wordsworth and Dorothy had paid their visit to Coleridge, who was sojourning at Keswick; during this visit Coleridge, on April 4, had written "Dejection: an Ode," very probably after he had read what was already in existence of the "Immortality Ode." Coleridge's mental state was very bad—still, not so bad as to keep him from writing a great poem—and the Wordsworths were much distressed. A month later, on May 3, Wordsworth began to compose "The Leech Gatherer," later known as "Resolution and Independence." It is this poem that is, I think, the timely utterance.

I follow Professor Garrod in assuming that the "utterance" was a poem, but of course it may have been a letter or a spoken word. And, as Jacques Barzun has suggested to me, it may refer to what the leech gatherer in the poem says to the poet, for certainly it is what the old man "utters" that gives the poet "relief."

"Resolution and Independence" is a poem about the fate of poets. It is also a poem about sullenness, in the sense that the people in the Fifth Circle are said by Dante to be sullen: " 'Sullen were we in the sweet air, that is gladdened by the sun, carrying lazy smoke within our hearts; now lie sullen here in the black mire!' This hymn they gurgle in their throats, for they cannot speak it in full words"—that is, they cannot now have relief by timely utterance, as they would not on earth. And "sullenness" I take to be the creation of difficulties where none exist, the working of a self-injuring imagination such as a modern mental physician would be quick to recognize as a neurotic symptom. Wordsworth's poem is about a sudden unmotivated anxiety after a mood of great exaltation. He speaks of his reversal of feeling as something experienced by himself before and known to all. In this mood he is the prey of "fears and fancies," of "dim sadness" and "blind thoughts." These feelings have reference to two imagined catastrophes. One of them—natural enough in a man under the stress of approaching marriage, for Wordsworth was to be married in October—is economic destitution. He reproaches himself for his past indifference to the means of getting a living and thinks of what may follow from this carefree life: "solitude, pain of heart, distress, and poverty." His black thoughts are led to the fate of poets "in their misery dead," among them Chatterton and Burns. The second specific fear is of mental distress:

*We Poets in our youth begin in gladness;*
*But thereof come in the end despondency and madness.*

Coleridge, we must suppose, was in his thoughts after the depressing Keswick meeting, but he is of course thinking chiefly of himself. It will be remembered how the poem ends, how with some difficulty of utterance the poet brings himself to speak with an incredibly old leech gatherer, and, taking heart from the man's resolution and independence, becomes again "strong."

This great poem is not to be given a crucial meaning in Wordsworth's life. It makes use of a mood to which everyone, certainly every creative person, is now and again a victim. It seems to me more likely that it, rather than the rainbow poem, is the timely utterance of which the "Ode" speaks because in it, and not in the rainbow poem, a sullen feeling occurs and is relieved. But whether or not it is actually the timely utterance, it is an autobiographical and deeply felt poem written at the time the "Ode" was being written and seeming to have an emotional connection with the first part of the "Ode." (The meeting with the old man had taken place two years earlier and it is of some significance that it should have come to mind as the subject of a poem at just this time.) It is a very precise and hardheaded account of a mood of great fear and it deals in a very explicit way with the dangers that beset the poetic life. But although Wordsworth urges himself on to think of all the bad things that can possibly happen to a poet, and mentions solitude, pain of heart, distress and poverty, cold, pain and labor, all fleshly ills, and then even madness, he never says that a poet stands in danger of losing his talent. It seems reasonable to suppose that if Wordsworth were actually saying farewell to his talent in the "Ode," there would be some hint of an endangered or vanishing talent in "Resolution and Independence." But there is none; at the end of the poem Wordsworth is resolute in poetry.

Must we not, then, look with considerable skepticism at such interpretations of the "Ode" that suppose without question that the "gleam," the "glory," and the "dream" constitute the power of making poetry?—especially when we remember that at a time still three years distant Wordsworth in *The Prelude* will speak of himself as becoming a "*creative* soul" (book XII, line 207; the italics are Wordsworth's own) despite the fact that, as he says (book XII, line 281), he "sees by glimpses now."

The second half of the "Ode" is divided into two large movements, each of which gives an answer to the question with which the first part ends. The two answers seem to contradict each other. The first issues in despair, the second in hope; the first uses a language strikingly supernatural, the second is entirely naturalistic. The two parts even differ in the statement of fact, for the first says that the gleam is gone, whereas the second says that it is not gone, but only transmuted. It is necessary to understand this contradiction, but it is not necessary to resolve it, for from the circuit between its two poles comes much of the power of the poem.

The first of the two answers (stanzas five through eight) tells us where the visionary gleam has gone by telling us where it came from. It is a remnant of a pre-existence in which we enjoyed a way of seeing and knowing now almost wholly gone from us. We come into the world, not with minds that are merely *tabulae rasae*, but with a kind of attendant light, the vestige of an existence otherwise obliterated from our memories. In infancy and childhood the recollection is relatively strong, but it fades as we move forward into earthly life. Maturity, with its habits and its cares and its increase of distance from our celestial origin, wears away the light of recollection. Nothing could be more poignantly sad than the conclusion of this part with the heavy sonority of its last line as Wordsworth addresses the child in whom the glory still lives:

> *Full soon thy Soul shall have her earthly freight,*
> *And custom lie upon thee with a weight,*
> *Heavy as frost, and deep almost as life!*

Between this movement of despair and the following movement of hope there is no clear connection save that of contradiction. But between the question itself and the movement of hope there is an explicit verbal link, for the question is: "Whither is *fled* the visionary gleam?" and the movement of hope answers that "nature yet remembers / What was so *fugitive*."

The second movement of the second part of the "Ode" tells us again what has happened to the visionary gleam: it has not wholly fled, for it is remembered. This possession of childhood has been passed on as a legacy to the child's heir, the adult man; for the mind, as the rainbow epigraph also says, is one and continuous, and what was so intense a light in childhood becomes "the fountain-light of all our day" and a "master-light of all our seeing," that is, of our adult day and our mature seeing. The child's recollection of his heavenly home exists in the recollection of the adult.

But what exactly is this fountain-light, this master-light? I am sure that when we understand what it is we shall see that the glory that Wordsworth means is very different from Coleridge's glory, which is joy. Wordsworth says that what he holds in memory as the guiding heritage of childhood is exactly not the joy of childhood. It is not "delight," not "liberty," not even "hope"—not for these, he says, "I raise / The song of thanks and praise." For what then does he raise the song? For this particular experience of childhood:

> . . . *those obstinate questionings*
> *Of sense and outward things,*
> *Fallings from us, vanishings;*
> *Blank misgivings of a Creature*
> *Moving about in worlds not realized.*

He mentions other reasons for gratitude, but here for the moment I should like to halt the enumeration.

We are told, then, that light and glory consist, at least in part, of "questionings," "fallings from us," "vanishings," and "blank misgivings" in a world not yet *made real*, for surely Wordsworth uses the word "realized" in its most literal sense. In his note on the poem he has this to say of the experience he refers to:

> . . . I was often unable to think of external things as having external existence, and I communed with all that I saw as something not apart from, but inherent in, my own material nature. Many times while going to school have I grasped at a wall or tree to recall myself from this abyss of idealism to the reality. At this time I was afraid of such processes.

He remarks that the experience is not peculiar to himself, which is of course true, and he says that it was connected in his thoughts with a potency of spirit which made him believe that he could never die.

The precise and naturalistic way in which Wordsworth talks of this experience of his childhood must cast doubt on Professor Garrod's statement that Wordsworth believed quite literally in the notion of pre-existence, with which the "vanishings" experience is connected. Wordsworth is very careful to delimit the extent of his belief; he says that it is "too shadowy a notion to be recommended to faith" as an evidence of immortality. He says that he is using the idea to illuminate another idea—using it, as he says, "for my purpose" and "as a poet." It has as much validity for him as any "popular" religious idea might have, that is to say, a kind of suggestive validity. We may regard pre-existence as being for Wordsworth a very serious conceit, vested with relative belief, intended to give a high value to the natural experience of the "vanishings."

The naturalistic tone of Wordsworth's note suggests that we shall be doing no violence to the experience of the "vanishings" if we consider it scientifically. In a well-known essay, "Stages in the Development of the Sense of Reality," the distinguished psychoanalyst Ferenczi speaks of the child's reluctance to distinguish between himself and the world and of the slow growth of objectivity which differentiates the self from external things. And Freud himself, dealing with the "oceanic" sensation of "being at one with the universe," which a literary friend had supposed to be the source of all religious emotions, conjectures that it is a vestige of the infant's state of feeling before he has learned to distinguish between the stimuli of his own sensations and those of the world outside. In *Civilization and Its Discontents* he writes:

> Originally the ego includes everything, later it detaches from itself the outside world. The ego-feeling we are aware of now is thus only a shrunken vestige of a more extensive feeling—a feeling which embraced the universe and expressed an inseparable connection of the ego with the external world. If we may suppose that this primary ego-feeling has been preserved in the minds of many people—to a greater or lesser extent—it would co-exist like a sort of counterpart with the narrower and more sharply outlined ego-feeling of maturity, and the ideational content belonging to it would be precisely the notion of limitless extension and oneness with the universe—the same feeling as that described by my friend as "oceanic."

This has its clear relation to Wordsworth's "worlds not realized." Wordsworth, like Freud, was preoccupied by the idea of reality, and, again like Freud, he knew that the child's way of apprehension was but a stage that in the course of nature would give way to another. If we understand that

Wordsworth is speaking of a period common to the development of everyone, we are helped to see that we cannot identify the vision of that period with his peculiar poetic power.

But in addition to the experience of the "vanishings" there is another experience for which Wordsworth is grateful to his childhood and which, I believe, goes with the "vanishings" to make up the "master-light," the "fountain-light." I am not referring to the

> *High instincts before which our mortal Nature*
> *Did tremble like a guilty Thing surprised,*

but rather to what Wordsworth calls "those first affections."

I am inclined to think that with this phrase Wordsworth refers to a later stage in the child's development which, like the earlier stage in which the external world is included within the ego, leaves vestiges in the developing mind. This is the period described in a well-known passage in Book II of *The Prelude,* in which the child learns about the world in his mother's arms:

> *Blest the infant Babe,*
> *(For with my best conjecture I would trace*
> *Our Being's earthly progress), blest the Babe,*
> *Nursed in his Mother's arms, who sinks to sleep,*
> *Rocked on his Mother's breast; who with his soul*
> *Drinks in the feelings of his Mother's eye!*
> *For him, in one dear Presence, there exists*
> *A virtue which irradiates and exalts*
> *Objects through widest intercourse of sense.*
> *No outcast he, bewildered and depressed:*
> *Along his infant veins are interfused*
> *The gravitation and the filial bond*
> *Of nature that connect him with the world.*
> *Is there a flower, to which he points with hand*
> *Too weak to gather it, already love*
> *Drawn from love's purest earthly fount for him*
> *Hath beautified that flower; already shades*
> *Of pity cast from inward tenderness*
> *Do fall around him upon aught that bears*
> *Unsightly marks of violence or harm.*
> *Emphatically such a Being lives,*
> *Frail creature as he is, helpless as frail,*
> *An inmate of this active universe:*
> *For feeling has to him imparted power*

*That through the growing faculties of sense,*
*Doth like an agent of the one great Mind*
*Create, creator and receiver both,*
*Working but in alliance with the works*
*Which it beholds.—Such, verily, is the first*
*Poetic spirit of our human life,*
*By uniform control of after years,*
*In most, abated or suppressed; in some,*
*Through every change of growth and of decay*
*Pre-eminent till death.*

The child, this passage says, does not perceive things merely as objects; he first sees them, because maternal love is a condition of his perception, as objects-and-judgments, as valued objects. He does not learn about a flower, but about the pretty-flower, the flower-that-I-want-and-that-mother-will-get-for-me; he does not learn about the bird and a broken wing but about the poor-bird-whose-wing-was-broken. The safety, warmth, and good feeling of his mother's conscious benevolence is a circumstance of his first learning. He sees, in short, with "glory"; not only is he himself not in "utter nakedness" as the "Ode" puts it, but the objects he sees are not in utter nakedness. The passage from *The Prelude* says in naturalistic language what stanza five of the "Ode" expresses by a theistical metaphor. Both the *Prelude* passage and the "Ode" distinguish a state of exile from a state of security and comfort, of at-homeness; there is (as the *Prelude* passage puts it) a "filial bond," or (as in stanza ten of the "Ode") a "primal sympathy," which keeps man from being an "outcast . . . bewildered and depressed."

The "Ode" and *The Prelude* differ about the source of this primal sympathy of filial bond. The "Ode" makes heavenly pre-existence the source, *The Prelude* finds the source in maternal affection. But the psychologists tell us that notions of heavenly pre-existence figure commonly as representations of physical prenatality—the womb is the environment which is perfectly adapted to its inmate and compared to it all other conditions of life may well seem like "exile" to the (very literal) "outcast." Even the security of the mother's arms, although it is an effort to re-create for the child the old environment, is but a diminished comfort. And if we think of the experience of which Wordsworth is speaking, the "vanishings," as the child's recollection of a condition in which it was very nearly true that he and his environment were one, it will not seem surprising that Wordsworth should compound the two experiences and figure them in the single metaphor of the glorious heavenly pre-existence.

I have tried to be as naturalistic as possible in speaking of Wordsworth's childhood experiences and the more-or-less Platonic notion they suggested to him. I believe that naturalism is in order here, for what we must now see is that Wordsworth is talking about something common to us all, the development of the sense of reality. To have once had the visionary gleam of the perfect union of the self and the universe is essential to and definitive of our human nature, and it is in that sense connected with the making of poetry. But the visionary gleam is not in itself the poetry-making power, and its diminution is right and inevitable.

That there should be ambivalence in Wordsworth's response to this diminution is quite natural, and the two answers, that of stanzas five through eight and that of stanzas nine through eleven, comprise both the resistance to and the acceptance of growth. Inevitably we resist change and turn back with passionate nostalgia to the stage we are leaving. Still, we fulfill ourselves by choosing what is painful and difficult and necessary, and we develop by moving toward death. In short, organic development is a hard paradox which Wordsworth is stating in the discrepant answers of the second part of the "Ode." And it seems to me that those critics who made the "Ode" refer to some particular and unique experience of Wordsworth's and who make it relate only to poetical powers have forgotten their own lives and in consequence conceive the "Ode" to be a lesser thing than it really is, for it is not about poetry, it is about life. And having made this error, they are inevitably led to misinterpret the meaning of the "philosophic mind" and also to deny that Wordsworth's ambivalence is sincere. No doubt it would not be a sincere ambivalence if Wordsworth were really saying farewell to poetry, it would merely be an attempt at self-consolation. But he is not saying farewell to poetry, he is saying farewell to Eden, and his ambivalence is much what Adam's was, and Milton's, and for the same reasons.

To speak naturalistically of the quasi-mystical experiences of his childhood does not in the least bring into question the value Wordsworth attached to them, for, despite its dominating theistical metaphor, the "Ode" is largely naturalistic in its intention. We can begin to see what that intention is by understanding the force of the word "imperial" in the sixth stanza. This stanza is the second of the four stanzas in which

Wordsworth states and develops the theme of the reminiscence of the light of heaven and its gradual evanescence through the maturing years. In stanza five we are told that the infant inhabits it; the boy beholds it, seeing it "in his joy"; the youth is still attended by it; "the Man perceives it die away, / And fade into the light of common day." The sixth stanza speaks briefly of the efforts made by earthly life to bring about the natural and inevitable amnesia:

> *Earth fills her lap with pleasures of her own;*
> *Yearnings she hath in her own natural kind,*
> *And even with something of a mother's mind,*
> *And no unworthy aim,*
> *The homely Nurse doth all she can*
> *To make her Foster-child, her Inmate Man,*
> *Forget the glories he hath known,*
> *And that imperial palace whence he came.*

"Imperial" suggests grandeur, dignity, and splendor, everything that stands in opposition to what, in *The Excursion*, Wordsworth was to call "littleness." And "littleness" is the result of having wrong notions about the nature of man and his connection with the universe; its outcome is "deadness." The melancholy and despair of the Solitary in *The Excursion* are the signs of the deadness that resulted from his having conceived of man as something less than imperial. Wordsworth's idea of splendid power is his protest against all views of the mind that would limit and debase it. By conceiving, as he, does, an intimate connection between mind and universe, by seeing the universe fitted to the mind and the mind to the universe, he bestows upon man a dignity that cannot be derived from looking at him in the actualities of common life, from seeing him engaged in business, in morality and politics.

Yet here we must credit Wordsworth with the double vision. Man must be conceived of as "imperial," but he must also be seen as he actually is in the field of life. The earth is not an environment in which the celestial or imperial qualities can easily exist. Wordsworth, who spoke of the notion of imperial pre-existence as being adumbrated by Adam's fall, uses the words "earth" and "earthly" in the common quasi-religious sense to refer to the things of this world. He does not make Earth synonymous with Nature, for although Man may be the true child of Nature, he is the "Foster-child" of Earth. But it is to be observed that the foster mother is a kindly one, that her disposition is at least quasi-maternal, that her aims are at least not unworthy; she is, in short, the foster mother who figures so often in the legend of the hero, whose real and unknown parents are noble or divine. Wordsworth, in short, is looking at man in a double way, seeing man both in his ideal nature and in his earthly activity. The two views do not so much contradict as supplement each other. If in stanzas five through eight Wordsworth tells us that we live by decrease, in the ninth, tenth, and eleventh he tells us of the everlasting connection of the diminished person with his own ideal personality. The child hands on to the hampered adult the imperial nature, the "primal sympathy / Which having been must ever be," the mind fitted to the universe, the universe to the mind. The sympathy is not so pure and intense in maturity as in childhood, but only because another relation grows up beside the relation of man to Nature—the relation of man to his fellows in the moral world of difficulty and pain. Given Wordsworth's epistemology, the new relation is bound to change the aspect of Nature itself: the clouds will "take a sober coloring from an eye / That hath kept watch o'er man's mortality," but a sober color is a color still.

There is sorrow in the "Ode," the inevitable sorrow of giving up an old habit of vision for a new one. In shifting the center of his interest from Nature to man in the field of morality, Wordsworth is fulfilling his own conception of the three ages of man that Professor Beatty has expounded so well. The shift in interest he called the coming of "the philosophic mind," but the word "philosophic" does not have here either of two of its meanings in common usage—it does not mean abstract and it does not mean apathetic. Wordsworth is not saying, and it is sentimental and unimaginative of us to say, that he has become less a feeling man and less a poet. He is only saying that he has become less a youth. Indeed, the "Ode" is so little a farewell to art, so little a dirge sung over departing powers, that it is actually the very opposite—it is a welcome of new powers and a dedication to a new poetic subject. For if sensitivity and responsiveness be among the poetic powers, what else is Wordsworth saying at the end of the poem except that he has a greater sensitivity and responsiveness than ever before? The "philosophic mind" has not decreased but, on the contrary, increased the power to feel.

> *The Clouds that gather round the setting sun*
> *Do take a sober coloring from an eye*

*That hath kept watch o'er man's mortality;*
*Another race hath been, and other palms are won.*

*Thanks to the human heart by which we live,*
*Thanks to its tenderness, its joys, and fears,*
*To me the meanest flower that blows can give*
*Thoughts that do often lie too deep for tears.*

The meanest flower is significant now not only because, like the small celandine, it speaks of age, suffering, and death, but because to a man who is aware of man's mortality the world becomes significant and precious. The knowledge of man's mortality—this must be carefully noted in a poem presumably about immortality—now replaces the "glory" as the agency which makes things significant and precious. We are back again at optics, which we have never really left, and the "Ode" in a very honest fashion has come full circle.

The new poetic powers of sensitivity and responsiveness are new not so much in degree as in kind; they would therefore seem to require a new poetic subject matter for their exercise. And the very definition of the new powers seems to imply what the new subject matter must be—thoughts that lie too deep for tears are ideally the thoughts which are brought to mind by tragedy. It would be an extravagant but not an absurd reading of the "Ode" that found it to be Wordsworth's farewell to the characteristic mode of his poetry, the mode that Keats called the "egotistical sublime" and a dedication to the mode of tragedy. But the tragic mode could not be Wordsworth's. He did not have the "negative capability" that Keats believed to be the source of Shakespeare's power, the gift of being able to be "content with half-knowledge," to give up the "irritable reaching after fact and reason," to remain "in uncertainties, mysteries, doubts." In this he was at one with all the poets of the romantic movement and after—negative capability was impossible for them to come by and tragedy was not for them. But although Wordsworth did not realize the new kind of art which seems implied by his sense of new powers, yet his bold declaration that he had acquired a new way of feeling makes it impossible for us to go on saying that the "Ode" was his "conscious farewell to his art, a dirge sung over his departing powers."

Still, was there not, after the composition of the "Ode," a great falling off in his genius which we are drawn to connect with the crucial changes the "Ode" records? That there was a falling off is certain, although we must observe that it was not so sharp as is commonly held and also that it did not occur immediately or even soon after the composition of the first four stanzas with their statement that the visionary gleam had gone; on the contrary, some of the most striking of Wordsworth's verse was written at this time. It must be remembered too that another statement of the loss of the visionary gleam, that made in "Tintern Abbey," had been followed by all the superb production of the "great decade" —an objection which is sometimes dealt with by saying that Wordsworth wrote his best work from his near memories of the gleam, and that, as he grew older and moved farther from it, his recollection dimmed and thus he lost his power: it is an explanation which suggests that mechanical and simple notions of the mind and of the poetic process are all too tempting to those who speculate on Wordsworth's decline. Given the fact of the great power, the desire to explain its relative deterioration will no doubt always be irresistible. But we must be aware, in any attempt to make this explanation, that an account of why Wordsworth ceased to write great poetry must at the same time be an account of how he once did write great poetry. And this latter account, in our present state of knowledge, we cannot begin to furnish.

## I Wandered Lonely as a Cloud

I wandered lonely as a cloud
   That floats on high o'er vales and hills,
When all at once I saw a crowd,
   A host, of golden daffodils;
Beside the lake, beneath the trees,       5
Fluttering and dancing in the breeze.

Continuous as the stars that shine
   And twinkle on the Milky Way,
They stretched in never-ending line
   Along the margin of a bay:       10
Ten thousand saw I at a glance,
Tossing their heads in sprightly dance.

The waves beside them danced, but they
   Out-did the sparkling waves in glee:
A poet could not but be gay,       15
   In such a jocund company:
I gazed—and gazed—but little thought
What wealth the show to me had brought:

For oft, when on my couch I lie
   In vacant or in pensive mood,       20
They flash upon that inward eye
   Which is the bliss of solitude;
And then my heart with pleasure fills,
And dances with the daffodils.

# Louis Coxe

## WORDSWORTH
### I WANDERED LONELY AS A CLOUD

This poem is Wordsworth pure and prime. It is one that had he not written it, would have had to be written for him, combining as it does all those obvious Wordsworthian characteristics that attract some readers and bore others. What Keats called Wordsworth's vein of the "egotistical sublime" is here in little, as are the characteristic language, visual awareness and the mnemonic scheme which lies as much at the heart of his work and thought and feeling as any other concept. To many readers, the poem is one of the clichés of romantic verse; to others, it exists only as one of those impossible "nature poems" that Our World has outgrown. Yet some readers find it new and exciting if only because it expresses what the poet puts down in another place as the experience of being "surprised by joy."

Joy, or delight, is the key. See how many words express pleasure and degrees of pleasure: *sprightly, gay, glee, jocund, bliss*. And then, of course, the whole movement of the poem, as of what the poem describes, is one of dance, the free play of the spirit, or what Wordsworth must have seen, by analogy, in the dance of the blossoms as his own "spontaneous overflow of powerful feeling." What more do you want? The flowers, in one sense, make us feel as they seem to feel and we are changed by the feeling. That is not to say that Wordsworth is saying, Flowers make you feel good like a poet should; not at all: he means, I think, that natural beauty can change us for the better and change us naturally.

It is just here that Wordsworth's theory and his mnemonics enter; the poem is, after all, a prime example of theory leading to practice and returning again to theory. The poet believes, as all poets must, that poems (not just Poetry) should delight and instruct and neither is more important than the other, though the delight must come first. A poem, says Robert Frost, "begins in delight and ends in wisdom," which Wordsworth would have agreed with—and well he might since it is practically his own phrase and is most certainly the heart of his aesthetic. Poetry teaches and it teaches by Memory, the mother of the muses.

Look how this poem moves: from loneliness to the visual shock, to the "crowd" or "host" and its dance, to the aftertime of recollection and the recreation of the feeling that at the time of the event itself was neither fully felt nor in any sense understood. The movement is from inside to outside and back to inside—with everything changed and with the assurance that the movement will return and recur. Significantly, the poet in stanza one is not only "lonely," he is "up in the clouds" as the old saying goes; and I for one take Wordsworth to mean that he is abstracted in mind, unseeing, until the sudden visual shock of the daffodils bumps him down to earth and he really *sees*—sees as few people ever do, has a way of seeing that is the end of all literature. Joseph Conrad said of literature, "It is to make you see. That is all and it is everything." The seeing brings delight, one's sense is stunned and pleased; but thus far there is no awareness or "wisdom." Wordsworth says ". . . but little thought / What wealth the show to me had brought." And we would be wrong to want that kind of sense at that time; the wisdom, the instruction, come later, "in vacant or in pensive mood."

Memory brings back the scene, inadvertently perhaps but equally the inadvertence can be used profitably by the conscious mind. Not just something to make poems out of—but something, as Wordsworth tells us in "Tintern Abbey," that can and must have an effect upon our conduct and upon character, if I may be permitted so old-fashioned a term. Memory—what and how and why we remember—has a vital influence on all that we are. In *The Prelude* he says that as natural beauty dies before the onslaught of civilization, education must move into the vacuum so that new generations will know beauty of another kind if they cannot have the natural. What we do, we are; we can remember only what we have done. If we can remember what brought delight and now brings wisdom, nature and nature's God have done well indeed by us. All we have to do is look, see, and love. The rest will take care of itself. But there is a great gap between the looking and the seeing, as we know very well.

Bernard Shaw observed that most people simply cannot associate pleasure with mental exertion of any sort. To bring to consciousness what is unconscious, then return it to unconsciousness where it properly belongs—that is an effort

of awareness and self-awareness that few people can associate
with pleasure and explains why not many people like good
poetry: one must be able to enter, at will, both realms, mingle
them, then let them return and resolve. Wordsworth spent
his life, or the best part of it, trying to do just that, and he
wrote poems that constitute both a record of the endeavor
and devices by means of which we can turn his experience
into our own. To be successful in both of these attempts, the
poet must take care to prepare his effects and to make certain
that nothing extraneous enters. There is a great difference
between fruitful ambiguity and mere noise. And because
Wordsworth was a careful and conscious artist, he makes
here the kind of poem that a strongly original poet, at his
best, can be depended upon to make: one that moves between
the poles of the poet's abstract theory and his practical
struggle with the recalcitrant medium.

As moderns, we are unlikely to find anything particularly
"original" in Wordsworth's diction or syntax or rhythms,
and in fact by any standard the language is eclectic. The poet
does not cleave stubbornly to doctrinaire notions of what
words or phrases or locutions are proper and what are not.
For example, he uses one of those adjectives that since Milton
had been overworked to a degree by the neoclassical poets,
the adjective *jocund*. Phrasing and word order are conventional. The novelty, the originality, reside in what the poet
sees and in his reaction to what he has seen. For him, the
visible world exists, feelings exist, thoughts about our feelings
should exist. Wordsworth here gives us a way of thinking
about these feelings and gives us feelings to have and to think
about. Of course, if he left us with a mere solipsistic, inturn-
ing "mood" that makes only for a moment's euphoria, we
would let the poem go and never bother with it again. But he
rejects the fragmented, purely personal notion of experience
in several ways. First, he presents the experience as a dramatic one, a confrontation and a response to a situation in the
real world, thereby involving others in the action. Second, he
contrasts the "loneliness" of abstraction with "the bliss of
solitude," a very different state and one which is simply the
natural recoil from a term of association with people. And
finally, he shows nature, not as a personified or sentimentalized sweetness, but as a totality which may or may not share
in a man's moods but at any rate is "continuous as the stars
that shine" and has a powerful effect, whatever her own

mood, on the nature of human kind. Man and nature are parts of a whole—parts that differ but that also are inseparable from the total scheme. We do not, Wordsworth says, "conquer" nature or even destroy her; we only despoil ourselves if we try. Obviously. We are a part of her.

# Lines Composed a Few Miles Above
# Tintern Abbey

## ON REVISITING THE BANKS OF THE WYE
## DURING A TOUR

Five years have past; five summers, with the length
Of five long winters! and again I hear
These waters, rolling from their mountain-springs
With a soft inland murmur.—Once again
Do I behold these steep and lofty cliffs,　　　　5
That on a wild secluded scene impress
Thoughts of more deep seclusion; and connect
The landscape with the quiet of the sky.
The day is come when I again repose
Here, under this dark sycamore, and view　　　　10
These plots of cottage-ground, these orchard-tufts,
Which at this season, with their unripe fruits,
Are clad in one green hue, and lose themselves
'Mid groves and copses. Once again I see
These hedge-rows, hardly hedge-rows, little lines　　　　15
Of sportive wood run wild: these pastoral farms,
Green to the very door; and wreaths of smoke
Sent up, in silence, from among the trees!
With some uncertain notice, as might seem
Of vagrant dwellers in the houseless woods,　　　　20
Or of some Hermit's cave, where by his fire
The Hermit sits alone.
　　　　　　　　　These beauteous forms,
Through a long absence, have not been to me
As is a landscape to a blind man's eye:　　　　25
But oft, in lonely rooms, and 'mid the din
Of towns and cities, I have owed to them
In hours of weariness, sensations sweet,
Felt in the blood, and felt along the heart;
And passing even into my purer mind,　　　　30
With tranquil restoration:—feelings too

Of unremembered pleasure: such, perhaps,
As have no slight or trivial influence
On that best portion of a good man's life,
His little, nameless, unremembered, acts                        35
Of kindness and of love. Nor less, I trust,
To them I may have owed another gift,
Of aspect more sublime; that blessed mood,
In which the burthen of the mystery,
In which the heavy and the weary weight                        40
Of all this unintelligible world,
Is lightened:—that serene and blessed mood,
In which the affections gently lead us on,—
Until, the breath of this corporeal frame
And even the motion of our human blood                          45
Almost suspended, we are laid asleep
In body, and become a living soul:
While with an eye made quiet by the power
Of harmony, and the deep power of joy,
We see into the life of things.                                 50
                                    If this
Be but a vain belief, yet, oh!—how oft—
In darkness and amid the many shapes
Of joyless daylight; when the fretful stir
Unprofitable, and the fever of the world,                       55
Have hung upon the beatings of my heart—
How oft, in spirit, have I turned to thee,
O sylvan Wye! thou wanderer thro' the woods,
How often has my spirit turned to thee!
    And now, with gleams of half-extinguished thought,          60
With many recognitions dim and faint,
And somewhat of a sad perplexity,
The picture of the mind revives again:
While here I stand, not only with the sense
Of present pleasure, but with pleasing thoughts                 65
That in this moment there is life and food
For future years. And so I dare to hope,
Though changed, no doubt, from what I was when first
I came among these hills; when like a roe
I bounded o'er the mountains, by the sides                      70
Of the deep rivers, and the lonely streams,
Wherever nature led: more like a man
Flying from something that he dreads, than one
Who sought the thing he loved. For nature then
(The coarser pleasures of my boyish days,                       75
And their glad animal movements all gone by)

To me was all in all.—I cannot paint
What then I was. The sounding cataract
Haunted me like a passion: the tall rock,
The mountain, and the deep and gloomy wood,                    80
Their colours and their forms, were then to me
An appetite; a feeling and a love,
That had no need of a remoter charm,
By thought supplied, nor any interest
Unborrowed from the eye.—That time is past,                    85
And all its aching joys are now no more,
And all its dizzy raptures. Not for this
Faint I, nor mourn nor murmur; other gifts
Have followed; for such loss, I would believe,
Abundant recompense. For I have learned                        90
To look on nature, not as in the hour
Of thoughtless youth; but hearing oftentimes
The still, sad music of humanity,
Nor harsh nor grating, though of ample power
To chasten and subdue. And I have felt                         95
A presence that disturbs me with the joy
Of elevated thoughts; a sense sublime
Of something far more deeply interfused,
Whose dwelling is the light of setting suns,
And the round ocean, and the living air,                      100
And the blue sky, and in the mind of man;
A motion and a spirit, that impels
All thinking things, all objects of all thought,
And rolls through all things. Therefore am I still
A lover of the meadows and the woods,                         105
And mountains; and of all that we behold
From this green earth; of all the mighty world
Of eye, and ear,—both what they half create,
And what perceive; well pleased to recognize
In nature and the language of the sense,                      110
The anchor of my purest thoughts, the nurse,
The guide, the guardian of my heart, and soul
Of all my moral being.                Nor perchance,
If I were not thus taught, should I the more                  115
Suffer my genial spirits to decay:
For thou art with me here upon the banks
Of this fair river; thou my dearest Friend,
My dear, dear Friend; and in thy voice I catch
The language of my former heart, and read                     120
My former pleasures in the shooting lights

Of thy wild eyes. Oh! yet a little while
May I behold in thee what I was once,
My dear, dear Sister! and this prayer I make,
Knowing that Nature never did betray                           125
The heart that loved her; 'tis her privilege,
Through all the years of this our life, to lead
From joy to joy: for she can so inform
The mind that is within us, so impress
With quietness and beauty, and so feed                         130
With lofty thoughts, that neither evil tongues,
Rash judgments, nor the sneers of selfish men,
Nor greetings where no kindness is, nor all
The dreary intercourse of daily life,
Shall e'er prevail against us, or disturb                      135
Our cheerful faith that all which we behold
Is full of blessings. Therefore let the moon
Shine on thee in thy solitary walk;
And let the misty mountain-winds be free
To blow against thee: and, in after years,                     140
When these wild ecstasies shall be matured
Into a sober pleasure; when thy mind
Shall be a mansion for all lovely forms,
Thy memory be as a dwelling-place
For all sweet sounds and harmonies; oh! then,                  145
If solitude, or fear, or pain, or grief,
Should be thy portion, with what healing thoughts
Of tender joy wilt thou remember me,
And these my exhortations! Nor, perchance—
If I should be where I no more can hear                        150
Thy voice, nor catch from thy wild eyes these gleams
Of past existence—wilt thou then forget
That on the banks of this delightful stream
We stood together; and that I, so long
A worshipper of Nature, hither came                            155
Unwearied in that service: rather say
With warmer love—oh! with far deeper zeal
Of holier love. Nor wilt thou then forget,
That after many wanderings, many years
Of absence, these steep woods and lofty cliffs,               160
And this green pastoral landscape, were to me
More dear, both for themselves and for thy sake!

*Richard Eberhart*

WORDSWORTH
TINTERN ABBEY

On rereading Wordsworth's "Tintern Abbey" I was impressed with its density. It is like entering a dense thicket rather than walking in a light wood. It was the density, the fullness, the heaviness and richness of the language that impressed me with the wholeness of the work while I held in mind at the same time its difference, due to these qualities, from almost every poem one reads in contemporary literature.

I also felt immediately a density of meaning, but not in a pejorative sense. Quite the contrary. By density here I mean richness and fullness, a heaviness as of the utterance of oracular truth, a justice being conveyed without fault. The language is so rich and pure, the meaning so clear, the passion behind the poem so strong, even, and harmonious, that I was carried along upon the poem with recognition and ardor.

The considerable length of the poem gives it part of its weight and dignity. The lines demand and compel complete attention. There are 162 lines of the poem, covering four pages in the text I was reading. The complexity and subtlety of the emotions behind the poem are conveyed with a masterly finality of language.

At the same time that I was feeling what I have called the density of the poem, its rare heaviness, complete conviction, and startling honesty, I was aware of the profundity and nobility of the language. I was aware, again and again, that it was not only truth of a personal passion that was coming to me, but that greatness of absolute statement was pervasive throughout the poem, a purity of words, phrases, and whole sentences and passages so marked and final as not only to be captivating and enthralling, but to induce a feeling of universality. This only the greatest poetry can achieve.

While the whole force and brunt of Wordsworth was coming to one, the language was so exalted, pure, steady, deep, harmonious, and totally meaningful, it was as if nature itself were speaking. One knew it was Wordsworth, and yet it seemed that the poet so far transcended himself that he was uttering universal truths of nature, that somehow the poem was a message of nature speaking to man, rather than man speaking about nature and life.

I do not know how else to put it but that in some of the highest forms of poetry, of which "Tintern Abbey" is an example, the poem becomes not only an example of the genius of a man but exists as an example of the genius of a race. It exemplifies the heart, the core, the depth, the particularity and the peculiarity, the very essence of a people and a time.

At the same time that I was enjoying the poem, not having read it for years, and while it was making its massive, cumulative effect on me, giving me a slow but exciting pleasure in which one was directly with the words and did not wander, while reading, beyond them, except that in this very one-to-one relationship and strong restraint there were outleapings of instantaneous connotations, all delighting and exhilarating—at the same time, I recognized that the poem is beyond criticism.

There is a sense in which great poetry is beyond criticism. It is so whole, so final, so perfectly-communicated, so totally meaningful, that indeed the poem is its own criticism and needs no other. I pay the poem so great a tribute as to say that the best criticism I could offer of it would be to read it, without comment, to my reader. For how could, in fact, my criticism exceed the poem itself? How could it state the meaning of the poem better than the poem does itself?

For instance, there are so many magnificent phrases and passages in this poem that I would like to quote them all! But to quote them all would approach what I have said above, reading the poem in its entirety as an entirety of criticism.

There are many ways of approaching a poem, however, and there are many modes of critical awareness. One mode would be in the nature of a paraphrase, where the critic would bring the reader up into his most intimate, delicately balanced, and subtle reactions as he is experiencing the poem. I like this idea of criticism, that it should lead the reader along into the intimate insights of the critic, in some kind of excellence of praise. No criticism can destroy a great poem. The critic can only modify a conception of it due to his uniqueness of reaction and the necessary feeling of his own time. The greatest criticism should be that of praise, which is

elicited by a great poem. One is reminded of Ben Jonson's
praise of Shakespeare.

As a young man I went once to Tintern Abbey. I stood
among the ruins and thought of Wordsworth. I knew many,
if not all, of his poems, and felt a kinship with the spirit of
the poet. Through him "we see into the life of things." The
soul and the body are one and these are one with nature. Life
is deeply "a feeling and a love." It is

> *A motion and a spirit, that impels*
> *All thinking things, all objects of all thought,*
> *And rolls through all things.* [102–104]

But I promised myself not to quote! It is to be noted that
Wordsworth composed his poem a few miles above Tintern
Abbey. He was not standing in it. He first visited the banks
of the Wye in 1793, when he was twenty-three. It was five
years later, 1798, when he was twenty-eight, that he wrote
the poem. There is a natural progression of his deep contemplation from scenes of nature revisited to direct address to his
sister Dorothy, his "dearest Friend," whom he begins to
address at line 118 of the 162 lines of the poem and who
becomes the locus of his "holier love." Part of the humanity
of the poem is that it moves thus from contemplation of
nature to contemplation of the significance of a human
person, in this case his own sister as the vehicle of his expression of love.

Upon the absolute grace and control of the language there
are only a few of what a modern critic might call verbal
blemishes, a slight inversion here, or an awkwardness there,
but these are hardly worth mentioning while the whole
massive concretion and outpouring of truth remains seemingly as enduring as nature itself. Words such as grandeur,
depth, and greatness have to be used to describe it.

Why is the poem great? Because it deals uniquely with
awareness central to man, his relation to the earth. Man is a
creature on the earth living with fellow creatures. Wordsworth reflects upon an earlier passion for nature when the
things of nature were "An appetite; a feeling and a love, /
That had no need of a remoter charm, / By thought supplied. . . ." Now, under the necessity of thought from awareness of the passing of time, awareness of the inevitability of
change and death, he hears "the still, sad music of humanity"
(which our age is too noisy to hear in his way: it is all harsh
and grating), which brings a "sense sublime" of "something

far more deeply interfused." It is a spiritual power in nature that he feels. It is this deep spiritual power that he announces in plain, economic, but fervent speech. He transposes this meditative love to his sister, his fellow creature on the earth and in nature, expressing the power of nature to ennoble and enhance mankind as it did "our cheerful faith" when nature led on "from joy to joy" and "never did betray / The heart that loved her."

## Resolution and Independence

Written at Town-end, Grasmere. This old Man I met a few
hundred yards from my cottage; and the account of him is taken
from his own mouth. I was in the state of feeling described in the
beginning of the poem, while crossing over Barton Fell from Mr.
Clarkson's, at the foot of Ullswater, towards Askham. The image
of the hare I then observed on the ridge of the Fell.

There was a roaring in the wind all night;
The rain came heavily and fell in floods;
But now the sun is rising calm and bright;
The birds are singing in the distant woods;
Over his own sweet voice the Stock-dove broods;          5
The Jay makes answer as the Magpie chatters;
And all the air is filled with pleasant noise of waters.

All things that love the sun are out of doors;
The sky rejoices in the morning's birth;
The grass is bright with rain-drops;—on the moors        10
The hare is running races in her mirth;
And with her feet she from the plashy earth
Raises a mist, that, glittering in the sun,
Runs with her all the way, wherever she doth run.

I was a Traveller then upon the moor,                    15
I saw the hare that raced about with joy;
I heard the woods and distant waters roar;
Or heard them not, as happy as a boy:
The pleasant season did my heart employ:
My old remembrances went from me wholly;                 20
And all the ways of men, so vain and melancholy.

But, as it sometimes chanceth, from the might
Of joy in minds that can no further go
As high as we have mounted in delight
In our dejection do we sink as low;                      25
To me that morning did it happen so;

And fears and fancies thick upon me came;
Dim sadness—and blind thoughts, I knew not, nor could name.

I heard the sky-lark warbling in the sky;
And I bethought me of the playful hare:     30
Even such a happy Child of earth am I;
Even as these blissful creatures do I fare;
Far from the world I walk and from all care;
But there may come another day to me—
Solitude, pain of heart, distress, and poverty.     35

My whole life I have lived in pleasant thought
As if life's business were a summer mood;
As if all needful things would come unsought
To genial faith still rich in genial good;
But how can He expect that others should     40
Build for him, sow for him, and at his call
Love him, who for himself will take no heed at all?

I thought of Chatterton, the marvellous Boy,
The sleepless Soul that perished in his pride;
Of Him who walked in glory and in joy     45
Following his plough, along the mountain-side:
By our own spirits are we deified:
We Poets in our youth begin in gladness;
But thereof come in the end despondency and madness.

Now, whether it were by peculiar grace,     50
A leading from above, a something given,
Yet it befell, that, in this lonely place,
When I with these untoward thoughts had striven,
Beside a pool bare to the eye of heaven
I saw a Man before me unawares:     55
The oldest man he seemed that ever wore grey hairs.

As a huge stone is sometimes seen to lie
Couched on the bald top of an eminence;
Wonder to all who do the same espy,
By what means it could thither come, and whence;     60
So that it seems a thing endued with sense:
Like a sea-beast crawled forth, that on a shelf
Of rock or sand reposeth, there to sun itself;

Such seemed this man, not all alive nor dead,
Nor all asleep—in his extreme old age:     65
His body was bent double, feet and head
Coming together in life's pilgrimage;
As if some dire constraint of pain, or rage

Of sickness felt by him in times long past,
A more than human weight upon his frame had cast.    70

Himself he propped, limbs, body, and pale face,
Upon a long grey staff of shaven wood:
And, still as I drew near with gentle pace,
Upon the margin of that moorish flood
Motionless as a cloud the old Man stood,    75
That heareth not the loud winds when they call;
And moveth all together, if it move at all.

At length, himself unsettling, he the pond
Stirred with his staff, and fixedly did look
Upon the muddy water, which he conned,    80
As if he had been reading in a book:
And now a stranger's privilege I took;
And, drawing to his side, to him did say,
"This morning gives us promise of a glorious day."

A gentle answer did the old Man make,    85
In courteous speech which forth he slowly drew:
And him with further words I thus bespake,
"What occupation do you there pursue?
This is a lonesome place for one like you."
Ere he replied, a flash of mild surprise    90
Broke from the sable orbs of his yet-vivid eyes.

His words came feebly, from a feeble chest,
But each in solemn order followed each,
With something of a lofty utterance drest—
Choice word and measured phrase, above the reach    95
Of ordinary men; a stately speech;
Such as grave Livers do in Scotland use,
Religious men, who give to God and man their dues.

He told that to these waters he had come
To gather leeches, being old and poor:    100
Employment hazardous and wearisome!
And he had many hardships to endure:
From pond to pond he roamed, from moor to moor;
Housing, with God's good help, by choice or chance;
And in this way he gained an honest maintenance.    105

The old Man still stood talking by my side;
But now his voice to me was like a stream
Scarce heard; nor word from word could I divide;
And the whole body of the Man did seem
Like one whom I had met with in a dream;    110

Or like a man from some far region sent,
To give me human strength, by apt admonishment.

My former thoughts returned: the fear that kills;
And hope that is unwilling to be fed;
Cold, pain, and labour, and all fleshly ills;     115
And mighty Poets in their misery dead.
—Perplexed, and longing to be comforted,
My question eagerly did I renew,
"How is it that you live, and what is it you do?"

He with a smile did then his words repeat;     120
And said that, gathering leeches, far and wide
He travelled; stirring thus about his feet
The waters of the pools where they abide.
"Once I could meet with them on every side;
But they have dwindled long by slow decay;     125
Yet still I persevere, and find them where I may."

While he was talking thus, the lonely place,
The old Man's shape, and speech—all troubled me:
In my mind's eye I seemed to see him pace
About the weary moors continually,     130
Wandering about alone and silently.
While I these thoughts within myself pursued,
He, having made a pause, the same discourse renewed.

And soon with this he other matter blended,
Cheerfully uttered, with demeanour kind,     135
But stately in the main; and when he ended,
I could have laughed myself to scorn to find
In that decrepit Man so firm a mind.
"God," said I, "be my help and stay secure;
I'll think of the Leech-gatherer on the lonely moor!"     140

# Geoffrey Grigson

---

## WORDSWORTH
### RESOLUTION AND INDEPENDENCE

On a midsummer occasion in 1868, "in all likelihood"—in his
own words—"after a time of mental depression over his
work and prospects," Thomas Hardy at the age of twenty-
eight years old wrote down three cures for despair. The first
was "To read Wordsworth's 'Resolution and Independence.'"
Written when he was four years older than Thomas Hardy,
in May, in the vegetative time of the year, this poem was
Wordsworth's cure in a like condition. But it is not to be
taken as no more than a Purple Heart. Finding for his poem
as he worked on it a stanza that will contain both exultation
and depression, both beginning and end of life, both quickness and lightness and sobriety, both the hare of the opening
exultation, which runs in her luminous mist, and the old man,
bent double, with feet and head coming together toward the
end of his travel, both unself-awareness and the later consolation of knowledge, Wordsworth made "Resolution and Independence" out of his experience, his reflection and the power
of his character. The lines move with quick variation,
quickly pivoted on rhymes. Then at the end of lines 4 and 5
in each stanza, the rhyme is repeated; and this doubling
makes the stanza pause, gathers and emphasizes the meaning;
a deeper pause coming when the kernel of sound is doubled
at the end of the sixth line and the seventh—that closing line,
which lengthens always and is enabled to carry, when required, the most expressive gravity, "Solitude, pain of heart,
distress, and poverty," or "The oldest man he seemed that
ever wore grey hairs," or "But thereof come in the end
despondency and madness." As you read, it is not necessary
to know about this poet's thought or the circumstances of
this poem: which is complete and self-subsistent, and explains
itself. Wordsworth, it has been said, is to be deduced from
his own poetry. But knowledge of him does not hinder
enjoyment. A strong-bodied man, ruthless and direct in his
emotional and mental attack, Wordsworth had been in his

childhood, by his own confession, of a "stiff, moody and
violent temper." He had made himself happy. Not long after
the composition of "Resolution and Independence," his dearest friend Coleridge confirmed how Wordsworth had
suffered "occasional fits of hypochondriacal uncomfortable-
ness—from which, more or less, and at longer or shorter
intervals, he has never been wholly free from his very childhood." Yet "he both deserves to be and is a happy man; and a
happy man not from natural temperament, for there lies his
main obstacle . . . but . . . because he is a Philosopher, because he knows the intrinsic value of the different objects of
human pursuit, and regulates his wishes in strict subordina-
tion to that knowledge." Making himself happy, he was independently William Wordsworth; and then resolute, against
the difficulties and dangers inherent in his being.

> *As high as we have mounted in delight*
> *In our dejection do we sink as low*

The dangers were exceedingly real; and they recurred. And
in this poem the most famous lines, too often true, are the
rhyme-coupled pair, shorter and longer, that compel a pause
of extra solemnity at the end of the seventh stanza:

> *We Poets in our youth begin in gladness;*
> *But thereof come in the end despondency and madness*

In his end Wordsworth became melancholy, if not mad. The
right set of the words also deserted him, and the fineness of
response coarsened, the thought became dogma, the poems
hardened like calcium carbonate around a stick into official
verse; and his sister who had been his twin in gladness,
became altogether mad. But in May 1802, realizing what
might be head of him, he was all the same—taking comfort
from the grave independence and resolution of the old man
by the moorland pool, poor and decrepit, on the bare upland
of existence and from his stately speech—himself resolved.
*Thereof*, he admits,—of the gladness, come the despondency
and the madness: of the gladness in which we begin; which is
yet, as in the second stanza, the sunny mist the hare by her
own act raises around herself, and that "Runs with her all the
way, wherever she doth run."

"By our own spirits are we deified": Wordsworth was firm
on the creative role of joy. The hare raced with joy, which
succeeded the roaring night of floods, and might be succeeded by them again. He thought of Burns (stanza VII
again)

*. . . who walked in glory and in joy*
*Following his plough, along the mountain-side*

Joy and our own spirits desert us: they let us down, they leave us unable to create. Then we need the firmness of the old man, catching leeches, which he sold, Dorothy Wordsworth recorded, at thirty shillings a hundred; who lost his joy long ago, yet lived, alone, by a hard, humble avocation that gave health to others, without despair. Then whatever firmness we have at our own command, we need stimulating by such exterior firmness; not being superhuman.

A poem that is self-instruction in this way, and not a release of self-deifying spirit, needs straight discourse and very simple language—"And in this way he gained an honest maintenance." Coleridge said within two months of reading "Resolution and Independence" that in Wordsworth's new poems he found "here and there a daring humbleness of language and versification, and a strict adherence to matter of fact, even to prolixity, that startled me." Yet the straight discourse of the poem is interspersed with its rhymes; with its variations of rhythm against measure; with the action of the encounter on the moor; with contrasts, the quick hare that raises her self-enveloping mist, the slow old man staring fixedly at muddy water; direct matter-of-fact speech from Wordsworth, and from the old man nothing directly recorded, but the reported *oratio obliqua* received into the narrator, whose poem this is; feebleness, and the life in the very old man's pale face, from "the sable orbs of his yet vivid eyes." And from straight discourse or daring humbleness of language, this poem lifts or descends without discord into its extra-memorably effective lines: up into "All things that love the sun are out of doors," down into "The sleepless soul that perished in his pride" (the bright Chatterton who killed himself at eighteen) or deeper down into that wider line, more inclusive, yet more naked: "And mighty Poets in their misery dead"; as this mighty poet was to be, in a body that continued to work.

# SAMUEL TAYLOR COLERIDGE

## [1772–1834]

## Kubla Khan: Or, a Vision in a Dream

### A FRAGMENT

The following fragment is here published at the request of a poet of great and deserved celebrity [Lord Byron], and, as far as the author's own opinions are concerned, rather as a psychological curiosity, than on the ground of any supposed *poetic* merits.

In the summer of the year 1797, the Author, then in ill health, had retired to a lonely farm-house between Porlock and Linton, on the Exmoor confines of Somerset and Devonshire. In consequence of a slight indisposition, an anodyne had been prescribed, from the effects of which he fell asleep in his chair at the moment he was reading the following sentence, or words of the same substance, in Purchas's *Pilgrimage:* "Here the Khan Kubla commanded a palace to be built, and a stately garden thereunto. And thus ten miles of fertile ground were inclosed with a wall." The Author continued for about three hours in a profound sleep, at least of the external senses, during which time he has the most vivid confidence, that he could not have composed less than from two to three hundred lines; if that indeed can be called composition in which all the images rose up before him as *things,* with a parallel production of the correspondent expressions, without any sensation or consciousness of effort. On awaking he appeared to himself to have a distinct recollection of the whole, and taking his pen, ink, and paper, instantly and eagerly wrote down the lines that are here preserved. At this moment he was unfortunately called out by a person on business from Porlock, and detained by him above an hour, and on his return to his room, found, to his no small surprise and mortification, that though he still retained some vague and dim recollection of the general purport of the vision, yet, with exception of some eight or ten scattered lines and images, all the rest had passed away like the images on the surface of a stream into which a stone had been cast, but, alas! without the after restoration of the latter!

> *Then all the charm*
> *Is broken—all that phantom-world so fair*
> *Vanishes, and a thousand circlets spread,*
> *And each mis-shape[s] the other. Stay awhile,*

*Poor youth! who scarcely dar'st lift up thine eyes—*
*The stream will soon renew its smoothness, soon*
*The visions will return! And lo, he stays,*
*And soon the fragments dim of lovely forms*
*Come trembling back, unite, and now once more*
*The pool becomes a mirror.*

[From "The Picture"]

Yet from the still surviving recollections in his mind, the Author
has frequently purposed to finish for himself what had been originally, as it were, given to him Σαμερον αδιον ασω but the to-morrow is yet to come.

In Xanadu did Kubla Khan
A stately pleasure-dome decree:
Where Alph, the sacred river, ran
Through caverns measureless to man
    Down to a sunless sea.                                    5
So twice five miles of fertile ground
With walls and towers were girdled round:
And there were gardens bright with sinuous rills,
Where blossomed many an incense-bearing tree;
And here were forests ancient as the hills,                        10
Enfolding sunny spots of greenery.

But oh! that deep romantic chasm which slanted
Down the green hill athwart a cedarn cover!
A savage place! as holy and enchanted
As e'er beneath a waning moon was haunted                          15
By woman wailing for her demon-lover!
And from this chasm, with ceaseless turmoil seething,
As if this earth in fast thick pants were breathing,
A mighty fountain momentarily was forced:
Amid whose swift half-intermitted burst                            20
Huge fragments vaulted like rebounding hail,
Or chaffy grain beneath the thresher's flail:
And 'mid these dancing rocks at once and ever
It flung up momently the sacred river.
Five miles meandering with a mazy motion                          25
Through wood and dale the sacred river ran,
Then reached the caverns measureless to man,
And sank in tumult to a lifeless ocean:
And 'mid this tumult Kubla heard from far
Ancestral voices prophesying war!                                  30
    The shadow of the dome of pleasure
    Floated midway on the waves;
    Where was heard the mingled measure

S. T. COLERIDGE

*The Bettmann Archive*

From the fountain and the caves.
It was a miracle of rare device,                        35
A sunny pleasure-dome with caves of ice!

A damsel with a dulcimer
In a vision once I saw:
It was an Abyssinian maid,
And on her dulcimer she played,                         40
Singing of Mount Abora.
Could I revive within me
Her symphony and song,
To such a deep delight 'twould win me,
That with music loud and long,                          45
I would build that dome in air,
That sunny dome! those caves of ice!
And all who heard should see them there,
And all should cry, Beware! Beware!
His flashing eyes, his floating hair!                   50
Weave a circle round him thrice,
And close your eyes with holy dread,
For he on honey-dew hath fed,
And drunk the milk of Paradise.

*Kenneth Burke*

COLERIDGE

KUBLA KHAN: OR, A VISION IN A DREAM

Let's begin at the heart of the matter, and take up the "prob-lems" afterwards. Count me among those who would view this poem both as a marvel, and as in principle *finished* (and here is a "problem," inasmuch as Coleridge himself refers to "Kubla Khan" as a fragment). Conceivably, details could be added, to amplify one or another of the three movements. And some readers (I am not among them) might especially feel the need of transitional lines to bridge the ellipsis between the middle and final stanzas. But the relationship among the three stages of the poem's development is unfolded with no less trim demarca-tion than the strophes of a Greek chorus, or (more rele-vantly) the Hegelian pattern of thesis, antithesis, and synthe-sis. Whatever may have got lost, the three stanzas in their overall progression tick off a perfect form, with beginning, middle, and end respectively. Thus:

Stanza one (thesis) amplifies the theme of the beatific vision. Stanza two (antithesis) introduces and develops the sinister, turbulent countertheme (plus, at the close, a recall of the contrasting first theme). And the third stanza fuses the two motives in terms of a beatific vision (the "damsel with a dulcimer") seen by a poetic "I," the mention of whom, despite the euphoria, leads to the cry, "Beware! Beware!" and to talk of a "dread" that, however "holy," in a sinister fashion is felt to befit the idealistic building of this particular air castle.

In "The Road to Xanadu," John Livingston Lowes brought an infectious combination of research and spirited delight to the tracking down of possible literary sources behind Cole-ridge's great "poems of fascination" (an enterprise further justified by the fact that Coleridge was so notoriously om-nivorous a reader, and one of his memorandum books listed texts containing many references to caverns, chasms, mazes, sunken rivers, fountains, and the like). By consulting Lowes, the reader will discover that nearly every notable term or reference in the poem appeared (often with quite relevant applications and combinations) in passages that Coleridge is quite likely to have seen. But though greatly enjoying the charm of Lowes's presentation, and having on many occasions consulted his book when working on Coleridge, I should begin by pointing out that our present job involves a quite different trend of investigation—an investigation in which Lowes's book can be of great help, though his interest is directed otherwise.

There is a sense in which poets can be said to have special nomenclatures, just as scientists or philosophers do. But this situation is concealed from us by the fact that, rather than inventing a special word for some particular conceptual purpose, or pausing to define some particular application he is giving to a word in common usage, a poet leaves the process implicit, even though he uses the common idiom in his peculiar way. For instance, the term "fish" in Theodore Roethke's poems would have little in common with the article of food we might buy in a market or order in a restaurant. And by collating all the contexts that help define a word as it figures in a given poet's work, we can discern respects in which it is part of a nomenclature essentially as specialized as *entelechy* in the philosophy of Aristotle, or *relativity* with particular reference to the theories of Einstein. So, thinking along those lines, insofar as I'd risk looking up from the immediate text, I'd tend to ask about uses of a given term in other works *by Coleridge* rather than asking (like Lowes) about possible sources in *other* writers. For instance, people have doubtless talked about fountains since they could talk at all. And Coleridge's reference to the sacred river, Alph, does unquestionably suggest the ancient myth of the river Alpheus that sank into the ground and emerged as the fountain Arethusa (a belief that Lowes shows to have merged with notions about the sources of the Nile). I'd tend to start matters from a concern with the themes of submergence and emergence, with the Alpheus-Arethusa *pattern* as a symbolizing of *rebirth*, regardless of who else happened to speak of it. Or take this comment in Lowes:

> In April, 1798, Coleridge who had been suffering from an infected tooth, wrote as follows, in a letter to his brother George: "Laudanum gave me repose, not sleep; but you, I believe, know how divine that repose is, *what a spot of enchantment, a green spot of foun-*

*tain and flowers and trees in the very heart of a waste of sands!"* Now when Coleridge wrote that, he was recalling and echoing, consciously or unconsciously, something else. For in the Note Book (which, as we know, belongs to this same period) appears this memorandum: "*—some wilderness-plot, green and fountainous* and unviolated by Man."

Lowes then asks, "Is it possible to discover what lies behind this note?" He proceeds to discover, in Bartram's *Travels*, the expressions, "blessed unviolated spot of earth!" and "the enchanting spot." And he notes that two pages earlier Bartram had written: "the dew-drops twinkle and play . . . on the tips of the lucid, green savanna, sparkling" beside a "serpentine rivulet, meandering over the meadows." Approached from Lowes' point of view, the serpentine, meandering rivulet would seem to touch upon the "sacred river, / Five miles meandering with a mazy motion"; the "dew-drops" might impinge upon "honey-dew"; and so on.

But of primary importance for our present investigations is not the question of where Coleridge may have read words almost identical with "spot of enchantment," but the fact that he used the expression in this particular context—in association with laudanum. And the reference to "honey-dew" would lead us, not to such a reference as Bartram's "dew-drops," but rather to a pair of quite contrasting references in "The Ancient Mariner," the first a dew like the sweat of anguish ("From the sails the dew did drip"), the second the dew of refreshment after release from the dreadful drought ("I dreamt that they were filled with dew; / And when I awoke, it rained"). Or we might recall the voice "As soft as honey-dew" that, though gentle, pronounced a fatal sentence: "The man hath penance done, / And penance more will do." And above all, I should rejoice to encounter in another poem ("Youth and Age") an explicit recognition of this term's convertibility: "Dew-drops are the gems of morning, / But the tears of mournful eve." In a juvenile poem, there is a related expression, "inebriate with dew." And I should never feel wholly content until I could also fit in one of the jottings from *Anima Poetae* that widens the circle of associations by reference to "a voice that suits a dream, a voice in a dream, a voice soundless and yet for the *ear* and not for the *eye* of the soul" (for often eye and ear can represent quite different orders of motivation).

In brief, the student of any one poet's nomenclature has

more to learn from a concordance of his work (a purely *internal* inspection of a term's "sources" in its own range of contexts) than from an inspection of possible borrowings (except in the broadest sense, as when a scholar cites usages by an older writer's contemporaries to help establish the likelihood that a given term was being used in a sense local to that period but now obsolete).

In fact, the many interesting documents that Lowes assembles as inductive proof of expressions Coleridge derived or adapted from his reading, might with much justice be interpreted quite differently, as indication that Coleridge was but responding "naturally" to the implications of such imagery. For instance, one might conceivably not require a prior text to help him discover that the image of a maze can adequately stand for a certain kind of emotional entanglement or "amazement," and that the greenery of an oasis in a desert provides an adequate image for an idea of refuge. And presumably travel books select such things to talk about for the very reason that their sheer "factuality" follows along the grooves of man's spontaneous imagination. Be that as it may, Lowes's study of possible derivation with regard to possible private literary sources contains much material that can be applied to the study of "associations" in two senses that Lowes was not concerned with: (1) their relation to "mythic" or "archetypal" forms of thought that do not rely on historical sources for their derivation; and (2) their relation to a nomenclature that, at notable points, may be uniquely Coleridgean (in that they possess personal connotations not to be found in any dictionary, and not precisely appreciated by us who read them, as it were, without quite the proper accent).

In any case, for the most part, we shall interpret the poem by looking rather for what now would often be called "archetypal" sources than Lowes's possible derivations from other sources (while occasionally considering the areas at which the two kinds of inquiry seem to overlap).

Even if we choose to accept without question Coleridge's statement that the poem is the spontaneous product of a dream (and thus arose without artistic purpose), when viewing it as a work of art we must ask what kind of effect it "aims" to produce. I'd propose to answer that question roundabout, thus:

In Aristotle's *Poetics*, among the resources he says contribute to the effectiveness of tragedy as a literary species he lists a sense of the "marvellous" (*to thaumaston*). The overall purpose involved in tragedy is "catharsis," while various other resources serve in one way or another to make the sense of purgation most effective. The Cornelian "theater of admiration" played down the principle of catharsis as exemplified in the Attic plays. And it so altered the proportions of the tragic ingredients that one particular kind of the "marvellous" (the cortége-like neoclassic pomp of such plays' courtly style) rose in the scale from a means to an end. The appeal to our sense of the marvellous takes many other forms, and among the variations I would include Coleridge's great "mystery poems" (or "poems of fascination"): "Kubla Khan," *The Ancient Mariner*, and "Christabel." Indeed, they come closer to a sense of the marvellous that Aristotle had in mind, since he was discussing ways whereby the playwright might endow a plot with the aura of supernatural fatality; and in his *Biographia Literaria* Coleridge says of his part in the volume of *Lyrical Ballads* containing work by him and Wordsworth:

> It was agreed, that my endeavours should be directed to persons and characters supernatural, or at least romantic; yet so as to transfer from our inward nature a human interest and a semblance of truth sufficient to procure for these shadows of imagination that willing suspension of disbelief for the moment, which constitutes poetic faith.

And previously in the same text:

> The incidents and agents were to be, in part at least, supernatural; and the excellence aimed at was to consist in the interesting of the affections by the dramatic truth of such emotions, as would naturally accompany such situations, supposing them real. And real in *this* sense they have been to every human being who, from whatever source of delusion, has at any time believed himself under supernatural agency.

Though Coleridge does not mention "Kubla Khan" in this connection (it was not published at that time), when judged as a poem it obviously appeals by producing much the same kind of effect. That is, its *mystery* endows it with a feeling of *fatality*. Presumably "The Ancient Mariner" also had its "archetypal" origins in a dream, told to Coleridge by a friend of his, though greatly modified, as Wordsworth testifies, by Coleridge's own additions. And few works have a more

strangely dreamlike quality than "Christabel." The sinister
element that lies about their edges attains its blunt documen-
tary completion in the nightmares of guilt, remorse, or woe
that he describes in "The Pains of Sleep" with such clinical
testimony as the lines:

> The third night, when my own loud scream
> Had waked me from the fiendish dream,
> O'ercome with sufferings strange and wild,
> I wept as I had been a child;
> And having thus by tears subdued
> My anguish to a milder mood,
> My punishments, I said, were due
> To natures deepliest stained with sin,—
> For aye entempesting anew
> The unfathomable hell within,
> The horror of their deeds to view,
> To know and loathe, yet wish and do!
> Such griefs with such men well agree,
> But wherefore, wherefore fall on me?

Before considering "Kubla Khan" in detail, I cite this piece
(which Coleridge himself specifically mentions as a "contrast") because of my conviction that it brings out the full
implication of the sinister potentialities one finds but traces of
in the predominantly euphoric state symbolized by pleasure-
dome, Edenic garden, and "a damsel with a dulcimer" (surely
one of the most euphonious lines in the language). And now,
to the poem in detail:

The first stanza, obviously, is the beatific vision of an
Edenic garden, enclosed ("girdled round") in a circle of
protection. In the third stanza the idea of encirclement will
take on quite different connotations ("Weave a circle round
him thrice"). To the generally recognized connotations of
"Alph" as both "Alpheus" and "alpha," I would offer but one
addition; yet I submit that it is essential to an understanding
of many notable details in the poem. As I have tried to show
in my *Grammar of Motives* (pp. 430–440 on "the temporizing of essence") and in my *Rhetoric of Religion* (particularly the section on "The First Three Chapters of *Genesis*"),
the proper narrative, poetic, or "mythic" way to deal with
fundamental motives is in terms of *temporal* priority. In this
mode of expression, things deemed most basic are said to be
first in time. So a river whose name suggests the first letter of
the alphabet in an ancient language (one can as well hear the

Hebrew form, "Aleph") is indeed well named. And fittingly, therefore, the forests are called "ancient as the hills." For this stanza is designed to convey in narrative, or "mythic" or "archetypal" terms the very *essence* of felicity (the creative "joy" that, in his poignant ode, "Dejection," written about two years later, Coleridge will bemoan the permanent loss of, since his "genial spirits fail," and he "may not hope from outward forms to win / The passion and the life, whose fountains are within").

True, in the first stanza, there is no specific reference to a fountain. But when we recall the passage already quoted from a letter to his brother (concerning a "divine repose" that is like "a spot of enchantment, a green spot of fountain and flowers and trees in the very heart of a waste of sands"), we can see how, as far as the associations within Coleridge's private nomenclature were concerned, the reference to "sunny spots of greenery" (plus the connotations of Alph) had already set the terministic conditions for the explicit emergence of a fountain. And the thought might also induce us to ask whether, beyond such a "spot of enchantment," there might also be lurking some equivalent to the "waste of sands" for which it is medicinal.

In any case, given what we now know about the imagery of man's ideal beginnings, would we not take it for granted that the "caverns" traversed by the river are leading us "back" to such a "sunless sea" as the womb-heaven of the amniotic fluid by which the foetus was once "girdled round" in Edenic comfort? (In one of his fragments, Coleridge characteristically depicts a "sot" luxuriating on a couch and exclaiming: "Would that this were work—*utinam hoc esset laborare!*") In Lowes you can find literary "sources" for the fact that the caverns are "measureless." It is also a fact that they *should* be measureless for the simple reason that they connote an ideal time wholly alien to the knowledge of numbers. On the other hand, the garden spot is measured ("twice five miles") since such finiteness helps suggest connotations of protective enclosure, as with the medieval ideal of the *hortus conclusus*, which Leo Spitzer has discussed in his monograph on "Milieu and Ambiance."

How far should we carry such speculations? We need not insist on it, but inasmuch as forests are of *wood* (thereby bringing us into the fate-laden Greek-Roman line of thought that commingles ideas of wood, matter, and mother: *hyle, dynamis, mater, materia, potentia*), the reference to them reinforces the feminine connotations of such a guarded garden. So far as Coleridgean terminology in general is concerned, we might also note that green is not an unambiguous color. Christabel is to Geraldine as a dove is to a green snake coiled about her ("Swelling its neck as she swelled hers"). And when reading that Alph is a "sacred river," we might bear in mind the well-known but sometimes neglected etymological fact that in Latin usage either a priest or a criminal was *sacer*, as with the fluctuancies between French *sacre* and *sacré* (the same ambiguities applying to Greek *hagios* and to the Hebrew concept of the "set apart," *qodesh, qadesh*).

As for "stately": We might recall that Geraldine's bare neck was "stately" (line 62). And cutting in from another angle, I might cite a prose passage that I consider so basic to Coleridge's thinking, I keep finding all sorts of uses for it. (See, for instance, *Permanence and Change*, Hermes edition, pp. 279–80.) It is from "The Friend," where the exposition is divided into what he calls "landing-places." He is here discussing the sheer *form* of his presentation (the emphasis is mine):

> Among my *earliest* impressions I still distinctly remember that of my *first* entrance into the *mansion* of a neighboring baronet, *awefully* known to me by the name of the great house, its exterior having been long *connected in my childish imagination* with the *feelings and fancies* stirred up in me by the perusal of the Arabian Nights' Entertainments. Beyond all other objects, I was most struck with the magnificent staircase, relieved at well-proportioned intervals by spacious landing-places, this adorned with grand or showy plants, the next looking out on an extensive prospect through the STATELY window . . . while from the last and highest the eye commanded the *whole spiral ascent* with the marble pavement of the great hall; from which it seemed to spring up as if it merely used the ground on which it rested. My readers will find no difficulty in *translating these forms of the outward senses into their intellectual analogies.*

In sum, I'd say that references to the "decreeing" of this "stately pleasure-dome" combine connotations of infantile ("first" or "essential") felicity with concepts of hierarchal wonder. Though on its face the term fits well with the euphoria that so strikingly pervades the whole first stanza, and we shall later see the term applied to a hero, there is also the fact, as regards Coleridge's nomenclature in general, that it also applies to the sinister serpent-woman, Geraldine. Viewed in this light, it might be said to possess latent possibilities of trouble, an ambiguous announcement of a "problematical" theme that would become explicit later.

Similarly, despite my interpretation of "sunless" as uterine, I must concede its deathly connotations, particularly in view of the fact that the "sunless sea" will later be redefined as the "lifeless ocean." At best, we are on the edges of that midway, life-in-death stage, which played so important a part in the sufferings of the Ancient Mariner. Or, otherwise put, any connotations of *rebirth* also imply connotations of *dying*.

In any case, the overall benign tenor of the first stanza is so pronounced, the poetic conditions are set for a contrast, if the imaginative logic of the poem makes such a turn desirable. Thus, the second stanza is an amplification of the sinister meanings subsumed in the opening outcry: "But oh! that deep romantic chasm which slanted / Down the green hill athwart a cedarn cover!" On their face, chasms are cataclysmic, ghastly, and chaotic. "Athwart" on its face is troublous, to the extent that it has "thwart" in it. And in discerning Coleridge's particular nomenclature, we might well adduce as evidence, from "Fears in Solitude," the lines, "the owlet Atheism, / Sailing on obscene wings athwart the noon," though part of the damage here may be associated also with the time of day, since it was "the bloody Sun, at noon" that visited such torture on the Ancient Mariner. (More on these lines later.)

Though you may have felt that I was straining the ambiguities of "sacred" in the first stanza, surely you will grant that in this middle stanza such disturbances come to the fore: note the synonym "holy" with reference to "A savage place! . . . enchanted" (recall the "spot of enchantment") and "haunted / By woman wailing for her demon-lover!" I take it that the theme of the demon lover will return in a slightly transformed state near the end of the poem. As for the phase of the moon, Lowes notes that it was under the aegis of the "waning moon" that the Mariner's cure began. (It would be more accurate to say his *partial* cure; for we should always remember that that "grey-beard loon" was subject to periodic relapses, and then his anguish again drove him to confess his sense of guilt.)

Coleridge has so beautifully interwoven description of

*natural motions* with words for *human actions*, one is hardly
aware of the shifts between the two kinds of verbs (beginning as early as the pleasure dome, which is described as
being decreed). Thus one hardly notes the "as if" in his
reference to the "fast quick pants" with which the fountain is
"breathing." All the descriptions are so saturated with *narrative*, one inevitably senses in them a principle of *personality*.
(Ruskin's "pathetic fallacy" is carried to the point where
everything is as active as in a picture by Breughel.) Though
the observation applies to the poem throughout, we might
illustrate the point by listing only the more obvious
instances in the middle stanza: *slanted, athwart, enchanted,
waning, haunted, wailing, seething, breathing, forced, half-
intermitted, vaulted, rebounding, flung up, meandering, ran,
sank, heard, prophesying.*

I would view this general hubbub as something more than
a way of making descriptions vivid (though it certainly is at
least that). I would take it also to indicate that this inde-
terminate mixture of motion and action is in effect a poetized
*psychology*, detailing not what the reader is to *see* but what
*mental states* he is thus empathically and sympathetically
*imitating* as he reads.

I stress the notion because of my belief that it provides the
answer to the problem of the "sunless sea" synonymized in
the second stanza as a "lifeless ocean." Though the reciprocal
relation between the destination of the river and the emergence of the fountain justifies one in looking upon them as
standing for aspects of a life force that bursts into creativity
and sinks into death, I would contend that the central significance of this stream is somewhat more specific. The poem is
figuring stages in a *psychology*—and in this sense the river is,
first of all, the "stream of consciousness" (which is in turn
inextricably interwoven with the river of *time*). That is, the
design is not just depicting in general the course of *life and
death*, plus connotations of rebirth. Rather, the poem is tracing in terms of imagery the very *form* of thinking (which is
necessarily integral with a time process, inasmuch as the form
of thinking must unfold through time). It is as though, like
Kantian transcendentalism, Coleridge were speculating epistemologically on the nature of consciousness, *except* that he is
in effect talking of intuition in terms that are themselves the
embodiment of what he is talking *about*. That's why Coleridge could say in his introduction to the poem:

The Author . . . could not have composed less than from two to three hundred lines; if that indeed can be called composition in which all the images rose up before him as *things*. . . .

In this respect, I repeat, the poem could be viewed as a highly personal, *poetic* analogue of Kantian transcendentalism, which sought *conceptually* to think about itself until it ended in a schematization of the forms necessarily implicit in its very act of thinking.

I have several reasons for wanting to insist that the image of the sacred river, in its journey to and from an ultimate reservoir of the "sunless" or "lifeless," is to be viewed thus, as more specifically tied to the *psychology of idealism* than just a figuring of life and death in general. For one thing (as per my paper, "Thanatopsis for Critics: a Brief Thesaurus of Deaths and Dyings," *Essays in Criticism*, October 1952), since poets at their best write only what they profoundly know (and beyond all doubt, "Kubla Khan" is one kind of poetry at its best) and inasmuch as no living poet has experienced death, I take it for granted that, when a poet speaks of death, he is necessarily talking about something else, something witnessed *from without*, like a funeral, whereas this poem is wholly *from within*. Similarly, as regards fictions about the "supernatural," we need but consider the conduct of the "dead" sailors in "The Ancient Mariner" to realize that in the realm of the supernatural there *is* no death. Even in the "double death" of the orthodox Christian's hell, the miserable wretches somehow carry on eternally. Or Whitman's paeans to death indicate how death becomes rather like the ultimate, maternal repository from which the forms of conscious life emerge (a pattern that also infuses thoughts on the ultimate end and source of things, in the second part of Goethe's *Faust*). Or think of the similar return to the "button-moulder," in *Peer Gynt*. And to cap things, recall Coleridge's "Epitaph," asking the reader to pray "That he who many a year with toil of breath / Found death in life, may here find life in death!"

Further, the realm of "essence" can never "die." For instance, what destruction of all existing life in the universe could alter the essential "fact" that, if $a$ is greater than $b$ and $b$ is greater than $c$, then $a$ is greater than $c$? And what obliteration can be so total as to alter the fact that Napoleon's character, or "essence," must go on having been exactly what it was?

If, on the other hand, we think of the river as more specifically interweaving the stream of time and the stream of
consciousness (what Coleridge called the "streamy nature of
association"), all comes clear. For there *is* a sense in which
both time and thought continually hurry to their "death," yet
are continually "reborn," since the death of one moment is
incorporated in the moment that arises out of it, and the early
stages of a thought process are embedded in its fulfillment.
Nor should we forget Coleridge's original declared intention
with regard to the "supernatural, or at least romantic" as a
device to transfer from our "inward nature" various "shadows of imagination."

For these reasons, if you choose to see the river and the
fountain as figuring ultimately the course of life and death,
I'd ask you at least to think of these more specific "transcendental" qualifications as relevant adjectives to your
nouns. And certainly a note like this, in the *Gutch Memorandum Notebook*, is on our side: "There is not a new or
strange opinion—Truth returns from banishment—a river
run underground—fire beneath embers—." Also, in his
*Notebooks*, when saying that in the best part of one's
nature man must be solitary, he adds: "Man exists herein to
himself & to God alone—Yea, in how much only to God—
how much lies *below* his own Consciousness."

In any case, there is no questioning the fact that the
Coleridgean nomenclature elsewhere does clearly give us
personal (moral, psychological) equivalents for fountains and
streams with mazy motion. The most relevant for our purposes is in "Dejection," a poem specifically concerned with
the loss of such impulsive poetic ability as distinguishes
"Kubla Khan":

> *My genial spirits fail;*
> *And what can these avail*
> *To lift the smothering weight from off my breast?*
> *It were a vain endeavour,*
> *Though I should gaze for ever*
> *On that green light that lingers in the west:*
> *I may not hope from outward forms to win*
> *The passion and the life, whose fountains are within.*

In an expression some years later, he gives the word a
decidedly moral twist, in referring to "my conscience, the
sole fountain of certainty." In one letter, he refers to "the
pure fountain of all my moral religious feelings and com-

forts,—I mean the absolute Impersonality of the Deity." And in a formal letter of condolence, written before the production of "Kubla Khan," he had given us a related moral significance for "chaff": "The pestilence of our lusts must be scattered, the strong-layed Foundations of our Pride blown up, and the stubble and chaff of our Vanities burnt, ere we can give ear to the inspeaking Voice of Mercy, 'Why *will* ye die?' " True, Lowes finds references to fountains that hurled forth various kinds of fragments, but he also cites a reference to an "inchanting and amazing chrystal fountain"; hence so far as "sources," in his sense, are concerned, Coleridge could just as well have given us a fountain *without* "chaff." Thus, from the standpoint of "mythic" or "archetypal" sources, I'd say that Coleridge's creative fountain was a bit "problematical," as with the countertheme of this stanza generally; in effect this spirited (or breathy) upheaval had not yet separated the wheat from the tares, though it was intensely involved in the process of doing so.

In *Anima Poetae* there is an apostrophe "to a former friend" who, Coleridge says, was once a part of him, "even as the chaff to corn." The note ends bitterly: "But since that time, through whose fault I will be mute, I have been thrashed out by the flail of experience. Because you have been, therefore, never more can you be a part of the grain." May we thus take the spurt of the fountain to symbolize a personal condition prior to such dissociative "flailing"? (One might also mention some discarded lines from "The Ancient Mariner," regarding the tempest: "For days and weeks it play'd us freaks— / Like Chaff we drove along.")

"Mazy" is a word that turns up often in Coleridge. It's as characteristically his as "dim." (Though there is no "dim" in the poem itself, the introduction quotes lines that refer to "the fragments dim of lovely forms.") And if you want the range of troublous moral connotations that are packed into that word "mazy," consult a passage in "Religious Musings" (an earlier, somewhat bombastic poem that Charles Lamb greatly admired). Here Enmity, Mistrust, "listening Treachery," and War are said to falsely defend the "Lamb of God" and "Prince of Peace," whom

> *(in their songs*
> *So bards of elder times had haply feigned)*
> *Some Fury fondled in her hate of man,*
> *Bidding her serpent hair in mazy surge*

*Lick his young face, and at his mouth imbreathe*
*Horrible sympathy!*

"Religious Musings" is quite a storehouse for expressions
that reveal the moral implications in many of the most
characteristic images found in the "fascination poems."
Though Lowes cites a text that refers to the prophecy of
war (and in connection with "Abyssinia" even, an associative
preparation, if you will, of the corresponding adjective in the
final stanza), I'd view the line, "Ancestral voices prophesying
war," as a narrative way of saying in effect: This tumultuous
scene is *essentially* interwoven with such motives as we
connote by the term "war." Or, otherwise put: The war that
is to break out *subsequently* is *already implicit* in the nature
of things *now*. That is, I would interpret it as a typical
stylistic device for the "temporizing of essence." Such is
always the significance of "portents," that detect the *presence*
of the future.

The stanza does not conclude by a simple return to the
pleasure dome of the opening: three notable details are added.
We now learn of the dome's "shadow"; it is said to have
"floated midway" on the waves; and the caves are said to be
"of ice." Let us consider these additions.

In "The Ancient Mariner" we read that "where the ship's
huge shadow lay, / The charmèd water burnt alway / A still
and awful red." In a letter to Southey, written about three
years after the probable production of "Kubla Khan," Coleridge says regarding troubles with his wife that his sleep
"became the valley of the shadows of Death." (The same
letter refers to "her inveterate habits of puny thwarting," a
phrase which please bear in mind for later reference, "and
unintermitting dyspathy"; the reader must decide for himself
whether the participle throws connotative light upon the
poem's reference to the fountain's "half-intermitted burst.")
In the explicitly moralistic use of imagery in "Religious
Musings," we are told that "Life is a vision shadowy of
Truth; / And vice, and anguish, and the wormy grave, /
Shapes of a dream!"

At this point it's almost imperative that we introduce an
aside. For the pejorative reference to "shapes" all but *demands* our attention. "Shape" is characteristically a troublous
word in Coleridgese. Thus, in "Religious Musings," see "pale
Fear / Haunted by ghastlier shapings than surround / Moon-
blasted Madness when he yells at midnight." Likewise, the
ominous supernatural specter-bark of "The Ancient Mari-

ner" was "A speck, a mist, a shape." In "The Pains of Sleep" he refers to "the fiendish crowd / Of shapes and thoughts" that "tortured" him. Many other usages could be adduced here. And though, in "Dejection," Coleridge explicitly regrets that he has lost his "shaping Spirit of Imagination," in one of his letters written during the same *annus mirabilis* when the first version of "The Ancient Mariner" and the first part of "Christabel" came into being, he speaks of his body as "diseased and fevered" by his imagination. Nor should we forget the essentially ironic situation underlying "The Eolian Harp," a poem that begins as an address to his wife, but develops into a vision of beatific universal oneness; whereupon he forgets all about his "pensive Sara," until he sees her "mild reproof"—and four lines after the appearance of his characteristic word "dim," he apologizes for "These shapings of the unregenerate mind."

So much for "shadow," and its membership in a cluster of terms that include pejorative or problematical connotations of "shape." "Float" is much less strongly weighted on the "bad" side than "shadow" and "shape." Things can float either malignly or benignly, as with the Mariner's boat at different stages in its journey. In Coleridge's play, *Remorse*, there is a passage that suggests Shelley's typical kind of idealistically easy-going boat:

> *It were a lot divine in some small skiff*
> *Along some ocean's boundless solitude*
> *To float forever with a careless course*
> *And think myself the only being alive!*

Thus, in "Religious Musings," we read of Edenic delights that "float to earth." But in the same text there are "floating mists of dark idolatry" that "Broke and misshaped the omnipresent Sire." The poem itself has an interesting ambiguous usage, where talk of "Moulding Confusion" with "plastic might" (the Greek derivative *plastic* being his consistently "good" word for *shaping*) leads into talk of "bright visions" that "float." And somewhere in between, there is a letter: "My thoughts are floating about in an almost chaotic state." So, when in the next stanza you come to the "floating hair," you are presumably on a ridge that slopes both ways. And the only fairly sure grounds for deciding which way it slopes is given to us on the surface: the accompanying cry, "Beware! Beware!"

We shall consider later the strategic term *midway*. But

before leaving it for the present, I'd like to suggest that in Coleridge's poem "Love" (which transforms his troubled courtship of Sara Hutchinson into an allegory of knighthood), I doubt whether, under the modern dispensation, he'd have included the line, "When midway on the mount I lay."

We now have only the ice to deal with, and we shall have finished our consideration of the ways in which the closing lines of the second stanza are not just a return to the theme of stanza one, but a return *with a difference*. And that difference resides *precisely* in the addition of details more in keeping with the countertheme, though ambiguously so (yet not quite so ambiguously, if we read the poem not just as English, but as one particular poetic dialect of English, one vatic nomenclature subtly or implicitly, different from all others).

Lowes (as might be expected!) turns up some caverns of ice in another text that Coleridge presumably read (even a quite rare kind of ice that waxes and wanes with the phases of the moon). But we still contend that a "source" in that sense is not relevant to our present problem. For we need but assume that the source chose to talk about ice for the same reason that Coleridge incorporated what had been said in the source; namely: because "ice" has a set of mythic or archetypal connotations that recommend it to a poet's attention. And we are concerned with "derivation" in that nonhistoric but poetically principled sense.

It is obvious enough what kind of attitude is linked with the iciness of ice in "The Ancient Mariner." There, ice is purely and simply a horror. And ice is unambiguously unpleasant, insofar as it stands for coldness in the sense that Coleridge had in mind when, in the letter to Southey about his wife's "puny thwarting," he characterized her as "cold in sympathy." And we are still to discuss Coleridge's play, *Remorse*, where "fingers of ice" are located in a "chasm" within a "cavern." (Here the sound of water dropping in the darkness is likened to "puny thwartings.") But regardless of what ominous implications may lurk in the ice, on its face the reference is euphoric.

We are now ready for the wind-up. In terms of the Hegelian pattern, we should expect the final stanza (a kind of poem-within-a-poem) to synthesize the two movements that have gone before. It does so. For the vision of the "Abyssinian maid" is clearly *beatific*, yet the beholder of the vision (as presented in terms of the poem) is also to be identified with *sinister* connotations (as with those that explicitly emerge just after a recurrent reference to "those caves of ice"). I refer to the cry, "Beware! Beware!"—and to the development that malignly transforms the principle of encirclement (introduced benignly in stanza one). Of course, this "synthesis" might also be viewed as a belated or misplaced "prothesis," which is Coleridge's own word for the kind of unity that precedes a division into thesis and antithesis.

The maid in the vision is said to be Abyssinian: derive her as you will along the lines of sources in other books, there's still a tonal likelihood that the lady is Abyssinian because, among other things, as so designated she contains within this name for her essence the syllables that spell *abyss*. There, roundabout, would be the "chasm," euphorically transmuted for the last phase. And regardless of the possible derivation of "Mount Abora" from other texts (as Lowes suggests), in accordance with theories of "musicality in verse" that I have discussed elsewhere (in connection with Coleridge, an essay in *The Philosophy of Literary Form*), I would lay great stress upon the fact that *m* and *b* are close tonal cognates— hence these vocables come very close to "Singing of Mount Amora," which is understandable enough.

As for the lines, "Could I revive within me / Her symphony and song," I see in them the euphorically tinged adumbration of the outcry that was to turn up in "Dejection" only a few years later.

For some reason that it's hard to be clear about, though in a letter Coleridge admonished his son Hartley "not to speak so loud," again and again he applies this epithet to music (even to the bassoon, in "The Ancient Mariner," though that instrument cannot be loud so far as sheer decibels go). All I can offer, along these lines, is the possibility of a submerged pun, as indicated by an early poem in which Coleridge speaks of "loud, lewd Mirth." Might "loud" *deflectively* connote "lewd," in the depths of the Coleridgean nomenclature? I won't assert so, but there does seem to be the possibility— though it would be a tough one to prove, even if it were absolutely true. In the meantime, we must simply await further advices.

The cavern scenes in Act IV of *Remorse* might well be mentioned in greater detail, since they help so greatly to reveal the sinister possibilities lurking beneath the surface of the terms in "Kubla Khan." Seen in a dream, the cave is "haunted," the villain appearing to his victim in "a thousand fearful shapes." There is a morbid dalliance with "shadows." The threat implicit in the very idea of a chasm is brought out explicitly by the nature of the plot, as the villain hurls his victim "down the chasm." (Chasms, that is, are implicitly a to-be-bewared-of, a to-be-hurled-into.) And whereas we are told that the "romantic chasm" of the euphoric poem "slanted / Down," these apparently innocuous words are seen to have contained, about their edges, malign connotations, for in the victim's premonitory dream of his destruction in *Remorse*, we learn that his foot hung "aslant adown" the edge. At the end of the act, the woman who is to be the *avenger* announces, "The moon hath moved in Heaven, and I am here," a remarkable transformation of the prime motivating line in "The Ancient Mariner": "The moving Moon went up the sky." (Is the work of "moved" and "moving" done by "momently" in "Kubla Khan"?) At the start of the last act, the circle appears at its worst: "Circled with evil." A previous reference to a threatening circle of people surrounding the villain had appeared in the stage directions. A reference to the "fascination" in the eye of the hero (whom the loving heroine calls "stately") marks the spot from which I would derive the term "fascination poems" as an alternative to "mystery poems."

In the light of our analysis, it should be easy to understand why, in the closing poem-within-a-poem, the references to the poet (who is ambiguously one with both the dream and the dreamer) should be so surrounded with connotations of admonition. Yet the poem is essentially euphoric. Hence, even though we are told to "beware," and to view with "holy dread" (or rather, to deflect our eyes from) the poet who both is this marvel and has conceived it, we end on *Paradise*.

Returning now to a point we postponed when considering "midway on the waves," should we not take into consideration the fact that in the *middle stanza* the notion appears not once but four times? The other explicit places are: "Amid whose swift half-intermitted burst"; "And 'mid these dancing rocks"; "And 'mid this tumult"—while a strong trace of the pattern is also observable in "half-intermitted" and "the mingled measure / From the fountain and the caves." (I take it that "measure," in contrast with "measureless," includes connotations of poetic measure.)

At the risk of being charged with oversubtlety, I'd propose to view that design (a kind of *spatial fixity* in these many

motions and actions and actionlike motions) as a matter of
basic significance. These conflicting elements, the beatific and
the sinister, are but what we might Spinozistically call two
attributes of a single substance, the essence of the poem as a
whole. Thus, in the last analysis, the stages of its unfolding
melt into a simultaneity, a nodus of motivation that stands
"midway" between the extremes. (A stanza of "Religious
Musings" where Saints "sweep athwart" the poet's "gaze"
develops into agitation thus: "For who of woman born may
paint the hour, / When seized in his mid course, the Sun
shall wane / Making noon ghastly!" I'd hardly dare press the
point; but we might at least recall that the midday sun trans-
fixed the Mariner's boat, and Christabel's troubles took place
at midnight. And anyone who is concerned with the strange
magic of reversal, as in formulae like "ave Eva," might also
pause to note however uneasily that, quite as Cummings saw
*God* as *dog* spelled backwards, so *mid* is but a chiastic
form of Coleridge's ubiquitous *dim*.)

However, even if there is a sense in which the generating
principle represented by this poem's action is itself as much
an unmoved mover as Aristotle's God (with even an analogue of "negative theology" in "sunless," "lifeless," and
"measureless"), there is also the fact that, as "broken down"
into a quasi-temporal sequence, the translation of this essential unity into a series of successive revelations (or tiny
"apocalypses") can *begin* with reference to an Edenic garden, and *end* on the word *Paradise*. In this sense, despite the
intrinsic immobility of the poem's organizing principle (a
"midway" situation that found more explicit dissociative
expression in "The Ancient Mariner," both in the figure of
the motionless boat, and in the specter, "The Night-mare Life-
in-Death"); despite the fact that while the narrative relation
between rising fountain and sinking river goes on "turning,"
the *principle* behind the unfolding is "forever still"; despite
these ups and downs en route, the poem as a whole can be
called "euphoric."

We are now ready to take up the problem that arises from
our insistence upon calling the poem *finished* whereas the
author himself called it a "fragment." Here I can best make
my point by quoting a passage from my *Philosophy of
Literary Form* (Vintage edition, pp. 26–27):

Imagine an author who had laid out a five-act drama of
the rational, intricate, intrigue sort—a situation that was
wound up at the start, and was to be unwound, step by

step, through the five successive acts. Imagine that this plot was scheduled, in Act V, to culminate in a scene of battle. Dramatic consistency would require the playwright to "foreshadow" this battle. Hence, in Act III, he might give us the battle incipiently, or implicitly, in a vigorous battle of words between the antagonists. But since there was much business still to be transacted, in unwinding the plot to its conclusion he would treat Act III as a mere foreshadowing of Act V, and would proceed with his composition until the promises emergent in Act III had been fulfilled in Act V.

On the other hand, imagine a "lyric" plot that had reduced the intrigue business to a minimum. When the poet had completed Act III, his job would be ended, and despite his intention to write a work in five acts, he might very well feel a loss of inclination to continue into Acts IV and V. For the act of foreshadowing, in Act III, would already *implicitly contain* the culmination of the promises. The battle of words would itself be the *symbolic equivalent* of the mortal combat scheduled for Act V. Hence, it would *serve as surrogate* for the *quality* with which he had intended to end Act V, whereat the poet would have no good reason to continue further. He would "lose interest"—and precisely because the quality of Act V had been "telescoped" into the quality of Act III that foreshadowed it (and in foreshadowing it, was of the same substance or essence). Act III would be a kind of ejaculation too soon, with the purpose of the composition forthwith dwindling.

Does not this possibility solve our problem? I believe that, in principle at least, Coleridge actually did dream all those lines, and transcribed them somewhat as an amanuensis might have done. For nearly every writer has jotted down a few bits that he woke up with, and there's no reason why someone couldn't wake up with more. And Mozart apparently could conceive of a work all finished before he wrote it down, so that in effect the act of composition was but the translating of a timeless unity (like a painting or piece of sculpture) into a temporal progression (quite as the observer reads histories into a static form when he lets his eye wander from place to place across it, thereby "improvising" developments within its parts). And even a long and complex structure that one works out painfully step by step

may involve but the progressive "discovery" of implications
already present in the "germ" that set him off in the first
place. Why had it even struck him as worth working on, if it
had not been for him like a knotted bundle of possibilities—
which he would untie one by one, as the loosening of each
knot set the conditions for the loosening of the next (like a
psychoanalyst's patient discovering by free association things
that he somehow already knew but didn't know he knew)?

But "Kubla Khan" was the kind of poem that Coleridge's
own aesthetic theories were not abreast of. His very attempts
to distinguish between "imagination" and "fancy" at the
expense of the latter serve to indicate my point. "Fancy"
wouldn't come into its own until the time of Rimbaud, when
it would take on dimensions that Coleridge never explicitly
attributed to it. For his concept of fancy got mixed up with
purely mechanical doctrines of associationism, which he
strongly rejected (a kind of resistance that was probably also
tied up with his moralistic attempts to resist the compulsive
aspects of his addiction to opium, when it became integrated
with the fountain of his creativity). In any case, at the very
start of his collaboration with Wordsworth in plans for the
lyrical ballads, the kind of job he set himself really involved
an ideal of "fancy" (but not in the partly pejorative sense
that the term took on, in the dialectic of his *Biographia
Literaria*). And as an integral aspect of such possibilities
there would be the kind of imagistic short-circuiting to which
I have referred in my quotation from *Philosophy of Literary Form*.

Thus, when one contemporary critic finds that the expression, "ancestral voices prophesying war" is "too pointless,"
since "no further use is made of it," the objection would be
like contending that, in Eliot's "Gerontion," a line such as
"By Hakagawa, bowing among the Titians" is "pointless"
because we learn nothing more about Hakagawa. On the
contrary, as I have tried to show, the line does to perfection
exactly what it is there for, as a narrative way of stating a
motivational essence. Yvor Winters' label, "Reference to a
nonexistent plot," to characterize such usages as Eliot's, helps
us see that Coleridge's poem was already moving towards a
later elliptical manner, at a time when Southey could have
turned "Kubla Khan" into a work as long as "The Ring and
the Book." In this sense, the poem was a "fragment." But it is
complete insofar as no further movements are needed (or
even possible, without the poem's becoming something else,

as when one dream fades into another). The most one can
imagine is the addition of a few details that amplify what is
already sufficiently there. By the same token, there is the
embarrassing fact that the more efficient the poet's brevity,
the greater is the need for the critic to expatiate in trying to
show how condensed the work really is.

All told, the more closely we study the poem in the light of
Coleridge's particular nomenclature, the more fully we realize how many of the terms have sinister connotations. Imagery lends itself well to such shiftiness, and readily transcends
the law of excluded middle. In fact, such susceptibility doubtless accounts for much of its appeal, since it can so spontaneously bridge the gulfs of dispute, and can simultaneously
confess and be reticent. In line with contemporary interests,
one might note that Coleridge explicitly equates the image of
the fountain with the principle of what would now be called
"creativity." On this point, in addition to references already
cited, we might recall his objections, in his preface to "Christabel," to "a set of critics . . . who have no notion that there
are such things as fountains in the world, small as well as
great." At another place he distinguishes between "springs"
and "tanks" ("two Kinds of Heads in the world of literature"). Elsewhere, when on the subject of "knowing" and
"being," he sums up by thoughts on "the common fountain-
head of both, the mysterious source whose being is knowledge, whose knowledge is being—the adorable I AM IN THAT I
AM." In *Anima Poetae* he writes: *"Nota bene* to make a
detailed comparison, in the manner of Jeremy Taylor, between the searching for the first cause of a thing and the
seeking the fountains of the Nile—so many streams, each
with its particular fountains—and, at last, it all comes to a
name." Another note beautifully illustrates how the image
takes on other connotations of delight: "Some wilderness-
plot—green and fountainous and unviolated by Man." But
"creativity" also has its *risks*. And whether or not you would
agree that the "problematic" element was heightened in Coleridge's case by the interweaving of the mystery poems with
the early stages of opium addiction, it still remains a fact that
in "Kubla Khan" as enacted in detail, the principle of inspiration is simultaneously welcomed and feared (a secular attitude properly analogous to the theologians' doubts whether a
vision of the divine is truly from God or from the Devil in
disguise).

In later years, in his theological work, *Aids to Reflection*,
when on the subject of mysticism (a term that he explicitly

says he is using in "a bad sense"), it is interesting to see how Coleridge allegorizes his theories by reapplying the imagery of his mystery poems (thus in effect saying that mystery is to poetry as mysticism is to religion). However, the mystics to whom he is objecting are men for whom he had great affection (such as Boehme and Fenelon). He explicitly refers to "The Ancient Mariner," "Christabel," and "The Wanderings of Cain" in connection with his allegory, using the "creations" of his youthful fancy to illustrate the "errors" of mysticism. (Note *fancy*, not *imagination*, though he had already published his *Biographia Literaria* in which *fancy* was downgraded.) There is "an oasis or Islet of Verdure on the Sea of Sand"; a pilgrim here "wanders at leisure in its maze of beauty and sweetness." Moonshine is "the imaginative poesy of nature" that spreads "its soft shadowy form over all." Thus, if you "interpret the moonlight and the shadows as the peculiar genius and sensibility of the individual's own spirit," you get but "a dream of truth," while in another connection there is "truth mingled with the dream." There is a wanderer who has "eaten of the fruits and drunk of the fountain," has been "scared by the roar and howl from the desert," and is confused because "shadows and imperfect beholdings and vivid fragments of things distinctly seen blend with the past and present shapings of his brain." There is a narrator whose "craving for sympathy . . . impels him to unbosom himself to abstract auditors." There is talk of an "enchanted land" and "refreshing caves." Throughout, the reservations on mysticism are thus spoken of mildly and sympathetically. But the mood grows harsh when the subject shifts from mysticism to materialism, whereupon Coleridge says of materialism and subjective idealism: "the one obtruding on us a World of Spectres and Apparitions; the other a mazy Dream!"

In *Confessions of an Inquiring Spirit*, there is a passage that faintly suggests the kind of imagery with which "Kubla Khan" was concerned. But here the strong stress upon the fountainheads of creativity has definitely given way to image-tinged thoughts on life in general: "The unsubstantial, insulated Self passes away as a stream; but these are the shadows and reflections of the Rock of Ages, and of the Tree of Life that starts forth from its side."

I have here given the paper as written prior to a discussion of the poem in a seminar at the University of California (Santa Barbara Division), in the fall of 1964. I presented the substance of these pages in a lecture there, on the same day when members of the class submitted their own analyses, worked out independently of my observations. Some of their papers, and the discussion that followed, have led me to sharpen up the overall outline of the poem thus:

The fountain is so obviously scandalous when its behavior is considered from the psychoanalytic point of view, it prompts students to offer many ingenious speculations along those lines, ranging between extremes of heterosexual and homosexual motivations. The tendency is to lay great stress upon the orgastic aspects of the fountain's ejaculatory ways. I would but ask that any such interpretations do not confine themselves to the *erotic*, but also deal with the *familial* aspects of the imagination. Viewed in such wider terms, the steps in the poem could be summed up thus:

Kubla Khan's decree is the romantic counterpart of God's authoritative (parental, creative) fiat. The pleasure dome and encircled garden are the analogue of happily enclosed Edenic *innocence*.

The fountain and the chasm figure the *fall*, as personalized in the wailing woman (the erotic woman) and the demon lover.

When the lines that revert to the first theme add the shadow and the ice, the stage of "innocence" has been radically modified. It now confronts a conscience-laden way of life overshadowed by connotations of frigidity, or castration. Innocence being lost, there can at best be the straining after virtue.

The final synthesis (the song-within-a-song) reveals the personal figure that was missing in the garden (perhaps because the garden did itself stand for that figure in being inchoately maternal). If Kubla Khan is the father, and the poet is the child who had left the garden and erred, then the "damsel" is the counterpart of Mary, the heavenly mother, *gratia plena*, the erotic woman replaced by the maternal woman (*eros* replaced by *agape*), plus romantic ambiguities. The poet, now grown up, is "set apart" by his profession, a role at once sacred and criminal. And appropriately the *hoi polloi* of everyday society are apostrophized and admonished with regard to him. (The poem, in brief, is a "breakdown" of the romantic passion, involving analogues of the concern with "beginnings" in the book of Genesis. The principles of what, in current cant, is called *creativity*, are here stated narratively. Though they all imply one another (as a cycle of interrelated terms) they are here reduced to a sequence. There is a "problematical" element implicit in such romantically spontaneous waywardness; and biographical data permit us to speculate on the further possibility (lying outside the realm of poetics proper) that the fountain of productivity had also become interwoven with the instabilities of drug addiction (though in this particular poem, the admonitory element is present but the stress is predominantly euphoric).

In general, the papers that favored psychoanalytic modes of interpretation omitted what I have called the important *familial* aspect of the poem's development, and thus slighted the problem of accounting for the *successive stages* of the poem. Also, one member of the class contended that the poem could not be fully developed because a fuller development would have involved too much "self-revelation." To this notion I would only add the fact that there is a sheerly *formal* reason why any such implications could not be made explicit: for they would necessarily introduce doctrinal terms alien to the work's nature as a poetic species—somewhat as a scientific theory of guilt is alien to the experience of guilt in its intuitive immediacy. True, one might go back a bit farther, and note that all poems relying strongly upon imagery permit of much reticence, even in the midst of *implied* "confession." But by the same token, any *explicit* step outside this charmed circle is the fault of the reader or critic, not of the poet, intrinsic to whose "reticently" ambiguous medium is the rejoinder, *honi soit qui mal y pense.*

In closing I should also refer to a delightful article on "Kubla Khan" by Miss Kathleen Raine in the autumn, 1964, issue of *The Sewanee Review.* I am happy to note that she allows for the "abyss" in "Abyssinia," hence I can retreat behind her authority. Also, she rightly points to Abyssinia's association with the symbolic motives implicit in Coleridge's thoughts on the source of the Nile.

And her remarks on the dulcimer are a major contribution. I refer to her reminding us that it is "a one-stringed instrument, the monochord," upon which the Pythagoreans worked out their theory of the diatonic scale, and their application of it to the structure of the universe. Accordingly, when Coleridge's damsel plays a dulcimer, "she plays upon the chords of harmony which underlie all creation." It is most exciting to realize that Coleridge's line, so lovely as sheer music, has this added "doctrinal" backing.

But when Miss Raine comments on the Platonic doctrine of anamnesis, I dare avow that, until critics get my point about the "temporizing of essence" (as discussed particularly in my *Grammar of Motives* and *Rhetoric of Religion*) they will not grasp the sheerly *linguistic* principle underlying the relationship between "mythic" and "philosophic" terms for "beginnings." Such analysis is needed to explain the position of the quasi-narrative "archetypes" that Plato's nomenclature situates midway between terms for logical priority and terms for temporal priority. It involves the step from a mythological to what I would call a "logological" study of such poetic structures as "Kubla Khan," with its obvious *bearing upon the very rudiments of poetic genesis.*

# The Rime of the Ancient Mariner

## IN SEVEN PARTS

Facile credo, plures esse Naturas invisibiles quam visibiles in rerum universitate. Sed horum omnium familiam quis nobis enarrabit? et gradus et cognationes et discrimina et singulorum munera? Quid agunt? quae loca habitant? Harum rerum notitiam semper ambivit ingenium humanum, nunquam attigit. Juvat, interea, non diffiteor, quandoque in animo, tanquam in tabulà, majoris et melioris mundi imaginem contemplari: ne mens assuefacta hodiernae vitae minutiis se contrahat nimis, et tota subsidat in pusillas cogitationes. Sed veritati interea invigilandum est, modusque servandus, ut certa ab incertis, diem a nocte, distinguamus.

T. BURNET, *Archaeol. Phil., p. 68*

### ARGUMENT

How a Ship having passed the Line was driven by storms to the cold Country towards the South Pole; and how from thence she made her course to the tropical Latitude of the Great Pacific Ocean; and of the strange things that befell; and in what manner the Ancyent Marinere came back to his own Country.

### PART I

*An ancient Mariner meeteth three Gallants bidden to a wedding-feast, and detaineth one.*

It is an ancient Mariner,
And he stoppeth one of three.
"By thy long grey beard and glittering eye,
Now wherefore stopp'st thou me?

The Bridegroom's doors are opened wide,      5
And I am next of kin;
The guests are met, the feast is set:
May'st hear the merry din."

He holds him with his skinny hand,
"There was a ship," quoth he.      10

"Hold off! unhand me, grey-beard loon!"
Eftsoons his hand dropt he.

The Wedding-Guest is spellbound by the eye of the old seafaring man, and constrained to hear his tale.

He holds him with his glittering eye—
The Wedding-Guest stood still,
And listens like a three years' child:          15
The Mariner hath his will.

The Wedding-Guest sat on a stone:
He cannot choose but hear;
And thus spake on that ancient man,
The bright-eyed Mariner.                        20

The Mariner tells how the ship sailed southward with a good wind and fair weather, till it reached the line.

"The ship was cheered, the harbour cleared,
Merrily did we drop
Below the kirk, below the hill,
Below the lighthouse top

The Sun came up upon the left,                  25
Out of the sea came he!
And he shone bright, and on the right
Went down into the sea.

Higher and higher every day,
Till over the mast at noon—"                     30
The Wedding-Guest here beat his breast,
For he heard the loud bassoon.

The Wedding-Guest heareth the bridal music; but the Mariner continueth his tale.

The bride hath paced into the hall,
Red as a rose is she;
Nodding their heads before her goes             35
The merry minstrelsy.

The Wedding-Guest he beat his breast,
Yet he cannot choose but hear;
And thus spake on that ancient man,
The bright-eyed Mariner.                         40

The ship driven by a storm toward the south pole.

"And now the STORM-BLAST came and he
Was tyrannous and strong:
He struck with his o'ertaking wings,
And chased us south along.

With sloping masts and dipping prow,            45
As who pursued with yell and blow
Still treads the shadow of his foe,
And forward bends his head,
The ship drove fast, loud roared the blast,
And southward aye we fled.                      50

And now there came both mist and snow,
And it grew wondrous cold:

And ice, mast-high, came floating by,
As green as emerald.

The land
of ice, and
of fearful
sounds
where no
living
thing was
to be seen.

And through the drifts the snowy clifts    55
Did send a dismal sheen:
Nor shapes of men nor beasts we ken—
The ice was all between.

The ice was here, the ice was there,
The ice was all around:    60
It cracked and growled, and roared and howled,
Like noises in a swound!

Till a great
seabird,
called the
Albatross,
came
through
the snow-
fog, and
was re-
ceived
with great
joy and
hospitality.

At length did cross an Albatross,
Thorough the fog it came;
As if it had been a Christian soul,    65
We hailed it in God's name.

It ate the food it ne'er had eat,
And round and round it flew.
The ice did split with a thunderfit;
The helmsman steered us through!    70

And lo!
the Alba-
tross prov-
eth a bird
of good
omen, and
followeth
the ship as
it returned
northward
through
fog and
floating
ice.

And a good south wind sprung up behind;
The Albatross did follow,
And every day, for food or play,
Came to the mariner's hollo!

In mist or cloud, on mast or shroud,    75
It perched for vespers nine;
Whiles all the night, through fog-smoke white,
Glimmered the white Moonshine."

The
ancient
Mariner in-
hospitably
killeth the
pious bird
of good
omen.

"God save thee, ancient Mariner!
From the fiends, that plague thee thus!—    80
Why look'st thou so?"—With my crossbow
I shot the ALBATROSS.

PART II

The Sun now rose upon the right:
Out of the sea came he,
Still hid in mist, and on the left    85
Went down into the sea.

And the good south wind still blew behind,
But no sweet bird did follow,
Nor any day for food or play
Came to the mariners' hollo!                                    90

His ship-
mates cry
out against
the ancient
Mariner,
for killing
the bird of
good luck.

And I had done a hellish thing,
And it would work 'em woe:
For all averred, I had killed the bird
That made the breeze to blow.
Ah wretch! said they, the bird to slay,          95
That made the breeze to blow!

But when
the fog
cleared off,
they justify
the same,
and thus
make
themselves
accom-
plices in the crime.

Nor dim nor red, like God's own head,
The glorious Sun uprist:
Then all averred, I had killed the bird
That brought the fog and mist.                    100
'Twas right, said they, such birds to slay,
That bring the fog and mist.

The fair
breeze
continues;
the ship
enters the
Pacific
Ocean, and
sails north-
ward, even
till it reaches the Line.

The fair breeze blew, the white foam flew,
The furrow followed free;
We were the first that ever burst              105
Into that silent sea.

The ship
hath been
suddenly
becalmed.

Down dropt the breeze, the sails dropt down,
'Twas sad as sad could be;
And we did speak only to break
The silence of the sea!                           110

All in a hot and copper sky,
The bloody Sun, at noon,
Right up above the mast did stand,
No bigger than the Moon.

Day after day, day after day,                     115
We stuck, nor breath nor motion;
As idle as a painted ship
Upon a painted ocean.

And the
Albatross
begins to
be avenged

Water, water, every where,
And all the boards did shrink;                    120
Water, water, every where,
Nor any drop to drink.

The very deep did rot: O Christ!
That ever this should be!
Yea, slimy things did crawl with legs     125
Upon the slimy sea.

About, about, in reel and rout
The death-fires danced at night;
The water, like a witch's oils,
Burnt green, and blue and white.     130

And some in dreams assurèd were
Of the Spirit that plagued us so;
Nine fathom deep he had followed us
From the land of mist and snow.

And every tongue, through utter drought,     135
Was withered at the root;
We could not speak, no more than if
We had been choked with soot.

*A Spirit had followed them; one of the invisible inhabitants of this planet, neither departed* souls nor angels; concerning whom the learned Jew, Josephus, and the Platonic Constantinopolitan, Michael Psellus, may be consulted. They are very numerous, and there is no climate or element without one or more.

Ah! well a-day! what evil looks
Had I from old and young!     140
Instead of the cross, the Albatross
About my neck was hung.

*The shipmates, in their sore distress, would fain throw the* whole guilt on the ancient Mariner: in sign whereof they hang the dead seabird round his neck.

## PART III

There passed a weary time. Each throat
Was parched, and glazed each eye.
A weary time! a weary time!     145
How glazed each weary eye,
When looking westward, I beheld
A something in the sky.

At first it seemed a little speck,
And then it seemed a mist;     150
It moved and moved, and took at last
A certain shape, I wist.

A speck, a mist, a shape, I wist!
And still it neared and neared:
As if it dodged a water-sprite,     155
It plunged and tacked and veered.

*The ancient Mariner beholdeth a sign in the element afar off.*

At its
nearer
approach,
it seemeth
him to be a
ship; and
at a dear
ransom he
freeth his
speech
from the
bonds of
thirst.

With throats unslaked, with black lips baked,
We could nor laugh nor wail;
Through utter drought all dumb we stood!
I bit my arm, I sucked the blood,          160
And cried, A sail! a sail!

With throats unslaked, with black lips baked,
Agape they heard me call:

A flash of
joy;

Gramercy! they for joy did grin,
And all at once their breath drew in,      165
As they were drinking all.

And
horror
follows.
For can it
be a ship
that comes
onward
without
wind or
tide?

See! see! (I cried) she tacks no more!
Hither to work us weal;
Without a breeze, without a tide,
She steadies with upright keel!            170

The western wave was all a-flame.
The day was well nigh done!
Almost upon the western wave
Rested the broad bright Sun;
When that strange shape drove suddenly     175
Betwixt us and the Sun.

It seemeth
him but
the skcle-
ton of a
ship.

And straight the Sun was flecked with bars,
(Heaven's Mother send us grace!)
As if through a dungeon-grate he peered
With broad and burning face.               180

And its
ribs are
seen as
bars on the
face of the
setting
Sun. The
Spectre-
Woman

Alas! (thought I, and my heart beat loud)
How fast she nears and nears!
Are those *her* sails that glance in the Sun,
Like restless gossameres?

Are those *her* ribs through which the Sun   185
Did peer, as through a grate?
And is that Woman all her crew?

Is that a DEATH? and are there two?
Is DEATH that woman's mate?

and her
Death-
mate, and
no other
on board
the skele-
ton ship.

Like vessel,
like crew!

*Her* lips were red, *her* looks were free,        190
Her locks were yellow as gold:
Her skin was as white as leprosy,
The Night-mare LIFE-IN-DEATH was she,
Who thicks man's blood with cold.

Death and
Life-in-
Death have
diced for
the ship's
crew, and
she (the
latter)
winneth
the ancient
Mariner.

The naked hulk alongside came,        195
And the twain were casting dice;
"The game is done! I've won! I've won!"
Quoth she, and whistles thrice.

No twi-
light
within the
courts of
the Sun.

The Sun's rim dips; the stars rush out:
At one stride comes the dark;        200
With far-heard whisper, o'er the sea,
Off shot the spectre-bark.

At the
rising of
the Moon,

We listened and looked sideways up!
Fear at my heart, as at a cup,
My life-blood seemed to sip!        205
The stars were dim, and thick the night,
The steersman's face by his lamp gleamed white;

From the sails the dew did drip—
Till clomb above the eastern bar
The hornèd Moon, with one bright star        210
Within the nether tip.

One after
another,

One after one, by the star-dogged Moon,
Too quick for groan or sigh,
Each turned his face with a ghastly pang,
And cursed me with his eye.        215

His ship-
mates drop
down
dead.

Four times fifty living men,
(And I heard nor sigh nor groan)
With heavy thump, a lifeless lump,
They dropped down one by one.

But Life-
in-Death
begins her
work on
the ancient
Mariner.

The souls did from their bodies fly,—        220
They fled to bliss or woe!
And every soul, it passed me by,
Like the whizz of my cross-bow!

## PART IV

The Wed-
ding-Guest
feareth
that a
Spirit is
talking to
him;

"I fear thee, ancient Mariner!
I fear thy skinny hand!     225
And thou art long, and lank, and brown,
As is the ribbed sea-sand.

I fear thee and thy glittering eye,
And thy skinny hand, so brown."—
Fear not, fear not, thou Wedding-Guest!     230
This body dropt not down.

But the
ancient
Mariner
assureth
him of his
bodily life,
and pro-
ceedeth to
relate his
horrible
penance.

Alone, alone, all, all alone,
Alone on a wide wide sea!
And never a saint took pity on
My soul in agony.     235

He de-
spiseth the
creatures
of the
calm,

The many men, so beautiful!
And they all dead did lie:
And a thousand thousand slimy things
Lived on; and so did I.

And envi-
eth that
*they*
should
live, and
so many
lie dead.

I looked upon the rotting sea,     240
And drew my eyes away;
I looked upon the rotting deck,
And there the dead men lay.

I looked to heaven, and tried to pray;
But or ever a prayer had gusht,     245
A wicked whisper came, and made
My heart as dry as dust.

I closed my lids, and kept them close,
And the balls like pulses beat;
For the sky and the sea, and the sea and the sky 250
Lay like a load on my weary eye,
And the dead were at my feet.

But the
curse
liveth for
him in the
eye of the
dead men.

The cold sweat melted from their limbs,
Nor rot nor reek did they:
The look with which they looked on me     255
Had never passed away.

An orphan's curse would drag to hell
A spirit from on high;
But oh! more horrible than that
Is the curse in a dead man's eye!                     260
Seven days, seven nights, I saw that curse,
And yet I could not die.

In his lone-
liness and     The moving Moon went up the sky,
fixedness      And no where did abide:
he yearn-      Softly she was going up,                            265
eth to-        And a star or two beside—
wards the
journeying     Her beams bemocked the sultry main,
Moon, and      Like April hoar-frost spread;
the stars      But where the ship's huge shadow lay,
that still     The charmèd water burnt alway               270
sojourn,       A still and awful red.
yet still
move on-
ward; and every where the blue sky belongs to them, and is their
appointed rest, and their native country and their own natural
homes, which they enter unannounced, as lords that are certainly
expected and yet there is a silent joy at their arrival.

By the         Beyond the shadow of the ship,
light of the   I watched the water-snakes:
Moon he        They moved in tracks of shining white,
beholdeth       And when they reared, the elfish light             275
God's          Fell off in hoary flakes.
creatures
of the
great calm.

               Within the shadow of the ship
               I watched their rich attire:
               Blue, glossy green, and velvet black,
               They coiled and swam; and every track          280
               Was a flash of golden fire.

Their
beauty and     O happy living things! no tongue
their hap-     Their beauty might declare:
piness.        A spring of love gushed from my heart,

He bless-      And I blessed them unaware:                         285
eth them       Sure my kind saint took pity on me,
in his         And I blessed them unaware.
heart.

The spell      The self-same moment I could pray;
begins to      And from my neck so free
break.         The Albatross fell off, and sank                    290
               Like lead into the sea.

### PART V

Oh sleep! it is a gentle thing,
Beloved from pole to pole!
To Mary Queen the praise be given!
She sent the gentle sleep from Heaven,     295
That slid into my soul.

By grace
of the holy
Mother,
the ancient
Mariner is
refreshed
with rain.

The silly buckets on the deck,
That had so long remained,
I dreamt that they were filled with dew;
And when I awoke, it rained.     300

My lips were wet, my throat was cold,
My garments all were dank;
Sure I had drunken in my dreams,
And still my body drank.

I moved, and could not feel my limbs:     305
I was so light—almost
I thought that I had died in sleep,
And was a blessèd ghost.

He heareth
sounds and
seeth
strange
sights and
commo-
tions in the
sky and
the ele-
ment.

And soon I heard a roaring wind:
It did not come anear;     310
But with its sound it shook the sails,
That were so thin and sere.

The upper air burst into life!
And a hundred fire-flags sheen,
To and fro they were hurried about!     315
And to and fro, and in and out,
The wan stars danced between.

And the coming wind did roar more loud,
And the sails did sigh like sedge;
And the rain poured down from one black
          cloud;     320
The Moon was at its edge.

The thick black cloud was cleft, and still
The Moon was at its side:
Like waters shot from some high crag,
The lightning fell with never a jag,     325
A river steep and wide.

The bodies
of the
ship's crew
are in-
spired and
the ship
moves on;

The loud wind never reached the ship,
Yet now the ship moved on!
Beneath the lightning and the Moon
The dead men gave a groan.     330

They groaned, they stirred, they all uprose,
Nor spake, nor moved their eyes;
It had been strange, even in a dream,
To have seen those dead men rise.

The helmsman steered, the ship moved on;    335
Yet never a breeze up-blew;
The mariners all 'gan work the ropes,
Where they were wont to do;
They raised their limbs like lifeless tools—
We were a ghastly crew.    340

The body of my brother's son
Stood by me, knee to knee:
The body and I pulled at one rope,
But he said nought to me.

"I fear thee, ancient Mariner!"    345
Be calm, thou Wedding-Guest!
'Twas not those souls that fled in pain,
Which to their corses came again,
But a troop of spirits blest:

For when it dawned—they dropped their
    arms,    350
And clustered round the mast;
Sweet sounds rose slowly through their mouths,
And from their bodies passed.

Around, around, flew each sweet sound,
Then darted to the Sun;    355
Slowly the sounds came back again,
Now mixed, now one by one.

Sometimes a-dropping from the sky
I heard the sky-lark sing;
Sometimes all little birds that are,    360
How they seemed to fill the sea and air
With their sweet jargoning!

And now 'twas like all instruments,
Now like a lonely flute;
And now it is an angel's song,    365
That makes the heavens be mute.

It ceased; yet still the sails made on
A pleasant noise till noon,
A noise like of a hidden brook
In the leafy month of June,    370

But not by the souls of the men, nor by dæmons of earth or middle air, but by a blessed troop of angelic spirits, sent down by the invocation of the guardian saint.

That to the sleeping woods all night
Singeth a quiet tune.

Till noon we quietly sailed on,
Yet never a breeze did breathe:
Slowly and smoothly went the ship,                    375
Moved onward from beneath.

The lone-
some
Spirit from
the south-
pole car-
ries on the
ship as far
as the Line,
in obedi-
ence to the
angelic
troop, but
still re-
quireth
vengeance.

Under the keel nine fathom deep,
From the land of mist and snow,
The spirit slid: and it was he
That made the ship to go.                             380
The sails at noon left off their tune,
And the ship stood still also.

The Sun, right up above the mast,
Had fixed her to the ocean:
But in a minute she 'gan stir,                        385
With a short uneasy motion—
Backwards and forwards half her length
With a short uneasy motion.

Then like a pawing horse let go,
She made a sudden bound:                              390
It flung the blood into my head,
And I fell down in a swound.

The Polar
Spirit's fel-
low-dæ-
mons, the
invisible
inhabitants
of the ele-
ment, take
part in his
wrong;
and two of
them re-
late, one to
the other,
that pen-
ance long
and heavy
for the
ancient
Mariner
hath been
accorded
to the
Polar
Spirit, who
returneth
southward.

How long in that same fit I lay,
I have not to declare;
But ere my living life returned,                      395
I heard and in my soul discerned
Two voices in the air.

"Is it he?" quoth one, "Is this the man?
By him who died on cross,
With his cruel bow he laid full low                   400
The harmless Albatross.

The spirit who bideth by himself
In the land of mist and snow,
He loved the bird that loved the man
Who shot him with his bow."                           405

The other was a softer voice,
As soft as honey-dew:
Quoth he, "The man hath penance done,
And penance more will do."

PART VI

FIRST VOICE

"But tell me, tell me! speak again,     410
Thy soft response renewing—
What makes that ship drive on so fast?
What is the ocean doing?"

SECOND VOICE

"Still as a slave before his lord,
The ocean hath no blast;     415
His great bright eye most silently
Up to the Moon is cast—

If he may know which way to go;
For she guides him smooth or grim.
See, brother, see! how graciously     420
She looketh down on him."

FIRST VOICE

The Mariner hath been cast into a trance; for the angelic power causeth the vessel to drive northward faster than human life could endure.

"But why drives on that ship so fast,
Without or wave or wind?"

SECOND VOICE

"The air is cut away before,
And closes from behind.     425

Fly, brother, fly! more high, more high!
Or we shall be belated:
For slow and slow that ship will go,
When the Mariner's trance is abated."

The supernatural motion is retarded; the Mariner awakes, and his penance begins anew.

I woke, and we were sailing on     430
As in a gentle weather:
'Twas night, calm night, the moon was high;
The dead men stood together.

All stood together on the deck,
For a charnel-dungeon fitter:     435
All fixed on me their stony eyes,
That in the Moon did glitter.

The pang, the curse, with which they died,
Had never passed away:

I could not draw my eyes from theirs, 440
Nor turn them up to pray.

*The curse
is finally
expiated.*

And now this spell was snapt: once more
I viewed the ocean green,
And looked far forth, yet little saw
Of what had else been seen— 445

Like one, that on a lonesome road
Doth walk in fear and dread,
And having once turned round walks on,
And turns no more his head;
Because he knows, a frightful fiend 450
Doth close behind him tread.

But soon there breathed a wind on me,
Nor sound nor motion made:
Its path was not upon the sea,
In ripple or in shade. 455

It raised my hair, it fanned my cheek
Like a meadow-gale of spring—
It mingled strangely with my fears,
Yet it felt like a welcoming.

Swiftly, swiftly flew the ship, 460
Yet she sailed softly too:
Sweetly, sweetly blew the breeze—
On me alone it blew.

*And the
ancient
Mariner
beholdeth
his native
country.*

Oh! dream of joy! is this indeed
The light-house top I see? 465
Is this the hill? is this the kirk?
Is this mine own countree?

We drifted o'er the harbour-bar,
And I with sobs did pray—
O let me be awake, my God! 470
Or let me sleep alway.

The harbour-bay was clear as glass,
So smoothly it was strewn!
And on the bay the moonlight lay,
And the shadow of the Moon. 475

The rock shone bright, the kirk no less,
That stands above the rock:
The moonlight steeped in silentness
The steady weathercock.

And the bay was white with silent light,          480
Till rising from the same,
Full many shapes, that shadows were,
In crimson colours came.

The an-
gelic spirits
leave the
dead
bodies,

A little distance from the prow
Those crimson shadows were:          485
I turned my eyes upon the deck—
Oh, Christ! what saw I there!

And ap-
pear in
their own
forms of
light.

Each corse lay flat, lifeless and flat,
And, by the holy rood!
A man all light, a seraph-man,          490
On every corse there stood.

This seraph-band, each waved his hand:
It was a heavenly sight!
They stood as signals to the land,
Each one a lovely light;          495

This seraph-band, each waved his hand,
No voice did they impart—
No voice; but oh! the silence sank
Like music on my heart.

But soon I heard the dash of oars,          500
I heard the Pilot's cheer;
My head was turned perforce away
And I saw a boat appear.

The Pilot and the Pilot's boy,
I heard them coming fast:          505
Dear Lord in Heaven! it was a joy
The dead men could not blast.

I saw a third—I heard his voice:
It is the Hermit good!
He singeth loud his godly hymns          510
That he makes in the wood.
He'll shrieve my soul, he'll wash away
The Albatross's blood.

PART VII

The Her-
mit of the
Wood,

This Hermit good lives in that wood
Which slopes down to the sea.          515
How loudly his sweet voice he rears!

He loves to talk with marineres
That come from a far countree.

He kneels at morn, and noon, and eve—
He hath a cushion plump:                                   520
It is the moss that wholly hides
The rotted old oak-stump.

The skiff-boat neared: I heard them talk,
"Why, this is strange, I trow!
Where are those lights so many and fair,   525
That signal made but now?"

Approach-<br>eth the<br>ship with<br>wonder.

"Strange, by my faith!" the Hermit said—
"And they answered not our cheer!
The planks looked warped! and see those
    sails,
How thin they are and sere!                               530
I never saw aught like to them,
Unless perchance it were

Brown skeletons of leaves that lag
My forest-brook along;
When the ivy-tod is heavy with snow,                      535
And the owlet whoops to the wolf below,
That eats the she-wolf's young."

"Dear Lord! it hath a fiendish look—
(The Pilot made reply)
I am a-feared"—"Push on, push on!"                        540
Said the Hermit cheerily.

The boat came closer to the ship,
But I nor spake nor stirred;
The boat came close beneath the ship,
And straight a sound was heard.                           545

The ship<br>suddenly<br>sinketh.

Under the water it rumbled on,
Still louder and more dread:
It reached the ship, it split the bay;
The ship went down like lead.

The<br>ancient<br>Mariner is<br>saved in<br>the Pilot's<br>boat.

Stunned by that loud and dreadful sound,   550
Which sky and ocean smote,
Like one that hath been seven days drowned
My body lay afloat;
But swift as dreams, myself I found
Within the Pilot's boat.                                  555

Upon the whirl, where sank the ship,
The boat spun round and round;
And all was still, save that the hill
Was telling of the sound.

I moved my lips—the Pilot shrieked     560
And fell down in a fit;
The holy Hermit raised his eyes,
And prayed where he did sit.

I took the oars: the Pilot's boy,
Who now doth crazy go,     565
Laughed loud and long, and all the while
His eyes went to and fro.
"Ha! ha!" quoth he, "full plain I see,
The Devil knows how to row."

And now, all in my own countree,     570
I stood on the firm land!
The Hermit stepped forth from the boat,
And scarcely he could stand.

The
ancient
Mariner
earnestly
entreateth
the Hermit
to shrieve
him; and
the pen-
ance of life
falls on
him.

"O shrieve me, shrieve me, holy man!"
The Hermit crossed his brow.     575
"Say quick," quoth he, "I bid thee say—
What manner of man art thou?"

Forthwith this frame of mine was wrenched
With a woful agony,
Which forced me to begin my tale;     580
And then it left me free.

And ever
and anon
through-
out his
future life
an agony
constrain-
eth him to
travel
from land
to land;

Since then, at an uncertain hour,
That agony returns:
And till my ghastly tale is told,
This heart within me burns.     585

I pass, like night, from land to land;
I have strange power of speech;
That moment that his face I see,
I know the man that must hear me:
To him my tale I teach.     590

What loud uproar bursts from that door!
The wedding-guests are there:
But in the garden-bower the bride
And bride-maids singing are:

And hark the little vesper bell,                    595
Which biddeth me to prayer!

O Wedding-Guest! this soul hath been
Alone on a wide wide sea:
So lonely 'twas, that God himself
Scarce seemèd there to be.                          600

O sweeter than the marriage-feast,
'Tis sweeter far to me,
To walk together to the kirk
With a goodly company!—

To walk together to the kirk,                       605
And all together pray,
While each to his great Father bends,
Old men, and babes, and loving friends
And youths and maidens gay!

*And to teach, by his own example, love and reverence to all things that God made and loveth.*

Farewell, farewell! but this I tell                 610
To thee, thou Wedding-Guest!
He prayeth well, who loveth well
Both man and bird and beast.

He prayeth best, who loveth best
All things both great and small;                    615
For the dear God who loveth us,
He made and loveth all.

The Mariner, whose eye is bright,
Whose beard with age is hoar,
Is gone: and now the Wedding-Guest                  620
Turned from the bridegroom's door.

He went like one that hath been stunned,
And is of sense forlorn:
A sadder and a wiser man,
He rose the morrow morn.                            625

# E. M. W. Tillyard

---

COLERIDGE

THE RIME OF THE ANCIENT MARINER

. . . first let me explain that I shall not try to criticize the poem in the sense of conveying something of the total effect. It is a rich and complicated poem, and to put in words the total effect issuing from this complication would be at once surpassingly difficult and unnecessary for the humbler objects I have in view. All I seek to do is to enumerate some of the layers of significance that go to make up the whole.

First, it is an exciting story, imitated from the old ballads, drawing much of its material from old books of travel, enlivened by touches of realistic natural description, yet partly appealing to that part of our natures that delights in superstitions and in the supernatural. Second, in spite of the supernatural happenings, of which no rational explanation is given, the main events of the story happen logically in a sequence of cause and effect. In such a sequence the moral motive naturally enters, and the question arises of what this amounts to. Late in his life, Coleridge censured the presence of a motivating morality. In reply to an objection of Mrs. Barbauld that the poem lacked a moral, he answered that it had too much.

> It ought to have had no more moral than the Arabian Nights' tale of the merchant's sitting down to eat dates by the side of a well, and throwing the shells aside, and lo! a genie starts up, and says he must kill the aforesaid merchant, because one of the date shells had, it seems, put out the eye of the genie's son.—*Table Talk*, May 31, 1830

Probably Coleridge was stung to perversity by Mrs. Barbauld's being so stupid, and did not mean what he said. In truth, the moral story, the punishment of a crime, is the core of the poem: each part ends with a reference to the crime, the killing of the albatross; remove the moral and the poem collapses. Granted the moral, we must beware of narrowing it to the familiar modern doctrine of kindness to animals. If the albatross had been a crow or vulture or other bird of ill omen, there would have been no crime in shooting it; yet by humanitarian standards the act would have been just as bad. The reasons for not shooting the albatross were superstitious or at least primitive. By standards of superstition, animals are good or bad. It is unlucky to kill the good; the bad (the toad, for instance) can be persecuted to any extent. The albatross was a good bird, and they "hailed it in God's name." It was also their guest, and in a primitive world treachery to a guest was a terrible crime. Coleridge's gloss sums the matter up: "The ancient Mariner inhospitably killeth the pious bird of good omen." Whether the act itself apart from its consequences can be motivated is a matter of opinion. Should we simply accept it as a piece of plot-mechanism, like Lear's resolution to divide his kingdom, or should we detect a reason? Certainly there is a very simple reason to hand. The act could be interpreted as the essential act of devilment, the act of pride, of the unbridled assertion of the self. It was what Satan did when he rebelled and what Defoe made Crusoe do when he thrice rejected God's offer of a virtuous middle way of life. Whatever the answer, we are suitably impressed by the enormity of the mariner's crime and readily accept the straits into which he falls. The way he gets out of these straits is also motivated, but with a richness that makes it difficult not to encroach here on other layers of the poem's meaning. One reason for his escape is the sheer fulfilment of a frightful penance: he issues out of his prison like a prisoner who has served his time, whether repentant or not. And this punitive motive corresponds well enough to the purely superstitious crime of killing a bird of good omen. But there is the further reason of his blessing the water snakes. And this was an act of repentance, a moral reversal of his grossly self-regarding act of killing the albatross, a forgetfulness of self in recognizing the beauty of something quite independent. The crime, however, is not expiated at once. One of the two voices in the air says there is more penance to do. It is the one defect in the poem's structure that this further penance hardly exists and that the final expiation in line 442 ("And now this spell was snapt . . .") comes in very casually. Having learnt to expect motivation, we are disappointed when it is lacking. Even if we assume that the penance is now really complete, we still miss a further act of repentance to correspond to the blessing of the water snakes. Thenceforward everything is credible in its context. The crime has been such that we accept the mariner's final doom of having periodically to relive his old experience through recounting his tale.

I have spoken of the simple narrative interest and of the moral motivation together because the second helps the first along: a logical is more emphatic than a mere casual sequence. As Lowes says in his *Road to Xanadu* (p. 299): "The sequence which follows the Mariner's initial act accomplishes two ends: it unifies and it 'credibilizes' the poem." But Lowes notices something more about the morality: its truth to the ordinary experience of life. He writes (p. 298):

> The train of cause and consequence is more than a consolidating factor of the poem. It happens to be life, as every human being knows it. You do a foolish or an evil deed, and its results come home to you. And they are apt to fall on others too. You repent, and a load is lifted from your soul. But you have not thereby escaped your deed. You attain forgiveness, but cause and effect work on unmoved, and life to the end may be the continued reaping of the repented deed's results.

Though this is not how we think of the poem when we read it, we do ratify Lowes's words on reflection. And they are important, for they convey a part of the meaning that is too often forgotten. And it is precisely the blend of this sheer truth to human experience with the narrative power, the fantastic happenings, and the brilliant pictures, that makes the *Ancient Mariner* so rich and so surprising.

But the *Ancient Mariner* is more than a fascinating story with a moral. It may be that H. I'A. Fausset is right in seeing it as an allegory of Coleridge's own life: his strange mind, his terror, his loquacity. The mariner, repeating his tale, may well be Coleridge, "seeking relief throughout his life in endless monologues." But even if Fausset is right, he is indicating a very minor layer of the poem's meaning. What matters is not that Coleridge should be speaking for himself but that he should be speaking for many others. Miss Bodkin, in her *Archetypal Patterns in Poetry*, chooses the *Ancient Mariner* as one of the poems "the ground of whose appeal is most evidently the impression of the inner life," but she rightly does not confine the inner life to Coleridge's. And if, as I think we should, we take the mariner's voyage as a mental one, it should figure the adventures not of Coleridge alone but of all mental voyagers.

Once we postulate an allegory we are beset with dangers,

above all with the temptation to grow excited, to see too
much, to mistake a simple picturesque detail for a complicated moral truth. I will try to keep to the more obvious and
plausible significances.

The general drift of the poem in its mental action can
readily be recognized by two passages from other poets:
Webster,

> *My soul like to a ship in a black storm*
> *Is driven I know not whither*

and Shelley,

> *The breath whose might I have invoked in song*
> *Descends on me; my spirit's bark is driven*
> *Far from the shore, far from the trembling throng*
> *Whose sails were never to the tempest given;*
> *The massy earth and sphered skies are riven.*
> *I am borne darkly, fearfully, afar!*

The sea voyage, then, indicates spiritual adventure, as the
ordinary journey or pilgrimage indicates the course of normal life. And it is not everyone who goes out of his way to
seek adventure. There is a passage in Coleridge's prose
(*Biographia Literaria*, xii) that both says this and has its
bearing on the "Ancient Mariner."

> The first range of hills, that encircles the scanty vale of
> human life, is the horizon for the majority of its in-
> habitants. On its ridges the common sun is born and
> departs. From them the stars rise, and touching them
> they vanish. By the many, even this range, the natural
> limit and bulwark of the vale, is but imperfectly known.
> Its higher ascents are too often hidden by mists and
> clouds from uncultivated swamps, which few have
> courage or curiosity to penetrate. To the multitude be-
> low these vapours appear, now as the dark haunts of
> terrific agents, on which none may intrude with im-
> punity; and now all aglow, with colours not their own,
> they are gazed at as the splendid palaces of happiness
> and power. But in all ages there have been a few, who
> measuring and sounding the rivers of the vale at the
> feet of their furthest inaccessible falls have learned,
> that the sources must be far higher and far inward; a
> few, who even in the level streams have detected ele-
> ments, which neither the vale itself nor the surrounding
> mountains contained or could supply . . . It is the es-
> sential mark of the true philosopher to rest satisfied

with no imperfect light, as long as the impossibility of attaining a fuller knowledge has not been demonstrated.

The ancient mariner and his ship represent the small but persisting class of mental adventurers who are not content with the appearances surrounding them but who attempt to get behind. (It may be added that though the class is small it stands for a universal impulse, which is dormant in most minds and not absent from them.) Further, and here I recognize the danger of seeing too much, it is possible that the different degrees of nearness to normality represented in the poem do correspond to the apprehension of such degrees in actual life. The harbor town, occurring in a narrative, is less real than the wedding guest and the wedding, but more so than the realms visited in the voyage; and these degrees of reality can hardly be without their effect.

Granted that the mariner and his voyage signify the mental adventure of an unusually inquiring spirit, the outline of that adventure becomes tolerably clear, while it would be senseless to seek more than an outline. From the social point of view these spiritual adventurers are criminals: they disturb the existing order and they imply a criticism of the accepted round of life: they are self-appointed outcasts. The shooting of the albatross in the present context was an anti-social act: something that by everyday rules would not be done. And the avenging spirit takes the mariner into a region and a situation the utter loneliness of which is both the logical consequence and the avengement of his revolt against society. This same region is one more version of that aridity that besets all isolated mental voyagers at one stage of their voyage. Other versions are Donne's conceit of himself in "A Nocturnal upon St. Lucy's Day" as the quintessence of the primeval nothingness out of which God created the world; the emptiness experienced by the poet in Shelley's Alastor, who, when he awakes from his dreams, sees the "garish hills" and "vacant woods," while his "wan eyes"

> *Gaze on the empty scene as vacantly*
> *As ocean's moon looks on the moon in heaven*

and the landscape in Browning's "Childe Roland." The mariner escapes from his isolation by the enlargement of his sympathies in the manner least expected and he is allowed to return to common life. And he does so as a changed man. He has repented of his isolation; his greatest satisfaction is to worship in company with his fellows of all ages. But he is still

the marked man, the outcast, the Wandering Jew, the victim
of his own thoughts. Further, although he has been judged by
society, he has the reward of the courage that propels the
mental adventurer: that of arresting and disturbing and
teaching those who have had no such experiences. And this
ambivalent criterion enriches the poem incalculably.

But there may be yet one more important layer of meaning; something so simple and fundamental that it extends
beyond the rarer sphere of self-imposed mental adventure to
the common inevitable workings of the human mind. Miss
Bodkin sees in the *Ancient Mariner* a rendering of the
pattern of rebirth (*Archetypal Patterns in Poetry*, chapter
II), which is at once the theme of tragedy and a very law of
human life: the process of renovation through destruction.
This theme is certainly present. It was only through the
destruction of his old state of mind that the mariner was able
to achieve the new, enlarged state of mind that could include
the water snakes in its sympathies. But the "Ancient Mariner" is unlike the most satisfying works that render the
theme, for instance the "Oresteia" or "Lycidas," in that the
renovation brought about is less powerful than the thing
from whose destruction it has sprung. There is nothing to
correspond to the thrust of energy that ends "Lycidas" with

*Tomorrow to fresh Woods, and Pastures new.*

The ancient mariner has been born again into a ghostly
existence, not rejuvenated. And the haunting terror of the
destructive experience remains the dominant theme of the
poem:

*O Wedding-Guest! this soul hath been*
*Alone on a wide wide sea.*

## Dejection: An Ode

[WRITTEN APRIL 4, 1802]

*Late, late yestreen I saw the new Moon,*
*With the old Moon in her arms;*
*And I fear, I fear, my Master dear!*
*We shall have a deadly storm.*

BALLAD OF SIR PATRICK SPENCE

I

Well! If the Bard was weather-wise, who made
The grand old ballad of Sir Patrick Spence,
This night, so tranquil now, will not go hence
Unroused by winds, that ply a busier trade
Than those which mould yon cloud in lazy flakes,     5
Or the dull sobbing draft, that moans and rakes
Upon the strings of this Æolian lute,
    Which better far were mute.
For lo! the New-moon winter-bright!
And overspread with phantom light,     10
(With swimming phantom light o'erspread
But rimmed and circled by a silver thread)
I see the old Moon in her lap, foretelling
The coming-on of rain and squally blast.
And oh! that even now the gust were swelling,     15
And the slant night-shower driving loud and fast!
Those sounds which oft have raised me, whilst they awed,
    And sent my soul abroad,
Might now perhaps their wonted impulse give,
Might startle this dull pain, and make it move and live!     20

II

A grief without a pang, void, dark, and drear,
    A stifled, drowsy, unimpassioned grief,

Which finds no natural outlet, no relief,
   In word, or sigh, or tear—
O Lady! in this wan and heartless mood,         25
To other thoughts by yonder throstle woo'd,
   All this long eve, so balmy and serene,
Have I been gazing on the western sky,
   And its peculiar tint of yellow green:
And still I gaze—and with how blank an eye!     30
And those thin clouds above, in flakes and bars,
That give away their motion to the stars;
Those stars, that glide behind them or between,
Now sparkling, now bedimmed, but always seen:
Yon crescent Moon, as fixed as if it grew     35
In its own cloudless, starless lake of blue;
I see them all so excellently fair,
I see, not feel, how beautiful they are!

### III

   My genial spirits fail;
   And what can these avail         40
To lift the smothering weight from off my breast?
   It were a vain endeavour,
   Though I should gaze for ever
On that green light that lingers in the west:
I may not hope from outward forms to win     45
The passion and the life, whose fountains are within.

### IV

O Lady! we receive but what we give,
And in our life alone does Nature live:
Ours is her wedding garment, ours her shroud!
   And would we aught behold, of higher worth,     50
Than that inanimate cold world allowed
To the poor loveless ever-anxious crowd,
   Ah! from the soul itself must issue forth
A light, a glory, a fair luminous cloud
   Enveloping the Earth—         55
And from the soul itself must there be sent
   A sweet and potent voice, of its own birth,
Of all sweet sounds the life and element!

### V

O pure of heart! thou need'st not ask of me
What this strong music in the soul may be!     60

What, and wherein it doth exist,
This light, this glory, this fair luminous mist,
This beautiful and beauty-making power.
Joy, virtuous Lady! Joy that ne'er was given,
Save to the pure, and in their purest hour,                    65
Life, and Life's effluence, cloud at once and shower,
Joy, Lady! is the spirit and the power,
Which wedding Nature to us gives in dower
    A new Earth and new Heaven,
Undreamt of by the sensual and the proud—                      70
Joy is the sweet voice, Joy the luminous cloud—
    We in ourselves rejoice!
And thence flows all that charms or ear or sight,
    All melodies the echoes of that voice,
All colours a suffusion from that light.                       75

VI

There was a time when, though my path was rough,
    This joy within me dallied with distress,
And all misfortunes were but as the stuff
    Whence Fancy made me dreams of happiness:
For hope grew round me, like the twining vine,                 80
And fruits, and foliage, not my own, seemed mine.
But now afflictions bow me down to earth:
Nor care I that they rob me of my mirth;
    But oh! each visitation
Suspends what nature gave me at my birth,                      85
    My shaping spirit of Imagination.
For not to think of what I needs must feel,
    But to be still and patient, all I can;
And haply by abstruse research to steal
    From my own nature all the natural man—                    90
    This was my sole resource, my only plan:
Till that which suits a part infects the whole,
And now is almost grown the habit of my soul.

VII

Hence, viper thoughts, that coil around my mind,
    Reality's dark dream!                                      95
I turn from you, and listen to the wind,
    Which long has raved unnoticed. What a scream
Of agony by torture lengthened out
That lute sent forth! Thou Wind, that rav'st without,
    Bare crag, or mountain-tairn, or blasted tree,            100

Or pine-grove whither woodman never clomb,
Or lonely house, long held the witches' home,
   Methinks were fitter instruments for thee,
Mad Lutanist! who in this month of showers,
Of dark-brown gardens, and of peeping flowers,     105
Mak'st Devils' yule, with worse than wintry song,
The blossoms, buds, and timorous leaves among.
   Thou Actor, perfect in all tragic sounds!
Thou mighty Poet, e'en to frenzy bold!
    What tell'st thou now about?     110
    'Tis of the rushing of an host in rout,
  With groans, of trampled men, with smarting wounds—
At once they groan with pain, and shudder with the cold!
But hush! there is a pause of deepest silence!
   And all that noise, as of a rushing crowd,     115
With groans, and tremulous shudderings—all is over—
  It tells another tale, with sounds less deep and loud!
    A tale of less affright,
    And tempered with delight,
As Otway's self had framed the tender lay,—     120
    'Tis of a little child
    Upon a lonesome wild,
Not far from home, but she hath lost her way:
And now moans low in bitter grief and fear,
And now screams loud, and hopes to make her mother
  hear.     125

### VIII

'Tis midnight, but small thoughts have I of sleep:
Full seldom may my friend such vigils keep!
Visit her, gentle Sleep! with wings of healing,
   And may this storm be but a mountain-birth,
May all the stars hang bright above her dwelling,     130
   Silent as though they watched the sleeping Earth!
    With light heart may she rise,
    Gay fancy, cheerful eyes,
  Joy lift her spirit, joy attune her voice;
To her may all things live, from pole to pole,     135
Their life the eddying of her living soul!
  O simple spirit, guided from above,
Dear Lady! friend devoutest of my choice,
Thus mayest thou ever, evermore rejoice.

# Sir Herbert Read

## COLERIDGE
## DEJECTION: AN ODE

The ode which Coleridge first published in the *Morning Post* on the 4th of October, 1802, had been composed six months earlier in a form very different from that given to the public. The full version was first published as recently as 1937 by Ernest de Selincourt in Volume XXII of *Essays and Studies by Members of the English Association*. It was republished ten years later in a collection of Professor de Selincourt's essays (*Wordsworthian and Other Studies*, pp. 57–76), but the poem in its completeness is not well known. Yet the original version is a great and moving poem, and a comparison of the two versions, with a consideration of the reasons which led Coleridge to revise the poem before publication, raises a problem of the greatest critical importance.

The original version is a continuous poem of 340 lines. What might be called the standard version, first published by Coleridge in a collection of his poems called *Sibylline Leaves* in 1817, is merely 139 lines long, and the *Morning Post* version of 1802 is even shorter still. In its ruthlessly lopped state the poem is no longer a continuous train of thought, and is therefore divided into eight numbered and rearranged sections. Apart from these larger structural changes, numerous small revisions have been made in the remaining text which completely disguise its origin and alter its tone. The considerations that led Coleridge to make these alterations were partly personal and partly critical. But before we can discuss them profitably we must take into account the circumstances in which the poem was composed.

As is generally known, Coleridge had married in haste and repented at leisure. For our present purposes it is not necessary to take sides in the quarrel, for we are concerned only with Coleridge's feelings in the matter, and of these there is no doubt. He gave full expression to them in a letter written in October of this same year, 1802, to his friend and benefactor, Thomas Wedgwood. Let me quote a few sentences from this revealing document:

After my return to Keswick, I was, if possible, more miserable than before. Scarce a day passed without such a scene of discord between me and Mrs. Coleridge, as quite incapacitated me from any worthy exertion of my faculties by degrading me in my own estimation. I found my temper injured, and daily more so; the good and pleasurable thoughts, which had been the support of my moral character, departed from my solitude—I determined to go abroad—but alas! the less I loved my wife, the more dear and necessary did my children seem to me. I found no comfort except in the driest speculations. . . . About two months ago after a violent quarrel I was taken suddenly ill with spasms in my stomach—I expected to die—Mrs. C. was, of course, shocked and frightened beyond measure—and two days after, I still being very weak and pale as death, she threw herself upon me and made a solemn promise of amendment—and she has kept her promise beyond any hope I could have flattered myself with. . . . If any woman wanted an exact and copious Recipe, 'How to make a Husband compleatly miserable,' I could furnish her with one—with a Probatum est, tacked to it.—Ill-tempered Speeches sent after me when I went out of the House, ill-tempered Speeches on my return, my friends received with freezing looks, the least opposition or contradiction occasioning screams of passion, and the sentiments which I held most base, ostentatiously avowed—all this added to the utter negation of all, which a Husband expects from a Wife—especially, living in retirement—and the consciousness that I was myself growing a worse man. O dear Sir! no one can tell what I have suffered. I can say with strict truth, that the happiest half-hours I have had, were when all of a sudden, as I have been sitting alone in my Study, I have burst into Tears.

—*Collected Letters of Samuel Coleridge*,
ed. E. L. Griggs

Such was Coleridge's state of mind when he wrote "Dejection." But he did not tell Tom Wedgwood the whole truth—he did not tell him that the passion he had once felt for Sarah Fricker, his wife, he now felt for Sara Hutchinson, the sister of Mary who was to become Wordsworth's wife.

> *All thoughts, all passions, all delights,*
> *Whatever stirs this mortal frame*

> *All are but ministers of Love,*
> *And feed his sacred flame* . . .

The lovely ballad that opens with these lines had been inspired by this new and deep and hopeless passion, and had been written three years before the letter to Wedgwood. It had been written in December 1799, and the following summer, in order to be near the object of his new passion, Coleridge had moved to the Lake District, and during the next few years Coleridge and Sara saw much of each other. During all this time Coleridge's health was rapidly deteriorating—apart from the spasms in the stomach mentioned to Wedgwood he suffered from giddiness and rheumatic pains, and it was then that he first had fatal recourse to opium. He was indeed a miserable man, but he was also a deeply religious man, and his convictions forbade him any thought of a divorce. He had three women to minister to him in his sickness, to sympathize with his misery—Mary and Sara Hutchinson, and Dorothy Wordsworth, who was as hopelessly in love with him as he was with Sara. It was in a mood induced by the tenderness of these ministering angels that he wrote the ode, "Dejection."

It is such an intimate poem, so self-revealing and so revealing of a complex passionate situation affecting others, that no other excuse would be necessary for the considerable excisions which Coleridge made in the published version. But there was another consideration, to which I have already referred, of a more theoretical nature. Coleridge held the view, which I think we ought to share with him, that the best poetry is not written out of what we might call private situations. The best poetry is *objective*—it is aloof. In the *Biographia Literaria*, Coleridge praises Shakespeare for possessing this quality. A sign of his genius, he says,

> . . . is the choice of subjects very remote from the private interests and circumstances of the writer himself. At least I have found, that where the subject is taken immediately from the author's personal sensations and experiences, the excellence of a particular poem is but an equivocal mark, and often a fallacious pledge, of genuine poetic power.

I think there is no doubt that Coleridge had this particular poem of his own in mind when making such a statement. This general principle of objectivity or aloofness (or "aesthetic distance," as the aestheticians call it) is one that might be discussed at length, but for the moment it is perhaps sufficient to note that it is a principle recognized in all the arts, and it is perhaps a distinguishing mark between certain schools of art—the idealist school, for example, accepts it as a matter of course, but the realist, and more particularly the expressionist artist, goes to the opposite extreme and makes personal experiences the basis of his work.

We will consider presently what, if anything, was lost in this particular case of the "depersonalization" of a poem, but let us first ask how we are to square this principle of objectivity with the romantic principle itself—with Coleridge's own demand that form should proceed from the intuitive experience of the poet. Schelling and Coleridge provide the answer: the "squaring" takes place within that dialectical process whereby the external is reconciled with the internal, the conscious with the unconscious.

The two factors that Coleridge himself did in fact reconcile in "Dejection" were on one hand a full private confession of his feelings, and on the other hand a public expression of generalized sentiments. Let us observe in the first place that there is no distinction of technique involved—at least, none of poetic diction. The original version of the poem has a closer sequence or continuity, and is only broken by an organic paragraphing, demanded by the transitions of the thought. In the final version the excisions require an arrangement of the fragments in numbered stanzas, which makes a virtue of the necessary gaps in the thought. I do not suppose that anyone who remained ignorant of the original continuity of the poem would complain of this division of the poem into separate "movements." This quality of continuity apart, there is no doubt that in cutting the poem and disguising its personal nature, Coleridge managed to salvage all the heat and fire of the original text. He may have been actuated by personal motives, but at the same time his critical powers were at work, and what he kept and what he sacrificed were determined by literary judgment no less than by social prudence. There are passages of moving simplicity, which we must regret:

> *It was as calm as this, that happy night*
> *When Mary, thou, and I together were,*
> *The low decaying fire our only Light,*
> *And listen'd to the Stillness of the Air.*

There is at least one passage of confessional pathos which must always be remembered when we are considering Coleridge's tragic life:

*I speak not now of those habitual Ills*
*That wear out Life, when two unequal Minds*
*Meet in one House and two discordant Wills—*
*This leaves me, where it finds,*
*Past Cure, and past Complaint,—a fate austere*
*Too fix'd and hopeless to partake of Fear!*

Passages such as these indicate, perhaps, that something essential was lost—something we might call emotional integrity; something was sacrificed to a higher integrity. The two versions differ as the course of a river running through a virgin landscape, and the still waters and divided lawns of a public garden. But both grew in the same light of nature, both were organic in their substance and of living beauty. There is neither imprisonment nor death in the final form given to the poem: that form still proceeds from the core of the artist's consciousness. The reconciliation that has been effected is not a formal one at all, in the immediate sense of poetic expression; rather it is a generalization of personal experience—and in that sense a reconciliation of the internal with the external. The two most significant lines in the poem make this clear:

*I may not hope from outward forms to win*
*The passion and the life, whose fountains are within.*

But the whole poem bears witness to the fact that those fountains are impeded by a too conscious or direct expression of personal emotions. We now see why Schelling's theory of a necessary retreat into the unconscious appealed to Coleridge, for his own creative experience had taught him that the material of sensational experience must be transmuted in some mental alembic before it can emerge in poetic form. Such is the process of reconcilement of the external with the internal effected by the poet, and "Dejection" is a poem in which we can see the poet consciously distinguishing between what had, and what had not, passed through the alembic and thereby acquired universal significance. The weakness of the poem, as compared with a poem like Wordsworth's "Ode: Intimations of Immortality," springs from this conscious dichotomy. This is openly, beautifully confessed in the sixth section of the final version:

*There was a time when . . .*
*. . . all misfortunes were but as the stuff*
*Whence Fancy made me dreams of happiness . . .*
*But now . . .*

> . . . *each visitation*
> *Suspends what nature gave me at my birth,*
> *My shaping spirit of Imagination.*

In the original version there then intervened some twenty
lines descriptive of his "coarse domestic life," and of his
resolve

> . . . *not to think of what I needs must feel,*
> *But to be still and patient, all I can;*
> *And haply by abstruse research to steal*
> *From my own nature all the natural man—*

a resolve, it will be seen, to turn away from the direct
contemplation of his own affliction, and to send forth from
the soul

> *A light, a glory, a faint luminous cloud*
> *. . .*
> *A sweet and potent voice, of its own birth,*
> *Of all sweet sounds the life and element!*

"Of its own birth"—here again, in the heart of Coleridge's
most intimate poem, is the essential idea: the voice of the
natural man proceeding from his own nature, and formed
under laws of its own origination.

# GEORGE GORDON, LORD BYRON
## [1788–1824]

## The Vision of Judgment

Saint Peter sat by the celestial gate:
   His keys were rusty, and the lock was dull,
So little trouble had been given of late;
   Not that the place by any means was full,
But since the Gallic era "eighty-eight"       5
   The devils had ta'en a longer, stronger pull,
And "a pull altogether," as they say
At sea—which drew most souls another way.

The angels all were singing out of tune,
   And hoarse with having little else to do,       10
Excepting to wind up the sun and moon,
   Or curb a runaway young star or two,
Or wild colt of a comet, which too soon
   Broke out of bounds o'er th' ethereal blue,
Splitting some planet with its playful tail,       15
As boats are sometimes by a wanton whale.

The guardian seraphs had retired on high,
   Finding their charges past all care below;
Terrestrial business fill'd nought in the sky
   Save the recording angel's black bureau;       20
Who found, indeed, the facts to multiply
   With such rapidity of vice and woe,
That he had stripp'd off both his wings in quills,
And yet was in arrear of human ills.

His business so augmented of late years,       25
   That he was forced, against his will no doubt,
(Just like those cherubs, earthly ministers,)
   For some resource to turn himself about,
And claim the help of his celestial peers,
   To aid him ere he should be quite worn out       30
By the increased demand for his remarks:
Six angels and twelve saints were named his clerks.

This was a handsome board—at least for heaven;
   And yet they had even then enough to do,
So many conquerors' cars were daily driven,      35
   So many kingdoms fitted up anew;
Each day too slew its thousands six or seven,
   Till at the crowning carnage, Waterloo,
They threw their pens down in divine disgust—
The page was so besmear'd with blood and dust.     40

This by the way; 'tis not mine to record
   What angels shrink from: even the very devil
On this occasion his own work abhorr'd,
   So surfeited with the infernal revel:
Though he himself had sharpen'd every sword,     45
   It almost quench'd his innate thirst of evil.
(Here Satan's sole good work deserves insertion—
'Tis, that he has both generals in reversion.)

Let's skip a few short years of hollow peace,
   Which peopled earth no better, hell as wont,     50
And heaven none—they form the tyrant's lease,
   With nothing but new names subscribed upon't;
'Twill one day finish: meantime they increase,
   "With seven heads and ten horns," and all in front,
Like Saint John's foretold beast; but ours are born     55
Less formidable in the head than horn.

In the first year of freedom's second dawn
   Died George the Third; although no tyrant, one
Who shielded tyrants, till each sense withdrawn
   Left him nor mental nor external sun:     60
A better farmer ne'er brush'd dew from lawn,
   A worse king never left a realm undone!
He died—but left his subjects still behind,
One half as mad—and t'other no less blind.

He died! his death made no great stir on earth:     65
   His burial made some pomp; there was profusion
Of velvet, gilding, brass, and no great dearth
   Of aught but tears—save those shed by collusion.
For these things may be bought at their true worth;
   Of elegy there was the due infusion—     70
Bought also; and the torches, cloaks, and banners,
Heralds, and relics of old Gothic manners,

Form'd a sepulchral melodrame. Of all
   The fools who flock'd to swell or see the show,

GEORGE GORDON, LORD BYRON

*The Bettmann Archive*

Who cared about the corpse? The funeral                              75
  Made the attraction, and the black the woe.
There throbb'd not there a thought which pierced the pall;
  And when the gorgeous coffin was laid low,
It seem'd the mockery of hell to fold
  The rottenness of eighty years in gold.                            80

So mix his body with the dust! It might
  Return to what it *must* far sooner, were
The natural compound left alone to fight
  Its way back into earth, and fire, and air;
But the unnatural balsams merely blight                              85
  What nature made him at his birth, as bare
As the mere million's base unmummied clay—
Yet all his spices but prolong decay.

He's dead—and upper earth with him has done;
  He's buried; save the undertaker's bill,                           90
Or lapidary scrawl, the world is gone
  For him, unless he left a German will:
But where's the proctor who will ask his son?
  In whom his qualities are reigning still,
Except that household virtue, most uncommon,                         95
Of constancy to a bad, ugly woman.

"God save the king!" It is a large economy
  In God to save the like; but if he will
Be saving, all the better; for not one am I
  Of those who think damnation better still:                         100
I hardly know too if not quite alone am I
  In this small hope of bettering future ill
By circumscribing, with some slight restriction,
The eternity of hell's hot jurisdiction.

I know this is unpopular; I know                                     105
  'Tis blasphemous; I know one may be damn'd
For hoping no one else may e'er be so;
  I know my catechism; I know we're cramm'd
With the best doctrines till we quite o'erflow;
  I know that all save England's church have shamm'd,                110
And that the other twice two hundred churches
And synagogues have made a *damn'd* bad purchase.

God help us all! God help me too! I am,
  God knows, as helpless as the devil can wish,
And not a whit more difficult to damn,                              115
  Than is to bring to land a late-hook'd fish,

Or to the butcher to purvey the lamb;
   Not that I'm fit for such a noble dish,
As one day will be that immortal fry
Of almost everybody born to die.          120

Saint Peter sat by the celestial gate,
   And nodded o'er his keys; when, lo! there came
A wondrous noise he had not heard of late—
   A rushing sound of wind, and stream, and flame;
In short, a roar of things extremely great,        125
   Which would have made aught save a saint exclaim;
But he, with first a start and then a wink,
Said, "There's another star gone out, I think!"

But ere he could return to his repose,
   A cherub flapp'd his right wing o'er his eyes—    130
At which St. Peter yawn'd, and rubb'd his nose:
   "Saint porter," said the angel, "prithee rise!"
Waving a goodly wing, which glow'd, as glows
   An earthly peacock's tail, with heavenly dyes:
To which the saint replied, "Well, what's the matter?   135
Is Lucifer come back with all this clatter?"

"No," quoth the cherub; "George the Third is dead."
   "And who *is* George the Third?" replied the apostle:
"*What George? what Third?*" "The king of England," said
   The angel. "Well! he won't find kings to jostle   140
Him on his way; but does he wear his head?
   Because the last we saw here had a tustle,
And ne'er would have got into heaven's good graces,
Had he not flung his head in all our faces.

"He was, if I remember, king of France;     145
   That head of his, which could not keep a crown
On earth, yet ventured in my face to advance
   A claim to those of martyrs—like my own:
If I had had my sword, as I had once
   When I cut ears off, I had cut him down;   150
But having but my *keys*, and not my brand,
I only knock'd his head from out his hand.

"And then he set up such a headless howl,
   That all the saints came out and took him in;
And there he sits by St. Paul, cheek by jowl;   155
   That fellow Paul—the parvenù! The skin
Of St. Bartholomew, which makes his cowl
   In heaven, and upon earth redeem'd his sin,

So as to make a martyr, never sped
Better than did this weak and wooden head.                160

"But had it come up here upon its shoulders,
    There would have been a different tale to tell:
The fellow-feeling in the saint's beholders
    Seems to have acted on them like a spell,
And so this very foolish head heaven solders        165
    Back on its trunk: it may be very well,
And seems the custom here to overthrow
Whatever has been wisely done below."

The angel answer'd, "Peter! do not pout:
    The king who comes has head and all entire,        170
And never knew much what it was about—
    He did as doth the puppet—by its wire,
And will be judged like all the rest, no doubt:
    My business and your own is not to inquire
Into such matters, but to mind our cue—        175
Which is to act as we are bid to do."

While thus they spake, the angelic caravan,
    Arriving like a rush of mighty wind,
Cleaving the fields of space, as doth the swan
    Some silver stream (say Ganges, Nile, or Inde,        180
Or Thames, or Tweed), and 'midst them an old man
    With an old soul, and both extremely blind,
Halted before the gate, and in his shroud
Seated their fellow traveller on a cloud.

But bringing up the rear of this bright host        185
    A Spirit of a different aspect waved
His wings, like thunder-clouds above some coast
    Whose barren beach with frequent wrecks is paved;
His brow was like the deep when tempest-toss'd;
    Fierce and unfathomable thoughts engraved        190
Eternal wrath on his immortal face,
And *where* he gazed a gloom pervaded space.

As he drew near, he gazed upon the gate
    Ne'er to be enter'd more by him or Sin,
With such a glance of supernatural hate,        195
    As made Saint Peter wish himself within;
He patter'd with his keys at a great rate,
    And sweated through his apostolic skin:
Of course his perspiration was but ichor,
Or some such other spiritual liquor.        200

The very cherubs huddled all together,
  Like birds when soars the falcon; and they felt
A tingling to the tip of every feather,
  And form'd a circle like Orion's belt
Around their poor old charge; who scarce knew whither   205
  His guards had led him, though they gently dealt
With royal manes (for by many stories,
And true, we learn the angels all are Tories).

As things were in this posture, the gate flew
  Asunder, and the flashing of its hinges   210
Flung over space an universal hue
  Of many-colour'd flame, until its tinges
Reach'd even our speck of earth, and made a new
  Aurora borealis spread its fringes
O'er the North Pole; the same seen, when ice-bound,   215
By Captain Parry's crew, in "Melville's Sound."

And from the gate thrown open issued beaming
  A beautiful and mighty Thing of Light,
Radiant with glory, like a banner streaming
  Victorious from some world-o'erthrowing fight:   220
My poor comparisons must needs be teeming
  With earthly likenesses, for here the night
Of clay obscures our best conceptions, saving
Johanna Southcote, or Bob Southey raving.

'Twas the archangel Michael; all men know   225
  The make of angels and archangels, since
There's scarce a scribbler has not one to show,
  From the fiends' leader to the angels' prince;
There also are some altar-pieces, though
  I really can't say that they much evince   230
One's inner notions of immortal spirits;
But let the connoisseurs explain *their* merits.

Michael flew forth in glory and in good;
  A goodly work of him from whom all glory
And good arise; the portal past—he stood;   235
  Before him the young cherubs and saints hoary—
(I say *young*, begging to be understood
  By looks, not years; and should be very sorry
To state, they were not older than St. Peter,
But merely that they seem'd a little sweeter).   240

The cherubs and the saints bow'd down before
  That arch-angelic hierarch, the first
Of essences angelical, who wore

The aspect of a god; but this ne'er nursed
Pride in his heavenly bosom, in whose core                      245
  No thought, save for his Master's service, durst
Intrude, however glorified and high;
He knew him but the viceroy of the sky.

He and the sombre, silent Spirit met—
  They knew each other both for good and ill;                   250
Such was their  power, that neither could forget
  His former friend and future foe; but still
There was a high, immortal, proud regret
  In either's eye, as if 'twere less their will
Than destiny to make the eternal years                          255
Their date of war, and their "champ clos" the spheres.

But here they were in neutral space: we know
  From Job, that Satan hath the power to pay
A heavenly visit thrice a year or so;
  And that the "sons of God," like those of clay,               260
Must keep him company; and we might show
  From the same book, in how polite a way
The dialogue is held between the Powers
Of Good and Evil—but 'twould take up hours.

And this is not a theologic tract,                              265
  To prove with Hebrew and with Arabic,
If Job be allegory or a fact,
  But a true narrative; and thus I pick
From out the whole but such and such an act
  As sets aside the slightest thought of trick.                 270
'Tis every tittle true, beyond suspicion,
And accurate as any other vision.

The spirits were in neutral space, before
  The gate of heaven; like eastern thresholds is
The place where Death's grand cause is argued o'er,             275
  And souls despatch'd to that world or to this;
And therefore Michael and the other wore
  A civil aspect: though they did not kiss,
Yet still between his Darkness and his Brightness
There pass'd a mutual glance of great politeness.               280

The Archangel bow'd, not like a modern beau,
  But with a graceful Oriental bend,
Pressing one radiant arm just where below
  The heart in good men is supposed to tend;
He turn'd as to an equal, not too low,                          285

But kindly; Satan meet his ancient friend
With more hauteur, as might an old Castilian
Poor noble meet a mushroom rich civilian.

He merely bent his diabolic brow
    An instant; and then raising it, he stood        290
In act to assert his right or wrong, and show
    Cause why King George by no means could or should
Make out a case to be exempt from woe
    Eternal, more than other kings, endued
With better sense and hearts, whom history mentions,    295
Who long have "paved hell with their good intentions."

Michael began: "What wouldst thou with this man,
    Now dead, and brought before the Lord? What ill
Hath he wrought since his mortal race began,
    That thou canst claim him? Speak! and do thy will,    300
If it be just: if in this earthly span
    He hath been greatly failing to fulfil
His duties as a king and mortal, say,
And he is thine; if not, let him have way."

"Michael!" replied the Prince of Air, "even here,    305
    Before the Gate of him thou servest, must
I claim my subject: and will make appear
    That as he was my worshipper in dust,
So shall he be in spirit, although dear
    To thee and thine, because nor wine nor lust    310
Were of his weaknesses; yet on the throne
He reign'd o'er millions to serve me alone.

"Look to *our* earth, or rather *mine;* it was,
    *Once, more* thy master's: but I triumph not
In this poor planet's conquest; nor, alas!    315
    Need he thou servest envy me my lot:
With all the myriads of bright worlds which pass
    In worship round him, he may have forgot
Yon weak creation of such paltry things:
I think few worth damnation save their kings,—    320

"And these but as a kind of quit-rent, to
    Assert my right as lord: and even had
I such an inclination, 'twere (as you
    Well know) superfluous; they are grown so bad,
That hell has nothing better left to do    325
    Than leave them to themselves: so much more mad
And evil by their own internal curse,
Heaven cannot make them better, nor I worse.

"Look to the earth, I said, and say again:
    When this old, blind, mad, helpless, weak, poor worm    330
Began in youth's first bloom and flush to reign,
    The world and he both wore a different form,
And much of earth and all the watery plain
    Of ocean call'd him king: through many a storm
His isles had floated on the abyss of time;    335
For the rough virtues chose them for their clime.

"He came to his sceptre young; he leaves it old:
    Look to the state in which he found his realm,
And left it; and his annals too behold,
    How to a minion first he gave the helm;    340
How grew upon his heart a thirst for gold,
    The beggar's vice, which can but overwhelm
The meanest hearts; and for the rest, but glance
Thine eye along America and France.

"'Tis true, he was a tool from first to last    345
    (I have the workmen safe); but as a tool
So let him be consumed. From out the past
    Of ages, since mankind have known the rule
Of monarchs—from the bloody rolls amass'd
    Of sin and slaughter—from the Cæsar's school,    350
Take the worst pupil; and produce a reign
More drench'd with gore, more cumber'd with the slain.

"He ever warr'd with freedom and the free:
    Nations as men, home subjects, foreign foes,
So that they utter'd the word 'Liberty!'    355
    Found George the Third their first opponent. Whose
History was ever stain'd as his will be
    With national and individual woes?
I grant his household abstinence; I grant
His neutral virtues, which most monarchs want;    360

"I know he was a constant consort; own
    He was a decent sire, and middling lord.
All this is much, and most upon a throne;
    As temperance, if at Apicius' board,
Is more than at an anchorite's supper shown.    365
    I grant him all the kindest can accord;
And this was well for him, but not for those
Millions who found him what oppression chose.

"The New World shook him off; the Old yet groans
    Beneath what he and his prepared, if not    370

Completed: he leaves heirs on many thrones
    To all his vices, without what begot
Compassion for him—his tame virtues; drones
    Who sleep, or despots who have now forgot
A lesson which shall be re-taught them, wake          375
Upon the thrones of earth; but let them quake!

"Five millions of the primitive, who hold
    The faith which makes ye great on earth, implored
A *part* of that vast *all* they held of old,—
    Freedom to worship—not alone your Lord,          380
Michael, but you, and you, Saint Peter! Cold
    Must be your souls, if you have not abhorr'd
The foe to Catholic participation
In all the license of a Christian nation.

"True! he allow'd them to pray God; but as          385
    A consequence of prayer, refused the law
Which would have placed them upon the same base
    With those who did not hold the saints in awe."
But here Saint Peter started from his place,
    And cried, "You may the prisoner withdraw:          390
Ere heaven shall ope her portals to this Guelph,
While I am guard, may I be damn'd myself!

"Sooner will I with Cerberus exchange
    My office (and *his* is no sinecure)
Than see this royal Bedlam bigot range          395
    The azure fields of heaven, of that be sure!"
"Saint!" replied Satan, "you do well to avenge
    The wrongs he made your satellites endure;
And if to this exchange you should be given,
I'll try to coax *our* Cerberus up to heaven!"          400

Here Michael interposed: "Good saint! and devil!
    Pray, not so fast; you both outrun discretion.
Saint Peter! you were wont to be more civil!
    Satan! excuse this warmth of his expression,
And condescension to the vulgar's level:          405
    Even saints sometimes forget themselves in session.
Have you got more to say?"—"No."—"If you please,
I'll trouble you to call your witnesses."

Then Satan turn'd and waved his swarthy hand,
    Which stirr'd with its electric qualities          410
Clouds farther off than we can understand,
    Although we find him sometimes in our skies;

Infernal thunder shook both sea and land
  In all the planets, and hell's batteries
Let off the artillery, which Milton mentions                415
  As one of Satan's most sublime inventions.

This was a signal unto such damn'd souls
  As have the privilege of their damnation
Extended far beyond the mere controls
  Of worlds past, present, or to come; no station          420
Is theirs particularly in the rolls
  Of hell assign'd; but where their inclination
Or business carries them in search of game,
They may range freely—being damn'd the same.

They're proud of this—as very well they may,               425
  It being a sort of knighthood, or gilt key
Stuck in their loins; or like to an "entré"
  Up the back stairs, or such freemasonry.
I borrow my comparisons from clay,
  Being clay myself. Let not those spirits be              430
Offended with such base low likenesses;
We know their posts are nobler far than these.

When the great signal ran from heaven to hell—
  About ten million times the distance reckon'd
From our sun to its earth, as we can tell                  435
  How much time it takes up, even to a second,
For every ray that travels to dispel
  The fogs of London, through which, dimly beacon'd,
The weathercocks are gilt some thrice a year,
If that the *summer* is not too severe:                    440

I say that I can tell—'twas half a minute;
  I know the solar beams take up more time
Ere, pack'd up for their journey, they begin it;
  But then their telegraph is less sublime,
And if they ran a race, they would not win it              445
  'Gainst Satan's couriers bound for their own clime.
The sun takes up some years for every ray
To reach its goal—the devil not half a day.

Upon the verge of space, about the size
  Of half-a-crown, a little speck appear'd                 450
(I've seen a something like it in the skies
  In the Ægean, ere a squall); it near'd,
And, growing bigger, took another guise;
  Like an aërial ship it tack'd, and steer'd,

Or *was* steer'd (I am doubtful of the grammar 455
Of the last phrase, which makes the stanza stammer;—
But take your choice): and then it grew a cloud;
And so it was—a cloud of witnesses.
But such a cloud! No land e'er saw a crowd
Of locusts numerous as the heavens saw these; 460
They shadow'd with their myriads space; their loud
And varied cries were like those of wild geese
(If nations may be liken'd to a goose),
And realised the phrase of "hell broke loose."

Here crash'd a sturdy oath of stout John Bull, 465
Who damn'd away his eyes as heretofore:
There Paddy brogued "By Jasus!"—"What's your wull?"
The temperate Scot exclaim'd: the French ghost swore
In certain terms I shan't translate in full,
As the first coachman will; and 'midst the war, 470
The voice of Jonathan was heard to express,
"*Our* president is going to war, I guess."

Besides there were the Spaniard, Dutch, and Dane;
In short, an universal shoal of shades,
From Otaheite's isle to Salisbury Plain, 475
Of all climes and professions, years and trades,
Ready to swear against the good king's reign,
Bitter as clubs in cards are against spades:
All summon'd by this grand "subpœna," to
Try if kings mayn't be damn'd like me or you. 480

When Michael saw this host, he first grew pale,
As angels can; next, like Italian twilight,
He turn'd all colours—as a peacock's tail,
Or sunset streaming through a Gothic skylight
In some old abbey, or a trout not stale, 485
Or distant lightning on the horizon *by* night,
Or a fresh rainbow, or a grand review
Of thirty regiments in red, green, and blue.

Then he address'd himself to Satan: "Why—
My good old friend, for such I deem you, though 490
Our different parties make us fight so shy,
I ne'er mistake you for a *personal* foe;
Our difference is *political*, and I
Trust that, whatever may occur below,
You know my great respect for you: and this 495
Makes me regret whate'er you do amiss—

"Why, my dear Lucifer, would you abuse
    My call for witnesses? I did not mean
That you should half of earth and hell produce;
    'Tis clean superfluous, since two honest, clean,      500
True testimonies are enough: we lose
    Our time, nay, our eternity, between
The accusation and defence: if we
Hear both, 'twill stretch our immortality."

Satan replied, "To me the matter is                       505
    Indifferent, in a personal point of view:
I can have fifty better souls than this
    With far less trouble than we have gone through
Already; and I merely argued his
    Late majesty of Britain's case with you              510
Upon a point of form: you may dispose
Of him; I've kings enough below, God knows!"

Thus spoke the Demon (late call'd "multi-faced"
    By multo-scribbling Southey). "Then we'll call
One or two persons of the myriads placed                  515
    Around our congress, and dispense with all
The rest," quoth Michael: "Who may be so graced
    As to speak first? there's choice enough—who shall
It be?" Then Satan answer'd, "There are many;
But you may choose Jack Wilkes as well as any."           520

A merry, cock-eyed, curious-looking sprite
    Upon the instant started from the throng,
Dress'd in a fashion now forgotten quite;
    For all the fashions of the flesh stick long
By people in the next world; where unite                  525
    All the costumes since Adam's, right or wrong,
From Eve's fig-leaf down to the petticoat,
Almost as scanty, of days less remote.

The spirit look'd around upon the crowds
    Assembled, and exclaim'd, "My friends of all          530
The spheres, we shall catch cold amongst these clouds;
    So let's to business: why this general call?
If those are freeholders I see in shrouds,
    And 'tis for an election that they bawl,
Behold a candidate with unturn'd coat!                    535
Saint Peter, may I count upon your vote?"

"Sir," replied Michael, "you mistake; these things
    Are of a former life, and what we do

Above is more august; to judge of kings
   Is the tribunal met: so now you know."      540
"Then I presume those gentlemen with wings,"
   Said Wilkes, "are cherubs; and that soul below
Looks much like George the Third, but to my mind
   A good deal older—Bless me! is he blind?"

"He is what you behold him, and his doom      545
   Depends upon his deeds," the Angel said;
"If you have aught to arraign in him, the tomb
   Gives licence to the humblest beggar's head
To lift itself against the loftiest."—"Some,"
   Said Wilkes, "don't wait to see them laid in lead,      550
For such a liberty—and I, for one,
   Have told them what I thought beneath the sun."

"*Above* the sun repeat, then, what thou hast
   To urge against him," said the Archangel, "Why,"
Replied the spirit, "since old scores are past,      555
   Must I turn evidence? In faith, not I.
Besides, I beat him hollow at the last,
   With all his Lords and Commons: in the sky
I don't like ripping up old stories, since
   His conduct was but natural in a prince.      560

"Foolish, no doubt, and wicked, to oppress
   A poor unlucky devil without a shilling;
But then I blame the man himself much less
   Than Bute and Grafton, and shall be unwilling
To see him punish'd here for their excess,      565
   Since they were both damn'd long ago, and still in
Their place below: for me, I have forgiven,
And vote his 'habeas corpus' into heaven."

"Wilkes," said the Devil, "I understand all this;
   You turn'd-to half a courtier ere you died,      570
And seem to think it would not be amiss
   To grow a whole one on the other side
Of Charon's ferry; you forget that *his*
   Reign is concluded; whatsoe'er betide,
He won't be sovereign more: you've lost your labour,      575
For at the best he will but be your neighbour.

"However, I knew what to think of it,
   When I beheld you in your jesting way,
Flitting and whispering round about the spit
   Where Belial, upon duty for the day,      580

With Fox's lard was basting William Pitt,
  His pupil; I knew what to think, I say:
That fellow even in hell breeds farther ills;
  I'll have him *gagg'd*—'twas one of his own bills.

"Call Junius!" From the crowd a shadow stalk'd,        585
  And at the name there was a general squeeze,
So that the very ghosts no longer walk'd
  In comfort, at their own aërial ease,
But were all ramm'd, and jamm'd (but to be balk'd,
  As we shall see), and jostled hands and knees,        590
Like wind compress'd and pent within a bladder,
Or like a human colic, which is sadder.

The shadow came—a tall, thin, grey-hair'd figure,
  That look'd as it had been a shade on earth;
Quick in its motions, with an air of vigour,            595
  But nought to mark its breeding or its birth;
Now it wax'd little, then again grew bigger,
  With now an air of gloom, or savage mirth;
But as you gazed upon its features, they
Changed every instant—to *what*, none could say.       600

The more intently the ghosts gazed, the less
  Could they distinguish whose the features were;
The Devil himself seem'd puzzled even to guess;
  They varied like a dream—now here, now there;
And several people swore from out the press,           605
  They knew him perfectly; and one could swear
He was his father: upon which another
Was sure he was his mother's cousin's brother:

Another, that he was a duke, or knight,
  An orator, a lawyer, or a priest,                     610
A nabob, a man-midwife; but the wight
  Mysterious changed his countenance at least
As oft as they their minds; though in full sight
  He stood, the puzzle only was increased;
The man was a phantasmagoria in                         615
Himself—he was so volatile and thin.

The moment that you had pronounced him *one*,
  Presto! his face changed, and he was another;
And when that change was hardly well put on,
  It varied, till I don't think his own mother          620
(If that he had a mother) would her son
  Have known, he shifted so from one to t'other;

Till guessing from a pleasure grew a task,
At this epistolary "Iron Mask."

For sometimes he like Cerberus would seem—
    "Three gentlemen at once" (as sagely says
Good Mrs. Malaprop); then you might deem
    That he was not even *one;* now many rays
Were flashing round him; and now a thick steam
    Hid him from sight—like fogs on London days:
Now Burke, now Tooke, he grew to people's fancies,
And certes often like Sir Philip Francis.

I've an hypothesis—'tis quite my own;
    I never let it out till now, for fear
Of doing people harm about the throne,
    And injuring some minister or peer,
On whom the stigma might perhaps be blown;
    It is—my gentle public, lend thine ear!
'Tis, that what Junius we are wont to call
Was *really*, *truly*, nobody at all.

I don't see wherefore letters should not be
    Written without hands, since we daily view
Them written without heads; and books, we see,
    Are fill'd as well without the latter too:
And really till we fix on somebody
    For certain sure to claim them as his due,
Their author, like the Niger's mouth, will bother
The world to say if *there* be mouth or author.

"And who and what art thou?" the Archangel said.
    "For *that* you may consult my title-page,"
Replied this mighty shadow of a shade:
    "If I have kept my secret half an age,
I scarce shall tell it now."—"Canst thou upbraid,"
    Continued Michael, "George Rex, or allege
Aught further?" Junius answer'd, "You had better
First ask him for *his* answer to my letter:

"My charges upon record will outlast
    The brass of both his epitaph and tomb."
"Repent'st thou not," said Michael, "of some past
    Exaggeration? something which may doom
Thyself if false, as him if true? Thou wast
    Too bitter—is it not so?—in thy gloom
Of passion?"—"Passion!" cried the phantom dim,
"I loved my country, and I hated him.

625

630

635

640

645

650

655

660

"What I have written, I have written: let                                   665
    The rest be on his head or mine!" So spoke
Old "Nominis Umbra"; and while speaking yet,
    Away he melted in celestial smoke.
Then Satan said to Michael, "Don't forget
    To call George Washington, and John Horne Tooke,    670
And Franklin";—but at this time there was heard
    A cry for room, though not a phantom stirr'd.

At length with jostling, elbowing, and the aid
    Of cherubim appointed to that post,
The devil Asmodeus to the circle made                                      675
    His way, and look'd as if his journey cost
Some trouble. When his burden down he laid,
    "What's this?" cried Michael; "why, 'tis not a ghost?"
"I know it," quoth the incubus; "but he
    Shall be one, if you leave the affair to me.                           680

"Confound the renegado! I have sprain'd
    My left wing, he's so heavy; one would think
Some of his works about his neck were chain'd.
    But to the point; while hovering o'er the brink
Of Skiddaw (where as usual it still rain'd),                               685
    I saw a taper, far below me, wink,
And stooping, caught this fellow at a libel—
No less on history than the Holy Bible.

"The former is the devil's scripture, and
    The latter yours, good Michael: so the affair                         690
Belongs to all of us, you understand.
    I snatch'd him up just as you see him there,
And brought him off for sentence out of hand:
    I've scarcely been ten minutes in the air—
At least a quarter it can hardly be:                                       695
I dare say that his wife is still at tea."

Here Satan said, "I know this man of old,
    And have expected him for some time here;
A sillier fellow you will scarce behold,
    Or more conceited in his petty sphere:                                700
But surely it was not worth while to fold
    Such trash below your wing, Asmodeus dear:
We had the poor wretch safe (without being bored
With carriage) coming of his own accord.

"But since he's here, let's see what he has done."                        705
    "Done!" cried Asmodeus, "he anticipates

The very business you are now upon,
 And scribbles as if head clerk to the Fates.
Who knows to what his ribaldry may run,
 When such an ass as this, like Balaam's, prates?"    710
"Let's hear," quoth Michael, "what he has to say:
You know we're bound to that in every way."

Now the bard, glad to get an audience, which
 By no means often was his case below,
Began to cough, and hawk, and hem, and pitch    715
 His voice into that awful note of woe
To all unhappy hearers within reach
 Of poets when the tide of rhyme's in flow;
But stuck fast with his first hexameter,
Not one of all whose gouty feet would stir.    720

But ere the spavin'd dactyls could be spurr'd
 Into recitative, in great dismay
Both cherubim and seraphim were heard
 To murmur loudly through their long array;
And Michael rose ere he could get a word    725
 Of all his founder'd verses under way,
And cried, "For God's sake stop, my friend! 'twere best—
*Non Di, non homines*—you know the rest."

A general bustle spread throughout the throng,
 Which seem'd to hold all verse in detestation;    730
The angels had of course enough of song
 When upon service; and the generation
Of ghosts had heard too much in life, not long
 Before, to profit by a new occasion:
The monarch, mute till then, exclaim'd, "What! what!    735
*Pye* come again? No more—no more of that!"

The tumult grew; an universal cough
 Convulsed the skies, as during a debate,
When Castlereagh has been up long enough
 (Before he was first minister of state,    740
I mean—the *slaves hear now*); some cried "Off, off!"
 As at a farce; till, grown quite desperate,
The bard Saint Peter pray'd to interpose
(Himself an author) only for his prose.

The varlet was not an ill-favour'd knave;    745
 A good deal like a vulture in the face,
With a hook nose and a hawk's eye, which gave
 A smart and sharper-looking sort of grace

To his whole aspect, which, though rather grave,
   Was by no means so ugly as his case;           750
But that, indeed, was hopeless as can be,
   Quite a poetic felony "*de se.*"

Then Michael blew his trump, and still'd the noise
   With one still greater, as is yet the mode
On earth besides; except some grumbling voice,        755
   Which now and then will make a slight inroad
Upon decorous silence, few will twice
   Lift up their lungs when fairly overcrow'd;
And now the bard could plead his own bad cause,
   With all the attitudes of self-applause.        760

He said—(I only give the heads)—he said,
   He meant no harm in scribbling; 'twas his way
Upon all topics; 'twas, besides, his bread,
   Of which he butter'd both sides; 'twould delay
Too long the assembly (he was pleased to dread),    765
   And take up rather more time than a day,
To name his works—he would but cite a few—
   "Wat Tyler"—"Rhymes on Blenheim"—"Waterloo."

He had written praises of a regicide;
   He had written praises of all kings whatever;    770
He had written for republics far and wide,
   And then against them bitterer than ever;
For pantisocracy he once had cried
   Aloud, a scheme less moral than 'twas clever;
Then grew a hearty anti-jacobin—        775
   Had turn'd his coat—and would have turn'd his skin.

He had sung against all battles, and again
   In their high praise and glory; he had call'd
Reviewing "the ungentle craft," and then
   Become as base a critic as e'er crawl'd—    780
Fed, paid, and pamper'd by the very men
   By whom his muse and morals had been maul'd:
He had written much blank verse, and blanker prose,
   And more of both than anybody knows.

He had written Wesley's life:—here turning round    785
   To Satan, "Sir, I'm ready to write yours,
In two octavo volumes, nicely bound,
   With notes and preface, all that most allures
The pious purchaser; and there's no ground
   For fear, for I can choose my own reviewers:    790

So let me have the proper documents,
That I may add you to my other saints."

Satan bow'd, and was silent. "Well, if you,
    With amiable modesty, decline
My offer, what says Michael? There are few          795
    Whose memoirs could be render'd more divine.
Mine is a pen of all work; not so new
    As it was once, but I would make you shine
Like your own trumpet. By the way, my own
Has more of brass in it, and is as well blown.      800

"But talking about trumpets, here's my Vision!
    Now you shall judge, all people; yes, you shall
Judge with my judgment, and by my decision
    Be guided who shall enter heaven or fall.
I settle all these things by intuition,             805
    Times present, past, to come, heaven, hell, and all,
Like King Alfonso. When I thus see double,
I save the Deity some worlds of trouble."

He ceased, and drew forth an MS.; and no
    Persuasion on the part of devils, saints,        810
Or angels, now could stop the torrent; so
    He read the first three lines of the contents;
But at the fourth, the whole spiritual show
    Had vanish'd, with variety of scents,
Ambrosial and sulphureous, as they sprang,          815
Like lightning, off from his "melodious twang."

Those grand heroics acted as a spell:
    The angels stopp'd their ears and plied their pinions;
The devils ran howling, deafen'd, down to hell;
    The ghosts fled, gibbering, for their own dominions—  820
(For 'tis not yet decided where they dwell,
    And I leave every man to his opinions);
Michael took refuge in his trump—but, lo!
His teeth were set on edge, he could not blow!

Saint Peter, who has hitherto been known            825
    For an impetuous saint, upraised his keys,
And at the fifth line knock'd the poet down;
    Who fell like Phaeton, but more at ease,
Into his lake, for there he did not drown;
    A different web being by the Destinies           830
Woven for the Laureate's final wreath, whene'er
Reform shall happen either here or there.

He first sank to the bottom—like his works,
   But soon rose to the surface—like himself;
For all corrupted things are buoy'd like corks,        835
   By their own rottenness, light as an elf,
Or wisp that flits o'er a morass: he lurks,
   It may be, still, like dull books on a shelf,
In his own den, to scrawl some "Life" or "Vision,"
As Welborn says—"the devil turn'd precisian."       840

As for the rest, to come to the conclusion
   Of this true dream, the telescope is gone
Which kept my optics free from all delusion,
   And show'd me what I in my turn have shown;
All I saw farther, in the last confusion,         845
   Was, that King George slipp'd into heaven for one;
And when the tumult dwindled to a calm,
I left him practising the hundredth psalm.

# Peter Quennell

## BYRON
### THE VISION OF JUDGMENT

The death of King George III, on January 29, 1820, was not an event that much disturbed his subjects. He had been their nominal sovereign for nearly six decades; but he had suffered a preliminary bout of madness as long ago as 1780, had been judged permanently insane thirty years later, and since that time had led a twilit existence among the fantastic creations of his own disordered mind, a bearded patriarch immured in his palace-asylum, who, during his last days, said one of his undutiful sons, bore a strange resemblance to an ancient rabbi. Few regretted him now that his consort was dead: his relations with other members of his large, ill-behaved family had never been harmonious; and with his heir and successor, the Prince Regent, he had had many violent public quarrels. In 1820 the *de facto* ruler formally assumed the crown; while George III, already a living ghost, moved off quietly into the realm of shadows.

His body was laid to rest, however, with the proper royal pomp; and the ceremony was followed by a no less pompous effusion from the middle-aged Poet Laureate Robert Southey. When it was published, under the title *Vision of Judgment*, Southey added an appropriately solemn and sententious preface, where, after paying some effusive compliments to the new monarch and explaining why the English hexameter line was the metrical mode that he had chosen, he made a stern reference to the so-called Satanic School, and to "those monstrous combinations of horror and mockery, lewdness and impiety, with which English poetry has, in our days, first been polluted." Clearly the Laureate's shafts were directed at Byron and at the opening cantos of his "Don Juan."

The *Vision* itself was a delightfully absurd affair. Previous Laureates had set a high standard; but Southey's description of the old king's apotheosis was one of the most unintentionally amusing works yet written in the English language. Thomas Shadwell could not have done better; every detail has a burlesque extravagance. First, Southey pictures "The Awakening":

> *Ho! he exclaim'd, King George of England cometh to*
> *judgement!*
> *Hear Heaven! Ye Angels hear! Souls of the Good and*
> *the wicked*
> *Whom it concerns, attend! Thou, Hell, bring forth his*
> *accusers!*

Prominent among "The Accusers" who arrive is the brilliant, impudent demagogue, John Wilkes. But Southey, recognizing him and his notorious squint, the "cast of his eye oblique," briskly drives him back to Hell. Chief of "The Absolvers," oddly enough, is the heroic spirit of George Washington, purged of his errors since he has crossed the heavenly threshold and prepared at length to pay the good King homage. Washington's help is blandly acknowledged:

> *Washington! said the Monarch, well has thou spoken*
> *and truly . . .*

But there are still five sections to come before the *Vision* reaches a sonorous close; George is reunited with "our late-lost Queen, the nation's example of virtue," with his beloved daughter, the Princess Amelia, and his short-lived grand-daughter, the Princess Charlotte, and the "happy company" joins the celestial throng, accompanied by "loud hosannahs of welcome." At this point, Southey's vision dissolves and the poet is abruptly returned to Keswick. Instead of the "rapturous sound of hosannahs," he hears the evening chimes of a prosaic English churchbell.

Such were the verses with which, in April 1821, Southey improved the occasion of the King's demise. He had done his best; he always did his best. He was not only a studious, but an astonishingly prolific writer. A government pension of £170 a year had had the usual salutary effect; and little now remained of the free-thinking youth whom his friend Coleridge had with some difficulty converted from deism to unitarianism, or of the revolutionary dramatist who had once written "Wat Tyler" to air his boldly democratic views. His former allies now voted him an apostate. Nor had he much endeared himself to his fellow poets by his animadversions on their disreputable private lives, as when he had suggested that Byron and Shelley were united in "a league of incest"—a spitefully misleading jibe at Byron's liaison with Claire Clairmont and Shelley's romantic attachment to Mary Godwin.

Byron had once admired Southey, and had praised his fine poetic head. But he was a man who could rarely forget an insult; and the appearance of *The Vision* provided an opportunity far too good to miss. It was not the first time he had belabored the handsome apostate: in his appendix to "The Two Foscari" and his suppressed dedication to *Don Juan* he had administered a series of savage blows. The "Epic Renegade's" new publication, however, presented an especially attractive target. Byron had an incorrigible sense of fun, which underlay even his darkest and gloomiest moods, and must have enjoyed Southey's limping hexameters for their own absurd sake. Better still, the Laureate's use and misuse of his supernatural machinery set his mind working in a similar direction. He had always been preoccupied with thoughts of death, and with the vague, bewildering possibility of an existence after death; and here was a chance of depicting the next world and its imaginary denizens in his "finest, ferocious, Caravaggio style," in a work that would be a blend of the sublime and the grotesque, of epic poetry and personal and social satire. His poem was begun during the early summer of 1821, and was published in the opening issue of Leigh Hunt's ill-fated paper, *The Liberal*, which Shelley had persuaded him to support, on October 15th, 1822.

*The Vision of Judgment* is not a mere parody, though it becomes doubly entertaining if we compare it with Southey's original production; not simply a headlong attack on the existing British government, or on the "old stupid system" of monarchical rule reinstated in Europe since the Congress of Vienna by Castlereagh, Talleyrand, Metternich and their legitimist and ultra-conservative allies. Satire, when it achieves poetic excellence, invariably transcends its object; and just as important to Byron as Southey, George III, or the odious principles for which they stood, was his personal vision of human life and death, and of the pathetic contrast between "unaccommodated man" and the adventitious trappings of a royal personage:

> *In the first year of freedom's second dawn*
> *Died George the Third; although no tyrant, one*
> *Who shielded tyrants, till each sense withdrawn*
> *Left him nor mental nor external sun:*
> *A better farmer ne'er brush'd dew from lawn,*
> *A worse king never left a realm undone!*

*He died! his death made no great stir on earth:*
*His burial made some pomp; there was profusion*
*Of velvet, gilding, brass, and no great dearth*
*Of aught but tears—save those shed by collusion.*
*. . .*
*It seem'd the mockery of hell to fold*
*The rottenness of eighty years in gold.*

"Of the Immortality of the Soul," Byron wrote during the same year in a collection of *Detached Thoughts*, "it appears to me that there can be little doubt. . . ." He had never entirely cast off the influence of the grim Calvinist upbringing that had helped to mold his youth; and, if he jokes about Christian heaven and hell, he does so in a half-mocking, yet somehow half-respectful, fashion. As an imaginative writer, Byron is at his best when his method is apparently least consistent, and he can give free expression to all the varying impulses of his radically divided nature. "The Vision of Judgment," like "Don Juan" (of which five cantos had been written by the end of 1820), is a comic poem haunted throughout by profoundly serious undertones; and among its finest qualities is the majestic assurance with which its author swings from mood to mood. Thus the splendid passage that describes the encounter of Michael and the fallen archangel:

*He and the sombre, silent Spirit met—*
*They knew each other both for good and ill;*
*Such was their power, that neither could forget*
*His former friend and future foe; but still*
*There was a high, immortal, proud regret*
*In either's eye . . .*

—is completed and suddenly brought down to earth by an inimitable serio-comic couplet:

*Yet still between his Darkness and his Brightness*
*There pass'd a mutual glance of great politeness*

—whence the narrative smoothly and swiftly reverts to the plane of social satire:

*The Archangel bow'd, not like a modern beau,*
*But with a graceful Oriental bend,*
*Pressing one radiant arm just where below*
*The heart in good men is supposed to tend;*
*He turn'd as to an equal, not too low,*
*But kindly; Satan met his ancient friend*

*With more hauteur; as might an old Castilian*
*Poor noble meet a mushroom rich civilian*

From a stylistic point of view, *The Vision of Judgment* occupies a crucial midway point in the history of Byron's genius. He was already well launched upon his greatest poem, *Don Juan,* and had discovered that he could be as "facetious" as he pleased without any loss of real gravity. But *Don Juan* is a diffuse and rambling masterpiece; and the subject and scope of his new work obliged him to adopt a more compact form. In each poem he achieved an early ambition. The romantic adventurer par excellence, he disliked and distrusted most romantic writing; Pope was the literary forebear whom he never ceased to worship; and, although his own demonic inclinations were constantly pulling him the other way, his avowed aim was to follow Pope's example, injecting modern literature, which he considered slipshod and jejune, with the Augustan virtues of intellectual clarity, lyrical harmony, and incisive masculine common sense.

*The Vision of Judgment* shows him both as a disciple of Pope and as an irrepressibly romantic poet. His canvas is as large as that of "The Dunciad"; but whereas Pope peoples his verse with a vast assembly of insignificant figures—publishers and versifiers nowadays only remembered because they had incurred the poet's hatred—Byron's subject is the unending conflict between the gigantic social forces, reborn liberalism and obscurantist monarchical conservatism, then at war in nineteenth-century Europe. Wilkes emerges from among the King's accusers, "a merry, cock-eyed, curious-looking sprite," who makes a singularly sensible and generous speech and casts his vote against damnation; and Wilkes is followed by the enigmatic Junius, a protean apparition whose features "varied like a dream"—he still preserves his anonymity—and who refuses doggedly to withdraw his previous charges—

*I loved my country, and I hated him.*

—and thereupon, secretive and elusive as ever, vanishes in a puff of smoke.

Finally, it is the turn of Southey, dunce to beat all dunces, literary turncoat on the grand scale. Characteristic of the renegade laureate was his imperturbable self-confidence; surrounded by the hosts of heaven and hell, this, he judges, is a good moment to read aloud his latest manuscript—which provokes the impetuous St. Peter to raise his keys and knock the scribbler head over heels into the waters of his native lake:

> *He first sank to the bottom—like his works,*
> *But soon rose to the surface—like himself;*
> *For all corrupted things are buoyed like corks*

Byron's vision was alike poetic and prophetic; it is less difficult to damage a good writer than to annihilate a bad one. Byron died seventeen months after the publication of his satire, a disappointed and exhausted exile; Southey, self-important to the last, lived on until 1843.

# PERCY BYSSHE SHELLEY
## [1792–1822]

## Adonais

### AN ELEGY ON THE DEATH OF JOHN KEATS,
### AUTHOR OF ENDYMION, HYPERION ETC.

Αστήρ πρὶν μὲν ἐγαμπες ενι ζωοισιν εωος.
Νῦν δε θανῶν, γαμπεις ἑσπερος εν Φθίμενοις.

PLATO.

I weep for Adonais—he is dead!
Oh, weep for Adonais! though our tears
Thaw not the frost which binds so dear a head!
And thou, sad Hour, selected from all years
To mourn our loss, rouse thy obscure compeers, 5
And teach them thine own sorrow, say: with me
Died Adonais; till the Future dares
Forget the Past, his fate and fame shall be
An echo and a light unto eternity!

Where wert thou mighty Mother, when he lay, 10
When thy Son lay, pierced by the shaft which flies
In darkness? where was lorn Urania
When Adonais died? With veiled eyes,
'Mid listening Echoes, in her Paradise
She sate, while one, with soft enamoured breath, 15
Rekindled all the fading melodies,
With which, like flowers that mock the corse beneath,
He had adorned and hid the coming bulk of death.

Oh, weep for Adonais—he is dead!
Wake, melancholy Mother, wake and weep! 20
Yet wherefore? Quench within their burning bed
Thy fiery tears, and let thy loud heart keep
Like his, a mute and uncomplaining sleep;
For he is gone, where all things wise and fair
Descend:—oh, dream not that the amorous Deep 25
Will yet restore him to the vital air;
Death feeds on his mute voice, and laughs at our despair.

Most musical of mourners, weep again!
Lament anew, Urania!—He died,
Who was the Sire of an immortal strain,                30
Blind, old, and lonely, when his country's pride,
The priest, the slave, and the liberticide,
Trampled and mocked with many a loathed rite
Of lust and blood; he went, unterrified,
Into the gulf of death; but his clear Sprite          35
Yet reigns o'er earth; the third among the sons of light.

Most musical of mourners, weep anew!
Not all to that bright station dared to climb;
And happier they their happiness who knew,
Whose tapers yet burn through that night of time      40
In which suns perished; others more sublime,
Struck by the envious wrath of man or God,
Have sunk, extinct in their refulgent prime;
And some yet live, treading the thorny road,
Which leads, through toil and hate, to Fame's serene abode.   45

But now, thy youngest, dearest one, has perished,
The nursling of thy widowhood, who grew,
Like a pale flower by some sad maiden cherished,
And fed with true love tears, instead of dew;
Most musical of mourners, weep anew!                  50
Thy extreme hope, the loveliest and the last,
The bloom, whose petals nipt before they blew
Died on the promise of the fruit, is waste;
The broken lily lies—the storm is overpast.

To that high Capital, where kingly Death              55
Keeps his pale court in beauty and decay,
He came; and bought, with price of purest breath,
A grave among the eternal.—Come away!
Haste, while the vault of blue Italian day
Is yet his fitting charnel-roof! while still          60
He lies, as if in dewy sleep he lay;
Awake him not! surely he takes his fill
Of deep and liquid rest, forgetful of all ill.

He will awake no more, oh, never more!—
Within the twilight chamber spreads apace,            65
The shadow of white Death, and at the door
Invisible Corruption waits to trace
His extreme way to her dim dwelling-place;
The eternal Hunger sits, but pity and awe
Soothe her pale rage, nor dares she to deface         70

PERCY BYSSHE SHELLEY

*Watercolor by William Blake*

*The Bettmann Archive*

So fair a prey, till darkness and the law
Of change, shall o'er his sleep the mortal curtain draw.

Oh, weep for Adonais!—The quick Dreams,
The passion-winged Ministers of thought,
Who were his flocks, whom near the living streams        75
Of his young spirit he fed, and whom he taught
The love which was its music, wander not,—
Wander no more, from kindling brain to brain,
But droop there, whence they sprung; and mourn their lot
Round the cold heart, where, after their sweet pain,       80
They ne'er will gather strength, or find a home again.

And one with trembling hand clasps his cold head,
And fans him with her moonlight wings, and cries,
"Our love, our hope, our sorrow, is not dead;
See, on the silken fringe of his faint eyes,       85
Like dew upon a sleeping flower, there lies
A tear some Dream has loosened from his brain."
Lost Angel of a ruined Paradise!
She knew not 'twas her own; as with no stain
She faded, like a cloud which had outwept its rain.       90

One from a lucid urn of starry dew
Washed his light limbs as if embalming them;
Another clipt her profuse locks, and threw
The wreath upon him, like an anadem,
Which frozen tears instead of pearls begem;       95
Another in her wilful grief would break
Her bow and winged reeds, as if to stem
A greater loss with one which was more weak;
And dull the barbed fire against his frozen cheek.

Another Splendour on his mouth alit,       100
That mouth, whence it was wont to draw the breath
Which gave it strength to pierce the guarded wit,
And pass into the panting heart beneath
With lightning and with music: the damp death
Quenched its caress upon its icy lips;       105
And, as a dying meteor stains a wreath
Of moonlight vapour, which the cold night clips,
It flushed through his pale limbs, and passed to its eclipse.

And others came . . . Desires and Adorations,
Winged Persuasions and veiled Destinies,       110
Splendours, and Glooms, and glimmering Incarnations
Of hopes and fears, and twilight Phantasies;

And Sorrow, with her family of Sighs,
And Pleasure, blind with tears, led by the gleam
Of her own dying smile instead of eyes,                    115
Came in slow pomp;—the moving pomp might seem
Like pageantry of mist on an autumnal stream.

All he had loved, and moulded into thought
From shape, and hue, and odour, and sweet sound,
Lamented Adonais. Morning sought                           120
Her eastern watch-tower, and her hair unbound,
Wet with the tears which should adorn the ground,
Dimmed the aerial eyes that kindle day;
Afar the melancholy thunder moaned,
Pale Ocean in unquiet slumber lay,                         125
And the wild winds flew round, sobbing in their dismay.

Lost Echo sits amid the voiceless mountains,
And feeds her grief with his remembered lay,
And will no more reply to winds or fountains,
Or amorous birds perched on the young green spray,         130
Or herdsman's horn, or bell at closing day;
Since she can mimic not his lips, more dear
Than those for whose disdain she pined away
Into a shadow of all sounds:—a drear
Murmur, between their songs, is all the woodmen hear.      135

Grief made the young Spring wild, and she threw down
Her kindling buds, as if she Autumn were,
Or they dead leaves; since her delight is flown
For whom should she have waked the sullen year?
To Phœbus was not Hyacinth so dear,                        140
Nor to himself Narcissus, as to both
Thou Adonais; wan they stand and sere
Amid the faint companions of their youth,
With dew all turned to tears; odour, to sighing ruth.

Thy spirit's sister, the lorn nightingale,                 145
Mourns not her mate with such melodious pain;
Not so the eagle, who like thee could scale
Heaven, and could nourish in the sun's domain
Her mighty youth, with morning, doth complain,
Soaring and screaming round her empty nest,                150
As Albion wails for thee: the curse of Cain
Light on his head who pierced thy innocent breast,
And scared the angel soul that was its earthly guest!

Ah woe is me! Winter is come and gone,
But grief returns with the revolving year;                 155

The airs and streams renew their joyous tone;
The ants, the bees, the swallows reappear;
Fresh leaves and flowers deck the dead Seasons' bier;
The amorous birds now pair in every brake,
And build their mossy homes in field and brere;          160
And the green lizard, and the golden snake,
Like unimprisoned flames, out of their trance awake.

Through wood and stream and field and hill and Ocean,
A quickening life from the Earth's heart has burst
As it has ever done, with change and motion,          165
From the great morning of the world when first
God dawned on Chaos; in its stream immersed
The lamps of Heaven flash with a softer light;
All baser things plant with life's sacred thirst;
Diffuse themselves; and spend in love's delight,          170
The beauty and the joy of their renewed might.

The leprous corpse touched by this spirit tender
Exhales itself in flowers of gentle breath;
Like incarnations of the stars, when splendour
Is changed to fragrance, they illumine death          175
And mock the merry worm that wakes beneath;
Nought we know, dies. Shall that alone which knows
Be as a sword consumed before the sheath
By sightless lightning?—th' intense atom glows
A moment, then is quenched in a most cold repose.          180

Alas! that all we loved of him should be,
But for our grief, as if it had not been.
And grief itself be mortal! Woe is me!
Whence are we, and why are we? of what scene
The actors or spectators? Great and mean          185
Meet massed in death, who lends what life must borrow.
As long as skies are blue, and fields are green,
Evening must usher night, night urge the morrow,
Month follow month with woe, and year wake year to sorrow.

*He* will awake no more, oh, never more!          190
"Wake thou," cried Misery, "childless Mother, rise
Out of thy sleep, and slake, in thy heart's core,
A wound more fierce than his with tears and sighs."
And all the Dreams that watched Urania's eyes,
And all the Echoes whom their sister's song          195
Had held in holy silence, cried, "Arise!"
Swift as a Thought by the snake Memory stung,
From her ambrosial rest the fading Splendour sprung.

She rose like an autumnal Night, that springs
Out of the East, and follows wild and drear          200
The golden Day, which, on eternal wings,
Even as a ghost abandoning a bier,
Has left the Earth a corpse. Sorrow and fear
So struck, so roused, so rapt; Urania
So saddened round her like an atmosphere          205
Of stormy mist; so swept her on her way
Even to the mournful place where Adonais lay.

Out of her secret Paradise she sped,
Through camps and cities rough with stone, and steel,
And human hearts, which to her aery tread          210
Yielding not, wounded the invisible
Palms of her tender feet where'er they fell:
And barbed tongues, and thoughts more sharp than they
Rent the soft Form they never could repel,
Whose sacred blood, like the young tears of May,          215
Paved with eternal flowers that undeserving way.

In the death-chamber for a moment Death,
Shamed by the presence of that living Might
Blushed to annihilation, and the breath
Revisited those lips, and life's pale light          220
Flashed through those limbs, so late her dear delight.
"Leave me not wild and drear and comfortless,
As silent lightning leaves the starless night!
Leave me not!" cried Urania: her distress
Roused Death: Death rose and smiled, and met her vain
          caress.          225

"Stay yet awhile! speak to me once again;
Kiss me, so long but as a kiss may live;
And in my heartless breast and burning brain
That word, that kiss shall all thoughts else survive,
With food of saddest memory kept alive,          230
Now thou art dead, as if it were a part
Of thee, my Adonais! I would give
All that I am to be as thou now art,
But I am chained to Time, and cannot thence depart!

"Oh gentle child, beautiful as thou wert,          235
Why didst thou leave the trodden paths of men
Too soon, and with weak hands though mighty heart
Dare the unpastured dragon in his den?
Defenceless as thou wert, oh! where was then
Wisdom the mirror'd shield, or scorn the spear?          240

Or hadst thou waited the full cycle, when
Thy spirit should have filled its crescent sphere,
The monsters of life's waste had fled from thee like deer.

"The herded wolves, bold only to pursue;
The obscene ravens, clamorous oer the dead;　　　　245
The vultures, to the conqueror's banner true,
Who feed where Desolation first has fed,
And whose wings rain contagion;—how they fled,
When like Apollo, from his golden bow,
The Pythian of the age one arrow sped　　　　250
And smiled!—The spoilers tempt no second blow,
They fawn on the proud feet that spurn them lying low.

"The sun comes forth, and many reptiles spawn;
He sets, and each ephemeral insect then
Is gathered into death without a dawn,　　　　255
And the immortal stars awake again;
So is it in the world of living men:
A godlike mind soars forth, in its delight
Making earth bare and veiling heaven, and when
It sinks, the swarms that dimmed or shared its light　　　　260
Leave to its kindred lamps the spirit's awful night."

Thus ceased she: and the mountain shepherds came
Their garlands sere, their magic mantles rent;
The Pilgrim of Eternity, whose fame
Over his living head like Heaven is bent,　　　　265
An early but enduring monument,
Came, veiling all the lightnings of his song
In sorrow; from her wilds Ierne sent
The sweetest lyrist of her saddest wrong,
And love taught grief to fall like music from his tongue.　　　　270

Midst others of less note, came one frail Form,
A phantom among men; companionless
As the last cloud of an expiring storm,
Whose thunder is its knell; he, as I guess,
Had gazed on Nature's naked loveliness,　　　　275
Actæon-like, and now he fled astray
With feeble steps o'er the world's wilderness,
And his own thoughts, along that rugged way,
Pursued, like raging hounds, their father and their prey.

A pardlike Spirit beautiful and swift—　　　　280
A Love in desolation masked;—a Power
Girt round with weakness;—it can scarce uplift
The weight of the superincumbent hour;

It is a dying lamp, a falling shower,
A breaking billow;—even whilst we speak 285
Is it not broken? On the withering flower
The killing sun smiles brightly: on a cheek
The life can burn in blood, even while the heart may break.

His head was bound with pansies overblown,
And faded violets, white, and pied, and blue; 290
And a light spear topped with a cypress cone,
Round whose rude shaft dark ivy-tresses grew
Yet dripping with the forest's noon-day dew,
Vibrated, as the ever-beating heart
Shook the weak hand that grasped it; of that crew 295
He came the last, neglected and apart;
A herd-abandoned deer, struck by the hunter's dart.

All stood aloof, and at his partial moan
Smiled through their tears; well knew that gentle band.
Who in another's fate now wept his own; 300
As in the accents of an unknown land,
He sung new sorrow; sad Urania scanned
The Stranger's mien, and murmured: "Who art thou?"
He answered not, but with a sudden hand
Made bare his branded and ensanguined brow, 305
Which was like Cain's or Christ's.—Oh! that it should be so!

What softer voice is hushed over the dead?
Athwart what brow is that dark mantle thrown?
What form leans sadly o'er the white death-bed,
In mockery of monumental stone, 310
The heavy heart heaving without a moan?
If it be He, who, gentlest of the wise,
Taught, soothed, loved, honoured the departed one;
Let me not vex, with inharmonious sighs,
The silence of that heart's accepted sacrifice. 315

Our Adonais has drunk poison—oh!
What deaf and viperous murderer could crown
Life's early cup with such a draught of woe?
The nameless worm would now itself disown:
It felt, yet could escape the magic tone 320
Whose prelude held all envy, hate and wrong,
But what was howling in one breast alone,
Silent with expectation of the song,
Whose master's hand is cold, whose silver lyre unstrung.

Live thou, whose infamy is not thy fame! 325
Live! fear on heavier chastisement from me,

Thou noteless blot on a remembered name!
But be thyself, and know thyself to be!
And ever at thy season be thou free
To spill the venom when thy fangs o'erflow:                    330
Remorse and Self-contempt shall cling to thee;
Hot Shame shall burn upon thy secret brow,
And like a beaten hound tremble thou shalt—as now.

Not let us weep that our delight is fled
Far from these carrion kites that scream below;               335
He wakes or sleeps with the enduring dead;
Thou canst not soar where he is sitting now.—
Dust to the dust! but the pure spirit shall flow
Back to the burning fountain whence it came,
A portion of the Eternal, which must glow                     340
Through time and change, unquenchably the same,
Whilst thy cold embers choke the sordid hearth of shame.

Peace, peace! he is not dead, he doth not sleep—
He hath awakened from the dream of life—
'Tis we, who lost in stormy visions, keep                     345
With phantoms an unprofitable strife,
And in mad trance strike with our spirit's knife
Invulnerable nothings—*We* decay
Like corpses in a charnel; fear and grief
Convulse us and consume us day by day,                        350
And cold hopes swarm like worms within our living clay.

He has outsoared the shadow of our night;
Envy and calumny and hate and pain,
And that unrest which men miscall delight,
Can touch him not and torture not again;                      355
From the contagion of the world's slow stain
He is secure, and now can never mourn
A heart grown cold, a head grown grey in vain;
Nor, when the spirit's self has ceased to burn,
With sparkless ashes load an unlamented urn.                  360

He lives, he wakes—'tis Death is dead, not he;
Mourn not for Adonais.—Thou young Dawn,
Turn all thy dew to splendour, for from thee
The spirit thou lamentest is not gone;
Ye caverns and ye forests, cease to moan!                     365
Cease ye faint flowers and fountains, and thou Air,
Which like a morning veil thy scarf hadst thrown
O'er the abandoned Earth, now leave it bare
Even to the joyous stars which smile on its despair!

He is made one with Nature: there is heard      370
His voice in all her music, from the moan
Of thunder, to the song of night's sweet bird;
He is a presence to be felt and known
In darkness and in light, from herb and stone,
Spreading itself where'er that Power may move      375
Which has withdrawn his being to its own;
Which wields the world with never wearied love,
Sustains it from beneath, and kindles it above.

He is a portion of the loveliness
Which once he made more lovely: he doth bear      380
His part, while the one Spirit's plastic stress
Sweeps through the dull dense world, compelling there
All new successions to the forms they wear;
Torturing th' unwilling dross that checks its flight
To its own likeness, as each mass may bear;      385
And bursting in its beauty and its might
From trees and beasts and men into the Heaven's light.

The splendours of the firmament of time
May be eclipsed, but are extinguished not;
Like stars to their appointed height they climb,      390
And death is a low mist which cannot blot
The brightness it may veil. When lofty thought
Lifts a young heart above its mortal lair,
And love and life contend in it, for what
Shall be its earthly doom, the dead live there      395
And move like winds of light on dark and stormy air.

The inheritors of unfulfilled renown
Rose from their thrones, built beyond mortal thought,
Far in the Unapparent. Chatterton
Rose pale, his solemn agony had not      400
Yet faded from him; Sidney, as he fought
And as he fell and as he lived and loved
Sublimely mild, a Spirit without spot,
Arose; and Lucan, by his death approved:
Oblivion as they rose shrank like a thing reproved.      405

And many more, whose names on Earth are dark
But whose transmitted effluence cannot die
So long as fire outlives the parent spark,
Rose, robed in dazzling immortality.
"Thou art become as one of us," they cry,      410
"It was for thee yon kingless sphere has long
Swung blind in unascended majesty,

Silent alone amid an Heaven of Song.
Assume thy winged throne, thou Vesper of our throng!"

Who mourns for Adonais? oh come forth,     415
Fond wretch! and know thyself and him aright.
Clasp with thy panting soul the pendulous Earth;
As from a centre, dart thy spirit's light
Beyond all worlds, until its spacious might
Satiate the void circumference: then shrink     420
Even to a point within our day and night;
And keep thy heart light lest it make thee sink
When hope has kindled hope, and lured thee to the brink.

Or go to Rome, which is the sepulchre
Oh, not of him, but of our joy: 'tis nought     425
That ages, empires, and religions there
Lie buried in the ravage they have wrought;
For such as he can lend,—they borrow not
Glory from those who made the world their prey;
And he is gathered to the kings of thought     430
Who waged contention with their time's decay,
And of the past are all that cannot pass away.

Go thou to Rome,—at once the Paradise,
The grave, the city, and the wilderness;
And where its wrecks like shattered mountains rise,     435
And flowering weeds, and fragrant copses dress
The bones of Desolation's nakedness
Pass, till the Spirit of the spot shall lead
Thy footsteps to a slope of green access
Where, like an infant's smile, over the dead     440
A light of laughing flowers along the grass is spread,

And grey walls moulder round, on which dull Time
Feeds, like slow fire upon a hoary brand;
And one keen pyramid with wedge sublime,
Pavilioning the dust of him who planned     445
This refuge for his memory, doth stand
Like flame transformed to marble; and beneath,
A field is spread, on which a newer band
Have pitched in Heaven's smile their camp of death,
Welcoming him we lose with scarce extinguished breath.     450

Here pause: these graves are all too young as yet
To have outgrown the sorrow which consigned
Its charge to each; and if the seal is set,
Here, on one fountain of a mourning mind,

Break it not thou! too surely shalt thou find 455
Thine own well full, if thou returnest home,
Of tears and gall. From the world's bitter wind
Seek shelter in the shadow of the tomb.
What Adonais is, why fear we to become?

The One remains, the many change and pass; 460
Heaven's light forever shines, Earth's shadows fly;
Life, like a dome of many-coloured glass,
Stains the white radiance of Eternity,
Until Death tramples it to fragments.—Die,
If thou wouldst be with that which thou dost seek! 465
Follow where all is fled!—Rome's azure sky,
Flowers, ruins, statues, music, words, are weak
The glory they transfuse with fitting truth to speak.

Why linger, why turn back, why shrink, my Heart?
Thy hopes are gone before: from all things here 470
They have departed; thou shouldst now depart!
A light is past from the revolving year,
And man, and woman; and what still is dear
Attracts to crush, repels to make thee wither.
The soft sky smiles,—the low wind whispers near: 475
'Tis Adonais calls! oh, hasten thither,
No more let life divide what Death can join together.

That Light whose smile kindles the Universe,
That Beauty in which all things work and move,
That Benediction which the eclipsing Curse 480
Of birth can quench not, that sustaining Love
Which through the web of being blindly wove
By man and beast and earth and air and sea,
Burns bright or dim, as each are mirrors of
The fire for which all thirst; now beams on me, 485
Consuming the last clouds of cold mortality.

The breath whose might I have invoked in song
Descends on me; my spirit's bark is driven,
Far from the shore, far from the trembling throng
Whose sails were never to the tempest given; 490
The massy earth and sphered skies are riven!
I am borne darkly, fearfully, afar;
Whilst burning through the inmost veil of Heaven,
The soul of Adonais, like a star,
Beacons from the abode where the Eternal are. 495

*Edwin Honig*

---

### SHELLEY
#### ADONAIS

A very old way of memorializing the dead is to give them attributes of the gods or of great heroes—in other words, epithetical or mythological names. This makes them sacrosanct and endows them with certain aspects of eternal existence. In this famous elegy, written on the death of John Keats in 1821, a year before Shelley's own death, we witness the process of sanctifying the spirit, as Shelley saw it, of his great young contemporary. Keats has become Adonais—a name that partakes of Adonis, the youth slain by a wild boar and hence a sacrificed seasonal god, and Adonai, the Hebrew name for Supreme Being. The gradual deification or glorification of Adonais parallels the movement of the poem, which is a kind of image-making machine weaving together poetic myth and mourning into the heavy-threaded tapestry that we see taking form before our eyes.

There is a vast choral opening, with many voices announcing, reiterating and participating in the lament that extends itself over a hundred lines. "Weep for Adonais" becomes the refrain we hear throughout the poem—but a refrain that is to change significantly at the end, when Adonais attains eternal glory. We are made to attend while the forces of admiration, moral abstractions, and ceremonial processions of emotions pass in review. Then there is the pageantry of elements, sense effects, and the seasons, until Urania, the presiding goddess and muse, is summoned to address the corpse.

And so, much of what happens in the poem is not an expression of grief but a way of objectifying it. What we find is a strange, often profuse fiction, now in the form of a peroration like a funeral speech, now in a lovingly descriptive listing of decorative effects resembling the details carved on a bier. The poem is a pure artifice in which Keats, the subject, hardly appears as a person. He is the occasion and vehicle of the poet's mood—a mood that is strictly conventionalized in the elegiac tradition of the classical poets, Bion and Moschus, both of whom Shelley quotes at the head of his poem. "All things have perished in his death," wrote Bion on the passing of the nature god; and the season correspondingly is winter, dry, frozen, sterile. Shelley also adapts the Renaissance elegy, particularly that of Milton's "Lycidas" and of Spenser. But the guiding spirit is Spenserian rather than Miltonic; for Shelley uses not only Spenser's stanza, as did other Romantics, but takes over much of the pastoral paraphernelia, the allegorical devices and metaphorical habits, of Spenser's practice in "The Faerie Queene" and "The Shepherd's Calendar." Such adaptations of the elegiac tradition and of Spenserian devices result in a formal poem composed of a series of set attitudes conveying easily identifiable thematic progressions typical of all poems about mourning.

Yet certain differences appear that are pertinent to the kind of poem Shelley writes as a nineteenth-century poet. For what the Renaissance poet took for granted, a Christian dispensation and consolation, the Romantic poet has nothing to do with. The dead Adonais might have lived in the pre-Christian era or in a totally imaginary time and country where Christianity had never been heard of. The strict lack of personalized emotion and the lack of Christian consolation do not, however, result in a poem that is without feeling. In some sense "Adonais" is all feeling. The feeling appears to follow the direction that the mourning takes, in its progress and minute particulars, from the beginning to the end of the poem. This direction is from the estrangement and fear of death toward sympathy with the dead and identification with the glorification of Adonais, until Shelley sees himself at one with the dead Adonais. The initial lamentations, "I weep for Adonais—he is dead!" and "Oh, weep for Adonais—he is dead!" are converted into the sober joyousness of " 'tis Death is dead, not he; / Mourn not for Adonais." The soul of Adonais has become "like a star" toward which Shelley, the poet, journeys in order to join him "where the Eternal are."

What a twentieth-century reader may have to do in order to appreciate the feeling is to accept, if not enjoy, the artifice, the congeries of myth, personification, rhetoric, all the decorative and argumentative uses that count for so much in the poem. If he can take the expressive force, the pressured effect of the language, as a substitute for narrative or psychological analysis, the poem begins to have a savor and credibility it may otherwise lack. He must also discard most notions that the poem has anything to do with a realistic situation—but not quite all. For toward the end of the poem (lines 433–59) there occurs a description of the cemetery and grave where Keats is buried in Rome. Here the realistic note seems almost intrusive, if not startling; in effect it works well because it serves to introduce dramatically the transcendental resolution of a voyage to death, to join Adonais among the stars.

It is on this resolute note, so much in keeping with the artifice of the rest of the poem, that "Adonais" comes to an end.

# Carlos Baker

## SHELLEY
### ADONAIS

Two legends inform Shelley's "Adonais." One is the famous myth of Adonis from classical sources. The other is more or less adventitious, for Shelley appears to have been taken in by the widespread and long-lived fairy tale that Keats's death had been hastened if not caused by the malevolent attack on "Endymion" in the *Quarterly Review* for April, 1818. The Adonis story was of course equally effective in modifying Shelley's poem away from historical actuality. Having chosen Adonis as the poetic prototype of Keats, he followed to a degree the limited characterization of Adonis as he found it in Bion's "Lament," while altering the original story wherever it best suited his pseudo-biographical purpose.

It was characteristic of Shelley's mythopoetic approach to accept for his "ideal" poems only such situations as could be developed allegorically. Both by the use of a presumed variant of the name Adonis, and by the application to the Venus figure of only one of her innumerable Greek surnames, Shelley partly concealed his source-myth. But in modified form all the original elements are present: Venus' temporary absence from the side of her beloved, Adonis' daring of the boar, the beast's attack, the death of the hero, the arrival of mourners, the ministrations of various subdeities, Venus' attempt to revive her fallen lover, and finally, though this is merely suggested as one possible fate of Adonais, the victim's metamorphosis into a flower. The place of the boar in "Adonais" is of course occupied by the anonymous reviewer whom Shelley blamed for the death of Keats.

Urania herself is first of all what she is in the original fable, a goddess enamored of a mortal youth. But the epithet "Urania" immediately indicates that she is not to be confused with the lower or Cyprian Aphrodite of Bion and Moschus. She is rather a spiritual being at a much higher level, a goddess of heavenly love like Asia in Shelley's "Prometheus

*543*

Unbound." The obvious reason for showing her in love with Keats is that his poems had helped, as Shelley saw them, to spread the doctrine of divine love of which he himself was so ardent and consistent a champion. Urania, in fact, is both a symbol of heavenly love and, as her name would suggest to students of Milton, a muse who has in her charge the most sublime poetry. Among the nine muses of classical mythology, Urania is the overseer of astronomy. Shelley retained this conception in "Adonais" through the most precise development of a Lucifer-Hesper star-image derived from Plato. But he was likewise aware that Milton, in the proem to the seventh book of *Paradise Lost,* had invoked her as guide to his highest poetic effort, the literally astronomical task of describing the Creation. In making Keats the "nursling" of this most noble muse, Shelley was paying him a very high compliment indeed.

Besides Urania, Adonais has several mortal mourners, among them Byron, Moore, Hunt, and Shelley himself. They appear in the thin disguise of mountain shepherds, and the conceit is that (like Keats) they watch over the sheep of their thoughts. Their mount of habitation might well be Helicon, domain of the muses, on one of whose peaks lies the "secret paradise" from which Urania-as-muse first descended in her attempt to reanimate Adonais. In deference to the memory of their fellow poet, their magic mantles (signifying imagination, as with the cloak of Prospero in Shakespeare's *Tempest*) are rent in mourning, and the leaves in their garlands are sere and yellow like those imaged by the bereaved Macbeth.

The first two-thirds of the elegy is developed with one eye on the Adonis myth, though Shelley has broadened and deepened the significance of Aphrodite, emphasized the importance of the mourning shepherds, and charged the whole with angry vilification of the boorish reviewer whose attack precipitated the tragedy. But when one turns to the final third of the poem, a question of the unity of "Adonais" arises. As commonly broken down, the poem is in two parts: thirty-seven stanzas of narrative, and eighteen more in which the narrative element is apparently dropped in favor of philosophic consolations. E. B. Hungerford has argued, however, that the myth is not abandoned at all. It is rather carried along, at least by implication, to the time when Adonais enters the realm of the immortals to be permanently reunited with Urania, much as Shelley's Prometheus in the lyrical drama is enabled in the end to rejoin Asia, his long-lost bride.

Meantime Urania has been dissolved in light and transformed from an incarnated goddess into the mystical "One"—the Soul of the Universe. The muse of heavenly poetry is thus the goddess of heavenly love viewed in another aspect. It is fitting that Adonais, entering the immortal state, should be reunited with the divine light that infused his poetry during his earthly career.

According to this argument, then, "Adonais" is all of a piece. It is further unified by Shelley's use of star symbolism. Shelley is preoccupied with the notion of an astronomical hierarchy of dead poets. The clue to his intention here is provided by the Platonic epigram which he used as a head-note. In his translation:

*Thou wert a morning star among the living,*
*Ere thy clear light had fled;*
*Now, having died, thou art as Hesperus, giving*
*New splendor to the dead.*

The star alluded to is the planet Venus, which is both morning star (Lucifer: light-bearer) and evening star (Hesperus or Vesper). The conception is that when great poets die they become as stars fixed in the firmament of time, stars whose light (the poets' works) continues to shine down on the benighted earth. Shelley imagines that the same wonderful transformation has occurred with Keats. As a "morning star among the living" he was a bringer-of-light through his poetry. When he entered the immortal realm, the light continued undiminished. He is now one of the "splendors" of Time's firmament, having climbed like a star to his preappointed height. Other dead poets assembled there greet him as "thou Vesper of our throng." And it is as Vesper, or the evening star, that he shines like a beacon light for Shelley's aspiring spirit in the last stanza of the poem. In some such manner as this, the star-image of the Platonic epigram helps to unify the poem.

The last third of the elegy is filled with verbs ordinarily associated with fire and light: dazzling, burning, beaming, beneficently smiling, glowing, kindling, beaconing, and cold-consuming. Adonais's spirit has returned to the burning fountain of its origin. It has become a part, rather than only the earthly instrument, of that sublime fire, which continues forever to glow through time and change. Merged now with the divine fire, he can bear his part in the "plastic stress" which forces the unwilling dross of the temporal world toward, if never quite to, the condition and likeness of the eternal world. Yet immortality has a dual aspect. While functioning as agent, Adonais continues to serve as instrument through the powerful survival of his poetic works. All great poets, "the splendors of the firmament of time," may enter a temporary eclipse, but their light will never be extinguished. Their "transmitted effluence" cannot die out on earth, for it is a manifestation of the cosmic light whose smile unfailingly kindles the universe from within. The great poets are the "kings of thought" who strove against "their time's decay." They are the only parts of the past that will never pass away.

The substance of Shelley's informing vision is that the world as we know it is spiritually a Cimmerian desert, dark, storm-ridden, enveloped in mist. Far above it, arched beyond mortal sight, is the *primum mobile*, the divine light of the World-Soul, the "white radiance of Eternity"—a burning fountain like the sun. Its influences are felt throughout nature and in the mind of man. Its effectiveness corresponds exactly to the sensitiveness of that which receives it. As a vitalizing force, an *élan vital*, it impels all things in their degree to aspire towards the condition of immortality. In Shelley's precise phrasing, it "tortures the unwilling dross" toward "heaven's light." Idealistic poets are its most sensitive receivers, and in them the driving force, the *eros* or aspirational principle, is almost unendurably strong. For in a very real psychological sense, they are tortured by the wish to clarify and spread among mankind the wonders of their vision of eternity. As "splendors of the firmament of time," they reign immortal in the memories of men. But their souls rejoin the World-Soul, thus carrying a joyous double burden in the enlightenment of this dark realm where we would otherwise be permanently imprisoned. This is the essential burden of Shelley's idealistic elegy on the death of John Keats.

# The Triumph of Life

Swift as a spirit hastening to his task
Of glory and of good, the Sun sprang forth
Rejoicing in his splendour, and the mask

Of darkness fell from the awakened Earth—
The smokeless altars of the mountain snows     5
Flamed above crimson clouds, and at the birth

Of light, the Ocean's orison arose,
To which the birds tempered their matin lay.
All flowers in field or forest which unclose

Their trembling eyelids to the kiss of day,     10
Swinging their censers in the element,
With orient incense lit by the new ray

Burned slow and inconsumably, and sent
Their odorous sighs up to the smiling air;
And, in succession due, did continent,     15

Isle, ocean, and all things that in them wear
The form and character of mortal mould,
Rise as the sun their father rose, to bear

Their portion of the toil, which he of old
Took as his own and then imposed on them:     20
But I, whom thoughts which must remain untold

Had kept as wakeful as the stars that gem
The cone of night, now they were laid asleep
Stretched my faint limbs beneath the hoary stem

Which an old chestnut flung athwart the steep     25
Of a green Apennine: before me fled
The night; behind me rose the day; the deep

Was at my feet, and Heaven above my head,
When a strange trance over my fancy grew
Which was not slumber, for the shade it spread     30

Was so transparent that the scene came through
As clear as, when a veil of light is drawn
O'er evening hills, they glimmer; and I knew

That I had felt the freshness of that dawn
Bathe in the same cold dew my brow and hair,     35
And sate as thus upon that slope of lawn

Under the self-same tree, and heard as then

The birds, the fountains, and the sea still hold
Sweet talk in music through the enamoured air,
And see those clouds o'er the horizon rolled.     40

As in that trance of wondrous thought I lay,
This was the tenour of my waking dream:—
Methought I sate beside a public way

Thick strewn with summer dust, and a great stream
Of people there was hurrying to and fro,     45
Numerous as gnats upon the evening gleam,

All hastening onward, yet none seemed to know
Whither he went, or whence he came, or why
He made one of the multitude, and so

Was borne amid the crowd, as through the sky     50
One of the million leaves of summer's bier;
Old age and youth, manhood and infancy,

Mixed in one mighty torrent did appear:
Some flying from the thing they feared, and some
Seeking the object of another's fear;     55

And others as with steps towards the tomb,
Pored on the trodden worms that crawled beneath,
And others mournfully within the gloom

Of their own shadow walked and called it death;
And some fled from it as it were a ghost,     60
Half fainting in the affliction of vain breath:

But more, with motions which each other crost,
Pursued or shunned the shadows the clouds threw,
Or birds within the noon-day æther lost,

Upon that path where flowers never grew,—     65
And weary with vain toil and faint for thirst,
Heard not the fountains, whose melodious dew

Out of their mossy cells for ever burst;
Nor felt the breeze which from the forest told
Of grassy paths and wood-lawn interspersed,     70

With over-arching elms and caverns cold,
And violet banks where sweet dreams brood, but they
Pursued their serious folly as of old.

And as I gazed, methought that in the way
The throng grew wilder, as the woods of June          75
When the south wind shakes the extinguished day,

And a cold glare intenser than the noon,
But icy cold, obscured with blinding light
The sun, as he the stars. Like the young moon

When on the sunlit limits of the night          80
Her white shell trembles amid crimson air,
And whilst the sleeping tempest gathers might,

Doth, as the herald of its coming, bear
The ghost of its dead mother, whose dim form
Bends in dark æther from her infant's chair,—          85

So came a chariot on the silent storm
Of its own rushing splendour, and a Shape
So sate within, as one whom years deform,

Beneath a dusky hood and double cape,
Crouching within the shadow of a tomb;          90
And o'er what seemed the head a cloud-like crape

Was bent, a dun and faint æthereal gloom
Tempering the light. Upon the chariot beam
A Janus-visaged shadow did assume

The guidance of that wonder-wingèd team;          95
The shapes which drew it in thick lightnings
Were lost:—I heard alone on the air's soft stream

The music of their ever-moving wings.
All the four faces of that charioteer
Had their eyes banded; little profit brings,          100

Speed in the van and blindness in the rear,
Nor then avail the beams that quench the sun
Or that with banded eyes could pierce the sphere

Of all that is, has been, or will be done;
So ill was the car guided—but it past          105
With solemn speed majestically on.

The crowd gave way, and I arose aghast,
Or seemed to rise, so mighty was the trance,
And saw, like clouds upon the thunder-blast,

The million with fierce song and maniac dance          110
Raging around—such seemed the jubilee
As when, to meet some conqueror's advance,

Imperial Rome poured forth her living sea
From senate-house, and forum, and theatre,
When [                    ] upon the free          115

Had bound a yoke, which soon they stooped to bear.
Nor wanted here the just similitude
Of a triumphal pageant, for where'er

The chariot rolled, a captive multitude
Was driven;—all those who had grown old in power          120
Or misery,—all who had their age subdued

All those whose fame or infamy must grow          125
Till the great winter lay the form and name
Of this green earth with them for ever low;—

By action or by suffering, and whose hour
Was drained to its last sand in weal or woe,
So that the trunk survived both fruit and flower;—

All but the sacred few who could not tame
Their spirits to the conquerors—but as soon
As they had touched the world with living flame,          130

Fled back like eagles to their native noon,
Or those who put aside the diadem
Of earthly thrones or gems till the last

Were there, of Athens or Jerusalem,
Were neither 'mid the mighty captives seen,          135
Nor 'mid the ribald crowd that followed them,

Nor those who went before fierce and obscene.
The wild dance maddens in the van, and those
Who lead it—fleet as shadows on the green,

Outspeed the chariot, and without repose          140
Mix with each other in tempestuous measure
To savage music, wilder as it grows,

They, tortured by their agonizing pleasure,
Convulsed, and on the rapid whirlwinds spun
Of that fierce Spirit whose unholy leisure          145

Was soothed by mischief since the world begun,—
Throw back their heads and loose their streaming hair;
And in their dance round her who dims the sun,

Maidens and youths fling their wild arms in air;
As their feet twinkle; they recede, and now 150
Bending within each other's atmosphere

Kindle invisibly—and as they glow,
Like moths by light attracted and repelled,
Oft to their bright destruction come and go,

Till like two clouds into one vale impelled 155
That shake the mountains when their lightnings mingle
And die in rain—the fiery band which held

Their natures, snaps—while the shock still may tingle;
One falls and then another in the path
Senseless—nor is the desolation single, 160

Yet ere I can say 'Ware,—the chariot hath
Past over them—nor other trace I find
But as of foam after the ocean's wrath

Is spent upon the desert shore;—behind,
Old men and women foully disarrayed, 165
Shake their grey hairs in the insulting wind,

And follow in the dance, with limbs decayed,
Seeking to reach the light which leaves them still
Farther behind and deeper in the shade.

But not the less with impotence of will 170
They wheel, though ghastly shadows interpose
Round them and round each other, and fulfil

Their work, and in the dust from whence they rose
Sink, and corruption veils them as they lie,
And past in these performs what [      ] in those. 175

Struck to the heart by this sad pageantry,
Half to myself I said—"And what is this?
Whose shape is that within the car? And why"—

I would have added—"Is all here amiss?"—
But a voice answered—"Life!"—I turned, and knew 180
(O Heaven, have mercy on such wretchedness!)

That what I thought was an old root which grew
To strange distortion out of the hill side,
Was indeed one of those deluded crew,

And that the grass, which methought hung so wide 185
And white, was but his thin discoloured hair,
And that the holes he vainly sought to hide,

Were or had been eyes:—"If thou canst, forbear
To join the dance, which I had well forborne!"
Said the grim Feature (of my thought aware;)          190

"I will unfold that which to this deep scorn
Led me and my companions, and relate
The progress of the pageant since the morn;

"If thirst of knowledge shall not then abate,
Follow it thou even to the night, but I          195
Am weary."—Then like one who with the weight

Of his own words is staggered, wearily
He paused; and ere he could resume, I cried,
"First, who art thou?"—"Before thy memory,

"I feared, loved, hated, suffered, did and died,          200
And if the spark with which Heaven lit my spirit
Had been with purer nutriment supplied,

"Corruption would not now thus much inherit
Of what was once Rousseau,—nor this disguise
Stained that which ought to have disdained to wear it;          205

"If I have been extinguished, yet there rise
A thousand beacons from the spark I bore"—
"And who are those chained to the car?"—"The wise,

"The great, the unforgotten,—they who wore
Mitres and helms and crowns, or wreaths of light,          210
Signs of thought's empire over thought—their lore

"Taught them not this, to know themselves; their might
Could not repress the mystery within,
And, for the morn of truth they feigned, deep night

"Caught them ere evening."—"Who is he with chin          215
Upon his breast, and hands crost on his chain?"—
"The Child of a fierce hour; he sought to win

"The world, and lost all that it did contain
Of greatness, in its hope destroyed; and more
Of fame and peace than virtue's self can gain          220

"Without the opportunity which bore
Him on its eagle pinions to the peak
From which a thousand climbers have before

"Fallen, as Napoleon fell."—I felt my cheek
Alter to see the shadow pass away,          225
Whose grasp had left the giant world so weak,

That every pigmy kicked it as it lay;
And much I grieved to think how power and will
In opposition rule our mortal day,

And why God made irreconcilable                                    230
Good and the means of good; and for despair
I half disdained mine eyes' desire to fill

With the spent vision of the times that were
And scarce have ceased to be.—"Dost thou behold,"
Said my guide, "those spoilers spoiled, Voltaire,                  235

"Frederick, and Paul, Catherine, and Leopold,
And hoary anarchs, demagogues, and sage—
[    ] names which the world thinks always old,

"For in the battle Life and they did wage,
She remained conqueror. I was overcome                            240
By my own heart alone, which neither age,

"Nor tears, nor infamy, nor now the tomb
Could temper to its object."—"Let them pass,"
I cried, "the world and its mysterious doom

"Is not so much more glorious than it was,                         245
That I desire to worship those who drew
New figures on its false and fragile glass

"As the old faded."—"Figures ever new
Rise on the bubble, paint them as you may;
We have but thrown, as those before us threw,                     250

"Our shadows on it as it past away.
But mark how chained to the triumphal chair
The mighty phantoms of an elder day;

"All that is mortal of great Plato there
Expiates the joy and woe his master knew not:                     255
The star that ruled his doom was far too fair,

"And life, where long that flower of Heaven grew not,
Conquered that heart by love, which gold, or pain,
Or age, or sloth, or slavery, could subdue not.

"And near him walk the [        ] twain,                          260
The tutor and his pupil, whom Dominion
Followed as tame as vulture in a chain.

"The world was darkened beneath either pinion
Of him whom from the flock of conquerors
Fame singled out for her thunder-bearing minion;                  265

"The other long outlived both woes and wars,
Throned in the thoughts of men, and still had kept
The jealous key of Truth's eternal doors,

"If Bacon's eagle spirit had not leapt
Like lightning out of darkness—he compelled          270
The Proteus shape of Nature, as it slept

"To wake, and lead him to the caves that held
The treasure of the secrets of its reign.
See the great bards of elder time, who quelled

"The passions which they sung, as by their strain          275
May well be known: their living melody
Tempers its own contagion to the vein

"Of those who are infected with it—I
Have suffered what I wrote, or viler pain,
And so my words have seeds of misery——          280

"Even as the deeds of others, not as theirs."[1]

And then he pointed to a company,

'Midst whom I [quickly] recognised the heirs
Of Cæsar's crime, from him to Constantine;
The anarch [chiefs], whose force and murderous snares          285

Had founded many a sceptre-bearing line,
And spread the plague of gold and blood abroad:
And Gregory and John, and men divine,

Who rose like shadows between man and God;
Till that eclipse, still hanging over heaven,          290
Was worshipped by the world o'er which they strode,

For the true sun it quenched—"Their power was given
But to destroy," replied the leader:—"I
Am one of those who have created, even

"If it be but a world of agony."—          295
"Whence camest thou? and whither goest thou?
How did thy course begin?" I said, "and why?

"Mine eyes are sick of this perpetual flow
Of people, and my heart sick of one sad thought—
Speak!"—"Whence I am, I partly seem to know,          300

[1] There is a chasm here in the MS, which it is impossible to fill
up. It appears from the context, that other shapes pass, and that
Rousseau still stood beside the dreamer. [Mrs. Shelley's Note.]

"And how and by what paths I have been brought
To this dread pass, methinks even thou may'st guess;—
Why this should be, my mind can compass not;

"Whither the conqueror hurries me, still less;—
But follow thou, and from spectator turn                         305
Actor or victim in this wretchedness,

"And what thou wouldst be taught I then may learn
From thee. Now listen:—In the April prime,
When all the forest tips began to burn

"With kindling green, touched by the azure clime                 310
Of the young season, I was laid asleep
Under a mountain, which from unknown time

"Had yawned into a cavern, high and deep;
And from it came a gentle rivulet,
Whose water, like clear air, in its calm sweep                   315

"Bent the soft grass, and kept for ever wet
The stems of the sweet flowers, and filled the grove
With sounds, which whoso hears must needs forget

"All pleasure and all pain, all hate and love,
Which they had known before that hour of rest;                   320
A sleeping mother then would dream not of

"Her only child who died upon the breast
At eventide—a king would mourn no more
The crown of which his brows were dispossest

"When the sun lingered o'er his ocean floor,                     325
To gild his rival's new prosperity.
Thou wouldst forget thus vainly to deplore

"Ills, which, if ills, can find no cure from thee,
The thought of which no other sleep will quell,
Nor other music blot from memory,                                330

"So sweet and deep is the oblivious spell;
And whether life had been before that sleep
The heaven which I imagine, or a hell

"Like this harsh world in which I wake to weep,
I know not. I arose, and for a space                             335
The scene of woods and waters seemed to keep,

"Though it was now broad day, a gentle trace
Of light diviner than the common sun
Sheds on the common earth, and all the place

"Was filled with magic sounds woven into one 340
Oblivious melody, confusing sense
Amid the gliding waves and shadows dun;

"And, as I looked, the bright omnipresence
Of morning through the orient cavern flowed,
And the sun's image radiantly intense 345

"Burned on the waters of the well that glowed
Like gold, and threaded all the forest's maze
With winding paths of emerald fire; there stood

"Amid the sun,—as he amid the blaze
Of his own glory, on the vibrating 350
Floor of the fountain paved with flashing rays,—

"A Shape all light, which with one hand did fling
Dew on the earth, as if she were the dawn,
And the invisible rain did ever sing

"A silver music on the mossy lawn; 355
And still before me on the dusky grass,
Iris her many-coloured scarf had drawn:

"In her right hand she bore a crystal glass,
Mantling with bright Nepenthe; the fierce splendour
Fell from her as she moved under the mass 360

"Out of the deep cavern, with palms so tender,
Their tread broke not the mirror of its billow;
She glided along the river, and did bend her

"Head under the dark boughs, till, like a willow,
Her fair hair swept the bosom of the stream 365
That whispered with delight to be its pillow.

"As one enamoured is upborne in dream
O'er lily-paven lakes, 'mid silver mist,
To wondrous music, so this shape might seem

"Partly to tread the waves with feet which kissed 370
The dancing foam; partly to glide along
The air which roughened the moist amethyst,

"Or the faint morning beams that fell among
The trees, or the soft shadows of the trees;
And her feet, ever to the ceaseless song 375

"Of leaves, and winds, and waves, and birds, and bees,
And falling drops moved to a measure new,
Yet sweet, as on the summer evening breeze,

"Up from the lake a shape of golden dew
Between two rocks, athwart the rising moon,          380
Dances i' the wind, where never eagle flew;

"And still her feet, no less than the sweet tune
To which they moved, seemed as they moved to blot
The thoughts of him who gazed on them; and soon

"All that was, seemed as if it had been not;          385
And all the gazer's mind was strewn beneath
Her feet like embers; and she, thought by thought,

"Trampled its sparks into the dust of death,
As day upon the threshold of the east
Treads out the lamps of night, until the breath          390

"Of darkness re-illumine even the least
Of heaven's living eyes! like day she came,
Making the night a dream; and ere she ceased

"To move, as one between desire and shame
Suspended, I said—If, as it doth seem,          395
Thou comest from the realm without a name,

"Into this valley of perpetual dream,
Show whence I came, and where I am, and why—
Pass not away upon the passing stream.

"Arise and quench thy thirst, was her reply.          400
And as a shut lily, stricken by the wand
Of dewy morning's vital alchemy,

"I rose; and, bending at her sweet command,
Touched with faint lips [      ] the cup she raised,
And suddenly my brain became as sand          405

"Where the first wave had more than half erased
The track of deer on desert Labrador;
Whilst the [      ] wolf, from which they fled amazed,

"Leaves his stamp visibly upon the shore,
Until the second bursts;—so on my sight          410
Burst a new vision, never seen before,

"And the fair Shape waned in the coming light,
As veil by veil the silent splendour drops
From Lucifer, amid the chrysolite

"Of sunrise, ere it tinge the mountain tops;          415
And as the presence of that fairest planet,
Although unseen, is felt by one who hopes

"That his day's path may end, as he began it,
In that star's smile, whose light is like the scent
Of a jonquil when evening breezes fan it,                    420

"Or the soft note in which his dear lament
The Brescian shepherd breathes, or the caress
That turned his weary slumber to content;[1]

"So knew I in that light's severe excess
The presence of that Shape which on the stream           425
Moved, as I moved along the wilderness,

"More dimly than a day-appearing dream,
The ghost of a forgotten form of sleep;
A light of heaven, whose half-extinguished beam

"Through the sick day in which we wake to weep,          430
Glimmers, for ever sought, for ever lost;
So did that shape its obscure tenour keep

"Beside my path, as silent as a ghost;
But the new Vision, and the cold bright car,
With solemn speed and stunning music, crost              435

"The forest, and as if from some dread war
Triumphantly returning, the loud million
Fiercely extolled the fortune of her star.

"A moving arch of victory, the vermilion
And green and azure plumes of Iris had                   440
Built high over her wind-wingèd pavilion,

"And underneath ethereal glory clad
The wilderness, and far below her flew
The tempest of the splendour, which forbade

"Shadow to fall from leaf and stone; the crew            445
Seemed in that light, like atomies to dance
Within a sunbeam;—some upon the new

"Embroidery of flowers, that did enhance
The grassy vesture of the desert, played,
Forgetful of the chariot's swift advance;                450

"Others stood gazing, till within the shade
Of the great mountain its light left them dim;
Others outspeeded it; and others made

[1] The favourite song, "Stanco di pascolar le pecorelle," is a
Brescian national air. [Mrs. Shelley's note.]

"Circles around it, like the clouds that swim
Round the high moon in a bright sea of air;                    455
And more did follow, with exulting hymn,

"The chariot and the captives fettered there:—
But all like bubbles on an eddying flood
Fell into the same track at last, and were

"Borne onward. I among the multitude                          460
Was swept—me, sweetest flowers delayed not long;
Me, not the shadow nor the solitude;

"Me, not that falling stream's Lethean song;
Me, not the phantom of that early form,
Which moved upon its motion—but among                         465

"The thickest billows of that living storm
I plunged, and bared my bosom to the clime
Of that cold light, whose airs too soon deform.

"Before the chariot had begun to climb
The opposing steep of that mysterious dell,                   470
Behold a wonder worthy of the rhyme

"Of him whom from the lowest depths of hell,
Through every paradise and through all glory,
Love led serene, and who returned to tell

"In words of hate and awe, the wondrous story                 475
How all things are transfigured except Love;
For deaf as is a sea, which wrath makes hoary,

"The world can hear not the sweet notes that move
The sphere whose light is melody to lovers:
A wonder worthy of his rhyme. The grove                       480

"Grew dense with shadows to its inmost covers,
The earth was grey with phantoms, and the air
Was peopled with dim forms, as when there hovers

"A flock of vampire-bats before the glare
Of the tropic sun, bringing, ere evening,                     485
Strange night upon some Indian isle;—thus were

"Phantoms diffused around; and some did fling
Shadows of shadows, yet unlike themselves,
Behind them; some like eaglets on the wing

"Were lost in the white day; others like elves                490
Danced in a thousand unimagined shapes
Upon the sunny streams and grassy shelves;

"And others sate chattering like restless apes
In vulgar bands,
Some made a cradle of the ermined capes                    495

"Of kingly mantles; some across the tiar
Of pontiffs sate like vultures; others played
Under the crown which girt with empire

"A baby's or an idiot's brow, and made
Their nests in it. The old anatomies                       500
Sate hatching their bare broods under the shade

"Of demon wings, and laughed from their dead eyes
To re-assume the delegated power,
Arrayed in which those worms did monarchise,

"Who made this earth their charnel. Others more           505
Humble, like falcons, sat upon the fist
Of common men, and round their heads did soar;

"Or like small gnats and flies, as thick as mist
On evening marshes, thronged about the brow
Of lawyers, statesmen, priest, and theorist;—             510

"And others, like discoloured flakes of snow
On fairest bosoms and the sunniest hair,
Fell, and were melted by the youthful glow

"Which they extinguished; and, like tears, they were
A veil to those from whose faint lids they rained         515
In drops of sorrow. I became aware

"Of whence those forms proceeded which thus stained
The track in which we moved. After brief space,
From every form the beauty slowly waned;

"From every firmest limb and fairest face                 520
The strength and freshness fell like dust, and left
The action and the shape without the grace

"Of life. The marble brow of youth was cleft
With care; and in those eyes where once hope shone,
Desire, like a lioness bereft                             525

"Of her last cub, glared ere it died; each one
Of that great crowd sent forth incessantly
These shadows, numerous as the dead leaves blown

"In autumn evening from a poplar tree,
Each like himself and like each other were                530
At first; but some distorted seemed to be

"Obscure clouds, moulded by the casual air;
And of this stuff the car's creative ray
Wrought all the busy phantoms that were there,

"As the sun shapes the clouds; thus on the way          535
Mask after mask fell from the countenance
And form of all; and long before the day

"Was old, the joy which waked like heaven's glance
The sleepers in the oblivious valley died;
And some grew weary of the ghastly dance,          540

"And fell, as I have fallen, by the way-side;—
Those soonest from whose forms most shadows past,
And least of strength and beauty did abide.

"Then, what is life?" I cried.—The cripple cast
His eye upon the car, which now had rolled          545
Onward, as if that look must be the last,

And answered, "Happy those for whom the gold
Of"

# Carlos Baker

---

## SHELLEY
## THE TRIUMPH OF LIFE

The long poem on which Shelley was working when he died was called "The Triumph of Life." Although he did not live to see it through, the lengthy fragment that precedes indicates that it might have been—indeed, it is—one of his greatest poems. It is filled with solemn music, charged with deep melancholy, mature in its inward control, and majestic in its quiet outward demeanor. The movement throughout is *andante*, as befits a poem which might be thought of as a return from the Paradiso of Act IV of "Prometheus Unbound" or the ineffable heights at the close of "Adonais," to a kind of Purgatorio of life in this world. To many, on this account, it has seemed a palinode to Shelley's previous philosophic affirmations.

Yet it is rather a reaffirmation than a palinode. In the course of his narrative Shelley looks again, from a different point of view, at the poet's relation to the life around him and his connections with the divine light that must always infuse the best work of the best poets.

The theme of the poem is well summarized in Wordsworth's lines about the light of heaven in the ode, "Intimations of Immortality" (lines 75 and 76):

> At length the Man perceives it die away,
> And fade into the light of common day.

For the icy glare that emanates from the chariot of life in Shelley's "triumphal" procession is a more intensely felt and withering version of the older poet's "light of common day" which supersedes the "vision splendid" by which the youth in the "Ode" was once "on his way attended."

The dramatic method employed in the poem is analogous to that of Dante's "Inferno," with Shelley and Rousseau in the place of Dante and Virgil. Instead of journeying, as in *The Divine Comedy*, Shelley and his companion stand in one place to watch the approach and departure of the car of the worldly life along a dusty highroad where millions of blind and aimless people hurry to and fro. In this bacchic rout, young and old are either crushed beneath or fall behind the moving chariot, like barbarian captives in a Roman *triumphus*. Only the "sacred few" of Athens and Jerusalem escape the malign influence of the worldly life to which the others have succumbed. They are those who established and never lost contact with the "living flame" of heavenly light. Evidently Jesus and Socrates are foremost among this small band of the truly elect.

Shelley's poem consists of a prologue, three unnumbered sections, and a final unanswered question. The opening forty lines provide a superb description of the physical setting, with the seer lying under a chestnut tree on a slope of the Apennines, facing westward toward the sea, with the sunrise behind him. Now comes the waking trance, which overspreads his mind as the sunlight of morning advances across the mountains. The first part (lines 41–175) is a detailed and graphic description of the visionary pageant of the worldly life. The second part (176–300) discovers the commentator Rousseau, who first identifies himself and then points to various famous victims as they drag past in the long procession. Part three (300–543) is Rousseau's "idealized history" of his "life and feelings" and occupies all the rest of the poem except the final question of line 544: "Then, what is life?"

In a series of personifications—Asia in "Prometheus Unbound" and Urania in "Adonais" are examples—Shelley had earlier incarnated in woman's shape his conception of the source of true poetic power. This time she appears as Iris, many-colored rainbow goddess, prismatic reflector of the rays of the supernal sun. Rousseau says that on an April morning long ago he was laid asleep under a mountain. Through its base ran a tunnel-like cavern, which caught the rays of the rising sun. Out of this cavern flowed a westward-running brook along whose surface "a Shape all light" like Iris seemed to beckon him onwards. But the fleeting tryst was interrupted by the chariot of the worldly life, the vision faded, and the "half-extinguished beam" of the "light of heaven" was at last reduced to a glimmer—"for ever sought, for ever lost."

The fragmentary state of "The Triumph" leaves uncertain the identity of the asker of the final question, "What is life?" Whether we conclude that the asker is Shelley or Rousseau, the answer is the same. For the "life" of the question is that which has been spoken of during the greater part of the poem: worldly life as a corrupting force, a slow stain, a cold light "whose airs too soon deform." In his "Defence of Poetry," Shelley had recently argued that "the end of social corruption is to destroy all sensibility to pleasure." It spreads like a "paralysing venom" through imagination, intellect, affections, and even "into the very appetites"—until the whole complex is reduced to "a torpid mass in which hardly sense survives." On the other hand, the true poetic principle wages perpetual war against social corruption, and a poet is susceptible to decay only to the degree that he has cut himself off from his best source of power. The decadent shade of Jean Jacques Rousseau serves as an exemplum: one who turned his back on the splendor of his vision and followed the millions in the wake of the chariot of the worldly life.

The poet who would avoid "the contagion of the world's slow stain" ("Adonais") must follow his vision to the last. It is probable that Shelley would have succeeded in doing so, given his adamant determination not to succumb to the blandishments of the corrupt and corrupting forces that spread abroad, as he thought, wherever human beings congregate in any numbers. If there were dangers on the other side, and there were, his death by drowning in a sailing accident in the Gulf of Spezzia preserved him from the fate of those who followed the chariot in his last great poem.

Less than a year before his death he had quoted the first two lines from the following passage of Goethe's *Faust:*

> *Over the noblest gift, the spirit's splendour,*
> *There floods an alien, ever alien stream;*
> *When this world's wealth is won, our souls surrender,*
> *The larger hope we call a lying dream.*
> *Our life of life, the visions grave and glorious,*
> *Fade, and the earthly welter is victorious.*
> *Imagination once, fire-winged with hope,*
> *Filled all eternity, and flamed to heaven;*
> *But now it dwindles to a petty scope,*
> *While joy on joy falls round us, wrecked and riven.*

The theme of this passage is germane to "The Triumph of Life" as Shelley set it forth. For again and again he had addressed himself to the recurrent problem: the impingement of the mundane and the meretricious upon the higher life of the visionary mind. From the perhaps inevitable stain upon the spirit's splendor Shelley was saved, if he needed saving, in the late afternoon of July 8, 1822, when the boat in which he was a passenger collided with another and went down with all hands, including those that had set down all that survives of "The Triumph of Life."

JOHN KEATS

*Sketch by William Blake*
*The Bettmann Archive*

# JOHN KEATS

[1795–1821]

## Ode on a Grecian Urn

Thou still unravish'd bride of quietness,
   Thou foster-child of Silence and slow Time,
Sylvan historian, who canst thus express
   A flowery tale more sweetly than our rhyme:
What leaf-fringed legend haunts about thy shape      5
   Of deities or mortals, or of both,
      In Tempe or the dales of Arcady?
What men or gods are these? What maidens loth?
   What mad pursuit? What struggle to escape?
      What pipes and timbrels? What wild ecstasy?      10

Heard melodies are sweet, but those unheard
   Are sweeter; therefore ye soft pipes, play on;
Not to the sensual ear, but, more endear'd,
   Pipe to the spirit ditties of no tone:
Fair youth, beneath the trees, thou canst not leave      15
   Thy song, nor ever can those trees be bare;
      Bold lover, never, never canst thou kiss,
Though winning near the goal—yet, do not grieve;
   She cannot fade, though thou hast not thy bliss,
      For ever wilt thou love, and she be fair!      20

Ah, happy, happy boughs! that cannot shed
   Your leaves, nor ever bid the Spring adieu:
And, happy melodist, unwearièd,
   For ever piping songs for ever new;
More happy love! more happy, happy love!      25
   For ever warm, and still to be enjoy'd,
      For ever panting, and for ever young;
All breathing human passion far above,
   That leaves a heart high-sorrowful and cloy'd,
      A burning forehead, and a parching tongue.      30

Who are these coming to the sacrifice?
   To what green altar, O mysterious priest,

Lead'st thou that heifer lowing at the skies,
   And all her silken flanks with garlands drest?
What little town by river or sea-shore,       35
   Or mountain-built with peaceful citadel,
     Is emptied of this folk, this pious morn?
And, little town, thy streets for evermore
   Will silent be; and not a soul, to tell
     Why thou art desolate, can e'er return.    40

O Attic shape! Fair attitude! with brede
   Of marble men and maidens overwrought,
With forest branches and the trodden weed;
   Thou, silent form, dost tease us out of thought
As doth eternity: Cold Pastoral!      45
   When old age shall this generation waste,
     Thou shalt remain, in midst of other woe
Than ours, a friend to man, to whom thou say'st,
   "Beauty is truth, truth beauty,—that is all
     Ye know on earth, and all ye need to know."   50

# Kenneth Burke

## KEATS
### ODE ON A GRECIAN URN

We are here set to analyze the "Ode on a Grecian Urn" as a viaticum, a series of transformations, into the oracle, "Beauty is truth, truth beauty." We shall analyze the ode "dramatistically," in terms of symbolic action. To consider language as a means of *information* or *knowledge* is to consider it epistemologically, semantically, in terms of "science." To consider it as a mode of *action* is to consider it in terms of "poetry." For a poem is an act, the symbolic act of the poet who made it—an act of such a nature that, in surviving as a structure or object, it enables us as readers to re-enact it.

*Truth* being the essential word of knowledge (science) and *beauty* being the essential word of art or poetry, we might substitute accordingly. The oracle would then assert, "Poetry is science, science poetry." It would be particularly exhilarating to proclaim them one if there were a strong suspicion that they were at odds (as the assertion that "God's in his heaven, all's right with the world" is really a *counter* assertion to doubts about God's existence and suspicions that much is wrong). It was the dialectical opposition between the "aesthetic" and the "practical," with "poetry" on one side and utility (business and applied science) on the other, that was being ecstatically denied. The *relief* in this denial was grounded in the romantic philosophy itself, a philosophy that gave strong recognition to precisely the contrast between "beauty" and "truth."

Perhaps we might put it this way: If the oracle were to have been uttered in the first stanza of the poem rather than the last, its phrasing proper to that place would have been: "Beauty is *not* truth, truth *not* beauty." The five stanzas of successive transformation were necessary for the romantic philosophy of a romantic poet to transcend itself (raising its romanticism to a new order, or new dimension). An abolishing of romanticism through romanticism! (To transcend

romanticism through romanticism is, when all is over, to restore in one way what is removed in another.)
But to the poem, step by step through the five stanzas.

As a "way in," we begin with the sweeping periodic sentence that, before the stanza is over, has swiftly but imperceptibly been transmuted in quality from the periodic to the breathless, a cross between interrogation and exclamation. Even the last quick outcries retain somewhat the quality of the periodic structure with which the stanza began. The final line introduces the subject of "pipes and timbrels," which is developed and then surpassed in the second stanza.

If we had only the first stanza of this ode, and were speculating upon it from the standpoint of motivation, we could detect there tentative indications of two motivational levels. For the lines express a doubt whether the figures on the urn are "deities or mortals"—and the motives of gods are of a different order from the motives of men. This bare hint of such a possibility emerges with something of certainty in the second stanza's development of the "pipes and timbrels" theme. For we explicitly consider a contrast between body and mind (in the contrast between "heard melodies," addressed "to the sensual ear," and "ditties of no tone," addressed "to the spirit").

Also, of course, the notion of inaudible sound brings us into the region of the mystic oxymoron (the term in rhetoric for "the figure in which an epithet of a contrary significance is added to a word: e.g., *cruel kindness; laborious idleness*"). And it clearly suggests a concern with the level of motives-behind-motives, as with the paradox of the prime mover that is itself at rest, being the unmoved ground of all motion and action. Here the poet whose sounds are the richest in our language is meditating upon *absolute* sound, the *essence* of sound, which would be soundless as the prime mover is motionless, or as the "principle" of sweetness would not be sweet, having transcended sweetness, or as the sub-atomic particles of the sun are each, in their isolate purity, said to be devoid of temperature.

Contrast Keats's unheard melodies with those of Shelley:

> *Music, when soft voices die,*
> *Vibrates in the memory—*
> *Odours, when sweet violets sicken,*
> *Live within the sense they quicken.*

*Rose leaves, when the rose is dead,*
*Are heaped for the beloved's bed;*
*And so thy thoughts, when thou art gone,*
*Love itself shall slumber on.*

Here the futuristic Shelley is anticipating retrospection; he is looking forward to looking back. The form of thought is naturalistic and temporalistic in terms of *past* and *future*. But the form of thought in Keats is mystical, in terms of an *eternal present*. The "Ode" is striving to move beyond the region of becoming into the realm of *being*. (This is another way of saying that we are here concerned with two levels of motivation.)

In the last four lines of the second stanza, the state of immediacy is conveyed by a development peculiarly Keatsian. I refer not simply to translation into terms of the erotic, but rather to a quality of *suspension* in the erotic imagery, defining an eternal prolongation of the state just prior to fulfilment—not exactly arrested ecstasy, but rather an arrested pre-ecstasy. (Mr. G. Wilson Knight, in *The Starlit Dome*, refers to "that recurring tendency in Keats to image a poised form, a stillness suggesting motion, what might be called a 'tiptoe' effect.")

Suppose that we had but this one poem by Keats, and knew nothing of its author or its period, so that we could treat it only in itself, as a series of internal transformations to be studied in their development from a certain point, and without reference to any motives outside this ode. Under such conditions, I think, we should require no further observations to characterize (from the standpoint of symbolic action) the main argument in the second stanza. We might go on to make an infinity of observations about the details of the stanza; but as regards major deployments, we should deem it enough to note that the theme of "pipes and timbrels" is developed by the use of mystic oxymoron, and then surpassed (or given a development-atop-the-development) by the stressing of erotic imagery (that had been ambiguously adumbrated in the references to "maidens loth" and "mad pursuit" of the first stanza.) And we could note the quality of *incipience* in this imagery, its state of arrest not at fulfilment, but at the point just prior to fulfilment.

Add, now, our knowledge of the poem's place as an enactment in a particular cultural scene, and we likewise note in this second stanza a variant of the identification between death and sexual love that was so typical of nineteenth century romanticism and was to attain its musical monument in the Wagnerian *Liebestod*. On a purely dialectical basis, to die in love would be to be born to love (the lovers dying as individual identities that they might be transformed into a common identity). Adding historical factors, one can note the part that capitalist individualism plays in sharpening this consummation (since a property structure that heightens the sense of individual identity would thus make it more imperiously a "death" for the individual to take on the new identity made by a union of two). We can thus see why the love-death equation would be particularly representative of a romanticism that was the reflex of business.

Fortunately, the relation between private property and the love-death equation is attested on unimpeachable authority, concerning the effect of consumption and consummation in a "mutual flame":

> *So between them love did shine,*
> *That the turtle saw his right*
> *Flaming in the phoenix' sight;*
> *Either was the other's mine.*

> *Property was thus appall'd,*
> *That the self was not the same;*
> *Single nature's double name*
> *Neither two nor one was called.*

The addition of fire to the equation, with its pun on sexual burning, moves us from purely dialectical considerations into psychological ones. In the lines of Shakespeare, fire is the third term, the ground term for the other two (the synthesis that ends the lovers' roles as thesis and antithesis). Less obviously, the same movement from the purely dialectical to the psychological is implicit in any imagery of a *dying* or a *falling* in common, which when woven with sexual imagery signalizes a "transcendent" sexual consummation. The figure appears in a lover's compliment when Keats writes to Fanny Brawne, thus:

> I never knew before, what such a love as you have made me feel, was; I did not believe in it; my Fancy was afraid of it lest it should burn me up. But if you will fully love me, though there may be some fire, 'twill not be more than we can bear when moistened and be-dewed with pleasures.

Our primary concern is to follow the transformations of the poem itself. But to understand its full nature as a symbolic act, we should use whatever knowledge is available. In the case of Keats, not only do we know the place of this poem in his work and its time, but also we have material to guide our speculations as regards correlations between poem and poet. I grant that such speculations interfere with the symmetry of criticism as a game. (Criticism as a game is best to watch, I guess, when one confines himself to the single unit, and reports on its movements like a radio commentator broadcasting the blow-by-blow description of a prize fight.) But linguistic analysis has opened up new possibilities in the correlating of producer and product—and these concerns have such important bearing upon matters of culture and conduct in general that no sheer conventions or ideals of criticism should be allowed to interfere with their development.

From what we know of Keats's illness, with the peculiar inclination to erotic imaginings that accompany its fever (as with the writings of D.H. Lawrence) we can glimpse a particular bodily motive expanding and intensifying the lyric state in Keats's case. Whatever the intense *activity* of his thoughts, there was the material *pathos* of his physical condition. Whatever transformations of mind or body he experienced, his illness was there as a kind of constitutional substrate, whereby all aspects of the illness would be imbued with their derivation from a common ground (the phthisic fever thus being at one with the phthisic chill, for whatever the clear contrast between fever and chill, they are but modes of the same illness, the common underlying substance).

The correlation between the state of agitation in the poems and the physical condition of the poet is made quite clear in the poignant letters Keats wrote during his last illness. In 1819 he complains that he is "scarcely content to write the best verses for the fever they leave behind." And he continues: "I want to compose without this fever." But a few months later he confesses, "I am recommended not even to read poetry, much less write it." Or: "I must say that for 6 Months before I was taken ill I had not passed a tranquil day. Either that gloom overspre[a]d me or I was suffering under some passionate feeling, or if I turn'd to versify that exacerbated the poison of either sensation." Keats was "like a sick eagle looking at the sky," as he wrote of his mortality in a kindred poem, "On Seeing the Elgin Marbles."

But though the poet's body was a *patient*, the poet's mind was an *agent*. Thus, as a practitioner of poetry, he could *use* his fever, even perhaps encouraging, though not deliberately, esthetic habits that, in making for the perfection of his lines, would exact payment in the ravages of his body (somewhat as Hart Crane could write poetry only by modes of living that made for the cessation of his poetry and so led to his dissolution).

Speaking of agents, patients, and action here, we might pause to glance back over the centuries thus: in the Aristotelian grammar of motives, action has its reciprocal in passion, hence *passion* is the property of a *patient*. But by the Christian paradox (which made the martyr's action identical with his passion, as the accounts of the martyrs were called both Acts and Passionals), *patience* is the property of a moral *agent*. And this Christian view, as secularized in the philosophy of romanticism, with its stress upon creativeness, leads us to the possibility of a bodily suffering redeemed by a poetic act.

In the third stanza, the central stanza of the "Ode" (hence properly the fulcrum of its swing) we see the two motives, the action and the passion, in the process of being separated. The possibility raised in the first stanza (which was dubious whether the level of motives was to be human or divine), and developed in the second stanza (which contrasts the "sensual" and the "spirit"), becomes definitive in the third. The poem as a whole makes permanent, or fixes in a state of arrest, a peculiar agitation. But within this fixity, by the nature of poetry as a progressive medium, there must be development. Hence, the agitation that is maintained throughout (as a mood absolutized so that it fills the entire universe of discourse) will at the same time undergo internal transformations. In the third stanza, these are manifested as a clear division into two distinct and contrasted realms. There is a transcendental fever, which is felicitous, divinely above "all breathing human passion." And this "leaves" the other level, the level of earthly fever, "a burning forehead and a parching tongue." From the bodily fever, which is a passion, and malign, there has split off a spiritual activity, a wholly benign aspect of the total agitation.

Clearly, a movement has been finished. The poem must, if it is well formed, take a new direction, growing out of and surpassing the curve that has by now been clearly established by the successive stages from "is there the possibility of two motivational levels?" through "there are two motivational levels" to "the 'active' motivational level 'leaves' the 'passive' level."

Prophesying, with the inestimable advantage that goes with having looked ahead, what should we expect the new direction to be? First, let us survey the situation. Originally, before the two strands of the fever had been definitely drawn apart, the bodily passion could serve as the scene or ground of the spiritual action. But at the end of the third stanza, we abandon the level of bodily passion. The action is "far above" the passion, it "leaves" the fever. What then would this transcendent act require, to complete it?

It would require a scene of the same quality as itself. An act and a scene belong together. The nature of the one must be a fit with the nature of the other. (I like to call this the "scene-act ratio," or "dramatic ratio.") Hence, the act having now transcended its bodily setting, it will require, as its new setting, a transcendent scene. Hence, prophesying *post eventum*, we should ask that, in the fourth stanza, the poem *embody* the transcendental act by endowing it with an appropriate scene.

The scene-act ratio involves a law of dramatic consistency whereby the quality of the act shares the quality of the scene in which it is enacted (the synecdochic relation of container and thing contained). Its grandest variant was in supernatural cosmogonies wherein mankind took on the attributes of gods by acting in cosmic scenes that were themselves imbued with the presence of godhead.

Or we may discern the logic of the scene-act ratio behind the old controversy as to whether "God willed the good because it is good," or "the good is good because God willed it." This strictly theological controversy had political implications. But our primary concern here is with the *dramatistic* aspects of this controversy. For you will note that the whole issue centers in the problem of the *grounds* of God's creative act.

Since, from the purely dramatic point of view, every act requires a scene in which it takes place, we may note that one of the doctrines (that "God willed the good because it is good") is more symmetrical than the other. For by it, God's initial act of creation is itself given a ground, or scene (the objective existence of goodness, which was so real that God himself did not simply make it up, but acted in conformity with its nature when willing it to be the law of his creation). In the scholastic formulas taken over from Aristotle, God was defined as "pure act" (though this pure act was in turn the ultimate ground or *scene* of human acting and willing). And from the standpoint of purely dramatic symmetry, it would be desirable to have some kind of "scene" even for God. This requirement is met, we are suggesting, in the doctrine that "God willed the good *because* it is good." For this word, "because," in assigning a reason for God's willing, gives us in principle a kind of scene, as we may discern in the pun of our word, "ground," itself, which indeterminately applies to either "place" or "cause."

If even theology thus responded to the pressure for dramatic symmetry, by endowing God, as the transcendent act, with a transcendent scene of like quality, we should certainly expect to find analogous tactics in this ode. For as we have noted that the romantic passion is the secular equivalent of the Christian passion, so we may recall Coleridge's notion that poetic action itself is a "dim analogue of Creation." Keats, in his way confronting the same dramatistic requirement that the theologians confronted in theirs, when he has arrived at his transcendent act at the end of the third stanza (that is, when the benign fever has split away from the malign bodily counterpart, as a divorcing of spiritual action from sensual passion), is ready in the next stanza for the imagining of a scene that would correspond in quality to the quality of the action as so transformed.

His fourth stanza will concretize, or "materialize," the act, by dwelling upon its appropriate ground. It is a vision, as you prefer, of "death" or of "immortality." "Immortality," we might say, is the "good" word for "death," and must necessarily be conceived in terms of death (the necessity that Donne touches upon when he writes, ". . . but thinke that I / Am, by being dead, immortall"). This is why, when discussing the second stanza, I felt justified in speaking of the variations of the love-death equation, though the poem spoke not of love and *death*, but of love *for ever*. We have a deathy-deathless scene as the corresponding ground of our transcendent act. The urn itself, as with the scene upon it, is not merely an immortal act in our present mortal scene; it was originally an immortal act in a mortal scene quite different. The imagery, of sacrifice, piety, silence, desolation, is that of communication with the immortal or the dead.

Incidentally, we might note that the return to the use of rhetorical questions in the fourth stanza serves well, on a purely technical level, to keep our contact with the mood of the opening stanza, a music that now but vibrates in the memory. Indeed, one even gets the impression that the form of the rhetorical question had never been abandoned; that the poet's questings had been couched as questions throughout. This is tonal felicity at its best, and something much like unheard tonal felicity. For the actual persistence of the rhetorical questions through these stanzas would have been wearisome, whereas their return now gives us an inaudible variation, by making us feel that the exclamations in the second and third stanzas had been questions, as the questions in the first stanza had been exclamations.

But though a lyric greatly profits by so strong a sense of continuousness, or perpetuity, I am trying to stress the fact that in the fourth stanza we *come upon* something. Indeed, this fourth stanza is related to the three foregoing stanzas quite as the sestet is related to the octave in Keats's sonnet, "On First Looking into Chapman's Homer":

> *Much have I travell'd in the realms of gold,*
> *And many goodly states and kingdoms seen;*
> *Round many western islands have I been*
> *Which bards in fealty to Apollo hold.*
> *Oft of one wide expanse had I been told*
> *That deep-brow'd Homer ruled as his demesne;*
> *Yet did I never breathe its pure serene*
> *Till I heard Chapman speak out loud and bold;*
>
> *Then felt I like some watcher of the skies*
> *When a new planet swims into his ken;*
> *Or like stout Cortez when with eagle eyes*
> *He stared at the Pacific—and all his men*
> *Look'd at each other with a wild surmise—*
> *Silent, upon a peak in Darien.*

I am suggesting that just as the sestet in this sonnet *comes upon a scene,* so it is with the fourth stanza of the ode. In both, likewise, we end on the theme of silence; and is not the ode's reference to the thing that "not a soul can tell" quite the same in quality as the sonnet's reference to a "wild surmise"?

Thus, with the urn as viaticum (or rather, with the *poem* as viaticum, and *in the name* of the urn), having symbolically enacted a kind of act that transcends our mortality, we round out the process by coming to dwell upon the transcendental ground of this act. The dead world of ancient Greece, as immortalized on an urn surviving from that period, is the vessel of this deathy-deathless ambiguity. And we have gone dialectically from the "human" to the "divine" and thence to the "ground of the divine" (here tracing in poetic imagery

the kind of "dramatistic" course we have considered, on the
purely conceptual plane, in the theological speculations about
the "grounds" for God's creative act). Necessarily, there
must be certain inadequacies in the conception of this
ground, precisely because of the fact that immortality can
only be conceived in terms of death. Hence the reference to
the "desolate" in a scene otherwise possessing the benignity
of the eternal.

The imagery of pious sacrifice, besides its fitness for such
thoughts of departure as when the spiritual act splits from
the sensual pathos, suggests also a bond of communication
between the levels (because of its immortal character in a
mortal scene). And finally, the poem, in the name of the urn,
or under the aegis of the urn, is such a bond. For we readers,
by re-enacting it in the reading, use it as a viaticum to
transport us into the quality of the scene that it depicts on
its face (the scene containing as a fixity what the poem as act
extends into a process). The scene *on* the urn is really the
scene *behind* the urn; the urn is literally the ground of this
scene, but transcendentally the scene is the ground of the
urn. The urn contains the scene out of which it arose.

We turn now to the closing stanza. In the third stanza we
were at a moment of heat, emphatically sharing an imagery
of love "panting" and "for ever warm" that was, in the
transcendental order, companionate to "a burning forehead,
and a parching tongue" in the order of the passions. But in
the last stanza, as signalized in the marmoreal utterance,
"Cold Pastoral!" we have gone from transcendental fever to
transcendental chill. Perhaps, were we to complete our exegesis, we should need reference to some physical step from
phthisic fever to phthisic chill, that we might detect here a
final correlation between bodily passion and mental action. In
any event we may note that, the mental action having departed from the bodily passion, the change from fever to
chill is not a sufferance. For, as only the *benign* aspects of the
fever had been left after the split, so it is a wholly benign
chill on which the poem ends. In a letter to Fanny Brawne,
by the way, Keats touches upon the fever-chill contrast in a
passage that also touches upon the love-death equation,
though here the chill figures in an untransfigured state:

I fear that I am too prudent for a dying kind of Lover.
Yet, there is a great difference between going off in

warm blood like Romeo; and making one's exit like a frog in a frost.

I wonder whether anyone can read the reference to "brede of marble men and maidens overwrought" without thinking of "breed" for "brede" and "excited" for "overwrought." (Both expressions would thus merge notions of sexuality and craftsmanship, the erotic and the poetic.) As for the designating of the urn as an "attitude," it fits in admirably with our stress upon symbolic action. For an attitude is an arrested, or incipient *act*—not just an *object*, or *thing*.

Yeats, in "A Vision," speaks of "the diagrams in Law's *Boehme*, where one lifts a paper to discover both the human entrails and the starry heavens." This equating of the deeply without and the deeply within (as also with Kant's famous remark) might well be remembered when we think of the sky that the "watcher" saw in Keats's sonnet. It is an internal sky, attained through meditations induced by the reading of a book. And so the oracle, whereby truth and beauty are proclaimed as one, would seem to derive from a profound inwardness.

Otherwise, without these introductory mysteries, "truth" and "beauty" were at odds. For whereas "beauty" had its fulfillment in romantic poetry, "truth" was coming to have its fulfillment in science, technological accuracy, accountancy, statistics, actuarial tables, and the like. Hence, without benefit of the rites which one enacts in a sympathetic reading of the "Ode" (rites that remove the discussion to a different level), the enjoyment of "beauty" would involve an esthetic kind of awareness radically in conflict with the kind of awareness deriving from the practical "truth." And as regards the tactics of the poem, this conflict would seem to be solved by "estheticizing" the true rather than by "verifying" the beautiful.

Earlier in our essay, we suggested reading *poetry* for *beauty* and *science* for *truth*, with the oracle deriving its *liberating* quality from the fact that it is uttered at a time when the poem has taken us to a level where earthly contradictions do not operate. But we might also, in purely conceptual terms, attain a level where "poetry" and "science" cease to be at odds; namely: by translating the two terms into the "grammar" that lies behind them. That is: we could generalize the term "poetry" by widening it to the point where we could substitute for it the term "act." And we could widen "science" to the point where we could substitute "scene." Thus we have:

"beauty"   equals   "poetry"   equals   "act"
"truth"    equals   "science"  equals   "scene"

We would equate "beauty" with "act," because it is not
merely a decorative thing, but an assertion, an affirmative, a
creation, hence in the fullest sense an act. And we would
equate "truth" or "science" with the "scenic" because science
is a knowledge of *what is*—and *all that is* comprises the
overall universal *scene*. Our corresponding transcendence,
then, got by "translation" into purely grammatical terms,
would be: "Act is scene, scene act." We have got to this
point by a kind of purely conceptual transformation that
would correspond, I think, to the transformations of imagery
leading to the oracle in the "Ode."

"Act is scene, scene act." Unfortunately, I must break the
symmetry a little. For poetry, as conceived in idealism
(romanticism), could not quite be equated with *act* but
rather with *attitude*. For idealistic philosophies, with their
stress upon the subjective, place primary stress upon the
*agent* (the individual, the ego, the will, etc.). It was medieval
scholasticism that placed primary stress upon the *act*. And in
the "Ode" the urn (which is the vessel or representative of
poetry) is called an "attitude," which is not outright an act,
but an incipient or arrested act, a *state of mind*, the property
of an *agent*. Keats, in calling the urn an attitude, is *personify-
ing* it. Or we might use the italicizing resources of dialectic
by saying that for Keats, beauty (poetry) was not so much
"the *act* of an agent" as it was "the act of an *agent*."

Perhaps we can re-enforce this interpretation by examining
kindred strategies in Yeats, whose poetry similarly derives
from idealistic, romantic sources. Indeed, as we have noted
elsewhere,[1] Yeats's vision of immortality in his Byzantium
poems but carries one step further the Keatsian identification
with the Grecian urn:

> *Once out of nature I shall never take*
> *My bodily form from any natural thing,*
> *But such a form as Grecian goldsmiths make*
> *Of hammered gold and gold enamelling*

Here certainly the poet envisions immortality as "estheti-
cally" as Keats. For he will have immortality as a golden bird,
a fabricated thing, a work of Grecian goldsmiths. Here we
go in the same direction as the "overwrought" urn, but
farther along in that direction.

[1] "On Motivation in Yeats," *The Southern Review*, Winter 1942.

The ending of Yeats's poem, "Among School Children," helps us to make still clearer the idealistic stress upon agent:

> *Labour is blossoming or dancing where*
> *The body is not bruised to pleasure soul,*
> *Nor beauty torn out of its own despair,*
> *Nor blear-eyed wisdom out of midnight oil.*
> *O chestnut tree, great rooted blossomer,*
> *Are you the leaf, the blossom or the bole?*
> *O body swayed to music, O brightening glance,*
> *How can we know the dancer from the dance?*

Here the chestnut tree (as personified agent) is the ground of unity or continuity for all its scenic manifestations; and with the agent (dancer) is merged the act (dance). True, we seem to have here a commingling of act, scene, and agent, all three. Yet it is the *agent* that is "foremost among the equals." Both Yeats and Keats, of course, were much more "dramatistic" in their thinking than romantic poets generally, who usually center their efforts upon the translation of *scene* into terms of *agent* (as the materialistic science that was the dialectical counterpart of romantic idealism preferred conversely to translate *agent* into terms of *scene*, or in other words, to treat "consciousness" in terms of "matter," the "mental" in terms of the "physical," "people" in terms of "environment").

To review briefly: The poem begins with an ambiguous fever which in the course of the further development is "separated out," splitting into a bodily fever and a spiritual counterpart. The bodily passion is the malign aspect of the fever, the mental action its benign aspect. In the course of the development, the malign passion is transcended and the benign active partner, the intellectual exhilaration, takes over. At the beginning, where the two aspects were ambiguously one, the bodily passion would be the "scene" of the mental action (the "objective symptoms" of the body would be paralleled by the "subjective symptoms" of the mind, the bodily state thus being the other or ground of the mental state). But as the two become separated out, the mental action transcends the bodily passion. It becomes an act in its own right, making discoveries and assertions not grounded in the bodily passion. And this quality of action, in transcending the merely physical symptoms of the fever, would thus require a different ground or scene, one more suited in quality to the quality of the transcendent act.

The transcendent act is concretized, or "materialized," in

the vision of the "immortal" scene, the reference in the fourth stanza to the original scene of the urn, the "heavenly" scene of a dead, or immortal, Greece (the scene in which the urn was originally enacted and which is also fixed on its face). To indicate the internality of this vision, we referred to a passage in Yeats relating the "depths" of the sky without to the depths of the mind within; and we showed a similar pattern in Keats's account of the vision that followed his reading of Chapman's Homer. We suggested that the poet is here coming upon a new internal sky, through identification with the urn as act, the same sky that he came upon through identification with the enactments of Chapman's translation.

This transcendent scene is the level at which the earthly laws of contradiction no longer prevail. Hence, in the terms of this scene, he can proclaim the unity of truth and beauty (of science and art), a proclamation that he needs to make precisely because here was the basic split responsible for the romantic agitation (in both poetic and philosophic idealism). That is, it was gratifying to have the oracle proclaim the unity of poetry and science because the values of technology and business were causing them to be at odds. And from the perspective of a "higher level" (the perspective of a dead or immortal scene transcending the world of temporal contradictions) the split could be proclaimed once more a unity.

At this point, at this stage of exaltation, the fever has been replaced by chill. But the bodily passion has completely dropped out of account. All is now mental action. Hence, the chill (as in the ecstatic exclamation, "Cold Pastoral!") is proclaimed only in its benign aspect.

We may contrast this discussion with explanations such as a materialist of the Kretschmer school might offer. I refer to accounts of motivation that might treat disease as cause and poem as effect. In such accounts, the disease would not be "passive," but wholly active; and what we have called the mental action would be wholly passive, hardly more than an epiphenomenon, a mere symptom of the disease quite as are the fever and the chill themselves. Such accounts would give us no conception of the essential matter here, the intense linguistic activity.

## Ode to a Nightingale

My heart aches, and a drowsy numbness pains
　　My sense, as though of hemlock I had drunk,
Or emptied some dull opiate to the drains
　　One minute past, and Lethe-wards had sunk:
'Tis not through envy of thy happy lot,           5
　　But being too happy in thine happiness,
　　　　That thou, light-wingèd Dryad of the trees,
　　　　　　In some melodious plot
　　Of beechen green, and shadows numberless,
　　Singest of summer in full-throated ease.      10

O, for a draught of vintage! that hath been
　　Cool'd a long age in the deep-delvèd earth,
Tasting of Flora and the country-green,
　　Dance, and Provençal song, and sunburnt mirth!
O for a beaker full of the warm South!        15
　　Full of the true, the blushful Hippocrene,
　　　　With beaded bubbles winking at the brim,
　　　　　　And purple-stainèd mouth;
　　That I might drink, and leave the world unseen,
　　And with thee fade away into the forest dim:    20

Fade far away, dissolve, and quite forget
　　What thou among the leaves hast never known,
The weariness, the fever, and the fret
　　Here, where men sit and hear each other groan;
Where palsy shakes a few, sad, last grey hairs,    25
　　Where youth grows pale, and spectre-thin, and dies;
　　　　Where but to think is to be full of sorrow
　　　　　　And leaden-eyed despairs,
　　Where Beauty cannot keep her lustrous eyes,
　　Or new Love pine at them beyond to-morrow.    30

Away! away! for I will fly to thee,
　　Not charioted by Bacchus and his pards,

But on the viewless wings of Poesy,
    Though the dull brain perplexes and retards:
Already with thee! tender is the night,          35
    And haply the Queen-Moon is on her throne,
        Cluster'd around by all her starry Fays;
            But here there is no light,
    Save what from heaven is with the breezes blown
        Through verdurous glooms and winding mossy ways.     40

I cannot see what flowers are at my feet,
    Nor what soft incense hangs upon the boughs,
But, in embalmèd darkness, guess each sweet
    Wherewith the seasonable month endows
The grass, the thicket, and the fruit-tree wild:          45
    White hawthorn, and the pastoral eglantine;
        Fast-fading violets cover'd up in leaves;
            And mid-May's eldest child,
    The coming musk-rose, full of dewy wine,
        The murmurous haunt of flies on summer eves.     50

Darkling I listen; and, for many a time
    I have been half in love with easeful Death,
Call'd him soft names in many a musèd rhyme,
    To take into the air my quiet breath;
Now more than ever seems it rich to die,          55
    To cease upon the midnight with no pain,
        While thou art pouring forth thy soul abroad
            In such an ecstasy!
    Still wouldst thou sing, and I have ears in vain—
        To thy high requiem become a sod.          60

Thou wast not born for death, immortal Bird!
    No hungry generations tread thee down;
The voice I hear this passing night was heard
    In ancient days by emperor and clown:
Perhaps the self-same song that found a path          65
    Through the sad heart of Ruth, when, sick for home,
        She stood in tears amid the alien corn;
            The same that oft-times hath
    Charm'd magic casements, opening on the foam
        Of perilous seas, in faery lands forlorn.          70

Forlorn! the very word is like a bell
    To toll me back from thee to my sole self!
Adieu! the fancy cannot cheat so well
    As she is fam'd to do, deceiving elf.

Adieu! adieu! thy plaintive anthem fades    75
　　Past the near meadows, over the still stream,
　　Up the hill-side; and now 'tis buried deep
　　　　In the next valley-glades:
Was it a vision, or a waking dream?
　　Fled is that music:—Do I wake or sleep?    80

# Cleanth Brooks

---

## KEATS
### ODE TO A NIGHTINGALE

This poem is essentially a reverie induced by the poet's listening to the song of the nightingale. In the first stanza the poet is just sinking into the reverie; in the last stanza, he comes out of the reverie and back to a consciousness of the actual world in which he and all other human beings live. The first lines of the poem and the last, therefore, constitute a sort of frame for the reverie proper.

The poet has chosen to present his reverie largely in terms of imagery—imagery drawn from nature—the flowers and leaves, etc., associated with the bird actually, or imaginatively in myth and story. The images are elaborate and decorative and the poet dwells upon them lovingly and leisurely, developing them in some detail as pictures. It is not the sort of method that would suit a poem exhibiting a rapid and dramatic play of thought; but one remembers the general character of the poem. The loving elaboration and slowed movement resemble the slowed movement of meditative trance, or dream, and therefore is appropriate to the general mood of this poem. The imagery, then, in its elaboration is not merely beautifully decorative, but has a relation to the general temper of the whole poem.

The poet, with his desire to escape from the world of actuality, calls for a drink of wine

*That I might drink, and leave the world unseen*

but the wish for the draught of wine is half fancy. The poet lingers over the description of the wine, making it an idealized and lovingly elaborated thing, too. We know that it is not a serious and compelling request. The grammar of the passage itself tells us this: after "O, for a draught of vintage!" the poet interposes seven lines of rich description identifying the wine with the spirit of summer and pastoral joys and with the romantic associations of Provence, and finally gives a concrete picture of a bubbling glass of the wine itself before he goes on to tell us why he wishes the draught of wine.

The third stanza amplifies the desire to get away from the world of actuality. The word *fade* in the last line of the second stanza is echoed in the next stanza in "Fade far away, dissolve. . . ." The implication is that the poet wishes for a dissolution of himself; a wish that later in the poem becomes an explicit pondering on death as something attractive and desirable. The principal aspects of the actual world the poet would like to escape are just those aspects of it that seem opposed to the world conjured up by the bird's song: its feverish hurry, the fact that in it youth dies and beauty fades. The world that the nightingale seems to inhabit is one of deathless youth and beauty. This idea, too, is to be developed explicitly by the poet in the seventh stanza.

In the fourth stanza the poet apparently makes a sudden decision to attempt to leave actual life and penetrate to the world of the imagination. The apparent suddenness of the decision is reflected in the movement of the first line of the stanza,

*Away! away! for I will fly to thee*

But he will fly to it by exciting his mind not with wine but with poetry. And in line 35 the poet has apparently been successful: "already with thee," he says. There follows down to the opening of the sixth stanza a very rich description of the flowery, darkened thicket in which the nightingale is singing.

The poet's wish for dissolution, which he expresses in the third stanza, becomes in the sixth a wish for death itself, an utter dissolution. But the idea as repeated receives an additional twist. Earlier, his wish to fade away was a desire to escape the sorrow and sordidness of the real world. Now even death itself seems to the poet an easy and attractive thing; and, more than that, it seems even a sort of positive fulfillment to die to the sound of the nightingale's high requiem.

But the nightingale at the height of its singing does not seem to be subject to death. The poet describes the effect of the nightingale's song by two incidents drawn from the remote past—as if he believed that the nightingale he now hears had literally lived forever. The two incidents are chosen also to illustrate two different aspects of the bird's song. The first, the song as heard by Ruth, is an incident taken from biblical literature, and gives the effect of the song as it reminded the homesick girl of her native land. The second, hinting at some unnamed romance of the Middle Ages, gives the unearthly magic of the song.

With the first word of the last stanza, the poet breaks out of his reverie. He catches up the word "forlorn," which he has just used in describing one of the imagined scenes induced by his reverie, and suddenly realizes that it applies all too accurately to himself. The effect is almost that of an abrupt stumbling: the chance employment of a particular word in one of the richly imaginative scenes induced by the bird's song suddenly comes home to him—with altered weight and tone, of course—to remind him that it is he who is forlorn, whose plight is hopeless. With the new and chilling meaning of "forlorn" the song of the nightingale itself alters: what had a moment before been an ecstatic "high requiem" becomes a "plaintive anthem." The song becomes fainter: what had had power to make the sorrowing man "fade . . . away" (lines 20, 21) from a harsh and bitter world, now itself "fades" (line 75), and the speaker is left alone in the silence.

The vitality of the poem, of course, lies in its imagery. The imagery is so rich and resonant, taken line by line, that it is a temptation to treat it as amazingly rich decoration. Consider, for example, the description of the wine in the second stanza. The poet uses the term *vintage* rather than *wine* because of the associations of vintage with age and excellence. It tastes of Flora (goddess of flowers) and the country green (a land predominantly fruitful and rich) and of dance and Provençal song (associations with the merry country of the troubadours and associations with the period of the troubadours) and sunburnt mirth. Mirth cannot, of course, be literally sunburnt, but the sensitive reader will not be troubled by this. The phrase is a condensation of the fuller phrase: mirth of hearty folk who live close to nature and to the earth and whose sunburnt faces and arms indicate that they live close to nature. These associations of the wine with Provence and with all that Provence implies are caught up and corroborated by another bold and condensed phrase: "full of the warm South." For the word South carries not only its associations of warmth but also of the particular South that the poet has just been describing: the south of France.

This, for a rather inadequate account of only one item of the sort of description that fills the poem. One who examines other of the poem's passages in this way will notice that Keats does not sacrifice sharpness of perception to mere

prettiness. Again and again it is the sharp and accurate observation that gives the richness a validity. For example,

> *The coming musk-rose, full of dewy wine,*
> *The murmurous haunt of flies on summer eves*

The passage is not merely beautiful and rich: it embodies
acute observation. We feel that the poet knows what he is
talking about. A poorer poet would try only for the decorative effect and would fail. Moreover, much of the suggestiveness resides also in the choice of precise details. Many a poet
feels that, because the stimulus to the imagination makes for
an indefinite richness of association, this indefiniteness is
aroused by vague, general description. On the contrary, the
force of association is greatest when it is aroused by precise
detail. For example, consider the passage most famous for its
suggestiveness.

> *Charmed magic casements, opening on the foam*
> *Of perilous seas, in faery lands forlorn*

After all, these lines present a scene that is precisely visual-
ized. If the casements opening on the seas and framing the
scene were omitted, the general, vague words, *perilous, faery,*
and *forlorn,* would not be sufficient to give the effect actually
transmitted.

One may, however, read the "Ode to a Nightingale" at a
deeper level. Indeed, if we are to do full justice to the general
architecture of the poem and to the intensity of many of the
individual passages, one must read it at this deeper level.

A basic problem—already hinted at in earlier paragraphs of
this analysis—has to do with the speaker's attitude toward
death. If he wishes to escape from a world overshadowed by
death, why then does he go on to conceive of that escape as a
kind of death? The nightingale's song makes him yearn to
leave a world where "youth grows pale . . . and dies," yet,
as we remember, the highest rapture that he can conceive of
is to die—"to cease upon the midnight with no pain." The
last phrase, "with no pain," offers only a superficial resolution
of our problem. We shall not find our answer in distinguishing between the "easeful Death" of line 52 and some agonizing death. The speaker in this poem is not saying merely that
he would like to die if he could be sure that his death would
be painless.

The death with which he falls "half in love" is not a negative thing, but is conceived of as a rich and positive experi-

ence. To see how Keats brings this about will require a re-examination of the whole poem. We might well begin with the beginning of the poem, for the ambiguous relationship between life and death, joy and pain, intensity of feeling and numb lack of feeling, runs through the poem, and is to be found even in the opening lines.

The song of the nightingale has a curious double effect. The speaker's "heart aches" through the very intensity of pleasure—by "being too happy in thy happiness." But the song also acts as an opiate, making the listener feel drowsy and numbed. Now, an opiate is used to deaden pain, and the song of the bird does deaden (see stanzas three and four) the pain of the mortal world in which "to think is to be full of sorrow." A reader may be tempted therefore to say that the nightingale's song gives to the sorrowing man a little surcease from his unhappiness. But the experience is more complex than this: the song itself causes the pain. Thus, though the song means to the hearer life, freedom, and ease, its effect is to deaden him and render him drowsy.

Are we to say, then, that the poet is confused in this first stanza? No, because the apparent contradictions are meaningful and justified in terms of the poem as a whole. First, as to the realistic basis of the opiate metaphor: the initial effect of a heavy opiate may be painfully numbing. Second, as to the psychological basis: what is pleasurable, if carried to an extreme degree, becomes painful. The nightingale's song, which suggests a world beyond mortality, gives the hearer happiness, but by reminding him of his own mortal state, gives him pain. But the full implications of this paradox of pleasure-pain, life-death, immortal-mortal require the whole of the poem for their full development.

We have commented upon what the speaker wishes to escape from; he has himself made clear the primary obstacle to his escape. It is the "dull brain" that "perplexes and retards." The opiate, the draught of vintage for which the speaker has called, the free play of the imagination—all have this in common: they release one from the tyranny of the "dull brain." The brain insists upon clarity and rigid order; it is an order that must be "dissolved" if the speaker is to escape into, and merge with, the richer world for which he longs.

But the word that the speaker uses to describe this process is "fade," and his entry into this world of the imagination is symbolized by a fading into the rich darkness out of which the nightingale sings. We associate darkness with death, but this darkness is instinct with the most intense life. How is the darkness insisted upon—and thus defined? The nightingale sings in a plot of "shadows numberless"; the speaker would leave the world "unseen" and join the bird in "the forest dim"; he would "fade far away"—would "dissolve"; and when he feels that he is actually with the nightingale, he is in a place of "verdurous glooms."

Having attained to that place, he "cannot see." Though the poem abounds in sensuous detail, and appeals so powerfully to all the senses, most of the images of sight are *fancied* by the speaker. He does not actually see the Queen-Moon or the stars. He guesses at what flowers are at his feet. He has found his way into a warm "embalmed darkness." The last adjective means primarily "filled with incense," "sweet with balm," but it must also have suggested death—in Keats's day as well as in ours. In finding his way imaginatively into the dark covert from which the bird is singing, the speaker has approached death. He has wished to fade far away, "dissolve, and quite forget"; but the final dissolution and the ultimate forgetting are death. True, death here is apprehended in a quite different fashion from the death depicted in stanza three: here the balm is the natural perfume of growing flowers and the gloom is "verdurous," with suggestions of rich organic growth. But the fading has been complete—he is completely encompassed with darkness.

It is worth remarking that Keats has described the flowery covert with full honesty. If his primary emphasis is on fertility and growth, still he recognizes that death and change have their place here too: the violets, for instance, are thought of as "fast-fading." But the atmosphere of this world of nature is very different, to be sure, from that of the human world haunted by death, where "men sit and hear each other groan." The world of nature is a world of cyclic change (the "seasonable month," "the coming musk-rose," etc.) and consequently can seem fresh and immortal, like the bird whose song seems to be its spirit.

The poem, then, is not only about death and deathlessness, or about the actual and the ideal; it is also about alienation and wholeness. It is man's necessary alienation from nature that invests death with its characteristic horror. To "dissolve" —to "fade"—into the warm darkness is to merge into the eternal pattern of nature. Death itself becomes something positive—a flowering—a fulfillment. Keats has underlined this suggestion very cunningly in the sixth stanza. The ancients thought that at death, a man's soul was breathed out with his last breath. Here the nightingale is pouring forth its "soul" and at this high moment the man listening in the darkness would be glad to die. Soul and breath become interchangeable. The most intense expression of life (the nightingale's ecstatic song) invites the listener to breathe forth his soul (death).

The foregoing paragraphs may suggest the sense in which the speaker calls the nightingale immortal. The nightingale symbolizes the immortality of nature, which, harmonious with itself, remains through all its myriad changes unwearied and beautiful. We need not suppose that the speaker, even in his tranced reverie, thinks of the particular biological mechanism of flesh and bone and feathers as deathless—any more than he thinks of the "fast-fading violets" and the "coming musk-rose" as unwithering. Keats has clearly specified the sense in which the bird is immortal: it is in harmony with its world—not, as man is, in competition with his ("No hungry generations tread thee down"); and the bird cannot even conceive of its separation from the world which it knows and expresses and of which it is a part ("Thou wast not born for death"). Man knows that he was born to die—"What thou among the leaves hast never known"—and that knowledge overshadows man's life, and necessarily all his songs.

That knowledge overshadows this song, and gives it its special poignance. As the poem ends, the speaker's attempt to enter the world of the nightingale breaks down. The music by means of which he hoped to flee from his mortal world has itself fled—"fled is that music." The music that almost succeeded in making him "fade far away" now itself "fades / Past the near meadows" and in a moment is "buried deep / In the next valley-glades." The word "buried" here suggests a view of death very different from that conjured up by "embalmed darkness" in the fifth stanza. Death here is bleak and negative. The poem has come full circle.

## La Belle Dame sans Merci

"O what can ail thee, knight-at-arms,
    Alone and palely loitering?
The sedge is wither'd from the lake,
    And no birds sing!

"O what can ail thee, knight-at-arms       5
    So haggard and so woe-begone?
The squirrel's granary is full
    And the harvest's done.

"I see a lily on thy brow
    With anguish moist and fever dew,     10
And on thy cheek a fading rose
    Fast withereth too."

"I met a Lady in the meads,
    Full beautiful—a faery's child;
Her hair was long, her foot was light,     15
    And her eyes were wild.

"I made a garland for her head,
    And bracelets too, and fragrant zone
She look'd at me as she did love,
    And made sweet moan.     20

"I set her on my pacing steed,
    And nothing else saw all day long,
For sideways would she lean, and sing
    A faery's song.

"She found me roots of relish sweet,     25
    And honey wild, and manna dew,
And sure in language strange she said—
    'I love thee true!'

"She took me to her elfin grot,
    And there she wept and sighed full sore;    30
And there I shut her wild, wild eyes
    With kisses four.

"And there she lullèd me asleep
    And there I dream'd—Ah! woe betide!
The latest dream I ever dream'd                                            35
    On the cold hill's side.

"I saw pale kings and princes too,
    Pale warriors, death-pale were they all;
Who cried—'La belle dame sans merci
    Thee hath in thrall!'                                   40

"I saw their starved lips in the gloam,·
    With horrid warning gapèd wide,
"And there I shut her wild, wild eyes
    On the cold hill's side.

"And this is why I sojourn here,                                           45
    Alone and palely loitering;
Though the sedge is wither'd from the lake,
    And no birds sing."

# Robert Graves

---

LA BELLE DAME SANS MERCI

O what can ail thee Knight at arms
    Alone and palely loitering?
The sedge is withered from the Lake
    And no birds sing!

O what can ail thee Knight at arms        5
    So haggard, and so woe begone?
The squirrel's granary is full
    And the harvest's done.

I see a lily on thy brow
    With anguish moist and fever dew,    10
And on thy cheeks a fading rose
    Fast withereth too—

I met a Lady in the Meads
    Full beautiful, a faery's child
Her hair was long, her foot was light    15
    And her eyes were wild—

I made a Garland for her head,
    And bracelets too, and fragrant Zone
She look'd at me as she did love
    And made sweet moan—    20

I set her on my pacing steed
    And nothing else saw all day long
For sidelong would she bend and sing
    A faery's song—

She found me roots of relish sweet    25
    And honey wild and manna dew
And sure in language strange she said
    I love thee true—

She took me to her elfin grot
    And there she wept and sigh'd full sore,    30

And there I shut her wild wild eyes
   With kisses four—

And there she lulled me asleep
   And there I dream'd Ah Woe betide!
The latest dream I ever dreamt                    35
   On the cold hill side

I saw pale Kings, and Princes too
   Pale warriors death pale were they all
Who cried La belle dame sans merci
   Thee hath in thrall.                           40

I saw their starv'd lips in the gloam
   With horrid warning gaped wide,
And I awoke, and found me here
   On the cold hill's side

And this is why I sojourn here                    45
   Alone and palely loitering;
Though the sedge is withered from the Lake
   And no birds sing—

The Psalmist records: "I kept silent, yea, even from good words. My heart was hot within me and, while I was thus musing, the fire kindled and at the last I spake with my tongue." The same thing seems to have happened when Keats wrote this ballad, in a poetic trance, knowing deep in his heart what it was about, yet unwilling to interpret the symbolism even for his own enlightenment.

Sir Sidney Colvin in his *Life of Keats* suggests that he had recently read a translation, ascribed to Chaucer, from Alain Chartier's French poem of the same title, "La Belle Dame sans Merci":

I came into a lustie green vallay
Full of floures . . . Riding an easy paas
I fell in thought of joy full desperate
With greate disease and paine, so that I was
Of all lovers the most unfortunate

Death separated this lover from his mistress.

Keats's heart had been "hot within him" for a long while, and the mental disturbances that made him keep silence and muse in the "loitering indolence" that had lately overtaken his writing were as painful as they were complicated. "Greate disease and paine" attacked him: body, mind and heart all at once. He felt a growing passion for his next-door neighbor, the "beautiful and elegant, graceful, silly, fashionable and

strange . . . MINX," Fanny Brawne (his own description
after their first meeting), who was "looking on him as she
did love," and "sighing full sore." He fought against this
entanglement in self-defense. The fear that she must be making eyes at him from mere cruelty demanded suppression, as
also did another worse fear—not yet certainty—of his own
fated death by consumption, the then incurable disease that
had just taken off his brother, Tom. Suppressed at the normal
thought level, these fears surged up in poetic fantasia: the
"Merciless Lady" thus representing both love and death.

Keats, writing a journal-letter to his brother George in
America, sent him the draft which I have printed above. The
poem begins abruptly under the heading "Wednesday Evening," and shows every sign of recent conposition. He jokes
at the close:

> Why four kisses—you will say—why four because I
> wish to restrain the headlong impetuosity of the Muse—
> she would have fain said "score" without hurting the
> rhyme—but we must temper the Imagination as the
> Critics say with Judgement. I was obliged to choose an
> even number that both eyes might have fair play, and to
> speak truly I think two a piece quite sufficient. Suppose
> I had said seven there would have been three and a half
> a piece—a very awkward affair and well got out of on
> my side—

Such light-heartedness can be accepted as genuine only if,
when he emerged from his poetic trance, Keats did not
recognize the terrible double sense of shutting those wild
eyes with kisses. This journal-letter was the last place where
Keats could parade his troubles. George being in low water
financially, and needing cheering up, John felt bound to hide
the serious condition of his own health. Their brother Tom's
recent death made matters worse for both—George had sailed
to America without realizing the extent of his sickness, and
John, off in Scotland for an arduous walking tour, came back
to find Tom in his death agony. He saw the lily on Tom's
brow, the hectic rose on his cheek, his starved lips agape in
horrid warning; and, as the final terrible duty, shut those
wild, wild eyes with coins, not kisses. Now Fanny's mocking
smile and Tom's trembling lips play hide and seek through
Keats's dreams: Fanny's lovely life-mask has the wild, wild
eyes of cruelty; Tom's death-mask has the wild, wild eyes of
horror and pain. . . .

About this time Keats met Coleridge walking by Highgate

Ponds; and "wishing to carry away the memory" of meeting Coleridge, asked leave to press his hand. When Keats had gone, Coleridge told his friend Green: "There is death in that hand." He described it afterwards as "a heat and a dampness"—but "fever-dew" is Keats's own word.

We can accept Sir Sidney Colvin's view that "La Belle Dame" symbolizes death by consumption: the poem includes numerous phrases suggesting phthisic symptoms. That the same character also represents Fanny Brawne need not offend the logical-minded; a double metaphor often occurs in poems and psychopathic dreams where two emotional conflicts are aggravating each other. Here Keats's love for Fanny could not alleviate his own physical distress; for the fear of consumption implied a despair of never being able to marry her—even if she gave surer proofs of love than hitherto. . . .

Comparing Keats's two pen-pictures of Fanny with "La Belle Dame" and noting the "tolerable" foot, the agreeable hair, the elfin grace and elfish manners in transformation, we wonder: did the knight-at-arms set her on his steed as it took to its "easy pass through the green valley" in order to see her commended profile at the best advantage? Did her natural paleness and thinness—as he has described it—form an easy link with the fear of consumption?

It would be wrong to omit facts about Keats's health clearly given in Rossetti's *Life*, but hushed up by most textbooks. His consumption was aggravated by another malady, of the most mind-torturing kind: venereal disease, which he had contracted at Oxford in 1817, two years before, and which even more prejudiced his hopes of Fanny.

Keats's main solace was his assurance of being included "among the English Poets," and "La Belle Dame sans Merci" contains numerous poetic reminiscences confirming this: from Spenser's "Faery Queene," the ballad of "Thomas the Rhymer," Malory's "Lady of the Lake," Coleridge's "Kubla Khan" (with its singing maiden and poetic honey-dew, traceable in Keats's "honey wild, and manna dew"), an echo from William Browne, "Let no bird sing," and from Wordsworth—"her eyes are wild." All these references suggest poetic ambition.

Yet even poetry had proved cruel to Keats: he was now overtaken by a period of poetic dumbness, so that "La Belle Dame" may also represent the figure of Poetry. Sickness threatened him with only a short life in which to get his thoughts on paper; and this new love affair, coming close after his infatuation for Isabella Jones, plunged him in such uncertainty that he could make no progress with the long poems from which he hoped most reputation. Fanny Brawne, Keats knew, was the sort of girl to be greatly impressed by poetic fame; thus poetry, if he could write it, would be not merely a solace but a weapon for clearing the way to her love. Nevertheless, his pen failed him. He felt that "the squirrel's granary is full and the harvest done"—Keats was squirrellike in his harvesting and storing of poetic provender.

I know no simple ballad that opens up longer vistas of torment, horror, self-reproach and despair. The restlessness of Keats's mind has forbidden him to marshal his thoughts carefully and logically; the pain, if it ever found any better expression than a beating of the breast and a tearing of the hair, could be satisfied only with phrases of the most condensed and perverse imagery—such as Lear, Hamlet, and Shakespeare's other grief-maddened heroes pour out. Indeed, if "La Belle Dame sans Merci" had not been bound both by Keats's tenderness for George's feelings and his regard for established poetic convention, it might have disintegrated into pure nightmare.

# The Eve of St. Agnes

St. Agnes' Eve—Ah, bitter chill it was!
The owl, for all his feathers, was a-cold;
The hare limp'd trembling through the frozen grass,
And silent was the flock in woolly fold:
Numb were the Beadsman's fingers, while he told          5
His rosary, and while his frosted breath,
Like pious incense from a censer old,
Seem'd taking flight for heaven without a death,
Past the sweet Virgin's picture, while his prayer he saith.

His prayer he saith, this patient, holy man;          10
Then takes his lamp, and riseth from his knees,
And back returneth, meagre, barefoot, wan,
Along the chapel aisle by slow degrees:
The sculptur'd dead, on each side, seem to freeze,
Emprison'd in black, purgatorial rails:          15
Knights, ladies, praying in dumb orat'ries,
He passeth by; and his weak spirit fails
To think how they may ache in icy hoods and mails.

Northward he turneth through a little door,
And scarce three steps, ere Music's golden tongue          20
Flatter'd to tears this agèd man and poor;
But no—already had his deathbell rung;
The joys of all his life were said and sung:
His was harsh penance on St. Agnes' Eve:
Another way he went, and soon among          25
Rough ashes sat he for his soul's reprieve,
And all night kept awake, for sinners' sake to grieve.

That ancient Beadsman heard the prelude soft;
And so it chanc'd, for many a door was wide,
From hurry to and fro. Soon, up aloft,          30
The silver, snarling trumpets 'gan to chide:
The level chambers, ready with their pride,
Were glowing to receive a thousand guests:

The carved angels, ever eager-eyed,
Star'd, where upon their heads the cornice rests, 35
With hair blown back, and wing put cross-wise on their breasts.

At length burst in the argent revelry,
With plume, tiara, and all rich array,
Numerous as shadows, haunting fairily
The brain, new stuff'd, in youth, with triumphs gay 40
Of old romance. These let us wish away,
And turn, sole-thoughted, to one Lady there,
Whose heart had brooded, all that wintry day,
On love, and wing'd St. Agnes' saintly care,
As she had heard old dames full many times declare. 45

They told her how, upon St. Agnes' Eve,
Young virgins might have visions of delight,
And soft adorings from their loves receive
Upon the honey'd middle of the night,
If ceremonies due they did aright; 50
As, supperless to bed they must retire,
And couch supine their beauties, lily white;
Nor look behind, nor sideways, but require
Of Heaven with upward eyes for all that they desire.

Full of this whim was thoughtful Madeline: 55
The music, yearning like a God in pain,
She scarcely heard: her maiden eyes divine,
Fix'd on the floor, saw many a sweeping train
Pass by—she heeded not at all: in vain
Came many a tiptoe, amorous cavalier, 60
And back retir'd: not cool'd by high disdain,
But she saw not: her heart was otherwhere:
She sigh'd for Agnes' dreams, the sweetest of the year.

She danc'd along with vague, regardless eyes,
Anxious her lips, her breathing quick and short: 65
The hallow'd hour was near at hand: she sighs
Amid the timbrels, and the throng'd resort
Of whisperers in anger, or in sport;
'Mid looks of love, defiance, hate, and scorn,
Hoodwink'd with faery fancy; all amort, 70
Save to St. Agnes and her lambs unshorn,
And all the bliss to be before to-morrow morn.

So, purposing each moment to retire,
She linger'd still. Meantime, across the moors,
Had come young Porphyro, with heart on fire 75
For Madeline. Beside the portal doors,

Buttress'd from moonlight, stands he, and implores
All saints to give him sight of Madeline,
But for one moment in the tedious hours,
That he might gaze and worship all unseen;      80
Perchance speak, kneel, touch, kiss—in sooth such things have
    been.

He ventures in: let not buzz'd whisper tell:
All eyes be muffled, or a hundred swords
Will storm his heart, Love's fev'rous citadel:
For him, those chambers held barbarian hordes,      85
Hyena foemen, and hot-blooded lords,
Whose very dogs would execrations howl
Against his lineage: not one breast affords
Him any mercy, in that mansion foul,
Save one old beldame, weak in body and in soul.      90

Ah, happy chance! the agèd creature came,
Shuffling along with ivory-headed wand,
To where he stood, hid from the torch's flame,
Behind a broad hall-pillar, far beyond
The sound of merriment and chorus bland:      95
He startled her; but soon she knew his face,
And grasp'd his fingers in her palsied hand,
Saying, "Mercy, Porphyro! hie thee from this place;
They are all here to-night, the whole blood-thirsty race!

"Get hence! get hence! there's dwarfish Hildebrand;      100
He had a fever late, and in the fit
He cursèd thee and thine, both house and land:
Then there's that old Lord Maurice, not a whit
More tame for his grey hairs—Alas me! flit!
Flit like a ghost away."—"Ah, Gossip dear,      105
We're safe enough; here in this arm-chair sit,
And tell me how"—"Good Saints! not here, not here;
Follow me, child, or else these stones will be thy bier."

He follow'd through a lowly archèd way,
Brushing the cobwebs with his lofty plume,      110
And as she mutter'd "Well-a—well-a-day!"
He found him in a little moonlight room,
Pale, lattic'd, chill, and silent as a tomb.
"Now tell me where is Madeline," said he,
"O tell me, Angela, by the holy loom      115
Which none but secret sisterhood may see,
When they St. Agnes' wool are weaving piously."

"St. Agnes! Ah! it is St. Agnes' Eve—
Yet men will murder upon holy days;
Thou must hold water in a witch's sieve,                    120
And be liege-lord of all the Elves and Fays,
To venture so: it fills me with amaze
To see thee, Porphyro!—St. Agnes' Eve!
God's help! my lady fair the conjuror plays
This very night: good angels her deceive!                    125
But let me laugh awhile, I've mickle time to grieve."

Feebly she laugheth in the languid moon,
While Porphyro upon her face doth look,
Like puzzled urchin on an agèd crone
Who keepeth clos'd a wond'rous riddle-book,                    130
As spectacled she sits in chimney nook.
But soon his eyes grew brilliant, when she told
His lady's purpose; and he scarce could brook
Tears, at the thought of those enchantments cold
And Madeline asleep in lap of legends old.                    135

Sudden a thought came like a full-blown rose,
Flushing his brow, and in his painèd heart
Made purple riot: then doth he propose
A stratagem, that makes the beldame start:
"A cruel man and impious thou art:                    140
Sweet lady, let her pray, and sleep, and dream
Alone with her good angels, far apart
From wicked men like thee. Go, go!—I deem
Thou canst not surely be the same that thou didst seem."

"I will not harm her, by all saints I swear,"                    145
Quoth Porphyro: "O may I ne'er find grace
When my weak voice shall whisper its last prayer,
If one of her soft ringlets I displace,
Or look with ruffian passion in her face:
Good Angela, believe me by these tears;                    150
Or I will, even in a moment's space,
Awake, with horrid shout, my foemen's ears,
And beard them, though they be more fang'd than wolves
    and bears."

"Ah! why wilt thou affright a feeble soul?
A poor, weak, palsy-stricken, churchyard thing,                    155
Whose passing-bell may ere the midnight toll;
Whose prayers for thee, each morn and evening,
Were never miss'd."—Thus plaining, doth she bring
A gentler speech from burning Porphyro;
So woful, and of such deep sorrowing,                    160

That Angela gives promise she will do
Whatever he shall wish, betide her weal or woe.

Which was, to lead him, in close secrecy,
Even to Madeline's chamber, and there hide
Him in a closet, of such privacy                          165
That he might see her beauty unespied,
And win perhaps that night a peerless bride,
While legion'd fairies pac'd the coverlet,
And pale enchantment held her sleepy-eyed.
Never on such a night have lovers met,                    170
Since Merlin paid his Demon all the monstrous debt.

"It shall be as thou wishest," said the Dame:
"All cates and dainties shall be storèd there
Quickly on this feast-night: by the tambour frame
Her own lute thou wilt see; no time to spare,            175
For I am slow and feeble, and scarce dare
On such a catering trust my dizzy head.
Wait here, my child, with patience; kneel in prayer
The while: Ah! thou must needs the lady wed,
Or may I never leave my grave among the dead."           180

So saying, she hobbled off with busy fear.
The lover's endless minutes slowly pass'd;
The Dame return'd, and whisper'd in his ear
To follow her; with agèd eyes aghast
From fright of dim espial. Safe at last,                 185
Through many a dusky gallery, they gain
The maiden's chamber, silken, hush'd, and chaste;
Where Porphyro took covert, pleas'd amain.
His poor guide hurried back with agues in her brain.

Her falt'ring hand upon the balustrade,                  190
Old Angela was feeling for the stair,
When Madeline, St. Agnes' charmèd maid,
Rose, like a mission'd spirit, unaware:
With silver taper's light, and pious care,
She turn'd, and down the agèd gossip led                 195
To a safe level matting. Now prepare,
Young Porphyro, for gazing on that bed;
She comes, she comes again, like ring-dove fray'd and fled.

Out went the taper as she hurried in;
Its little smoke, in pallid moonshine, died:             200
She clos'd the door, she panted, all akin
To spirits of the air, and visions wide:
No uttered syllable, or, woe betide!
But to her heart, her heart was voluble,

Paining with eloquence her balmy side;                      205
As though a tongueless nightingale should swell
Her throat in vain, and die, heart-stifled, in her dell.

A casement high and triple-arched there was,
All garlanded with carven imag'ries
Of fruits, and flowers, and bunches of knot-grass,          210
And diamonded with panes of quaint device,
Innumerable of stains and splendid dyes,
As are the tiger-moth's deep-damask'd wings;
And in the midst, 'mong thousand heraldries,
And twilight saints, and dim emblazonings,                  215
A shielded scutcheon blush'd with blood of queens and kings.

Full on this casement shone the wintry moon,
And threw warm gules on Madeline's fair breast,
As down she knelt for heaven's grace and boon;
Rose-bloom fell on her hands, together prest,               220
And on her silver cross soft amethyst,
And on her hair a glory, like a saint:
She seem'd a splendid angel, newly drest,
Save wings, for heaven:—Porphyro grew faint:
She knelt, so pure a thing, so free from mortal taint.      225

Anon his heart revives: her vespers done,
Of all its wreathèd pearls her hair she frees;
Unclasps her warmèd jewels one by one;
Loosens her fragrant boddice; by degrees
Her rich attire creeps rustling to her knees:               230
Half-hidden, like a mermaid in sea-weed,
Pensive awhile she dreams awake, and sees,
In fancy, fair St. Agnes in her bed,
But dares not look behind, or all the charm is fled.

Soon, trembling in her soft and chilly nest,                235
In sort of wakeful swoon, perplex'd she lay,
Until the poppied warmth of sleep oppress'd
Her soothèd limbs, and soul fatigued away;
Flown, like a thought, until the morrow-day;
Blissfully haven'd both from joy and pain;                  240
Clasp'd like a missal where swart Paynims pray;
Blinded alike from sunshine and from rain,
As though a rose should shut, and be a bud again.

Stol'n to this paradise, and so entranced,
Porphyro gazed upon her empty dress,                        245
And listen'd to her breathing, if it chanced
To wake into a slumberous tenderness;
Which when he heard, that minute did he bless,

And breath'd himself: then from the closet crept,
Noiseless as fear in a wide wilderness,                          250
And over the hush'd carpet, silent, stept,
And 'tween the curtains peep'd, where, lo!—how fast she slept.

Then by the bed-side, where the faded moon
Made a dim, silver twilight, soft he set
A table, and, half anguish'd, threw thereon                      255
A cloth of woven crimson, gold, and jet:—
O for some drowsy Morphean amulet!
The boisterous, midnight, festive clarion,
The kettle-drum, and far-heard clarionet,
Affray his ears, though but in dying tone:—                      260
The hall door shuts again, and all the noise is gone.

And still she slept an azure-lidded sleep,
In blanchèd linen, smooth, and lavender'd,
While he from forth the closet brought a heap
Of candied apple, quince, and plum, and gourd;                   265
With jellies soother than the creamy curd,
And lucent syrops, tinct with cinnamon;
Manna and dates, in argosy transferr'd
From Fez; and spicèd dainties, every one,
From silken Samarcand to cedar'd Lebanon.                        270

These delicates he heap'd with glowing hand
On golden dishes and in baskets bright
Of wreathèd silver: sumptuous they stand
In the retirèd quiet of the night,
Filling the chilly room with perfume light.—                     275
"And now, my love, my seraph fair, awake!
Thou art my heaven, and I thine eremite:
Open thine eyes, for meek St. Agnes' sake,
Or I shall drowse beside thee, so my soul doth ache."

Thus whispering, his warm, unnervèd arm                          280
Sank in her pillow. Shaded was her dream
By the dusk curtains:—'twas a midnight charm
Impossible to melt as icèd stream:
The lustrous salvers in the moonlight gleam;
Broad golden fringe upon the carpet lies:                        285
It seem'd he never, never could redeem
From such a steadfast spell his lady's eyes;
So mus'd awhile, entoil'd in woofèd phantasies.

Awakening up, he took her hollow lute,—
Tumultuous,—and, in chords that tenderest be,                    290
He play'd an ancient ditty, long since mute,
In Provence call'd, "La belle dame sans merci":

Close to her ear touching the melody:—
Wherewith disturb'd, she utter'd a soft moan:
He ceased—she panted quick—and suddenly          295
Her blue affrayèd eyes wide open shone:
Upon his knees he sank, pale as smooth-sculptured stone.

Her eyes were open, but she still beheld,
Now wide awake, the vision of her sleep:
There was a painful change, that nigh expell'd          300
The blisses of her dream so pure and deep
At which fair Madeline began to weep,
And moan forth witless words with many a sigh;
While still her gaze on Porphyro would keep;
Who knelt, with joinèd hands and piteous eye,          305
Fearing to move or speak, she look'd so dreamingly.

"Ah, Porphyro!" said she, "but even now
Thy voice was at sweet tremble in mine ear,
Made tuneable with every sweetest vow;
And those sad eyes were spiritual clear:          310
How chang'd thou art! how pallid, chill, and drear!
Give me that voice again, my Porphyro,
Those looks immortal, those complainings dear!
Oh leave me not in this eternal woe,
For if thou diest, my Love, I know not where to go."          315

Beyond a mortal man impassion'd far
At these voluptuous accents, he arose,
Ethereal, flush'd, and like a throbbing star
Seen mid the sapphire heaven's deep repose
Into her dream he melted, as the rose          320
Blendeth its odor with the violet,—
Solution sweet: meantime the frost-wind blows
Like Love's alarum pattering the sharp sleet
Against the window-panes; St. Agnes' moon hath set.

'Tis dark: quick pattereth the flaw-blown sleet:          325
"This is no dream, my bride, my Madeline!"
'Tis dark: the iced gusts still rave and beat:
"No dream, alas! alas! and woe is mine!
Porphyro will leave me here to fade and pine.—
Cruel! what traitor could thee hither bring?          330
I curse not, for my heart is lost in thine
Though thou forsakest a deceivèd thing;—
A dove forlorn and lost with sick unprunèd wing."

"My Madeline! sweet dreamer! lovely bride!
Say, may I be for aye thy vassal blest?          335

Thy beauty's shield, heart-shap'd and vermeil dyed?
Ah, silver shrine, here will I take my rest
After so many hours of toil and quest,
A famish'd pilgrim,—saved by miracle.
Though I have found, I will not rob thy nest          340
Saving of thy sweet self; if thou think'st well
To trust, fair Madeline, to no rude infidel.

"Hark! 'tis an elfin-storm from faery land
Of haggard seeming, but a boon indeed:
Arise—arise! the morning is at hand;—              345
The bloated wassaillers will never heed:—
Let us away, my love, with happy speed;
There are no ears to hear, or eyes to see,—
Drown'd all in Rhenish and the sleepy mead:
Awake! arise! my love, and fearless be,           350
For o'er the southern moors I have a home for thee."

She hurried at his words, beset with fears,
For there were sleeping dragons all around,
At glaring watch, perhaps, with ready spears—
Down the wide stairs a darkling way they found.—   355
In all the house was heard no human sound.
A chain-droop'd lamp was flickering by each door;
The arras, rich with horseman, hawk, and hound,
Flutter'd in the besieging wind's uproar;
And the long carpets rose along the gusty floor.    360

They glide, like phantoms, into the wide hall;
Like phantoms, to the iron porch, they glide;
Where lay the Porter, in uneasy sprawl,
With a huge empty flaggon by his side:
The wakeful bloodhound rose, and shook his hide,    365
But his sagacious eye an inmate owns:
By one, and one, the bolts full easy slide:—
The chains lie silent on the footworn stones;—
The key turns, and the door upon its hinges groans.

And they are gone: ay, ages long ago                370
These lovers fled away into the storm.
That night the Baron dreamt of many a woe,
And all his warrior-guests, with shade and form
Of witch, and demon, and large coffin-worm,
Were long be-nightmar'd. Angela the old            375
Died palsy-twitch'd, with meagre face deform;
The Beadsman, after thousand aves told,
For aye unsought-for slept among his ashes cold.

# William Stafford

## KEATS
### THE EVE OF ST. AGNES

As everyone knows, running ahead of an artist as he works is a line of hope or faith: somewhere in the realm of possibility there waits a story or tune or scene that, once realized, will spring into immediate reverberation with its matching human state. Out there, in the transformations of art, intensest needs project a vision of what they demand: the starving most vividly know what food means; those who are freezing glow in sudden knowledge of what they lack; the young who glimpse love are quick in an opulent dream which others can faintly understand. So, for an adept in art, the world is illuminated at intervals. With photo-flash suddenness a strong potential of experience leaps into intensified existence. The genius marks the place of these flashes for us, and when he brings word back he cannot fully explain the sweet and unbearable burden he has.

For John Keats in 1819, twenty-three years old, poor, sick, in love—and possessed of a gust of that glimpsing kind of genius—an all-at-once blaze of possibility had blown open before him, and for an interval in his short life he burned with realizations he did not have time to capture. In that one year he committed to paper an avalanche of perception: "On a Grecian Urn," "On Melancholy," "Ode to Autumn," "Lamia," "La Belle Dame sans Merci," "Hyperion," "The Eve of St. Agnes." And in this last a particular intensification was present: the lover had recently discovered in medieval romance a great liberating line of possibility. In his poem he lavished at full tide the stored riches that medieval romanticism could afford.

In the romance as Keats used it, the quality that first strikes the reader is immediacy. The reader is drafted into the scenario; he limps trembling through the frozen grass; and in quick, sharp focus he is with the owl in its feathers, crowded into the woolly fold, numbed like a finger, and swept into the whole radial presence of the stormed castle as it turns itself to offer glimpses while the lanterned eyes twitch it bit by bit into view. By the time the story ends even the walls and floor are alive, their tapestries and rugs animated by the gusts of wind that have besieged the castle through the night. The empathy for which Keats is celebrated is evident everywhere, even as he pushes his material into a distance of time and place. The power of language to overcome distance, and in fact to use distance as inverse perspective, looms throughout the poem.

Meanwhile, the immediacy of experience is seconded by another kind of intensification: every part of the scene stands out in contrast with another part, by a series of dimensioned extremes. Paired opposites hold the poem apart in a wide clarity—old-young, then-now, enemies-lovers, heavenly-earthly, outside-inside, sacred-profane. It is all one wide, sustained flourish of pattern. Even the elements within each pair are further intensified; there are occult resemblances among these elements—the angels who cross their wings in front of them are strangely related to Madeline when she disrobes; the worshiper ("another way he went") in the cold ashes contrasts to the secular worshiper Porphyro, a direct and immediate devotee by the warm bed.

Doors that open and close throughout the story make music burst in, fade out, make the storm remind of how small and inner the warmth is, and make a fine, diminishing groan of hinges as the lovers escape into the storm. These doors allow the reader near or shut him far from events accumulating toward the close of that last door; and in lines 316 through 333 the reader experiences quick, decisive maneuvers like the opening and shutting of doors, as the lovers are near each other, distant as heaven, blended into one dream, distanced by the convention of flowers, enclosed in the storm, set over the scene with the moon, brought back through the sleeted window, and confronted with each other, to say, "No dream." But after this for the reader the story again distances, goes into a long time ago, immortalized as a part of any storm.

Several considerations help in accounting for Keats's excellence. One consideration would note his typical trading of duration for intensity: brief things burn bright. He died at the age of twenty-six, and he lived in the presence of dissolving time. His writings recur to the theme: "When I have fears that I may cease to be." He often bolsters a lack with a linked compensation: "There is a triple sight in blindness keen." He is often as direct as can be on this topic: "I know this Being's lease, / My fancy to its utmost blisses spreads." And of course the odes catch into lasting forms the anguish of experience that passes: "Forever piping songs forever new."

But stating this theme—the brevity of life—is common; and even to be one obsessed by it is no great distinction. It is in the quality of his perception of it that Keats is distinguished. To identify this quality it is necessary to refer to what happens in a poetic use of language. Every human state exists in circumstances that identify with it—the sound, the sight, the sensations that are the experience of living; language enables us to refer with our consciousness to these triggering circumstances and to do so in such sequences and accompanied by such considerations as the spaciousness and the quality of our attention will allow. Poetry derives from the exercise of an intense and spacious attention on timed and sequenced references in such a way as to maximize our self-discoveries and to reinforce them by reminders of naturally accepted harmonies in experience. In attaining his goal, the poet stoops to use any slight means; his justification comes from the total effect of strictly congruent means, all helping each other, no matter how small the part each element plays. And it happens that language lends itself to these infinitely multiplying opportunities for little gains in the service of a developing meaning. Language grows by accretions of nuances, and it is therefore available to exploitation by a writer or speaker who can mobilize these nuances already built into his material. When a poet to whom language is so very available attains to his best work, it sometimes seems that the language must have been formed in such a way, and seasoned by earlier uses in such a way, as to provide him with exactly what he needs. It is as if some power had conditioned us all and had delivered to Keats a language tailored for maximum effect on us. Of course, the practice goes the other way: the writer is widely aware in the language which in turn lends itself to his adaptations.

To read slowly the first four or five lines of "The Eve of St. Agnes" is enough to show how the language chimes along for Keats, and the occasional deliberately archaic words establish the distance of the story at the same time as they weather the surface of it; the stanza form, too, reduplicates the meaning—Spenser's extreme medievalism is used again, from a greater distance, to echo the lavish tales Elizabethans drew from yet earlier times of exuberant faith and Gothic elaboration.

Sustained by many such reinforcements the story reaches us. It is a dream, in olden times, in a storm, in a castle, in a room—in a dream; it is charmed to a stillness of the past, and held out in immediacy for our eternal contemplation.

# EDWARD FITZGERALD

[1809–1883]

## *Rubáiyát of Omar Khayyám of Naishápúr*

Wake! For the Sun who scattered into flight
The Stars before him from the Field of Night,
    Drives Night along with them from Heav'n, and strikes
The Sultán's Turret with a Shaft of Light.

Before the phantom of False morning died,      5
Methought a Voice within the Tavern cried,
    "When all the Temple is prepared within,
Why nods the drowsy Worshipper outside?"

And, as the Cock crew, those who stood before
The Tavern shouted—"Open then the door!      10
    You know how little while we have to stay,
And, once departed, may return no more."

Now the New Year reviving old Desires,
The thoughtful Soul to Solitude retires,
    Where the WHITE HAND OF MOSES on the Bough      15
Puts out, and Jesus from the Ground suspires.

Iram indeed is gone with all his Rose,
And Jamshyd's Sev'n-ringed Cup where no one knows;
    But still a Ruby kindles in the Vine,
And many a Garden by the Water blows.      20

And David's lips are lockt; but in divine
High-piping Pehleví, with "Wine! Wine! Wine!
    Red Wine!"—the Nightingale cries to the Rose
That sallow cheek of hers to incarnadine.

Come, fill the Cup, and in the fire of Spring      25
Your Winter-garment of Repentance fling:
    The Bird of Time has but a little way
To flutter—and the Bird is on the Wing.

Whether at Naishápúr or Babylon,
Whether the Cup with sweet or bitter run,      30
    The Wine of Life keeps oozing drop by drop,
The Leaves of Life keep falling one by one.

Each Morn a thousand Roses brings, you say;
Yes, but where leaves the Rose of Yesterday?
And this first Summer month that brings the Rose          35
Shall take Jamshyd and Kaikobád away.

Well, let it take them! What have we to do
With Kaikobád the Great, or Kaikhosrú?
Let Zál and Rustum bluster as they will,
Or Hátim call to Supper—heed not you.                     40

With me along the strip of Herbage strown
That just divides the desert from the sown,
    Where name of Slave and Sultán is forgot—
And Peace to Mahmúd on his golden Throne!

A Book of Verses underneath the Bough,                    45
A Jug of Wine, a Loaf of Bread—and Thou
    Besides me singing in the Wilderness—
Oh, Wilderness were Paradise enow!

Some for the Glories of This World; and some
Sigh for the Prophet's Paradise to come;                  50
    Ah, take the Cash, and let the Credit go,
Nor heed the rumble of a distant Drum!

Look to the blowing Rose about us—"Lo,
Laughing," she says, "into the world I blow,
    At once the silken tassel of my Purse                 55
Tear, and its Treasure on the Garden throw."

And those who husbanded the Golden grain,
And those who flung it to the winds like Rain,
    Alike to no such aureate Earth are turned
As, buried once, Men want dug up again.                   60

The Worldly Hope men set their Hearts upon
Turns Ashes—or it prospers; and anon,
    Like Snow upon the Desert's dusty Face,
Lighting a little hour or two—is gone.

Think, in this battered Caravanserai                      65
Whose Portals are alternate Night and Day,
    How Sultán after Sultán with his Pomp
Abode his destined Hour, and went his way.

They say the Lion and the Lizard keep
The Courts where Jamshyd gloried and drank deep:          70
    And Bahrám, that great Hunter—the Wild Ass
Stamps o'er his Head, but cannot break his Sleep.

EDWARD FITZGERALD

*The Bettmann Archive*

I sometimes think that never blows so red
The Rose as where some buried Cæsar bled;
   That every Hyacinth the Garden wears 75
Dropt in her Lap from some once lovely Head.

And this reviving Herb whose tender Green
Fledges the River-Lip on which we lean—
   Ah, lean upon it lightly! for who knows
From what once lovely Lip it springs unseen! 80

Ah, my Belovéd, fill the cup that clears
To-DAY of past Regrets and future Fears:
   *To-morrow!*—Why, To-morrow I may be
Myself with Yesterday's Sev'n thousand Years.

For some we loved, the loveliest and the best 85
That from his Vintage rolling Time hath prest,
   Have drunk their Cup a Round or two before,
And one by one crept silently to rest.

And we, that now make merry in the Room
They left, and Summer dresses in new bloom, 90
   Ourselves must we beneath the Couch of Earth
Descend—ourselves to make a Couch—for whom?

Ah, make the most of what we yet may spend,
Before we too into the Dust descend;
   Dust into Dust, and under Dust, to lie, 95
Sans Wine, sans Song, sans Singer, and—sans End!

Alike for those who for TO-DAY prepare,
And those that after some TO-MORROW stare,
   A Muezzín from the Tower of Darkness cries,
"Fools! your Reward is neither Here nor There." 100

Why, all the Saints and Sages who discussed
Of the Two Worlds so wisely—they are thrust
   Like foolish Prophets forth; their Words to Scorn
Are scatter'd, and their Mouths are stopt with Dust.

Myself when young did eagerly frequent 105
Doctor and Saint, and heard great argument
   About it and about: but evermore
Came out by the same door where in I went.

With them the seed of Wisdom did I sow,
And with mine own hand wrought to make it grow; 110
   And this was all the Harvest that I reap'd—
"I came like Water, and like Wind I go."

Into this Universe, and *Why* not knowing,
Nor *Whence*, like Water willy-nilly flowing;
    And out of it, as Wind along the Waste,
I know not *Whither*, willy-nilly blowing.

What, without asking, hither hurried *Whence?*
And, without asking, *Whither* hurried hence!
    Oh, many a Cup of this forbidden Wine
Must drown the memory of that insolence!

Up from Earth's Centre through the Seventh Gate
I rose, and on the Throne of Saturn sate;
    And many a Knot unravel'd by the Road;
But not the Master-knot of Human Fate.

There was the Door to which I found no Key;
There was the Veil through which I might not see:
    Some little talk awhile of ME AND THEE
There was—and then no more of THEE AND ME.

Earth could not answer; nor the Seas that mourn
In flowing Purple, of their Lord forlorn;
    Nor rolling Heaven, with all his Signs revealed
And hidden by the sleeve of Night and Morn.

Then of the THEE IN ME who works behind
The Veil, I lifted up my hands to find
    A Lamp amid the Darkness; and I heard,
As from Without—"THE ME WITHIN THEE BLIND!"

Then to the Lip of this poor earthen Urn
I lean'd, the Secret of my Life to learn:
    And Lip to Lip it murmur'd—"While you live,
Drink!—for, once dead, you never shall return."

I think the Vessel, that with fugitive
Articulation answer'd, once did live,
    And drink; and Ah! the passive Lip I kiss'd,
How many Kisses might it take—and give!

For I remember stopping by the way
To watch a Potter thumping his wet Clay:
    And with its all-obliterated Tongue
It murmured—"Gently, Brother, gently pray!"

And has not such a Story from of Old
Down Man's successive generations roll'd,
    Of such a clod of saturated Earth
Cast by the Maker into Human mould?

And not a drop that from our Cups we throw
For Earth to drink of, but may steal below
   To quench the fire of Anguish in some Eye
There hidden—far beneath, and long ago.       155

As then the Tulip for her morning sup
Of Heav'nly Vintage from the soil looks up,
   Do you devoutly do the like, till Heav'n
To Earth invert you—like an empty Cup.

Perplext no more with Human or Divine,       160
To-morrow's tangle to the winds resign,
   And lose your fingers in the tresses of
The Cypress-slender Minister of Wine.

And if the Wine you drink, the Lip you press,
End in what All begins and ends in—Yes;       165
   Think then you are TO-DAY what YESTERDAY
You were—TO-MORROW you shall not be less.

So when the Angel of the darker Drink
At last shall find you by the river-brink,
   And, offering his Cup, invite your Soul       170
Forth to your Lips to quaff—you shall not shrink.

Why, if the Soul can fling the Dust aside,
And naked on the Air of Heaven ride,
   Were't not a Shame—were't not a Shame for him
In this clay carcase crippled to abide?       175

'Tis but a Tent where takes his one-day's rest
A Sultán to the realm of Death addrest;
   The Sultán rises, and the dark Ferrásh
Strikes, and prepares it for another Guest.

And fear not lest Existence closing your       180
Account, and mine, should know the like no more;
   The Eternal Sákí from that Bowl has pour'd
Millions of Bubbles like us, and will pour.

When You and I behind the Veil are past,
Oh but the long, long while the World shall last,       185
   Which of our Coming and Departure heeds
As the SEA's SELF should heed a pebble-cast.

A Moment's Halt—a momentary taste
Of BEING from the Well amid the Waste—
   And Lo!—the phantom Caravan has reach'd       190
The NOTHING it set out from—Oh, make haste!

Would you that spangle of Existence spend
About THE SECRET—quick about it, Friend!
A Hair perhaps divides the False and True—
And upon what, prithee, may Life depend?     195

A Hair perhaps divides the False and True;
Yes; and a single Alif were the clue—
Could you but find it—to the Treasure-house,
And peradventure to THE MASTER too;

Whose secret Presence, through Creation's veins     200
Running Quicksilver-like eludes your pains;
Taking all shapes from Máh to Máhi; and
They change and perish all—but He remains;

A moment guess'd—then back behind the Fold
Immerst of Darkness round the Drama roll'd     205
Which, for the Pastime of Eternity,
He does Himself contrive, enact, behold.

But if in vain, down on the stubborn floor
Of Earth, and up to Heav'n's unopening door,
You gaze TO-DAY, while You are You—how then     210
TO-MORROW, You when shall be You no more?

Waste not your Hour, nor in the vain pursuit
Of This and That endeavour and dispute;
Better be jocund with the fruitful Grape
Then sadden after none, or bitter, Fruit.     215

You know, my Friends, with what a brave Carouse
I made a Second Marriage in my house;
Divorced old barren Reason from my Bed,
And took the Daughter of the Vine to Spouse.

For "IS" and "IS-NOT" though with Rule and Line,     220
And "UP-AND-DOWN" by Logic I define,
Of all that one should care to fathom, I
Was never deep in anything but—Wine.

Ah, but my Computations, People say,
Reduced the Year to better reckoning?—Nay,     225
'Twas only striking from the Calendar
Unborn To-morrow, and dead Yesterday.

And lately, by the Tavern Door agape,
Came shining through the Dusk an Angel Shape
Bearing a Vessel on his Shoulder; and     230
He bid me taste of it; and 'twas—the Grape!

The Grape that can with Logic absolute
The Two-and-Seventy jarring Sects confute:
   The sovereign Alchemist that in a trice
Life's leaden metal into Gold transmute:     235

The mighty Mahmúd, Allah-breathing Lord,
That all the misbelieving and black Horde
   Of Fears and Sorrows that infest the Soul
Scatters before him with his whirlwind Sword.

Why, be this Juice the growth of God, who dare     240
Blaspheme the twisted tendril as a Snare?
   A Blessing, we should use it, should we not?
And if a Curse—why, then, Who set it there?

I must abjure the Balm of Life, I must,
Scared by some After-reckoning ta'en on trust,     245
   Or lured with Hope of some Diviner Drink,
To fill the Cup—when crumbled into Dust!

O threats of Hell and Hopes of Paradise!
One thing at least is certain,—This Life flies;
   One thing is certain and the rest is Lies;     250
The Flower that once has blown for ever dies.

Strange, is it not? that of the myriads who
Before us passed the door of Darkness through
   Not one returns to tell us of the Road
Which to discover we must travel too.     255

The Revelations of Devout and Learn'd
Who rose before us, and as Prophets burn'd,
   Are all but Stories, which, awoke from Sleep
They told their fellows, and to Sleep return'd.

I sent my Soul through the Invisible,     260
Some letter of that After-life to spell:
   And by and by my Soul return'd to me,
And answered "I Myself am Heav'n and Hell":

Heav'n but the Vision of fulfill'd Desire,
And Hell the Shadow from a Soul on fire,     265
   Cast on the Darkness into which Ourselves,
So late emerged from, shall so soon expire.

We are no other than a moving row
Of Magic Shadow-shapes that come and go
   Round with this Sun-illumined Lantern held     270
In Midnight by the Master of the Show;

But helpless Pieces of the Game He plays
Upon this Chequer-board of Nights and Days;
  Hither and thither moves, and checks, and slays,
And one by one back in the Closet lays.     275

The Ball no question makes of Ayes and Noes,
But Here or There as strikes the Player goes;
  And He that tossed you down into the Field,
*He* knows about it all—HE knows—HE knows!

The Moving Finger writes; and, having writ,     280
Moves on; nor all your Piety nor Wit
  Shall lure it back to cancel half a Line,
Nor all your Tears wash out a Word of it.

And that inverted Bowl they call the Sky,
Whereunder crawling coop'd we live and die,     285
  Lift not your hands to *It* for help—for It
As impotently rolls as you or I.

With Earth's first Clay They did the Last Man knead,
And there of the Last Harvest sowed the Seed:
  And the first Morning of Creation wrote     290
What the Last Dawn of Reckoning shall read.

YESTERDAY *This* Day's Madness did prepare;
To-MORROW's Silence, Triumph, or Despair:
  Drink! for you know not whence you came, nor why:
Drink, for you know not why you go, nor where.     295

I tell you this—When, started from the Goal,
Over the flaming shoulders of the Foal
  Of Heav'n Parwín and Mushtarí they flung,
In my predestined Plot of Dust and Soul

The Vine had struck a fibre: which about     300
If clings my Being—let the Dervish flout;
  Of my Base metal may be filed a Key,
That shall unlock the Door he howls without.

And this I know: whether the one True Light
Kindle to Love, or Wrath-consume me quite,     305
  One Flash of It within the Tavern caught
Better than in the Temple lost outright.

What! out of senseless Nothing to provoke
A conscious Something to resent the yoke
  Of unpermitted Pleasure, under pain     310
Of Everlasting Penalties, if broke!

What! from his helpless Creature be repaid
Pure Gold for what he lent him dross-allayed—
    Sue for a Debt we never did contract,
And cannot answer—Oh the sorry trade!                    315

Oh Thou, who didst with pitfall and with gin
Beset the Road I was to wander in,
    Thou wilt not with Predestined Evil round
Enmesh, and then impute my Fall to Sin!

Oh Thou, who Man of baser Earth didst make             320
And ev'n with Paradise devise the Snake:
    For all the Sin wherewith the Face of Man
Is blacken'd—Man's Forgiveness give—and take!

        .    .    .    .    .    .

As under cover of departing Day
Slunk hunger-stricken Ramazán away,                      325
    Once more within the Potter's house alone
I stood, surrounded by the Shapes of Clay.

Shapes of all Sorts and Sizes, great and small,
That stood along the floor and by the wall;
    And some loquacious Vessels were; and some          330
Listen'd perhaps, but never talk'd at all.

Said one among them—"Surely not in vain
My substance of the common Earth was ta'en
    And to this Figure moulded, to be broke,
Or trampled back to shapeless Earth again."             335

Then said a Second—"Ne'er a peevish Boy
Would break the Bowl from which he drank in joy;
    And He that with his hand the Vessel made
Will surely not in after Wrath destroy."

After a momentary silence spake                          340
Some Vessel of a more ungainly Make;
    "They sneer at me for leaning all awry:
What! did the Hand then of the Potter shake?"

Whereat some one of the loquacious Lot—
I think a Súfi pipkin—waxing hot—                        345
    "All this of Pot and Potter—Tell me, then,
Who is the Potter, pray, and who the Pot?"

"Why," said another, "Some there are who tell
Of one who threatens he will toss to Hell
    The luckless Pots he marr'd in making—Pish!         350
He's a Good Fellow, and 'twill all be well."

"Well," murmur'd one, "Let whoso make or buy,
My Clay with long Oblivion is gone dry:
But fill me with the old familiar Juice,
Methinks I might recover by and by."                   355

So while the Vessels one by one were speaking,
The little Moon look'd in that all were seeking:
And then they jogg'd each other, "Brother! Brother!
Now for the Porter's shoulder-knot a-creaking!"

 . . . . . .

Ah, with the Grape my fading Life provide,              360
And wash the Body whence the Life has died,
And lay me, shrouded in the living Leaf,
By some not unfrequented Garden-side.

That ev'n my buried Ashes such a snare
Of Vintage shall fling up into the Air                 365
As not a True-believer passing by
But shall be overtaken unaware.

Indeed the Idols I have loved so long
Have done my credit in this World much wrong:
Have drown'd my Glory in a shallow Cup,                370
And sold my Reputation for a Song.

Indeed, indeed, Repentance oft before
I swore—but was I sober when I swore?
And then and then came Spring, and Rose-in-hand
My thread-bare Penitence apieces tore.                375

And much as Wine has play'd the Infidel,
And robb'd me of my Robe of Honour—Well,
I wonder often what the Vintners buy
One half so precious as the stuff they sell.

Yet Ah, that Spring should vanish with the Rose!       380
That Youth's sweet-scented manuscript should close!
The Nightingàle that in the branches sang,
Ah whence, and whither flown again, who knows!

Would but the Desert of the Fountain yield
One glimpse—if dimly, yet indeed, reveal'd,            385
To which the fainting Traveller might spring,
As springs the trampled herbage of the field!

Would but some wingèd Angel ere too late
Arrest the yet unfolded Roll of Fate,
And make the stern Recorder otherwise                 390
Enregister, or quite obliterate!

Ah Love! could you and I with Him conspire
To grasp this sorry Scheme of Things entire,
    Would not we shatter it to bits—and then
Re-mould it nearer to the Heart's Desire!     395

. . . . . .

Yon rising Moon that looks for us again—
How oft hereafter will she wax and wane;
    How oft hereafter rising look for us
Through this same Garden—and for *one* in vain!

And when like her, oh Sákí, you shall pass     400
Among the Guests Star-scatter'd on the Grass,
    And in your joyous errand reach the spot
Where I made One—turn down an empty Glass!

                              TAMÁM

# C. M. Bowra

## FITZGERALD
### RUBÁIYÁT OF OMAR KHAYYÁM OF NAISHÁPÚR

Poetry was the art FitzGerald most loved and admired and wished to practice. Recognizing that he could not be a great poet in his own right, he decided to devote himself to the translation of poetry, and with this for the rest of his life he was mainly occupied. The three languages that concerned him were Greek, Spanish and, above all, Persian. Greek he had studied at school and at Cambridge, and knew with the thoroughness inculcated by a well-established discipline; Spanish and Persian he learned with the help of his friend Edward Byles Cowell, who was a man of most unusual gifts and, despite the lack of a formal education, took up Persian, Sanskrit, Norse, Italian, and Spanish, to end up as Professor of Sanskrit at Cambridge University. FitzGerald met him in 1846 and formed with him a friendship that lasted until his own death. Cowell was an excellent scholar, who combined a very wide range of reading with a thorough knowledge of the languages he read and a real enthusiasm for their literatures, and though FitzGerald was never to know Spanish or Persian so well as Cowell, he inspired FitzGerald with his own excitement, taught him how to study new languages, engaged in a long and scholarly correspondence on points of detail, and put him on to new topics when his ardor began to flag. It is a pity that in translating Greek, on which FitzGerald could so easily have got expert advice, he relied on his own judgment and sought for no Cowell to assist him. Cowell's direct contribution to Persian studies in England was not nearly so great as that of Sir William Jones or Browne or Nicholson, but indirectly, in his own sphere, he may have had more influence than any of them, since it is through him that one Persian poet became an established English classic.

In translating from Spanish and Greek, FitzGerald's methods were very much his own. He translated eight plays of Calderon, the *Agamemnon* of Aeschylus, and the *King*

*Oedipus* and the *Oedipus at Colonus* of Sophocles. The results are always readable, even distinguished, but the methods are certainly eccentric. First, FitzGerald thought nothing
of omitting passages that did not appeal to him. This might
not matter if the omitted passages were unimportant either
for their own sake or because they did not contribute to the
structure of a complete work of art. However, if they bored
FitzGerald, or for some reason he did not like them, they
were left out. Second, he took more than legitimate liberties
with the text when he fused two separate and quite different
plays of Sophocles' into a single play. The two plays about
Oedipus differ in manner, in intention, in tragic interest, in
the actual quality of their poetry, and to make them one,
FitzGerald had to leave out important characters, soften the
asperities of the first play, obscure the age of Oedipus, who is
a young man in one play and an old man in the other, spoil
the detective interest of the first play and the religious interest of the second. Third, FitzGerald disliked anything too
elaborate and mannered. If complexities got in the way,
FitzGerald pushed them aside. Fourth, FitzGerald was not a
lyrical poet, and the more melodious passages were beyond
his reach. His gift was much more for philosophic or reflective verse than for lyrical or even dramatic poetry, and
though his translations have always a noble resonance and
often a real sweep and splendor, they are not dramatic.

At the same time, FitzGerald needed the persona of some
other poet in order to discover and express himself, and at
least he saw that, whatever else a translation must do, it must
live as poetry in its own right. "Better a live sparrow than a
stuffed eagle" was his own comment on his work, and there is
much to be said for it. He did not necessarily have to accept
the views of the authors whom he translated; what really
stirred him was the kind of poetry that deals with general
ideas, but in such a way that they are transmuted and transfigured by an individual, imaginative treatment of them.
FitzGerald felt at home with this and made it fit his own
more troubled ideas; his error was to try to find it in Greek
and Spanish. He had still to find what he really needed, and it
came to him unexpectedly.

To realize himself as he wished, FitzGerald had to set
himself at some distance from his own life and society. In a
foreign language, in a distant past, in ways of thought that
had not been touched by Christianity, in ideas and ideals not
familiar to western Europe, in poetry richer and more

heavily loaded than any other known to him, FitzGerald found his release and his means of self-expression, and his final, complete, satisfying and inspiring refuge was the poetry of Persia.

As with Spanish, the first impulse came from Cowell, in the winter of 1852. Cowell later said of it; "I suggested Persian to him and guaranteed to teach the grammar in a day. The book was Jones' grammar, the illustrations in which are nearly all from Hafiz. FitzGerald was interested in these and went on to read Hafiz closely." FitzGerald carried the grammar, which was that published by William Jones in 1771, about with him for a year, translating the passages in it and writing to Cowell in January 1853: "The Persian is really a great amusement to me. . . . As to Jones' grammar, I have a sort of love for it." For the next eighteen months, he studied poems by Sa'di, Ferdowsi, Hafiz, Jāmi, and Attār, and read many books about Persia and its people. Then in the summer of 1854, with Cowell's help, he read Jāmi's "Salāmān and Absāl," and began to translate it, very much according to his own rules, omitting what did not interest him, elaborating what did, and giving much more care to some passages than to others. He told Cowell that he had "compacted the story into a producible drama and reduced the rhetoric into perhaps too narrow a compass." Yet though he thought his version the best thing that he had yet done, it did not meet all his inner needs. He did not like its more complex thoughts and said of it: "I shall bundle up the celestial and earthly shah so neatly that neither can be displeased, and no reader know which is which. Trust an Irishman where any confusion is wanted." But what he himself really wanted was not confusion but a clarity and firmness, which the poem did not give him, at least in the form that he desired: "I wanted to secure a palpable image of the deity *scrutinizing* the world he made and moves in *through the eyes* of his master-work, Man, and to edge and clench it with the sharp corner-stone of rhyme in that very word scrutinize." In the end, Fitz-Gerald produced a version of a poem whose actual story he found boring, but there was much else in it to excite him, and it has more sustained power than his translations from Greek and Spanish. Moreover, it tells much about himself, especially when he deals with its speculative and metaphysical passages. In his first version he translated the opening lines not only with an unusual power but with an unexpected fidelity to the original.

> *Oh Thou, whose memory quickens Lovers' souls,*
> *Whose fount of joy renews the Lover's tongue,*
> *Thy Shadow falls across the world, and they*
> *Bow down to it, and of the rich in beauty*
> *Thou art the riches that make Lovers sad.*
> *Not till thy secret beauty through the cheek*
> *Of Laila smite does she inflame Majnun,*
> *And not till thou have sugar'd Shirin's lip,*
> *The hearts of those two Lovers fill with blood.*

The mystical concept of love has caught FitzGerald's imagination, and he breaks out into words that would have been beyond his scope but for the Persian text in front of him. Over twenty years later, FitzGerald published a revised version of the poem, and his new translation of these opening lines shows how much he has thought about them and how much further he has moved from them:

> *Oh Thou, whose Spirit through this universe*
> *In which Thou doest involve thyself diffused,*
> *Shall so perchance irradiate human clay*
> *That men, suddenly dazzled, lose themselves*
> *In ecstasy before a mortal shrine*
> *Whose Light is but a shade of the Divine;*
> *Not till thy Secret Beauty through the cheek*
> *Of Laila smite doth she inflame Majnùn;*
> *And not till Thou have kindled Shirin's Eyes*
> *The hearts of those two Rivals swell with blood.*

Some of the first sweep and power and ecstasy have gone, and yet FitzGerald is more at home in his new version, more at ease with the idea of love as a divine power working through the universe. "Salāmān and Absāl" opened new vistas to him, and, as he slowly grew accustomed to them, he made them fit his inner longings more closely.

For FitzGerald the trouble with "Salāmān and Absāl" is that he was not equally interested in the whole poem throughout. He conscientiously translated much of it, but the narrative portions called for talents that he did not possess, and he made a grave error of judgment when, for the sake of variety, he put some passages into the jaunty meter of "Hiawatha," for which his original provided no excuse. The poem introduced him to a new kind of religious poetry, and it was this that fascinated him and kept him to it, but meanwhile he had found something else of a different kind, which was to satisfy much more of his nature and to excite the full

exercise of his genius. In July 1856, FitzGerald told Tennyson: "I have been the last fortnight with the Cowells. We
read some curious infidel and Epicurean tetrastichs by a
Persian of the eleventh century—as savage against destiny,
etc., as Manfred—but mostly of Epicurean pathos of this
kind—'drink for the moon will often come round to look for
us in this garden and find us not.'" Behind this lay Cowell's
discovery, in the Bodleian Library at Oxford, of a manuscript
of Omar Khayyám written in 1460 on thick yellow paper, in
purple-black ink, profusely powdered with gold. It contains
158 quatrains, which Cowell copied out and sent to Fitz-
Gerald. FitzGerald was fascinated by them, collected more
information from the French scholar Garcin de Tassy, got
hold of a Calcutta text of them, and in the summer of 1857
could read no other books. At first he played with the idea of
translating it into rhymed Latin verse in the medieval manner, and a specimen of this was sent to Cowell. It was probably no more than a joke, though FitzGerald wrote to
Cowell: "You will think me a perfectly Aristophanic old man
when I tell you how many lines of Omar I could not help
running into such bad Latin." By the autumn of the same
year he had finished the first draft of his translation into
rhymed English verse, and in 1859 he published anonymously, in an edition of 250 copies, bound in brown paper,
his "Rubáiyát of Omar Khayyám," at the price of one
shilling a copy.

At first it attracted no notice whatsoever. For two years it
lay on the shelves of Quaritch, the publisher, who, giving up
all hope of selling it, dumped the copies into his bargain box
at the price of one penny each. Some unknown man of great
perception saw it there, bought a copy, and showed it to
Dante Gabriel Rossetti, who returned to the shop with his
friend Swinburne, to find themselves charged two pence a
copy. As Swinburne wrote: "We were extravagant enough
to invest in a few more copies at that scandalous price." From
Swinburne and Rossetti news of the book was passed to
William Morris, Burne Jones and Ruskin, and by 1868 the
book appeared as a rarity in Quaritch's catalogue at the price
of three shillings and sixpence, and FitzGerald wrote to him
to say that the price made him blush. While the pre-Raphaelites took up the poem in England, the American scholar
and critic, Charles Eliot Norton, saw Burne Jones' copy and
made the poem known in the United States. In all this,
nobody was more surprised than FitzGerald, who had not
attached his name to the book and read with pleasure the

statement in a newspaper that it was the work of "a certain Reverend Edward FitzGerald, who lived somewhere in Norfolk and was fond of boating." Off and on the poem was to occupy FitzGerald for the rest of his life. He published new editions of it, each greatly revised, in 1868, 1872, and 1879. It made his name in select circles, but he did not live to see the enormous popularity it had in the last ten years of the last century and the first twenty years of this. Produced in every shape and size and print, ornamented often with the most startling or most inappropriate illustrations, given freely as a Christmas present by elderly relations to their nephews and nieces, parodied and copied and maltreated from comic papers to Rudyard Kipling, it shared a strange popularity with other vastly inferior works which were thought to make no claims on the intelligence of their recipients. It was set to music with luscious accompaniments suited to contralto voices and thought to reflect all the lure and luxury of the East. It even became a symbol for those who paid more than serious attention to food and drink, and the Omar Khayyám Club in London, with its ceremonious and carefully chosen dinners, passes far beyond the poet's own satisfaction with a loaf of bread and a jug of wine. FitzGerald would have been amazed, amused, perhaps even a little shocked. It was not in the expectation of such a future that he translated the quatrains of the astronomer-poet of Persia.

FitzGerald was himself somewhat surprised that Omar should appeal to him so much as he did. Omar was a man of strong appetites and a strong predilection for wine; FitzGerald was a vegetarian and seldom drank anything stronger than beer. Omar did not attempt to hide his taste for women; FitzGerald was shy of them and liked them only for their conversation. Omar played a large part in public affairs; FitzGerald was a recluse even in his own small section of rural society. Omar speculated boldly about the universe; FitzGerald, at least outwardly, conformed to the Church of England, though it must be admitted that his local clergyman remonstrated with him about his laxity. FitzGerald was attracted to Omar as to a poet quite outside his previous experience, and all the more seductive because he lived in a world so unlike FitzGerald's own and had so marked and so powerful a personality. He wrote to Cowell: "I thought him from the first the most remarkable of the Persian poets, and you keep finding out in him evidences of logical fancy which I had not dreamed of." That FitzGerald should prefer Omar to Hafiz or Ferdowsi indicates that this usually balanced and sagacious critic had been swept off his feet, and it was not only the quality of Omar's poetry that had done it. Fitz-Gerald had a strong taste for what he here calls "logical fancy," and by it he means something akin to metaphysical poetry, which treats ideas imaginatively and enriches and expounds them through symbols and images. He had liked this in Calderon, and he liked it in Omar, but behind it was something else, which exerted a stronger attraction on him and about which he was not quite so happy.

FitzGerald owed his knowledge of Omar to Cowell, but he knew that Cowell, who was a devout member of the Church of England, could not take Omar entirely to his heart. He was quite frank about it and wrote to Cowell in December 1857: "In truth, I take old Omar more as my property than yours; he and I are more akin, are we not? You see all his beauty, you don't feel with him in some respects as I do. I think you would almost feel obliged to leave out the part of Hamlet in representing him to your audience, for fear of mischief. Now I do not wish to show Hamlet at his maddest; but mad he must be shown, or he is no Hamlet at all . . . I think these free opinions are less dangerous in an old Mahometan or an old Roman (like Lucretius) than when they are returned to by those who have lived on happier food." FitzGerald was right in thinking that Cowell felt some responsibility for introducing Omar to FitzGerald: many years later, in 1898, after FitzGerald's death, when the Persian scholar, Edward Heron-Allen, proposed to dedicate to him a book on Omar and FitzGerald, Cowell wrote:

> I yield to no one in my admiration of Omar's poetry as literature, but I cannot join in the Omar cult, and it would be wrong in me to pretend to profess it. So I am deeply interested in Lucretius . . . but here again I only admire Lucretius as "literature." I feel this especially about Omar Khayyám, as I unwittingly incurred a grave responsibility when I introduced his poems to my old friend in 1856. I admire Omar as I admire Lucretius, but I cannot take him as a guide. In these grave matters I prefer to go to Nazareth, not to Naishápúr.

Cowell was quite right. What fascinated FitzGerald in Omar was not merely its strangeness, nor its purely literary quality, nor even its metaphysical ingenuity, but its point of view. This appealed to him more deeply than the Olympian grandeur of Sophocles or the mystical fervor of Calderon, or the philosophic sweep of "Salāmān and Absāl." No doubt he had many serious reservations about Omar's philosophy and would certainly neither admit nor think that he accepted it in its entirety. No doubt he believed that he liked it simply for its purely poetical qualities, irrespective of its sentiments, though this is not an easy position to maintain and usually conceals an element of self-deception somewhere. Yet Omar fascinated FitzGerald in more than one way, and the fascination was by no means merely aesthetic. FitzGerald was at heart a practicing epicurean, in his love of a quiet life with its tranquil consolations, and untroubled security, enjoying the passing moment and not looking beyond it, free alike from action and from the decisions that action demands. More than this, as a modern epicurean, FitzGerald could not but speculate about the nature of the universe and its government. His Christian upbringing and allegiance meant little to him, and in some moods he saw an encompassing darkness, to whose central mystery there was no clue, but which raised awkward questions and prompted various answers. The inconsistencies and the contradictions in his agnosticism found an echo in Omar, and when he turned the quatrains into English, the strength and the passion of his words show how fully Fitz-Gerald was at home. On one side there is a profound skepticism, which asserts that it is useless to ask questions because no answers can be found to them:

> Why, all the Saints and Sages who discussed
> Of the Two Worlds so wisely—they are thrust
>     Like foolish Prophets forth; their Words to Scorn
>     Are scatter'd, and their Mouths are stopt with Dust

On the other side is a positive conviction that the universe has its own ghostly guidance, which is indeed alien to any teaching of religion. In an early edition we find:

> Then to the rolling heav'n itself I cried,
> Asking, 'What Lamp has Destiny to guide
>     Her little Children stumbling in the Dark?'
>     And—'A blind Understanding!' Heav'n replied.

FitzGerald may have had reservations and qualifications, and certainly did not treat literally all that Omar said and he himself translated, but how seriously he treated him and liked him can be seen from his association of Omar with Lucretius: "Men of subtle, strong and cultivated intellect, fine imagination, and hearts passionate for truth and justice, who justly revolted from their country's false religion and . . .

with no better revelation to guide them, had yet made a law to themselves." The words "with no better revelation to guide them" are a saving clause, which FitzGerald no doubt puts in sincerely, but equally there is no doubt about his admiration of Omar, as of Lucretius, for his bold and independent outlook, and though he does not say that he himself shares it, he would hardly display this degree of admiration if it did not in some respects appeal to him.

FitzGerald's treatment of Omar has its characteristic idiosyncrasies. He has been accused of adding and falsifying, of making too much or too little of what he found before him. He certainly treated Omar on his usual principles of translation, determined that "at all cost a thing must live," but in his curious way he was more faithful than he is commonly thought to have been. In the final form his poem has 101 stanzas, and it has been calculated that of these:

> Forty-nine are faithful translations of single quatrains to be found in the Bodleian MS., copied for him by Cowell, or in the copy of the text which he got from Calcutta.
>
> Forty-four are traceable to more than one quatrain and may be called composite, but not in the last resort unfaithful.
>
> Two are inspired by quatrains found by FitzGerald in the French version of J. B. Nicholas, published in 1867.
>
> Two are quatrains reflecting the whole spirit of the original poem, but may be classed as FitzGerald's own inventions.
>
> Four are traceable to other poems by other poets, notably Attār and Hafiz.

At least FitzGerald treated Omar with more respect than he treated Sophocles, and even his additions have been skillfully adapted to the dominating tone and temper.

Examples of FitzGerald's methods will illustrate what he had in mind and what success he achieved. First, he took from Hafiz the quatrain:

> *Before the phantom of False morning died,*
> *Methought a Voice within the Tavern cried,*
> *"When all the temple is prepared within,*
> *Why nods the drowsy Worshipper outside?"*

FitzGerald has completely changed the context and therefore the intention of the lines, but they fit very well into his scheme, and he puts them in at this point because they provide a useful link to get his subject going at the start. Secondly, from Attār comes:

> Earth could not answer; not the Seas that mourn
> In flowing Purple, of their Lord forlorn;
> Nor rolling Heaven, with all his signs revealed
> And hidden by the sleeve of Night and Morn.

This gives a new strength and majesty to the sense of utter ignorance that afflicts mankind, and fits very well in Fitz-Gerald's presentation of it. Thirdly, FitzGerald composed verses of his own, which reflect and summarize the general spirit of Omar, but are not based on his actual words. Such is the quatrain:

> Iram indeed is gone with all his Rose,
> And Jamshyd's Seven-ringed Cup where no one knows;
> But still a Ruby kindles in the Vine,
> And many a Garden by the Water blows.

This little distillation of poetry in the master's manner is needed in its place to provide a transition to the theme of wine, and FitzGerald's words are a remarkable example of *pastiche*. He has so absorbed Omar that he speaks like him in his own voice.

Apart from these small and successful aberrations from the text, FitzGerald treated it in other ways, which may seem to be high-handed but are also justified by success. First, he chose from a larger number available 101 quatrains, and omitted those that did not appeal to him. He then arranged his selection to suit his own design. This was permissible because the original quatrains were single, separate poems, which could be arranged in any order because each stood in its own right and was not part of any unifying design. But FitzGerald, who treated Omar seriously, decided to make a single poem of the various quatrains, because this would stress their underlying philosophy. There is a real development through the poem from the dawn, with which it starts, to the resigned melancholy of the end. This development has not the logic of an argument or an apology; it follows a natural sequence of emotional states, as the poem passes from the ignorance and insecurity of man to the consolations of the grape. FitzGerald's "Rubáiyát" is by his own choice and skill not a mere string of stanzas, of which almost any might take the place of any other, but, as he himself calls it, "something of an Eclogue, with perhaps less than an equal proportion of the 'drink and make merry,' which (genuine or not) recurs over frequently in the original." Secondly, FitzGerald reduced all the stanzas to the same shape and to the same scheme of rhyme. He kept the unit of four lines, made all of them the same length, and rhymed the first, second, and fourth lines, leaving the third unrhymed. The result is remarkably effective, and we can see what FitzGerald means when he says that "the penultimate line seems to lift and suspend the wave that falls over into the last." The stanza so formed is irrevocably associated with the names of Omar and FitzGerald and has found a lasting place in English poetry, being used even for so unexpected a task as Mackail's translation of the "Odyssey."

At the same time FitzGerald certainly played some minor tricks with the text, and these throw some light on his ulterior intentions. Take, for instance, a famous and much quoted stanza:

> *Oh Thou, who Man of baser Earth didst make,*
> *And ev'n with Paradise devise the Snake:*
> *For all the Sin wherewith the Face of Man*
> *Is blacken'd—Man's Forgiveness give—and take!*

Asked much later about the last line, Cowell wrote in 1903:

> There is no original for the line about the snake; I have looked for it in vain in Nicholas. FitzGerald mistook the meaning of *giving* and *accepting* . . . and so invented his last line out of his own mistake. I wrote to him about it when I was in Calcutta, but he never cared to alter it.

Fortunately we have FitzGerald's answer at the time to Cowell's criticism:

> I have certainly an idea that this *is* said somewhere in the Calcutta manuscript. But it is very likely I may have construed, or remembered, erroneously. But I do not *add* dirt to Omar's face.

In fact FitzGerald got the idea not from Omar but from Attār, and so absorbed it that he forgot the source. But it is exactly the kind of effect that he seeks and loves, and we can understand that, having done it, he was not going to withdraw or alter it.

FitzGerald altered his poem greatly in the four editions of it which he published at intervals, and though we may feel that many of his corrections take away some of the first freshness, there is no doubt that FitzGerald, who was an

excellent critic of his own work, made them with due de-
liberation because they represented more closely the poetical
effect that he wished to produce. In each he tends to get
farther away from the original text and to speak more
confidently in his own voice. Take, for instance, one quatrain
on the theme of drinking while we may. In the first edition it
runs:

> *While the Rose blows along the River Brink*
> *With old Khayyám the Ruby Vintage drink:*
> *And when the Angel with the darker Draught*
> *Draws up to Thee—take that, and do not shrink.*

In the second edition this has been remodelled:

> *So when at last the Angel of the Drink*
> *Of Darkness finds you by the river-brink,*
> *And, proffering his cup, invites your Soul*
> *Forth to your lips to quaff it—do not shrink.*

The rose by the river and the whole conception of drinking
with old Khayyám have disappeared, and the stanza is
devoted to the single, powerful image of the draught offered
by the angel of death. It is more sombre, more pointed, more
concentrated. Then in the fourth and final form the quatrain
reads:

> *So when that Angel of the darker Drink*
> *At last shall find you by the river-brink,*
> *And, offering his cup, invite your Soul*
> *Forth to your lips to quaff—you shall not shrink.*

The Angel has become more remote and more mysterious,
and the last line is now not a command but a prophecy. This
is what will happen, and there is no gainsaying it. FitzGerald
has hardened and condensed his style to get this effect, and
there is no doubt that he rewrote it because it said what he
really wished to say.

In making his alterations FitzGerald had a clear notion of
what the style of his poem should be, and in this he presents a
marked independence from any Victorian practice. The
Victorians suffered from a taste for archaic, literary words.
In their rejection of the neatness and point sought so ardently
by the eighteenth century, they sought to convey an air of
romance by certain affectations of speech—not merely medieval words long passed out of currency, but inversions, such
as putting the adjective after the nouns, or twisting the order
of words to make them look more impressive. They did this

because they thought that the poetry of their immediate predecessors was unduly prosaic, and they thought that this was a good way to counter and correct its influence. Fitz-Gerald did not agree with them. He was no great admirer of Victorian poetry, and thought that most of it compared poorly with even such work as that of Crabbe. On the other hand, though he saw much to admire in Pope and Cowper, he felt that they did not belong to his world and could not teach him anything, and in this he was certainly right so far as his love of exotic situations and striking fancies was concerned. The result was that he stood in a middle position between the dominating styles of the eighteenth and nineteenth century, and instead of being perplexed and defeated by this, he took triumphant advantage of it. He was a man of the nineteenth century in his romantic affection for the past, for strange places and strange names, for flaunting statements about the nature of reality, for rich, decorative effects, for the graces and subtleties of nature. But he had his roots in the eighteenth century—in his love of point and paradox, of sharp epigram and lyrical wit, of personal statements that tell the truth in a concise and striking way without any adventitious ornament. His peculiar, indeed his unique success was that he fused these two sides of his nature into a single style. At one time the nineteenth century seems to dominate in such a stanza as:

> *One Moment in Annihilation's Waste,*
> *One Moment, of the Well of Life to taste—*
> *The Stars are setting and the Caravan*
> *Starts for the Dawn of Nothing—Oh, make haste!*

or

> *I sometimes think that never blows so red*
> *The Rose as where some buried Caesar bled;*
> *That every Hyacinth the Garden wears*
> *Dropt in her Lap from some once lovely Head.*

Here indeed FitzGerald speaks with the luxurious melancholy of his time and finds an imagery that suggests vast distances in space or long tracts of time, but he casts his words in a strict and economical mold. Nothing is otiose or flabby. At other times the eighteenth century comes to the fore, and in the background we hear the disciplined march of the heroic couplet:

> *Myself when young did eagerly frequent*
> *Doctor and Saint, and heard great argument*

> *About it and about: but evermore*
> *Came out by the same door where in I went.*

or

> *Indeed, indeed Repentance oft before*
> *I swore—but was I sober when I swore?*
> *And then and then came Spring, and Rose-in-hand*
> *My thread-bare Penitence apieces tore.*

In such cases there is much that Pope would have liked, but FitzGerald is richer and warmer and less self-conscious. And though we may distinguish the two strands in him, the important fact is that he unites them in a style that is at once highly colored and strictly drilled, bold in its sweep and yet careful of every step that it takes, straightforward as common speech and yet loaded with imaginative association at every point, reckless and ironical, outspoken and controlled, passionate and witty. All this FitzGerald learned from Omar, but he learned it so well and made it so intimate a part of himself that he stands in his own right as a unique poetical personality.

Through Omar, FitzGerald found the deliverance that he needed from certain misgivings and uncertainties. Of course he did not take everything that Omar said at its face value, and was very far from preaching a gospel of drink. For him no doubt the vine and its products were symbols of the happiness that he hoped to find, and indeed often found, by avoiding the troubles and entanglements of an active life. As such they enabled him to state with unusual power the troubles that gnawed his spirit, as indeed they gnawed the spirits of other men, but were not easily publicized in Victorian England. The complacent religion of his time forced him into opposition because he saw that it did not meet his real spiritual needs, and, though in his daily life he treated it with a polite tolerance, in his inner self rebellious powers were at work, urging him to complain about the scheme of things that aroused not merely his discontent but his condemnation. He felt, as the Greeks felt, that human life was a shadowy affair at the mercy of dark, incalculable forces, and he found in Omar his instrument to speak of his disillusion and his distress. In this respect he was the forerunner and almost the guide of some Victorian rebels, who did not share the current optimism and reverted to those denunciations that Shakespeare gives to some of his characters when their worlds are shattered around them. Yet he differs greatly from them. He has much more tenderness and love of life than James Thomson in the prolonged gloom of "The City of Dreadful Night"; his outlook is much gentler and easier to understand than Housman's acrid and disdainful vision:

> *It is in truth iniquity on high*
> *To cheat our sentenced souls of aught they crave,*
> *And mar the merriment as you and I*
> *Fare on our long fool's-errand to the grave;*

he gives far more scope to human effort and choice than do Thomas Hardy's Spirits of the Years:

> *O Immanence, That reasonest not*
> *In putting forth all things begot,*
> *Thou build'st thy house in space—for what?*
>
> *O loveless, hateless! past the sense*
> *Of kindly eyed benevolence,*
> *To what tune danceth this immense?*

FitzGerald felt the force of these questions, but shrank from answering them in his own voice or with any final assurance. His translation of Omar is the record of his quarrel with himself, of the conflict between his natural desire to take things as they come and not complain, and something that forced him to look away from the creeds and assurances of his youth and to find some sort of answer in Omar's epicurean nihilism. At least this left the human affections intact and gave ·a brief, if precarious, dignity to his pleasures. If pressed about his views, FitzGerald would have said that he did not know what they were, and that much of Omar was not really acceptable to him. Yet in his inner self, away from the compromises and falsities of his time, he found something that caught his heart and his imagination. In him the Victorian melancholy was set on a philosophic basis, where it could be exorcized only by a recognition that what we have is after all worth having, even if its career is brief and uncertain. At times he might wish to get more than this, to break out into complaint and denunciation, but in the end he knew that it was useless, and it is this sense of his human limitations which gives a special tenderness to some of his darker foreboding and doubts:

> *Ah Love! could thou and I with Him conspire*
> *To grasp this sorry Scheme of Things entire,*
> *Would not we shatter it to bits, and then*
> *Re-mould it nearer to the Heart's Desire!*

Yet Omar taught him that such questions, and the desires that made him ask them, were in the end futile, and that it was better to enjoy things as they come. This was the lesson that FitzGerald, certainly an apt and ready pupil, learned from his master and transformed into his own high poetry. It was because he was able to identify himself with Omar on this central issue that he wrote his masterpiece, and fulfilled a wish which he had expressed in 1851 before he had heard of the "Rubáiyát":

> I was thinking . . . to myself how it was fame enough to have written but one song—air, or words—which should in after days solace the sailor at the wheel, or the soldier in foreign places! to be taken up into the life of England.

His prayer was answered on a scale he could never have imagined, and it was Persia that answered it for him.

# ALFRED, LORD TENNYSON
## [1809–1892]

## The Two Voices

A still small voice spake unto me,
"Thou art so full of misery,
Were it not better not to be?"

Then to the still small voice I said:
"Let me not cast in endless shade     5
What is so wonderfully made."

To which the voice did urge reply;
"To-day I saw the dragon-fly
Come from the wells where he did lie.

"An inner impulse rent the veil     10
Of his old husk: from head to tail
Came out clear plates of sapphire mail.

"He dried his wings: like gauze they grew;
Thro' crofts and pastures wet with dew
A living flash of light he flew."     15

I said, "When first the world began,
Young Nature thro' five cycles ran,
And in the sixth she moulded man.

"She gave him mind, the lordliest
Proportion, and, above the rest,     20
Dominion in the head and breast."

Thereto the silent voice replied;
"Self-blinded are you by your pride;
Look up thro' night; the world is wide.

"This truth within thy mind rehearse,     25
That in a boundless universe
Is boundless better, boundless worse.

"Think you this mould of hopes and fears
Could find no statelier than his peers
In yonder hundred million spheres?"     30

It spake, moreover, in my mind:
"Tho' thou wert scatter'd to the wind,
Yet is there plenty of the kind."

Then did my response clearer fall:
"No compound of this earthly ball     35
Is like another, all in all."

To which he answer'd scoffingly:
"Good soul! suppose I grant it thee,
Who'll weep for thy deficiency?

"Or will one beam be less intense,     40
When thy peculiar difference
Is cancell'd in the world of sense?"

I would have said, "Thou canst not know,"
But my full heart, that work'd below,
Rain'd thro' my sight its overflow.     45

Again the voice spake unto me:
"Thou art so steep'd in misery,
Surely 't were better not to be.

"Thine anguish will not let thee sleep,
Nor any train of reason keep;     50
Thou canst not think, but thou wilt weep."

I said, "The years with change advance;
If I make dark my countenance,
I shut my life from happier chance.

"Some turn this sickness yet might take,     55
Ev'n yet." But he: "What drug can make
A wither'd palsy cease to shake?"

I wept, "Tho' I should die, I know
That all about the thorn will blow
In tufts of rosy-tinted snow;     60

"And men, thro' novel spheres of thought
Still moving after truth long sought,
Will learn new things when I am not."

"Yet," said the secret voice, "some time,
Sooner or later, will gray prime     65
Make thy grass hoar with early rime.

"Not less swift souls that yearn for light,
Rapt after heaven's starry flight,
Would sweep the tracts of day and night.

"Not less the bee would range her cells,     70
The furzy prickle fire the dells,
The foxglove cluster dappled bells."

ALFRED, LORD TENNYSON

*This photograph he referred to as*
*"The Dirty Monk"*

*The Bettmann Archive*

I said that "All the years invent;
Each month is various to present
The world with some development.                          75

"Were this not well, to bide mine hour,
Tho' watching from a ruin'd tower
How grows the day of human power?"

"The highest-mounted mind," he said,
"Still sees the sacred morning spread                     80
The silent summit overhead.

"Will thirty seasons render plain
Those lonely lights that still remain,
Just breaking over land and main?

"Or make that morn, from his cold crown                   85
And crystal silence creeping down,
Flood with full daylight glebe and town?

"Forerun thy peers, thy time, and let
Thy feet, millenniums hence, be set
In midst of knowledge, dream'd not yet.                   90

"Thou hast not gain'd a real height,
Nor art thou nearer to the light,
Because the scale is infinite.

" 'T were better not to breathe or speak,
Than cry for strength, remaining weak,                    95
And seem to find, but still to seek.

"Moreover, but to seem to find
Asks what thou lackest, thought resign'd,
A healthy frame, a quiet mind."

I said, "When I am gone away,                             100
'He dared not tarry,' men will say,
Doing dishonor to my clay."

"This is more vile," he made reply,
"To breathe and loathe, to live and sigh,
Than once from dread of pain to die.                      105

"Sick art thou—a divided will
Still heaping on the fear of ill
The fear of men, a coward still.

"Do men love thee? Art thou so bound
To men, that how thy name may sound                       110
Will vex thee lying underground?

"The memory of the wither'd leaf
In endless time is scarce more brief
Than of the garner'd Autumn-sheaf.

"Go, vexed Spirit, sleep in trust;
The right ear, that is fill'd with dust,
Hears little of the false or just."

"Hard task, to pluck resolve," I cried,
"From emptiness and the waste wide
Of that abyss, or scornful pride!

"Nay—rather yet that I could raise
One hope that warm'd me in the days
While still I yearn'd for human praise.

"When, wide in soul and bold of tongue,
Among the tents I paused and sung,
The distant battle flash'd and rung.

"I sung the joyful Pæan clear,
And, sitting, burnish'd without fear
The brand, the buckler, and the spear—

"Waiting to strive a happy strife,
To war with falsehood to the knife,
And not to lose the good of life—

"Some hidden principle to move,
To put together, part and prove,
And mete the bounds of hate and love—

"As far as might be, to carve out
Free space for every human doubt,
That the whole mind might orb about—

"To search thro' all I felt or saw,
The springs of life, the depths of awe,
And reach the law within the law;

"At least, not rotting like a weed,
But, having sown some generous seed,
Fruitful of further thought and deed,

"To pass, when Life her light withdraws,
Not void of righteous self-applause,
Nor in a merely selfish cause—

"In some good cause, not in mine own,
To perish, wept for, honor'd, known,
And like a warrior overthrown;

"Whose eyes are dim with glorious tears,
When, soil'd with noble dust, he hears
His country's war-song thrill his ears:

"Then dying of a mortal stroke,
What time the foeman's line is broke,                155
And all the war is roll'd in smoke."

"Yea!" said the voice, "thy dream was good,
While thou abodest in the bud.
It was the stirring of the blood.

"If Nature put not forth her power                   160
About the opening of the flower,
Who is it that could live an hour?

"Then comes the check, the change, the fall,
Pain rises up, old pleasures pall.
There is one remedy for all.                         165

"Yet hadst thou, thro' enduring pain,
Link'd month to month with such a chain
Of knitted purport, all were vain.

"Thou hadst not between death and birth
Dissolved the riddle of the earth.                   170
So were thy labor little-worth.

"That men with knowledge merely play'd,
I told thee—hardly nigher made,
Tho' scaling slow from grade to grade;

"Much less this dreamer, deaf and blind,             175
Named man, may hope some truth to find,
That bears relation to the mind.

"For every worm beneath the moon
Draws different threads, and late and soon
Spins, toiling out his own cocoon.                   180

"Cry, faint not; either Truth is born
Beyond the polar gleam forlorn,
Or in the gateways of the morn.

"Cry, faint not, climb: the summits slope
Beyond the furthest flights of hope,                 185
Wrapt in dense cloud from base to cope.

"Sometimes a little corner shines,
As over rainy mist inclines
A gleaming crag with belts of pines.

"I will go forward, sayest thou,                    190
I shall not fail to find her now.
Look up, the fold is on her brow.

"If straight thy track, or if oblique,
Thou know'st not. Shadows thou dost strike,
Embracing cloud, Ixion-like;                        195

"And owning but a little more
Than beasts, abidest lame and poor,
Calling thyself a little lower

"Than angels. Cease to wail and brawl!
Why inch by inch to darkness crawl?                 200
There is one remedy for all."

"O dull, one-sided voice," said I,
"Wilt thou make everything a lie,
To flatter me that I may die?

"I know that age to age succeeds,                   205
Blowing a noise of tongues and deeds,
A dust of systems and of creeds.

"I cannot hide that some have striven,
Achieving calm, to whom was given
The joy that mixes man with Heaven;                 210

"Who, rowing hard against the stream,
Saw distant gates of Eden gleam,
And did not dream it was a dream;

"But heard, by secret transport led,
Ev'n in the charnels of the dead,                   215
The murmur of the fountain-head—

"Which did accomplish their desire,
Bore and forebore, and did not tire,
Like Stephen, an unquenched fire.

"He heeded not reviling tones,                      220
Nor sold his heart to idle moans,
Tho' cursed and scorn'd, and bruised with stones;

"But looking upward, full of grace,
He pray'd, and from a happy place
God's glory smote him on the face."                 225

The sullen answer slid betwixt:
"Not that the grounds of hope were fix'd,
The elements were kindlier mix'd."

I said, "I toil beneath the curse,
But, knowing not the universe,        230
I fear to slide from bad to worse.

"And that, in seeking to undo
One riddle, and to find the true,
I knit a hundred others new.

"Or that this anguish fleeting hence,    235
Unmanacled from bonds of sense,
Be fix'd and froz'n to permanence:

"For I go, weak from suffering here;
Naked I go, and void of cheer:
What is it that I may not fear?"        240

"Consider well," the voice replied,
"His face, that two hours since hath died;
Wilt thou find passion, pain or pride?

"Will he obey when one commands?
Or answer should one press his hands?    245
He answers not, nor understands.

"His palms are folded on his breast;
There is no other thing express'd
But long disquiet merged in rest.

"His lips are very mild and meek;        250
Tho' one should smite him on the cheek,
And on the mouth, he will not speak.

"His little daughter, whose sweet face
He kiss'd, taking his last embrace,
Becomes dishonor to her race—          255

"His sons grow up that bear his name,
Some grow to honor, some to shame,—
But he is chill to praise or blame.

"He will not hear the north-wind rave,
Nor, moaning, household shelter crave    260
From winter rains that beat his grave.

"High up the vapors fold and swim;
About him broods the twilight dim;
The place he knew forgetteth him."

"If all be dark, vague voice," I said,    265
"These things are wrapt in doubt and dread,
Nor canst thou show the dead are dead.

"The sap dries up: the plant declines.
A deeper tale my heart divines.
Know I not Death? the outward signs?     270

"I found him when my years were few;
A shadow on the graves I knew,
And darkness in the village yew.

"From grave to grave the shadow crept;
In her still place the morning wept;     275
Touch'd by his feet the daisy slept.

"The simple senses crown'd his head:
'Omega! thou art Lord,' they said,
'We find no motion in the dead.'

"Why, if man rot in dreamless ease,     280
Should that plain fact, as taught by these,
Not make him sure that he shall cease?

"Who forged that other influence,
That heat of inward evidence,
By which he doubts against the sense?     285

"He owns the fatal gift of eyes,
That read his spirit blindly wise,
Not simple as a thing that dies.

"Here sits he shaping wings to fly;
His heart forebodes a mystery;     290
He names the name Eternity.

"That type of Perfect in his mind
In Nature can he nowhere find.
He sows himself on every wind.

"He seems to hear a Heavenly Friend,     295
And thro' thick veils to apprehend
A labor working to an end.

"The end and the beginning vex
His reason: many things perplex,
With motions, checks, and counterchecks.     300

"He knows a baseness in his blood
At such strange war with something good,
He may not do the thing he would.

"Heaven opens inward, chasms yawn,
Vast images in glimmering dawn,     305
Half shown, are broken and withdrawn.

"Ah! sure within him and without,
Could his dark wisdom find it out,
There must be answer to his doubt.

"But thou canst answer not again.              310
With thine own weapon art thou slain,
Or thou wilt answer but in vain.

"The doubt would rest, I dare not solve,
In the same circle we revolve.
Assurance only breeds resolve."              315

As when a billow, blown against,
Falls back, the voice with which I fenced
A little ceased, but recommenced.

"Where wert thou when thy father play'd
In his free field, and pastime made,              320
A merry boy in sun and shade?

"A merry boy they call'd him then,
He sat upon the knees of men
In days that never come again.

"Before the little ducts began              325
To feed thy bones with lime, and ran
Their course, till thou wert also man:

"Who took a wife, who rear'd his race,
Whose wrinkles gather'd on his face,
Whose troubles number with his days.              330

"A life of nothings, nothing worth,
From that first nothing ere his birth
To the last nothing under earth!"

"These words," I said, "are like the rest,
No certain clearness, but at best              335
A vague suspicion of the breast:

"But if I grant, thou might'st defend
The thesis which thy words intend—
That to begin implies to end;

"Yet how should I for certain hold,              340
Because my memory is so cold,
That I first was in human mould?

"I cannot make this matter plain,
But I would shoot, howe'er in vain,
A random arrow from the brain.              345

"It may be that no life is found,
Which only to one engine bound
Falls off, but cycles always round.

"As old mythologies relate,
Some draught of Lethe might await      350
The slipping thro' from state to state.

"As here we find in trances, men
Forget the dream that happens then,
Until they fall in trance again.

"So might we, if our state were such      355
As one before, remember much,
For those two likes might meet and touch.

"But, if I lapsed from nobler place,
Some legend of a fallen race
Alone might hint of my disgrace;      360

"Some vague emotion of delight
In gazing up an Alpine height,
Some yearning toward the lamps of night;

"Or if thro' lower lives I came—
Tho' all experience past became      365
Consolidate in mind and frame—

"I might forget my weaker lot;
For is not our first year forgot?
The haunts of memory echo not.

"And men, whose reason long was blind,      370
From cells of madness unconfined,
Oft lose whole years of darker mind.

"Much more, if first I floated free,
As naked essence, must I be
Incompetent of memory;      375

"For memory dealing but with time,
And he with matter, could she climb
Beyond her own material prime?

"Moreover, something is or seems,
That touches me with mystic gleams,      380
Like glimpses of forgotten dreams—

"Of something felt, like something here;
Of something done, I know not where;
Such as no language may declare."

The still voice laugh'd. "I talk," said he,                385
"Not with thy dreams. Suffice it thee
Thy pain is a reality."

"But thou," said I, "hast miss'd thy mark,
Who sought'st to wreck my mortal ark,
By making all the horizon dark.                            390

"Why not set forth, if I should do
This rashness, that which might ensue
With this old soul in organs new?

"Whatever crazy sorrow saith,
No life that breathes with human breath          395
Has ever truly long'd for death.

" 'Tis life, whereof our nerves are scant,
O life, not death, for which we pant;
More life, and fuller, that I want."

I ceased, and sat as one forlorn.                          400
Then said the voice, in quiet scorn,
"Behold, it is the Sabbath morn."

And I arose, and I released
The casement, and the light increased
With freshness in the dawning east.                        405

Like soften'd airs that blowing steal,
When meres begin to uncongeal,
The sweet church bells began to peal.

On to God's house the people prest;
Passing the place where each must rest,                    410
Each enter'd like a welcome guest.

One walk'd between his wife and child,
With measured footfall firm and mild,
And now and then he gravely smiled.

The prudent partner of his blood                           415
Lean'd on him, faithful, gentle, good,
Wearing the rose of womanhood.

And in their double love secure,
The little maiden walk'd demure,
Pacing with downward eyelids pure.                         420

These three made unity so sweet,
My frozen heart began to beat,
Remembering its ancient heat.

I blest them, and they wander'd on;
I spoke, but answer came there none;    425
The dull and bitter voice was gone.

A second voice was at mine ear,
A little whisper silver-clear,
A murmur, "Be of better cheer."

As from some blissful neighborhood,    430
A notice faintly understood,
"I see the end, and know the good."

A little hint to solace woe,
A hint, a whisper breathing low,
"I may not speak of what I know."    435

Like an Æolian harp that wakes
No certain air, but overtakes
Far thought with music that it makes;

Such seem'd the whisper at my side:
"What is it thou knowest, sweet voice?" I cried.⁴⁴⁰
"A hidden hope," the voice replied;

So heavenly-toned, that in that hour
From out my sullen heart a power
Broke, like the rainbow from the shower,

To feel, altho' no tongue can prove,    445
That every cloud, that spreads above
And veileth love, itself is love.

And forth into the fields I went,
And Nature's living motion lent
The pulse of hope to discontent.    450

I wonder'd at the bounteous hours,
The slow result of winter showers;
You scarce could see the grass for flowers.

I wonder'd, while I paced along;
The woods were fill'd so full with song,    455
There seem'd no room for sense of wrong.

So variously seem'd all things wrought,
I marvell'd how the mind was brought
To anchor by one gloomy thought;

And wherefore rather I made choice    460
To commune with that barren voice,
Than him that said, "Rejoice! rejoice!"

*George Barker*

---

TENNYSON
THE TWO VOICES

Being invited to write an essay on "The Two Voices" is
rather like being invited to write an essay to the month of
September. Briefly, it needs no explanation. Like that melancholy and lovely month, this poem is a thing that happens
for the joy of people. To those for whom knowledge of a
fine poem constitutes a serious delight, this particular poem
could provide a pleasure comparable with that, say, of meeting the adolescent Hamlet.

Perhaps the principal distinction of "The Two Voices" is
how naturally it obeys the dictation of Milton's apothegm
that poems should be simple, sensuous and passionate. The
simplicity of "The Two Voices" is the simplicity of an
honest despair, its sensuousness the sensuousness of the hedonistic imagination, its passion that of a tormented moralist in
love with a world of unpardonable temptations. For this
poem speaks more clearly than most other Victorian poetry
of the seizures of conscience undergone by those who found
themselves inheriting an imperial destiny, a long and disreputable legacy of social and ethical injustice, and a religious
tradition worn down to the lip service of a liturgy. "The
Two Voices" is a poem of guilt.

When Tennyson balances the issue of suicide in this poem
the echo of the voice of Hamlet is, perhaps, fortuitous. But it
is nevertheless present. The suicide speech of Hamlet is
superior (or so it seems to me) only insofar as Hamlet uses
few words better. But then, not many poets and even fewer
people have described this particular crisis of self-consciousness with such pithiness as Hamlet. Tennyson's poem is the
soliloquy of a lyrical poet—where that of Hamlet is the
soliloquy of a dramatic poet. And since this situation, this
crisis of self-consciousness, is dramatic before it is lyrical, the
sword of Hamlet dominates the lyre of Tennyson.

The intellect of this sinister and passionate man does not
operate happily among abstractions: but then, neither does

the intellect of the normal man. And it is for and to the normal man that Tennyson speaks.

The subject of this poem, which is the morality or immorality of suicide, may sound a bit abstract, but, clearly, it is not so. The question of whether you propose to get rid of yourself is not an abstract question. For if it arises seriously at all (and if it is not serious the question has not arisen), then it is very much a matter of fact. Either you do it or you don't. And it is in presenting the analogical argument of these alternatives that the poem coruscates with magnificent specifics and unforgettable instances. This is that passion for the particular, the unforgettable instances, that deluded Verlaine into perpetrating his impertinent solecism on Tennyson: "When he should have been brokenhearted he had reminiscences." For this is precisely what constitutes the poetic response: when it is brokenhearted, it has reminiscences.

For the reminiscences are specific. They speak. They are the tribute the memory pays to its pathetic impotence, and from these reminiscences arise the figures and instances of the poem. The memory is the seat or source of the poem, not a locket-shaped muscle with a crack down the middle. And it is in the multiplicity of these instances of reminiscence or image of memory in "The Two Voices" that Tennyson reveals the richness of his imagination.

It was, I think, Mr. T.S. Eliot who first pointed out that the truly remarkable element in the poetry of Tennyson is the quality of its doubt. And this doubt lies right at the heart of "The Two Voices." What distinguished much of Tennyson's poetry in the statuesque posing of so much Victorian literature is this tragic ambivalence at its heart. And in this particular poem the ambivalence, the very poignant self-accusation, the continually uncurling question mark of doubt, is delineated, harped upon, and even celebrated. It is, in truth, a huge Ode to Unknowing. And thus this statement of intellectual and spiritual humility is not without its cogency nowadays. I think it admirable that from a poet who could be called the advocate emperor of Victorian imperialism, we can derive the lesson of a virtuous unknowing, the morality of a salutary doubt, the hygiene of a deep self-questioning.

When Tennyson finished composing this poem he had circumscribed an area of the spirit that had never before been so clearly defined. This area of the spirit had not, indeed, truly existed until the aftermath of the Industrial Revolution invented it. For this area of the spirit could be said to be the dark landscape of the Satanic Mill: it was inhabited by the wage-slave, the underprivileged and the gin-addict: thus one of the sources from which Tennyson's doubt—his despair—arises, can be seen to be that guilt brought upon the conscience by the contemplation of such unholy things as social injustice and ethical anarchy.

But it is never possible (and this should go without saying) to equate the statements of poetry by analyzing their ostensible propositions in prose: the emotional atmosphere in which a poem exists and operates produces a chemical effect upon these propositions in such a degree as to seem to allegorize them. They become susceptible to a plurality of interpretations. Thus I was once told by Eliot that he wrote "The Waste Land" about that dreary and dangerous thoroughfare in West London called Edgware Road: but the poem has been understood, since, to describe the miserable condition of the world at large following upon the First World War. And so, I think, this poem of Tennyson's, seeming to speak of a personal crisis, speaks also of an historical crisis. This historical crisis is the doubt and despair brought upon the conscience when, like a scapegoat, it perceives that it has inherited that hideous wilderness of the spirit created by the Industrial Revolution, and called Prosperity. In "The Two Voices" Tennyson anticipates, but darkly, some of the tergiversations of "The Waste Land":

> *And wherefore rather I made choice*
> *To commune with that barren voice*
> *Than him that said: "Rejoice! Rejoice!"*

Between such lines lies that mysterious No Man's Land where the personal judgment takes on the authority of a law and the momentary exultations of the mind or speculations of the heart are seen to be monuments of the unaging intellect.

And so in "The Two Voices" what one is witnessing is the continual transformation of the personal into the historical, and of the sow's ear into the silk purse:

> *To search thro' all I felt or saw,*
> *The springs of life, the depths of awe,*
> *And reach the law within the law*

Furthermore, it is in the philosophical quality of his doubt that Tennyson, in this particular poem, reveals the aristocracy of his spirit. For the doubt, the questioning, the Cloud of Unknowing, is accepted as a natural (and by this I mean also inevitable) and even as an elevating condition of existence. It brings to my mind that marvellous sentence of John Keats's on Shakespeare:

> I had not a dispute but a disquisition with Dilke, on various subjects; several things dovetailed in my mind and at once it struck me what quality went to form a Man of Achievement especially in Literature and which Shakespeare possessed so enormously—I mean *Negative Capability*, that is when man is capable of being in uncertainties, Mysteries, doubts, without any irritable reaching after fact or reason—Coleridge, for instance, would let go by a fine isolated verisimilitude caught from the Penetralium of mystery, from being incapable of remaining content with half knowledge.

For this doubt, like a ball suspended between the pull of equal forces, permits itself to be moved by the smallest of instances; at the wave of a hand a mile away it trembles; and this is the condition also of the poetic imagination, to be agitated into poems by the wave of a vanished hand or the echo of two voices that never existed. For such a doubt is like that supreme neutrality in which the mind and heart may labor, conscious that only in such neutrality are they subject to the smallest as well as to the greatest of influences.

## Tears, Idle Tears

Tears, idle tears, I know not what they mean,
Tears from the depth of some divine despair
Rise in the heart, and gather to the eyes,
In looking on the happy Autumn-fields,
And thinking of the days that are no more.     5

Fresh as the first beam glittering on a sail,
That brings our friends up from the underworld,
Sad as the last which reddens over one
That sinks with all we love below the verge;
So sad, so fresh, the days that are no more.     10

Ah, sad and strange as in dark summer dawns
The earliest pipe of half-awaken'd birds
To dying ears, when unto dying eyes
The casement slowly grows a glimmering square;
So sad, so strange, the days that are no more.     15

Dear as remember'd kisses after death,
And sweet as those by hopeless fancy feign'd
On lips that are for others; deep as love,
Deep as first love, and wild with all regret;
O Death in Life, the days that are no more.     20

# Cleanth Brooks

## TENNYSON
### TEARS, IDLE TEARS

Tennyson is perhaps the last English poet one would think of associating with the subtleties of paradox and ambiguity. He is not the thoughtless poet, to be sure: he grapples—particularly in his later period—with the "big" questions that were up for his day; and he struggles manfully with them. But the struggle, as Tennyson conducted it, was usually kept out of the grammar and symbolism of the poetry itself. Like his own protagonist in "In Memoriam," Tennyson "fought his doubts"—he does not typically build them into the structure of the poetry itself as enriching ambiguities.

Yet substantially true as this generalization is, Tennyson was not always successful in avoiding the ambiguous and the paradoxical; and indeed, in some of his poems his failure to avoid them becomes a saving grace. The lyric "Tears, Idle Tears" is a very good instance. It is a poem that from a strictly logical point of view Tennyson may be thought to have blundered into. But, whether he blundered into it or not, the poem gains from the fact that it finds its unity in a principle of organization higher than the principle that seems to be operative in many of Tennyson's more "thoughtful" poems.

Any account of the poem may very well begin with a consideration of the nature of the tears. Are they *idle* tears? Or are they not rather the most meaningful of tears? Does not the very fact that they are "idle" (that is, tears occasioned by no immediate grief) become in itself a guarantee of the fact that they spring from a deeper, more universal cause?

It would seem so, and that the poet is thus beginning his poem with a paradox. For the third line of the poem indicates that there is no doubt in the speaker's mind about the origin of the tears in some divine despair. They "rise in the heart"— for all that they have been first announced as "idle."

But the question of whether Tennyson is guilty of (or to

be complimented upon) a use of paradox may well wait upon further discussion. At this point in our commentary, it is enough to observe that Tennyson has chosen to open his poem with some dramatic boldness—if not with the bold step of equating "idle" with "from the depth of some divine despair," then at least with a bold and violent reversal of the speaker's first characterization of his tears.

The tears "rise in the heart" as the speaker looks upon a scene of beauty and tranquillity. Does looking on the "happy Autumn-fields" bring to mind the days that are no more? The poet does not say so. The tears rise to the eyes in looking on the "happy Autumn-fields" *and* thinking of the days that are no more. The poet himself does not stand responsible for any closer linkage between these actions, though, as a matter of fact, most of us will want to make a closer linkage here. For, if we change "happy Autumn-fields," to say, "happy April-fields," the two terms tend to draw apart. The fact that the fields are autumn fields that though happy, point back to something that is over—that is finished—*does* connect them with the past and therefore properly suggests to the observer thoughts about that past.

To sum up: The first stanza has a unity, but it is not a unity that finds its sanctions in the ordinary logic of language. Its sanctions are to be found in the dramatic context, and, to my mind, there alone. Indeed, the stanza suggests the play of the speaker's mind as the tears unexpectedly start, tears for which there is no apparent occasion, and as he searches for an explanation of them. He calls them "idle," but, even as he says "I know not what they mean," he realizes that they must spring from the depths of his being—is willing, with his very next words, to associate them with "some divine despair." Moreover, the real occasion of the tears, though the speaker himself comes to realize it only as he approaches the end of the stanza, is the thought about the past. It is psychologically and dramatically right, therefore, that the real occasion should be stated explicitly only with the last line of the stanza.

This first stanza, then, recapitulates the surprise and bewilderment in the speaker's own mind, and sets the problem that the succeeding stanzas are to analyze. The dramatic effect may be described as follows: the stanza seems, not a meditated observation, but a speech begun impulsively—a statement the speaker has begun before he knows how he will end it.

In the second stanza we are not surprised to have the poet characterize the days that are no more as "sad," but there is some shock in hearing him apply to them the adjective "fresh." Again, the speaker does not pause to explain: the word "fresh" actually begins the stanza. Yet the adjective justifies itself.

The past is fresh as with a dawn freshness—as fresh as the first beam glittering on the sail of an incoming ship. The ship is evidently expected; it brings friends, friends "up from the underworld." On the surface, the comparison is innocent: the "underworld" is merely the antipodes, the world that lies below the horizon—an underworld in the sense displayed in old-fashioned geographies with their sketches illustrating the effects of the curvature of the earth. The sails, which catch the light and glitter, will necessarily be the part first seen of any ship coming "up" over the curve of the earth.

But the word underworld will necessarily suggest the underworld of Greek mythology, the realm of the shades, the abode of the dead. The attempt to characterize the freshness of the days that are no more has, thus, developed almost imperceptibly into a further characterization of the days themselves as belonging, not to our daylight world, but to an "underworld." This suggestion is, of course, strengthened in the lines that follow, in which the ship metaphor is reversed so as to give us a picture of sadness: evening, the last glint of sunset light on the sail of a ship

*That sinks with all we love below the verge*

The conjunction of the qualities of sadness and freshness is reinforced by the fact that the same basic symbol—the light on the sails of a ship—has been employed to suggest both qualities. With the third stanza, the process is carried one stage further: the two qualities (with the variant of "strange" for "fresh") are explicitly linked together:

*Ah, sad and strange as in dark summer dawns*

And here the poet is not content to suggest the qualities of sadness and strangeness by means of two different, even if closely related, figures. In this third stanza the special kind of sadness and strangeness is suggested by one and the same figure.

It is a figure developed in some detail. It, too, involves a dawn scene, though ironically so, for the beginning of the new day is to be the beginning of the long night for the dying man. The dying eyes, the poem suggests, have been for some time awake—long enough to have had time to watch as the "casement slowly grows a glimmering square." The dying man, soon to sleep the lasting sleep, is more fully awake than the "half-awaken'd birds" whose earliest pipings come to his dying ears. We know why these pipings are sad; but why are they *strange?* Because to the person hearing a bird's song for the last time, it will seem that he has never before really heard one. The familiar sound will take on a quality of un-reality—of strangeness.

If this poem were merely a gently melancholy reverie on the sweet sadness of the past, stanzas two and three would have no place in the poem. But the poem is no such reverie: the images from the past rise up with a strange clarity and sharpness that shock the speaker. Their sharpness and fresh-ness account for the sudden tears and for the psychological problem with which the speaker wrestles in the poem. If the past would only remain melancholy but dimmed, sad but worn and familiar, we should have no problem and no poem. At least, we should not have *this* poem; we should certainly not have the intensity of the last stanza.

That intensity, if justified, must grow out of a sense of the apparent nearness and intimate presence of what is irre-vocably beyond reach: the days that are no more must be more than the conventional "dear, dead days beyond recall." They must be beyond recall, yet alive—tantalizingly vivid and near. It is only thus that we can feel the speaker justified in calling them

> *Dear as remember'd kisses after death,*
> *And sweet as those by hopeless fancy feign'd*
> *On lips that are for others . . .*

It is only thus that we can accept the culminating paradox of

> *O Death in Life, the days that are no more*

We have already observed, in the third stanza, how the speaker compares the strangeness and sadness of the past to the sadness of the birds' piping as it sounds to dying ears. There is a rather brilliant ironic contrast involved in the comparison. The speaker, a living man, in attempting to indicate how sad and strange to him are the days of the past, says that they are as sad and strange as is the natural activity of the awakening world to the man who is dying: the dead past seems to the living man as unfamiliar and fresh in its sadness as the living present seems to the dying man. There is more here, however, than a mere, ironic reversal of roles; in each case there is the sense of being irrevocably barred from the known world.

This ironic contrast, too, accounts for the sense of desperation that runs through the concluding lines of the poem. The kisses feigned by "hopeless fancy" are made the more precious because of the very hopelessness; but memory takes on the quality of fancy. It is equally hopeless—the kisses can as little be renewed as those "feign'd / On lips that are for others" can be obtained. The realized past has become as fabulous as the unrealizable future. The days that are no more are as dear as the one, as sweet as the other, the speaker says; and it does not matter whether we compare them to the one or to the other or to both: it comes to the same thing.

But the days that are no more are not merely "dear" and "sweet"; they are "deep" and "wild." Something has happened to the grammar here. How can the *days* be "deep as love" or "wild with all regret"? And what is the status of the exclamation "O Death in Life"? Is it merely a tortured cry like "O God! the days that are no more"? Or is it a loose appositive: "the days that are no more are a kind of death in life"?

The questions are not asked in a censorious spirit, as if there were no justification for Tennyson's license here. But it is important to see how much license the poem requires, and the terms on which the reader decides to accord it justification. What one finds on closer examination is not muddlement but richness. But it is a richness achieved through principles of organization that many an admirer of the poet has difficulty in allowing to the "obscure" modern poet.

For example, how can the days of the past be *deep?* Here, of course, the problem is not very difficult. The past is buried within one: the days that are no more constitute the deepest level of one's being, and the tears that arise from thinking on them may be said to come from the "depth of some divine despair." But how can the days be "wild with all regret"? The extension demanded here is more ambitious. In matter of fact, it is the speaker, the man, who is made wild with regret by thinking on the days.

One can, of course, justify the adjective as a transferred epithet on the model of Vergil's *maestum timorem;* and perhaps this was Tennyson's own conscious justification (if, indeed, the need to justify it ever occurred to him). But one can make a better case than a mere appeal to the authority of an established literary convention. There is a sense in which the man and the remembered days are one and the same. A man is the sum of his memories. The adjective which applies to the man made wild with regret can apply to those memories that make him wild with regret. For, does the man charge the memories with his own passion, or is it the memories that give the emotion to him? If we pursue the matter far enough, we come to a point where the distinction lapses. Perhaps I should say, more accurately, adopting the metaphor of the poem itself, we *descend* to a depth where the distinction lapses. The days that are no more are *deep* and *wild*, buried but not dead—below the surface and unthought of, yet at the deepest core of being, secretly alive.

The past *should* be tame, fettered, brought to heel; it is not. It is capable of breaking forth and coming to the surface. The word "wild" is bold, therefore, but justified. It reasserts the line of development that has been maintained throughout the earlier stanzas: "fresh," "strange," and now "wild"—all adjectives that suggest passionate, irrational life. The word "wild," thus, not only pulls into focus the earlier paradoxes, but is the final stage in the preparation for the culminating paradox, "O Death in Life."

The last stanza evokes an intense emotional response from the reader. The claim could hardly be made good by the stanza taken in isolation. The stanza leans heavily upon the foregoing stanzas, and the final paradox draws heavily upon the great metaphors in the second and third stanzas. This is as it should be. The justification for emphasizing the fact here is this: the poem, for all its illusion of impassioned speech—with the looseness and *apparent* confusion of unpremeditated speech—is very tightly organized. It represents an organic structure; and the intensity of the total effect is a reflection of the total structure.

When the poet is able, as in "Tears, Idle Tears," to analyze his experience, and in the full light of the disparity and even apparent contradiction of the various elements, bring them into a new unity, he secures not only richness and depth but dramatic power as well. Our conventional accounts of poetry, which oppose emotion to intellect, "lyric simplicity" to "thoughtful meditation," have done no service to the cause of poetry. The opposition is not only superficial: it falsifies the real relationships. For the lyric quality, if it be genuine, is not the result of some transparent and "simple" redaction of a theme or a situation that is somehow poetic in itself; it is, rather, the result of an imaginative grasp of diverse materials but an imaginative grasp so sure that it may show itself to the reader as unstudied and unpredictable without for a moment relaxing its hold on the intricate and complex stuff it carries.

# ROBERT BROWNING
## [1812–1889]

## Rabbi Ben Ezra

### I

Grow old along with me!
The best is yet to be,
The last of life, for which the first was made:
    Our times are in His hand
    Who saith "A whole I planned,        5
Youth shows but half; trust God: see all, nor be afraid!"

### II

Not that, amassing flowers,
Youth sighed "Which rose make ours,
Which lily leave and then as best recall?"
    Not that, admiring stars,        10
    It yearned "Nor Jove, nor Mars;
Mine be some figured flame which blends, transcends them all!"

### III

Not for such hopes and fears
Annulling youth's brief years,
Do I remonstrate: folly wide the mark!        15
    Rather I prize the doubt
    Low kinds exist without,
Finished and finite clods, untroubled by a spark.

### IV

Poor vaunt of life indeed,
Were man but formed to feed        20
On joy, to solely seek and find and feast:
    Such feasting ended, then
    As sure an end to men;
Irks care the crop-full bird? Frets doubt the maw-crammed
       beast?

### V

Rejoice we are allied                                          25
To That which doth provide
And not partake, effect and not receive!
A spark disturbs our clod;
Nearer we hold of God
Who gives, than of His tribes that take, I must believe.       30

### VI

Then, welcome each rebuff
That turns earth's smoothness rough,
Each sting that bids nor sit nor stand but go!
Be our joys three-parts pain!
Strive, and hold cheap the strain;                             35
Learn, nor account the pang; dare, never grudge the throe!

### VII

For thence,—a paradox
Which comforts while it mocks,—
Shall life succeed in that it seems to fail:
What I aspired to be,                                          40
And was not, comforts me:
A brute I might have been, but would not sink i' the scale.

### VIII

What is he but a brute
Whose flesh has soul to suit,
Whose spirit works lest arms and legs want play?               45
To man, propose this test—
Thy body at its best,
How far can that project thy soul on its lone way?

### IX

Yet gifts should prove their use:
I own the Past profuse                                         50
Of power each side, perfection every turn:
Eyes, ears took in their dole,
Brain treasured up the whole;
Should not the heart beat once "How good to live and
    learn"?

### X

Not once beat "Praise be Thine!                                55
I see the whole design,

ROBERT BROWNING

*Portrait by his son in 1882*
*The Bettmann Archive*

I, who saw Power, see now Love perfect too:
    Perfect I call Thy plan:
    Thanks that I was a man!
Maker, remake, complete,—I trust what Thou shalt do!"    60

### XI

    For pleasant is this flesh;
    Our soul, in its rose-mesh
Pulled ever to the earth, still yearns for rest;
    Would we some prize might hold
    To match those manifold    65
Possessions of the brute,—gain most, as we did best!

### XII

    Let us not always say
    "Spite of this flesh to-day
I strove, made head, gained ground upon the whole!"
    As the bird wings and sings,    70
    Let us cry "All good things
Are ours, nor soul helps flesh more, now, than flesh helps soul!"

### XIII

    Therefore I summon age
    To grant youth's heritage,
Life's struggle having so far reached its term:    75
    Thence shall I pass, approved
    A man, for aye removed
From the developed brute; a God though in the germ.

### XIV

    And I shall thereupon
    Take rest, ere I be gone    80
Once more on my adventure brave and new:
    Fearless and unperplexed,
    When I wage battle next,
What weapons to select, what armor to indue.

### XV

    Youth ended, I shall try    85
    My gain or loss thereby;
Leave the fire ashes, what survives is gold:
    And I shall weigh the same,
    Give life its praise or blame:
Young, all lay in dispute; I shall know, being old.    90

### XVI

For note, when evening shuts,
  A certain moment cuts
The deed off, calls the glory from the grey:
  A whisper from the west
  Shoots—"Add this to the rest, 95
Take it and try its worth: here dies another day."

### XVII

So, still within this life,
  Though lifted o'er its strife,
Let me discern, compare, pronounce at last,
  "This rage was right i' the main, 100
  That acquiescence vain:
The Future I may face now I have proved the Past."

### XVIII

For more is not reserved
  To man, with soul just nerved
To act to-morrow what he learns to-day: 105
  Here, work enough to watch
  The Master work, and catch
Hints of the proper craft, tricks of the tool's true play.

### XIX

As it was better, youth
  Should strive, through acts uncouth, 110
Toward making, than repose on aught found made:
  So, better, age, exempt
  From strife, should know, than tempt
Further. Thou waitedest age: wait death nor be afraid!

### XX

Enough now, if the Right 115
  And Good and Infinite
Be named here, as thou callest thy hand thine own,
  With knowledge absolute,
  Subject to no dispute
From fools that crowded youth, nor let thee feel alone. 120

### XXI

Be there, for once and all,
  Severed great minds from small,

Announced to each his station in the Past!
    Was I, the world arraigned,
    Were they, my soul disdained,        125
Right? Let age speak the truth and give us peace at last!

### XXII

    Now, who shall arbitrate?
    Ten men love what I hate,
Shun what I follow, slight what I receive;
    Ten, who in ears and eyes        130
    Match me: we all surmise,
They this thing, and I that: whom shall my soul believe?

### XXIII

    Not on the vulgar mass
    Called "work," must sentence pass,
Things done, that took the eye and had the price;    135
    O'er which, from level stand,
    The low world laid its hand,
Found straightway to its mind, could value in a trice:

### XXIV

    But all, the world's coarse thumb
    And finger failed to plumb,        140
So passed in making up the main account;
    All instincts immature,
    All purposes unsure,
That weighed not as his work, yet swelled the man's amount:

### XXV

    Thoughts hardly to be packed    145
    Into a narrow act,
Fancies that broke through language and escaped;
    All I could never be,
    All, men ignored in me,
This, I was worth to God, whose wheel the pitcher
    shaped.        150

### XXVI

    Aye, note that Potter's wheel,
    That metaphor! and feel
Why time spins fast, why passive lies our clay,—
    Thou, to whom fools propound,

When the wine makes its round,                                    155
"Since life fleets, all is change; the Past gone, seize to-day!"

### XXVII

Fool! All that is, at all,
Lasts ever, past recall;
Earth changes, but thy soul and God stand sure:
What entered into thee,                                          160
*That* was, is, and shall be:
Time's wheel runs back or stops: Potter and clay endure.

### XXVIII

He fixed thee 'mid this dance
Of plastic circumstance,
This Present, thou, forsooth, wouldst fain arrest:               165
Machinery just meant
To give thy soul its bent,
Try thee and turn thee forth, sufficiently impressed.

### XXIX

What though the earlier grooves
Which ran the laughing loves                                      170
Around thy base, no longer pause and press?
What thought, about thy rim,
Skull-things in order grim
Grow out, in graver mood, obey the sterner stress?

### XXX

Look not thou down but up!                                       175
To uses of a cup,
The festal board, lamp's flash, and trumpet's peal,
The new wine's foaming flow,
The Master's lips a-glow!
Thou, heaven's consummate cup, what need'st thou with
       earth's wheel?                                            180

### XXXI

But I need, now as then,
Thee, God, who mouldest men;
And since, not even while the whirl was worst,
Did I,—to the wheel of life
With shapes and colors rife,                                     185
Bound dizzily,—mistake my end, to slake Thy thirst:

### XXXII

So, take and use Thy work:
Amend what flaws may lurk,
What strain o' the stuff, what warpings past the aim!
    My times be in Thy hand!        190
    Perfect the cup as planned!
Let age approve of youth, and death complete the same!

# Roy P. Basler

## BROWNING
## RABBI BEN EZRA

As the opening lines suggest, "Rabbi Ben Ezra" is an exhortation to youth not to be shortsighted in setting guidelines for living and goals for achievement. It examines closely two apparently opposing philosophies of life, one of which may be considered pagan because it derives from the Greek philosophy known as hedonism, advocated by various Greek philosophers, but in its cruder form by Aristippus, who taught that pleasure is the highest good, to be achieved by gratification of sensual desires. The other may be considered Judeo-Christian, with its emphasis on knowledge, particularly the quest for recognition of God's purpose in creation, as the highest good, because derived from biblical teachings and elaborated by both Christian and Hebrew philosophers. Among the latter was the twelfth century Hebrew poet-preacher-scholar, Ibn Ezra, whom Browning chose as his imaginary speaker for this dramatic monologue.

The opposition of pagan and Judeo-Christian points of view in these two philosophies is not by any means an absolute one, however, for the quest for knowledge as the highest good was taught by Socrates and other Greek philosophers, and not a few Christian churchmen, on the other hand, have tried to adapt some of the hedonistic point of view into their religious attitude. A fine English poetical expression of this effort is the famous "To the Virgins, to Make Much of Time," written by the seventeenth century English clergyman, Robert Herrick. Browning probably assumed that his readers would be familiar with Herrick's famous poem, beginning "Gather ye Rose-buds while ye may," and thus had Rabbi Ben Ezra address himself to it immediately in the second stanza, not wholly anachronistically either, since the metaphor of gathering flowers is from antiquity.

We may dismiss at once the question whether Browning was trying to any considerable extent to represent the teaching of the historical Ibn Ezra, by saying that although there

are general similarities to be observed in the writings of Ibn
Ezra—such as his adherence to a mystic theory of a double
creation, spiritual and material—there is little more in Browning's adoption of Rabbi Ben Ezra as his dramatic character
than a disguise for the nineteenth century scholar-poet who
wrote the poem, and who needed this disguise, not so much
to bolster his own convictions as to lend poetic authority to
what were already in the 1860's somewhat shaky religious
convictions. Whether a Robert Browning or a T.S. Eliot, the
poet who writes in dramatic form does so for his own very
good reasons, and although the reader-critic cannot prove,
neither can he ignore, what they were. Even at his best
(which he is frequently in this poem) and his subtlest (less
frequently here), Browning never dared speak in his own
person so authoritatively as the mouthpiece of the Almighty.
But this did not prevent his creating a true masterpiece of
nineteenth century whistling in the dark. To appreciate what
Browning accomplished, one should try to discover any
poem written during the century that has elapsed since 1864
whose "eternal verities" better withstand the onslaught described by Browning's contemporary, Matthew Arnold, in a
memorable metaphor:

> And we are here as on a darkling plain
> Swept by confused alarms of struggle and flight,
> Where ignorant armies clash by night.

What the modern reader should beware above all in
reading "Rabbi Ben Ezra" is his own sophistication, accumulated from a century of scientific agnosticism, or perhaps
equally from the reading of pessimistic modern poets who
have covered the nakedness of their natural intellectual condition with tags and tatters ripped from the gown of tradition, and sewn into a motley of obfuscating allusion, to hide
the "poor, bare, forked animal" of natural intellect. Not even
a further accumulation of footnotes to tags and tatters should
be permitted to mislead us into the belief that such as these,
to clip a phrase from the good rabbi's sermon, have "severed
great minds from small." Intellection is a tool not by any
means reserved for scientists, but in the hands of poetic
magicians it may become a wand to charm us into spiritual
bughouses of sophistication. If one is not moved by the fifth
stanza of "Rabbi Ben Ezra," then he should watch out! If, on
the other hand, he is moved, then also he should watch out,
especially for something better than the rabbi's "I shall
know, being old."

For although "Rabbi Ben Ezra" is an indubitable master-piece of didactic poetry, there are deeper realms than Browning penetrated. Perhaps he had too much bounce to the ounce to plumb the depths reached by the preacher in *Ecclesiastes*—"Remember now thy Creator in the days of thy youth, while the evil days come not, nor the years draw nigh, when thou shalt say, I have no pleasure in them." The specific gravity of *Ecclesiastes*, however, has seldom been equalled in English poetry. Likewise perhaps, living in the nineteenth century, Browning lacked the poetic thrust to penetrate so far as Dante had in the thirteenth, into the now obsolete outer space of the anthropomorphic conception of "His glory, by whose might all things are moved." Or again perhaps, like many of his contemporaries and more of ours, he had sensed just enough of what a modern scientist-poet, Buckminster Fuller, has dubbed "anticipatory design science," to doubt "God as noun," and yet not enough adequately to imagine "God as verb." And hence he did the best he could with the metaphor of an obsolescent anthropomorphism, which had so utterly sufficed for both *Ecclesiastes* and Dante.

In either case, what Browning "aspired to be, and was not" may or may not comfort you or me, whatever it did for him, but it most certainly should instruct us in how "a man's reach should exceed his grasp," as another of Browning's dramatic characters, the artist Andrea Del Sarto, bitterly phrased his own recognition of failure. For Browning could not, even by impersonating Rabbi Ben Ezra, preach with conviction, "Let age speak the truth and give us peace at last," in any terms save a poet's metaphor.

The poem's conclusion shows the good rabbi as poet more than as preacher, escaping from the consequences of his somewhat arrogant avowal of absolute moral and intellectual certitude, by a flight into an Old Testament metaphorical fantasy of potter and clay (see *Isaiah* 64:8), in which he symbolizes himself as God's cup, the vessel created by God for the purpose of celebrating God's own everlasting thirst—but not a thirst for *knowing* so much as for *being*. This is an artist's conception of God as one who creates art for art's sake, with man the noblest creation of the Master, and as such perhaps absolved even of the presumption of playing at God's game of artistic creation himself, as poet-preacher, somewhat mystically using his reason (the tool of the true Judeo-Christian ego) instead of his senses (the tool of the pagan id) on the assumption that there is a higher achievement of being than the biological, in the realm of spirit rather than in the realm of matter.

Even without benefit of this Freudian frame of reference, it may be seen that Browning makes the most of the artist's sublimation, for religious purpose, in his elaboration of the metaphor of potter and clay, saying to God in effect that he is sorry to have appeared so presumptuous as to assume he is himself any more than a metaphor in God's own poem, life, a spiritual as well as a material entity, created by God merely for his own delectation.

Whether this interpretation is fair to Browning, or to the poem, from either a religious or a poetical point of view, the reader will judge for himself; but it is significant that in the last two stanzas Rabbi Ben Ezra no longer addresses the reader, but speaks to God, somewhat apologetically,

> *But I need, now as then*
> *Thee, God, who mouldest men*

and prays, rather than preaches,

> *Let age approve of youth, and death complete the same!*

This is the ground on which the metaphysically, as well as the physically, arrogant human being must at last prostrate himself, along with the meek.

# My Last Duchess

### FERRARA

That's my last Duchess painted on the wall,
Looking as if she were alive. I call
That piece a wonder, now; Frà Pandolf's hands
Worked busily a day, and there she stands.
Will't please you sit and look at her? I said          5
"Frà Pandolf" by design, for never read
Strangers like you that pictured countenance,
The depth and passion of its earnest glance,
But to myself they turned (since none puts by
The curtain I have drawn for you, but I)              10
And seemed as they would ask me, if they durst,
How such a glance came there; so, not the first
Are you to turn and ask thus. Sir, 't was not
Her husband's presence only, called that spot
Of joy into the Duchess' cheek; perhaps            15
Frà Pandolf chanced to say, "Her mantle laps
Over my lady's wrist too much," or "Paint
Must never hope to reproduce the faint
Half-flush that dies along her throat;" such stuff
Was courtesy, she thought, and cause enough        20
For calling up that spot of joy. She had
A heart . . . how shall I say? . . . too soon made glad,
Too easily impressed; she liked whate'er
She looked on, and her looks went everywhere.
Sir, 't was all one! My favour at her breast,      25
The dropping of the daylight in the West,
The bough of cherries some officious fool
Broke in the orchard for her, the white mule
She rode with round the terrace—all and each
Would draw from her alike the approving speech,    30
Or blush, at least. She thanked me,—good; but thanked
Somehow . . . I know not ho` . . . as if she ranked

My gift of a nine-hundred-years-old name
With anybody's gift. Who'd stoop to blame
This sort of trifling? Even had you skill      35
In speech—(which I have not)—to make your will
Quite clear to such an one, and say, "Just this
Or that in you disgusts me; here you miss,
Or there exceed the mark"—and if she let
Herself be lessoned so, nor plainly set      40
Her wits to yours, forsooth, and made excuse,
—E'en then would be some stooping, and I chuse
Never to stoop. Oh, Sir, she smiled, no doubt,
Whene'er I passed her; but who passed without
Much the same smile? This grew; I gave commands;      45
Then all smiles stopped together. There she stands
As if alive. Will't please you rise? We'll meet
The company below, then. I repeat,
The Count your Master's known munificence
Is ample warrant that no just pretence      50
Of mine for dowry will be disallowed;
Though his fair daughter's self, as I avowed
At starting, is my object. Nay, we'll go
Together down, Sir! Notice Neptune, though,
Taming a sea-horse, thought a rarity,      55
Which Claus of Innsbruck cast in bronze for me.

# Edwin Honig

## BROWNING
## MY LAST DUCHESS

Next to "Rabbi Ben Ezra," "My Last Duchess" is Browning's
best-known poem. If the "Rabbi" bounces along with moralistic optimism, the other exults in being amoral and brutal.
The poet enjoyed striking poses, though modern readers
probably prefer his immoralist to his good gray sage.

Ferrara, the narrator of "My Last Duchess," is like the
other wicked personae we hear speaking through "The
Bishop Orders his Tomb at St. Praxed's Church" and "Porphyria's Lover." These three poems are serviceable examples
of the type Browning is reputed to have done best—the
dramatic monologue. As character studies they certainly
belong in the same rogues' gallery. While the bishop is a
monumental hypocrite and Porphyria's lover a towering
romantic psychotic, the marrying duke is more of a successful big businessman: investor in handsome dowries, cold fish,
art collector. Such attributes go with being a tycoon. By
putting him in Renaissance Italy, Browning eludes the ethical
stricture against making wicked characters sympathetic and
discourages possible identification with any contemporary
Victorian analogue.

But if "My Last Duchess" is a monologue, it is something
more than a soliloquy. It is one side of a conversation of
which the other side is silent, or taken for granted. We are
aware of the count's envoy, the listener, sitting or standing
nearby as the duke addresses him. This is a bit like what
happens in Strindberg's short play *The Stronger*, where the
wife does all the talking while the other woman mutely
attends. What makes such a speech dramatic and the villainous duke attractive is that we find ourselves eavesdrop-
ping, like a theatre audience, on the duke's casual but deliberate self-revelation. Through his own words the duke makes
us believe in him as a person, no matter how much we may
disapprove of his behavior. It should be added that Browning
uses this stock theatrical device more successfully here than

in his lengthy poetic plays that were intended for the theater. We are intrigued by the character. He is demonic—a close and jealous observer, a destroyer of innocence, ruthless in his possessiveness, polite, murderously obtuse, a technician par excellence. The poem glides along through fifty-six lines of run-on couplets, skillfully turned, now to unobtrusive echoes and modulations, now to emphases on rhyme words. On one such turn the key to the poem's underlying life is disclosed. It occurs with the terse, climactic phrases:

> *. . . This grew; I gave commands;*
> *Then all smiles stopped together. There she stands*
> *As if alive . . .*

The emotional scheme of the poem clicks open, revealing how much of it has to do with the elements of pose, posture, placement, aloofness, servility.

There is the duke's sadism in his first remark about the duchess, where she is viewed as an inanimate object, as though, appearing "painted on the wall, / Looking as if she were alive," he had *nailed* her there. Also, we may now see why the painter's *hands* had to be employed upon the duchess: in order to dignify her with the only kind of life the duke could tolerate. "Frà Pandolf's hands / Worked busily a day, and there she stands." Meanwhile the envoy has been asked to take a position of servile admiration before the frozen art work: "Will't please you sit and look at her?" And, though privileged by the duke's hospitality, the envoy must not regard his unspoken question as unique, for "not the first / Are you to turn and ask thus." In not appreciating the duke's rank or his "nine-hundred-years-old name," the duchess exceeded her place; the duke would not "stoop" to tell her so. Therefore she had to be cut down so that she might stand afterward only in the painting. With this observation the duke bids his visitor rise—as though having been taught his lesson for the day the envoy had been shown his place, so that now they can go down together to "meet / The company below."

The count ought to be forewarned—the villainous duke is up to no good. By his own admission he is no romanticist but one interested in hard cash:

> *The Count your Master's known munificence*
> *Is ample warrant that no just pretence*
> *Of mine for dowry will be disallowed;*

> *Though his fair daughter's self, as I avowed*
> *At starting, is my object . . .*

And, as if to remind himself and the envoy of how completely objective (i.e., object-fixated) he is, the duke moves
on from the effigy of the duchess on the wall to a sculpture,
typically combative in subject:

> *. . . Notice Neptune, though,*
> *Taming a sea-horse, thought a rarity,*
> *Which Claus of Innsbruck cast in bronze for me*

The man who makes the comment disapproves of flesh and
blood blushes and smiles—"the spot of joy" in his wife's
cheek was a stain, unlike the admirable "faint / Half-flush
that dies along her throat" in the portrait. He does not warm
to the red-and-white of love (and the poem goes on to
associate the dead duchess with "The dropping of the daylight in the West," a "bough of cherries" broken off, and "the
white mule / She rode with") but to the dead simulacrum of
the original and the bronze mythological subject a bit farther
down the stairs.

Is the duke an art lover or just a collector of objects—and
of wives who must be stopped, silenced, and converted into
objects before they can be enjoyed? If the latter is true then
he is, like all exploiters, simply a gross materialist. And it is
this grossness, his acquisitive zeal, that makes his amoralism
so extreme, so self-insistent.

Can it be that Ferrara, the self-confessed immoralist, is a
moralist in disguise, the other face of the good gray Rabbi
Ben Ezra? At any rate, this histrionic scoundrel and poseur,
for all his flashing boasts and casual, mirror-watching exhibitionism, is tolerable only for the length of the fifty-six lines
devoted to him—not one line more.

EMILY BRONTË

*From a drawing by Charlotte Brontë*
*Brown Brothers*

# EMILY BRONTË
[1818–1848]

## Remembrance

*[R. Alcona to J. Brenzaida]*

Cold in the earth, and the deep snow piled above thee!
Far, far removed, cold in the dreary grave!
Have I forgot, my Only Love, to love thee,
Severed at last by Time's all-wearing wave?

Now, when alone, do my thoughts no longer hover      5
Over the mountains on Angora's shore;
Resting their wings where heath and fern-leaves cover
That noble heart for ever, ever more?

Cold in the earth, and fifteen wild Decembers
From those brown hills have melted into spring—      10
Faithful indeed is the spirit that remembers
After such years of change and suffering!

Sweet Love of youth, forgive if I forget thee
While the World's tide is bearing me along:
Sterner desires and darker hopes beset me,      15
Hopes which obscure but cannot do thee wrong.

No other Sun has lightened up my heaven;
No other Star has ever shone for me:
All my life's bliss from thy dear life was given—
All my life's bliss is in the grave with thee.      20

But when the days of golden dreams had perished
And even Despair was powerless to destroy,
Then did I learn how existence could be cherished,
Strengthened and fed without the aid of joy;

Then did I check the tears of useless passion,      25
Weaned my young soul from yearning after thine;
Sternly denied its burning wish to hasten
Down to that tomb already more than mine!

And even yet, I dare not let it languish,
Dare not indulge in Memory's rapturous pain;      30
Once drinking deep of that divinest anguish,
How could I seek the empty world again?

# Reed Whittemore

## BRONTË
## REMEMBRANCE

"Remembrance" is what is known to Brontë scholars as a Gondal poem. As children Emily and Anne Brontë created a whole fictional world around a fictional island in the North Pacific called Gondal; then in maturity Emily wrote a great number of poems with the old fictions as background. Not only are most of the details of these fictions now missing (see Miss Fannie E. Ratchford's reconstruction of them in C.W. Hatfield's edition of Emily's poems: Columbia University Press, 1941), but they would probably not add much to the poem even if we had them. All we really need to know is that a queen in a gothic fairyland is grieving over the loss of her gothic-fairyland king, and that, being such a queen, she has earned the poetic right to a fifteen-year term of "divinest anguish."

If we add to the elaborate Gondal fiction the fact that Emily's poems as well as her sisters' were originally published pseudonymously under the title "Poems by Currer, Ellis and Acton Bell" (Emily was Ellis), we find ourselves looking through a double mask to find out Emily's relationship to the expressed anguish. And since the lofty art of fiction is sometimes hard to distinguish from the lower art of hoax we might at this point, if we were not sensitive to the proprieties, even come to question poor Emily's integrity.

But conventions in poetry, like conventions in clothes, are constantly changing. Such masking, if undertaken at all in our time, would probably not be undertaken by a person of Emily's somber temperament and talent, and would indeed be hoax. Realism is our fictional staple; the time for medieval romance and its near equivalents is past even though Sir Walter Scott and other nineteenth century antiquarians still thrive in our high schools. Accordingly our poets tend to steer clear of such fantasies, which are no longer an attractive vehicle for the expression of basic human emotions. How many poets of this century are going to commune with the installment-plan sorrows of an impossible Queen of Gondal? Few, but that is not to say that Emily didn't.

To put this another way, "Remembrance," though a most accomplished piece, is probably too much of a period piece of an eccentrically mannered period to be more than an eccentricity for us. It represents Victorian bustledom too well, partaking too earnestly of the funny mixture of propriety and emotional indulgence the Victorians achieved, to work except for lingering Victorians. A cynic might describe the poem as a beautiful anachronism. Yet, for Emily, the Queen of Gondal and her sorrows, though certainly fantasy, must have appeared to be a reasonable, not outlandish device for the expression of the feelings of Emily. Not only were there plenty of literary precedents for such indirection, but also there was an unhappy childhood of suppression and frustration to encourage Emily to speak, if she spoke at all, only through tubes from underground. Emily, like the Brownings, makes a fine case study—as if that could be of any consolation to her or to literature—of what happens when somebody fed on Keats and Shelley and all the vitamins of romantic expressionism has a moral tyrant for a father, is brought up in a society of sinister rural righteousness, and attends a hell-fire institution called the Clergy Daughters' School. Her impulse as a child was to get away from all that and create Gondal. As she matured she grew bolder and finally produced a relatively unmasked romance, *Wuthering Heights*, where the characters of her father and her brother, and Emily too, are clearly visible, though a great deal of transposition has been effected, and though sex remains a sort of rhetorical rather than physical passion. But in "Remembrance," while apparently written at about the time of *Wuthering Heights*, Gondal still looms darkly out of the mists of the North Pacific. To imagine, for example, that Emily is *really* talking in the poem about her beloved and depraved brother Branwell, and contemplating not his death —for he did not die until after the poem's publication—but his long and depressing physical and mental decline, and thinking back on the times when he was still an arrogant young "king," precocious, poetic and ambitious—such imaginings are possibly of interest but they have very little bearing upon the poem as it stands. The poem as it stands has a hidden violence to it which it certainly does not get from Gondal, and it is rhetorically as beautifully controlled as anything of Tennyson's (Tennyson was also a sort of Gondal poet); yet its wild Decembers and golden dreams are not substantiated as wild or golden in the poem, and Rosina of Alcona in her anguish is much too reticent about the real sources of that anguish to be a persuasive mourner unless we become biographical and introduce Emily's own griefs to sustain her.

Could not a good bit of nineteenth century verse be discarded on similar grounds? Yes. But in making this sweeping complaint I still have, I think, my wits about me. One cannot after all either discard or save the past; it pretty much goes its own way in our parlors and libraries and museums despite our ravings about it. The most we can do is to try to understand it and participate vicariously in it since it is a part, though not a growing part, of us. Therefore to complain here is not to try to discard the poem but to place it, and by placing it to suggest its distance from where we are now in poetry.

Which is where? I am sure there are some readers of "Remembrance" who will assert that "Remembrance" is where we are—or if not, so much the worse for modern poetry. I don't think so, and that is my point. While one cannot place precisely any contemporary art, and while modern poetry is now sallying forth in so many directions that it is probably the most difficult of all our arts to place, still even of it one can surely say in this instance where it is not: it is not in Gondal.

# WALT WHITMAN
## [1819–1892]

## *Memories of President Lincoln: When Lilacs Last in the Dooryard Bloom'd*

### I

When lilacs last in the dooryard bloom'd,
And the great star early droop'd in the western sky in the
    night,
I mourn'd, and yet shall mourn with ever-returning spring.

Ever-returning spring, trinity sure to me you bring,
Lilac blooming perennial and drooping star in the west,    5
And thought of him I love.

### II

O powerful western fallen star!
O shades of night—O moody, tearful night!
O great star disappear'd—O the black murk that hides the
    star!
O cruel hands that hold me powerless—O helpless soul
    of me!    10
O harsh surrounding cloud that will not free my soul.

### III

In the dooryard fronting an old farm-house near the white-
    wash'd palings,
Stands the lilac-bush tall-growing with heart-shaped leaves of
    rich green,
With many a pointed blossom rising delicate, with the per-
    fume strong I love,
With every leaf a miracle—and from this bush in the door-
    yard,    15
With delicate-color'd blossoms and heart-shaped leaves of
    rich green,
A sprig with its flower I break.

### IV

In the swamp in secluded recesses,
A shy and hidden bird is warbling a song.

Solitary the thrush,                                                    20
The hermit withdrawn to himself, avoiding the settlements,
Sings by himself a song.

Song of the bleeding throat,
Death's outlet song of life, (for well dear brother I know,
If thou wast not granted to sing thou would'st
    surely die.)                                                        25

### V

Over the breast of the spring, the land, amid cities,
Amid lanes and through old woods, where lately the violets
    peep'd from the ground, spotting the gray debris,
Amid the grass in the fields each side of the lanes, passing the
    endless grass,
Passing the yellow-spear'd wheat, every grain from its shroud
    in the dark-brown fields uprisen,
Passing the apple-tree blows of white and pink in the
    orchards,                                                           30
Carrying a corpse to where it shall rest in the grave,
Night and day journeys a coffin.

### VI

Coffin that passes through lanes and streets,
Through day and night with the great cloud darkening
    the land,
With the pomp of the inloop'd flags with the cities draped in
    black,                                                             35
With the show of the States themselves as of crape-veil'd
    women standing,
With processions long and winding and the flambeaus of the
    night,
With the countless torches lit, with the silent sea of faces and
    the unbared heads,
With the waiting depot, the arriving coffin, and the sombre
    faces,
With dirges through the night, with the thousand voices
    rising strong and solemn,                                          40
With all the mournful voices of the dirges pour'd around the
    coffin,

WALT WHITMAN

*The Bettmann Archive*

The dim-lit churches and the shuddering organs—where amid
    these you journey,
With the tolling bells' perpetual clang,
Here, coffin that slowly passes,
I give you my sprig of lilac.                 45

### VII

(Nor for you, for one alone,
Blossoms and branches green to coffins all I bring,
For fresh as the morning, thus would I chant a song for you O
    sane and sacred death.

All over bouquets of roses,
O death, I cover you over with roses and early lilies,     50
But mostly and now the lilac that blooms the first,
Copious I break, I break the sprigs from the bushes,
With loaded arms I come, pouring for you,
For you and the coffins all of you O death.)

### VIII

O western orb sailing the heaven,           55
Now I know what you must have meant as a month since I
    walk'd,
As I walk'd in silence the transparent shadowy night,
As I saw you had something to tell as you bent to me night
    after night,
As you droop'd from the sky low down as if to my side,
    (while the other stars all look'd on,)
As we wander'd together the solemn night, (for something I
    know not what kept me from sleep,)     60
As the night advanced, and I saw on the rim of the west how
    full you were of woe,
As I stood on the rising ground in the breeze in the cool
    transparent night,
As I watch'd where you pass'd and was lost in the nether-
    ward black of the night,
As my soul in its trouble dissatisfied sank, as where you sad orb,
Concluded, dropt in the night, and was gone.     65

### IX

Sing on there in the swamp,
O singer bashful and tender, I hear your notes, I hear your
    call,
I hear, I come presently, I understand you,

But a moment I linger, for the lustrous star has detain'd me,
The star my departing comrade holds and detains me.     70

### X

O how shall I warble myself for the dead one there I loved?
And how shall I deck my song for the large sweet soul that
    has gone?
And what shall my perfume be for the grave of him I love?

Sea-winds blown from east and west,
Blown from the Eastern sea and blown from the Western sea,
    till there on the prairies meeting,     75
These and with these and the breath of my chant,
I'll perfume the grave of him I love.

### XI

O what shall I hang on the chamber walls?
And what shall the pictures be that I hang on the walls,
To adorn the burial-house of him I love?     80

Pictures of growing spring and farms and homes,
With the Fourth-month eve at sundown, and the gray smoke
    lucid and bright,
With floods of the yellow gold of the gorgeous, indolent,
    sinking sun, burning, expanding the air,
With the fresh sweet herbage under foot, and the pale green
    leaves of the trees prolific,

In the distance the flowing glaze, the breast of the river,
    with a wind-dapple here and there,     85
With ranging hills on the banks, with many a line against the
    sky, and shadows,
And the city at hand with dwellings so dense, and stacks of
    chimneys,
And all the scenes of life and the workshops, and the work-
    men homeward returning.

### XII

Lo, body and soul—this land,
My own Manhattan with spires, and the sparkling and hurry-
    ing tides, and the ships,     90
The varied and ample land, the South and the North in the
    light, Ohio's shores and flashing Missouri,
And ever the far-spreading prairies cover'd with grass and
    corn.

Lo, the most excellent sun so calm and haughty,
The violet and purple morn with just-felt breezes,
The gentle soft-born measureless light,                          95
The miracle spreading bathing all, the fulfill'd noon,
The coming eve delicious, the welcome night and the stars,
Over my cities shining all, enveloping man and land.

XIII

Sing on, sing on you gray-brown bird,
Sing from the swamps, the recesses, pour your chant from the
    bushes,                                                      100
Limitless out of the dusk, out of the cedars and pines.

Sing on dearest brother, warble your reedy song,
Loud human song, with voice of uttermost woe.

O liquid and free and tender!
O wild and loose to my soul—O wondrous singer!                  105
You only I hear—yet the star holds me, (but will soon depart,)
Yet the lilac with mastering odor holds me.

XIV

Now while I sat in the day and look'd forth,
In the close of the day with its light and the fields of spring,
    and the farmers preparing their crops,
In the large unconscious scenery of my land with its lakes and
    forests,                                                     110
In the heavenly aerial beauty, (after the perturb'd winds and
    the storms,)
Under the arching heavens of the afternoon swift passing, and
    the voices of children and women,
The many-moving sea-tides, and I saw the ships how they
    sail'd,
And the summer approaching with richness, and the fields all
    busy with labor,
And the infinite separate houses, how they all went on, each
    with its meals and minutia of daily usages,                 115
And the streets how their throbbings throbb'd, and the cities
    pent—lo, then and there,
Falling upon them all and among them all, enveloping me with
    the rest,
Appear'd the cloud, appear'd the long black trail,
And I knew death, its thought, and the sacred knowledge of
    death.

Then with the knowledge of death as walking one side of
    me,        120
And the thought of death close-walking the other side of me,
And I in the middle as with companions, and as holding the
    hands of companions,
I fled forth to the hiding receiving night that talks not,
Down to the shores of the water, the path by the swamp in
    the dimness,
To the solemn shadowy cedars and ghostly pines so still.  125

And the singer so shy to the rest receiv'd me,
The gray-brown bird I know receiv'd us comrades three,
And he sang the carol of death, and a verse for him I love.

From deep secluded recesses,
From the fragrant cedars and the ghostly pines so still,   130
Came the carol of the bird.

And the charm of the carol rapt me,
As I held as if by their hands my comrades in the night,
And the voice of my spirit tallied the song of the bird.

*Come lovely and soothing death,*   135
*Undulate round the world, serenely arriving, arriving,*
*In the day, in the night, to all, to each,*
*Sooner or later delicate death.*

*Prais'd be the fathomless universe,*
*For life and joy, and for objects and knowledge curious,*  140
*And for love, sweet love—but praise! praise! praise!*
*For the sure-enwinding arms of cool-enfolding death.*

*Dark mother always gliding near with soft feet,*
*Have none chanted for thee a chant of fullest welcome?*
*Then I chant it for thee, I glorify thee above all,*  145
*I bring thee a song that when thou must indeed come,*
    *come unfalteringly.*

*Approach strong deliveress,*
*When it is so, when thou hast taken them I joyously sing the*
    *dead,*
*Lost in the loving floating ocean of thee,*
*Laved in the flood of thy bliss O death.*  150

*From me to thee glad serenades,*
*Dances for thee I propose saluting thee, adornments and feast-*
    *ings for thee,*
*And the sights of the open landscape and the high-spread sky*
    *are fitting,*
*And life and the fields, and the huge and thoughtful night.*

*The night in silence under many a star,*                                    155
*The ocean shore and the husky whispering wave whose
    voice I know,*
*And the soul turning to thee O vast and well-veil'd death,*
*And the body gratefully nestling close to thee.*

*Over the tree-tops I float thee a song,*
*Over the rising and sinking waves, over the myriad fields
    and the prairies wide,*                                                  160
*Over the dense-pack'd cities all and the teeming wharves and
    ways,*
*I float this carol with joy, with joy to thee O death.*

### XV

To the tally of my soul,
Loud and strong kept up the gray-brown bird,
With pure deliberate notes spreading filling the night.                      165

Loud in the pines and cedars dim,
Clear in the freshness moist and the swamp-perfume,
And I with my comrades there in the night.

While my sight that was bound in my eyes unclosed,
As to long panoramas of visions.                                             170

And I saw askant the armies,
I saw as in noiseless dreams hundreds of battle-flags,
Borne through the smoke of the battles and pierc'd with
    missiles I saw them,
And carried hither and yon through the smoke, and torn and
    bloody,
And at last but a few shreds left on the staffs, (and all in
    silence,)                                                                175
And the staffs all splinter'd and broken.

I saw battle-corpses, myriads of them,
And the white skeletons of young men, I saw them,
I saw the debris and debris of all the slain soldiers of the war,
But I saw they were not as was thought,                                      180
They themselves were fully at rest, they suffer'd not,
The living remain'd and suffer'd, the mother suffer'd,
And the wife and the child and the musing comrade suffer'd,
And the armies that remain'd suffer'd.

### XVI

Passing the visions, passing the night,                                      185
Passing, unloosing the hold of my comrades' hands,

Passing the song of the hermit bird and the tallying song of
    my soul,
Victorious song, death's outlet song, yet varying ever-altering
    song,
As low and wailing, yet clear the notes, rising and falling,
    flooding the night,
Sadly sinking and fainting, as warning and warning, and yet
    again bursting with joy,                   190
Covering the earth and filling the spread of the heaven,
As that powerful psalm in the night I heard from recesses,
Passing, I leave thee lilac with heart-shaped leaves,
I leave thee there in the dooryard, blooming, returning with
    spring.

I cease from my song for thee,                195
From my gaze on thee in the west, fronting the west,
    communing with thee,
O comrade lustrous with silver face in the night.

Yet each to keep and all, retrievements out of the night,
The song, the wondrous chant of the gray-brown bird,
And the tallying chant, the echo arous'd in my soul,     200
With the lustrous and drooping star with the countenance full
    of woe,
With the holders holding my hand nearing the call of the bird,
As low and wailing, yet clear the notes, rising and falling,
Comrades mine and I in the midst, and their memory ever
    to keep, for the dead I loved so well,
For the sweetest, wisest soul of all my days and lands—and this
    for his dear sake,
Lilac and star and bird twined with the chant of my soul,     205
There in the fragrant pines and the cedars dusk and dim.

# Geoffrey Grigson

## WHITMAN
### MEMORIES OF PRESIDENT LINCOLN:
### WHEN LILACS LAST IN THE DOORYARD BLOOM'D

It subsists, this great carol, not in history, but in the sprig of
lilac:

> *Here, coffin that slowly passes,*
> *I give you my sprig of lilac,*

in the meeting of April and death. Familiar with the poem, a
reader and user of English from birth who is not American
may require to remind himself that its occasion was the death
of Abraham Lincoln, in the April of 1865. And it is arguable
that only such a reader can see this poem clear and clean. He
can read it without historical or national emotion. The
history of it is someone else's history. Whitman wrote "Dear
to the Muse—thrice dear to Nationality—to the whole human race—precious to this Union—precious to Democracy—
unspeakably and for ever precious—their first great Martyr
Chief." He exaggerated. The victory, "the million dead,
too, summ'd up," belong to America, but not to those other
readers. If they know the scraggy form and features, the
beard, the smile, the Adam's apple from the photographs, the
shock and the scene, when the body fell in Ford's theater, and
and Booth called out "*Sic semper tyrannis*" and the soldiers of
the President's guard (says Whitman) burst in, "literally
charging the audience with fix'd bayonets, muskets and
pistols, shouting *Clear out! clear out! You sons of—*" (presumably bitches)—all these affect them only as an *Et tu,
Brute*. Not being their grand death, or their "most important
inheritance-value," the historical death drops from the poem;
leaving behind something altogether first-hand and immediate, as poetry; which is its measure as a masterpiece.

The lilac usurps the poem. Lincoln is not named except in
the title. Whitman smelt the lilac on the day of the assassina-
tion. Early herbage, early flowers were out: "I remember
where I was stopping at the time, the season being advanced,

there were many lilacs in full bloom. By one of those caprices that enter and give tinge to events without being at all a part of them, I find myself always reminded of the great tragedy of that day by the sight and odour of these blossoms." Lilac is named; Lincoln, through the poem, is the unnamed corpse of the loved man, in the coffin, who is made—but without the anemia of an idea arising out of generalization—into all death, straightaway. First the lilac, in its particular place, "when lilacs last in the dooryard bloom'd," then the evening star in the west after day, then mourning, then the cause of mourning, the "thought of him I love." If black night obtrudes in the five lines of the second section, and returns, the song of the bird enters it; and fourteen sections follow that are a sequence of variations on lilac, star, and death, and the song of the withdrawn hermit thrush, which is added in the fourth section.

Senses are quickly engaged, sight, scent, sound. The poem proceeds in a great movement of contraction that demands expansion, expansion that counterdemands the necessary strength of the single image. After the thrush of the fourth section, in the fifth and sixth sections a universe of the spring season and a billion of mourners, and flambeaux, and dirges and bells and shuddering organs attend the one coffin, which is given the one sprig of lilac; and this one coffin in the next section—section seven—multiplies to all coffins and all death; one sprig of lilac multiplies to blossoms and branches and roses and early lilies, and lilac now broken off and loading the arms.

> *With loaded arms I come, pouring for you,*
> *For you and the coffins all of you O death*

Star-night—all stars. Thrush: and songs of eastern and western sea winds meeting on the prairies, and combining song or sound with perfume. The interplay goes on of single, or few, with multitude. Pictures for the room of death become all country and city that can be pictured, all sun over an infinity of the particularized; then narrow again to the grey-brown bird singing, "Limitless out of the dusk, out of the cedars and pines," and to the setting star, and to the lilac with mastering odor; and to Whitman—but Whitman who sat in the close of the day

> *In the large unconscious scenery of my land*
> *with its lakes and forests,*

and saw himself and everything enveloped in death; but in death as, after all, rest, which embraced the armies of the dead, the white skeletons, "the debris and debris" of the slain.

So, a resolution. After this great review or parade, Whitman, involved in comradeship (one recalls D.H. Lawrence in *Studies in Classic American Literature* celebrating in this poet "the love of comrades: a recognition of souls, and a communion of worship," which are here, "a glad recognition of souls, and a gladder worship of great and greater souls, because they are the only riches"), returns from all death to the one death: since he makes his poem end on its beginning. "For the sweetest, wisest soul of all my days and lands," for the sake of the one dead "lilac and star and bird twined with the chant of my soul."

A poet, or his poem, is sometimes definable in a central phrase from another poet of the same nature. Gerard Manley Hopkins, not without apprehension, since he was a priest and Whitman was a sensualist like himself but without his canonical discipline, saw that Whitman was his closest affinity; and he named in one sonnet the characteristics he wanted, but then lacked, in his own verse: *The roll, the rise, the carol, the creation.* Here are these four in Whitman, the result in this poem of receiving a reality—the death of Abraham Lincoln—into dream or vision.

Notice, incidentally, one not insignificant item in Whitman's presentation: that nowhere in this poem is the recurrent blossom of the dooryard lilac given its color. Its scent only. Otherwise the force of it is left in the word, in the name.

## I Sing the Body Electric

I

I sing the body electric,
The armies of those I love engirth me and I engirth them,
They will not let me off till I go with them, respond to them,
And discorrupt them, and charge them full with the charge of
    the soul.         5
Was it doubted that those who corrupt their own bodies con-
    ceal themselves?
And if those who defile the living are as bad as they who de-
    file the dead?
And if the body does not do fully as much as the soul?
And if the body were not the soul, what is the soul?

II

The love of the body of man or woman balks account, the
    body itself balks account,         10
That of the male is perfect, and that of the female is perfect.
The expression of the face balks account,
But the expression of a well-made man appears not only in
    his face,
It is in his limbs and joints also, it is curiously in the joints of
    his hips and wrists,
It is in his walk, the carriage of his neck, the flex of his waist
    and knees, dress does not hide him,
The strong sweet quality he has strikes through the cotton
    and broadcloth,         15
To see him pass conveys as much as the best poem, perhaps
    more,
You linger to see his back, and the back of his neck and shoul-
    der-side.
The sprawl and fulness of babes, the bosoms and heads of
    women, the folds of their dress, their style as
    we pass in the street, the contour of their
    shape downwards,

The swimmer naked in the swimming-bath, seen as he swims
        through the transparent green-shine, or lies
        with his face up and rolls silently to and fro
        in the heave of the water,
The bending forward and backward of rowers in row-boats,
        the horseman in his saddle,        20
Girls, mothers, house-keepers, in all their performances,
The group of laborers seated at noon-time with their open
        dinner kettles, and their wives waiting,
The female soothing a child, the farmer's daughter in the gar-
        den or cow-yard,
The young fellow hoeing corn, the sleigh-driver driving his
        six horses through the crowd,
The wrestle of wrestlers, two apprentice-boys, quite grown,
        lusty, good-natured, native-born, out on the
        vacant lot at sundown after work,      25
The coats and caps thrown down, the embrace of love and
        resistance,
The upper-hold and under-hold, the hair rumpled over and
        blinding the eyes;
The march of firemen in their own costumes, the play of mas-
        culine muscle through clean-setting trowsers
        and waist-straps,
The slow return from the fire, the pause when the bell
        strikes suddenly again, and the listening on the
        alert,
The natural, perfect, varied attitudes, the bent head, the
        curv'd neck and the counting;        30
Such-like I love—I loosen myself, pass freely, am at the
        mother's breast with the little child,
Swim with the swimmers, wrestle with wrestlers, march in
        line with the firemen, and pause, listen, count.

### III

I knew a man, a common farmer, the father of five sons,
And in them the fathers of sons, and in them the fathers
        of sons.
This man was of wonderful vigor, calmness, beauty of
        person,        35
The shape of his head, the pale yellow and white of his hair
        and beard, the immeasurable meaning of his
        black eye, the richness and breadth of his
        manners,
These I used to go and visit him to see, he was wise also,

He was six feet tall, he was over eighty years old, his sons
      were massive, clean, bearded, tan-faced, hand-
      some,
They and his daughters loved him, all who saw him loved him,
They did not love him by allowance, they loved him with
      personal love,          40
He drank water only, the blood show'd like scarlet through
      the clear-brown skin of his face,
He was a frequent gunner and fisher, he sail'd his boat him-
      self, he had a fine one presented to him by a
      ship-joiner, he had fowling-pieces presented to
      him by men that loved him,
When he went with his five sons and many grand-sons to
      hunt or fish, you would pick him out as the
      most beautiful and vigorous of the gang,
You would wish long and long to be with him, you would
      wish to sit by him in the boat that you and he
      might touch each other.

### IV

I have perceiv'd that to be with those I like is enough,     45
To stop in company with the rest at evening is enough,
To be surrounded by beautiful, curious, breathing, laughing
      flesh is enough,
To pass among them or touch any one, or rest my arm
      ever so lightly round his or her neck for a
      moment, what is this then?
I do not ask any more delight, I swim in it as in a sea.
There is something in staying close to men and women and
      looking on them, and in the contact and
      odor of them, that pleases the soul well,     50
All things please the soul, but these please the soul well.

### V

This is the female form,
A divine nimbus exhales from it from head to foot,
It attracts with fierce undeniable attraction,
I am drawn by its breath as if I were no more than a helpless
      vapor, all falls aside but myself and it,     55
Books, art, religion, time, the visible and solid earth, and what
      was expected of heaven or fear'd of hell, are
      now consumed,
Mad filaments, ungovernable shoots play out of it, the re-
      sponse likewise ungovernable,

Hair, bosom, hips, bend of legs, negligent falling hands all dif-
fused, mine too diffused,
Ebb stung by the flow and flow stung by the ebb, love-
flesh swelling and deliciously aching,
Limitless limpid jets of love hot and enormous, quivering jelly
of love, white-blow and delirious juice,　　60
Bridegroom night of love working surely and softly into the
prostrate dawn,
Undulating into the willing and yielding day,
Lost in the cleave of the clasping and sweet-flesh'd day.
This the nucleus—after the child is born of woman, man is
born of woman,
This the bath of birth, this the merge of small and large,
and the outlet again.　　65
Be not ashamed women, your privilege encloses the rest, and
is the exit of the rest,
You are the gates of the body, and you are the gates of the
soul.
The female contains all qualities and tempers them,
She is in her place and moves with perfect balance,
She is all things duly veil'd, she is both passive and active,　70
She is to conceive daughters as well as sons, and sons as well
as daughters.
As I see my soul reflected in Nature,
As I see through a mist, One with inexpressible completeness,
sanity, beauty,
See the bent head and arms folded over the breast, the Female
I see.

### VI

The male is not less the soul nor more, he too is in his
place,　　75
He too is all qualities, he is action and power,
The flush of the known universe is in him,
Scorn becomes him well, and appetite and defiance become
him well,
The wildest largest passions, bliss that is utmost, sorrow that is
utmost become him well, pride is for him,
The full-spread pride of man is calming and excellent to the
soul,　　80
Knowledge becomes him, he likes it always, he brings every
thing to the test of himself,
Whatever the survey, whatever the sea and the sail he strikes
soundings at last only here,

(Where else does he strike soundings except here?)
The man's body is sacred and the woman's body is sacred,
No matter who it is, it is sacred—is it the meanest one in the laborers' gang? 85
Is it one of the dull-faced immigrants just landed on the wharf?
Each belongs here or anywhere just as much as the well-off, just as much as you,
Each has his or her place in the procession.
(All is a procession,
The universe is a procession with measured and perfect motion.)
Do you know so much yourself that you call the meanest ignorant? 90
Do you suppose you have a right to a good sight, and he or she has no right to a sight?
Do you think matter has cohered together from its diffuse float, and the soil is on the surface, and water runs and vegetation sprouts,
For you only, and not for him and her?

### VII

A man's body at auction,
(For before the war I often go to the slave-mart and watch the sale,) 100
I help the auctioneer, the sloven does not half know his business.
Gentlemen look on this wonder,
Whatever the bids of the bidders they cannot be high enough for it,
For it the globe lay preparing quintillions of years without one animal or plant,
For it the revolving cycles truly and steadily roll'd. 105
In this head the all-baffling brain,
In it and below it the makings of heroes.
Examine these limbs, red, black, or white, they are cunning in tendon and nerve,
They shall be stript that you may see them.
Exquisite senses, life-lit eyes, pluck, volition, 110
Flakes of breast-muscle, pliant backbone and neck, flesh not flabby, good-sized arms and legs,
And wonders within there yet.
Within there runs blood,
The same old blood! the same red-running blood!

There swells and jets a heart, there all passions, desires, reach-
    ings, aspirations, 115
(Do you think they are not there because they are not ex-
    press'd in parlors and lecture-rooms?)
This is not only one man, this the father of those who
    shall be fathers in their turns,
In him the start of populous states and rich republics,
Of him countless immortal lives with countless embodiments
    and enjoyments.
How do you know who shall come from the offspring of
    his offspring through the centuries? 120
(Who might you find you have come from yourself, if you
    could trace back through the centuries?)

### VIII

A woman's body at auction,
She too is not only herself, she is the teeming mother of
    mothers,
She is the bearer of them that shall grow and be mates to the
    mothers.
Have you ever loved the body of a woman? 125
Have you ever loved the body of a man?
Do you not see that these are exactly the same to all in all
    nations and times all over the earth?
If anything is sacred the human body is sacred,
And the glory and sweet of a man is the token of manhood
    untainted,
And in man or woman a clean, strong, firm-fibred body,
    is more beautiful than the most beautiful
    face. 130
Have you seen the fool that corrupted his own live body? or
    the fool that corrupted her own live body?
For they do not conceal themselves, and cannot conceal
    themselves.

### IX

O my body! I dare not desert the likes of you in other men
    and women, nor the likes of the parts of you,
I believe the likes of you are to stand or fall with the likes
    of the soul, (and that they are the soul,)
I believe the likes of you shall stand or fall with my poems,
    and that they are my poems, 135
Man's, woman's, child's, youth's, wife's, husband's, mother's,
    father's, young man's, young woman's poems,

Head, neck, hair, ears, drop and tympan of the ears,
Eyes, eye-fringes, iris of the eye, eyebrows, and the waking
 or sleeping of the lids,
Mouth, tongue, lips, teeth, roof of the mouth, jaws, and the
 jaw-hinges,
Nose, nostrils of the nose, and the partition,      140
Cheeks, temples, forehead, chin, throat, back of the neck,
 neck-slue,
Strong shoulders, manly beard, scapula, hind-shoulders, and
 the ample side-round of the chest,
Upper-arm, armpit, elbow-socket, lower-arm, arm-sinews,
 arm-bones,
Wrist and wrist-joints, hand, palm, knuckles, thumb, fore-
 finger, finger-joints, finger-nails,
Broad breast-front, curling hair of the breast, breast-bone,
 breast-side,      145
Ribs, belly, backbone, joints of the backbone,
Hips, hip-sockets, hip-strength, inward and outward round,
 man-balls, man-root,
Strong set of thighs, well carrying the trunk above,
Leg-fibres, knee, knee-pan, upper-leg, under-leg,      150
Ankles, instep, foot-ball, toes, toe-joints, the heel;
All attitudes, all the shapeliness, all the belongings of my or
 your body or of any one's body, male or
 female,
The lung-sponges, the stomach-sac, the bowels sweet and
 clean,
The brain in its folds inside the skull-frame,
Sympathies, heart-valves, palate-valves, sexuality, mater-
 nity,      155
Womanhood and all that is a woman, and the man that comes
 from woman,
The womb, the teats, nipples, breast-milk, tears, laughter,
 weeping, love-looks, love-perturbations and
 risings,
The voice, articulation, language, whispering, shouting aloud,
Food, drink, pulse, digestion, sweat, sleep, walking, swim-
 ming,
Poise on the hips, leaping, reclining, embracing, arm-curving
 and tightening,      160
The continual changes of the flex of the mouth, and around
 the eyes,
The skin, the sunburnt shade, freckles, hair,

The curious sympathy one feels when feeling with the hand
    the naked meat of the body,
The circling rivers the breath, and breathing it in and out,
The beauty of the waist, and thence of the hips, and thence
    downward toward the knees,       165
The thin red jellies within you or within me, the bones and
    the marrow in the bones,
The exquisite realization of health;
O I say these are not the parts and poems of the body
    only, but of the soul,
O I say now these are the soul!       170

# Mark Strand

## WHITMAN
### I SING THE BODY ELECTRIC

Psalmic in its praise of the flesh, "I Sing the Body Electric" is central to Whitman's conception of the New America. We have only to glance at the first poem in the group called "Children of Adam," in which Whitman has cast himself as Adam, and then at the first section of "I Sing the Body Electric," to catch the drift of his thought.

Typical of Whitman is the preacher's journey he takes among men and women in order to "discorrupt them, and charge them full with the charge of the soul." What he preaches is not the body itself, but the "body electric," the body which *is* soul. For without this new sense of the body's divinity there can be no Eden, and it is to Eden that the newly awakened Adamic poet is leading his children. If he preaches sex, it is because through sex the body's spirituality is most firmly established. And those who shrink from it must be "discorrupted." "Undrape!" he tells them in "Song of Myself." "You are not guilty to me, nor stale nor discarded. . . ." The romantic impulse for nakedness runs deep in Whitman.

In section III, the beauty of the old man is in his paternity. Able to hunt or fish with his sons and grandsons, and still vigorous, still able to forcefully project himself physically, he is the Adamic prototype. "You would wish to sit by him," the poet tells us, "that you and he might touch each other." If some of the stridency that characterizes the first two sections of the poem is diminished in this account of the old man, it is lacking altogether in section IV, which resembles, in tone, the intimacy of the "Calamus" poems. A different, more modest contact with people provides fulfillment. "To be with those I like is enough," says the poet. "To be surrounded by beautiful, curious, breathing, laughing flesh is enough."

Whitman's characteristic inability to describe women extends to the more abstract "female form" as well. Its "fierce undeniable attraction" draws the poet almost immediately into "singing the phallus . . . the song of procreation." He and the "female form" rapidly dissolve in the act of love.

*Hair, bosom, hips, bend of legs, negligent falling hands*
*all diffused, mine too diffused,*
*Ebb stung by the flow and flow stung by the ebb, love-*
*flesh swelling and deliciously aching,*
*Limitless limpid jets of love hot and enormous, quiver-*
*ing jelly of love, white-blow and delirious juice,*
*Bridegroom night of love working surely and softly into*
*the prostrate dawn,*
*Undulating into the willing and yielding day,*
*Lost in the cleave of the clasping and sweet-flesh'd day.*

The sexual performance is not limited. As natural as daybreak
or the sea, it operates on all levels, one has only to recognize it.

Though Whitman claims equal status for men and women,
it is clear that woman's role is functional, her "place" an
agency of man's becoming. In a moment of bland biblical
rhetoric he tells us that "she is to conceive daughters as well as
sons, and sons as well as daughters." In "A Woman Waits for
Me" he is clear in describing for women their role in the
future of democracy:

*I pour the stuff to start sons and daughters fit for these*
*States, I press with slow rude muscle*

And then, without making any apparent distinction between
the two, he shifts from his patriotic calling to personal
craving:

*I brace myself effectually, I listen to no entreaties,*
*I dare not withdraw till I deposit what has so long accu-*
*mulated within me.*

*Through you I drain the pent-up rivers of myself*

When the poet takes over at a slave auction, in section VII
of "I Sing the Body Electric," his democratic ideals are made
even more manifest. He ironically assumes the voice of the
auctioneer—"look on this wonder," "examine these limbs"—
but his point is the pricelessness of human life. For even the
slave has "in him the start of populous states and rich republics." The body does not observe class distinctions. "If anything is sacred the human body is sacred."

The children of Adam will live in a perfect democracy.
Whitman's ability to be so many things, to extend himself in
so many directions, is necessary to his preaching the gospel of
the new America. His acceptance of others and his ability to
identify with them, as are clearly demonstrated in sections II
and VII, is a form of democratization. In him all men are
equal, and through him they speak:

*I speak the pass-word primeval, I give the sign of de-
   mocracy.*
*By God! I will accept nothing which all cannot have
   their counterpart of in the same terms.*

An exhaustive and passionate hymn to the parts of the
body, section IX is a fitting climax to the poem. For Whitman is not merely naming the parts of the body, he is naming
the parts of the body into being, creating a body uncorrupted
and divine, a body which is soul.

"I Sing the Body Electric" is extraordinary in the energetic
and relentless way it makes its point. The loud adoration of
the body never flags. Long, fragmented, easy to read, it shifts
rapidly back and forth between the closely observed and the
unobservable. Through a unifying parallelism and clusters of
short vigorous phrases, a strong cadence is established. If, as I
have noted before, the poem seems at times strident, it is to its
ultimate advantage. Whitman is fighting fire with fire, pitting
his rhetoric against that of an established and corrupting
Puritanism. Adam, according to Whitman, is still unfallen,
and must lead his children back to the garden. Natural, unfallen man must be re-established; and Puritanism that denies
men and women the free use of their bodies and therefore, in
Whitman's words, their souls, denies America its future.

Reading the "Children of Adam" poems, we are convinced
of the peculiar strength of Whitman's democratized mysticism, but we are not convinced that he is really doing more
than exhorting whoever will listen to take his advice. What
we hear is the voice, but not the man. Instead, the man is
heard clearly and poignantly in the love poems in the
"Calamus" group. To read the "Children of Adam" is ultimately to be absorbed by a voice that has only one position
and one general purpose. In "Calamus" the experience is more
complex because the voice is determined by the need to speak
truthfully about Walt Whitman the man.

Nevertheless, "I Sing the Body Electric" is a powerful,
prophetic poem; it has as much immediacy as the best sections
of "Song of Myself." In excitement of language, in urgency of
metaphor and rhythm, it is Whitman at his most incandescent
—the good gray poet turned on.

MATTHEW ARNOLD

*The Bettmann Archive*

# MATTHEW ARNOLD
## [1822–1888]

## *Dover Beach*

The sea is calm to-night,
The tide is full, the moon lies fair
Upon the straits;—on the French coast, the light
Gleams, and is gone; the cliffs of England stand,
Glimmering and vast, out in the tranquil bay.　　　　　5
Come to the window, sweet is the night-air!
Only, from the long line of spray
Where the sea meets the moon-blanch'd land,
Listen! you hear the grating roar
Of pebbles which the waves draw back, and fling,　　　10
At their return, up the high strand,
Begin, and cease, and then again begin,
With tremulous cadence slow, and bring
The eternal note of sadness in.

Sophocles long ago　　　　　15
Heard it on the Aegean, and it brought
Into his mind the turbid ebb and flow
Of human misery; we
Find also in the sound a thought,
Hearing it by this distant northern sea.　　　　　20

The Sea of Faith
Was once, too, at the full, and round earth's shore
Lay like the folds of a bright girdle furled.
But now I only hear
Its melancholy, long, withdrawing roar,　　　　　25
Retreating, to the breath
Of the night-wind, down the vast edges drear
And naked shingles of the world.

Ah, love, let us be true
To one another! for the world, which seems　　　　　30
To lie before us like a land of dreams,
So various, so beautiful, so new,

Hath really neither joy, nor love, nor light,
Nor certitude, nor peace, nor help for pain;
And we are here as on a darkling plain                    35
Swept with confused alarms of struggle and flight,
Where ignorant armies clash by night.

# James Dickey

### ARNOLD

### DOVER BEACH

"Dover Beach" has been called the first modern poem. If this is true, it is modern not so much in diction and technique—for its phrasing and its Miltonic inversions are obvious carry-overs from a much older poetry—but in psychological orientation. Behind the troubled man standing at the lover's conventional moon-filled window looking on the sea, we sense—more powerfully because our hindsight confirms what Arnold only began to intuit—the shift in the human viewpoint from the Christian tradition to the impersonal world of Darwin and the nineteenth century scientists. The way the world is seen, and thus the way men live, is conditioned by what men know about it, and they know more now than they ever have before. Things themselves—the sea, stars, darkness, wind—have not changed; it is the perplexed anxiety and helplessness of the newly dispossessed human being that now come forth from his mind and transmute the sea, the night air, the French coast, and charge them with the sinister implications of the entirely alien. What begins as a rather conventional—but very good—description of scenery turns slowly into quite another thing: a recognition of where the beholder stands in relation to these things; where he *really* stands. It is this new and comfortless knowledge as it overwhelms for all time the old and does away with the place where he thought he stood, where his tradition told him he stood, that creates the powerful and melancholy force of the poem.

In statement, "Dover Beach" goes very easily and gravely, near prose and yet not too near. It has something of the effect of overheard musing, though it is addressed, or half-addressed, to someone present. Its greatest technical virtue, to my mind, is its employment of sound-imagery, particularly in the deep, sustained vowels of lines like "Its melancholy, long, withdrawing roar." The lines also seem to me to *break* beautifully: ". . . on the French coast, the light / Gleams, and is gone." I have tried many times to rearrange Arnold's lines, and have never succeeded in doing anything but diminish their subtlety, force and conviction.

The one difficulty of the poem, it seems to me, is in the famous third strophe wherein the actual sea is compared to the Sea of Faith. If Arnold means that the Sea of Faith was formerly at high tide, and he hears now only the sound of the tide going out, one cannot help thinking also of the cyclic nature of tides, and the consequent coming of another high tide only a few hours after the present ebb. In other words, the figure of speech appears valid only on one level of the comparison; the symbolic half fails to sustain itself. Despite the magnificence of the writing in this section, I cannot help believing that it is the weakest part of the poem when it should be the strongest; the explicitness of the comparison seems too ready-made. Yet I have the poem as it is so deeply in memory that I cannot imagine it changed, and would not have it changed even if I knew it would be a better poem thereby.

In the sound of waves rolling pebbles, an eternal senseless motion, unignorable and meaningless, Arnold hears—as we ever afterwards must hear—human sadness, the tears of things. It links us to Sophocles and to all men at all times who have discovered in such a sound an expression of their own unrest, and have therefore made of it "the eternal note of sadness." Yet our sadness has a depth that no other era has faced: a certainty of despair based upon our own examination of empirical evidence and the conclusions drawn by our rational faculty. These have revealed not God but the horror and emptiness of things, including those that we cannot help thinking beautiful: that *are* beautiful. By its direct, slow-speaking means, the poem builds toward its last nine lines, when the general resolves into the particular, divulging where *we* stand, what these things mean to *us*. The implication is that if love, morality, constancy and the other traditional Western virtues are not maintained without supernatural sanction, there is nothing. The world that lies before us in such beauty that it seems to have come instantaneously from God's hand does not include, guarantee or symbolize the qualities that men have assumed were also part of it. It is beautiful and impersonal, but we must experience it—and now suffer it—as persons. Human affection is revealed as a completely different thing than what we believed it to be; as different, in fact, as the world we were mistaken about. It is a different thing but also a new thing, with new possibilities of terror, choice and meaning. The moment between the lovers thus takes on the qualities of a new expulsion from Eden: they tremble with fear but also with terrible freedom; they look eastward. The intense vulnerability of the emotional life takes place in an imperiled darkness among the sounds of the sea and against the imminence of violence, wars, armies blundering blindly into each other for no reason. Yet there is a new, fragile center to things: a man and a woman. In a word, it is love in what we have come to call the existential predicament. Nearly a hundred years ago, Arnold fixed unerringly and profoundly on the quality that more than any other was to characterize the emotion of love in our own century: desperation.

# The Scholar-Gipsy

Go, for they call you, Shepherd, from the hill;
  Go, shepherd, and untie the wattled cotes:
    No longer leave thy wistful flock unfed,
    Nor let thy bawling fellows rack their throats,
    Nor the cropp'd grasses shoot another head.      5
      But when the fields are still,
    And the tired men and dogs all gone to rest,
      And only the white sheep are sometimes seen
      Cross and recross the strips of moon-blanch'd green,
  Come, shepherd, and again begin the quest.      10

Here, where the reaper was at work of late,
  In this high field's dark corner, where he leaves
    His coat, his basket, and his earthen cruise,
    And in the sun all morning binds the sheaves,
    Then here, at noon, comes back his stores to use;      15
      Here will I sit and wait,
    While to my ear from uplands far away
      The bleating of the folded flocks is borne,
      With distant cries of reapers in the corn—
  All the live murmur of a summer's day.      20

Screen'd is this nook o'er the high, half-reap'd field,
  And here till sun-down, Shepherd, will I be.
    Through the thick corn the scarlet poppies peep,
    And round green roots and yellowing stalks I see
      Pale pink convolvulus in tendrils creep:      25
      And air-swept lindens yield
    Their scent, and rustle down their perfumed showers
      Of bloom on the bent grass where I am laid,
      And bower me from the August sun with shade;
  And the eye travels down to Oxford's towers:      30

And near me on the grass lies Glanvil's book—
  Come, let me read the oft-read tale again:
    The story of the Oxford scholar poor,

Of pregnant parts and quick inventive brain,
  Who, tired of knocking at Preferment's door,      35
    One summer morn forsook
His friends, and went to learn the Gipsy-lore
And roam'd the world with that wild brotherhood,
And came, as most men deem'd, to little good,
But came to Oxford and his friends no more.      40

But once, years after, in the country lanes,
  Two scholars, whom at college erst he knew,
    Met him, and of his way of life enquired;
Whereat he answer'd that the Gipsy-crew,
  His mates, had arts to rule as they desired      45
    The workings of men's brains;
And they can bind them to what thoughts they will:
"And I," he said, "the secret of their art,
When fully learn'd, will to the world impart;
But it needs Heaven-sent moments for this skill."      50

This said, he left them, and return'd no more,
  But rumours hung about the country-side,
    That the lost Scholar long was seen to stray,
Seen by rare glimpses, pensive and tongue-tied,
  In hat of antique shape, and cloak of grey,      55
    The same the Gipsies wore.
Shepherds had met him on the Hurst in spring;
  At some lone alehouse in the Berkshire moors,
  On the warm ingle-bench, the smock-frock'd boors
Had found him seated at their entering,      60

But, 'mid their drink and clatter, he would fly.
  And I myself seem half to know thy looks,
    And put the shepherds, Wanderer, on thy trace;
And boys who in lone wheatfields scare the rooks
  I ask if thou hast pass'd their quiet place;      65
    Or in my boat I lie
Moor'd to the cool bank in the summer heats,
  'Mid wide grass meadows which the sunshine fills,
  And watch the warm green-muffled Cumner hills,
And wonder if thou haunt'st their shy retreats.      70

For most, I know, thou lov'st retirèd ground.
  Thee, at the ferry, Oxford riders blithe,
    Returning home on summer-nights, have met
Crossing the stripling Thames at Bablock-hithe,
  Trailing in the cool stream thy fingers wet,      75
    As the slow punt swings round;
And leaning backwards in a pensive dream,

And fostering in thy lap a heap of flowers
Pluck'd in shy fields and distant Wychwood bowers,
And thine eyes resting on the moonlit stream:                80

And then they land, and thou art seen no more.
Maidens who from the distant hamlets come
    To dance around the Fyfield elm in May,
Oft through the darkening fields have seen thee roam,
    Or cross a stile into the public way.                   85
        Oft thou hast given them store
Of flowers—the frail-leaf'd, white anemone—
    Dark bluebells drench'd with dews of summer eves,
    And purple orchises with spotted leaves—
But none has words she can report of thee.                   90

And, above Godstow Bridge, when hay-time's here
In June, and many a scythe in sunshine flames,
    Men who through those wide fields of breezy grass
Where black-wing'd swallows haunt the glittering Thames,
    To bathe in the abandon'd lasher pass,                  95
        Have often pass'd thee near
Sitting upon the river bank o'ergrown;
    Mark'd thine outlandish garb, thy figure spare,
    Thy dark vague eyes, and soft abstracted air;
But, when they came from bathing, thou wert gone.            100

At some lone homestead in the Cumner hills,
    Where at her open door the housewife darns,
    Thou hast been seen, or hanging on a gate
To watch the threshers in the mossy barns.
    Children, who early range these slopes and late          105
        For cresses from the rills,
Have known thee watching, all an April day,
    The springing pastures and the feeding kine;
    And mark'd thee, when the stars come out and shine,
Through the long dewy grass move slow away.                  110

In autumn, on the skirts of Bagley Wood,
    Where most the Gipsies by the turf-edged way
    Pitch their smoked tents, and every bush you see
With scarlet patches tagg'd and shreds of grey,
    Above the forest-ground call'd Thessaly—                 115
        The blackbird picking food,
Sees thee, nor stops his meal, nor fears at all;
    So often has he known thee past him stray
    Rapt, twirling in thy hand a wither'd spray,
And waiting for the spark from Heaven to fall.               120

And once, in winter, on the causeway chill
  Where home through flooded fields foot-travellers go,
    Have I not pass'd thee on the wooden bridge,
  Wrapt in the cloak and battling with the snow,
      Thy face towards Hinksey and its wintry ridge?          125
        And thou hast climb'd the hill
  And gain'd the white brow of the Cumner range;
    Turn'd once to watch, while thick the snowflakes fall,
    The line of festal light in Christ Church hall—
  Then sought thy straw in some sequester'd grange.           130

But what—I dream! Two hundred years are flown
  Since first thy story ran through Oxford halls,
    And the grave Glanvil did the tale inscribe
  That thou wert wander'd from the studious walls
      To learn strange arts, and join a Gipsy-tribe:          135
        And thou from earth art gone
  Long since, and in some quiet churchyard laid—
    Some country nook, where o'er thy unknown grave
    Tall grasses and white flowering nettles wave—
  Under a dark red-fruited yew-tree's shade.                  140

—No, no, thou hast not felt the lapse of hours.
  For what wears out the life of mortal men?
    'Tis that from change to change their being rolls:
    'Tis that repeated shocks, again, again,
      Exhaust the energy of strongest souls                   145
        And numb the elastic powers.
  Till having used our nerves with bliss and teen,
    And tired upon a thousand schemes our wit,
    To the just-pausing Genius we remit
  Our worn-out life, and are—what we have been.               150

Thou hast not lived, why should'st thou perish, so?
  Thou hadst *one* aim, *one* business, *one* desire:
    Else wert thou long since number'd with the dead!
  Else hadst thou spent, like other men, thy fire!
      The generations of thy peers are fled,                  155
        And we ourselves shall go;
  But thou possessest an immortal lot,
    And we imagine thee exempt from age
    And living as thou liv'st on Glanvil's page,
  Because thou hadst—what we, alas! have not.                 160

For early didst thou leave the world, with powers
  Fresh, undiverted to the world without,

Firm to their mark, not spent on other things;
Free from the sick fatigue, and languid doubt,
   Which much to have tried, in much been baffled, brings.
     O life unlike to ours!          166
Who fluctuate idly without term or scope,
   Of whom each strives, nor knows for what he strives,
   And each half lives a hundred different lives;
Who wait like thee, but not, like thee, in hope.    170

Thou waitest for the spark from heaven! and we,
   Light half-believers of our casual creeds,
     Who never deeply felt, nor clearly will'd,
   Whose insight never has borne fruit in deeds,
     Whose vague resolves never have been fulfill'd;   175
       For whom each year we see
   Breeds new beginnings, disappointments new;
     Who hesitate and falter life away,
     And lose to-morrow the ground won to-day—
Ah! do not we, Wanderer, await it too?    180

Yes, we await it, but it still delays,
   And then we suffer! and amongst us One,
     Who most has suffer'd, takes dejectedly
His seat upon the intellectual throne;
     And all his store of sad experience he    185
       Lays bare of wretched days;
   Tells us his misery's birth and growth and signs,
     And how the dying spark of hope was fed,
     And how the breast was soothed, and how the head,
And all his hourly varied anodynes.    190

This for our wisest: and we others pine,
   And wish the long unhappy dream would end,
   And waive all claim to bliss, and try to bear,
With close-lipp'd Patience for our only friend,
     Sad Patience too near neighbour to Despair;   195
       But none has hope like thine.
Thou through the fields and through the woods dost stray,
   Roaming the country-side, a truant boy,
   Nursing thy project in unclouded joy,
And every doubt long blown by time away.    200

O born in days when wits were fresh and clear,
   And life ran gaily as the sparkling Thames;
   Before this strange disease of modern life,
With its sick hurry, its divided aims,
     Its heads o'ertax'd, its palsied hearts, was rife—   205
       Fly hence, our contact fear!

Still fly, plunge deeper in the bowering wood!
  Averse, as Dido did with gesture stern
  From her false friend's approach in Hades turn,
  Wave us away, and keep thy solitude.                       210

Still nursing the unconquerable hope,
  Still clutching the inviolable shade,
    With a free, onward impulse brushing through,
    By night, the silver'd branches of the glade—
  Far on the forest-skirts, where none pursue;               215
      On some mild pastoral slope
  Emerge, and resting on the moonlit pales
  Freshen thy flowers, as in former years
  With dew, or listen with enchanted ears,
  From the dark dingles, to the nightingales.                220

But fly our paths, our feverish contact fly!
  For strong the infection of our mental strife,
    Which, though it gives no bliss, yet spoils for rest;
    And we should win thee from thy own fair life,
  Like us distracted, and like us unblest.                   225
      Soon, soon thy cheer would die,
  Thy hopes grow timorous, and unfix'd thy powers,
  And thy clear aims be cross and shifting made;
  And then thy glad perennial youth would fade,
  Fade, and grow old at last, and die like ours.             230

Then fly our greetings, fly our speech and smiles!
  —As some grave Tyrian trader, from the sea,
    Descried at sunrise an emerging prow
    Lifting the cool-hair'd creepers stealthily,
  The fringes of a southward-facing brow                     235
      Among the Ægæan isles;
  And saw the merry Grecian coaster come,
    Freighted with amber grapes, and Chian wine,
    Green bursting figs, and tunnies steep'd in brine;
  And knew the intruders on his ancient home,                240

The young light-hearted Masters of the waves;
  And snatch'd his rudder, and shook out more sail;
    And day and night held on indignantly
  O'er the blue Midland waters with the gale,
    Betwixt the Syrtes and soft Sicily,                      245
      To where the Atlantic raves
  Outside the Western Straits, and unbent sails
    There, where down cloudy cliffs, through sheets of foam,
    Shy traffickers, the dark Iberians come;
  And on the beach undid his corded bales.                   250

*Arthur Mizener*

---

ARNOLD

THE SCHOLAR-GIPSY

Matthew Arnold was the first great English poet to know the kind of divided consciousness that has become characteristic of the experience of the twentieth century. Like us, Arnold felt profoundly dissatisfied with the conventional life of his time, the "multitudinousness," the mechanical uniformity, the deadness of the everyday world: he was anxious to escape its influence. At the same time he was convinced that to alienate the world by defiance and eccentricity or to retire from it in order to cultivate one's soul in private was self-indulgent and self-defeating. He felt great—though strictly limited—respect for certain of his immediate predecessors, such as Wordsworth, Byron, and Keats, and for a few of his contemporaries such as Tennyson; but in his essential attitude he differed from them all. At its most characteristic his poetry is a quietly eloquent, melancholy, frequently ironic expression of a sense of experience far closer to ours than to that of most of the great Victorians or the romantics, and "The Scholar-Gipsy" is probably his most considerable expression of this feeling.

Like its complement in the twentieth century, "The Waste Land," which Mr. Eliot has called structureless in a futile way, "The Scholar-Gipsy" is not all Arnold had hoped to make it. Its inadequacy begins for him in its disproportionate though beautiful description of the scholar gypsy wandering in the Cumner country near Oxford, that home of all the beloved causes Arnold knew to be lost. Arnold loved the Cumner country deeply. There as an undergraduate, feeling as much optimism about the human situation as he ever would, he too had wandered with his closest friend, Arthur Hugh Clough, who later became for him an example of the man destroyed by the multitudinousness of the world, a victim of "storms that rage outside our happy ground; / He could not wait their passing, he is dead!" In the Cumner country, too, Arnold was always reminded of his father, the great

Victorian schoolmaster Thomas Arnold, who had plunged so vigorously into the world to espouse the social reforms of his time and to oppose the backward-looking Tractarianism of Newman, a man whom Arnold in his unexpected way also admired (it seems to have been Newman's unfailing self-possession, what one might almost call his worldliness, that Arnold admired). Ten years after the publication of "The Scholar-Gipsy" Arnold could still say of the Cumner country, "I got up alone into one of those little coombs that papa was so fond of and which I had in mind in the 'Gipsy-Scholar,' and felt the peculiar *sentiment* of this country and neighborhood as deeply as ever." Even longer after, when he recalled it again in "Thyrsis," his elegy for Clough, he still felt it.

"The Scholar-Gipsy's" description of the Cumner country is so exact that one can use it as a guidebook. At the same time, by introducing into his description delicate echoes of traditional pastoral poetry, Arnold makes it an image of timeless peace. Is the shepherd of the opening stanzas an actual Cumner shepherd, or a stylized figure from the world of pastoral poetry? Is the scholar gypsy a figure of fancy from an "oft-read tale" or an actual presence at Bablock-hithe, above Godstow Bridge, on the skirts of Bagley Wood? At the beginning of stanza seven, Arnold stops calling the scholar gypsy (two hundred years dead) "he" and begins to call him "thee," as if he were present and could be addressed directly; and though from stanza six to stanza thirteen we move through time from spring to winter, the scholar's wandering seems to take place in a charmed and endless now. We are awakened from this "dream" in stanza fourteen, but Arnold counts on it to support his prompt assertion that the scholar gypsy has "not felt the lapse of hours"; with him as with the nightingale of Keats's poem, which evidently influenced this part of "The Scholar-Gipsy," "no hungry generations tread thee down." No poet of the last two hundred years except Wordsworth has so successfully made the physical world both vividly actual and alive with human meaning. Arnold deeply admired Wordsworth, though he was convinced that "Wordsworth's eyes avert their ken / From half of human fate" (the half that consists in action), and he did not cease to measure with some amusement Wordsworth's provincial eccentricity, remarking, for example, that your devout Wordsworthians—of which he was one—"can read with pleasure and edification" all of Wordsworth, even " '*Peter Bell*' . . . and the address to Mr. Wil-kinson's spade."

The description of the Cumner country in "The Scholar-Gipsy," a great triumph in itself, is also an important aspect of the poem, for that was Arnold's country of the mind, an image of freedom from the busy, futile world of power and profit with all its philistinism, its pitiful half-grasped dis-satisfaction with the way we live now. That world, he felt, was a brazen prison,

> *Where in the sun's hot eye,*
> *With heads bent o'er their toil, [men] languidly*
> *Their lives to some unmeaning taskwork give;*

it was a darkling plain

> *Swept with confused alarms of struggle and flight*
> *Where ignorant armies clash by night*

From all that the scholar gypsy was free. He could wander through the Cumner country, his soul intact, waiting for the spark from heaven, the living knowledge of the truth that would unite the divided consciousness and make it possible for men to live meaningful lives in the world because they could be completely true to their innermost selves.

Yet Arnold was not satisfied with this image of the man who had escaped "the sick fatigue, and languid doubt" of those "who fluctuate idly without term or scope" into a pastoral world where he could dedicate himself to heaven-sent moments of insight. He wrote to Clough:

> I am glad you like the Gipsy Scholar, but what does it *do* for you? . . .
>
> > *The complaining millions of men*
> > *Darken in labour and pain—*
>
> what they want is something to *animate* and *ennoble* them—not merely to add zest to their melancholy or grace to their dreams.

He did not mean to deny the need for the gypsy scholar's art, the spark from heaven. But commitment to action, an actual, effective life, was as important to Arnold as having the right grounds for action. That is why he surprises us by admiring the Duke of Wellington, who, he thought, "saw *one* clue to life, and *follow'd* it" (the second italics are mine). That is why he sympathized with the fierce restlessness of romantics like Byron. He could see very well the futility of their impractical and even purposeless violence:

*What helps it now, that Byron bore*
*With haughty scorn which mock'd the smart,*
*Through Europe to the Aetolian shore*
*The pageant of his bleeding heart?*

Yet at least Byron had got free of the "brazen prison" of conventional life's deadly routine, and his life had at least the dignity of its heroism, however purposeless, of

*. . . the pale Master on his spar-strewn deck*
*With anguish'd face and flying hair*
*Grasping the rudder hard,*
*Still bent to make some port he knows not where,*
*Still standing for some false impossible shore.*

Yet commitment to action in the ordinary world is almost wholly ignored by the scholar gypsy; at most he may be said to refer to it scantily and indirectly in " 'And I,' he said, 'the secret of their art, / When fully learn'd, will to the world impart' " and the poem's speaker urges him to avoid even that much contact with the world. As a result "The Scholar-Gipsy," Arnold thought, fails to provide any image of the animating and ennobling life of action and so gives excessive emphasis to the quiescent and—when it becomes one's exclusive object—self-indulgent process of acquiring wisdom. In fact the contrast set up at the beginning of the poem between the pastoral Cumner country and the busy world of preferment forces Arnold, at the end of the poem, to insist that the scholar reject the world permanently. How can he hope to survive there when even "our wisest" has not escaped its fever and fret? (Arnold told an American newspaperman that "our wisest" was Goethe, but that was almost certainly a polite evasion of the truth that he was Tennyson: Goethe had been dead twenty-one years when the poem was published; "In Memoriam" appeared just three years before.) Thus "The Scholar-Gipsy" is logically forced to conclude by urging the scholar to continue forever to "fly our paths, our feverish contact fly!"—even though that leaves him, in his complete commitment to thought at the expense of action,

*Still nursing the unconquerable hope,*
*Still clutching the inviolable shade*

as futile in his way as Byron, with his commitment to action at the expense of thought, was in his.

This limitation on the poem's main argument is what makes the Homeric simile of the last two stanzas puzzlingly obscure. It is clear enough that the "Masters" of "the merry

Grecian coaster" with their light hearts and luxurious cargo are analogous with "us" who suffer from "this strange disease of modern life, / With its sick hurry, its divided aims," and that the "grave Tyrian trader" is analogous with the scholar gypsy who escapes this contamination. But we do not easily think of the merry Greek as dangerous (have we not just been told that "life ran gaily" in the scholar gypsy's Cumner country?) or of the scholar gypsy as a trader preoccupied with the business of the world, however shy the traffickers for whom he undoes his corded bales. But Arnold was not by any means unqualifiedly enthusiastic about the Greeks: men needed, he thought, as much Hebraism as Hellenism ("merry Greek" has had ominous overtones ever since Elizabethan times). Nor is it the Tyrian trader who is at fault in the other analogy, but the scholar gypsy, who would have committed himself to the right kind of worldly traffic—shy and grave— had Arnold known how to conceive him doing so, as he did know how to conceive the Tyrian trader's doing so in the slightly pastoralized classical world of the Victorian imagination.

Behind "The Scholar-Gipsy" lies, then, a complex and moving conception of a dilemma only beginning to be felt in Arnold's time that has come to bulk large in ours, how to live in a world where "the best lack all conviction, while the worst / Are full of passionate intensity." Arnold knew that, to be whole, men must act in the world and, if they are to do so purposefully, must have a passionate, controlled commitment—the disciplined ardor of a Byron who knows what port he sails for, the intense, unstrident assurance of a Newman. He was convinced that such unfanatical dedication was possible only if a spark from heaven had fallen to show one the clue to life that would unite the private and the public selves in a common meaning. When that happens,

> *A bolt is shot back somewhere in our breast*
> *And a lost pulse of feeling stirs again:*
> *The eye sinks inward, and the heart lies plain,*
> *And what we mean, we say, and what we would, we*
>      *know.*
> *A man becomes aware of his life's flow*
> *And hears its winding murmur, and he sees*
> *The meadows where it glides, the sun, the breeze*

as the young Arnold and the immortal scholar gipsy had heard "the stripling Thames" flow through the Cumner country like their own buried lives.

Like "The Waste Land," "The Scholar-Gipsy" can tell us only what it is like not to live so—what it is like to hear life's flow somewhere far from the busy haunts of men, where the sweet Thames runs softly still, and what it is like to live somewhere round behind the gashouse, where the river of the buried life is inaudible. For clearly as Arnold saw the need to live both in the world and with "the knowledge of our buried life," he never had succeeded in doing so. He knew the melancholy of faith preserved in isolation from life at the Grande Chartreuse, the wild despair of the master on his spar-strewn deck, the icy despair of "Obermann"—and the innocent, lost enthusiasm of the scholar gypsy. Like Mr. Eliot, who did not want to express the "disillusionment" of his age, Arnold did not want merely to add zest to the melancholy or grace to the dream of his. But that was all he honestly could do, because all he had actually experienced was the nightmare pastoral of his own

> *Wandering between two worlds, one dead,*
> *The other powerless to be born.*

DANTE GABRIEL ROSSETTI

*Photographed by Lewis Carroll, 1863*
*The Bettmann Archive*

# DANTE GABRIEL ROSSETTI

## [1828–1882]

## *The Blessèd Damozel*

The blessèd damozel lean'd out
  From the gold bar of Heaven;
Her eyes were deeper than the depth
  Of waters still'd at even;
She had three lilies in her hand,        5
  And the stars in her hair were seven.

Her robe, ungirt from clasp to hem,
  No wrought flowers did adorn,
But a white rose of Mary's gift,
  For service meetly worn;        10
Her hair that lay along her back
  Was yellow like ripe corn.

Herseem'd she scarce had been a day
  One of God's choristers;
The wonder was not yet quite gone        15
  From that still look of hers;
Albeit, to them she left, her day
  Had counted as ten years.

(To one, it is ten years of years.
  . . . Yet now, and in this place,        20
Surely she lean'd o'er me—her hair
  Fell all about my face. . . .
Nothing: the autumn-fall of leaves.
  The whole year sets apace.)

It was the rampart of God's house        25
  That she was standing on;
By God built over the sheer depth
  The which is Space begun;
So high, that looking downward thence
  She scarce could see the sun.        30

It lies in Heaven, across the flood
  Of ether, as a bridge.

Beneath, the tides of day and night
    With flame and darkness ridge
The void, as low as where this earth        35
    Spins like a fretful midge.

Around her, lovers, newly met
    'Mid deathless love's acclaims,
Spoke evermore among themselves
    Their heart-remember'd names;        40
And the souls mounting up to God
    Went by her like thin flames.

And still she bow'd herself and stoop'd
    Out of the circling charm;
Until her bosom must have made        45
    The bar she lean'd on warm,
And the lilies lay as if asleep
    Along her bended arm.

From the fix'd place of Heaven she saw
    Time like a pulse shake fierce        50
Through all the worlds. Her gaze still strove
    Within the gulf to pierce
Its path; and now she spoke as when
    The stars sang in their spheres.

The sun was gone now; the curl'd moon        55
    Was like a little feather
Fluttering far down the gulf; and now
    She spoke through the still weather.
Her voice was like the voice the stars
    Had when they sang together.        60

(Ah sweet! Even now, in that bird's song,
    Strove not her accents there,
Fain to be hearkened? When those bells
    Possess'd the mid-day air,
Strove not her steps to reach my side        65
    Down all the echoing stair?)

"I wish that he were come to me:
    For he will come," she said.
"Have I not pray'd in Heaven?—on earth,
    Lord, Lord, has he not pray'd?        70
Are not two prayers a perfect strength?
    And shall I feel afraid?

"When round his head the aureole clings,
    And he is clothed in white,

I'll take his hand and go with him          75
   To the deep wells of light;
As unto a stream we will step down,
   And bathe there in God's sight.

"We two will stand beside that shrine,
   Occult, withheld, untrod,          80
Whose lamps are stirred continually
   With prayer sent up to God;
And see our old prayers, granted, melt
   Each like a little cloud.

"We two will lie i' the shadow of          85
   That living mystic tree,
Within whose secret growth the Dove
   Is sometimes felt to be,
While every leaf that His plumes touch
   Saith His Name audibly.          90

"And I myself will teach to him,
   I myself, lying so,
The songs I sing here; which his voice
   Shall pause in, hush'd and slow,
And find some knowledge at each pause,          95
   Or some new thing to know."

(Alas! We two, we two, thou say'st!
   Yea, one wast thou with me
That once of old. But shall God lift
   To endless unity          100
The soul whose likeness with thy soul
   Was but its love for thee?)

"We two," she said, "will seek the groves
   Where the lady Mary is,
With her five handmaidens, whose names          105
   Are five sweet symphonies,
Cecily, Gertrude, Magdalen,
   Margaret and Rosalys.

"Circlewise sit they, with bound locks
   And foreheads garlanded;          110
Into the fine cloth white like flame
   Weaving the golden thread,
To fashion the birth-robes for them
   Who are just born, being dead.

"He shall fear, haply, and be dumb:          115
   Then will I lay my cheek

To his, and tell about our love,
  Not once abash'd or weak:
And the dear Mother will approve
  My pride, and let me speak.                    120

"Herself shall bring us, hand in hand,
  To Him round whom all souls
Kneel, the clear-ranged unnumbered heads
  Bowed with their aureoles:
And angels meeting us shall sing                 125
  To their citherns and citoles.

"There will I ask of Christ the Lord
  Thus much for him and me:—
Only to live as once on earth
  With Love,—only to be,                         130
As then awhile, for ever now
  Together, I and he."

She gazed and listen'd and then said,
  Less sad of speech than mild,—
"All this is when he comes." She ceased.         135
  The light thrill'd towards her, fill'd
With angels in strong level flight.
  Her eyes prayed, and she smiled.

(I saw her smile.) But soon their path
  Was vague in distant spheres:                  140
And then she cast her arms along
  The golden barriers,
And laid her face between her hands,
  And wept. (I heard her tears.)

# David Daiches

## D. G. ROSSETTI
### THE BLESSÈD DAMOZEL

"I saw that Poe had done the utmost it was possible to do with the grief of the lover on earth, and so I determined to reverse the conditions, and give utterance to the yearning of the loved one in heaven." So Rossetti described the theme of "The Blessèd Damozel," a reversal of the situation evoked in Poe's "Raven." But of course Rossetti's poem is more than a soliloquy of a heavenly soul separated from her earthly lover: it is a deliberate attempt to render the spiritual in concrete sensuous terms and in doing so to suggest a primitive equation of the spiritual and the physical. In a sense, one might call this a subversive poem, for it sets out to subvert traditional Christian teaching of the basic difference between the earthly, mortal state and the heavenly, immortal state. In dressing his heroine in a simple pre-Raphaelite "robe, ungirt from clasp to hem" decorated with a single white rose, Rossetti is suggesting that in an earlier, more innocent, less sophisticated age the spiritual and the physical were interchangeable. The stylized imagery of the poem has indeed a suggestion of primitive art with its unconscious confusing of such categories as the formal and the representational. But there is nothing unconscious about this poem: it is a very guileful piece of work. The very title, with its use of the old form "damozel" ("now used by poets, etc., as more stately than *damsel*"—O.E.D.), has implications of early chivalry and of the medieval world of courtly love. And the three lilies and seven stars of the first stanzas suggest medieval symbolism without being really symbolic. The particularization of the mystic numbers three and seven is almost a trick: an atmosphere of symbolic reference is set up without any precise reference being made.

The slow, even movement of the six-line stanza with its three rhyming words (the second, fourth, and sixth lines: note that the first, third, and fifth lines do not rhyme either with each other or with anything else) helps to achieve a dreamlike effect. It is the extra two lines that achieve this. Four lines alone in this meter, with the second and fourth rhyming, constitute simple ballad measure; it is remarkable how this is changed with two more lines and the third rhyme. The reader can test this for himself by reading the first few stanzas omitting the last two lines of each (the essential meaning is hardly changed).

"Herseem'd" in stanza three is a deliberate archaism, in keeping with the poet's general intention of creating an early-medieval atmosphere. Yet in spite of this and similar devices, the tone of modern sophistication is dominant in the poem. It's all, we feel, a beautiful trick—a splendid poem in its way, with its melodious rhythm and language, its subdued sacramental imagery, its mingling of grief and desire, religion and sex, beauty and spirituality, yet there is no genuine union of the physical symbol with its spiritual reference, as there is for example in Dante, because in the last analysis the poem is quite decisively on the side of the flesh. In spite of such bits of spiritual suggestiveness as

> *And the souls mounting up to God*
> *Went by her like thin flames*

and

> *From the fix'd place of Heaven she saw*
> *Time like a pulse shake fierce*
> *Through all the worlds*

the poem is anchored to the sensuous concrete to which in the end everything else is reduced:

> *And still she bow'd herself and stoop'd*
> *Out of the circling charm;*
> *Until her bosom must have made*
> *The bar she lean'd on warm,*
> *And the lilies lay as if asleep*
> *Along her bended arm.*

That flesh-warmed bar of heaven is the compelling image in the poem; it dominates everything, and shows what Rossetti is really doing.

The occasional shift from the damozel herself to the lover on earth having glimpses of her longing for him (fourth, eleventh, seventeenth, and twenty-fourth stanzas) seem at first sight to emphasize the difference between the heavenly and the earthly:

*(To one, it is ten years of years,*
*. . . Yet now, and in this place,*
*Surely she lean'd o'er me—her hair*
*Fell all about my face . . .*
*Nothing: the autumn-fall of leaves.*
*The whole year sets apace.)*

The earth is bound to time and the movement of the seasons, whereas heaven belongs to eternity and is timeless. The contrast is moving: the ten desolate years of the living lover compared with the single day of the damozel bring for a moment a new human dimension into the poem. But the contrast is neither fully developed nor adequately sustained. The damozel, too, is in a world of time, though her time moves at a different speed. As a relatively recent arrival in heaven she still wears a look of wonder, which time will presumably remove, and she is waiting for the time to come when her lover will join her in heaven. She is not outside time at all. This is perhaps not very important in itself, but it is related to the perfunctoriness of the attempt to translate earthly love into its heavenly counterpart that in turn reveals the lack of true symbolic or visionary quality in the poem and its trick use of religious imagery:

*When round his head the aureole clings,*
*And he is clothed in white,*
*I'll take his hand and go with him*
*To the deep wells of light;*
*As unto a stream we will step down,*
*And bathe there in God's sight.*

*. . .*

*We two will lie i' the shadow of*
*That living mystic tree*
*Within whose secret growth the Dove*
*Is sometimes felt to be,*
*While every leaf that His plumes touch*
*Saith His Name audibly.*

*And I myself will teach to him,*
*I myself, lying so,*
*The songs I sing here; . . .*

Heavenly mixed bathing and the use of images from the twenty-second chapter of *Revelation* to suggest a very special kind of open-air love-making can be said, if we are mischievously inclined, to suggest a tremendously superior travel

advertisement: "Come and make love beneath the mystic tree
in the wonderful climate of Heaven." This is unfair. The
poem, precisely because it does turn heaven into a superior
earth and preserve its tremulous sexual feeling and the heavy
sensual mood even in dealing with the immortal life of souls,
does have a strangely powerful impact, while the elegiac
tone, the sense of longing (hers confident in spite of the
sadness, his merely sad), comes across as genuinely moving.
The sense of collapse at the end, where the immortal soul
turns into a simple weeping girl, gives a new turn to the
poem, which ends with a girl's visible smile being followed
by a girl's audible tears. Both sight and sound testify to what
has happened: the senses provide the means of knowing what
happens even in heaven. We can see why a contemporary
critic attacked Rossetti's "fleshly school of poetry." But for
those who have faith in the flesh, this poem is a testament.

# CHRISTINA ROSSETTI

[1830–1894]

## *The Convent Threshold*

There's blood between us, love, my love,
There's father's blood, there's brother's blood;
And blood's a bar I cannot pass:
I choose the stairs that mount above,
Stair after golden skyward stair,      5
To city and to sea of glass.
My lily feet are soiled with mud,
With scarlet mud which tells a tale
Of hope that was, of guilt that was,
Of love that shall not yet avail;      10
Alas, my heart, if I could bare
My heart, this self-same stain is there:
I seek the sea of glass and fire
To wash the spot, to burn the snare;
Lo, stairs are meant to lift us higher:      15
Mount with me, mount the kindled stair.

Your eyes look earthward, mine look up.
I see the far-off city grand,
Beyond the hills a watered land,
Beyond the gulf a gleaming strand      20
Of mansions where the righteous sup;
Who sleep at ease among their trees,
Or wake to sing a cadenced hymn
With Cherubim and Seraphim;
They bore the Cross, they drained the cup,      25
Racked, roasted, crushed, wrenched limb from limb,
They the offscouring of the world:
The heaven of starry heavens unfurled,
The sun before their face is dim.

You looking earthward, what see you?      30
Milk-white, wine-flushed among the vines,
Up and down leaping, to and fro,
Most glad, most full, made strong with wines,
Blooming as peaches pearled with dew,

Their golden windy hair afloat,                                    35
Love-music warbling in their throat,
Young men and women come and go.

    You linger, yet the time is short:
Flee for your life, gird up your strength
To flee: the shadows stretched at length              40
Show that day wanes, that night draws nigh;
Flee to the mountain, tarry not.
Is this a time for smile and sigh,
For songs among the secret trees
Where sudden bluebirds nest and sport?               45
The time is short and yet you stay:
To-day, while it is called to-day,
Kneel, wrestle, knock, do violence, pray:
To-day is short, to-morrow nigh:
Why will you die? why will you die?                    50

    You sinned with me a pleasant sin:
Repent with me, for I repent.
Woe's me the lore I must unlearn!
Woe's me that easy way we went,
So rugged when I would return!                           55
How long until my sleep begin,
How long shall stretch these nights and days?
Surely, clean Angels cry, she prays;
She laves her soul with tedious tears:
How long must stretch these years and years?      60

    I turn from you my cheeks and eyes,
My hair which you shall see no more,—
Alas for joy that went before,
For joy that dies, for love that dies.
Only my lips still turn to you,                              65
My livid lips that cry, Repent!
O weary life, O weary Lent,
O weary time whose stars are few!

    How should I rest in Paradise,
Or sit on steps of Heaven alone?                          70
If Saints and Angels spoke of love
Should I not answer from my throne?
Have pity upon me, ye my friends,
For I have heard the sound thereof:
Should I not turn with yearning eyes,                   75
Turn earthwards with a pitiful pang?
O save me from a pang in Heaven!

CHRISTINA ROSSETTI

*The Bettmann Archive*

By all the gifts we took and gave,
Repent, repent, and be forgiven:
This life is long, but yet it ends; 80
Repent and purge your soul and save:
No gladder song the morning stars
Upon their birthday morning sang
Than Angels sing when one repents.

I tell you what I dreamed last night: 85
A spirit with transfigured face
Fire-footed clomb an infinite space.
I heard his hundred pinions clang,
Heaven-bells rejoicing rang and rang,
Heaven-air was thrilled with subtle scents, 90
Worlds spun upon their rushing cars:
He mounted shrieking: "Give me light!"
Still light was poured on him, more light;
Angels, Archangels he outstripped,
Exultant in exceeding might, 95
And trod the skirts of Cherubim.
Still "Give me light," he shrieked; and dipped
His thirsty face, and drank a sea,
Athirst with thirst it could not slake.
I saw him, drunk with knowledge, take 100
From arching brows the aureole crown,—
His locks writhed like a cloven snake,—
He left his throne to grovel down
And lick the dust of Seraphs' feet:
For what is knowledge duly weighed? 105
Knowledge is strong, but love is sweet;
Yea, all the progress he had made
Was but to learn that all is small
Save love, for love is all in all.

I tell you what I dreamed last night: 110
It was not dark, it was not light,
Cold dews had drenched my plenteous hair
Through clay; you came to seek me there.
And "Do you dream of me?" you said.
My heart was dust that used to leap 115
To you; I answered half asleep:
"My pillow is damp, my sheets are red,
There's a leaden tester to my bed:
Find you a warmer playfellow,
A warmer pillow for your head, 120
A kinder love to love than mine."

You wrung your hands; while I like lead
Crushed downwards through the sodden earth:
You smote your hands but not in mirth,
And reeled but were not drunk with wine.      125

For all night long I dreamed of you:
I woke and prayed against my will,
Then slept to dream of you again.
At length I rose and knelt and prayed:
I cannot write the words I said,             130
My words were slow, my tears were few;
But through the dark my silence spoke
Like thunder. When this morning broke,
My face was pinched, my hair was gray,
And frozen blood was on the sill             135
Where stifling in my struggle I lay.

If now you saw me you would say:
Where is the face I used to love?
And I would answer: Gone before;
It tarries veiled in Paradise.               140
When once the morning star shall rise,
When earth with shadow flees away
And we stand safe within the door,
Then you shall lift the veil thereof.
Look up, rise up: for far above              145
Our palms are grown, our place is set;
There we shall meet as once we met,
And love with old familiar love.

# William Stafford

## C. ROSSETTI
### THE CONVENT THRESHOLD

In our time, art inheres in the fragments that temporarily find themselves sustaining a pattern. Another way once thrived: an announced pattern, which could itself dignify, elevate, and intensify fragments that lived by their part in the traditional, the orthodox, the permanent. By focusing her references and committing herself fervently to such a pattern—the Christian view of salvation—Christina Rossetti provides in "The Convent Threshold" an internally consistent exemplar of the lasting power of this kind of art. An unfriendly reader may reject elements in the poem or may lump them as sentimental, but the direction of the whole work can gain the allegiance of all except those for whom art has to be a fragment in order to qualify as valid. And even for such an unfriendly critic, there must glimmer somewhere as a potential (always this is true for an artist) some coercive accomplishment that could hold lasting parts new-wrought into an accepted truth, and thus gain the utter allegiance of any—even the most desperately unfriendly—beholder. "The Convent Threshold" represents art of that ambitious, consistent kind.

At first reading, the poem heaps up too many fervent, irridescent elements to be convincing: the distraught lover, the hinted romantic broken hearts, the awful lapse over the threshold into the (stereotype) convent. And after all that renouncing, heaven is valued at the end as an occasion for re-uniting the lovers. Parts are sensationalized; an already charged situation is proclaimed and declaimed. But second thoughts can account for the poem's residual power, even after all charges are pressed to the limit. The extreme plot is the justification for lavish constructions. There is a spaciousness about the feelings here: big dimensions are whole-heartedly sought. Whatever the lack of realism, elements of the poem, it happens, offer maximum resonance for feelings, and these feelings—no matter how unfriendly the contemporary world is to their expression in particular poems or particular religions—endure as elements in man's life on the earth: people feel guilt, love, an impulse to renounce, a need to find security and permanence within the awful surges of fortune.

After all, even for the most phlegmatic among us, outside our comfortable but fleeting selves there are hints of finalities, terrible permanences; and as daily joys and small excitements may crescendo in the sensibilities of certain more imaginative people, those background permanences will often insist, too—more and more vividly present. Somewhere at the end of such a spiral of realization there could exist the kind of twang of broken pitch that Christina Rossetti cultivates in this poem. The poem seeks outward and upward, guided by what it seems to avoid—the unbearable degrees of realization: love barred by family, some kind of violence, mounting guilt (which grows from the potential of love subjected to contradictory requirements), and then by way of the unbearable toward the relieved turning to already-established emotional options in religion.

A story with this much intensity invites us to connect it to the life of the teller, and many readers have evaded the import of this poem by ascribing the emotions in it to a distant, curious, extreme character, Christina Rossetti, and assuming the materials of art to be simply equivalent to details of her life—someone else's life. But there is a more coercive way to see this poem. The drastic alternatives in the story, and the quick, contradictory options in the lines, and the rapid orders ("Kneel, wrestle, knock, do violence, pray") deliver, not the distant elements in the life of someone felt to be alien, but certain equivalents for any reader's submerged, permanent life pattern. Such a poem—offering either a sensational story of someone else or an available pattern for the attachment of the reader's own impulses—can in most eras give both effects without contradiction; that is, such poems can live most vividly in times when the reader lends a naive attention to them. The reader then accepts literally the religion in the poem, thus receiving that part of the poem with full effect, and he relishes the story as the immediate account of the teller's life, and the teller is someone like himself—thus he participates in a stunning experience. In our day we can hardly adopt either part of this stance, hence our plight. The more mistaken a reader today is about the provenance of such a poem, the more intensely he may experience it. One of the qualities of our time is that our analytical impulse destroys this ability to merge with art in a helpful and innocent way; as a consequence, a poem like this one dulls considerably in our salt air. We ascribe it quickly to the ravings of a distracted foreigner.

Luckily, even today there is a chance to sustain the value of such a poem, by lending it the kind of attention that recognizes its formal accomplishments. The resulting experience can provide the inner life with sustenance, without leading in overt conduct to such irrelevancies as the indictment of Christina Rossetti or the forsaking of one's mate. But the balance of commitment and reserve required in our day is difficult. Strangely, skeptical as we think ourselves, there have been examples in plenty in our time of persons whose commitment to literature was so great that they guided their lives by its formal elements—they have led crusades justified only by their accompanying elation, or have collapsed inwardly from the confluence of jarring literary styles; or in reaction they have turned philistine and persecuted writers who cultivate literary intensities. And the most common attitude of all is to turn utterly from anything emotional or "unreal"—to suppress the emotional life continually in the interest of maximum production or some other kind of physical accomplishment. Thus God and Caesar have divided most of mankind, leaving only a few free to lend their excited attention to ideas and feelings, and thus to live fully in their outer lives without damaging either heaven or earth— or perhaps even themselves. For such people the continued existence of such poems as "The Convent Threshold" is very important. Such a poem is like a graceful wild beast protected from fanatics of all kinds, and reminding us all of a style of literature that remained viable for long amidst the changes that brought about the world we know—and a style that might flourish, and even save us for a while, again.

# EMILY DICKINSON
## [1830–1886]

## *Death*

### A SEQUENCE OF POEMS

#### I

There's a certain slant of light,
Winter afternoons,
That oppresses like the heft
Of cathedral tunes.

Heavenly hurt it gives us.                     5
We can find no scar
But internal difference
Where the meanings are.

None may teach it any—
'Tis the seal despair,                         10
An imperial affliction
Sent us of the air.

When it comes the landscape listens,
Shadows hold their breath.
When it goes 'tis like the distance            15
On the look of death.

#### II

Because I could not stop for Death
He kindly stopped for me.
The carriage held but just ourselves
And immortality.

We slowly drove. He knew no haste,             5
And I had put away
My labor and my leisure too
For his civility.

We passed the school where children strove
At recess in the ring.                         10

We passed the fields of grazing grain;
We passed the setting sun—

Or rather, he passed us.
The dews drew quivering and chill,
For only gossamer my gown,                          15
My tippet only tulle.

We paused before a house that seemed
A swelling of the ground.
The roof was scarcely visible,
The cornice in the ground.                          20

Since then 'tis centuries, and yet
Feels shorter than the day
I first surmised the horses' heads
Were toward Eternity.

### III

I felt a funeral in my brain,
And mourners to and fro
Kept treading, treading, till it seemed
That sense was breaking through.

And when they all were seated,                      5
A service like a drum
Kept beating, beating, till I thought
My mind was going numb.

And then I heard them lift a box
And creak across my soul                            10
With those same boots of lead again,
Then space began to toll,

As all the Heavens were a bell,
And being but an ear,
And I and silence some strange race                 15
Wrecked solitary here.

And then a plank in reason broke,
And I dropped down and down
And hit a world at every plunge,
And finished knowing then.                          20

### IV

I heard a fly buzz when I died.
The stillness in the room

EMILY DICKINSON

*The Bettmann Archive*

Was like the stillness in the air
Between the heaves of storm.

The eyes around had wrung them dry,                    5
And breaths were gathering firm
For that last onset when the king
Be witnessed in the room.

I willed my keepsakes, signed away
What portion of me be                                 10
Assignable; and then it was
There interposed a fly

With blue uncertain stumbling buzz
Between the light and me;
And then the windows failed; and then                 15
I could not see to see.


                              v


Safe in their alabaster chambers,
Untouched by morning
And untouched by noon,
Sleep the meek members of the resurrection—
Rafter of satin,                                       5
And roof of stone.

Light laughs the breeze
In her castle above them,
Babbles the bee in a stolid ear,
Pipe the sweet birds in ignorant cadence—             10
Ah, what sagacity perished here!


                              VI


What inn is this
Where for the night
Peculiar traveller comes?
Who is the landlord?
Where the maids?                                       5
Behold, what curious rooms!
No ruddy fires on the hearth—
No brimming tankards flow.
Necromancer! Landlord!
Who are these below?                                   10

## VII

It was not death, for I stood up,
And all the dead lie down.
It was not night, for all the bells
Put out their tongues for noon.

It was not frost, for on my flesh                    5
I felt siroccos crawl;
Nor fire, for just my marble feet
Could keep a chancel cool—

And yet it tasted like them all.
The figures I have seen                               10
Set orderly for burial
Reminded me of mine,

As if my life were shaven
And fitted to a frame
And could not breathe without a key;                 15
And 'twas like midnight some

When everything that ticked has stopped
And space stares all around,
Or grisly frosts, first Autumn morns,
Repeal the beating ground,                            20

But most like chaos—stopless, cool,
Without a chance or spar,
Or even a report of land
To justify despair.

## VIII

I died for beauty, but was scarce
Adjusted in the tomb
When one who died for truth was lain
In an adjoining room.

He questioned softly why I failed,                   5
"For beauty" I replied.
"And I for truth. Themself are one.
We brethren are" he said.

And so, as kinsmen met a night,
We talked between the rooms,                          10
Until the moss had reached our lips
And covered up our names.

# D. S. Savage

## DICKINSON
### DEATH: A SEQUENCE OF POEMS

The poems of Emily Dickinson here selected from the voluminous body of her work and arranged into a sequence under the common title, "Death," are some of the most remarkable and impressive to have been written in the nineteenth century. As poetry, they fully justify themselves in their originality and in their internal consistency and completeness. They are also profoundly disquieting, striking the heart with an authentic chill. In one sense, therefore, they do not require elucidation: they stand on their own feet and are their own best argument. And yet because, like all great poetry, they are rooted deeply in the existence of the poet, and because that existence was shaped by an unusually rigorous inner direction, they compel, in our effort fully to comprehend them, some attempt to understand and evaluate the significance of the life they sprang from and expressed, however presumptuous such an attempt must seem.

Both historical and personal factors come into play here. Emily Dickinson was born into the last decades of the great Puritan-Protestant tradition that had formed and sustained North American culture for over two hundred years. The enthusiastic religious faith and practice of her grandfather, which in her father—a prosperous small-town lawyer and politician—had settled into a formal and somewhat repressive moralistic piety, had in her become by inheritance the implicit intellectual framework of a sensitive, skeptical and romantically individualistic mind. As is well known, living in the shadow of her awesome and quietly dominating father, she never married, and lived all her life in her childhood home, becoming more and more of an eccentric and recluse as her life advanced. The determining event of an outwardly uneventful life would appear to have been her meeting, falling irrevocably in love with, and conclusive separation from, a married clergyman, Edward Wadsworth, at about the thirtieth year of her age. Concerning the many poems of Emily Dickinson's that might be termed "love poems," a living poet, Mr. James Reeves, has written: "They are at times passionate, though rarely is there any indication of physical passion. Nevertheless, any reader examining the poems without external biographical knowledge gains the impression of a single all-mastering love frozen, as it were, in the moment of ecstasy by a supreme act of renunciation. Something like this was in fact the central event of Emily's life; but just how far it was actualized is still not clear." The poems in the present sequence (with the possible exception of the sixth) appear to have been written within a year or two of this crisis in her life.

But why death? As will be seen in a moment, Emily Dickinson was supremely the poet of death—and "immortality," with which death is (at first sight strangely) equated. As to death, there are two aspects to be distinguished here. There is death as the objective, factual, but still mysterious natural cessation of life and the silence and physical corruption of the grave. Emily was much preoccupied with death in this sense, and wrote many poems about it, of which the sixth in this sequence is only one. Although factual and inaccessible as such from within, this death may serve to symbolize death in the subjective sense. The fourth and eighth poems are attempts on the poet's part to think herself subjectively into the condition of objective death, although naturally an element of fantasy is present in both.

Then there is death experienced subjectively, as deprivation, the crushing burden of finitude, the extinction of hope, the loss of all possibility. As Mr. Reeves writes: "Whatever the outward facts of the situation, this [i.e., Wadsworth's departure from Philadelphia in 1862] was, in the inner drama of Emily's existence, death. It had been preceded by an agonized renunciation." This, it is very probable indeed, is what number seven is "about"; it is a triumph of articulation of the inexpressible. The third poem begins, quite explicitly, "I felt a funeral in my brain," and goes on to describe a mental state of acute and desperate anguish in images of which every one confirms and reinforces the others until the last extremity is reached and the mind plunges into the inexpressible chaos of insanity. The haunting cadences of the first poem express intimations of mortality in some of the most subtly eerie, most implacably disconsolate lines I know. The second and eighth, which have much in common, are among the best known of Emily Dickinson's work. Once read, they can never be forgotten. But what is their real theme and purport? And what does the whole sequence add up to?

It adds up, I think, to a vision of death in life, and life in death—of death as the content and meaning of life—which provokes the most chastening reflections. Let us look again at her situation.

Emily Dickinson became a recluse, and shut the door on a vulgar and trivial world, in order to lead a life of higher significance to her than any afforded by the society of a mid-century small town; a life in which she could, with the minimum of hindrance, act out her own interior drama of renunciation and self-commitment to that spiritual status to which she felt herself assigned, "by right of the white election," as "Queen of Calvary," scrupulously facing the facts of living and dying in this role. Despite, or because of her renunciation, she felt herself to be in some sense spiritually "married" to Edward Wadsworth, apparently believing or hoping that they would be united after death, in "immortality." In one poem she wrote explicitly that

> *The soul selects her own society*
> *Then shuts the door.*
> *To her divine majority*
> *Present no more.*
>
> *Unmoved she notes the chariots pausing*
> *At her low gate;*
> *Unmoved, an Emperor be kneeling*
> *Upon her mat.*
>
> *I've known her from an ample nation*
> *Choose one,*
> *Then close the valves of her attention*
> *Like stone.*

Besides remarking the astounding pride and arrogance here displayed, and the terrible implications of the final line, there is this to be said: an *exclusive* love, even when frozen in a perpetual renunciation, is an idolatry of a peculiarly sterile kind; for a love that holds obsessively to a particular object and fails to universalize itself (as life always requires) becomes a prison, or a grave, or a hell, from which there is no outlet. When she went upstairs and closed the door, Mr. Allen Tate has written in his fine essay on Emily Dickinson, "she mastered life by rejecting it." Similarly, she possessed her love by renouncing it, as, in a sense, she possessed her lover by renouncing *him*. But since the word "mystic" has more than once been loosely applied to Emily Dickinson, and her reclusion compared to that of a religious ("the Nun of Amherst," and so on), it should be made clear at once that what she could not, or would not do (and what a mystic or a religious would clearly have been required, in her place, to do) was to take the next step into life by renouncing her own renunciation. To master life by rejecting it is, no doubt, to achieve a kind of victory *over* life, as opposed to a generous giving of oneself *to* life; and thus to confer upon oneself a kind of "immortal" status; but it is at the same time, without any doubt at all, to choose death.

And this is what Emily did. If her subjective experience of death (*vide*, "My life closed twice before its close") became, by her own rigorously willed acceptance, the means by which she attained the regal or immortal estate, this achieved "immortality" itself was ambiguous; and the ambiguity persists in the poems in which the subjective experience of death in loss and renunciation fuses in a mental image with objective, physical dying and the grave. In her often quoted letter of 1862 to the journalist T.W. Higginson, Emily had characteristically written: "When a little girl, I had a friend who taught me Immortality; but venturing too near, himself, he never returned." This sentence of itself is enough to reveal that immortality—in Emily's mind an exalted, vaguely Emersonian concept for the highest, supramundane value—became readily assimilated to, and virtually identified with, death. Indeed, death itself held for her something of this highest value, in its awesome power to redeem life from accident and triviality: in the room of the dying (poem four) death appeared with majesty as "the king." In holding with great singleness of mind to her renunciation, or holding to herself in her renunciation (and we must not for one moment forget that this renunciation was in line with a temperamental timidity and introversion), and in thus "mastering" life, Emily became, not indeed a saint or mystic, but certainly a poet A poet of exclusion and confinement; of death, and "immortality."

But as to "immortality" (recalling that the *Revelation* was one of Emily's few chosen books), I am reminded forcibly of a sentence from a searching essay on "Apocalypse" by a little known modern thinker: "Infinity and immortality are death concepts which serve to define an unending homelessness."

Perhaps we can now turn to poem two, which Mr. Tate has called "one of the greatest in the English language." If it is so, it is because it brings into powerful focus all the issues of Emily's own life with the utmost precision, economy, and ruthlessness. Mr. Tate rightly says that, "The rhythm charges with movement the pattern of suspended action back of the poem. Every image is precise and, moreover, not merely beautiful, but fused with the central idea." (Mr. Richard Chase, in his indispensible monograph, has pointed out how her most impressive imagery tends to be kinaesthetic rather than visual or auditory: "One might almost say that at its deeper levels her typical experience is of motion—involving pain or terror—cessation, and an ensuing state of rest which either can be expressed by images or remains beyond perception. This fundamental trope tends to be the dramatic core of her best poems.") One can only agree with Mr. Tate when he points out, too, the "subtly interfused erotic motive, which the idea of death has presented to most romantic poets, love being a symbol interchangeable with death." But I have reluctantly to dissent when he goes on to say that "the terror of death is objectified through this figure of the genteel driver, *who is made ironically to serve the end of Immortality*," (my italics) and that "she has *presented a typical Christian theme* in its final irresolution, without making any final statements about it." There is nothing in the least ironical about Emily's assimilation—for that is what it is—of immortality to death; unless of course we choose to think it so; and there is here no "typical Christian theme" at all—far from it. The Christian theme would not concern death and immortality, but death and resurrection and eternal life; and ". . . Eternity and resurrection are life concepts."

This poem has elements of all of Emily's diverse preoccupations with death (and with immortality); with death as objective fact, with the morbidly fanciful attempt to think herself, in the present, into that future objective condition, and with "death" experienced subjectively as deprivation and loss of possibility, and symbolized by objective death, the grave. Death in this poem may be many things, and possibly many people (for instance, he might be presumed to wear the features or the costume of Edward Wadsworth, or of Edward Dickinson, or of both interchangeably); but he is certainly a bridegroom coming to take his bride to the nuptial chamber, where, as queen (for death is king), she will put on "immortal" status—in suspended animation, a living corpse. So much for the exaltation of an "immortality" that is held apart from, and in opposition to, the actual, living course of Life. (See also poem eight.) The journey, it should be remarked, is a retrogressive one. First childhood is passed (note the word *recess*—a going back or withdrawing), then the innocent seed-world of nature; then the sun, the giver of life, itself. The house that seemed "a swelling in the ground" suggests the prehistoric (this is emphasized by the subsequent: "since then 'tis centuries"), and this, in the context, is perfectly fitting. It also suggests the womb. Indeed, the poem is heavy with unlived life, Emily Dickinson's unlived life; but here, it is life going back on itself, reverting to its origins (in search of "immortality"), until the act of creation is undone, and life creeps back into the grave or womb from which it came. Life is death, and death, life. Against this backward movement to dissolution is counterposed the primly inflexible honesty of the poet's disciplined resolution to present *the facts* of her situation to her consciousness without deception, without sentimentality or cheating. A situation the most deeply and disturbingly unhappy it is possible to think of, in which the cherished "immortality" serves but to define an unending homelessness, and victory is swallowed up in death. Except, of course, the poetic victory, which the poem triumphantly sustains.

LEWIS CARROLL

*The Bettmann Archive*

# CHARLES L. DODGSON
# (LEWIS CARROLL)
### [1832–1898]

## *The Hunting of the Snark*

### AN AGONY IN EIGHT FITS

#### FIT THE FIRST
#### *The Landing*

"Just the place for a Snark!" the Bellman cried,
  As he landed his crew with care;
Supporting each man on the top of the tide
  By a finger entwined in his hair.

"Just the place for a Snark! I have said it twice:      5
  That alone should encourage the crew.
Just the place for a Snark! I have said it thrice:
  What I tell you three times is true."

The crew was complete: it included a Boots—
  A marker of Bonnets and Hoods—      10
A Barrister, brought to arrange their disputes—
  And a Broker, to value their goods.

A Billiard-marker, whose skill was immense,
  Might perhaps have won more than his share—
But a Banker, engaged at enormous expense,      15
  Had the whole of their cash in his care.

There was also a Beaver, that paced on the deck,
  Or would sit making lace in the bow:
And had often (the Bellman said) saved them from
    wreck,
  Though none of the sailors knew how.      20

There was one who was famed for the number of things
  He forgot when he entered the ship:
His umbrella, his watch, all his jewels and rings,
  And the clothes he had bought for the trip.

He had forty-two boxes, all carefully packed,　　　　　25
　　With his name painted clearly on each:
But, since he omitted to mention the fact,
　　They were all left behind on the beach.

The loss of his clothes hardly mattered, because
　　He had seven coats on when he came,　　　　　30
With three pair of boots—but the worst of it was,
　　He had wholly forgotten his name.

He would answer to "Hi!" or to any loud cry,
　　Such as "Fry me!" or "Fritter my wig!"
To "What-you-may-call-um!" or "What-was-his-name!"　35
　　But especially "Thing-um-a-jig!"

While, for those who preferred a more forcible word,
　　He had different names for these:
His intimate friends called him "Candle-ends,"
　　And his enemies "Toasted-cheese."　　　　　40

"His form is ungainly—his intellect small—"
　　(So the Bellman would often remark)
"But his courage is perfect! And that, after all,
　　Is the thing that one needs with a Snark."

He would joke with hyænas, returning their stare　45
　　With an impudent wag of the head:
And he once went a walk, paw-in-paw, with a bear,
　　"Just to keep up its spirits," he said.

He came as a Baker: but owned, when too late—
　　And it drove the poor Bellman half-mad—　　　　50
He could only bake Bride-cake—for which, I may state,
　　No materials were to be had.

The last of the crew needs especial remark,
　　Though he looked an incredible dunce:
He had just one idea—but, that one being "Snark,"　55
　　The good Bellman engaged him at once.

He came as a Butcher: but gravely declared,
　　When the ship had been sailing a week,
He could only kill Beavers. The Bellman looked scared,
　　And was almost too frightened to speak:　　　　60

But at length he explained, in a tremulous tone,
　　There was only one Beaver on board;
And that was a tame one he had of his own,
　　Whose death would be deeply deplored.

The Beaver, who happened to hear the remark,     65
  Protested, with tears in its eyes,
That not even the rapture of hunting the Snark
  Could atone for that dismal surprise!

It strongly advised that the Butcher should be
  Conveyed in a separate ship:     70
But the Bellman declared that would never agree
  With the plans he had made for the trip:

Navigation was always a difficult art,
  Though with only one ship and one bell:
And he feared he must really decline, for his part,     75
  Undertaking another as well.

The Beaver's best course was, no doubt, to procure
  A second-hand dagger-proof coat—
So the Baker advised it—and next, to insure
  Its life in some Office of note:     80

This the Banker suggested, and offered for hire
  (On moderate terms), or for sale,
Two excellent Policies, one Against Fire,
  And one Against Damage From Hail.

Yet still, ever after that sorrowful day,     85
  Whenever the Butcher was by,
The Beaver kept looking the opposite way,
  And appeared unaccountably shy.

FIT THE SECOND

*The Bellman's Speech*

The Bellman himself they all praised to the skies—
  Such a carriage, such ease and such grace!     90
Such solemnity, too! One could see he was wise,
  The moment one looked in his face!

He had bought a large map representing the sea,
  Without the least vestige of land:
And the crew were much pleased when they found it
    to be     95
  A map they could all understand.

"What's the good of Mercator's North Poles and
    Equators,
  Tropics, Zones, and Meridian Lines?"
So the Bellman would cry: and the crew would reply
  "They are merely conventional signs!     100

"Other maps are such shapes, with their islands and
    capes!
  But we've got our brave Captain to thank"
(So the crew would protest) "that he's bought *us* the
    best—
  A perfect and absolute blank!"

This was charming, no doubt: but they shortly found
    out                                    105
  That the Captain they trusted so well
Had only one notion for crossing the ocean,
  And that was to tingle his bell.

He was thoughtful and grave—but the orders he gave
  Were enough to bewilder a crew.                   110
When he cried "Steer to starboard, but keep her head
    larboard!"
  What on earth was the helmsman to do?

Then the bowsprit got mixed with the rudder sometimes:
  A thing, as the Bellman remarked,
That frequently happens in tropical climes,       115
  When a vessel is, so to speak, "snarked."

But the principal failing occurred in the sailing,
  And the Bellman, perplexed and distressed,
Said he *had* hoped, at least, when the wind blew due
    East,
  That the ship would *not* travel due West!    120

But the danger was past—they had landed at last,
  With their boxes, portmanteaus, and bags:
Yet at first sight the crew were not pleased with the
    view,
  Which consisted of chasms and crags.

The Bellman perceived that their spirits were low,   125
  And repeated in musical tone
Some jokes he had kept for a season of woe—
  But the crew would do nothing but groan.

He served out some grog with a liberal hand,
  And bade them sit down on the beach:         130
And they could not but own that their Captain looked
    grand,
  As he stood and delivered his speech.

"Friends, Romans, and countrymen, lend me your ears!"
  (They were all of them fond of quotations:

So they drank to his health, and they gave him three
    cheers,
  While he served out additional rations).
135

"We have sailed many months, we have sailed many
    weeks,
  (Four weeks to the month you may mark),
But never as yet ('tis your Captain who speaks)
  Have we caught the least glimpse of a Snark!
140

"We have sailed many weeks, we have sailed many days,
  (Seven days to the week I allow),
But a Snark, on the which we might lovingly gaze,
  We have never beheld till now!

"Come, listen, my men, while I tell you again
  The five unmistakable marks
By which you may know, wheresoever you go,
  The warranted genuine Snarks.
145

"Let us take them in order. The first is the taste,
  Which is meagre and hollow, but crisp:
Like a coat that is rather too tight in the waist,
  With a flavour of Will-o'-the-Wisp.
150

"Its habit of getting up late you'll agree
  That it carries too far, when I say
That it frequently breakfasts at five-o'clock tea,
  And dines on the following day.
155

"The third is its slowness in taking a jest.
  Should you happen to venture on one,
It will sigh like a thing that is deeply distressed:
  And it always looks grave at a pun.
160

"The fourth is its fondness for bathing-machines,
  Which it constantly carries about,
And believes that they add to the beauty of scenes—
  A sentiment open to doubt.

"The fifth is ambition. It next will be right
  To describe each particular batch:
Distinguishing those that have feathers, and bite,
  From those that have whiskers, and scratch.
165

"For, although common Snarks do no manner of harm,
  Yet I feel it my duty to say
Some are Boojums—" The Bellman broke off in alarm,
  For the Baker had fainted away.
170

### The Baker's Tale

They roused him with muffins—they roused him with
    ice—
    They roused him with mustard and cress—
They roused him with jam and judicious advice—    175
    They set him conundrums to guess.

When at length he sat up and was able to speak,
    His sad story he offered to tell;
And the Bellman cried "Silence! Not even a shriek!"
    And excitedly tingled his bell.    180

There was silence supreme! Not a shriek, not a scream,
    Scarcely even a howl or a groan,
As the man they called "Ho!" told his story of woe
    In an antediluvian tone.

"My father and mother were honest, though poor—"    185
    "Skip all that!" cried the Bellman in haste.
"If it once becomes dark, there's no chance of a Snark—
    We have hardly a minute to waste!"

"I skip forty years," said the Baker, in tears,
    "And proceed without further remark    190
To the day when you took me aboard of your ship
    To help you in hunting the Snark.

"A dear uncle of mine (after whom I was named)
    Remarked, when I bade him farewell—"
"Oh, skip your dear uncle!" the Bellman exclaimed,    195
    As he angrily tingled his bell.

"He remarked to me then," said that mildest of men,
    " 'If your Snark be a Snark, that is right:
Fetch it home by all means—you may serve it with
    greens,
    And it's handy for striking a light.    200

" 'You may seek it with thimbles—and seek it with care,
    You may hunt it with forks and hope;
You may threaten its life with a railway-share;
    You may charm it with smiles and soap—' "

("That's exactly the method," the Bellman bold    205
    In a hasty parenthesis cried,
"That's exactly the way I have always been told
    That the capture of Snarks should be tried!")

" 'But oh, beamish nephew, beware of the day,
      If your Snark be a Boojum! For then                   210
You will softly and suddenly vanish away,
      And never be met with again!'

"It is this, it is this that oppresses my soul,
      When I think of my uncle's last words:
And my heart is like nothing so much as a bowl     215
      Brimming over with quivering curds!

"It is this, it is this—" "We have had that before!"
      The Bellman indignantly said.
And the Baker replied "Let me say it once more.
      It is this, it is this that I dread!                  220

"I engage with the Snark—every night after dark—
      In a dreamy delirious fight:
I serve it with greens in those shadowy scenes,
      And I use it for striking a light:

"But if ever I meet with a Boojum, that day,             225
      In a moment (of this I am sure),
I shall softly and suddenly vanish away—
      And the notion I cannot endure!"

FIT THE FOURTH
*The Hunting*

The Bellman looked uffish, and wrinkled his brow.
      "If only you'd spoken before!                         230
It's excessively awkward to mention it now,
      With the Snark, so to speak, at the door!

"We should all of us grieve, as you well may believe,
      If you never were met with again—
But surely, my man, when the voyage began,               235
      You might have suggested it then?

"It's excessively awkward to mention it now—
      As I think I've already remarked."
And the man they called "Hi!" replied, with a sigh,
      "I informed you the day we embarked.                  240

"You may charge me with murder—or want of sense—
      (We are all of us weak at times):
But the slightest approach to a false pretence
      Was never among my crimes!

"I said it in Hebrew—I said it in Dutch—                 245
      I said it in German and Greek:

But I wholly forgot (and it vexes me much)
  That English is what you speak!"

" 'Tis a pitiful tale," said the Bellman, whose face
  Had grown longer at every word:                                  250
"But, now that you've stated the whole of your case,
  More debate would be simply absurd.

"The rest of my speech" (he exclaimed to his men)
  "You shall hear when I've leisure to speak it.
But the Snark is at hand, let me tell you again!                   255
  'Tis your glorious duty to seek it!

"To seek it with thimbles, to seek it with care;
  To pursue it with forks and hope;
To threaten its life with a railway-share;
  To charm it with smiles and soap!                                260

"For the Snark's a peculiar creature, that won't
  Be caught in a commonplace way.
Do all that you know, and try all that you don't:
  Not a chance must be wasted to-day!

"For England expects—I forbear to proceed:                         265
  'Tis a maxim tremendous, but trite:
And you'd best be unpacking the things that you need
  To rig yourselves out for the fight."

Then the Banker endorsed a blank cheque (which he
    crossed),
  And changed his loose silver for notes.                          270
The Baker with care combed his whiskers and hair.
  And shook the dust out of his coats.

The Boots and the Broker were sharpening a spade—
  Each working the grindstone in turn:
But the Beaver went on making lace, and displayed                  275
  No interest in the concern:

Though the Barrister tried to appeal to its pride,
  And vainly proceeded to cite
A number of cases, in which making laces
  Had been proved an infringement of right.                        280

The maker of Bonnets ferociously planned
  A novel arrangement of bows:
While the Billiard-marker with quivering hand
  Was chalking the tip of his nose.

But the Butcher turned nervous, and dressed himself
    fine,         285
  With yellow kid gloves and a ruff—
Said he felt it exactly like going to dine,
  Which the Bellman declared was all "stuff."

"Introduce me, now there's a good fellow," he said,
  "If we happen to meet it together!"     290
And the Bellman, sagaciously nodding his head,
  Said "That must depend on the weather."

The Beaver went simply galumphing about,
  At seeing the Butcher so shy:
And even the Baker, though stupid and stout,     295
  Made an effort to wink with one eye.

"Be a man!" cried the Bellman in wrath, as he heard
  The Butcher beginning to sob.
"Should we meet with Jubjub, that desperate bird,
  We shall need all our strength for the job!"     300

FIT THE FIFTH
*The Beaver's Lesson*

They sought it with thimbles, they sought it with care;
  They pursued it with forks and hope;
They threatened its life with a railway-share;
  They charmed it with smiles and soap.

Then the Butcher contrived an ingenious plan     305
  For making a separate sally;
And had fixed on a spot unfrequented by man,
  A dismal and desolate valley.

But the very same plan to the Beaver occurred:
  It had chosen the very same place:     310
Yet neither betrayed, by a sign or a word,
  The disgust that appeared in his face.

Each thought he was thinking of nothing but "Snark"
  And the glorious work of the day;
And each tried to pretend that he did not remark     315
  That the other was going that way.

But the valley grew narrow and narrower still,
  And the evening got darker and colder,
Till (merely from nervousness, not from good will)
  They marched along shoulder to shoulder.     320

Then a scream, shrill and high, rent the shuddering sky,
  And they knew that some danger was near:
The Beaver turned pale to the tip of its tail,
  And even the Butcher felt queer.

He thought of his childhood, left far far behind—          325
  That blissful and innocent state—
The sound so exactly recalled to his mind
  A pencil that squeaks on a slate!

" 'Tis the voice of the Jubjub!" he suddenly cried.
  (This man, that they used to call "Dunce.")          330
"As the Bellman would tell you," he added with pride,
  "I have uttered that sentiment once.

" 'Tis the note of the Jubjub! Keep count, I entreat.
  You will find I have told it you twice.
'Tis the song of the Jubjub! The proof is complete.          335
  If only I've stated it thrice."

The Beaver had counted with scrupulous care,
  Attending to every word:
But it fairly lost heart, and outgrabe in despair,
  When the third repetition occurred.          340

It felt that, in spite of all possible pains,
  It had somehow contrived to lose count,
And the only thing now was to rack its poor brains
  By reckoning up the amount.

"Two added to one—if that could but be done,"          345
  It said, "with one's fingers and thumbs!"
Recollecting with tears how, in earlier years,
  It had taken no pains with its sums.

"The thing can be done," said the Butcher, "I think
  The things must be done, I am sure.          350
The thing shall be done! Bring me paper and ink,
  The best there is time to procure."

The Beaver brought paper, portfolio, pens,
  And ink in unfailing supplies:
While strange creepy creatures came out of their dens,          355
  And watched them with wondering eyes.

So engrossed was the Butcher, he heeded them not,
  As he wrote with a pen in each hand,
And explained all the while in a popular style
  Which the Beaver could well understand.          360

"Taking Three as the subject to reason about—
    A convenient number to state—
We add Seven, and Ten, and then multiply out
    It never will look at a bribe:

"The result we proceed to divide, as you see,            365
    By Nine Hundred and Ninety and Two:
Then subtract Seventeen, and the answer must be
    Exactly and perfectly true.

"The method employed I would gladly explain,
    While I have it so clear in my head,                  370
If I had but the time and you had but the brain—
    But much yet remains to be said.

"In one moment I've seen what has hitherto been
    Enveloped in absolute mystery,
And without extra charge I will give you at large        375
    A Lesson in Natural History."

In his genial way he proceeded to say
    (Forgetting all laws of propriety,
And that giving instruction, without introduction,
    Would have caused quite a thrill in Society),         380

"As to temper the Jubjub's a desperate bird,
    Since it lives in perpetual passion:
Its taste in costume is entirely absurd—
    It is ages ahead of the fashion:

"But it knows any friend it has met once before:         385
    And in charity-meetings it stands at the door,
By One Thousand diminished by Eight.
    And collects—though it does not subscribe.

"Its flavour when cooked is more exquisite far
    Than mutton, or oysters, or eggs:                     390
(Some think it keeps best in an ivory jar,
    And some, in mahogany kegs:)

"You boil it in sawdust: you salt it in glue:
    You condense it with locusts and tape:
Still keeping one principal object in view—              395
    To preserve its symmetrical shape."

The Butcher would gladly have talked till next day,
    But he felt that the Lesson must end,
And he wept with delight in attempting to say
    He considered the Beaver his friend.                  400

While the Beaver confessed, with affectionate looks
  More eloquent even than tears,
It had learned in ten minutes far more than all books
  Would have taught it in seventy years.

They returned hand-in-hand, and the Bellman, unmanned 405
  (For a moment) with noble emotion,
Said "This amply repays all the wearisome days
  We have spent on the billowy ocean!"

Such friends, as the Beaver and Butcher became,
  Have seldom if ever been known;                         410
In winter or summer, 'twas always the same—
  You could never meet either alone.

And when quarrels arose—as one frequently finds
  Quarrels will, spite of every endeavour—
The song of the Jubjub recurred to their minds,          415
  And cemented their friendship for ever!

FIT THE SIXTH
*The Barrister's Dream*

They sought it with thimbles, they sought it with care;
  They pursued it with forks and hope;
They threatened its life with a railway-share;
  They charmed it with smiles and soap.                   420

But the Barrister, weary of proving in vain
  That the Beaver's lace-making was wrong,
Fell asleep, and in dreams saw the creature quite plain
  That his fancy had dwelt on so long.

He dreamed that he stood in a shadowy Court,             425
  Where the Snark, with a glass in its eye,
Dressed in gown, bands, and wig, was defending a pig
  On the charge of deserting its sty.

The Witnesses proved, without error or flaw,
  That the sty was deserted when found:                   430
And the Judge kept explaining the state of the law
  In a soft under-current of sound.

The indictment had never been clearly expressed,
  And it seemed that the Snark had begun,
And had spoken three hours, before any one guessed       435
  What the pig was supposed to have done.

The Jury had each formed a different view
  (Long before the indictment was read),

And they all spoke at once, so that none of them knew
    One word that the others had said.      440

"You must know—" said the Judge: but the Snark exclaimed
    "Fudge!
That statute is obsolete quite!
Let me tell you, my friends, the whole question depends
    On an ancient manorial right.

"In the matter of Treason the pig would appear    445
    To have aided, but scarcely abetted:
While the charge of Insolvency fails, it is clear,
    If you grant the plea 'never indebted.'

"The fact of Desertion I will not dispute:
    But its guilt, as I trust, is removed    450
(So far as relates to the costs of this suit)
    By the Alibi which has been proved.

"My poor client's fate now depends on your votes."
    Here the speaker sat down in his place,
And directed the Judge to refer to his notes    455
    And briefly to sum up the case.

But the Judge said he never had summed up before;
    So the Snark undertook it instead,
And summed it so well that it came to far more
    Than the Witnesses ever had said!    460

When the verdict was called for, the Jury declined,
    As the word was so puzzling to spell;
But they ventured to hope that the Snark wouldn't
    mind
    Undertaking that duty as well.

So the Snark found the verdict, although, as it owned,    465
    It was spent with the toils of the day:
When it said the word "GUILTY!" the Jury all
    groaned,
    And some of them fainted away.

Then the Snark pronounced sentence, the Judge being
    quite
    Too nervous to utter a word:    470
When it rose to its feet, there was silence like night,
    And the fall of a pin might be heard.

"Transportation for life" was the sentence it gave,
    "And *then* to be fined forty pound."

The Jury all cheered, though the Judge said he feared 475
That the phrase was not legally sound.

But their wild exultation was suddenly checked
When the jailer informed them, with tears,
Such a sentence would have not the slightest effect,
As the pig had been dead for some years. 480

The Judge left the Court, looking deeply disgusted:
But the Snark, though a little aghast,
As the lawyer to whom the defence was intrusted,
Went bellowing on to the last.

Thus the Barrister dreamed, while the bellowing seemed 485
To grow every moment more clear:
Till he woke to the knell of a furious bell,
Which the Bellman rang close at his ear.

FIT THE SEVENTH
*The Banker's Fate*

They sought it with thimbles, they sought it with care;
They pursued it with forks and hope; 490
They threatened its life with a railway-share;
They charmed it with smiles and soap.

And the Banker, inspired with a courage so new
It was matter for general remark,
Rushed madly ahead and was lost to their view 495
In his zeal to discover the Snark.

But while he was seeking with thimbles and care,
A Bandersnatch swiftly drew nigh
And grabbed at the Banker, who shrieked in despair,
For he knew it was useless to fly. 500

He offered large discount—he offered a cheque
(Drawn "to bearer") for seven-pounds-ten:
But the Bandersnatch merely extended its neck
And grabbed at the Banker again.

Without rest or pause—while those frumious jaws 505
Went savagely snapping around—
He skipped and he hopped, and he floundered and flopped,
Till fainting he fell to the ground.

The Bandersnatch fled as the others appeared
Led on by that fear-stricken yell: 510
And the Bellman remarked "It is just as I feared!"
And solemnly tolled on his bell.

He was black in the face, and they scarcely could trace
  The least likeness to what he had been:
While so great was his fright that his waistcoat turned
      white—                                                    515
  A wonderful thing to be seen!

To the horror of all who were present that day,
  He uprose in full evening dress,
And with senseless grimaces endeavoured to say
  What his tongue could no longer express.                     520

Down he sank in a chair—ran his hands through his hair—
  And chanted in mimsiest tones
Words whose utter inanity proved his insanity,
  While he rattled a couple of bones.

"Leave him here to his fate—it is getting so late!"            525
  The Bellman exclaimed in a fright.
"We have lost half the day. Any further delay,
  And we sha'n't catch a Snark before night!"

FIT THE EIGHTH
### The Vanishing

They sought it with thimbles, they sought it with care;
  They pursued it with forks and hope;                         530
They threatened its life with a railway-share;
  They charmed it with smiles and soap.

They shuddered to think that the chase might fail,
  And the Beaver, excited at last,
Went bounding along on the tip of its tail,                    535
  For the daylight was nearly past.

"There is Thingumbob shouting!" the Bellman said.
  "He is shouting like mad, only hark!
He is waving his hands, he is wagging his head,
  He has certainly found a Snark!"                             540

They gazed in delight, while the Butcher exclaimed
  "He was always a desperate wag!"
They beheld him—their Baker—their hero unnamed—
  On the top of a neighbouring crag,

Erect and sublime, for one moment of time,                    545
  In the next, that wild figure they saw
(As if stung by a spasm) plunge into a chasm,
  While they waited and listened in awe.

"It's a Snark!" was the sound that first came to their ears,
   And seemed almost too good to be true.         550
Then followed a torrent of laughter and cheers:
   Then the ominous words "It's a Boo—"

Then, silence. Some fancied they heard in the air
   A weary and wandering sigh
That sounded like "—jum!" but the others declare     555
   It was only a breeze that went by.

They hunted till darkness came on, but they found
   Not a button, or feather, or mark,
By which they could tell that they stood on the ground
   Where the Baker had met with the Snark.       560

In the midst of the word he was trying to say,
   In the midst of his laughter and glee,
He had softly and suddenly vanished away—
   For the Snark *was* a Boojum, you see.

# Richard Howard

## CARROLL
### THE HUNTING OF THE SNARK

In 1876, the same year a long ballad called "The Hunting of the Snark" was published in England, young Siegfried followed the voice of a mysterious forest bird that spoke to him in a language he alone could understand, killed a somnolent dragon, and sailed his boat up the Rhine on a still greater adventure—all this happening, for the very first time, on the stage of the Festspielhaus in Bayreuth. The impulse, of course, had been gathering momentum for a long time: from *Faust* to *Peer Gynt*, the century had delighted in heroic quests like the one Wagner's poem celebrated, voyages, crusades, hunts, all asking one question: What is the meaning of life, and what is the self? Vengefully, Tennyson's Maeldune "gathered his fellows together" and set out "for an island in the ocean [where] a score of wild birds cried from the topmost summit with human voices and words." Sick at heart, Browning's Childe Roland came to his Dark Tower: "This was the place! . . . at the thought, a great black bird sailed past, the guide I sought." Poe's Arthur Gordon Pym, as "gigantic and pallidly white birds flew continually from beyond the veil," dissolved into the embrace of a "figure of the perfect whiteness of snow"; and Melville's mariners beached on an enchanted wasteland where "no voice, no howl is heard: the chief sound of life here is a hiss. . . ." The list of such adventures bulges with solemn instances, and it may seem a disservice to Lewis Carroll's famous "nonsense poem" to offer it as the climax of such a series, but in defense of my tactic I should like to invoke the equally famous dictum of his contemporary, Karl Marx: "Everything of importance in history occurs twice, the first time as tragedy, the second as farce." The observation applies in literary history as well: after *La Recherche de l'Absolu* comes, outrageously, inevitably, "The Hunting of the Snark."

Carroll originally presented the poem—it appeared as an Easter volume, and was called by *The Atheneum* "the most

bewildering of modern poems"—with a subtitle and a preface. The subtitle was "An Agony, in Eight Fits," and
employed the first term in the archaic acceptation of a
struggle involving great anguish, physical pain, or death. *Fit*
has the double meaning of a convulsion and a canto, and in
this *agony* the fits grow shorter and shorter, their irregular
lengths and the occasional double rhymes within the quatrain
lines ("So the Bellman would cry and the crew would
reply") corresponding to the poet's impulse, not to a prede-
termined design.

That impulse, as exfoliated in Carroll's preface to the
poem, has three purposes: to insist on the autonomy of the
fable (as late as 1897, three years before his death, Carroll
wrote: "In answer to your question 'What did you mean the
Snark was?' will you tell your friend that I meant that the
Snark was a *Boojum*. I trust that she and you will now feel
quite satisfied and happy"); to relate its style to the "Lay of
the Jabberwock" ("The scene is laid," Carroll wrote to the
mother of the little girl to whom he dedicated the poem,
incredibly enough, "in memory of golden summer hours and
whispers of a summer sea"; the scene is laid, then, "in an
island frequented by the Jubjub and Bandersnatch—no doubt
the very island in which the Jabberwock was slain"); and to
explain certain "mechanical" procedures, particularly with
regard to the famous "portmanteau words" which occur in
both poems—words like *snark* itself ("snail," "snake" and
"shark" spoken together "with a perfectly balanced mind"),
*galumphing* ("galloping" and "triumphant") and *uffish* ("a
state of mind when the voice is gruffish, the manner roughish,
and the temper huffish"). But such entertainments to be
encountered in the verbal course of the poem, and indeed the
great felicity of image ("And my heart is like nothing so
much as a bowl / Brimming over with quivering curds!")
and music ("They roused him with jam and judicious advice") must not be allowed to distract the reader from the
work's full intent, the insistence of design that was first and
always Carroll's enterprise:

> I was walking on a hillside, alone, one bright summer
> day, when suddenly there came into my head one line of
> verse—one solitary line—"For the Snark *was* a Boojum,
> you see." I knew not what it meant then; I know not
> what it means, now; but I wrote it down; and, sometime
> afterwards, the rest of the stanza occurred to me, that
> being its last line: and so by degrees, at odd moments

during the next year or two, the rest of the poem pieced
itself together, that being the last stanza.

What, then, *was* the Boojum that was also the Snark, that
fatal equation, which occurred to Lewis Carroll in precisely
the fashion Paul Valéry tells us the initial verse of *"Le
Cimetière Marin"* was "given" to him? It was, as Auden has
pointed out, the realization that life might have no meaning,
that there might be no self. The dissolution and loss of self
into nothingness ("Then, silence") that haunted Peer Gynt in
the double form of the great Boyg and the threat of the
Button-Moulder—that is the modern horror (the horror of
Kurtz in *Heart of Darkness*) that faces and ultimately
overcomes the hunters of the Snark. These argonauts, an ill-
assorted band of businessmen (they have only trades, no
names; while the Snark has only identity—it *is* a Boojum—no
occupation): Bellman, Boots, Bonnet-maker, Barrister,
Broker, Billiard-marker, Banker, Baker, Butcher ("who can
only kill beavers") and a Beaver ("The Beaver's best course
was, no doubt, to procure / A second-hand dagger-proof
coat"). The alliteration turns out to be crucial to their enterprise, for by means of various premonitions, prophetic
dreams, and admonitory presentiments, the hunters are informed that the Snark may turn out to be, indeed, a Boojum.
By the logic that prevails in this poem—the logic that always
prevails in nightmare, nonsense, and wonder—the crew's fate
is already sealed.

The poem begins with the landing of these errant knights
of free enterprise on a desert island characterized by crags
and chasms, "a dismal and desolate valley [where] the evening gets darker and colder"; and their first task is to review
the identifying characteristics of their quarry (as—wrongly
—interpreted by the ten, these idiosyncrasies are all thoroughly bourgeois: the Snark's habit of getting up late, its
slowness in taking a jest, its fondness for bathing machines as
a means of beautifying the landscape, its ambition—in all, an
utterly middle-class monster). In the course of this briefing,
the Bellman feels it is his "duty" to point out that *some*
Snarks are Boojums. This intelligence has a terrible effect on
the Baker (who is not really a Baker, of course, but a nameless and notoriously unstable creature, identified by Auden
with The Artist, by Freudian Critics with Carroll himself).
He faints dead away, and upon being revived ("with mustard
and cress") he explains, over many interruptions and in "an
antediluvian tone," that if the Snark they are hunting *is*

indeed a Boojum, then he knows from ancestral evidence that its hunters are doomed, for upon meeting it they will "softly and suddenly vanish away." This, of course, happens precisely to "Thingumbob," as the others call the Baker, though they cannot find a single clue "by which they could tell that they stood on the ground / Where the Baker had met with the Snark," and by inference to the rest of the crew. To a society represented by the ten bourgeois knights (even the Beaver makes lace), the quarry (a quarry to be quested with all the allurements of commerce: thimbles, forks, railway shares, smiles and soap!) is indeed the question: to B or not to B. The Snark *is* a Boojum, you see, and they must cease to be.

# ALGERNON CHARLES SWINBURNE

[1837–1909]

## Two Choruses from *Atalanta in Calydon*

### WHEN THE HOUNDS OF SPRING

When the hounds of spring are on winter's traces,
   The mother of months in meadow or plain
Fills the shadows and windy places
   With lisp of leaves and ripple of rain;
And the brown bright nightingale amorous      5
Is half assuaged for Itylus,
For the Thracian ships and the foreign faces,
   The tongueless vigil, and all the pain.

Come with bows bent and with emptying of quivers,
   Maiden most perfect, lady of light,      10
With a noise of winds and many rivers,
   With a clamour of waters, and with might;
Bind on thy sandals, O thou most fleet,
Over the splendour and speed of thy feet;
For the faint east quickens, the wan west shivers,      15
   Round the feet of the day and the feet of the night.

Where shall we find her, how shall we sing to her,
   Fold our hands round her knees, and cling?
O that man's heart were as fire and could spring to her,
   Fire, or the strength of the streams that spring!      20
For the stars and the winds are unto her
As raiment, as songs of the harp-player;
For the risen stars and the fallen cling to her,
   And the southwest-wind and the west-wind sing.

For winter's rains and ruins are over,      25
   And all the season of snows and sins;
The days dividing lover and lover,

The light that loses, the night that wins;
And time remembered is grief forgotten,
And frosts are slain and flowers begotten,                    30
And in green underwood and cover
  Blossom by blossom the spring begins.

The full streams feed on flower of rushes,
  Ripe grasses trammel a travelling foot,
The faint fresh flame of the young year flushes              35
  From leaf to flower and flower to fruit;
And fruit and leaf are as gold and fire,
And the oat is heard above the lyre,
And the hoofèd heel of a satyr crushes
  The chestnut-husk at the chestnut-root.                    40

And Pan by noon and Bacchus by night,
  Fleeter of foot than the fleet-foot kid,
Follows with dancing and fills with delight
  The Maenad and the Bassarid;
And soft as lips that laugh and hide                         45
The laughing leaves of the trees divide,
And screen from seeing and leave in sight
  The god pursuing, the maiden hid.

The ivy falls with the Bacchanal's hair
  Over her eyebrows hiding her eyes;                         50
The wild vine slipping down leaves bare
  Her bright breast shortening into sighs;
The wild vine slips with the weight of its leaves,
But the berried ivy catches and cleaves
To the limbs that glitter, the feet that scare              55
  The wolf that follows, the fawn that flies.

ALGERNON CHARLES SWINBURNE

*The Bettmann Archive*

## BEFORE THE BEGINNING OF YEARS

Before the beginning of years
    There came to the making of man
Time, with a gift of tears;
    Grief, with a glass that ran;
Pleasure, with pain for leaven;          5
    Summer, with flowers that fell;
Remembrance fallen from heaven,
    And madness risen from hell;
Strength without hands to smite;
    Love that endures for a breath:        10
Night, the shadow of light,
    And life, the shadow of death.

And the high gods took in hand
    Fire, and the falling of tears,
And a measure of sliding sand        15
    From under the feet of the years;
And froth and drift of the sea;
    And dust of the labouring earth;
And bodies of things to be
    In the houses of death and of birth;    20
And wrought with weeping and laughter,
    And fashioned with loathing and love,
With life before and after
    And death beneath and above,
For a day and a night and a morrow,    25
    That his strength might endure for a span
With travail and heavy sorrow,
    The holy spirit of man.

From the winds of the north and the south
    They gathered as unto strife;    30
They breathed upon his mouth,
    They filled his body with life;
Eyesight and speech they wrought
    For the veils of the soul therein,
A time for labour and thought,    35
    A time to serve and to sin;
They gave him light in his ways,
    And love, and a space for delight,
And beauty and length of days,
    And night, and sleep in the night.    40
His speech is a burning fire;

With his lips he travaileth;
In his heart is a blind desire,
In his eyes foreknowledge of death;
He weaves, and is clothed with derision;    45
Sows, and he shall not reap;
His life is a watch or a vision
Between a sleep and a sleep.

## Bonamy Dobrée

### SWINBURNE
### TWO CHORUSES FROM ATALANTA IN CALYDON

About a hundred years ago young men would go about "chanting to one another the new astonishing melodies" of the choruses in "Atalanta in Calydon." This was not Swinburne's first production, for he had already, in 1860, published two dramas, "The Queen Mother" and "Rosamond," and in 1862 "Dead Love," works of great energy, and in blank verse which has been justly described as superb. But it was his Greek drama, "Atalanta in Calydon," 1865, that in its choruses revealed his astonishing lyrical gift, further exemplified in the next year by his first series of "Poems and Ballads." The surging rhythms, the immense variety of unfamiliar metrical forms freshly presented in these works, brought about a revolution in English poetry from which none of his successors has failed to benefit.

Apart from other reasons, such as what in those days seemed to be the daring nature of the thought, what moved the earliest readers of the play was the torrential vigor of the verse, its breaking away from the iambic measures then current both in rhyme and in blank verse, which, musical though it might be, lulled to contemplation rather than aroused excitement, and did not break the barriers between thought and imagination. Here the readers were compellingly invited to have their senses and their blood stirred by dactyls, anapaests, cretics, in a multitude of complex measures, and by all sorts of stress variants. After the smooth, mellifluous phrasing of "In Memoriam," in its own manner a great poem, how could they fail to respond to the pulse of, "When the hounds of spring are on winter's traces," and so on, with its gloriously unabashed use of alliteration and compulsive rhythm? Take only the next line—"The mother of months in meadow or plain"! Here was music, not altogether for its own sake, but as an integral part of the meaning the poem was wrought to convey.

The two poems here offered are, it will be at once apparent, choruses in a Greek tragedy. They express the general feelings of the onlookers at the drama, but they voice, also, the general sense of humanity in two respects: the first, the joy of life at the resurgence of spring, the great tide of self-renewing life; and second, the disillusion at the irony of existence—all made intensely real by the vivid imagery. Yet Swinburne felt intuitively that neither the vividness of poetic imagery, nor its impact by way of the unexpected, were wholly due to brilliant, realistic presentation. He knew, because he felt, that poetry does not make its effect merely through the mental approach, but through the intensified awareness, going below the level of the mind, produced by the sheer quality of its sound, its vowel-play and varied beat. He realized, with Keats, that poetry must be felt upon the pulses.

This is not to say that he believed that poetry had nothing but vague feelings to communicate. For example, both these choruses give one something to think about—nothing very original, perhaps, certainly nothing startlingly new by way of thought, but something expressing the universal feelings of humanity. So long as blood flows in our veins, so long as it comes upon us how small the effect is of our endeavors to shape the general course of things, so long will these splendid lyrical utterances arouse us by intensifying our awareness of our great joy in life, its energies and its hopes, tempered by the realization of its often defeating actualities. Man

> . . . *weaves, and is clothed in derision;*
> *Sows, and he shall not reap;*
> *His life is a watch or a vision*
> *Between a sleep and a sleep*

In the general fear of music prevalent among poets today, as though music were a symptom of what is regarded as the escapist sickness of "aestheticism" (a kind of "veil for the soul therein," which it is judged afflicted the Victorians) it is often said that Swinburne allowed words to run away with him, making sound more important than sense—as though sound were not part of the sense, the releasing medium through which sense can be conveyed, or even liberated. Overflowing as he was with imagery, he was far too good a craftsman to be mastered by his medium. It has been suggested that when he wrote:

> *Time, with a gift of tears;*
> *Grief, with a glass that ran*

he might just as well, even better, have transposed the words, since in common speech it is grief that brings tears, and time that governs the hourglass. But Swinburne knew perfectly well what he was saying. In due course, after the shock of a great sorrow, we can weep and gain relief: grief is in the end assuaged, and its sands run out in the glass. He is making you consider as well as feel. True, like most Victorians, he was overgenerous with words: the writers of his generation were nothing if not voluminous, in prose as well as in verse, believing in the power of a multitude of words, and they were not afraid to let themselves go.

To the modern reader, not brought up in the classical tradition, some references may prove baffling. When we read that

> *. . . the brown bright nightingale amorous*
> *Is half assuaged for Itylus*

he may pass this over, and so miss a significant implication. The reference is to the story of Aëdon, who was jealous of her brother's wife, Niobe, and decided to kill one of Niobe's sons. But by mistake Aëdon killed her own son, Itylus, and was later changed to a nightingale by Zeus, her song being a lament for her son. But now, so strong is the effect of spring, that she is almost assuaged for the death of her son. Other classical references are more a matter of common knowledge. We all know what a satyr is, that Pan is the great god of flocks and shepherds, Bacchus the god of wine, and Bacchanals his priestesses. Maenads, we will remember, are Bacchantes of Thrace, and Bassarids the followers of Dionysus, another name for Bacchus. In the prelude to "Songs Before Sunrise," Swinburne refers to "the blood-feasts of the Bassarid," and speaks of "the mirth the Maenads made."

The second chorus offers no such difficulties. It is nothing so simple as a song of joy, but a philosophic, almost a moral disquisition, a vision of the fate the gods imposed on man when they "filled his body with life." And as the choruses, in their variously complex meters, succeed one another throughout this drama, they become ever more solemn and foreboding, picturing more and more poignantly the tragic fate of man, where nothing can be said that will assuage the suffering,

> *For words divide and rend;*
> *But silence is most noble till the end.*

This is not to say that the choruses must be taken together. Each can be treated separately, imparting its individual sense to the reader, or, preferably, those read to, since Swinburne demands the actual sound of the voice, not merely the impact of print upon the eye and mind. Like much of Swinburne's verse, these poems are life-giving through their sheer energy.

THOMAS HARDY

*The Bettmann Archive*

# THOMAS HARDY

[1840–1928]

## The Darkling Thrush

I leant upon a coppice gate
  When Frost was spectre-grey,
And Winter's dregs made desolate
  The weakening eye of day.
The tangled bine-stems scored the sky      5
  Like strings of broken lyres,
And all mankind that haunted nigh
  Had sought their household fires.

The land's sharp features seemed to be
  The Century's corpse outleant,      10
His crypt the cloudy canopy,
  The wind his death-lament.
The ancient pulse of germ and birth
  Was shrunken hard and dry,
And every spirit upon earth      15
  Seemed fervourless as I.

At once a voice arose among
  The bleak twigs overhead
In a full-hearted evensong
  Of joy illimited;      20
An agèd thrush, frail, gaunt, and small,
  In blast-beruffled plume,
Had chosen thus to fling his soul
  Upon the growing gloom.

So little cause for carolings      25
  Of such ecstatic sound
Was written on terrestrial things
  Afar or nigh around,
That I could think there trembled through
  His happy good-night air      30
Some blessèd Hope, whereof he knew
  And I was unaware.

787

# John Berryman

## HARDY
### THE DARKLING THRUSH

Hardy's reputation has always been furiously unstable. So was his practice. I think we all loved, when young, three novels: *The Mayor of Casterbridge*, *Tess of the D'Urbervilles*, and *Jude the Obscure*—but it was with *The Return of the Native* that we were tortured in school. Hardy's novels not only were attacked, but were attacked by people like Henry James, with some justice since they are unreadable. Opinions about his poetry also differ, widely and strangely. We have violent comments on both sides. T.S. Eliot pronounced him a minor poet, whereas Mr. Lowell thinks that along with Rilke he is one of the greatest poets of the century. Surely they are both wrong. Yet, the author of "An Ancient to Ancients," "The Oxen," and "The Darkling Thrush" cannot, to my mind, bear to be regarded as minor; however there is the true fact that Hardy was quite unambitious: he once said that all he wanted was to place one or two poems in a good anthology like *The Golden Treasury*.

Now, ladies and gentlemen, ambition along with luck and health is a serious factor in artistic accomplishment. One has to *love* Hardy—Mr. Auden once remarked in print that he loved him, but that is a very different matter from critical judgment: just because he was so modest does not mean he was great. I love Hardy, too, but for his poetry: he took areas of dying rural England and made them permanent for us. He worked in three main modes as a poet. He was a lyric poet of genuine distinction. He also wrote meditative poems of great power like "The Darkling Thrush," with which at the new year in 1900 in *The London Times* he greeted the new century; and occasional poems like "The Convergence of the Twain."

In "The Darkling Thrush" we have an isolated bird. As in Walt Whitman, the term "alienation" would not be excessive. But the bird is very different from Whitman's. The bird is happy, and throughout the poem it *sounds* as if the poet were identifying with the bird as in Whitman; actually this is not so. The poet is in despair, whilst the bird feels fine.

Hardy kept proclaiming himself a meliorist—he refused the label pessimism; but when you begin to dig into his work anywhere—repeat anywhere—the mind involved is dark. Therefore let us suppose that the bird, the thrush, at dusk, represents a dream of Hardy's, not the dreamer. Does the dream succeed? Is the question worth asking? Men should be allowed their secrets. If we had this wonderful person on the telephone, would or could he tell us?

The truth of the matter is a presentiment out of the imagination, the author's opinions being irrelevant.

The nineteenth century with its fatal heritage to us comes on an end in this poem—so the bird thinks; the poet knows better. He sees that the insane nationalism and dreads of the nineteenth century will also dominate the twentieth, but he does not insist on this. It turns up almost by accident in the final line. So how shall we put the matter of emphasis—do we have one poem or two? Surely two: one called "The Darkling Thrush," the other called *Thomas Hardy explicat.* It is true that the second poem contains only one line, but it dominates the entire little masterpiece.

The poem occurs in the volume called *Poems of the Past and the Present* along with other bird songs, one of the closest being a villanelle called "The Caged Thrush, Freed and Home Again." The subject of the first line ("Men know but little more than we") is an inversion of the "The Darkling Thrush" theme in which the bird knows more. Of course, at a deeper level, the bird—of "The Darkling Thrush," that is—and the man are one. The bird, "aged," half-ruined, is *still* singing. So is the poet. Most poets at sixty, as Hardy then was, have quit. The bird's and man's messages differ, but here is the true motive of this matchless song.

For detailed analysis: it's an old man's poem—even the thrush is aged. Hence "leant," "spectre-grey," "dregs," "desolate," "weakening," "broken," "haunted," "outleant," "crypt," "death-lament." I do not like the second stanza, especially the end of it. May we inquire how it is that Hardy knew that "every spirit upon earth seem'd fervourless as I"? We may inquire in vain. This radar romanticism is incredibly boring. I thought it went out with Shelley, who is Hardy's actual master, different as they appear. Now for the sad old thrush who occupies the title and the last two stanzas, that is to say, half the poem. I will only say that to bring such brilliant joy out of such personal misery is, friends, not easily done.

Earlier I used the word "little" and I have quoted Eliot's word "minor" and I've seemed to be friendlier to these judgments than to Mr. Lowell's and to Mr. Ransom's. It is too soon to form an opinion about Hardy's ultimate place in our international English-speaking literature. He wrote one thousand pages of the worst short stories that the world has ever seen. He wrote some ridiculous novels. *The Dynasts* is a dud, fit only for graduate study. He wrote many atrocious poems, also, but the main novels will always be available for young people. As for the rest of us, I now change my position entirely and line up with Mr. Ransom—we are happy with a handful of magnificent, devoted poems, which that formidable little man has happened to leave to us as a legacy.

Hardy's most formidable disciple was W.H. Auden. Tell you a story. Mr. Ransom, who practically calls Hardy Mr. Hardy, once came and gave a chat to my little students. At one point he said, "In one of his poems Hardy is considering the thing as it will be after his death. One can imagine what Tennyson or Browning would have made of this theme; but all Hardy says is, 'after I'm gone will there be someone who, looking at a sunset, will think, well, he was the kind of man who liked sunsets.' Seems a pretty small thing to ask."

# GERARD MANLEY HOPKINS
## [1844–1889]

## *The Wreck of the Deutschland*

*To the*
*happy memory of five Franciscan Nuns*
*exiles by the Falk Laws*
*drowned between midnight and morning of*
*Dec. 7th, 1875*

I

Thou mastering me
God! giver of breath and bread;
World's strand, sway of the sea;
Lord of living and dead;
Thou has bound bones and veins in me, fastened me
flesh,                                                             5
And after it almost unmade, what with dread,
Thy doing: and dost thou touch me afresh?
Over again I feel thy finger and find thee.

I did say yes
O at lightning and lashed rod;                               10
Thou heardst me truer than tongue confess
Thy terror, O Christ, O God;
Thou knowest the walls, altar and hour and night:
The swoon of a heart that the sweep and the hurl of
thee trod
Hard down with a horror of height:                          15
And the midriff astrain with leaning of, laced with fire of
stress.

The frown of his face
Before me, the hurtle of hell
Behind, where, where was a, where was a place?
I whirled out wings that spell                               20
And fled with a fling of the heart to the heart of the Host.
My heart, but you were dovewinged, I can tell,

Carrier-witted, I am bold to boast.
To flash from the flame to the flame then, tower from the
grace to the grace.

I am soft sift                                    25
In an hourglass—at the wall
Fast, but mined with a motion, a drift,
And it crowds and it combs to the fall;
I steady as a water in a well, to a poise, to a pane,
But roped with, always, all the way down
from the tall                                     30
Fells or flanks of the voel, a vein
Of the gospel proffer, a pressure, a principle, Christ's gift.

I kiss my hand
To the stars, lovely-asunder
Starlight, wafting him out of it; and            35
Glow, glory in thunder;
Kiss my hand to the dappled-with-damson west:
Since, tho' he is under the world's splendour and wonder,
His mystery must be instressed, stressed;
For I greet him the days I meet him, and bless when I
understand.                                       40

Not out of his bliss
Springs the stress felt
Nor first from heaven (and few know this)
Swings the stroke dealt—
Stroke and a stress that stars and storms deliver,   45
That guilt is hushed by, hearts are flushed by and melt—
But it rides time like riding a river
(And here the faithful waver, the faithless fable and miss).

It dates from day
Of his going in Galilee;                          50
Warm-laid grave of a womb-life grey;
Manger, maiden's knee;
The dense and the driven Passion, and frightful sweat;
Thence the discharge of it, there its swelling to be,
Though felt before in high flood yet—             55
What none would have known of it, only the heart, being
hard at bay,

Is out with it! Oh,
We lash with the best or worst

GERARD MANLEY HOPKINS

*Brown Brothers*

Word last! How a lush-kept plush-capped sloe
   Will, mouthed to flesh-burst,         60
Gush!—flush the man, the being with it, sour or sweet
   Brim, in a flash, full!—Hither then, last or first,
      To hero of Calvary, Christ's feet—
Never ask if meaning it, wanting it, warned of it—men go.

      Be adored among men,         65
   God, three-numberèd form;
     Wring thy rebel, dogged in den,
      Man's malice, with wrecking and storm.
Beyond saying sweet, past telling of tongue,
Thou art lightning and love, I found it, a winter and
   warm;         70
     Father and fondler of heart thou hast wrung;
Hast thy dark descending and most art merciful then.

      With an anvil-ding
   And with fire in him forge thy will
     Or rather, rather then, stealing as Spring     75
      Through him, melt him but master him still:
Whether at once, as once at a crash Paul,
   Or as Austin, a lingering out swéet skíll,
     Make mercy in all of us, out of us all
Mastery, but be adored, but be adored King.     80

II

      "Some find me a sword; some
   The flange and the rail; flame,
     Fang, or flood" goes Death on drum,
      And storms bugle his fame.
But wé dream we are rooted in earth—Dust!     85
Flesh falls within sight of us, we, though our flower the
   same,
     Wave with the meadow, forget that there must
The sour scythe cringe, and the blear share come.

      On Saturday sailed from Bremen,
   American-outward-bound,     90
     Take settler and seamen, tell men with women,
      Two hundred souls in the round—
O Father, not under thy feathers nor ever as guessing
The goal was a shoal, of a fourth the doom to be
   drowned;

Yet did the dark side of the bay of thy blessing    95
Not vault them, the millions of rounds of thy mercy not
reeve even them in?

Into the snows she sweeps,
Hurling the haven behind,
The Deutschland, on Sunday; and so the sky keeps,
For the infinite air is unkind,    100
And the sea flint-flake, black-backed in the regular blow,
Sitting Eastnortheast, in cursed quarter, the wind;
Wiry and white-fiery and whirlwind-swivellèd snow
Spins to the widow-making unchilding unfathering deeps.

She drove in the dark to leeward,    105
She struck—not a reef or a rock
But the combs of a smother of sand: night drew her
Dead to the Kentish Knock;
And she beat the bank down with her bows and the ride
of her keel:
The breakers rolled on her beam with
ruinous shock;    110
And canvas and compass, the whorl and the wheel
Idle for ever to waft her or wind her with, these she endured.

Hope had grown grey hairs,
Hope had mourning on,
Trenched with tears, carved with cares,    115
Hope was twelve hours gone;
And frightful a nightfall folded rueful a day
Nor rescue, only rocket and lightship, shone,
And lives at last were washing away:
To the shrouds they took,—they shook in the hurling and
horrible airs.    120

One stirred from the rigging to save
The wild woman-kind below,
With a rope's end round the man, handy and
brave—
He was pitched to his death at a blow,
For all his dreadnought breast and braids of thew:    125
They could tell him for hours, dandled the to and fro
Through the cobbled foam-fleece, what could
he do
With the burl of the fountains of air, buck and the flood of
the wave?

They fought with God's cold—
And they could not and fell to the deck      130
(Crushed them) or water (and drowned them) or rolled
With the sea-romp over the wreck.
Night roared, with the heart-break hearing a heart-broke rabble,
The woman's wailing, the crying of child without check—
Till a lioness arose breasting the babble,      135
A prophetess towered in the tumult, a virginal tongue told.

Ah, touched in your bower of bone
Are you! turned for an exquisite smart,
Have you! make words break from me here all alone,
Do you!—mother of being in me, heart.      140
O unteachably after evil, but uttering truth,
Why tears! is it? tears; such a melting, a madrigal start!
Never-eldering revel and river of youth,
What can it be, this glee? the good you have there of your own?

Sister, a sister calling      145
A master, her master and mine!—
And the inboard seas run swirling and hawling;
The rash smart sloggering brine
Blinds her; but she that weather sees one thing, one;
Has one fetch in her: she rears herself to divine      150
Ears, and the call of the tall nun
To the men in the tops and the tackle rode over the storm's brawling.

She was first of a five and came
Of a coifèd sisterhood.
(O Deutschland, double a desperate name!      155
O world wide of its good!
But Gertrude, lily, and Luther, are two of a town,
Christ's lily and beast of the waste wood:
From life's dawn it is drawn down,
Abel is Cain's brother and breasts they have sucked the same.)      160

Loathed for a love men knew in them,
Banned by the land of their birth,

Rhine refused them. Thames would ruin them;
 Surf, snow, river and earth
Gnashed: but thou art above, thou Orion of light; 165
Thy unchancelling poising palms were weighing the
 worth,
 Thou martyr-master: in thy sight
Storm flakes were scroll-leaved flowers, lily showers—
sweet heaven was astrew in them.

 Five! the finding and sake
 And cipher of suffering Christ. 170
 Mark, the mark is of man's make
 And the word of it Sacrificed.
But he scores it in scarlet himself on his own bespoken,
Before-time-taken, dearest prizèd and priced—
 Stigma, signal, cinquefoil token
For lettering of the lamb's fleece, ruddying of the rose-
flake. 175

 Joy fall to thee, father Francis,
 Drawn to the Life that died;
With the gnarls of the nails in thee, niche of the
 lance, his
 Lovescape crucified
And seal of his seraph-arrival! and these
 thy daughters 180
And five-livèd and leavèd favour and pride,
 Are sisterly sealed in wild waters,
To bathe in his fall-gold mercies, to breathe in his all-fire
glances.

 Away in the loveable west,
 On a pastoral forehead of Wales, 185
I was under a roof here, I was at rest,
 And they the prey of the gales;
She to the black-about air, to the breaker, the thickly
Falling flakes, to the throng that catches and quails
 Was calling "O Christ, Christ, come quickly": 190
The cross to her she calls Christ to her, christens her wild-
worst Best.

 The majesty! what did she mean?
 Breathe, arch and original Breath.
 Is it love in her of the being as her lover had been?
 Breathe, body of lovely Death. 195
They were else-minded then, altogether, the men

Woke thee with a *we are perishing* in the weather of
    Gennesareth.
    Or is it that she cried for the crown then,
The keener to come at the comfort for feeling the combating
    keen?

    For how to the heart's cheering       200
    The down-dugged ground-hugged grey
Hovers off, the jay-blue heavens appearing
    Of pied and peeled May!
Blue-beating and hoary-glow height; or night, still
    higher,
With belled fire and the moth-soft Milky Way,    205
    What by your measure is the heaven of desire,
The treasure never eyesight got, nor was ever guessed what
    for the hearing?

    No, but it was not these.
    The jading and jar of the cart,
Time's tasking, it is fathers that asking
    for ease       210
    Of the sodden-with-its-sorrowing heart,
Nor danger, electrical horror; then further it finds
The appealing of the Passion is tenderer in prayer apart:
    Other, I gather, in measure her mind's
Burden, in wind's burly and beat of endragonèd seas.    215

    But how shall I . . . make me room there:
    Reach me a . . . Fancy, come faster—
Strike you the sight of it? look at it loom there,
    Thing that she . . . there then! the Master,
*Ipse*, the only one, Christ, King, Head:    220
He was to cure the extremity where he had cast her;
    Do, deal, lord it with living and dead;
Let him ride, her pride, in his triumph, despatch and have
    done with his doom there.

    Ah! there was a heart right!
    There was single eye!    225
Read the unshapeable shock night
    And knew the who and the why;
Wording it how but by him that present and past,
    Heaven and earth are word of, worded by?—
    The Simon Peter of a soul! to the blast    230
Tarpeian-fast, but a blown beacon of light.

Jesu, heart's light,
Jesu, maid's son,
What was the feast followed the night
Thou hadst glory of this nun?—                235
Feast of the one woman without stain.
For so conceivèd, so to conceive thee is done;
But here was heart-throe, birth of a brain,
Word, that heard and kept thee and uttered thee outright.

Well, she has thee for the pain, for the        240
Patience; but pity of the rest of them!
Heart, go and bleed at a bitterer vein for the
Comfortless unconfessed of them—
No not uncomforted: lovely-felicitous Providence
Finger of a tender of, O of a feathery delicacy, the breast
of the                                         245
Maiden could obey so, be a bell to, ring of it, and
Startle the poor sheep back! is the shipwrack then a harvest,
does tempest carry the grain for thee?

I admire thee, master of the tides,
Of the Yore-flood, of the year's fall;
The recurb and the recovery of the
gulf's sides,                                  250
The girth of it and the wharf of it and the wall;
Stanching, quenching ocean of a motionable mind;
Ground of being, and granite of it: past all
Grasp God, throned behind
Death with a sovereignty that heeds but hides, bodes but
abides;                                        255

With a mercy that outrides
The all of water, an ark
For the listener; for the lingerer with a love glides
Lower than death and the dark;
A vein for the visiting of the past-prayer,
pent in prison,                                260
The-last-breach penitent spirits—the uttermost mark
Our passion-plungèd giant risen,
The Christ of the Father compassionate, fetched in the
storm of his strides.

Now burn, new born to the world,
Doubled-naturèd name,                          265
The heaven-flung, heart-fleshed, maiden-furled
Miracle-in-Mary-of-flame,

Mid-numbered He in three of the thunder-throne!
Not a dooms-day dazzle in his coming nor dark as he
came;
Kind, but royally reclaiming his own;                          270
A released shower, let flash to the shire, not a lightning
of fire hard-hurled.

Dame, at our door
Drowned, and among our shoals,
Remember us in the roads, the heaven-haven of the
Reward:
Our King back, oh, upon English souls!          275
Let him easter in us, be a dayspring to the dimness of
us, be a crimson-cresseted east,
More brightening her, rare-dear Britain, as his reign rolls,
Pride, rose, prince, hero of us, high-priest,
Our hearts' charity's hearth's fire, our thoughts' chivalry's
throng's Lord.

# James Dickey

## HOPKINS
### THE WRECK OF THE DEUTSCHLAND

Hopkins' "Wreck of the Deutschland" represented a new direction, an entire new set of possibilities and techniques for English poetry. From the standpoint of influence—that is, considering what poetry after Hopkins really did become— it is probably the most important poem of the nineteenth century. Though he had been a fine traditional poet and an interesting and cautiously experimental writer before "The Wreck of the Deutschland," it is with this poem that he is first seen completely in the curious, breathtakingly original form which has since come to be identified as "Hopkinsian." Here for the first time came fully together his linguistic and prosodic experiments—of which the most famous and influential is the conscious employment of what the poet called "sprung rhythm," wherein only the stresses of a line are counted, and the line is allowed to have any number of unstressed syllables—the piety and agony of his Jesuitical faith, his personal suffering over the actuality and meaning of pain and death, and his intensely personal researches into nature, his "inscapes," his capacity to look at things as though time did not exist: as though he and that flower, that leaf, that formation of ice on a pond, that sunset or that drift of cloud were the only things in existence: as though he and the object were both placed in the world exclusively to meet and understand each other's essences.

Because these qualities came together in this way and were forged in Hopkins' mind as they were, the whole concept of what can be done with the English verse line, the English language, was changed. Hopkins is a poet of extremes, of the pushing of vision, the pushing of poetic devices beyond themselves, to a point one degree farther than the *reductio ad absurdum*, one degree higher than the ludicrous, which is in some cases the degree of sublimity. In no other poet, not even Shakespeare or Donne, is it quite so obvious to the un-warned reader that a new *dimension* has been added to poetry. All other poems, even some of those commonly called "great," are likely to seem linguistically thin, a little prosaic and easily satisfied with themselves, compared with Hopkins. On first encountering Hopkins' intense, peculiar, rapid idiom, a great many people have said to themselves that here, at long last, is a *complete* poetry, working power-fully at all levels, at once both wild and swift beyond all other wildness and swiftness and stringently, savagely dis-ciplined: a language *worked* for all it can give.

It is a poem about death at sea: a death that has to be *imagined* rather than suffered by a poet whose being, himself, at the time that "they fought with God's cold" "Away in the loveable west, / On a pastoral forehead of Wales" adds to the delirious guilt of the tone. In a fearsome and nearly miraculous metamorphosis, this guilt becomes a furious affir-mation of the role of suffering in life. The sea itself, the sea into which the *Deutschland* founders with its five nuns, is the most powerfully real and *active* sea in English literature, not surpassed even by the sea of *Beowulf, The Seafarer,* or any of the bardic poets who would seem able to render water, spray, and pain with a great deal more authority than could a withdrawn, scholarly, nineteenth century teach-ing Jesuit. And yet, through labors that made the writing of poetry so horrendously difficult as almost, but not quite, to make it impossible, Hopkins was able to catch the rhythms and terrors of the sea at its most murderous, as it surrounds the human spirit at its most hopeless. Hopkins' triumphant cry in the nun's "O Christ, Christ, come quickly" is a point from which English religious poetry has never risen. Christ is with the hopeless, even those *this* hopeless, even when they are blinded with snow and spray and their voice swallowed by the wind. The snow, the killing wind, are all God's: it is all part of the Way.

This assumption, this affirmation, is where some readers, as it were, "hang up." One cannot deny Hopkins the power and originality of his verse; these are too evident, too overwhelm-ing. Yet the continual recourse to the figure of Christ, not only in this poem but in most of Hopkins' others, to solve the problems of conflict implicit in the action of the poem, comes, after so much of it, to seem a calling of the god from the machine. Hopkins' repairing to Jesus and to God as the solution not only of every human problem but of every poem, strikes some readers as predictable and even a little complacent.

But the language, the rhythms, the desperate originality of

vision, the curious recklessness coupled with the marvelously wrought prosody, the sense of a disciplined outpour that is still, in every syllable, an outpour: these are Hopkins. His world, his work, are tight and compressed like a spring; they are feverish and a little hysterical. One cannot read too much of Hopkins at a time, for one cannot match his intensity. But "The Wreck of the Deutschland" introduced into the English literary tradition the idea of a *total* poetry. Consequently it represents a renewal of the language: a renewal from the region of the unforeseen, the unforeseeable, the triumphantly personal, the theoretically worked-out that works.

※

## The Leaden Echo and the Golden Echo
### (*Maidens' Song from St. Winefred's Well*)

##### THE LEADEN ECHO

How to keep—is there any any, is there none such, nowhere
    known some, bow or brooch or braid or brace, làce, latch
    or catch or key to keep
Back beauty, keep it, beauty, beauty, beauty, . . . from
    vanishing away?
O is there no frowning of these wrinkles, rankèd wrinkles
    deep,
Dòwn? no waving off of these most mournful messengers,
    still messengers, sad and stealing messengers of grey?
No there's none, there's none, O no there's none,        5
Nor can you long be, what you now are, called fair,
Do what you may do, what, do what you may,
And wisdom is early to despair:
Be beginning; since, no, nothing can be done
To keep at bay        10
Age and age's evils, hoar hair,
Ruck and wrinkle, drooping, dying, death's worst, winding
    sheets, tombs and worms and tumbling to decay;
So be beginning, be beginning to despair.
O there's none; no no no there's none:
Be beginning to despair, to despair,        15
Despair, despair, despair, despair.

##### THE GOLDEN ECHO

        Spare!
There is one, yes I have one (Hush there!);
Only not within seeing of the sun,
Not within the singeing of the strong sun,
Tall sun's tingeing, or treacherous the tainting of the
    earth's air,
Somewhere elsewhere there is ah well where! one,        5
One. Yes I càn tell such a key, I dò know such a place,

Where whatever's prized and passes of us, everything that's
  fresh and fast flying of us, seems to us sweet of us and
  swiftly away with, done away with, undone,
Undone, done with, soon done with, and yet dearly and dan-
  gerously sweet
Of us, the wimpled-water-dimpled, not-by-morning-matchèd
  face,
The flower of beauty, fleece of beauty, too too apt to, ah! to
  fleet,                                                                      10
Never fleets mòre, fastened with the tenderest truth
To its own best being and its loveliness of youth: it is an ever-
  lastingness of, O it is an all youth!
Come then, your ways and airs and looks, locks, maiden gear,
  gallantry and gaiety and grace,
Winning ways, airs innocent, maiden manners, sweet looks,
  loose locks, long locks, lovelocks, gaygear, going gallant,
  girlgrace—
Resign them, sign them, seal them, send them, motion them
  with breath,                                                               15
And with sighs soaring, soaring sìghs deliver
Them; beauty-in-the-ghost, deliver it, early now, long before
  death
Give beauty back, beauty, beauty, beauty, back to God,
  beauty's self and beauty's giver.
See; not a hair is, not an eyelash, not the least lash lost; every
  hair
Iș, hair of the head, numbered.                                             20
Nay, what we had lighthanded left in surly the mere mould
Will have waked and have waxed and have walked with the
  wind what while we slept,
This side, that side hurling a heavyheaded hundredfold
What while we, while we slumbered.
O then, weary then whỳ should we tread? O why are we so
  haggard at the heart, so care-coiled, care-killed, so fagged,
  so fashed, so cogged, so cumbered,                                        25
When the thing we freely fòrfeit is kept with fonder a care,
Fonder a care kept than we could have kept it, kept
Far with fonder a care (and we, we should have lost it) finer,
  fonder
A care kept.—Where kept? Do but tell us where kept,
  where.—
Yonder.—What high as that! We follow,
  now we follow.—                                                           30
  Yonder, yes yonder, yonder,
Yonder.

*Chad Walsh*

---

### HOPKINS
### THE LEADEN ECHO AND THE GOLDEN ECHO

The passing away of youthful charm and physical beauty has been a recurrent lament of poets, as of ordinary mortals who look apprehensively in the mirror to see new wrinkles and additional touches of grey. A vast industry has evolved to foster the illusion that beauty can stand still and never fade: cosmetics, face liftings, special diets. Mankind, and still less womankind, reconciles itself to the slow but sure destruction that nature wreaks on human beauty.

The normal impulse is to clutch and cling, to pretend that time can have a stop, to cover up and disguise its advances. In "The Leaden Echo and the Golden Echo" Gerard Manley Hopkins, a man as drunk with beauty as any who has ever lived, gives different advice. He says in effect, "Don't clutch. Give."

The poem itself is one of several fragments from a play, *St. Winefred's Well*, that Hopkins attempted to compose. The idea came to him during the three years, beginning in 1874, when he was studying theology at St. Beuno's College, in preparation for his ordination as a Jesuit priest. The college was set in the midst of a beautiful countryside in North Wales. Six miles away was the spring, and its healing waters, associated with the legend of St. Winefred; the college itself was named for her uncle. The spring, with all its associations of holiness, beauty, and old lore, was to haunt him after he had left the college. In 1879 he began the play he was never to finish, but which served as the framework for a poem, "The Leaden Echo and the Golden Echo," that mirrors as perfectly as anything he ever wrote his passionate conviction that human beauty, like all beauty, is from God and is a revelation of God; beauty is not something to be clutched but rather to be offered back to God, who in His mysterious way will ultimately return it to the giver, in greater radiance and splendor than ever.

The poem was originally written to be sung, and Hopkins

himself, who was keenly sensitive to music and even experimented at composing music, wrote to the poet, Richard W. Dixon: "I never did anything more musical." The first half, "The Leaden Echo," is one long cry of despair. To give it specific focus, the despair is that experienced by girls at the moment when they are at the peak of youthful beauty and are first becoming aware of the wreckage that time will bring. The despair is presented in the language, one might almost say, the shoptalk, of women, with such items as bows, brooches, braids, and braces serving as symbols of the effort to enhance and safeguard beauty:

> *How to kèep—is there àny any, is there none such, no-*
> *where known some, bow or brooch or braid or brace,*
> *làce, latch or catch or key to keep*
> *Back beauty, keep it, beauty, beauty, beauty, . . . from*
> *vanishing away?*

It is interesting to note that the first line gave Hopkins trouble in the writing. In a letter to Robert Bridges (who in 1918 published the first edition of Hopkins' poetry), he confessed: "I am somewhat dismayed about that piece and have laid it aside for a while. I cannot satisfy myself about the first line. You must know that words like *charm* and *enchantment* will not do; the thought is of beauty as of something that can be physically kept and lost and by physical things only, like keys; then the things must come from the *mundus muliebris.* . . ." Evidently he had started out with the general idea of "trying to lock beauty up and protect it from the pilfering of time" and had seen that for dramatic effectiveness the language needed to be made concrete and specific; hence he translated the general idea into the vocabulary of young girls as they first become aware of their own beauty, and spend endless hours discussing the physical aids to beauty.

The next two lines repeat the question of the opening lines, except that now the emphasis is on the visible signs of physical decay:

> *Ò is there no frowning of these wrinkles, rankèd wrinkles*
> *deep,*
> *Dòwn? no waving off of these most mournful messen-*
> *gers,*
> *still messengers, sad and stealing messengers of grey?*

The answer comes quickly: No. It comes in a line that reads like a slow lament, with its repetitions of the *n* sound, and the interweaving of the two negative words, *no* and *none*:

*No there's none, there's none, O no there's none*

The poem moves on with pitiless realism to picture the physical havoc wrought by time: hoar hair, wrinkles, winding sheets, tombs, worms; it offers only the sober wisdom:

*So be beginning, be beginning to despair*

The two themes, "there's none" and "despair," are now woven together in the three concluding lines, like dull words echoing back to the speaker:

*O there's none; no no no there's none:*
*Be beginning to despair, to despair,*
*Despair, despair, despair, despair.*

The Golden Echo now speaks in answer. The last word spoken by the Leaden Echo was "despair." The Golden Echo replies with the rhyme, "Spare!" There *is* a way that beauty can be made eternal. It is not the way of cosmetics and trying to frustrate the normal course of nature. The way is the way of giving, of self-offering. As the poem puts it—

*There is one, yes, I have one (Hush there!);*
*Only not within seeing of the sun,*
*Not within the singeing of the strong sun,*

. . .

*One. Yes I can tell such a key, I do know such a place*

The "One" is God. The poem next catalogues the beauties of youth—not-by-morning-matchèd face, the flower of beauty, ways and airs and looks, maiden gear, gallantry and gaity and grace, long locks, girlgrace—and counsels:

*Resign them, sign them, seal them, send them, motion them*
*with breath,*
*And with sighs soaring, soaring sighs deliver*
*Them; beauty-in-the-ghost, deliver it, early now, long before*
*death*
*Give beauty back, beauty, beauty, beauty, back to God,*
*beauty's self and beauty's giver*

The poem moves more and more toward the language of resurrection. Beauty freely offered to God, "beauty's self and beauty's giver," will not merely be restored, but will rise into new being with a glory that had previously been only a potentiality:

*See; not a hair is, not an eyelash, not the least lash lost; every*
*hair*
*Is, hair of the head, numbered.*
*Nay, what we had lighthanded left in surly the mere mould*
*Will have waked and have waxed and have walked with the*
*wind what while we slept,*
*This side, that side hurling a heavyheaded hundredfold*
*What while we, while we slumbered.*[1]

The language here is that of death and resurrection. But the reader senses a second level. The poem is speaking also of each present moment, and one's attitude toward God's gifts, such as beauty. They can be made the be-all and end-all, in which case they always turn to ashes. Or they can be gratefully viewed as the free gift of God, accepted with gratitude, given back to the giver as a voluntary offering of gratitude. Death and resurrection are a dramatic acting-out of the daily spiritual life of man with God.

The poem now moves swiftly to its conclusion. Despair has been conquered by hope—

*O then, weary then why should we tread? O why are we so*
*haggard at the heart, so care-coiled, care-killed, so fagged,*
*so fashed, so cogged, so cumbered,*
*When the thing we freely fòrfeit is kept with fonder a care,*
*Fonder a care kept than we could have kept it . . .*

And finally, the poem—which in its first half pointed from earthly beauty to inevitable decay—now focuses on the ultimate source of beauty:

*Yonder.—What high as that! We follow, now we follow.—*
  *Yonder, yes yonder, yonder,*
*Yonder.*

What began in the first half as an apprehensive lament over the passing of beauty has ended as a joyous affirmation. The poem has moved from "how to keep" to "despair" and on to "spare" and finally to the One who is to be sought "yonder" and who *is* the beauty and quickening life and resurrection.

Such are the bare bones of this poem, one of the greatest religious lyrics ever composed. The bare bones are its meaning. But what gives the poem flesh is the use of language, at

[1] In a letter to Bridges, Hopkins explains that this means "Nay more: the seed that we so carelessly and freely flung into the dull furrow, and then forgot it, will have come to ear meantime!" The passage seems to echo St. Paul's great affirmation of the resurrection of the body (*1 Corinthians* 15:35-58).

which Hopkins has few equals. In a riot of words, each carefully and lovingly chosen, there are created not merely the abstract ideas of beauty, decay, despair, salvation, but the taste and touch and smell of it all. This may not be evident if the poem is read silently. Read aloud—better still, chanted aloud—the richness and accuracy of the language will bring alive, as no paraphrase can, the full dramatic sweep of a poem that moves from poignant tears for the brevity of beauty to the joyful proclamation of Beauty Himself.

# FRANCIS THOMPSON
[1859–1907]

## The Hound of Heaven

I fled Him, down the nights and down the days;
I fled Him, down the arches of the years;
I fled Him, down the labyrinthine ways
    Of my own mind; and in the mist of tears
I hid from Him, and under running laughter.       5
      Up vistaed hopes I sped;
      And shot, precipitated,
Adown Titanic glooms of chasmèd fears,
  From those strong Feet that followed, followed after.
      But with unhurrying chase,       10
      And unperturbèd pace,
  Deliberate speed, majestic instancy,
    They beat—and a Voice beat
    More instant than the Feet—
"All things betray thee, who betrayest Me."       15

    I pleaded, outlaw-wise,
By many a hearted casement, curtained red,
  Trellised with intertwining charities;
(For, though I knew His love Who followèd,
    Yet was I sore adread       20
Lest, having Him, I must have naught beside);
But, if one little casement parted wide,
  The gust of His approach would clash it to.

Fear wist not to evade, as Love wist to pursue.
Across the margent of the world I fled,       25
  And troubled the gold gateways of the stars,
  Smiting for shelter on their clangèd bars;
    Fretted to dulcet jars
And silvern clatter the pale ports o' the moon.
I said to dawn, Be sudden; to eve, Be soon;      30
  With thy young skiey blossoms heap me over
    From this tremendous Lover!
Float thy vague veil about me, lest He see!
  I tempted all His servitors, but to find

My own betrayal in their constancy,                                    35
In faith to Him their fickleness to me,
   Their traitorous trueness, and their loyal deceit.
To all swift things for swiftness did I sue;
   Clung to the whistling mane of every wind.
      But whether they swept, smoothly fleet,                          40
      The long savannahs of the blue;
         Or whether, Thunder-driven,
         They clanged his chariot 'thwart a heaven
Plashy with flying lightnings round the spurn o' their feet:—
Fear wist not to evade as Love wist to pursue.                         45
         Still with unhurrying chase,
         And unperturbèd pace,
      Deliberate speed, majestic instancy,
         Came on the following Feet,
         And a Voice above their beat—                                 50
   "Naught shelters thee, who wilt not shelter Me."

I sought no more that after which I strayed
      In face of man or maid:
But still within the little children's eyes
      Seems something, something that replies;                         55
*They* at least are for me, surely for me!
I turned me to them very wistfully;
But, just as their young eyes grew sudden fair
      With dawning answers there,
Their angel plucked them from me by the hair.                          60
"Come then, ye other children, Nature's—share
With me" (said I) "your delicate fellowship;
      Let me greet you lip to lip,
      Let me twine with your caresses,
         Wantoning                                                     65
      With our Lady-Mother's vagrant tresses,
         Banqueting
      With her in her wind-walled palace,
      Underneath her azured daïs,
      Quaffing, as your taintless way is,                             70
         From a chalice
Lucent-weeping out of the dayspring."
         So it was done:
*I* in their delicate fellowship was one—
Drew the bolt of Nature's secrecies.                                  75
*I* knew all the swift importings
      On the wilful face of skies;
      I knew how the clouds arise

FRANCIS THOMPSON

*Drawn by V. Gribayedoff*
*New York Public Library*
*Picture Collection*

Spumèd of the wild sea-snortings;
 All that's born or dies     80
 Rose and drooped with—made them shapers
Of mine own moods, or wailful or divine—
 With them joyed and was bereaven.
 I was heavy with the even,
 When she lit her glimmering tapers   85
 Round the day's dead sanctities.
 I laughed in the morning's eyes.
I triumphed and I saddened with all weather,
 Heaven and I wept together,
And its sweet tears were salt with mortal mine;   90

Against the red throb of its sunset-heart
 I laid my own to beat,
 And share commingling heat;
But not by that, by that, was eased my human smart.
In vain my tears were wet on Heaven's grey cheek.   95
For ah! we know not what each other says,
 These things and I; in sound *I* speak—
*Their* sound is but their stir, they speak by silences.
Nature, poor stepdame, cannot slake my drouth;
 Let her, if she would owe me,    100
Drop yon blue bosom-veil of sky, and show me
 The breasts o' her tenderness:
Never did any milk of hers once bless
 My thirsting mouth.
 Nigh and nigh draws the chase,    105
 With unperturbèd pace,
Deliberate speed, majestic instancy;
 And past those noisèd Feet
 A voice comes yet more fleet—
"Lo! naught contents thee, who content'st not Me."   110

Naked I wait Thy love's uplifted stroke!
My harness piece by piece Thou hast hewn from me,
 And smitten me to my knee;
 I am defenceless utterly,
 I slept, methinks, and woke,    115
And, slowly gazing, find me stripped in sleep.
In the rash lustihead of my young powers,
 I shook the pillaring hours
And pulled my life upon me; grimed with smears,
I stand amid the dust o' the mounded years—   120
My mangled youth lies dead beneath the heap.
My days have crackled and gone up in smoke,

Have puffed and burst as sun-starts on a stream.
　　Yea, faileth now even dream
The dreamer, and the lute the lutanist;　　125
Even the linked fantasies, in whose blossomy twist
I swung the earth a trinket at my wrist,
Are yielding; cords of all too weak account
For earth with heavy griefs so overplussed.
　　Ah! is Thy love indeed　　130
A weed, albeit an amaranthine weed,
Suffering no flowers except its own to mount?
　　Ah! must—
　　Designer infinite!—
Ah! must Thou char the wood ere Thou canst limn with it?　135
My freshness spent its wavering shower i' the dust;
And now my heart is as a broken fount,
Wherein tear-drippings stagnate, spilt down ever
　　From the dank thoughts that shiver
Upon the sighful branches of my mind.　　140
　　Such is; what is to be?
The pulp so bitter, how shall taste the rind?
I dimly guess what Time in mists confounds;
Yet ever and anon a trumpet sounds
From the hid battlements of Eternity;　　145
Those shaken mists a space unsettle, then
Round the half-glimpsèd turrets slowly wash again.
　　But not ere him who summoneth
　　I first have seen, enwound
With glooming robes purpureal, cypress-crowned;　　150
His name I know, and what his trumpet saith.
Whether man's heart or life it be which yields
　　Thee harvest, must Thy harvest fields
　　Be dunged with rotten death?

　　　Now of that long pursuit　　155
　　　Comes on at hand the bruit;
　　That Voice is round me like a bursting sea:
　　　"And is thy earth so marred,
　　　Shattered in shard on shard?
　　Lo, all things fly thee, for thou fliest Me!　　160
　　Strange, piteous, futile thing,
Wherefore should any set thee love apart?
Seeing none but I makes much of naught?" (He said),
"And human love needs human meriting:
　　How hast thou merited—　　165
Of all man's clotted clay the dingiest clot?

Alack, thou knowest not
How little worthy of any love thou art!
Whom wilt thou find to love ignoble thee
    Save Me, save only Me?            170
All which I took from thee I did but take,
    Not for thy harms,
But just that thou might'st seek it in My arms.
    All which thy child's mistake
Fancies as lost, I have stored for thee at home:     175
    Rise, clasp My hand, and come!"

    Halts by me that footfall:
    Is my gloom, after all,
Shade of His hand, outstretched caressingly?
    "Ah, fondest, blindest, weakest,     180
    I am He Whom thou seekest!
Thou dravest love from thee, who dravest Me."

# James Dickey

## THOMPSON
## THE HOUND OF HEAVEN

Though a poet in the latter half of the twentieth century might write a poem with the same theme as "The Hound of Heaven"—the estrangement of the sinner from God's love and the devious and paradoxical ways in which he comes back to it—he would not be likely to conceive and write it in the way Thompson has done. If the mythological content has not entirely gone out of Christianity, at least it has greatly changed, and rhetoric of this particular grand, robed-seer kind has tended to disappear as well. There is a built-in hollowness in latter-day attempts at the sublime tone; many a swelling period has exploded in the face of the "Aw, come off it" that is one of our era's unique contributions to literary and other judgments. We welcome irony, indirection, a cool, in-group knowingness. But ecstasy? Well, no.

And yet the first thing to be noted about "The Hound of Heaven" is that it *is* grand: intentionally and grandly grand. It is also, *curiously* grand. And though it is unashamedly baroque it is also in part very daring linguistically; Hopkins or Joyce would have liked a coinage like "lustihead," and Hart Crane would surely have been excited by "the long savannahs of the blue." Yet it is the conception even more than the details that is daring, inspiring; it is the conception that takes the all-or-nothing chances, running the risk of toppling the whole poem into the frigidity and bombast that Longinus describes as being the pitfalls of the noble style that fails its intentions. Moreover, "The Hound" is not only grand, but *cosmically* grand. It is as if Thompson had taken the metaphysical conceit of Donne and Marvell literally, expanding it beyond all foreseeable bounds by inventing the most thrilling and monstrous figure of speech he could, and then not only come to believe it but leapt into it bodily. The poem is spectacularly far-fetched, but far-fetched with the excessiveness and total commitment that one feels instantly to be either the qualities of genuine inspiration or those of lunacy. Be this as it may, it is plain that Thompson has one charac-

teristic that visionary and mystical poets—certain kinds of
religious poets—must have: rapture. In its grip, he shows no
fear whatever of employing a scheme of imagery that involves, literally, the whole universe, with its star-systems,
winds, moons, clouds, suns, seas: he is not only unafraid of
his own conception but plunges triumphantly and giganti-
cally into it, for, though the sinner whose pursuit by the
celestial Hound is terrified, fleeing beautifully through sunsets, "wild sea-snortings" and the eyes of children, the poet
who writes of all this is gorgeously at home, revelling in the
metaphysical flight very much as if it were a physical one:
the cosmic and foredoomed paper-chase of a sinner who has
angelic powers. Since the universe is apprehended as the
sinner experiences it, and so in a sense is *in* him, "The Hound"
can also be read as a psychological poem, a study in religious
guilt-hysteria. But it is first and last a great—or near-great—
poem.

The structure of "The Hound" is superb, and the recklessness of its rushing imagery and rhetoric—things that start fast
and *cannot* slacken—will not fail to enthrall any reader who
will truly submit to them. Its pitch is high, nearly shrill, but
pure and beautifully modulated. Though its form is that of
the irregular Cowleyan ode, its dramatic force depends
mainly on its central paradox, which is that the pursued flees
as if damned, when capture would in fact be his salvation.
The "Hound" (and who but a man of Thompson's peculiar
baroque-mystic orientation would have used *this* as the figure
of God?) pursues simply by being the creator of and in-
dweller in everything that is, imbuing all things with His
essential quality of love. His gentle pursuit, which seems the
most dreadful possible one to the sinner desperate to keep his
youth and powers intact, does, however, take on something
of the truly ominous—pursuit, itself, is terrifying—and there
is something particularly terrible in the conviction that grows
in both sinner and reader that there is literally no escape. The
sinner flees, not through Kafka's dingy offices and bad telephone connections, but through the world, God being where
He has always been, in the stones and trees and grasses and
waves of the sea. It has always seemed to me to be indicative
of the angelic potential in the sinner himself that he can fly
upon winds, court stars, put his heart against that of the sunset and swing the earth a trinket at his wrist. This is in part
the reason that the flight is the most beautiful portion of the
poem, and fortunately it constitutes most of it. The capture
and reconciliation—the explanation—is, as it would almost

have to be, disappointing. And it is a measure of Thompson's accomplishment that the speech of God at the end disappoints us as much as it does, for one may have come to think that Thompson is a poet who might actually know—or guess—what God would say under these circumstances: that Thompson could speak with the tongues of angels as well as those of men, as he seems always about to do.

No matter; Thompson has entered, as well as created, his vision of the sinner-as-quarry, and turned the cosmos into a ritual hunt in some of the most frankly gorgeous imagery, some of the most resounding and yet curiously individual rhetoric, since Milton. For these reasons, "The Hound of Heaven" is a memorable poem, a poem like a theological nightmare, a Freudian or narcotic dream of excessive guilt where Existence itself, the ground of the flight, is really the protagonist of the poem, being in the sinner's and Thompson's hysterically heightened vision as excessive, unbelievable, haunted, and magnificent as it is whenever we choose or are compelled to bear the full brunt of its beauty and terror.

A. E. HOUSMAN

*Brown Brothers*

# A. E. HOUSMAN
[1859–1936]

## Selections From *A Shropshire Lad*

### I

Loveliest of trees, the cherry now
Is hung with bloom along the bough,
And stands about the woodland ride
Wearing white for Eastertide.

Now, of my threescore years and ten,     5
Twenty will not come again,
And take from seventy springs a score,
It only leaves me fifty more.

And since to look at things in bloom
Fifty springs are little room,     10
About the woodlands I will go
To see the cherry hung with snow.

### II

#### REVEILLE

Wake: the silver dusk returning
  Up the beach of darkness brims,
And the ship of sunrise burning
  Strands upon the eastern rims.

Wake: the vaulted shadow shatters,     5
  Trampled to the floor it spanned,
And the tent of night in tatters
  Straws the sky-pavilioned land.

Up, lad, up, 'tis late for lying:
  Hear the drums of morning play:     10
Hark, the empty highways crying
  "Who'll beyond the hills away?"

Towns and countries woo together,
  Forelands beacon, belfries call;
Never lad that trod on leather     15
  Lived to feast his heart with all.

Up, lad: thews that lie and cumber
   Sunlit pallets never thrive;
Morns abed and daylight slumber
   Were not meant for man alive.         20

Clay lies still, but blood's a rover;
   Breath's a ware that will not keep
Up, lad: when the journey's over
   There'll be time enough to sleep.

### III

When I watch the living meet,
   And the moving pageant file
Warm and breathing through the street
   Where I lodge a little while,

If the heats of hate and lust         5
   In the house of flesh are strong,
Let me mind the house of dust
   Where my sojourn shall be long.

In the nation that is not,
   Nothing stands that stood before;      10
There revenges are forgot,
   And the hater hates no more;

Lovers lying two and two
   Ask not whom they sleep beside,
And the bridegroom all night through    15
   Never turns him to the bride.

### IV

When I was one-and-twenty
   I heard a wise man say,
"Give crowns and pounds and guineas
   But not your heart away;
Give pearls away and rubies         5
   But keep your fancy free."
But I was one-and-twenty,
   No use to talk to me.

When I was one-and-twenty
   I heard him say again         10
"The heart out of the bosom
   Was never given in vain;
'Tis paid with sighs a plenty
   And sold for endless rue."

And I am two-and-twenty, 15
And oh, 'tis true, 'tis true.

V

TO AN ATHLETE DYING YOUNG

The time you won your town the race
We chaired you through the market-place;
Man and boy stood cheering by,
And home we brought you shoulder-high.

To-day, the road all runners come, 5
Shoulder-high we bring you home,
And set you at your threshold down,
Townsman of a stiller town.

Smart lad, to slip betimes away
From fields where glory does not stay 10
And early though the laurel grows
It withers quicker than the rose.

Eyes the shady night has shut
Cannot see the record cut,
And silence sounds no worse than cheers 15
After earth has stopped the ears:

Now you will not swell the rout
Of lads that wore their honours out,
Runners whom renown outran
And the name died before the man. 20

So set, before its echoes fade,
The fleet foot on the sill of shade,
And hold to the low lintel up
The still-defended challenge-cup

And round that early-laurelled head 25
Will flock to gaze the strengthless dead,
And find unwithered on its curls
The garland briefer than a girl's.

VI

The lads in their hundreds to Ludlow come in for the fair,
There's men from the barn and the
forge and the mill and the fold,
The lads for the girls and the lads for the liquor are there,
And there with the rest are the lads that will never be old.

There's chaps from the town and the
field and the till and the cart, 5

And many to count are the stalwart, and many the brave,
And many the handsome of face and the handsome of heart,
    And few that will carry their looks or
        their truth to the grave.

I wish one could know them, I wish there were tokens to tell
    The fortunate fellows that now you can never
        discern;                             10
And then one could talk with them
        friendly and wish them farewell
And watch them depart on the way
        that they will not return.

But now you may stare as you like and
        there's nothing to scan;
    And brushing your elbow unguessed-
        at and not to be told
They carry back bright to the coiner the mintage
        of man,                             15
    The lads that will die in their glory and never be old.

## VII

    Along the field as we came by
A year ago, my love and I,
The aspen over stile and stone
Was talking to itself alone.
"Oh who are these that kiss and pass?         5
A country lover and his lass;
Two lovers looking to be wed;
And time shall put them both to bed,
But she shall lie with earth above,
And he beside another love."           10

    And sure enough beneath the tree
There walks another love with me,
And overhead the aspen heaves
Its rainy-sounding silver leaves;
And I spell nothing in their stir,         15
But now perhaps they speak to her,
And plain for her to understand
They talk about a time at hand
When I shall sleep with clover clad,
And she beside another lad.           20

## VIII

On Wenlock Edge the wood's in trouble;
    His forest fleece the Wrekin heaves;

The gale, it plies the saplings double,
    And thick on Severn snow the leaves.

'Twould blow like this through holt and hanger      5
    When Uricon the city stood:
'Tis the old wind in the old anger,
    But then it threshed another wood.

Then, 'twas before my time, the Roman
    At yonder heaving hill would stare:      10
The blood that warms an English yeoman,
    The thoughts that hurt him, they were there.

There, like the wind through woods in riot,
    Through him the gale of life blew high;
The tree of man was never quiet:      15
    Then 'twas the Roman, now 'tis I.

The gale, it plies the saplings double,
    It blows so hard, 'twill soon be gone:
To-day the Roman and his trouble
    Are ashes under Uricon.      20

IX

Into my heart an air that kills
    From yon far country blows:
What are those blue remembered hills,
    What spires, what farms are those?

That is the land of lost content,      5
    I see it shining plain,
The happy highways where I went
    And cannot come again.

X

THE IMMORTAL PART

When I meet the morning beam
Or lay me down at night to dream,
I hear my bones within me say,
"Another night, another day.

"When shall this slough of sense be cast,      5
This dust of thoughts be laid at last,
The man of flesh and soul be slain
And the man of bone remain?

"This tongue that talks, these lungs that shout,
These thews that hustle us about,      10

This brain that fills the skull with schemes,
And its humming hive of dreams,—

"These to-day are proud in power
And lord it in their little hour:
The immortal bones obey control                    15
Of dying flesh and dying soul.

" 'Tis long till eve and morn are gone:
Slow the endless night comes on,
And late to fulness grows the birth
That shall last as long as earth.                  20

"Wanderers eastward, wanderers west,
Know you why you cannot rest?
'Tis that every mother's son
Travails with a skeleton.

"Lie down in the bed of dust;                      25
Bear the fruit that bear you must;
Bring the eternal seed to light,
And morn is all the same as night.

"Rest you so from trouble sore,
Fear the heat o' the sun no more,                  30
Nor the snowing winter wild,
Now you labour not with child.

"Empty vessel, garment cast,
We that wore you long shall last.
—Another night, another day."                      35
So my bones within me say.

Therefore they shall do my will
To-day while I am master still,
And flesh and soul, now both are strong,
Shall hale the sullen slaves along,                40

Before this fire of sense decay,
This smoke of thought blow clean away,
And leave with ancient night alone
The stedfast and enduring bone.

### XI

With rue my heart is laden
    For golden friends I had,
For many a rose-lipt maiden
    And many a lightfoot lad.

By brooks too broad for leaping  5
 The lightfoot boys are laid;
The rose-lipt girls are sleeping
 In fields where roses fade.

XII

"Terence, this is stupid stuff:
You eat your victuals fast enough;
There can't be much amiss, 'tis clear,
To see the rate you drink your beer.
But oh, good Lord, the verse you make,  5
It gives a chap the belly-ache.
The cow, the old cow, she is dead;
It sleeps well, the horned head:
We poor lads, 'tis our turn now
To hear such tunes as killed the cow.  10
Pretty friendship 'tis to rhyme
Your friends to death before their time
Moping melancholy mad:
Come, pipe a tune to dance to, lad."

Why, if 'tis dancing you would be,  15
There's brisker pipes than poetry.
Say, for what were hop-yards meant,
Or why was Burton built on Trent?
Oh many a peer of England brews
Livelier liquor than the Muse,  20
And malt does more than Milton can
To justify God's ways to man.
Ale, man, ale's the stuff to drink
For fellows whom it hurts to think:
Look into the pewter pot  25
To see the world as the world's not.
And faith, 'tis pleasant till 'tis past:
The mischief is that 'twill not last.
Oh I have been to Ludlow fair
And left my necktie God knows where,  30
And carried half-way home, or near,
Pints and quarts of Ludlow beer:
Then the world seemed none so bad,
And I myself a sterling lad;
And down in lovely muck I've lain,  35
Happy till I woke again.
Then I saw the morning sky:
Heigho, the tale was all a lie;

The world, it was the old world yet,
I was I, my things were wet,                                    40
And nothing now remained to do
But begin the game anew.

Therefore, since the world has still
Much good, but much less good than ill,
And while the sun and moon endure                              45
Luck's a chance, but trouble's sure,
I'd face it as a wise man would,
And train for ill and not for good.
'Tis true the stuff I bring for sale
Is not so brisk a brew as ale:                                 50
Out of a stem that scored the hand
I wrung it in a weary land.
But take it: if the smack is sour,
The better for the embittered hour;
It should do good to heart and head                           55
When your soul is in my soul's stead;
And I will friend you, if I may,
In the dark and cloudy day.

There was a king reigned in the East:
There, when kings will sit to feast,                          60
They get their fill before they think
With poisoned meat and poisoned drink.
He gathered all that springs to birth
From the many-venomed earth;
First a little, thence to more,                               65
He sampled all her killing store;
And easy, smiling, seasoned sound,
Sate the king when healths went round.
They put arsenic in his meat
And stared aghast to watch him eat;                           70
They poured strychnine in his cup
And shook to see him drink it up:
They shook, they stared as white's their shirt:
Them it was their poison hurt.
—I tell the tale that I heard told.                           75
Mithridates, he died old.

# A. J. M. Smith

## HOUSMAN
### SELECTIONS FROM A SHROPSHIRE LAD

The "poem" that follows has been selected with great skill by Oscar Williams from the lyrics that make up one of the most popular collections of poetry in the English language, *A Shropshire Lad*, published in 1896 by A. E. Housman, a somewhat withdrawn and retiring scholar, who held a chair of classics in the University of London. A slim volume of sixty-three short poems, *A Shropshire Lad* was so technically accomplished and so universal in its themes that it pleased both the fastidious critic and the general reader. On a first reading many of the verses seemed to have existed always, and the book was recognized as a classic at once. It has held its place in the affection of the public with a tenacity shared only by FitzGerald's translation of the *Rubáiyát* of Omar Khayyám. The special quality and peculiar flavor of Housman's poems lie in their simplicity and clarity—a clarity that is achieved, however, through verbal perfection and musical dexterity. Housman is a master of the technical devices of poetic language—alliteration, assonance, and meter. Furthermore, he has made use of a conventional, not to say artificial, poetic diction, derived from the old ballads and such poets as Herrick, Blake, and Tennyson, which gives people the comfortable feeling that what they are reading is indubitably poetry—nothing new, experimental, uncertain, or disturbing.

This might be thought by some a weakness, but actually it is a highly successful strategy—one that has enabled Housman to put across a philosophy as disillusioned and pessimistic as the Book of Ecclesiastes or Lucretius' *On the Nature of Things*. Nature is indifferent, and time is cruel; men are unstable and maids untrue; life is sweet, to be sure, but death is certain and unexpected and soon. A wry and disillusioned stoicism alone can answer.

The answer is given to an indifferent or hostile universe, and it is given in a voice that, though never impersonal, is the voice of all mankind. Its universality is unmistakable. There is nothing petty, egotistical, or self-pitying in Housman's pessimism, and it is this that gives it its classical validity:

> *They say my verse is sad: no wonder;*
> *Its narrow measure spans*
> *Tears of eternity, and sorrow,*
> *Not mine, but man's*

Another source of its strength is the fact that it does not deny the richness and beauty of nature but is based on a full acceptance of what is all the more precious because it is so fleeting. No poem in the English language more fully and intensely catches the loveliness of the springtime than the first lyric in the sequence given here—or of the dawn, than the wonderful image that opens the second poem.

All the poems in *A Shropshire Lad,* universal and concise as they are, are the product of excitement, and they communicate excitement. When after twenty-six years Housman published another small volume of lyrics, significantly titled *Last Poems,* he added a note that throws a little light on the state of mind in which he composed his poetry: "I publish these poems, few though they are, because it is not likely that I shall ever be impelled to write much more. I can no longer expect to be revisited by the continuous excitement under which in the early months of 1895 I wrote the greater part of my other book, nor indeed could I well sustain it if it came." After his death in April 1936, it should be added, a small volume of *More Poems* was published and in 1940 a *Collected Poems,* which contained a few additional unpublished pieces and fragments, some light and satiric in tone. It is a remarkable fact, and one that testifies to the careful technical craftsmanship with which Housman polished the productions of his inspiration, that none of the poems in the later books fall below the high level of excellence shown in *A Shropshire Lad.*

# WILLIAM BUTLER YEATS
[1865–1939]

## Sailing to Byzantium

That is no country for old men. The young
In one another's arms, birds in the trees
—Those dying generations—at their song,
The salmon-falls, the mackerel-crowded seas,
Fish, flesh, or fowl, commend all summer long      5
Whatever is begotten, born, and dies.
Caught in that sensual music all neglect
Monuments of unaging intellect.

An aged man is but a paltry thing,
A tattered coat upon a stick, unless      10
Soul clap its hands and sing, and louder sing
For every tatter in its mortal dress,
Nor is there singing school but studying
Monuments of its own magnificence;
And therefore I have sailed the seas and come      15
To the holy city of Byzantium.

O sages standing in God's holy fire
As in the gold mosaic of a wall,
Come from the holy fire, perne in a gyre,
And be the singing-masters of my soul.      20
Consume my heart away; sick with desire
And fastened to a dying animal
It knows not what it is; and gather me
Into the artifice of eternity.

Once out of nature I shall never take      25
My bodily form from any natural thing,
But such a form as Grecian goldsmiths make
Of hammered gold and gold enamelling
To keep a drowsy Emperor awake;
Or set upon a golden bough to sing      30
To lords and ladies of Byzantium
Of what is past, or passing, or to come.

WILLIAM BUTLER YEATS

*The Bettmann Archive*

## Elder Olson

<hr/>

### YEATS
### SAILING TO BYZANTIUM

In "Sailing to Byzantium," an old man faces the problem of old age, of death, and of regeneration, and gives his decision. Old age, he tells us, excludes a man from the sensual joys of youth; the world appears to belong completely to the young, it is no place for the old; indeed, an old man is scarcely a man at all—he is an empty artifice, an effigy merely, of a man; he is a tattered coat upon a stick. This would be very bad, except that the young also are excluded from something; rapt in their sensuality, they are ignorant utterly of the world of the spirit. Hence if old age frees a man from sensual passion, he may rejoice in the liberation of the soul; he is admitted into the realm of the spirit; and his rejoicing will increase according as he realizes the magnificence of the soul. But the soul can best learn its own greatness from the great works of art; hence he turns to those great works, but in turning to them, he finds that these are by no means mere effigies, or monuments, but things that have souls also; these live in the noblest element of God's fire, free from all corruption; hence he prays for death, for release from his mortal body; and since the insouled monuments exhibit the possibility of the soul's existence in some other matter than flesh, he wishes reincarnation, not now in a mortal body, but in the immortal and changeless embodiment of art.

There are thus the following terms, one might say, from which the poem suspends: the condition of the young, who are spiritually passive although sensually active; the condition of the merely old, who are spiritually and physically impotent; the condition of the old, who, although physically impotent, are capable of spiritual activity; the condition of art considered as inanimate—i.e., the condition of things that are merely monuments; and finally the condition of art considered as animate—as of such things as artificial birds that have a human soul. The second term, impotent and unspiritual old age, is a privative, a repugnant state, which causes the progression through the other various alternative terms until its contrary is encountered. The first and third terms are clearly contraries of each other: taken together as animate nature, they are further contrary to the fourth term, inanimate art. None of these terms represents a wholly desirable mode of existence; but the fifth term, which represents such a mode, amalgamates the positive elements and eliminates the negative elements of both nature and art, and effects thus a resolution of the whole, for now the soul is present, as it would not be in art, nor is it passive, as it would be in the young and sensual mortal body, nor is it lodged in a "dying animal," as it would be in the body of the aged man; the soul is now free to act in its own supremacy and in full cognizance of its own excellence, and its embodiment is now incorruptible and secure from all the ills of flesh.

About these several oppositions the poem forms. The whole turns on the old man's realization, now that he is in the presence of the images of Byzantium, that these images have souls; there are consequently two major divisions, which divide the poem precisely in half—the first two stanzas presenting art as inanimate, the second two, as animate. That this is the case can be seen from such signs as that in the first half of the poem the images are stated as passive objects—they are twice called "monuments," they are merely objects of contemplation, they may be neglected or studied, visited or not visited, whereas in the third and fourth stanzas they are treated as gods that can be prayed to for life or death, as beings capable of motion from sphere to sphere, as instructors of the soul, as sages possessed of wisdom; and the curious shift in the manner of consideration is signalized by the subtle phrasing of the first two lines of stanza three: "O sages standing in God's holy fire / As in the gold mosaic of a wall." According to the first part, the images at Byzantium were images, and one should have expected at most some figurative apostrophe to them: "O images set in the gold mosaic of a wall, much as the sages stand in God's holy fire": but here the similtude is reversed, and lest there should be any error, the sages are besought to come from the holy fire and begin the tuition of the soul, the destruction of the flesh.

Within these two halves of the poem, further divisions may be found, coincident with the stanzaic divisions. Stanza one presents a rejection of passion, stanza two an acceptance of intellection; then, turning on the realization that art is insouled, stanza three presents a rejection of the corruptible embodiment, and stanza four, an acceptance of the incorruptible. There is an alternation, thus, of negative and affirmative: out of passion into intellection, out of corruption into permanence, and what orders these sections is their dialectical sequence. That is, passion must be condemned before the intellect can be esteemed; the intellect must operate before the images can be known to be insouled; the realization that the images are insouled precedes the realization that the body may be dispensed with; and the reincarnation of the soul in some changeless medium can be recognized as a possibility only through the prior recognition that the flesh is not the necessary matter of the soul. The parallel opposition of contraries constitutes a sharp demarcation; in stanza one a mortal bird of nature amid natural trees sings a brief song of sensual joy in praise of mortal things, of "whatever is begotten, born, and dies"; in stanza four an immortal and artificial bird set in an artificial tree sings an eternal song of spiritual joy in praise of eternal things, of "what is past, or passing, or to come"; and similarly, in stanza two a living thing is found to be an inanimate artifice, "a tattered coat upon a stick," incapable of motion, speech, sense, or knowledge; whereas in stanza three what had appeared to be inanimate artifice is found to possess a soul, and hence to be capable of all these. A certain artificial symmetry in the argument serves to distinguish these parts even further; stanzas one and four begin with the conclusions of their respective arguments, whereas two and three end with their proper conclusions, and stanza one is dependent upon stanza two for the substantiation of its premises, as the fourth is dependent upon the third.

This much indication of the principal organization of the work permits the explication, in terms of this, of the more elementary proportions. The first line of the first stanza presents immediately, in its most simple statement, the condition that is the genesis of the whole structure: "That is no country for old men"; old men are shut out from something, and the remainder of the first six lines indicates precisely what it is from which they are excluded. The young are given over to sensual delight, in which old men can no longer participate. But a wall, if it shuts out, also shuts in; if the old are excluded from something, so are the young; lines 7 and 8, consequently, exhibit a second sense in which "that is no country for old men," for the young neglect all intellectual things. Further, the use of "that" implies a possible "this"; that is, there is a country for the old as for the young; and, again, the use of "that" implies that the separation from the country of the young is already complete. The occupation of the young is shrewdly stated: at first sight the human lovers "in one another's arms" have, like the birds at their song, apparently a romantic and sentimental aura; but the curious interpolation of "those dying generations" in the description of the birds foreshadows the significance they are soon to have; and the phrases immediately following remove all sentimentality: "the salmon-falls, the mackerel-crowded seas" intend the ascent of salmon to the headwaters, the descent of mackerel to the deep seas in the spawning season, and the ironic intention is clear: all—the human lovers, the birds, the fish, do but spawn, but copulate, and this is their whole being; and if the parallel statement does not make this sufficiently evident, the summation of all in terms merely of animal genera—"fish, flesh, or fowl"—is unmistakable. The country of the young, then, is in its air, in its waters, and on its earth, from headwaters to ocean, wholly given over to sensuality; its inhabitants "commend all summer long" anything whatsoever, so long as it be mortal and animal—they commend "whatever is begotten, born, and dies"; and while they "commend" because they have great joy, that which they praise, they who praise, and their praise itself are ephemeral, for these mortals praise the things of mortality, and their commendation, like their joy, lasts but a summer, a mating season. The concluding lines of the stanza remove all ambiguity, and cancel all possibility of a return to such a country; even if the old man could, he would not return to a land where "caught in that sensual music all neglect / Monuments of unaging intellect." The young are "caught," they are really passive and incapable of free action; and they neglect those things that are unageing.

Merely to end here, however, with a condemnation of youthful sensuality would be unsatisfactory; as the second stanza expounds, old age itself is no solution; the old man cannot justly say, like Sophocles when he was asked whether he regretted the loss of youth and love, "Peace; most gladly have I escaped the thing of which you speak; I feel as if I had escaped from a mad and furious master"; for merely to be old is merely to be in a state of privation, it is to be "a paltry thing, / A tattered coat upon a stick," it is to be the merest scarecrow, the merest fiction and semblance of a man, an inanimate rag upon a dead stick. A man merely old, then, is worse off than youth; if the souls of the young are captive, the old have, in this sense at least, no souls at all. Something positive must be added; and if the soul can wax and grow strong as the body wanes, then every step in the dissolution of the body—"every tatter in its mortal dress"—is cause for a further augmentation of joy. But this can occur only if the soul can rejoice in its own power and magnificence; this rejoicing is possible only if the soul knows of its own magnificence, and this knowledge is possible only through the contemplation of monuments that recall that magnificence. The soul of the aged must be strong to seek what youth neglects. Hence the old must seek Byzantium; that is the country of the old; it is reached by sailing the seas, by breaking utterly with the country of the young; all passion must be left behind, the soul must be free to study the emblems of unchanging things.

Here the soul should be filled with joy; it should, by merely "studying," commend changeless things with song, as youth commends the changing with song; it would seem that the problem has been resolved, and the poem hence must end; but the contemplation of the monuments teaches first of all that these are no mere monuments but living things, and that the soul cannot grow into likeness with these beings of immortal embodiment unless it cast off its mortal body utterly. Nor is joy possible until the body be dissolved; the heart is still sick with the impossible desires of the flesh, it is still ignorant of its circumstances, and no song is possible to the soul while even a remnant of passion remains. Hence the old man prays to the sages who really stand in God's holy fire and have merely the semblance of images in gold mosaic; let them descend, "perne in a gyre"—that is, move in the circular motion that is the only possible motion of eternal things—let them consume with holy fire the heart that is the last seat of passion and ignorance, let them instruct the soul, let them gather it into the artifice of eternity and make the old man like themselves; even Byzantium, so long as the flesh be present, is no country for old men.

What it is to be like these, the soul, as yet uninstructed, can only conjecture; at any rate, with the destruction of the flesh it will be free of its ills; and if, as in Plato's myth of Er, the soul after death is free to choose some new embodiment, it will never again elect the flesh, which is so quickly corruptible and which enslaves it to passion; it will choose some such form of art as that of the artificial birds in Theophilus' garden, it will be of incorruptible and passionless gold; and it will dwell among leaves and boughs that are also of incorruptible and passionless metal. And now all sources of conflict are resolved in this last: the old has become the ageless; impotency has been exchanged for a higher power; the soul is free of passion and free for its joy, and it sings as youth once sang, but now of "what is past, or passing, or to come"—of the divisions of eternity—rather than of "whatever is begotten, born, and dies"—of the divisions of mortal time. And it has here its country, its proper and permanent habitation.

## A Prayer for My Daughter

Once more the storm is howling, and half hid
Under this cradle-hood and coverlid
My child sleeps on. There is no obstacle
But Gregory's wood and one bare hill
Whereby the haystack- and roof-levelling wind,          5
Bred on the Atlantic, can be stayed;
And for an hour I have walked and prayed
Because of the great gloom that is in my mind.

I have walked and prayed for this young child an hour
And heard the sea-wind scream upon the tower,          10
And under the arches of the bridge, and scream
In the elms above the flooded stream;
Imagining in excited reverie
That the future years had come,
Dancing to a frenzied drum,          15
Out of the murderous innocence of the sea.

May she be granted beauty and yet not
Beauty to make a stranger's eye distraught,
Or hers before a looking-glass, for such,
Being made beautiful overmuch,          20
Consider beauty a sufficient end,
Lose natural kindness and maybe
The heart-revealing intimacy
That chooses right, and never find a friend.

Helen being chosen found life flat and dull          25
And later had much trouble from a fool,
While that great Queen, that rose out of the spray,
Being fatherless could have her way
Yet chose a bandy-leggèd smith for man.
It's certain that fine women eat          30
A crazy salad with their meat
Whereby the Horn of Plenty is undone.

In courtesy I'd have her chiefly learned;
Hearts are not had as a gift but hearts are earned
By those that are not entirely beautiful;                    35
Yet many, that have played the fool
For beauty's very self, has charm made wise,
And many a poor man that has roved,
Loved and thought himself beloved,
From a glad kindness cannot take his eyes.                   40

May she become a flourishing hidden tree
That all her thoughts may like the linnet be,
And have no business but dispensing round
Their magnanimities of sound,
Nor but in merriment begin a chase,                         45
Nor but in merriment a quarrel.
O may she live like some green laurel
Rooted in one dear perpetual place.

My mind, because the minds that I have loved,
The sort of beauty that I have approved,                    50
Prosper but little, has dried up of late,
Yet knows that to be choked with hate
May well be of all evil chances chief.
If there's no hatred in a mind
Assault and battery of the wind                             55
Can never tear the linnet from the leaf.

An intellectual hatred is the worst,
So let her think opinions are accursed.
Have I not seen the loveliest woman born
Out of the mouth of Plenty's horn,                          60
Because of her opinionated mind
Barter that horn and every good
By quiet natures understood
For an old bellows full of angry wind?

Considering that, all hatred driven hence,                  65
The soul recovers radical innocence
And learns at last that it is self-delighting,
Self-appeasing, self-affrighting,
And that its own sweet will is Heaven's will;
She can, though every face should scowl                     70
And every windy quarter howl
Or every bellows burst, be happy still.

And may her bridegroom bring her to a house
Where all's accustomed, ceremonious;
For arrogance and hatred are the wares                      75

Peddled in the thoroughfares.
How but in custom and in ceremony
Are innocence and beauty born?
Ceremony's a name for the rich horn,
And custom for the spreading laurel tree.          80

*Sarah Youngblood*

---

YEATS

A PRAYER FOR MY DAUGHTER

Yeats has described in his autobiography the most important event of his poetic career: his decision, in middle life, to recast his poetic style in order to achieve an expression at once traditional and distinctively personal. His wish to make a poetry that was intense and dramatic, that could illuminate the intricacies of human experience and yet (in a version of the Wordsworthian ideal) use the language of the common people, was most fully realized in the great meditative poems of his 1928 volume, *The Tower*. But the flowering of a great poetic gift is impressive at each stage of its unfolding, and a reader interested in Yeats's development finds a special interest in the meditative poems that he completed before 1928. "A Prayer for My Daughter" is one of these, and its relative simplicity of structure allows us to see in an especially clear way Yeats's use of a form that was to become distinctively his own: the monologue of a mind in "excited reverie," as it confronts, explores, and finally resolves some crisis or conflict. The experience generating the sense of crisis varies from poem to poem, but the paradigm of confrontation, exploration, and resolution is common to all of them.

The "Prayer," as well as illustrating the typical pattern of these poems, illustrates also Yeats's characteristic transformation of personal materials into subjects of public and universal consideration: it begins with the burden of a personal occasion, but concludes with a resolving generalization that extends far beyond the immediate poetic context. In the process by which the occasion is enlarged, Yeats scatters personal and autobiographical allusions: "Gregory's wood" refers to Lady Gregory's estate, which lay to the west of the Norman tower in which Yeats and his family were living; "the loveliest woman born" is Maud Gonne, the woman he first loved, whose violent political hatreds made her notorious in the Irish nationalist movement. But the precise reference

of these personal allusions is not so important as our sense
that they *are* personal, that they point to a living and real
world pressing upon the consciousness of the man whose
reverie is being dramatized. Yeats alludes in the same way—a
way that simulates the shorthand of memory—to larger areas
of general knowledge, as in his oblique reference to Helen's
abduction by Paris ("much trouble from a fool") and in his
easy colloquial reference to Aphrodite's choice of Hephais-
tos, the crippled blacksmith of the gods. When both of these
famous love matches are casually dismissed with the observation that "fine women eat / A crazy salad with their meat,"
the mythical events have been touched for us with a vivid
humanizing particularity which brings them into direct relation with the present and personal moment. Like Yeats's
references in other poems to Maud Gonne as a "Ledaean
body" or to Robert Gregory as "our Sidney," this technique
enacts the imagination's transcendence of the limits of space
and time: the present moment participates in the timelessness
of myth. By this means also, the personal is seen to participate
in some larger, impersonal and ceremonial pattern of events,
so that the allusions themselves prepare for the enlarged conclusion of the poem, when the meditation has been released
from the limitations of the time-bound occasion that
prompted it.

Yet the "Prayer" begins by being carefully set in space and
time. The setting is concretely detailed: the noise and movement of the wind, the sleeping child in the cradle, the pacing
father. By the end of the second stanza this setting begins to
merge into another, the internal world of the imagination,
and the objective scene expands, takes on new meanings
under the impress of the man's excited reverie, the force of
his symbolizing imagination. Now the real storm becomes
symbolic of the intangible storm of time; now the wind not
only levels the haystacks, but screams and dances out of a
"murderous" source. The real subject of the poem is not the
invocation of safety for the child, but the sense of crisis itself,
which gradually, within the movement of the meditation, will
find resolution. I use the word *movement* with special emphasis, for all of Yeats's meditative poems move, in many
senses of the word; each stanza is a larger and more inclusive
approach to resolution. This movement gives dramatic immediacy to his poems, for the reader is made to undergo the
same tentative search for conclusion, knowing at any moment
in the poem only as much as the poet knows of how it will be
found; and this in turn gives the conclusions of such poems

their power of liberation, their harmonious fitness and completion. Like the poet, the reader has "learned by going where he had to go," to paraphrase Roethke's fine line.

We can watch this movement beginning, almost as we watch the poet walking and praying, in the first two stanzas. The violence of the storm, so disturbing to the father, does not wake the child, who "sleeps on," ignorant of the threatening violence but vulnerable to it. The poet's sense of her vulnerability to time prompts his prayer for the protecting gifts he would have her carry into life. In invoking certain blessings for her life, his mind moves intuitively to images that will embody and clarify his sense of these blessings. The images are introduced, apparently spontaneously, and are then explored with a deepening recognition of their rightness as symbols for his thought. The horn of plenty is first introduced simply to stand for the abundance that Aphrodite and Helen could have chosen from, and it is here appropriately associated with food and appetite (appropriate for the sexual appetites of the women described, and appropriate for the original association of the cornucopia with the fruits of harvest). The image recurs later, in a kind of visual-association link with the "bellows full of angry wind," and dramatizes an even more extreme form of folly, for "the loveliest woman born" did not accept the horn but bartered it for a sterile and grotesque parody of itself. In the final stanza, the horn of plenty becomes an encompassing symbol for the plenitude of nature, and its hierarchies, that assures the possibility of right choices.

Likewise the first use of the laurel tree image is apparently fortuitous, intended merely to suggest the joy, natural spontaneity, and grace of the young girl; but as the poet explores the image he comes to see the most important implication of it, its rootedness, and the tree becomes a symbol of the stability that is the source of joy. At this point the poet recalls the first destructive image of his meditation, the wind, and he can now find, in the image of the stable tree unharmed by the wind, an emergent symbol for the child's safety against destroying time, a symbol that gradually shapes and coheres the meditation and makes possible the harmonious resolution of the final stanza. These two images come to stand for the two possibilities open to the child: one, the wind out of "the murderous innocence of the sea," which threatens her and which she may in time absorb into herself, as the remembered woman gave over her life to the "angry wind" of destruction; and the other, the "radical innocence," rooted

innocence, of the laurel tree, which insures stability and
creation. The poem, though it prays for blessings, is centrally
concerned with the choice the child must make, and the
prayer is, finally, that she may make the right choices and
having done so, may be brought home to a house where those
choices are confirmed and preserved.

The conclusion of the poem throws light on Yeats's famous
preference for "aristocratic" values, a preference for which
he has been often and wrongfully maligned. Custom and
ceremony, celebrated here as the source of personal as well as
social stability, are seen not as artificial structures imposed
upon natural impulse and inhibiting it, but as natural gifts in
themselves, being the enduring forms men give to their finest
natural instincts: kindness, joy, the impulse to create and
preserve life. The resolution of the poem is possible because
the poet's meditation has led him to reassess and reconfirm
those values upon which he feels life should be founded. The
prayer is a means by which he returns to his *own* roots, and
declares them.

## The Second Coming

Turning and turning in the widening gyre
The falcon cannot hear the falconer;
Things fall apart; the centre cannot hold;
Mere anarchy is loosed upon the world,
The blood-dimmed tide is loosed, and everywhere          5
The ceremony of innocence is drowned;
The best lack all conviction, while the worst
Are full of passionate intensity.

Surely some revelation is at hand;
Surely the Second Coming is at hand.                     10
The Second Coming! Hardly are those words out
When a vast image out of *Spiritus Mundi*
Troubles my sight: somewhere in sands of the desert
A shape with lion body and the head of a man,
A gaze blank and pitiless as the sun,                    15
Is moving its slow thighs, while all about it
Reel shadows of the indignant desert birds.
The darkness drops again; but now I know
That twenty centuries of stony sleep
Were vexed to nightmare by a rocking cradle,             20
And what rough beast, its hour come round at last,
Slouches towards Bethlehem to be born?

# Richard P. Blackmur

## YEATS
### THE SECOND COMING

One of the finest, because one of the most appropriate to our time and place, of all Yeats's poems, is his "The Second Coming." There is about it, to any slowed reading, the immediate conviction of pertinent emotion; the lines are stirring, separately and in their smaller groups, and there is a sensible life in them that makes them seem to combine in the form of an emotion. We may say at once then, for what it is worth, that in writing his poem Yeats was able to choose words that to an appreciable extent were the right ones to reveal or represent the emotion that was its purpose. The words deliver the meaning, which was put into them by the craft with which they were arranged, and that meaning is their own, not to be segregated or given another arrangement without diminution. Ultimately, something of this sort is all that can be said of this or any poem, and when it is said, the poem is known to be good in its own terms or bad because not in its own terms. But the reader seldom reaches an ulti- mate position about a poem; most poems fail, through craft or conception, to reach an ultimate or absolute position: parts of the craft remain machinery and parts of the conception remain in limbo. Or, as in this poem, close inspection will show something questionable about it. It is true that it can be read as it is, isolated from the rest of Yeats's work and iso- lated from the intellectual material it expresses, and a good deal got out of it, too, merely by submitting to it. That is because the words are mainly common, both in their emo- tional and intellectual senses; and if we do not know precisely what the familiar words drag after them into the poem, still we know vaguely what the weight of it feels like; and that seems enough to make a poem at one level of response. Yet if an attempt is made at a more complete response, if we wish to discover the precise emotion that the words mount up to, we come into trouble and uncertainty at once. There is an air of explicitness to each of the separate fragments of the poem.

Is it, in this line or that, serious? Has it a reference?—or is it
a rhetorical effect, a result only of the persuasive overtones of
words?—or is it a combination, a mixture of reference and
rhetoric?

Possibly the troubled attention will fasten first upon the
italicized phrase in the twelfth line, *Spiritus Mundi;* and the
question is whether the general, the readily available senses of
the words are adequate to supply the specific sense wanted
by the poem. Put another way, can the poet's own arbitrary
meaning be made, merely by discovering it, to participate in
and enrich what the "normal" meanings of the words in their
limiting context provide? The critic can only supply the
facts; the poem will in the end provide its own answer. Here
there are certain facts that may be extracted from Yeats's
prose writings that suggest something of what the words
symbolize for him. In one of the notes to the limited edition
of *Michael Robartes and the Dancer,* Yeats observes that
his mind, like another's, has been from time to time obsessed
by images that had no discoverable origin in his waking
experience. Speculating about their origin, he came to deny
both the conscious and the unconscious memory as their
probable seat, and finally invented a doctrine that traced the
images to sources of supernatural character. I quote only the
sentence that is relevant to the phrase in question: "Those
[images] that come in sleep are (1) from the state immediately preceding our birth; (2) from the *Spiritus Mundi*—
that is to say, from a general storehouse of images which
have ceased to be a property of any personality or spirit." It
apparently follows, for Yeats, that images so derived have
both an absolute meaning of their own and an operative force
in determining meaning and predicting events in this world.
In another place (the introduction to "The Resurrection" in
*Wheels and Butterflies*) he describes the image used in this
poem, which he had seen many times, "always at my left side
just out of the range of sight, a brazen winged beast that I
associated with laughing, ecstatic destruction." Ecstasy, it
should be added, comes for Yeats just before death, and at
death comes the moment of revelation, when the soul is
shown its kindred dead and it is possible to see the future.

Here we come directly upon that central part of Yeats's
magical beliefs that it is one purpose of this poem emotionally
to represent: the belief in what is called variously *magnus
annus,* the great year, the Platonic Year, and sometimes in a
slightly different symbolism, the Great Wheel. This belief,
with respect to the history of epochs, is associated with the

precession of the equinoxes, which bring, roughly every two thousand years, a "great year" of death and rebirth, and this belief seems to be associated with belief in the effect on individuals of the phases of the moon; although individuals may be influenced by the equinoxes and there may be a lunar interpretation of history. These beliefs have a scaffold of geometrical figures, gyres, cones, circles, etc., by the application of which exact interpretation is secured. Thus it is possible to predict, both in biography and history, and in time, both forward and backward, the character, climax, collapse, and rebirth in antithetical form of human types and cultures. There is a subordinate but helpful belief that signs, warnings, even direct messages, are always given, from *Spiritus Mundi* or elsewhere, which the poet and the philosopher have only to see and hear. As it happens, the Christian era, being nearly two thousand years old, is due for extinction and replacement, in short, for the Second Coming, which this poem heralds. In his note to its first publication (in *Michael Robartes and the Dancer*) Yeats expresses his belief as follows:

> At the present moment the life gyre is sweeping outward, unlike that before the birth of Christ which was narrowing, and has almost reached its greatest expansion. The revelation which approaches will however take its character from the contrary movement of the interior gyre. All our scientific, democratic, fact-accumulating, heterogeneous civilisation belongs to the outward gyre and prepares not the continuance of itself but the revelation as in a lightning flash, though in a flash that will not strike only in one place, and will for a time be constantly repeated, of the civilisation that must slowly take its place.

So much for a major gloss on the poem. Yeats combined, in the best verse he could manage, the beliefs that obsessed him with the image that he took to be a specific illustration of the beliefs. Minor and buttressing glosses are possible for many of the single words and phrases in the poem, some flowing from private doctrine and some from Yeats's direct sense of the world about him, and some from both at once. For example: the "ceremony of innocence" represents for Yeats one of the qualities that made life valuable under the dying aristocratic social tradition; and the meaning of the phrase in the poem requires no magic for completion but only a reading of other poems. The "falcon" and "falconer" in the second line have, besides the obvious symbolism, a doctrinal reference. A falcon is a hawk, and a hawk is symbolic of the active or intellectual mind; the falconer is perhaps the soul itself or its uniting principle. There is also the apposition, which Yeats has made several times, that "wisdom is a butterfly / And not a gloomy bird of prey." Whether the special symbolism has actually been incorporated in the poem, and in which form, or whether it is private debris merely, will take a generation of readers to decide. In the meantime it must be taken provisionally for whatever its ambiguity may seem to be worth. Literature is full of falcons, some that fly and some that lack immediacy and sit, archaic, on the poet's wrist; and it is not always illuminating to determine which is which. But when we come on such lines as

> *The best lack all conviction, while the worst*
> *Are full of passionate intensity*

we stop short, first to realize the aptness of the statement to every plane of life in the world about us, and then to connect the lines with the remote body of the poem they illuminate. There is a dilemma of which the branches grow from one trunk but which cannot be solved; for these lines have, not two meanings, but two sources for the same meaning. There is the meaning that comes from the summary observation that this is how men are—and especially men of power—in the world we live in; it is knowledge that comes from knowledge of the "fury and the mire in human veins"; a meaning the contemplation of which in April 1934 led Yeats to offer himself to any government or party that, using force and marching men, would "promise not this or that measure but a discipline, a way of life." And there is in effect the same meaning, at least at the time the poem was written—but from a different source, and one would think it would have very different consequences in prospective party loyalties: here the meaning has its source in the doctrines of the great year and the phases of the moon; whereby, to cut exegesis short, it is predicted as necessary that, at the time we have reached, the best minds, being subjective, should have lost all faith though desiring it, and the worst minds, being so nearly objective, have no need of faith and may be full of "passionate intensity" without the control of any faith or wisdom. Thus we have on the one side the mirror of observation, and on the other side an imperative, magically derived: both of which come to the conclusion of form in identical words.

## Nineteen Hundred and Nineteen

### I

Many ingenious lovely things are gone
That seemed sheer miracle to the multitude,
Protected from the circle of the moon
That pitches common things about. There stood
Amid the ornamental bronze and stone          5
An ancient image made of olive wood—
And gone are Phidias' famous ivories
And all the golden grasshoppers and bees.

We too had many pretty toys when young:
A law indifferent to blame or praise,          10
To bribe or threat; habits that made old wrong
Melt down, as it were wax in the sun's rays;
Public opinion ripening for so long
We thought it would outlive all future days.
O what fine thought we had because we thought   15
That the worst rogues and rascals had died out.

All teeth were drawn, all ancient tricks unlearned,
And a great army but a showy thing;
What matter that no cannon had been turned
Into a ploughshare? Parliament and king         20
Thought that unless a little powder burned
The trumpeters might burst with trumpeting
And yet it lack all glory; and perchance
The guardsmen's drowsy chargers would not prance.

Now days are dragon-ridden, the nightmare        25
Rides upon sleep: a drunken soldiery
Can leave the mother, murdered at her door,
To crawl in her own blood, and go scot-free;
The night can sweat with terror as before
We pieced our thoughts into philosophy,          30
And planned to bring the world under a rule,
Who are but weasels fighting in a hole.

He who can read the signs nor sink unmanned
Into the half-deceit of some intoxicant
From shallow wits; who knows no work can stand,                    35
Whether health, wealth or peace of mind were spent
On master-work of intellect or hand,
No honour leave its mighty monument,
Has but one comfort left: all triumph would
But break upon his ghostly solitude.                               40

But is there any comfort to be found?
Man is in love and loves what vanishes,
What more is there to say? That country round
None dared admit, if such a thought were his,
Incendiary or bigot could be found                                 45
To burn that stump on the Acropolis,
Or break in bits the famous ivories
Or traffic in the grasshoppers or bees.

### II

When Loie Fuller's Chinese dancers enwound
A shining web, a floating ribbon of cloth,                         50
It seemed that a dragon of air.
Had fallen among dancers, had whirled them round
Or hurried them off on its own furious path;
So the Platonic Year
Whirls out new right and wrong,                                    55
Whirls in the old instead;
All men are dancers and their tread
Goes to the barbarous clangour of a gong.

### III

Some moralist or mythological poet
Compares the solitary soul to a swan;                              60
I am satisfied with that,
Satisfied if a troubled mirror show it,
Before that brief gleam of its life be gone,
An image of its state;
The wings half spread for flight,                                  65
The breast thrust out in pride
Whether to play, or to ride
Those winds that clamour of approaching night.

A man in his own secret meditation
Is lost amid the labyrinth that he has made                        70
In art or politics;

Some Platonist affirms that in the station
Where we should cast off body and trade
The ancient habit sticks,
And that if our works could                        75
But vanish with our breath
That were a lucky death,
For triumph can but mar our solitude.

The swan has leaped into the desolate heaven:
That image can bring wildness, bring a rage        80
To end all things, to end
What my laborious life imagined, even
The half-imagined, the half-written page;
O but we dreamed to mend
Whatever mischief seemed                            85
To afflict mankind, but now
That winds of winter blow
Learn that we were crack-pated when we dreamed.

IV

We, who seven years ago
Talked of honour and of truth,                     90
Shriek with pleasure if we show
The weasel's twist, the weasel's tooth.

V

Come let us mock at the great
That had such burdens on the mind
And toiled so hard and late                         95
To leave some monument behind,
Nor thought of the levelling wind.

Come let us mock at the wise;
With all those calendars whereon
They fixed old aching eyes,                         100
They never saw how seasons run,
And now but gape at the sun.

Come let us mock at the good
That fancied goodness might be gay,
And sick of solitude                               105
Might proclaim a holiday:
Wind shrieked—and where are they?

Mock mockers after that
That would not lift a hand maybe

To help good, wise or great                                        110
To bar that foul storm out, for we
Traffic in mockery.


### VI

Violence upon the roads: violence of horses;
Some few have handsome riders, are garlanded
On delicate sensitive ear or tossing mane,                         115
But wearied running round and round in their courses
All break and vanish, and evil gathers head:
Herodias' daughters have returned again,
A sudden blast of dusty wind and after
Thunder of feet, tumult of images,                                 120
Their purpose in the labyrinth of the wind;
And should some crazy hand dare touch a daughter
All turn with amorous cries, or angry cries,
According to the wind, for all are blind.
But now wind drops, dust settles; thereupon                        125
There lurches past, his great eyes without thought
Under the shadow of stupid straw-pale locks,
That insolent fiend Robert Artisson
To whom the love-lorn Lady Kyteler brought
Bronzed peacock feathers, red combs of her cocks.                  130

# Robin Skelton

## YEATS
### NINETEEN HUNDRED AND NINETEEN

When Yeats first published this poem in *The Dial* of September 1921, he called it "Thoughts upon the Present State of the World," and it does attempt to outline the state of European culture and civilization in 1919. In that year Europe was reeling under the effects of the First World War, and Ireland was suffering from the persecutions of the Black and Tans, a militia drawn from the ranks of disillusioned British ex-servicemen, which was intended to combat the activities of the Irish rebels but which indulged in many acts of looting and terrorism.

The situation was perilous, and Yeats relates it in the first stanza of his poem to the downfall of Greek civilization; the reverence of the people for true religion (symbolized by the image of olive wood) and for the masterworks of art (symbolized by the ivories of Phidias and the golden grasshoppers and bees) has been destroyed. The poem progresses in terms of many such references. It is as if the speaker's richly endowed mind were ranging over the whole tangled complex of the social scene and finding images and echoes from the past that complement and explain the present, and lead him toward philosophic certainties.

The speaker's "voice" is also an important element of the poem. It contains both scholarly and vulgar cadences, and it includes the marketplace rhetoric of swinging iambs as well as the brusquer rhythms of the scholar forced into anti-rhetorical accuracies, and the more careless clumsiness of the honest speaker suspicious of an over-easy smoothness. Thus the "persona" is one who convinces us of his right to speak in all available tones of all available things.

The overall structure of the poem is that of a catena, a series of separate wise or crypto-religious statements strung together to form a pattern. The first section presents us with the ambiguity of a double perspective. The opening places us in Athens at the end of Greek civilization, and there are no

references in the remainder of the section that explicitly
contradict this placing, although it is clear that the descriptions of the false glories of war, of ideals betrayed, and of the
brutal soldiery, refer to the ideals of earlier Irish nationalism
and the current troubles as well as to the Athenian situation.
The return to Greece at the end of the section makes it clear
to us that a description of the one is also that of the other; the
Greeks facing ruin and the Irish struggling for freedom are
at the same point of the same dance.

I use the image of the dance because it is the next one to
take our attention. Loie Fuller's Chinese Dancers were an
attraction of the Folies Bergères in the Nineties; the main
feature of their performance was the colored silks they
whirled and manipulated under the electric light, thus presenting (to Yeats's mind) the very essence, the Platonic Idea
of Dance, for the individual bodies were less important than
the colored webs and scarves that, in their swathings and
circlings, suggested the possession of the dancers by some
overmastering impulse subduing and cancelling their subjective personalities in the service of a greater rhythm. This
image, therefore, relates the poem yet again to the rhythmic
and cyclic nature of history in which we are all involved and
by which we are all possessed.

It is not entirely illogical for the poem to move next to the
presentation of the swan symbol, for the swan in Greek
mythology must remind us of the myth of Leda and of her
possession by the spirit of Zeus that led both to the creation
of the ideal beauty of Helen and to the complete destruction
of a civilization. Just as the swan created Helen, so the lonely
soul possessed, though briefly, by a god, may, with one last
song before its sexual or absolute death, commit destruction
in a rage of purity. We, however, more usually busy ourselves in constructing imprisoning labyrinths by which we
may possibly continue to be troubled after death. Contemplating the surge of the swan into the desolate sky, we realize
that we were deluded when we imagined that our laborious
subtleties could mend anything. Our dreams—whether of a
triumphant Troy, a perpetual Athens, or a noble Dublin—
were mere folly.

Explication of this kind is hardly adequate, for Yeats was
not composing an allegory, and his symbolism is capable of
many complexities of interpretation. Nevertheless, such explication does indicate the tightly knitted intellectual pattern
of the poem and its world-encompassing rhetoric. The poem
itself indulges in cyclic repetitions, as do the civilizations to

which it refers. The weasels fighting in a hole, which image the civil strife in Ireland and its animal pettiness, recur in the fourth section, where much that has already been implied or stated is gathered together in one exact and passionate quatrain. This breaks the comparatively gentle, meditative flow of the poem with an outburst of anger, just as its short-lined epigrammatic form breaks the rhetorical flow of all that has preceded it.

Out of anger emerges mockery, and the speaker wakes from his meditative soliloquies and directly addresses an audience. He ridicules, one by one, the labors of the idealists; and then, reaching total nihilism, condemns also the act of ridicule, and curses those mockers who refuse to make any effort to bar out "the foul storm."

In the final section, the "foul storm" itself has arrived and is described. There is violence upon the roads of Ireland and Europe. The daughters of Herodias, those far-from-ideal dancers, who bring death to all prophets and all idealism, have returned. They are blindly caught up in the labyrinths of their own schemings, as are we with our petty considerations as described in the third section of the poem. They contrast, in their disorder, tumult, and dust, with the Chinese dancers—whose shining cloths suggested possession by a "dragon of air" rather than the dragon of nightmare described in the first section or the fiend to be described in this. As their dance fades the final draconic, grotesque image appears, that of the spirit, Robert Artisson, who in fourteenth century Kilkenny tormented and obsessed the Lady Kyteler. The names matter little, but the gesture is important, for the peacock feathers and cocks' combs (there is a play here upon the notion of coxcomb) she sacrifices to her demon lover are a parody of true religious ritual, and contrast with the opening reference to the image of olive wood and with all the other images of spiritual passion and intellectual purity. Here, again, we are given a double perspective by means of ambiguity, for the horses are at once those of the warring factions in Ireland and those of the apocalyptic riders foretelling the end of the world.

Such creatures as the daughters of Herodias and Robert Artisson are, however, all part of the cyclic movement of history, and Yeats himself related them to his own growing philosophic system as presented in *A Vision* (1925), and saw them, later, as significant in terms of Spengler's view in *The Decline of the West*. Indeed, the whole of Yeats's poem is part of a completely systematized politico-philosophical view of the nature of the growth and fall of civilizations. It is also, however, a dramatically personal poem.

In speaking of "Nineteen Hundred and Nineteen" as personal, I am not thinking of the autobiographical element, though this is clearly present in the first two sections. Nor do I mean the personal anguish, though this, too, is clear enough from the intensity of language and the sudden compulsive shifts in emotional level. I mean the voice—which is Yeats and Yeats alone. It is not the voice of a ventriloquial figure that has been given a valuably wide range of verbal characteristics: it is an individual man who speaks with an idiosyncratic style that may be comprehensively oracular, but is also human. Here are all Yeats's tricks of speech. We have the blandly unselfconscious oddity of such archaisms as *perchance*. We have sentences balanced weightily upon ponderous conditional clauses, and upon the gesticulatory use of *some* and *that*. We have the swift, easy, almost Marlovian swing of one line countered by the deliberate, near-pedantic clumsiness of the next. We have scholarly diction and literary image juxtaposed with vernacular directness and commonplace reference. These make up—in part, at least—the voice of Yeats. It is an individual voice, as "Nineteen Hundred and Nineteen" is an individual vision, but the individual is representative of the race, embodying the dream both of noble and of beggarman, fusing the subjective and the objective, the ideal and the pragmatic. In "Nineteen Hundred and Nineteen" W.B. Yeats contrived a poem "upon the present state of the world" as relevant to its time as Milton's "Areopagitica" and as timeless in its significance. This he must have realized when he altered his title, for the poem is not about the "present state" of the world, but about the world itself, and 1919 is simply the vantage point from which it is viewed.

# A Dialogue of Self and Soul

### I

*My Soul.* I summon to the winding ancient stair;
  Set all your mind upon the steep ascent,
  Upon the broken, crumbling battlement,
  Upon the breathless starlit air,
  Upon the star that marks the hidden pole;      5
  Fix every wandering thought upon
  That quarter where all thought is done:
  Who can distinguish darkness from the soul?

*My Self.* The consecrated blade upon my knees
  Is Sato's ancient blade, still as it was,      10
  Still razor-keen, still like a looking-glass
  Unspotted by the centuries;
  That flowering, silken, old embroidery, torn
  From some court-lady's dress and round
  The wooden scabbard bound and wound,      15
  Can, tattered, still protect, faded adorn.

*My Soul.* Why should the imagination of a man
  Long past his prime remember things that are
  Emblematical of love and war?
  Think of ancestral night that can,      20
  If but imagination scorn the earth
  And intellect its wandering
  To this and that and t'other thing,
  Deliver from the crime of death and birth.

*My Self.* Montashigi, third of his family, fashioned it      25
  Five hundred years ago, about it lie
  Flowers from I know not what embroidery—
  Heart's purple—and all these I set
  For emblems of the day against the tower
  Emblematical of the night,      30
  And claim as by a soldier's right
  A charter to commit the crime once more.

*My Soul.* Such fullness in that quarter overflows
   And falls into the basin of the mind
   That man is stricken deaf and dumb and blind,     35
   For intellect no longer knows
   *Is* from the *Ought*, or *Knower* from the *Known*—
   That is to say, ascends to Heaven;
   Only the dead can be forgiven;
   But when I think of that my tongue's a stone.     40

II

*My Self.* A living man is blind and drinks his drop.
   What matter if the ditches are impure?
   What matter if I live it all once more?
   Endure that toil of growing up;
   The ignominy of boyhood; the distress     45
   Of boyhood changing into man;
   The unfinished man and his pain
   Brought face to face with his own clumsiness;

   The finished man among his enemies?—
   How in the name of Heaven can he escape     50
   That defiling and disfigured shape
   The mirror of malicious eyes
   Casts upon his eyes until at last
   He thinks that shape must be his shape?
   And what's the good of an escape     55
   If honour find him in the wintry blast?

   I am content to live it all again
   And yet again, if it be life to pitch
   Into the frog-spawn of a blind man's ditch,
   A blind man battering blind men;     60
   Or into that most fecund ditch of all,
   The folly that man does
   Or must suffer, if he woos
   A proud woman not kindred of his soul.

   I am content to follow to its source     65
   Every event in action or in thought;
   Measure the lot; forgive myself the lot!
   When such as I cast out remorse
   So great a sweetness flows into the breast
   We must laugh and we must sing,     70
   We are blest by everything,
   Everything we look upon is blest.

# Reed Whittemore

## YEATS
### A DIALOGUE OF SELF AND SOUL

Any poet's collected works are potentially mines of the kind of data one feeds into an IBM machine. How many references to nature are there in Shakespeare? What wins out in Wordsworth, the hedge or the daffodil? How many of Faulkner's characters were not born in Yoknapatawpha County? And so on. But with Yeats the IBM machine would not be taxed: throughout his career he concentrated on just a few themes and landscapes, and he populated the latter with a relatively small cast of characters and images. As a result the number of factors involved in getting him properly programmed would be small, hopefully too small to interest a self-respecting machine.

Yeats has interested *people*, though, especially other poets. He is widely regarded as one of the great artists of modern times, and one of the reasons for this regard is that during his long career he tried his hand with such success at so many different kinds of verse. In the Nineties he turned out many poems and plays based in Irish mythology and having about them a fine but fuzzy air of romance, of heroic and idyllic affairs transacted long ago. A few years later he became deeply involved in contemporary social and political matters of Ireland, and produced a small body of poems that would grace any anthology dedicated to "engagement." Then he indulged his taste for astrology and the occult, and wrote, in conjunction with his eccentric and esoteric book, *A Vision*, a group of marvelous historical and prophetic poems describing cycles of human energy and apathy over the last several thousand years. Even as he was hard at these, however, he was doubting the validity of his mystical projections and busy at a number of works—of which "A Dialogue of Self and Soul" is one—in which he tried to synthesize the various forces and impulses—artistic, mystical, social, sexual —he had felt working within him all this time. And finally, in his old age, he set about writing a number of deceptively simple lyrics as if half a century of creative struggle could be summed up finally in dark apothegms. Now why would a machine not be interested in trying to chart and regularize such apparent diversity?

Maybe it would (and maybe it will be asked to do so in any case, for machines have been harnessed by a number of literary scholars for equally silly projects). Yet in spite of the diversity in Yeats, nothing is more apparent about him, rhetorically or thematically, than his obsessive drive for unity of understanding and being. Like most really dedicated poets, good and bad, he was always writing variations on a single poem. Over the years he naturally came at that unity, that One, from a number of different residences and in a number of different moods; and sometimes he hacked away at only a very small chunk of the One. Yet the One was never really out of sight as he wrote. No machine has ever mastered a human One.

"Dialogue of Self and Soul" is a relatively late poem (published in 1933 in a volume called *The Winding Stair and Other Poems*), and it is also among his more ambitious works, that is, a work in which he is working mightily toward the whole One. In it we see two of his most prized possessions of later life used, in characteristic fashion, as emblems or symbols to body forth a major conflict to be found in most of his verse, early or late: a conflict, roughly Platonic, between the real and the ideal, the flesh and the spirit, the worldly life and the artistic life. The tower was a Norman relic in Western Ireland he bought from his patroness Lady Gregory; the sword was a Japanese relic he received as a gift. Knowing his obsession for emblems or symbols, one can imagine that he originally coveted these not for themselves but for their symbolic potential. They were rich in suggestion for him; they were not merely illustrative appendages to his rather archaic dualistic philosophy but, mystically, the containers of their essences. Without the emblems, no philosophy.

The tower was an unusually happy purchase. Before acquiring it he had tested and tasted a number of other vaguely equivalent emblems—islands, swans, roses—and they had had their virtues and uses. But with the tower he had something all his own that, though not ivory, seemed physically to sum up for him the properties of one-half his poetic being. For two decades it appeared constantly in his writings; hence the rejection of it, and what it stands for, in "Dialogue of Self and Soul," is not a facile resolution in favor of life over art, or the flesh over the spirit, but a resolution by an artist who had literally experienced the tower's failure. It had failed him in life (he had wanted to repair it and live in it, but ill health drove him to warmer climates, leaving it still open to the winds or, as he put it, "half dead at the top"); and in a sense it had also failed him as art: the rumor of the permanence or immortality of art was one he found constantly being punctured as he grew older. One could say then that he began with the philosophy expressed by the soul in the "Dialogue" and ended with that expressed by the self, but retained throughout a sense of the interaction of both possibilities—tower and sword—in any human One.

Such indecisiveness is common among poets. They may reject the tower, as Yeats does in this poem, but the rejection is tentative and poetic rather than final and philosophic, since poets, unlike philosophers, cannot discard bits and pieces of their beings no matter how sensible it may appear to be to do so.

Possibly the difference between poetry and philosophy (or machinery) is at heart the difference hinted at above. Certainly the philosophy of Yeats, if abstracted from its emblems, comes to little; and his years of passionate addiction to finding the "right" image or symbol are years that a philosopher (or a machine) might well regard as wasted. Yet I think we see in "Dialogue of Self and Soul" that the energy of the poetry comes less from the soundness of the conclusions arrived at than from the drama of getting there. In the last lines, for example, the force of the conclusion is not so much in the recommendation that we cast out remorse or believe that everything we look upon is blessed (suggestions any homespun philosopher might throw at us at church or a ball game) as in the context of the conclusion, that is, in the *when such as I* of the passage. The *I* was desperately sick physically, and desperately oppressed artistically, when he wrote these lines; they show his trouble and at the same time magnificently assert his blessing.

To read Yeats is to discover the *such as I* of the "Dialogue," one of the great *I*'s to be such as.

EDWIN ARLINGTON ROBINSON

*The Bettmann Archive*

# EDWIN ARLINGTON ROBINSON
## [1869–1935]

### *Richard Cory*

Whenever Richard Cory went down town,
 We people on the pavement looked at him:
He was a gentleman from sole to crown,
 Clean favored, and imperially slim.

And he was always quietly arrayed,                          5
 And he was always human when he talked;
But still he fluttered pulses when he said,
 "Good-morning," and he glittered when he walked.

And he was rich—yes, richer than a king—
 And admirably schooled in every grace:                    10
In fine, we thought that he was everything
 To make us wish that we were in his place.

So on we worked, and waited for the light,
 And went without the meat, and cursed the bread;
And Richard Cory, one calm summer night,                   15
 Went home and put a bullet through his head.

## Mark Strand

---

ROBINSON

RICHARD CORY

Handsome, rich, well-bred, Richard Cory represents a conventional sort of success. This, of course, is how the townspeople see him. How he sees himself is not made manifest, and justly so, for the poem's power depends, in large part, on what is not known about Richard Cory. He has the same remoteness about him as Flammonde, another of E.A. Robinson's peripheral figures.

Put to more romantic uses, Flammonde inspires a mixture of pathos and awe while Richard Cory fills the townspeople with envy and admiration. Flammonde, too good, too otherworldly, has his true place in the collective memory or nostalgia of Tilbury Town.

"Richard Cory" does not provide so sentimental a story. It is a moral tale in which money is not only shown to be limited in what it can secure, but is shown to be blinding in relation to the truth. Thus the poem is as much about the townspeople who worship him as it is about Richard Cory himself. It is through their eyes that we see him. It is their values that operate in making him seem to be "everything to make us wish that we were in his place," and their values that are exposed as false in the poem's ironical close. They can only assess Richard Cory in material terms or by personal attributes wholly the product of class (his enormous wealth, his good manners). On the other hand, however, they are able to see themselves in religious terms. Theirs is a peculiar martyrdom as they wait for the light that will lead them, they hope, into the distant, glittering world of Richard Cory.

The enormous popularity of "Richard Cory" is in large part due to its spectacular ending. Suddenly we are told in flat, colloquial language that Richard Cory "went home and put a bullet through his head." The effectiveness of this finish could not have been achieved without skillful plotting. The poem never seems strained or cluttered, nor is its verbal surface complicated. In fact, the first three stanzas, because they contain similar information, seem almost to ramble. It is in the last stanza that the abbreviated character of the poem is established. In the first three stanzas the piling on of favorable attributes, one after the other, with the repeated use of "and," creates an illusion of more being said about Richard Cory than in fact there is and gives each attribute an importance it might not have had had it been mentioned in a simpler, less rhetorical series. When we get to the last "and" we expect more of the same praise for Richard Cory. The splendid effect of the ending hinges on the complete reversal of our expectations.

In "Flammonde," goodness takes the place of failure. In "Richard Cory," failure is absolute. Richard Cory, who seems to have "everything," commits suicide; and the townspeople fail to see, until it is too late, beyond the glitter of his public image. They are left at the poem's close without anything, it seems, to give their lives purpose.

If the poem has a major weakness it is that the moral looms larger and larger in retrospect and some of its elegance is sacrificed. A statement such as, "money isn't everything," seems too adequate a summation of the poem's meaning. This is not to say, however, that people will not continue to admire "Richard Cory," nor is it to say they will be wrong in doing so.

ROBERT FROST

*The Bettmann Archive*

# ROBERT FROST
## [1874–1963]

## *Two Tramps in Mud Time*

Out of the mud two strangers came
And caught me splitting wood in the yard.
And one of them put me off my aim
By hailing cheerily "Hit them hard!"
I knew pretty well why he dropped behind           5
And let the other go on a way.
I knew pretty well what he had in mind:
He wanted to take my job for pay.

Good blocks of beech it was I split,
As large around as the chopping block;            10
And every piece I squarely hit
Fell splinterless as a cloven rock.
The blows that a life of self-control
Spares to strike for the common good
That day, giving a loose to my soul,              15
I spent on the unimportant wood.

The sun was warm but the wind was chill.
You know how it is with an April day
When the sun is out and the wind is still,
You're one month on in the middle of May.        20
But if you so much as dare to speak,
A cloud comes over the sunlit arch,
A wind comes off a frozen peak,
And you're two months back in the middle of March.

A bluebird comes tenderly up to alight           25
And fronts the wind to unruffle a plume
His song so pitched as not to excite
A single flower as yet to bloom.
It is snowing a flake: and he half knew
Winter was only playing possum.                  30
Except in color he isn't blue,
But he wouldn't advise a thing to blossom.

The water for which we may have to look
In summertime with a witching-wand,
In every wheelrut's now a brook,     35
In every print of a hoof a pond.
Be glad of water, but don't forget
The lurking frost in the earth beneath
That will steal forth after the sun is set
And show on the water its crystal teeth.     40

The time when most I loved my task
These two must make me love it more
By coming with what they came to ask.
You'd think I never had felt before
The weight of an ax-head poised aloft,     45
The grip on earth of outspread feet.
The life of muscles rocking soft
And smooth and moist in vernal heat.

Out of the woods two hulking tramps
(From sleeping God knows where last night,     50
But not long since in the lumber camps).
They thought all chopping was theirs of right.
Men of the woods and lumberjacks,
They judged me by their appropriate tool.
Except as a fellow handled an ax,     55
They had no way of knowing a fool.

Nothing on either side was said.
They knew they had but to stay their stay
And all their logic would fill my head:
As that I had no right to play     60
With what was another man's work for gain.
My right might be love but theirs was need.
And where the two exist in twain
Theirs was the better right—agreed.

But yield who will to their separation,     65
My object in living is to unite
My avocation and my vocation
As my two eyes make one in sight.
Only where love and need are one,
And the work is play for mortal stakes,     70
Is the deed ever really done
For Heaven and the future's sakes.

---

FROST

TWO TRAMPS IN MUD TIME

"Two Tramps in Mud Time" is, at first glance, a very unpretentious poem—a simple episode in a simple world, with the episode simply moralized. In the first stanza we see the two tramps and are told that they want to do for pay the wood splitting that the poet is doing for fun. This is the germ of the episode, but after the first stanza, for five more stanzas, the poet seems to forget all about the tramps. He now whimsically toys with the indecisiveness of the weather, with the bluebird that half knew "winter was only playing possum," with the frost yet in the earth waiting to set, with nightfall, its crystal teeth in the little floods in wheel-rut and hoofprint. This is the season when, the poet says, he most loves his task, and after the lovingly rendered details of the place and season, he tells us why: now he rediscovers, in the heft of the axhead and the grip of feet on the earth, his relation to the external physical world, and in the "life of muscles rocking soft," his relation to an internal physical world. The inner and the outer worlds of physicality flow together; but more, his consciousness, his very self, flows into them. We have in such interpenetration a new sense of unity and fulfillment. And with this notion, we sense another reason why this moment in the year is right for loving the task: it is the moment when the polarities of the year, and the world, balance and interfuse. The bluebird, though the official harbinger of spring, "wouldn't advise a thing to bloom"; one moment you're forward a month "in the middle of May," and the next moment "two months back in the middle of March"; though the wheel-rut flows with the released waters, frost lurks in the earth, ready to "steal forth" at nightfall. Winter and summer, dark and light—even death and life, if you will—interpenetrate and embrace in the moment of fulfilling unity.

Now with stanza seven, the scene and its implications are set for us to return to the tramps, who impinge upon this moment of poise and the loving unity of poet and nature. The poet, as we have said, performs his task for love; the tramps propose, not by words but by their professional presence before the amateur, to do it for pay. Love against pay, play against work, love against need—in the face of these oppositions, the moment is shattered, and the Garden curse, as it were, is reaffirmed. The poet, as a matter of fact, is realistic enough to accept such terms for life, for when "need" and "love" exist "in twain"—in opposition—need must take priority, the physical base of life must be served. This is the "moralizing" dictated by the ordinary grinding process of life.

But with the last stanza, against this grinding process to which we seem committed, the poet proposes his own brand of moralizing for the episode, and asserts his will to live in all ways, as fully as possible, in the spirit of the moment of his springtime wood splitting, for only in such a moment when "work is play"—and play is "for mortal stakes" and therefore both serious and joyful—is life truly fulfilled.

The poem states a view of life, but it also embodies a certain "feel" for life, and is, in its very essence, a certain stance toward life. By embodying the feel, and in being the stance, the poem, in fact, becomes a poem—becomes in itself, in its details and ramifications, meaningful. For instance, the closely and lovingly observed details, the precision of phrase, the witty playfulness in the middle section of the poem, which comes as an intrusion on the narrative, incorporate by the closeness and lovingness and precision and playfulness the very attitude toward the whole world that the poem would celebrate—the acceptance of the wholeness of the world, winter and summer, the secret frost and the vernal sun. To go a little further with this line of thought, though the language is simple and familiar, and though, line by line, the rhythms are those of natural speech, the familiar language and natural rhythms enter into an overall rhythm, brisk and glittering, which, dominates the poem. This movement itself, with its briskness and glitter and gay assertiveness, is, in its interfusion with the other elements, an aspect of the stance toward life that is the poem.

Though, in one sense, a poem is a fulfillment of itself, a poem by a good poet is always a door to other poems by that poet, an invitation to enter into that poet's characteristic world. To change our image, the individual poem, with its own fulfillment, partakes of the other poems by that poet, echoes the other voices and mirrors the other scenes of the poet's world. This is particularly true of Frost's work, for with him, more truly than with many poets, the individual poems take on a richer tone and more disturbing resonance as we feel them part of a fuller utterance. The shadowy and subtly haunting doubleness, the glancing allusiveness to unspecified depths characteristic of individual poems by Frost, is accentuated when we think of the individual poems in relation to the body of his work. And "Two Tramps in Mud Time" is one of the poems that can take us to the center of Frost's world and inspiration.

Let us look for a moment at Frost's work in a broader perspective. Frost (like Faulkner, whom, despite obvious differences, he so deeply resembles) occupies a peculiarly strategic moment in our history—so strategic that, forgetting genius, one is apt to say that the moment is the man. Frost was firmly rooted in an old America, now dead; furthermore, in that America, he was a regionalist, a localist even, and clung with ferocious piety to the history as well as the present furniture of his chosen spot. His attitude toward the past as embodied in his place was not merely nostalgic. He was a realist, could look shrewdly at human nature, and believed in no Golden Age; and what his piety, with the abandoned apple orchards and tumbled chimneys of his characteristic landscape and the history of his characters, gave him, was primarily an image of the human condition, of vicissitude in time, of the tears of things, of human pity and endurance. His commitment to his world made him, despite all protestations, something of an outsider in the contemporary scene, never involved in the political, literary, and social fashions of modernity, and critical of such fashions. His commitment to his own world gave him a point of reference by which to criticize the ruling fashions of a moment. For one thing, in contrast to the abstracted man of megalopolis and technological triumph, man in his world bears an obviously significant relation to nature—not the relation of the sentimental tourist who might think the "phoebes wept" but a sense of participation in the great natural process that would give value to the contemplation of the smallest detail of nature and that, as in "Two Look at Two," might make men certain, for a moment anyway, that "earth returned their love." In "Two Tramps in Mud Time," as in so many other poems by Frost, the deep appreciation of nature and the acceptance of natural process appears; other poems we may think of are "After Apple Picking," "Goodbye and Keep Cold," "The Woodpile," and "Hyla Brook" with its unforgettable last line: "We love the things we love for what they are."

This soberly joyful fidelity to actuality leads to a further thought. Just as in "Two Tramps in Mud Time" the poet would have the reconciliation of love and need, so, in "Birches," he declares "earth the right place for love"—earth with its trials and toils, as contrasted with heaven. And in that masterpiece, "After Apple Picking," he would have the rewarding "dream" not a release from labor but a reliving of labor with the ache and sway of actuality fused with a more deliciously particularized, imaginative version of the harvest:

> *Magnified apples appear and disappear,*
> *Stem end and blossom end,*
> *And every fleck of russet showing clear.*

And in "Mowing" we find that "the fact is the sweetest dream that labor knows." In other words, as Frost said in contrasting himself with E.A. Robinson, he was no Platonist; he saw the ideal as a projection of the real, he saw man struggling nobly with his doom of being an ideal-creating animal, becoming worthy of his heaven only in the act of creating it.

Philosophically, Frost's anti-Platonism may strike one as characteristic of our age, but a great difference between our age and Frost lies in his conception of "work" as a joy and not merely something to be got through for the pension. To state it another way, in contrast with the world of Big Organization, and with the compartmentalization and fragmentation of life in the modern world, where the specialized function takes the place of a human being, Frost celebrates, for good or ill, the individual. "Two Tramps in Mud Time" is such a celebration, and the triumph of life it proclaims, against the professionals and specialists, is the unity of love and need, of vocation and avocation. This, of course, is at the furthest remove from what is tacitly accepted as the modern formula: technical function + hobby = man. Against this formula, Frost astonishingly proposes the notion that the living of life can partake of the nature of an art and of a religion—those approaches to life that share the assumption that all things may be significant. But the notion of the wholeness of life finds expression in poems seemingly very different from "Two Tramps in Mud Time." What else is at stake, we may ask, in such pieces as "The Code" and "The Ax-Helve"?

The dignity of man in his wholeness is related to Frost's special brand of stoicism. Frost, despite his joy in and acceptance of life, never denied the grinding diminishments and tragic shocks of life. In fact, we may take it that the ultimate joy, even in its grimness, is the willed confrontation of the diminishments and shocks. Despite the understating and the repudiation of heroics, such a theme is quite clear in "Desert Places," "Once by the Pacific," "Acquainted with the Night," "Canis Major," and "Bereft." The last poem ends:

> *Word [that] I was in the house alone*
> *Somehow must have gotten abroad,*
> *Word I was in my life alone,*
> *Word I had no one left but God.*

Though not often so explicitly put as in "Bereft," the willed confrontation is implicit in poem after poem, in "Stopping by Woods on a Snowy Evening" and "Come In," as well as in "Two Tramps in Mud Time," where beneath the spring thaw the frost lurks waiting for the night. In fact, in the deep coherence of Frost's work, even as we feel in any of his good poems the presence of all the others, we feel the weight of experience from which they all derive. For, after all, no good poem is merely a parlor trick or an acrostic; it is a voice of life.

## Stopping by Woods on a Snowy Evening

Whose woods these are I think I know.
His house is in the village though;
He will not see me stopping here
To watch his woods fill up with snow.

My little horse must think it queer          5
To stop without a farmhouse near
Between the woods and frozen lake
The darkest evening of the year.

He gives his harness bells a shake
To ask if there is some mistake.             10
The only other sound's the sweep
Of easy wind and downy flake.

The woods are lovely, dark and deep.
But I have promises to keep,
And miles to go before I sleep,              15
And miles to go before I sleep.

# James Wright

## FROST
### STOPPING BY WOODS ON A SNOWY EVENING

Robert Frost's little poem "Stopping by Woods on a Snowy Evening" is an awesome presence to my mind. It would be easy to be clever, and to proceed by deliberately building up a little verbal charm, for the purpose of translating the awesome presence of the strangely silent poem itself into a multitudinous plurality of other presences, themselves sufficiently awesome. They are the presences of Frost's critical interpreters, already awesomely numerous, forbiddingly articulate. I do not mean to imply that most of Frost's critics have published their commentaries with the intention of frightening the poet's readers away from the presence of his poems. As a matter of fact, among the several peculiarities that distinguish Frost individually among the other major poets of our century, surely one of the most noteworthy is his power of inspiring in so many professional critics of diverse philosophical persuasions the same singular and beautiful desire: to read the poet's poems with an intelligent love worthy of the nobility embodied in his several masterpieces. There are a number of good reasons why this generally sympathetic relation between Frost and the literary critics should give us pause. For one thing, unless my present reader is himself a professional student of literature, he might well be comparatively unfamiliar with the by no means predictable responses that some of the great poems have evoked from even the ablest literary critics of their time.

As Mr. James M. Cox has remarked, Frost "seems to have gathered his forces deliberately and bided his time until he was sure of not launching himself too soon." And when at last he did launch himself, at thirty-nine, his power of attracting serious critical admiration displayed itself almost immediately. Mr. Cox further notes, "when *North of Boston* appeared, both William Dean Howells, the aging patriarch of American letters, and Ezra Pound, the eccentric and rebellious exponent of the new poetry, reviewed and praised it."

These two early reviews signify a good deal more than mere variety of critical response. Both reviewers belong to the small handful of American periodical editors who have regarded the editorial position, as so many of their fellows have modestly accepted the same position, as some kind of sordid reward for services rendered, through an infernally long and murky intellectual lifetime, to some nebulous "great tradition of spiritual values" or other. It is utterly astonishing, and bottomlessly fascinating, to witness the same strange critical drama in a performance as recent as Frost's eighty-fifth birthday dinner on March 26, 1959. Mr. Lionel Trilling, the principal speaker, displeased many persons, apparently because of his having spoken of Frost as a "terrifying poet." The most spectacularly publicized expression of this displeasure was a column in *The New York Times Book Review* (April 12, 1959).

Mr. Trilling, in the course of the speech in question, confessed his "partisan devotion" to what he called the "essential work that is done by the critical intellect"—that is, "to create around itself the intensity and variety that traditionally characterize the intellectual life of the metropolis." One may disapprove of this critical viewpoint; but I believe one is bound to recognize in it a spirit akin to Pound's own in praising Frost: a disillusioned realism; a resignation to the self-conscious gracefulness of a deliberately studied style of prose whose very real simplicity is a severe achievement earned by labor and not snatched by spontaneous luck; and, finally, a stubbornness, almost a pigheadedness, in claiming a place for the urban intellectual in the life of the nation's spirit. I privately suspect that it was this sort of claim that Mr. J. Donald Adams in his column found as shocking as anything else in Mr. Trilling's speech, and that made him feel sincerely hurt. Our respectful sympathy belongs to any man whose intellectual vision of his country's ideals has been abruptly shaken and perhaps even flawed forever, even though it may be a vision in which the Founding Fathers brood, dreamy and immortal, above one another's quill-pens on the frieze of a postage-stamp, looking for all the world like plump and snuff-stained temperance fanatics whose ill-designed dentures have tortured their shrivelled gums into those heart-tugging little smiles of cruelty and despair. But it is unprofitable, and fortunately unnecessary, to subject Mr. Adams's critical powers to unkind scrutiny. He is a lover of Frost's poetry, which he wished to vindicate from what he thought an attack.

In effect, Mr. Trilling deplored (once and for all, it seems to me) the widespread attempt to castrate Frost's poetry by means of the intricate psychological tactic that we all are aware of by now: startled by the terrifying presence of a genuinely tragic imagination stubborn enough to cast its searchlights upon the most hysterically cherished of our American false pieties—our nostalgia for a personal and national childhood that never was, our cold-blooded hatred of man's intellectual life cunningly displaced and disguised as a modest, gentle affection for our virtuous great-grandfathers in rural areas—many literary journalists have praised their own lying public image of Frost, and denied his fierce greatness by lavishing upon him an unprecedented popularity. They have tried to flatter him into drowsing while they shear his locks. What Trilling did was to cry out to the poet in the very company of his flatterers, "The Philistines be upon thee!" The poet woke, and was not blind.

The best thing a reader can do at this moment is to follow Mr. Trilling's example by applying its principle to the reading of Frost's individual poems. They will respond to our intellectual respect by yielding up rich treasures of pleasure invisible to flatterers blinded by their own refusal to grant Frost his own poetic intelligence. The famous little poem "Stopping by Woods on a Snowy Evening" offers an occasion for putting these introductory speculations to the test. The poem is as appropriate an example of Frost's poetic power as one can imagine; and, if we are willing to grant the poem the intellectual respect that all of Frost's work deserved, I believe we can clearly identify at least one source of his power: his fantastic and yet self-concealed mastery of traditional lyric forms, and the secret boldness of his formal inventiveness.

I suspect that "Stopping by Woods on a Snowy Evening" is more widely known and loved than any other single poem in the English language at the present time. Grade-school children copy it into their notebooks for Nature Study. The late Prime Minister of India, Mr. Nehru, kept the poem on his desk as a kind of secret reminder, an emblem of steadfastness, during the last days of his life, when he realized perfectly well that he would have to carry his appalling burdens of public responsibility without relaxing for an instant, right up to the death itself. The poem privately nourished the energy of the late President Kennedy. Even the most vigorously self-assured of Frost's detractors during the thirties, Mr. Malcolm Cowley, chose "Stopping by Woods on a

Snowy Evening" as a characteristic example of Frost's political and social irresponsibility. According to this reading, the
poet is criticized for his habit of loitering for his mere
personal pleasure at the edge of the dark woods and then
blithely urging his little horse on toward home; whereas any
really mature, responsible person would have dismounted and
undertaken an exploration of the woods, which represent the
sinister realities of American life, both inward and external.
(What was Frost supposed to find in those dark woods, I
wonder. A hobo jungle? A snowman? The tar-paper hideout
shack of some American equivalent of Lenin's mother,
ladling out mulligan stew to fugitives from the Federal
Writers' Project?) The interpretations and misinterpretations
of this one short poem are as numerous and varied as its
readers. They all testify to its singularly powerful hold on its
reader's emotion.

I invite the reader to disregard, for a moment, the usual
tendency to view the poem either as a moral exhortation to
fulfill one's private duties or as a politico-social allegory. I
point to its lyrical craftsmanship, to its mastery of traditional
form, and, finally, to the hidden skill with which the poet has
combined two traditional lyric devices in such a way as to
create something entirely new.

The devices I mean are devices of sound, or rhyme. Consider the first of these: the rhyme scheme of the individual
stanzas. It is pleasing in itself, and even mildly odd: instead of
sustaining the promise of simplicity in rhymed couplets, the
poet gently surprises us in the fourth line of each stanza by
sidestepping his third-line rhyme and returning to the rhymes
of his first two lines: this is the first pattern. It is in the first
line of his second stanza that the musical secret is fully confessed. What seemed at first a mere pleasant deviation from
a strict and simple couplet pattern suddenly becomes itself a
principle of pattern, fully as strict as the first and, at the
same time, more complex: for the first pattern simply joined
together the two lines of the couplet, whereas the second
pattern joins together two entire stanzas. The poet creates his
interlocking pattern by returning to the end of his third line
and transforming what seemed an accident of sound, left
abandoned in mid-air, into the very principle of pattern, a
rhyme scheme whose principle is not simple repetition, as in a
couplet, but development, as in—in what?

Why, in the *terza rima* of Dante's *Divine Comedy*, no
less.

Stanza by stanza, Frost's brief poem, so modest in its diction, so obvious in its setting and action, so unambitious in its pattern of sound, turns out to be a devastatingly rich combination of two great traditional lyrical devices: the stanza form of the *Rubáiyát* of Omar Khayyám and the *terza rima* of Dante combined into a new harmony. The fourth line of each stanza of the *Rubáiyát* rebels against the couplet pattern into which it is being forced, and, instead of meekly completing the imperious sound of its syntactical counterpart in the third line, abandons that sound to fend for itself, and becomes a pathetic echo flowing constantly back to repeat the fulfilled rhymes of the first couplet. The effect of the sound in the *Rubáiyát* is to make one's ear constantly aware of a gentle yet persistent tugging, almost a faint undertone of yearning toward what is already perfected, already fulfilled in pattern, and already past. The principle of rhyme in the *terza rima* is, of course, just the opposite: the ear of the reader, after hearing at least one completed pattern of rhyme at the beginning, naturally listens with specially alerted interest to the sound of a new word introduced at the end of any line that in itself does not fit into any already established pattern of rhyme, and concentrates its listening attention in the only direction from which the fulfillment of a rhyming pattern can possibly come. That is the direction of the future: the next line, perhaps, or the line after the next.

So Frost in his poem combines two irresistibly strong currents of sound, one toward what is past and fulfilled, the other toward what may yet come into its own fulfillment; the two undertones of time become a single current, and the listener's yearning back toward the one flows into his yearning forward toward the other. These movements of rhyme give lyrical embodiment to two inescapably serious kinds of human music: the music of pathos that sings of our yearning to return, and the music of present energy that sings of our need to waken and discover, or even to create, what is alive and new. Frost has fused the two distinct principles of the elegiac and the philosopical lyric into a new lyrical principle, which he sings in a voice unmistakably his own. His syntax is so colloquial, his tone of voice modulates itself so casually back and forth between the murmur of speech and the humming of a solitary sleigh driver poised—for an eternal, absent-minded instant—between snowfall and night-fall—that his poem seems to record that strange moment when time pauses, whispers, and miraculously renews itself.

## Directive

Back out of all this now too much for us,
Back in a time made simple by the loss
Of detail, burned, dissolved, and broken off
Like graveyard marble sculpture in the weather,
There is a house that is no more a house                    5
Upon a farm that is no more a farm
And in a town that is no more a town.
The road there, if you'll let a guide direct you
Who only has at heart your getting lost,
May seem as if it should have been a quarry—           10
Great monolithic knees the former town
Long since gave up pretence of keeping covered.
And there's a story in a book about it:
Besides the wear of iron wagon wheels
The ledges show lines ruled southeast northwest,        15
The chisel work of an enormous Glacier
That braced his feet against the Arctic Pole.
You must not mind a certain coolness from him
Still said to haunt this side of Panther Mountain.
Nor need you mind the serial ordeal                          20
Of being watched from forty cellar holes
As if by eye pairs out of forty firkins.
As for the woods' excitement over you
That sends light rustle rushes to their leaves,
Charge that to upstart inexperience.                         25
Where were they all not twenty years ago?
They think too much of having shaded out
A few old pecker-fretted apple trees.
Make yourself up a cheering song of how
Someone's road home from work this once was,            30
Who may be just ahead of you on foot
Or creaking with a buggy load of grain.
The height of the adventure is the height

Of country where two village cultures faded
Into each other. Both of them are lost.                         35
And if you're lost enough to find yourself
By now, pull in your ladder road behind you
And put a sign up CLOSED to all but me.
Then make yourself at home. The only field
Now left's no bigger than a harness gall.                       40
First there's the children's house of make believe,
Some shattered dishes underneath a pine,
The playthings in the playhouse of the children.
Weep for what little things could make them glad.
Then for the house that is no more a house,                     45
But only a belilaced cellar hole,
Now slowly closing like a dent in dough.
This was no playhouse but a house in earnest.
Your destination and your destiny's
A brook that was the water of the house,                        50
Cold as a spring as yet so near its source,
Too lofty and original to rage.
(We know the valley streams that when aroused
Will leave their tatters hung on barb and thorn.)
I have kept hidden in the instep arch                           55
Of an old cedar at the waterside
A broken drinking goblet like the Grail
Under a spell so the wrong ones can't find it,
So can't get saved, as Saint Mark says they mustn't.
(I stole the goblet from the children's playhouse.)            60
Here are your waters and your watering place.
Drink and be whole again beyond confusion.

*Philip Booth*

---

FROST
DIRECTIVE

"Directive" reads to me like the height of Frost's poetry, the poem he climbed toward for perhaps forty years. Imagery and tone both tell that he's taken this road before: until its last six lines, there's only one image in "Directive" that doesn't appear in, or bear on, some earlier Frost poem. The "children's house" is new; but the apple trees, small animals, and outcrop rock of "Directive" are vintage Frost, here distilled to their metaphorical essence. As his didactic title implies, Frost is familiar with what he's up to. But only here does he newly play guide to his own metaphors and, climbing back to his poetry's wellspring, openly bid a reader to drink at their height.

"Directive" doesn't demand more knowledge of Frost than itself. But the poem gains stature if read as climaxing both the high inclination of, say, "Birches," and the dark temptations of "Stopping by Woods." "Directive" both walks *in* toward self-exploration and, all but simultaneously, works itself *up* toward a theologically marginal grace. The poem is simple to get into. But to be worthy of its final ascent a reader must, by Frost's own example, learn to read the nature with which this poem surrounds him. Earlier Frost poems can teach a reader what to make of deceptively simple natural images, but "Directive" must first be read by submitting to its insistence on "getting lost." Finding-in-losing is the poem's crucial paradox, and unless a reader has been scared by his own desert places he may not be "lost enough" to be guided by Frost through this high-country quest. As it tests a reader's earned humanity, not just his book-learning, "Directive" is in its own way a "serial ordeal"; it can't be read, and wasn't written, as a young man's poem. I remember my own undergraduate distrust of its tones, as Sidney Cox first taught me Frost in that year when it climaxed "Steeple Bush." I hadn't yet earned reading it. I still perhaps haven't. But now, at least, I know from the mountain poem in *North of Boston*, from the title poem of *West-Running Brook* (and the lesser piece in that book that involves "a broken drinking glass" beside a mountain spring), how much of Frost's writing life was committed to the poem that "Directive" would become. As I've grown older, it seems to me that one of the measures of "Directive" is how greatly Frost tried to make it come whole, how long it took him to discover the cumulative import of images he had always known.

"Directive" doesn't invite us to guess what human ordeals finally drove Frost to write it. Though his biography is full of serial possibilities, the poem asks only that we submit to discovering ourselves in its sense of our common experience. Against this world's temptations to seize the day, "Directive" bids us "back out of all this now too much for us." But Frost's strong stresses, roughened across that great iambic line, admit of no defeat. Precisely because he long knew that "the present / Is . . . / Too present to imagine," Frost begins "Directive" with his familiar gambit of a strategic retreat. As if with Thoreau, John Muir, John the Baptist, or whatever guide has grown wise through days and nights in the wilderness, "Directive" shares with us the possibility of a long perspective on our own emotional history.

Perspective is what the first thirty-five lines of the poem are about, and Frost—in them—is up to his old delight of preparing us for wisdom. There's more ice than fire in these early images of extinction; they notably begin with that "graveyard marble" which suggests our inability to imagine much beyònd death. But after its incantatory devastation of house-farm-town, "Directive" recovers our perspective by lending those close losses the context of geologic history. "Monolithic knees" might seem more native to Easter Island than Vermont; but they, like Panther Mountain's "enormous Glacier," lend scale to our mourning and personify those natural forces in whose universe we stand small. We may not know chapter and verse of this long story, but we begin to read ourselves as being part of its book. By Frost's directive, we find ourselves lost with laboring generations of men, exposed to those forty "eye pairs" which steal our courage from us. Unless we invent our own song in this strange land, as Frost requires, there's nothing "cheering" here. But just when our ordeal seems unbearable, Frost reminds us that beside the upstart trees we are comparatively experienced. By the time we climb line 36, we have, in fact, been initiated into the poem's strange lostness. Just as "two village cultures faded / Into each other," we become one with our guide in

having lost the accouterments of our civilization. By his
directive at this distance from our daily lives, we are mazed
in primitive fears, in a nature we see signs of but can't read,
in a history larger than our own.

> *And if you're lost enough to find yourself*
> *By now, pull in your ladder road behind you*
> *And put a sign up* CLOSED *to all but me*

"Directive" turns on these lines, not least as they restate
Frost's casual introduction of their crucial paradox. From
here on in, "Directive" climbs on that strange "ladder road"
by which we may find ourselves "at home." Frost's "harness
gall" metaphor implies, perhaps, how wearing is the burden
of paradox; it surely suggests how bitterly minimal our
"destination" will be. But here, at least, lostness gives way to
finding, the poem's perspective shortens to focus on those
few residual symbols by which our humanity is (if barely)
sustained. Frost's lines about the children's playthings are, I
think, the most heart-rending in all his poetry. "Make believe" though their house may have been, it is also the house
(of the farm and the town) in which we once vested belief.
This "house in earnest" is now only a "belilaced cellar hole,"
as impersonal as a "dent in dough"; its shelter may be lost to
us, but we find our hearts still in it. Newly children again, we
with Frost "weep for what little things could make them
glad."

Yet our tears now are more of empathy than of nostalgia;
we weep more in tragedy than in terror. Like figures suddenly legendary, we find ourselves become worthy to drink
from a "goblet like the Grail." Broken though that goblet is,
by the history we too have been lost in, we learn in drinking
from it both where we've been and where we've finally
arrived. We learn, in fact, to read "Directive" again, to
discover human directions in the natural world through
which we've been guided. Until its climactic references to the
Grail and to Saint Mark, "Directive" reads like an archeo-
logical field trip in Vermont (albeit without much compass).
The poem's greatness continues to reside in how painfully
native to us its least images seem. But as Frost's reference to
Mark challenges our memory of the book in which "Directive" is rooted, the reference further guides us to read Frost's
images as he would have them read. Frost long said that his
poetry was chiefly metaphor, "talking about one thing in
terms of another." Mark (4:11) is even more explicit: "Unto
you it is given to know the mystery of the kingdom . . . all
these things are done in parables." After a night of dark talk,

Mr. Frost once reassured me that verses eleven and twelve were his "Saint Mark gospel." (Whoever doubts Frost's salvational sense of metaphor could do worse than look up 4:12.)

"Directive" is, throughout, more metaphor than parable; Frost talks Christian in often secular terms. But its explicit biblical reference further directs us to the source of its chief thematic paradox (*Luke* 9:24): "For whosoever will save his life shall lose it: but whosoever will lose his life . . . the same shall save it." Frost's sense of being "saved" is as marginal as subsistence farming in Vermont: to sustain one's values, beyond sure losses, depends on being guided by natural signs. Only after we're lost in reading "Directive," and have thus earned a right to its wisdom, do its signs come metaphorically clear. The "cedar" of "Directive," for instance, is natural to Frost's New England; only in the context of the poem's climax does it seem to have been seeded by the cedars of biblical Lebanon. "Barb and thorn" or "ladder road" are similarly metaphors-in-retrospect; they are images of spring floods and steepness before they imply Gethsemane or Jacob. "Directive" is thick with Frost's delight in providing a context that illuminates simple images as the metaphors he intends them to be. The poem is typically Frost in its clear surfaces and complex depths; it's unusual in specifically initiating a reader to what "the wrong ones can't find."

"Under a spell" of metaphor though its ultimate image is, "Directive" is finally a secular poem rooted in residual Christianity. Its biblical references don't, as they might in Stevens, argue for reformation; they don't, as they might in Eliot, invite us back to a church. They measure, instead, both our distance from full redemption and our imaginative thirst for those wellsprings that revive our spirit. Though "Directive" guides us perilously through humanity's common ordeal, its country is no wasteland, there is no chapel at its height. Frost's goblet is merely *like* the Grail; in drinking from it we are still only "near its source." As with the contrary wave in "West-Running Brook," Frost shapes "Directive" as a "tribute of the current to the source," to the Christian drama in which his metaphors are steeped. But Frost is also asking, as he often does, "what to make of a diminished thing." However diminished its symbols may be, Frost seems to imply, our hearts need not let go the value of Christianity's crucial paradox. Yet to imagine our own ordeals as part of a larger drama is not to cast ourselves as heroes; it is simply to realize our share in the human condition. What is heroic in "Directive" is its quiet acceptance of the role to which experience

conditions us. Nothing in "Directive" has guided us to hope
(whether for a Grail, Redemption, or hope itself); we began
to climb without expectation, and end by quenching the
unexpected thirst we've earned in sweating uphill. Reality has
been our ordeal, and we drink what the poem finally offers
us: clear water from a real spring. We are "beyond confusion" not least in this; we are wholly ourselves both in
having wept for the children's playthings and in being gladdened by what we made-believe in drinking from their cup.
Our imaginative thirst may only be momentarily satisfied,
but the poem fulfills itself with a sacrament which redeems
our experience by completing our perspective on it.

I read "Directive" as one of those few rare poems that are,
by Frost's definitive hope, "a momentary stay against confusion." The margin of "a momentary stay" is the saving
grace of "Directive" and, greatly, its theme. Whoever demands a more ample margin had better be guided up Billy
Graham's public aisle; whoever can exist without metaphor
had best forget Frost. But whomever "Directive" privately
converts (Frost asks no less) can find his margin roughly
extended in that strangely unknown Frost poem, "An Empty
Threat":

> *Better defeat almost,*
> *If seen clear,*
> *Than life's victories of doubt*
> *That need endless talk talk*
> *To make them out.*

Terribly though doubt assailed him, nowhere in his work is
Frost defeated by it. Skeptically as a lot of poems talk,
nowhere in them is doubt victorious. Nor is there any poem
that argues "almost better defeat," whether seen clear or not.
What must be seen clear is the poised sequence of those
words I've just disordered. My misquote, "almost better
defeat," is narrowly, but wholly and perfectly, different from
"better defeat almost." The difference is as great as one man's
life might be from another's; the distinction in order is, as
Frost would have it, of the order of the distinction between
prose and poetry. *Defeat-almost* was the ordeal of Frost's life;
it is the narrow victory his major poems dramatize, and the
human margin of their greatness. As it climbs to marginal
redemption through a myth made local by image, through an
ordeal heightened by metaphor, "Directive" is one of the
greatest. It stays defeat by bettering being lost.

# WALLACE STEVENS
## [1879–1955]

## *Sunday Morning*

Complacencies of the peignoir, and late
Coffee and oranges in a sunny chair,
And the green freedom of a cockatoo
Upon a rug mingle to dissipate
The holy hush of ancient sacrifice.      5
She dreams a little, and she feels the dark
Encroachment of that old catastrophe,
As a calm darkens among water-lights.
The pungent oranges and bright, green wings
Seem things in some procession of the dead,      10
Winding across wide water, without sound.
The day is like wide water, without sound,
Stilled for the passing of her dreaming feet
Over the seas, to silent Palestine,
Dominion of the blood and sepulchre.      15

Why should she give her bounty to the dead?
What is divinity if it can come
Only in silent shadows and in dreams?
Shall she not find in comforts of the sun,
In pungent fruit and bright, green wings, or else      20
In any balm or beauty of the earth,
Things to be cherished like the thought of heaven?
Divinity must live within herself:
Passions of rain, or moods in falling snow;
Grievings in loneliness, or unsubdued      25
Elations when the forest blooms; gusty
Emotions on wet roads on autumn nights;
All pleasures and all pains, remembering
The bough of summer and the winter branch.
These are the measures destined for her soul.      30

Jove in the clouds had his inhuman birth.
No mother suckled him, no sweet land gave
Large-mannered motions to his mythy mind.

He moved among us, as a muttering king,
Magnificent, would move among his hinds,                    35
Until our blood, commingling, virginal,
With heaven, brought such requital to desire
The very hinds discerned it, in a star.
Shall our blood fail? Or shall it come to be
The blood of paradise? And shall the earth            40
Seem all of paradise that we shall know?
The sky will be much friendlier then than now,
A part of labor and a part of pain.
And next in glory to enduring love,
Not this dividing and indifferent blue.               45

She says, "I am content when wakened birds,
Before they fly, test the reality
Of misty fields, by their sweet questionings;
But when the birds are gone, and their warm fields
Return no more, where, then, is paradise?"            50
There is not any haunt of prophecy,
Nor any old chimera of the grave,
Neither the golden underground, nor isle
Melodious, where spirits gat them home,
Nor visionary south, nor cloudy palm                  55
Remote on heaven's hill, that has endured
As April's green endures; or will endure
Like her remembrance of awakened birds,
Or her desire for June and evening, tipped
By the consummation of the swallow's wings.           60

She says, "But in contentment I still feel
The need of some imperishable bliss."
Death is the mother of beauty; hence from her,
Alone, shall come fulfilment to our dreams
And our desires. Although she strews the leaves       65
Of sure obliteration on our paths,
The path sick sorrow took, the many paths
Where triumph rang its brassy phrase, or love
Whispered a little out of tenderness,
She makes the willow shiver in the sun                70
For maidens who were wont to sit and gaze
Upon the grass, relinquished to their feet.
She causes boys to pile new plums and pears
On disregarded plate. The maidens taste
And stray impassioned in the littering leaves.        75

Is there no change of death in paradise?
Does ripe fruit never fall? Or do the boughs

WALLACE STEVENS

*The New York Times*

Hang always heavy in that perfect sky,
Unchanging, yet so like our perishing earth,
With rivers like our own that seek for seas                80
They never find, the same receding shores
That never touch with inarticulate pang?
Why set the pear upon those river-banks
Or spice the shores with odors of the plum?
Alas, that they should wear our colors there,             85
The silken weavings of our afternoons,
And pick the strings of our insipid lutes!
Death is the mother of beauty, mystical,
Within whose burning bosom we devise
Our earthly mothers waiting, sleeplessly.                 90

Supple and turbulent, a ring of men
Shall chant in orgy on a summer morn
Their boisterous devotion to the sun,
Not as a god, but as a god might be,
Naked among them, like a savage source.                   95
Their chant shall be a chant of paradise,
Out of their blood, returning to the sky;
And in their chant shall enter, voice by voice,
The windy lake wherein their lord delights,
The trees, like seraphim, and echoing hills,              100
That choir among themselves long afterward.
They shall know well the heavenly fellowship
Of men that perish and of summer morn.
And whence they came and whither they shall go
The dew upon their feet shall manifest.                   105

She hears, upon that water without sound,
A voice that cries, "The tomb in Palestine
Is not the porch of spirits lingering.
It is the grave of Jesus, where He lay."
We live in an old chaos of the sun,                       110
Or old dependency of day and night,
Or island solitude, unsponsored, free,
Of that wide water, inescapable.
Deer walk upon our mountains, and the quail
Whistle about us their spontaneous cries;                 115
Sweet berries ripen in the wilderness;
And, in the isolation of the sky,
At evening, casual flocks of pigeons make
Ambiguous undulations as they sink,
Downward to darkness, on extended wings.                  120

# John Crowe Ransom

## STEVENS

### SUNDAY MORNING

Scholars of poetry are in the act of compiling a hundred essays, and a score of books, in praise of Wallace Stevens. Do they suspect that they may have to establish him as chief among the late poets in our language? And what short poem, among the five-hundred-odd of all sizes, is the masterpiece? Mr. Williams and his advisors did not go wrong; it is "Sunday Morning."

For one thing, it is mellifluous; it is where Stevens makes a very formal use of blank verse, the sinewy rhythm that the old Elizabethans brought to perfection as if anticipating Shakespeare the playwright, and Milton the heroic poet, and Wordsworth the nature poet; but now Stevens, another and better nature poet. Stevens does not transgress the tolerant laws of the rhythm, though he makes it suit his individual kind of eloquence. The form pleases especially the ears of common or general readers, who are schooled in it; it is as if they too were meant to be of its audience.

We come upon "Sunday Morning" in its final text in the opening *Harmonium* section, dated 1923, of the *Collected Poems*. It seems all of a sudden to jump and soar out of the exact middle pages of a miscellany as wide and gay and dazzling as a poet's first book could be. Nobody can miss its difference, as it goes on and on with an inexorable argument that has to be taken to its binding conclusion. There are many bits of fresh nature work in *Harmonium*, but perhaps Stevens never knew his destinate career till some of the phrases of this poem began to sound in his mind. But he knew it then, and he proclaims nothing less than a new gospel. This is its inaugural. He will establish it better hereafter, by attending to it more and more exclusively, till finally his office will seem like that of some old, learned Father of the Church. He will make necessary qualifications, and test a multitude of startling case-histories, and we shall admire his intellectual conscience as much as his teeming invention. But his voice will never stop being that of a poet.

He will not be trying to fix the letter of a determinate theology, but to find and hold onto a great though inconstant joy. The Sunday morning of the title used to be for us the hour appointed for meditating the crucifixion, and the resurrection afterwards in that heavenly paradise unto which we, like Jesus, would repair if we were worthy. But the logical honesty of intellectuals grows always more exacting. After the First World War, when this poem was written, many bright young men were having to reject the old faith, and be miserable in their desolation; as if, rather than violate their scruple, they had gone to surgery, and caused one of the favorite grandeurs of the mind to be sterilized. But Stevens had comfort for them. The poem is about the majesty of our planetary world, than which no greater majesty is available to the human senses; no world beyond nor world to come that perception can find or imagination invent. And what is specially hallowed as the price of this revelation is the thought of death itself, our own personal and final death. It is a thought that everybody has to live with in some fashion; perhaps it will bring fits of unmitigated loathing. But if we boldly and proudly embrace it? By the principle of equal action and reaction, the thought will cause us to fall all the more in love with life again, and as the weathers and the seasons roll, to indulge in planetary splendors and charms. These are actual, though the poet's imagination may heighten them till they exceed the fact a little, and dress them in adventitious but beautiful and irresistible phrases.

It is not a hard poem to read. But the structural pattern is strange; I have not found the like of it elsewhere in Stevens. The poem tells a story in the present tense. Therefore a "recapitulation" is needed, to acquaint us with the situation where action begins, and with the characters when they act. So a sophisticated but sweet-minded woman is presented; at home on Sunday morning, after the rites of the peignoir, and breakfast in the sunshine, and some watching of the green bird on the rug. No other character is objectively presented in the poem. What the woman does is only to think and dream, and twice to make small speeches, which are set in quotes, and later to hear from a mysterious monitor another small speech, again in quotes. But meantime a bigger action, a huge action, seems to be going on in the form of counterarguments made against her thoughts and speeches by some overwhelming antagonist, who is a man. How shall we identify him? I will take a long chance, because it is exciting, and because Stevens might just barely have thought so; he often takes giant strides and does not wait for us to catch up. This other actor is not the "omniscient" author who knows everything and takes us into his confidence but plays no part in the action. This is an "inside" reporter, and actor too, after the style of Henry James's fictions; and I have come to think I can see him there, sitting near her on the terrace and looking at her over his newspaper. So far as she is concerned he is clairvoyant, because he knows her habit of mind very well, and even her speeches as she makes them to herself. They must have had many battles about these Sunday mornings. His own arguments in turn are just his thoughts, which she can probably imagine and make the most of or the least of as she likes. We think she will make the most of them. He is very polite in referring to her, but we are sure this poet-evangelist will never loose his grip upon her till he has made her his convert.

Now some very brief comment upon a few of the shining texts of the poem. In stanza two:

> *The bough of summer and the winter branch.*
> *These are the measures destined for her soul.*

The leaves of summer cause "elations when the forest blooms," and the bare branch causes "grievings in loneliness," but there must be a principle of alternation if the elations are to enter into her consciousness.

We observe the delicacy of stanza three. Stevens does not care to speak disparagingly of the deity worshipped in the old churches, but substitutes a more primitive analogue, "Jove in the clouds," who could have had in himself no sense of the human experience. But finally "our blood," in the person of a virgin, mingled with his blood, and produced an earthly child heralded by a star. Now come three rhetorical questions:

> *Shall our blood fail? Or shall it come to be*
> *The blood of paradise? And shall the earth*
> *Seem all of paradise that we shall know?*

The answer to the first question is No, and to the other questions Yes.

But it is in number five that we come to the most arresting text in the poem: "Death is the mother of beauty." It is repeated with passion at the end of stanza six:

> *Death is the mother of beauty, mystical,*
> *Within whose burning bosom we devise*
> *Our earthly mothers waiting, sleeplessly*

There is no great concession of principle in indulging a dying woman who asks that her body be laid beside her mother's, as if the mother could not die completely till the daughter's dust returned to the mother dust. But in the boisterous opening of the seventh stanza, the interior reporter seems to forget the woman and to be thinking in utterly masculine terms; about chanting to an almost-god who is the sun, a "savage source"; and indeed the sun, among all agents planetary or agents visible from the planet, is the one who most created in his own good time the world as it is, including ourselves. This stanza was not in the original version.

In the final stanza Stevens returns to the woman, and it is now in her dream-thought that she hears the voice from across the seas, plagiarizing to be sure the reporter's own voice, which is probably adapting the words of the Angel of the Resurrection morning; at any rate somebody is crying,

> *"The tomb in Palestine*
> *Is not the porch of spirits lingering,*
> *It is the grave of Jesus, where He lay."*

She does not demur. Evidently the evangelist feels confident of her at last.

If the poem has moved us, it leaves us pondering. The new gospel pleases us because it suddenly simplifies the old intolerable confusion about the intention of poetry, through the happy stroke of one word: planetary. The term is so brilliantly strict in its limitation yet ample in its coverage that it could easily stand as the name of a new evangelism. There is always an irrational and indefinable element in natural beauty, but an instructed and planetary poet might tend thereafter to refrain from pushing as if by vocation into extraplanetary excursions.

I am obliged to observe that the word "gospel" does not appear in the poem. Stevens will play with the idea later, just as he has done in the inaugural poem, which is demanding and priestly. "Planetary" does not occur in our poem, either. But our planet is properly identified in the lines of stanza eight immediately following the cry from the tomb. And one of the very last in the *Collected Poems* is the poet's modest epilogue to his whole achievement, which has "planet" in the title and says of the poems in conclusion:

> *. . . What mattered was that they should bear*
> *Some lineament or character,*
>
> *Some affluence, if only half-perceived*
> *In the poverty of their words,*
> *Of the planet of which they were part*

We are dealing with a poet of unusual maganimity, and extreme diffidence in public. He would not have cared for my suggestions as to one potential of the legacy he left behind him.

As to its effect upon the old churches, we need hardly fear much upset there. Both privately (for priest and parishioner alike) and publicly or officially, the churchmen are adapting the credo to their human purposes. With that kind of exception only, the icons and rituals and articles of faith that the believers use remain conventional and reputable; and the believers themselves are the congregation of just men who mean to be made to obey the moral commandments. They are the salt of the earth. But man cannot live by bread alone, no, nor by bread and salt. What the poets do is to restore the appetite for living when there is no unspeakable rapture in it, nor even quiet joy. Poets are responsible for the delicacies and pungencies of the dietary.

WILLIAM CARLOS WILLIAMS

*John D. Schiff, New York*

## The Yachts

contend in a sea which the land partly encloses
shielding them from the too heavy blows
of an ungoverned ocean which when it chooses

tortures the biggest hulls, the best man knows
to pit against its beating, and sinks them pitilessly.      5
Mothlike in mists, scintillant in the minute

brilliance of cloudless days, with broad bellying sails
they glide to the wind tossing green water
from their sharp prows while over them the crew crawls

ant-like, solicitously grooming them, releasing,      10
making fast as they turn, lean far over and having
caught the wind again, side by side, head for the mark.

In a well guarded arena of open water surrounded by
lesser and greater craft which, sycophant, lumbering
and flittering follow them, they appear youthful, rare      15

as the light of a happy eye, live with the grace
of all that in the mind is feckless, free and
naturally to be desired. Now the sea which holds them

is moody, lapping their glossy sides, as if feeling
for some slightest flaw but fails completely.      20
Today no race. Then the wind comes again. The yachts

move, jockeying for a start, the signal is set and they
are off. Now the waves strike at them but they are too
well made, they slip through, though they take in canvas.

Arms with hands grasping seek to clutch at the prows.      25
Bodies thrown recklessly in the way are cut aside.
It is a sea of faces about them in agony, in despair

until the horror of the race dawns staggering the mind,
the whole sea become an entanglement of watery bodies
lost to the world bearing what they cannot hold. Broken,     30

beaten, desolate, reaching from the dead to be taken up
they cry out, failing, failing! their cries rising
in waves still as the skillful yachts pass over.

## James Dickey

### WILLIAMS
### THE YACHTS

In the daily lives of all human beings—as well as in the lives of poets—occur what might be called "instant symbols": moments when a commonplace event or object is transfigured without warning, as though by common consent of observed and observer, and becomes for the perceiver both itself and its meaning. Williams' "The Yachts" is that kind of vision, that kind of poem: a scene whose symbolic possibilities burst in upon—or out of—the observer. The poem dramatizes, rather than insists on this condition, but everywhere implicit in its matter-of-fact lines is the possibility that any of us in any situation may see not only the surface but the depth, the whole *intent* of the actions and people we live among: that at any moment anything we experience is likely to become more than what we had comfortably agreed with ourselves it is content to be, and that the world is perpetually capable of concretizing and *presenting* its most powerful, disturbing and profound symbols in an instant, and in ways known only to the private beholder.

In this case, the scene is a yacht race. The poet speaks of it matter-of-factly, in a sympathetic but curt, slightly impatient tone. Williams' voice, with its American bluntness, its imagistic concreteness, its dislike of rhetorical shows, is a convincing medium through which to feel the significance—the lightning-flash of import—that hits the poem about midway in its length. The first feeling that the reader has is one of vague unrest: it may be that the yachts are too perfect in their graceful appointments and movements, more perfect than their crews. They are like life on a greeting card, a life that no real human being has ever been able to live up to, though many have tried. Or it may be that poet and reader are troubled by the social implications that yachts usually carry: money, snobbery, privilege. Even so, none of these associations is *quite* enough to account for the feeling of unrest and dissatisfaction conveyed by the first lines of the poem. After all, why should someone so matter-of-fact as *this* poet be disturbed by an event as charming, exciting and graceful as a yacht race? And then—though no one explanation can account for it—the sea over which the yachts pass without seeming to be touched by it has suddenly changed into a sea of bodies terribly and uselessly beseeching the yachts for help, or even for notice; it has become a watery hell like something in Dante. The perfection of the yachts has something profound to do with all the loss, all the death and irrevocability in the world. It is the *cost* of this kind of perfection that makes the poet recoil in horror, as the meaning the yachts have for *him*, breaks free of the first troubling but vague connotations, and "the horror of the race dawns staggering the mind." And yet it is only the poet who sees the horror,˙only he whose mind is staggered by what, now that he *sees* it, the race suggests.

"The Yachts" is a symbolic rather than an allegorical poem, for the vessels do not mean *just* social and economic privilege, the exploitation of the working classes who made the yachts for the enjoyment of those who race them, but rather serve as an image that catches and binds in a central figure all human situations that have to do with these things, with oppression, greed, sloth, with perfection that human creatures can create but cannot attain in themselves, but also—on the other side of the figure—with rejection, with the demise of the body, with death, with the abject yearning of the dead to possess a *significance* once more, even if only for the one instant of a watery hand grasping the prow of an inhumanly beautiful hull and making an impression on it, having some effect, mattering. As Randall Jarrell has finely said, "The Yachts" is "a paradigm of all the unjust beauty, the necessary and unnecessary injustice of the world." To that I would add that it is also a wonderful and terrible witness to the fact that the things we see every day, the things we think we know, are at any moment likely to explode in our faces with meaning, and thence to *exist* for us most obsessively and necessarily in that connection: in that system of meaning that only we have discovered, and that we must exorcise, deal with or learn from in ways equally private, equally haunting, equally difficult.

# D. H. LAWRENCE
## [1885–1930]

## *The Ship of Death*

### I

Now it is autumn and the falling fruit
and the long journey towards oblivion.

The apples. falling like great drops of dew
to bruise themselves an exit from themselves.

And it is time to go, to bid farewell    5
to one's own self, and find an exit
from the fallen self.

### II

Have you built your ship of death, O have you?
O build your ship of death, for you will need it.

The grim frost is at hand, when the apples will fall  10
thick, almost thundrous, on the hardened earth.

And death is on the air like a smell of ashes!
Ah! can't you smell it?
And in the bruised body, the frightened soul
finds itself shrinking, wincing from the cold   15
that blows upon it through the orifices.

### III

And can a man his own quietus make
with a bare bodkin?

With daggers, bodkins, bullets, man can make
a bruise or break of exit for his life;    20
but is that a quietus, O tell me, is it quietus?

Surely not so! for how could murder, even self-murder,
ever a quietus make?

### IV

O let us talk of quiet that we know,
that we can know, the deep and lovely quiet          25
of a strong heart at peace!
How can we this, our own quietus, make?

### V

Build then the ship of death, for you must take
the longest journey, to oblivion.

And die the death, the long and painful death          30
that lies between the old self and the new.

Already our bodies are fallen, bruised, badly bruised,
already our souls are oozing through the exit
of the cruel bruise.

Already the dark and endless ocean of the end          35
is washing in through the breaches of our wounds,
already the flood is upon us.

O build your ship of death, your little ark
and furnish it with food, with little cakes, and wine
for the dark flight down oblivion.          40

### VI

Piecemeal the body dies, and the timid soul
has her footing washed away, as the dark flood rises.

We are dying, we are dying, we are all of us dying
and nothing will stay the death-flood rising within us
and soon it will rise on the world, on the outside world.          45

We are dying, we are dying, piecemeal our bodies are dying
and our strength leaves us,
and our soul cowers naked in the dark rain over the flood,
cowering in the last branches of the tree of our life.

### VII

We are dying, we are dying, so all we can do          50
is now to be willing to die, and to build the ship
of death to carry the soul on the longest journey.

A little ship, with oars and food
and little dishes, and all accoutrements
fitting and ready for the departing soul.          55

D . H . LAWRENCE

*Painting by Jan Juta,*
*National Portrait Gallery*

*The Bettmann Archive*

Now launch the small ship, now as the body dies
and life departs, launch out, the fragile soul
in the fragile ship of courage, the ark of faith
with its store of food and little cooking pans
and change of clothes,                                    60
upon the flood's black waste
upon the waters of the end
upon the sea of death, where still we sail
darkly, for we cannot steer, and have no port.

There is no port, there is nowhere to go              65
only the deepening blackness darkening still
blacker upon the soundless, ungurgling flood
darkness at one with darkness, up and down
and sideways utterly dark, so there is no direction any more
and the little ship is there; yet she is gone.        70
She is not seen, for there is nothing to see her by.
She is gone! gone! and yet
somewhere she is there.
Nowhere.

### VIII

And everything is gone, the body is gone              75
completely under, gone, entirely gone.
The upper darkness is heavy as the lower,
between them the little ship
is gone

It is the end, it is oblivion                          80

### IX

And yet out of eternity a thread
separates itself on the blackness,
a horizontal thread
that fumes a little with pallor upon the dark.

Is it illusion? or does the pallor fume               85
a little higher?
Ah wait, wait, for there's the dawn,
the cruel dawn of coming back to life
out of oblivion

Wait, wait, the little ship                            90
drifting, beneath the deathly ashly grey
of a flood-dawn.

Wait, wait! even so, a flush of yellow
and strangely, O chilled wan soul, a flush of rose.
A flush of rose, and the whole thing starts again. 95

### x

The flood subsides, and the body, like a worn sea-shell
emerges strange and lovely.
And the little ship wings home, faltering and lapsing
on the pink flood,
and the frail soul steps out, into the house again 100
filling the heart with peace.

Swings the heart renewed with peace
even of oblivion.

Oh build your ship of death. Oh build it!
for you will need it. 105
For the voyage of oblivion awaits you.

## Edwin Honig

### LAWRENCE
### THE SHIP OF DEATH

Written during Lawrence's last illness, this poem is a kind of testament of the poet's will to believe in a final healing of the rift between body and soul, the subject of many of his works.

The idea of a ship of death comes from the ancient Egyptians; outfitting oneself for the passage across in a tomb-ship provided with clothes and dishes and food helps soften the harshness of the journey in the imagination with the familiar domestic ritual. (Egyptian mythology is also the source of Lawrence's last long fiction, *The Man Who Died*, where a resurrected Christ marries the Egyptian goddess Isis and thereby reconciles the body with the soul.) The ship of death is also the piloted vessel the dying soul must board to cross the river Styx or Acheron in order to reach the nether world. Other traditional allusions in the poem are those suggesting the Biblical apocalypse—the references to "the ark of faith," "the falling apples," "the tree of our life" and the Creation imagery of a separation of eternity: "a thread / separates itself on the blackness." Such instances are particularly reminiscent of Lawrence's *Apocalypse*, where he writes about his bleak country childhood and the religious fundamentalism of the Nottinghamshire miner families.

Throughout the poem there is the injunction to the reader "to build your ship of death," to get ready to die. This is not death in the usual sense of a simple end to things. The reader is asked to imagine death as a passage into another self, a renewal of one's being, possibly a resurrection. This view is projected in the literal terms of the imagination's perceiving what it can and what it needs to know of a surpassing peace. And this is offered, we note, without the trappings of any religious consolation; the religious references underline not the dispensation but the imagery of belief.

Lawrence is saying how it must feel, what it must look like, to get through, to pass over from one state of being to another, from the self that is dying (that tries to "find an exit

/ from the fallen self") to the death that carries "the soul on the longest journey," going nowhere, to "the end," to "oblivion." But somehow, after reaching the end, one arrives, as after a flood the ship arrives, "and the frail soul steps out, into the house again" and there finds peace.

The poem is not about the afterlife or a belief in an afterlife; it is about the process of using the will to succumb, actively, to death in order to find peace, in body and spirit both. The poem lightly conceives and fills in the outline of an imaginable place, as if to say: This is how one must will it and how one needs it to be because dying and oblivion should conform with one's knowledge of the self in life, and be something like stepping "into the house again / filling the heart with peace."

Despite the looseness of line, typical of Lawrence's poetry, "The Ship of Death" has structure, form, and narrative movement; it even has a traditional content that suggests the classical elegy with its symbolic use of the seasonal gods and the main theme of the reconciliation of human aspirations and defeats with the changes of the natural world.

The first two sections of the poem state the condition of dying; the season is autumn, apples are falling, frost and death are everywhere. It is time to die, to prepare to take the body on its journey; and the soul, which inhabits the body, seems itself to dwell in a motionless, mechanical vehicle, like a ship. The second two sections are concerned with the question, How can a man enter into death without violating the sense of life that is strongest, most natural to him? The next two sections indicate the death of the old body and the birth of a new self, and picture the passage to death as a sequence from one state to the next, the ship as a temporary body and the time of passage as a period of flood, during which the body (the old self) comfortably takes its nourishment. Then, in section seven, the narrative movement quickens, the emotional interest rises. Everyone is dying, everyone inhabits his own small ship in passage. The adjectives "small" and "little" recur; it all seems like child's play—a toy ship, distinct and perishable, going into the blackness, the darkness, the oblivion of death. Section eight would seem briefly and immediately to present the end of which all along the poet has been warning us. Section nine introduces the new self, the birth of a new world, an arrival that seems almost unreal, more like a pictorial than a verbal creation. The final section imagines the resurrected self as a worn sea shell emerging from the flood, then as a frail soul re-entering its house, with the peace of oblivion achieved. The note is not entirely positive: "Is it illusion?" the poet asks in section nine; and here, in the last section, the word "even" indicates that there is still doubt: "Swings the heart renewed with peace / even of oblivion."

As in Shelley's elegy on the death of Keats, *Adonais*, the chief use of imagery here is that of personification in associative patterns. Autumn is the dying season with fruit falling, apples like drops of dew, like selves falling from the tree of life, body-bruised, frightened, hitting the hard cold earth, looking for a way out into another form, another being. And the journey to death is a passage in a ship, itself like the body in which the soul shrinks "from the cold / that blows upon it through the orifices."

It is surprising how sharply visual Lawrence makes this sense of departing life with a few simple tropes. He also relies upon other rhetorical effects, which one does not immediately notice. Again, there is the direct appeal to the reader throughout: What have you done to come to terms with your impending death? This stark and compelling question is followed by another: How can you make your own *quietus* with a *bare bodkin*? Before we realize that this question will introduce the matter of false (unnatural) ways of dying (violent death, murder, suicide), we are stopped, beguiled by the antiquated words. We soon see that they are devices that bring us closer to the theme of the poem. *Quietus* contains associations with acquittal, quietism: that is, with a quiet that has been activated by the will. And *bodkin*, a small sharp dagger, accentuates the idea of a willful action. Then, there is the phrase "strong heart" and later, "ship of courage," "ark of faith," and "tree of our life," all similarly evocative of a way of life lived according to the traditional sources of ceremony and strong daring. The value of these thematic allusions and evocations is seen when we come to the end of the poem. For there lies the challenge: what the poet has all along imagined and presented for himself he now asks the reader to take on similarly, individually. It is as much a plea to the will as to the imagination.

> *Oh build your ship of death. Oh build it!*
> *for you will need it.*
> *For the voyage of oblivion awaits you.*

The last stanza, as such, is not anticlimactic but a summing up of the poem's triumphant theme.

# EZRA POUND

## [b. 1885]

## Hugh Selwyn Mauberley

### (LIFE AND CONTENTS)

*"Vocat æstus in umbram"*
NEMESIANUS, EC. IV.

I

#### E. P. ODE POUR L'ELECTION DE SON SEPULCHRE

For three years, out of key with his time,
He strove to resuscitate the dead art
Of poetry; to maintain "the sublime"
In the old sense. Wrong from the start—

No, hardly, but seeing he had been born          5
In a half savage country, out of date;
Bent resolutely on wringing lilies from the acorn;
Capaneus; trout for factitious bait;

Ἴδμεν γάρ τοι πάνθ', ὅσ' ἐνὶ Τροίη
Caught in the unstopped ear;                      10
Giving the rocks small lee-way
The chopped seas held him, therefore, that year.

His true Penelope was Flaubert,
He fished by obstinate isles;
Observed the elegance of Circe's hair            15
Rather than the mottoes on sun-dials.

Unaffected by "the march of events,"
He passed from men's memory in *l'an trentiesme*
*De son eage;* the case presents
No adjunct to the Muses' diadem.                  20

II

The age demanded an image
Of its accelerated grimace,

Something for the modern stage,
Not, at any rate, an Attic grace;

Not, not certainly, the obscure reveries          25
Of the inward gaze;
Better mendacities
Than the classics in paraphrase!

The "age demanded" chiefly a mould in plaster,
Made with no loss of time,                        30
A prose kinema, not, not assuredly, alabaster
Or the "sculpture" of rhyme.

### III

The tea-rose tea-gown, etc.
Supplants the mousseline of Cos,
The pianola "replaces"                            35
Sappho's barbitos.

Christ follows Dionysus,
Phallic and ambrosial
Made way for macerations;
Caliban casts out Ariel.                          40

All things are a flowing,
Sage Heracleitus says;
But a tawdry cheapness
Shall outlast our days.

Even the Christian beauty                         45
Defects—after Samothrace;
We see τὸ καλὸν
Decreed in the market place.

Faun's flesh is not to us,
Nor the saint's vision.                           50
We have the press for wafer;
Franchise for circumcision.

All men, in law, are equals.
Free of Pisistratus,
We choose a knave or an eunuch                    55
To rule over us.

O bright Apollo,
τίν' ἄνδρα, τίν' ἥρωα, τίνα θεὸν,
What god, man, or hero
Shall I place a tin wreath upon!

E Z R A   P O U N D

*From a painting by Wyndham Lewis*
*The Bettmann Archive*
*(© Tate Gallery)*

IV

These fought in any case,                                        60
and some believing,
            pro domo, in any case . . .

Some quick to arm,
some for adventure,
some from fear of weakness,                                      65
some from fear of censure,
some for love of slaughter, in imagination,
learning later . . .
some in fear, learning love of slaughter;

Died some, pro patria,                                           70
            non "dulce" non "et decor" . . .
walked eye-deep in hell
believing in old men's lies, then unbelieving
came home, home to a lie,
home to many deceits,                                            75
home to old lies and new infamy;
usury age-old and age-thick
and liars in public places.

Daring as never before, wastage as never before.
Young blood and high blood,                                      80
fair cheeks, and fine bodies;

fortitude as never before

frankness as never before,
disillusions as never told in the old days,
hysterias, trench confessions,                                   85
laughter out of dead bellies.


                            V


There died a myriad,
And of the best, among them,
For an old bitch gone in the teeth,
For a botched civilization,                                      90

Charm, smiling at the good mouth,
Quick eyes gone under earth's lid,

For two gross of broken statues,
For a few thousand battered books.

### YEUX GLAUQUES

Gladstone was still respected,                                95
When John Ruskin produced
"King's Treasuries"; Swinburne
And Rossetti still abused.

Fœtid Buchanan lifted up his voice
When that faun's head of hers                                100
Became a pastime for
Painters and adulterers.

The Burne-Jones cartons
Have preserved her eyes;
Still, at the Tate, they teach                                105
Cophetua to rhapsodize;

Thin like brook-water,
With a vacant gaze.
The English Rubaiyat was still-born
In those days.                                                110

The thin, clear gaze, the same
Still darts out faun-like from the half-ruin'd face,
Questing and passive. . . .
"Ah, poor Jenny's case" . . .

Bewildered that a world                                       115
Shows no surprise
At her last maquero's
Adulteries.


### "SIENA MI FE'; DISFECEMI MAREMMA"

Among the pickled fœtuses and bottled bones,
Engaged in perfecting the catalogue,                          120
I found the last scion of the
Senatorial families of Strasbourg, Monsieur Verog.

For two hours he talked of Gallifet;
Of Dowson; of the Rhymers' Club;
Told me how Johnson (Lionel) died                             125
By falling from a high stool in a pub . . .

But showed no trace of alcohol
At the autopsy, privately performed—

Tissue preserved—the pure mind
Arose toward Newman as the whiskey warmed.                    130

Dowson found harlots cheaper than hotels;
Headlam for uplift; Image impartially imbued
With raptures for Bacchus, Terpsichore and the Church.
So spoke the author of "The Dorian Mood,"

M. Verog, out of step with the decade,                       135
Detached from his contemporaries,
Neglected by the young,
Because of these reveries.


### BRENNBAUM


The sky-like limpid eyes,
The circular infant's face,                                  140
The stiffness from spats to collar
Never relaxing into grace;

The heavy memories of Horeb, Sinai and the forty years,
Showed only when the daylight fell
Level across the face                                        145
Of Brennbaum "The Impeccable."


### MR. NIXON


In the cream gilded cabin of his steam yacht
Mr. Nixon advised me kindly, to advance with fewer
Dangers of delay. "Consider
          Carefully the reviewer.                            150

"I was as poor as you are;
When I began I got, of course,
Advance on royalties, fifty at first," said Mr. Nixon,
"Follow me, and take a column,
Even if you have to work free.                               155

"Butter reviewers. From fifty to three hundred
I rose in eighteen months;
The hardest nut I had to crack
Was Dr. Dundas.

"I never mentioned a man but with the view                   160
Of selling my own works.

The tip's a good one, as for literature
It gives no man a sinecure.

"And no one knows, at sight, a masterpiece.
And give up verse, my boy,                                    165
There's nothing in it."

.   .   .   .   .   .   .   .   .   .

Likewise a friend of Bloughram's once advised me:
Don't kick against the pricks,
Accept opinion. The "Nineties" tried your game
And died, there's nothing in it.                              170

X

Beneath the sagging roof
The stylist has taken shelter,
Unpaid, uncelebrated,
At last from the world's welter

Nature receives him;                                          175
With a placid and uneducated mistress
He exercises his talents
And the soil meets his distress.

The haven from sophistications and contentions
Leaks through its thatch;                                     180
He offers succulent cooking;
The door has a creaking latch.

XI

"Conservatrix of Milésien"
Habits of mind and feeling,
Possibly. But in Ealing                                       185
With the most bank-clerky of Englishmen?

No, "Milésien" is an exaggeration.
No instinct has survived in her
Older than those her grandmother
Told her would fit her station.                               190

XII

"Daphne with her thighs in bark
Stretches toward me her leafy hands,"—
Subjectively. In the stuffed-satin drawing-room
I await The Lady Valentine's commands,

Knowing my coat has never been                                195
Of precisely the fashion

To stimulate, in her,
A durable passion;

Doubtful, somewhat, of the value
Of well-gowned approbation                                    200
Of literary effort,
But never of The Lady Valentine's vocation:

Poetry, her border of ideas,
The edge, uncertain, but a means of blending
With other strata                                             205
Where the lower and higher have ending;

A hook to catch the Lady Jane's attention,
A modulation toward the theatre,
Also, in the case of revolution,
A possible friend and comforter.                              210

. . . . . . . . . .

Conduct, on the other hand, the soul
"Which the highest cultures have nourished"
To Fleet St. where
Dr. Johnson flourished;

Beside this thoroughfare                                      215
The sale of half-hose has
Long since superseded the cultivation
Of Pierian roses.

ENVOI
1919

*Go, dumb-born book,*
*Tell her that sang me once that song of Lawes:*             220
*Hadst thou but song*
*As thou hast subjects known,*
*Then were there cause in thee that should condone*
*Even my faults that heavy upon me lie,*
*And build her glories their longevity.*                     225

*Tell her that sheds*
*Such treasure in the air,*
*Recking naught else but that her graces give*
*Life to the moment,*
*I would bid them live*                                      230
*As roses might, in magic amber laid,*
*Red overwrought with orange and all made*
*One substance and one colour*
*Braving time.*

*Tell her that goes* 235
*With song upon her lips*
*But sings not out the song, nor knows*
*The maker of it, some other mouth,*
*May be as fair as hers,*
*Might, in new ages, gain her worshippers,* 240
*When our two dusts with Waller's shall be laid,*
*Siftings on siftings in oblivion,*
*Till change hath broken down*
*All things save Beauty alone.*

## MAUBERLEY

### 1920

*"Vacuos exercet aera morsus."*

### I

| | |
|---|---|
| Turned from the "eau-forte | Firmness, |
| Par Jaquemart" | Not the full smile,   10 |
| To the strait head | His art, but an art |
| Of Messalina: | In profile; |
| | |
| "His true Penelope   5 | Colourless |
| Was Flaubert," | Pier Francesca, |
| And his tool | Pisanello lacking the skill   15 |
| The engraver's. | To forge Achaia. |

### II

*"Qu'est ce qu'ils savent de l'amour, et qu'est ce qu'ils peuvent*
*comprendre?*
    *S'ils ne comprennent pas la poésie, s'ils ne sentent pas la*
*musique, qu'est ce qu'ils peuvent comprendre de cette passion*
*en comparaison avec laquelle la rose est grossière et le parfum*
*des violettes un tonnerre?"*     CAID ALI

For three years, diabolus in the scale,
He drank ambrosia,
All passes, ANANGKE prevails,
Came end, at last, to that Arcadia.   20

He had moved amid her phantasmagoria,
Amid her galaxies,
NUKTIS 'AGALMA

.  .  .  .  .  .  .  .  .

Drifted . . . drifted precipitate,
Asking time to be ride of . . .   25

Of his bewilderment; to designate
His new found orchid. . . .

To be certain . . . certain . . .
(Amid ærial flowers) . . . time for arrangements—
Drifted on
To the final estrangement;                          30

Unable in the supervening blankness
To sift TO AGATHON from the chaff
Until he found his sieve . . .
Ultimately, his seismograph:

—Given that is his "fundamental passion,"        35
This urge to convey the relation
Of eye-lid and cheek-bone
By verbal manifestations;

To present the series
Of curious heads in medallion—                     40

He had passed, inconscient, full gaze,
The wide-banded irides
And botticellian sprays implied
In their diastasis;

Which anæthesis, noted a year late,               45
And weighed, revealed his great affect,
(Orchid), mandate
Of Eros, a retrospect.

                .    .    .

Mouths biting empty air,
The still stone dogs,                               50
Caught in metamorphosis, were
Left him as epilogues.


                "THE AGE DEMANDED"
                  Vide Poem II.


For this agility chance found
Him of all men, unfit
As the red-beaked steeds of                         55
The Cytheræan for a chain bit.

The glow of porcelain
Brought no reforming sense
To his perception
Of the social inconsequence.                        60

Thus, if her colour
Came against his gaze,
Tempered as if
It were through a perfect glaze

He made no immediate application 65
Of this to relation of the state
To the individual, the month was more temperate
Because this beauty had been.

        The coral isle, the lion-colored sand
        Burst in upon the porcelain revery: 70
        Impetuous troubling
        Of his imagery.

Mildness, amid the neo-Nietzschean clatter,
His sense of graduations,
Quite out of place amid 75
Resistance to current exacerbations,

Invitation, mere invitation to perceptivity
Gradually led him to the isolation
Which these presents place
Under a more tolerant, perhaps, examination. 80

By constant elimination
The manifest universe
Yielded an armour
Against utter consternation,

A Minoan undulation, 85
Seen, we admit, amid ambrosial circumstances
Strengthened him against
The discouraging doctrine of chances,

And his desire for survival,
Faint in the most strenuous moods, 90
Became an Olympian *apathein*
In the presence of selected perceptions.

A pale gold, in the aforesaid pattern,
The unexpected palms
Destroying, certainly, the artist's urge, 95
Left him delighted with the imaginary
Audition of the phantasmal sea-surge,

Incapable of the least utterance or composition,
Emendation, conservation of the "better tradition,"
Refinement of medium, elimination of superfluities, 100
August attraction or concentration.

Nothing, in brief, but maudlin confession,
Irresponse to human aggression,
Amid the precipitation, down-float
Of insubstantial manna,                                    105
Lifting the faint susurrus
Of his subjective hosannah.

Ultimate affronts to
Human redundancies;

Non-esteem of self-styled "his betters"                    110
Leading, as he well knew,
To his final
Exclusion from the world of letters.


                            IV

Scattered Moluccas                  A consciousness disjunct,
Not knowing, day to day,  115       Being but this overblotted
The first day's end, in the         Series
    next noon;                      Of intermittences;
The placid water
Unbroken by the Simoon;             Coracle of Pacific voy-
                                        ages,                  130
Thick foliage                       The unforecasted beach;
Placid beneath warm suns,  120      Then on an oar
Tawn fore-shores                    Read this:
Washed in the cobalt of
    oblivions;                      "I was
                                    And I no more exist;      135
Or through dawn-mist                Here drifted
The grey and rose                   An hedonist."
Of the juridical
Flamingoes;                   125


                         MEDALLION


Luini in porcelain!
The grand piano
Utters a profane                                           140
Protest with her clear soprano.

The sleek head emerges
From the gold-yellow frock
As Anadyomene in the opening
Pages of Reinach.                                          145

Honey-red, closing the face-oval,
A basket-work of braids which seem as if they were
Spun in King Minos' hall
From metal, or intractable amber;

The face-oval beneath the glaze,                    150
Bright in its suave bounding-line, as,
Beneath half-watt rays,
The eyes turn topaz.

## William Van O'Connor

### POUND
### HUGH SELWYN MAUBERLEY

*Hugh Selwyn Mauberley* is a work of great virtuosity, the sort of virtuosity the later Pound would not achieve very often. There would be moments of great lyric beauty, but not of intellectual control. Yet as the years go by *Hugh Selwyn Mauberley* seems more and more a "period piece." Wallace Stevens' "Sunday Morning" and William Butler Yeats's "Byzantium" transcend their moments of creation. Pound's *Mauberley* does not. And the reason for this, quite probably, is that it is too personal, too autobiographical, too lacking in what Matthew Arnold called "disinterestedness." Even so, one can admire its wit and its metrical skill. For this, the poem still merits our attention as a masterpiece of its type. One does not have to admire its arcana, its sometimes impenetrable obscurity in order to admire the poem.

John Keats referred to Wordsworth's poetry as an example of the "egotistical sublime." Pound's poetry might be described as egotistical perverse. He reaches in all directions for quotations and allusions. There is a discreteness in them that will elude most readers. For example, *Mauberley* contains this quotation:

> *"Daphne with her thighs in bark*
> *Stretches toward me her leafy hands,"—*
> *Subjectively*

John Espey, the most careful student of the poem, has shown the lines come from Theophile Gautier's "Le Chateau du Souvenir":

> *Daphné, les banches dans l'écorce*
> *Etend toujours ses doigts touffus . . .*

In Gautier's poem Daphne is part of the décor of a salon. This is the use Pound makes of her:

> *"Daphne with her thighs in bark*
> *Stretches toward me her leafy hands,"—*

> *Subjectively. In the stuffed-satin drawing-room*
> *I await The Lady Valentine's commands*

Is the quotation simply afloat in Pound's mind, or is it suggested by the décor of the room *he* is in? The reader cannot tell.

Another such quotation comes at the beginning of the *Mauberley* section:

> *Turned from the "eau-forte*
> *Par Jaquemart"*
> *To the strait head*
> *Of Messalina:*

Espey says this can be understood if "one has at hand the 1884 edition of *Emaux et Camées* published by Charpentier, which has a title page:

Theophile Gautier

---

## EMAUX
## ET
## CAMÉES
Édition Définitive
## AVEC UNE EAU-FORTE PAR J. JACQUEMART

"Facing this," he continues, "and enclosed in a medallionlike border, is the etching itself, showing Gautier in three-quarter face, a portrait that looks not altogether unlike a weightier and more bravely bearded version of Pound's photograph by Alvin Langdon Coburn that serves as frontispiece to Lustra. 'Jaquemart' is clearly a casual error that has ridden unnoticed through several editions, like 'Bloughram' of which Pound wrote to [Kimon] Friar, 'reference to Browning's bishop, allegoric, thus requiring correction to 'Blougram' and eliminating all ingenious speculation on the possibility of a Joycean portmanteau cross of Blougram and Brougham."

Pound's allusions are excessively private. It is most unlikely that a reader would have the 1884 edition of *Emaux et Camées* at hand. One might also ask why Pound did not correct the name of Browning's bishop when he read galley or page proofs. Confusion is added to confusion.

Pound once wrote a review of a book called *The Dorian Mood*. It can hardly be called a book known to many readers, not even to those who have read the writers of the nineties. Yet Pound does not hesitate to devote a section of *Mauberley* to the author of *The Dorian Mood*. The nineties, including Whistler especially, were important in Pound's development as a poet—but private figures should not remain private. Yeats used people he knew, but he managed to universalize them; that is the only way they become viable for the reader.

There are memorable lines, such as

> *The age demanded an image*
> *Of its accelerated grimace*

or

> *There died a myriad,*
> *And of the best, among them,*
> *For an old bitch gone in the teeth,*
> *For a botched civilization*

Generally, however, the poem remains too private, too inward turning to be available to a reader unless he has the innumerable glosses provided by Espey and others.

In an essay on modern literature, William York Tindall writes, "Looking out of his window, Baudelaire was filled with the immense nausea of billboards. The rest follows from this." Mr. Tindall is referring to the alienation of modern writers. James Joyce fled from Ireland to the continent and exile; Ezra Pound and many of his compatriots fled from the United States. Alienation wasn't only geographical—it was a state of mind that found anything bourgeois or Philistine insufferable. Pound's *Hugh Selwyn Mauberley* is concerned with the alienated poet, himself and others like him.

It is also concerned with an active, gifted poet—Pound himself—and a less talented, passive poet, Mauberley. In the first half Pound writes about himself. Hugh Selwyn Mauberley, a contemporary esthete, appears only in the latter half of the poem. He is presented in contrast to Pound himself.

In part one, Pound, in an ironic manner, rehearses his own career. In part two he treats the "tawdry cheapness" of postwar England. In three, he assigns reasons for the cheapness: commercialization, a crass pursuit of money, a vulgar press. Such a society was willing to offer up its young men in the First World War. In part five, Pound traces recent esthetic history, the excesses of the pre-Raphaelites, the nineties, which caused writers to collapse or become tawdry themselves. Then he gives two portraits: Brennbaum gives up his heritage in order to be accepted, and Mr. Nixon gives up serious writing for commercial success. In part ten, the dedicated stylist lives in a run-down country cottage (Pound and Yeats each lived in such a cottage). In eleven, the educated woman inherits state traditions, which she doesn't even understand. In part twelve, Pound says he is unacceptable to the literary world of London. In *"Envoi"* he "sends" his book to a woman, in verses that capture some of the grace of Renaissance English love poems.

Pound's autobiography over, Hugh Selwyn Mauberley enters. Each of "his" poems develops in contrast to the poems in "E.P. Ode pour l'élection de son sépulchre." Mauberley is a poet *manqué*. In his part two, he speculates about a life of passion. In the part beginning, "Scattered Moluccas," his career is seen as awash. "Medallion" is his legacy, but it lacks the beauty of *"Envoi."*

John Espey points out that E. P. remains active—he leaves London, seeking new lands to investigate and conquer. Mauberley remains in London, and his career comes to very little.

Pound's poem is very "literary." There are references to and echoes from Bion, Theophile Gautier, Jules Laforgue, Henry James, Lionel Johnson, Ernest Dowson, and Remy de Gourmont. And there are, of course, many allusions to Greece and Rome. It is a poem that anticipates Pound's later work, the *Cantos,* and his view of culture.

Pound would come to see European culture as Ovidian nymphs, Ulysses's daring, memories of many passionate men now shades, literary tags, and economic theories. Pound's "culture" is not culture in the sense an historian or an anthropologist would use the term.

Ezra Pound, poet, confronts society—he would come to feel that society had betrayed him. *Hugh Selwyn Mauberley,* in this sense, is an augury of the fascinating and bitter later life of Ezra Pound. But, at thirty-five, when he finished the poem, neither he nor anyone else could say that this was one of the "meanings" of *Hugh Selwyn Mauberley.* Only in retrospect can we see that it was.

EDWIN MUIR

*The Estate of Oscar Williams*

# EDWIN MUIR

[1887–1959]

## *The Transfiguration*

So from the ground we felt that virtue branch
Through all our veins till we were whole, our wrists
As fresh and pure as water from a well,
Our hands made new to handle holy things,
The source of all our seeing rinsed and cleansed          5
Till earth and light and water entering there
Gave back to us the clear unfallen world.
We would have thrown our clothes away for lightness,
But that even they, though sour and travel stained,
Seemed, like our flesh, made of immortal substance,          10
And the soiled flax and wool lay light upon us
Like friendly wonders, flower and flock entwined
As in a morning field. Was it a vision?
Or did we see that day the unseeable
One glory of the everlasting world          15
Perpetually at work, though never seen
Since Eden locked the gate that's everywhere
And nowhere? Was the change in us alone,
And the enormous earth still left forlorn,
An exile or a prisoner? Yet the world          20
We saw that day made this unreal, for all
Was in its place. The painted animals
Assembled there in gentle congregations,
Or sought apart their leafy oratories,
Or walked in peace, the wild and tame together,          25
As if, also for them, the day had come.
The shepherds' hovels shone, for underneath
The soot we saw the stone clean at the heart
As on the starting-day. The refuse heaps
Were grained with that fine dust that made the world;          30
For he had said, "To the pure all things are pure."
And when we went into the town, he with us,
The lurkers under doorways, murderers,
With rags tied round their feet for silence, came

Out of themselves to us and were with us,                                35
And those who hide within the labyrinth
Of their own loneliness and greatness came,
And those entangled in their own devices,
The silent and the garrulous liars, all
Stepped out of their own dungeons and were free.            40
Reality or vision, this we have seen.
If it had lasted but another moment
It might have held for ever! But the world
Rolled back into its place, and we are here,
And all that radiant kingdom lies forlorn,                          45
As if it had never stirred; no human voice
Is heard among its meadows, but it speaks
To itself alone, alone it flowers and shines
And blossoms for itself while time runs on.

But he will come again, it's said, though not                      50
Unwanted and unsummoned; for all things,
Beasts of the field, and woods, and rocks, and seas,
And all mankind from end to end of the earth
Will call him with one voice. In our own time,
Some say, or at a time when time is ripe.                          55
Then he will come, Christ the uncrucified,
Christ the discrucified, his death undone,
His agony unmade, his cross dismantled—
Glad to be so—and the tormented wood
Will cure its hurt and grow into a tree                               60
In a green springing corner of young Eden,
And Judas damned take his long journey backward
From darkness into light and be a child
Beside his mother's knee, and the betrayal
Be quite undone and never more be done.                          65

*Anne Ridler*

---

## MUIR

### THE TRANSFIGURATION

"Our minds are possessed by three mysteries," Edwin Muir
wrote in his autobiography: "where we came from, where
we are going, and, since we are not alone, but members of a
countless family, how we should live with one another"; and
he affirmed that all three questions were involved in the
dream he had just been describing. A dream, yes, but Muir's
dreams are not the fragments of stuff that most of us retain
when we awake from sleep, but myth-making visions. Years
later, he used this dream as the basis of "The Transfiguration," and it seems a good choice to represent him in this
anthology: although it is not perfect in form and not so
entirely successful as some of his shorter poems, it is, I think,
the one among his best poems that is most inclusive of his
major themes.

To enrich our understanding, other poems are relevant to
this one—notably "The Animals," "The Fall," and "The
Dreamt-of Place"—but there is space here only to examine
the autobiographical passage. One would expect to discover
in a poet's life some of the raw material of his poetry, but
Muir's *Autobiography* gives us the material, not raw, but
transmuted into another kind of art. The dreams, or visions,
through which he discerned the meaning of life (the Fable, as
he called it, of his own life) did indeed sometimes find a
more perfect expression in prose—*Ballad of the Soul*, for
instance, is inferior to the prose "trance"—and when dream is
transmuted directly into poetry, the meaning is sometimes
obscure. In "The Transfiguration," the shaping effort of his
conscious mind has given the poem an ending and implied an
interpretation that does not exist in the prose version; no
obscurities remain, but also, something has been left out.

The dream begins thus:

A man was standing by my bedside. He was wearing a
long robe, which fell about him in motionless folds,
while he stood like a column. The light that filled the

room came from his hair, which rose straight up from
his head, burning, like a motionless brazier.

Muir follows him through the town, and they are joined
by,

> a dark, shabby man with a dagger in his hand . . .
> wearing rags bound round his feet, so that he walked
> quite soundlessly. . . . I took him to be a robber or a
> murderer and was afraid. But as he came nearer I saw
> that his eyes, which were fixed immovably on the figure
> beside me, were filled with a profound, violent adora-
> tion such as I had never seen in human eyes before.

A crowd then follows them,

> into a great plain dotted with little conical hills a little
> higher than a man's head. All over the plain animals
> were standing or sitting on their haunches on these little
> hills; lions, tigers, bulls, deer, elephants, were there . . .
> each was separate and alone, and each slowly lifted
> its head upward as if in prayer. . . . The elephant
> wreathed its trunk upward, and there was something
> pathetic and absurd in that indirect act of adoration.
> But the other animals raised their heads with the in-
> evitability of the sun's rising, as if they knew, like the
> sun, that a new day was about to begin, and were giving
> the signal for its coming. Then I saw a little dog busily
> running about with his nose tied to the ground, as if he
> did not know that the animals had been redeemed. He
> was a friendly little dog, officiously going about his
> business, and it seemed to me that he too had a place in
> this day, and that his oblivious concern with the earth
> was also a sort of worship.

Muir was not unfaithful to his dream in expressing it in terms
of a Christian myth, for he could trace the origin of the
figure appearing at his bedside to his childish image of Christ,
formed as he listened to the talk of his parents. But in the
poem the little hills, derived from the Orkney landscape of
his childhood, have disappeared; the animals are described
only collectively, and we miss the appealing figure of the
little dog—though he does have a share, perhaps, in the
mysterious brown animal of "The Combat," another poem in
the same volume—an image of pathetic, invincible and earth-
bound humanity.

The most important difference, however, is that there is no

description in the poem of Christ, who appeared in the dream with hair flaming upward like a figure from a Blake engraving. I can think of more than one reason for this. The poem begins at some moment after the sublime experience; moreover, it is concerned with metaphysics and the doubts of the thinking mind, where the dream was descriptive and direct. (The one visual detail taken over into the poem is that of the murderers, "with rags tied round their feet for silence.") But there are no doubts in the prophecy of the final coming, and here Muir rises to the height of his powers. Here the conscious mind has completed the vision (for Muir could not remember how his dream ended), and as earlier the horror of the bone factory, nightmare of Muir's early manhood, is to be redeemed into "that fine dust that made the world," so the final lines reach down to the depths of the Inferno and draw back Judas, symbol of ultimate treachery, into innocence again. The strength of these lines derives partly from a play on words, which is rare in Muir, with the double meanings of the words "undone" and "unmade," and the contrasted meanings of "uncrucified" and "discrucified."

The millennium as Muir imagined it has two attributes that are found in no one else's vision, so far as I know. First, Christ is to return only when earth calls him—not mankind only, but the whole universe. And second, his coming is to undo all hurts from the beginning of the world: not to redeem them merely, not to wipe out the memory of them as in Dante's Purgatorial Lethe, but to make them as though they had never been. I shall not attempt to discuss these ideas theologically, but both seem to me very characteristic of the gentle, compassionate but firmly independent nature of Muir. The Redeemer will not come unasked; and the earth he comes to has no need to go outside its own perfection. Muir's picture of the good life was not "a heaven on earth" but "a modest, peaceable life in this world," where the right relation between earth and heaven "gives proportion and meaning to the whole" (*The Story and the Fable,* 1st version of the *Autobiography,* p. 245).

It has often been pointed out that Muir was late to find himself as a poet—and he himself has explained why this was so, and has described the struggles by which he gained command of his medium. A comparison with the composer Ralph Vaughan Williams occurs to me, for with both men the struggles to attain what others more brilliantly gifted could reach with ease, gave their utterance its special sincerity and nobility. Muir said that he was not aware of "influences," but echoes of Eliot, Yeats, Wordsworth and Coleridge are to be heard in his poems—and the influence of *The Ancient Mariner* is deep and fruitful, in for instance "The Voyage." He is, as Helen Gardner has noticed in the 1960 W.D. Thomas Memorial Lecture, more skilful in the four-beat than in the five-beat line; and where he attempts a sequence of varied rhythms, as in "The Journey Back," the parts are unequally successful, though the conception is splendid, and some consider this his finest poem. One must admit that his blank verse is sometimes too level in tone, and monotonous in rhythm—as indeed is true of lines 14–18 of "The Transfiguration." But farther on in the poem, how admirably the inversion of stress is managed to bring out the sense:

> *And those entangled in their own devices,*
> *The silent and the garrulous liars, all*
> *Stepped out of their dungeons and were free*

Muir has a wonderful image in one of his last poems (*Collected Poems*, p. 284), which suggests to me the making-place of his own poetry:

> *About the well of life where we are made*
> *Spirits of earth and heaven together lie.*
> *They do not turn their bright heads at our coming,*
> *So deep their dream of pure commingled being . . .*

It is because his own gaze is bent so steadfastly and selflessly on the source of truth that his poetry has its lasting power to move us; intent on his vision, he could not always find adequate means to convey it, but never falsified: he speaks of what is eternal in man, and awakens in us the power to hear.

# MARIANNE MOORE
## [*b.* 1887]

## *Spenser's Ireland*

has not altered;—
   a place as kind as it is green,
   the greenest place I've never seen.
Every name is a tune.
Denunciations do not affect            5
     the culprit; nor blows, but it
is torture to him to not be spoken to.
They're natural—
     the coat, like Venus'
mantle lined with stars,            10
buttòned close at the neck—the sleeves new from disuse.

If in Ireland
   they play the harp backward at need,
   and gather at midday the seed
of the fern, eluding            15
their "giants all covered with iron," might
     there be fern seed for unlearn-
ing obduracy and for reinstating
the enchàntment?
     Hindered characters          20
seldom have mothers
in Irish stories, but they all have grandmothers.

It was Irish;
   a match not a marriage was made
   when my great great grandmother'd said     25
with native genius for
disunion, "although your suitor be
     perfection, one objection
is enough; he is not
Irish." Outwitting           30
     the fairies, befriending the furies,
whoever again
and again says, "I'll never give in," never sees

that you're not free
   until you've been made captive by                     35
   supreme belief—credulity
you say? When large dainty
fingers tremblingly divide the wings
   of the fly for mid-July
with a needle and wrap it with peacock-tail,          40
or tie wool and
         buzzard's wing, their pride,
like the enchanter's
is in care, not madness. Concurring hands divide

flax for damask                                        45
   that when bleached by Irish weather
   has the silvered chamois-leather
water-tightness of a
skin. Twisted torcs and gold new-moon-shaped
         lunulae aren't jewelry                        50
like the purple-coral fuchsia-tree's. If Eire—
the guillemot
         so neat and the hen
of the heath and the
linnet spinet-sweet—bespeak relentlessness? Then      55

they are to me
   like enchanted Earl Gerald who
   changed himself into a stag, to
a great green-eyed cat of
the mountain. Discommodity makes                       60
         them invisible; they've dis-
appeared. The Irish say your trouble is their
trouble and your
         joy their joy? I wish
I could believe it;                                    65
I am troubled, I'm dissatisfied, I'm Irish.

MARIANNE MOORE

*Henry Grossman*

*Josephine Miles*

---

MOORE

SPENSER'S IRELAND

The six stanzas of "Spenser's Ireland," with indented lines and with last lines long, look and sound airy yet solid in uniform repetition as if they would shape up for us a characterization of Ireland by touching lightly upon its traits and beliefs. And so they do. First, Ireland is natural, kind, and green; second and third, it is old and stubborn; fourth, it is skillful and full of care; fifth, if relentless, still, sixth, enchanted.

The poem begins, as do many of Marianne Moore's, with a straightforward statement about the subject: so direct as to prepare for the superlatives and negatives which follow. But then, *if*, and a question. Then instances, and another question. Finally, a doubt, and a wish. And in the last lines a new subject, *I*, which brings us to "I'm Irish" from "Spenser's Ireland," which has not altered.

So the reader may feel the sense of both lyrical objectivity and personal portrait, as well as some general truth about this Irish character. But do not the traits seem to contrast rather than to confirm? The stanzas are clear-cut, the tone is cool and steady, but the epithets are at odds. The enchantment is set against obduracy; mothers against grandmothers; fairies against furies; freedom against captivity; care against madness; relentlessly neat hen and linnet against disappearing stag and cat; dissatisfaction against belief. In the patterns of the verse the differences are interwoven by recurring threads, as, for example, by the repeated syllables of *di* and *dis: new from disuse; with native genius for disunion; divide the wings; divide the flax; discommodity; they've disappeared; I'm dissatisfied.* This is a character of division and change.

As in the sense and statement, so also in the sound, there is interweaving. In each stanza the first indented couplet lines are rhymed crisply and decisively, *green, seen;* but the next are hidden in internal rhyme, *culprit, it;* and the third indented rhyme *Venus* waits till the end of the extra long last line for its echo *disuse.* The regularities are put to difficulties. The reader's inner ear hears no easy beat, but an underlying sort of measure which he finally may recognize as a count of syllables. In each stanza, first a four syllable line, then eight and eight, then six, nine, seven, eleven, four, then five and five, and the long twelve. But, especially in the internally rhyming line, there are variations on these norms. And seldom does natural stress serve to support artistic stress, but rather the pattern is so steadily unstressed it almost disappears, like the stag and cat.

Throughout "Spenser's Ireland" we have therefore the delight of a mood, a subject, a sound, a structure mutually reinforcing, yet not resolving the difficulties of idea. The poem is not wholly accommodating. It both considers and uses superlative enchantment, but keeps the reader poised on its wish to believe.

If, so poised, the reader keeps asking more *whys*—why the pull and tug of feeling, of character, of measure, and of rhyme—and tries to follow out some of the strands of this meaning which has the silvered chamois-leather water-tight-ness of a skin, he may find guidance from a number of relevant sources: from other works by Marianne Moore, in which she comes out more explicitly for one side or another; from views of her by others; from her own specific clues and comments in her notes. Her poem, "To a Snail," is particularly helpful because it makes clear her principle of implicit-ness, of embodiment.

> If *"compression is the first grace of style,"*
> *you have it. Contractility is a virtue*
> *as modesty is a virtue.*
> *It is not the acquisition of any one thing*
> *that is able to adorn,*
> *or the incidental quality that occurs*
> *as a concomitant of something well said,*
> *that we value in style,*
> *but the principle that is hid:*

We have already seen that the principle of the metrics, of line length and stanza pattern, is hidden—in syllable count and in unstressed rhyme—and now we may see from poem to poem how ideas are hidden deep and how Miss Moore praises the look beneath the surface. In "He Digesteth Harde Yron," she says,

> *The power of the visible*
> *is the invisible;*

and in "Melancthon,"

*Will*
*depth be depth, thick skin be thick, to one who can see*
  *no*
*beautiful element of unreason under it?*

At the same time, she praises the obduracy of objects, the thickness of skin, the unaccommodation of a mule, the hindering of a Hercules. Accommodation and satisfaction are not all-important, as "Elephants" and "What are Years?" suggest; the mind in "The Mind is an Enchanting Thing" asserts its "conscientious inconsistency," and "In Distrust of Merits" asks,

*or am I what*
*I can't believe in?*

Though she has translated La Fontaine, Miss Moore's fables are not incidents like his. Rather, like objects, her animals and countries are to be scrutinized for their very complexity. Elephants, ostriches, wood-weasels, England, Ireland, Virginia, are objects of intense discernment through which we learn what we care about and that human nature "could not be pent within the bonds of the actual," as an earlier translator of the fables of La Fontaine once said.

William Carlos Williams too suggests about Miss Moore's poetry that: "in looking at some apparently small object one feels the swirl of great events." Even the manner of the person objectifies her feeling, as Mr. Williams describes her: "She would laugh with a gesture of withdrawal after making some able assertion, as if you yourself had said it and she were agreeing with you."

In the careful notes to "Spenser's Ireland," its principle is further hid, the principle of inner dialogue in the tradition of the owl and the nightingale and Yeats's self and soul. How so? Among the technical references to the *National Geographic Magazine*, Padraic Colum, and Maria Edgeworth, is one to Edmund Spenser, concerning the Irish mantle, like the cloak that Marianne Moore herself has worn. And this may remind us, though she does not, that Spenser's own *View of the Present State of Ireland*, his report to the English court in 1594, is put in the form of a dialogue between Eudoxus the civilizer and Irenius the wild and natural Irishman. In Miss Moore's terms, we hear Irenius argue, "Sure yt is yet a most bewtifull and sweete Countrie as any is under heaven," though there is "Morris of the ferne or weste wylde places . . . gatheringe unto him all the relicks of the discontented

Irishe" . . . and though "the Commodytie doth not counter-
vaile the discommoditie. . . ."

In the list of the families of Ireland are the Moores, and for
them the commodity does not countervail the discommodity.
This is the pull and tug to which there is no resolution, either
in sound or in sense. The long, unresolving, last alexandrine
line of the Spenserian stanza and of Miss Moore's stanza, the
Renaissance connoisseurship and protestantism of Spenser,
which she would admire to hark back to, and the enchanted
and mutable country of the last book of the *Faerie Queene*,
in which nature is finally victorious over mutability but
many of the beauties are mutabilities—all these provide the
tradition in support of the poem.

Because the principle that is hidden is the principle of
embodiment, of underemphasis, of qualification rather than
of statement or action, the reader of a poem by Marianne
Moore may read both over and under, both for less than it
says and for more. She allows, even encourages, conflicts of
imagination and reality, of art and artifice, of doubt and
belief. She allows the *you* of the poem to call belief credulity
and the hen relentless, yet allows your joy and trouble
almost to become hers. "Spenser's Ireland" is partly Spenser's,
wholly Moore's, and doubly Irish.

T . S . ELIOT

*The Bettmann Archive*

# T. S. ELIOT

[1888–1965]

## The Waste Land

### 1922

'Nam Sibyllam quidem Cumis ego ipse oculis meis vidi in ampulla pendere, et cum illi pueri dicerent: Σίβυλλα τί Θέλεις; respondebat illa: ἀποθανεῖν Θέλω.'

For Ezra Pound
*il miglior fabbro.*

### I. THE BURIAL OF THE DEAD

April is the cruellest month, breeding
Lilacs out of the dead land, mixing
Memory and desire, stirring
Dull roots with spring rain.
Winter kept us warm, covering                                    5
Earth in forgetful snow, feeding
A little life with dried tubers.
Summer surprised us, coming over the Starnbergersee
With a shower of rain; we stopped in the colonnade,
And went on in sunlight, into the Hofgarten,                    10
And drank coffee, and talked for an hour.
Bin gar keine Russin, stamm' aus Litauen, echt deutsch.
And when we were children, staying at the archduke's,
My cousin's, he took me out on a sled,
And I was frightened. He said, Marie,                           15
Marie, hold on tight. And down we went.
In the mountains, there you feel free.
I read, much of the night, and go south in the winter.

What are the roots that clutch, what branches grow
Out of this stony rubbish? Son of man,                          20
You cannot say, or guess, for you know only
A heap of broken images, where the sun beats,
And the dead tree gives no shelter, the cricket no relief,
And the dry stone no sound of water. Only
There is shadow under this red rock                             25

(Come in under the shadow of this red rock),
And I will show you something different from either
Your shadow at morning striding behind you
Or your shadow at evening rising to meet you;
I will show you fear in a handful of dust.　　　　　　30

> *Frisch weht der Wind*
> *Der Heimat zu*
> *Mein Irisch Kind,*
> *Wo weilest du?*

'You gave me hyacinths first a year ago;　　　　　　35
'They called me the hyacinth girl.'
—Yet when we came back, late, from the Hyacinth garden,
Your arms full, and your hair wet, I could not
Speak, and my eyes failed, I was neither
Living nor dead, and I knew nothing,　　　　　　40
Looking into the heart of light, the silence.
*Oed' und leer das Meer.*

Madame Sosostris, famous clairvoyante,
Had a bad cold, nevertheless
Is known to be the wisest woman in Europe,　　　　　　45
With a wicked pack of cards. Here, said she,
Is your card, the drowned Phoenician Sailor,
(Those are pearls that were his eyes. Look!)
Here is Belladonna, the Lady of the Rocks,
The lady of situations.　　　　　　50
Here is the man with three staves, and here the Wheel
And here is the one-eyed merchant, and this card,
Which is blank, is something he carries on his back,
Which I am forbidden to see. I do not find
The Hanged Man. Fear death by water.　　　　　　55
I see crowds of people, walking round in a ring.
Thank you. If you see dear Equitone,
Tell her I bring the horoscope myself:
One must be so careful these days.

Unreal City,　　　　　　60
Under the brown fog of a winter dawn,
A crowd flowed over London Bridge, so many,
I had not thought death had undone so many.
Sighs, short and infrequent, were exhaled,
And each man fixed his eyes before his feet.　　　　　　65
Flowed up the hill and down King William Street,
To where Saint Mary Woolnoth kept the hours
With a dead sound on the final stroke of nine.
There I saw one I knew, and stopped him, crying: 'Stetson!

You who were with me in the ships at Mylae!
That corpse you planted last year in your garden,
Has it begun to sprout? Will it bloom this year?
'Or has the sudden frost disturbed its bed?
'Oh keep the Dog far hence, that's friend to men,
'Or with his nails he'll dig it up again!        75
'You! hypocrite lecteur!—mon semblable,—mon frère!'

## II. A GAME OF CHESS

The Chair she sat in, like a burnished throne,
Glowed on the marble, where the glass
Held up by standards wrought with fruited vines
From which a golden Cupidon peeped out        80
(Another hid his eyes behind his wing)
Doubled the flames of sevenbranched candelabra
Reflecting light upon the table as
The glitter of her jewels rose to meet it,
From satin cases poured in rich profusion;        85
In vials of ivory and coloured glass
Unstoppered, lurked her strange synthetic perfumes,
Unguent, powdered, or liquid—troubled, confused
And drowned the sense in odours; stirred by the air
That freshened from the window, these ascended        90
In fattening the prolonged candle-flames,
Flung their smoke into the laquearia,
Stirring the pattern on the coffered ceiling.
Huge sea-wood fed with copper
Burned green and orange, framed by the coloured stone,        95
In which sad light a carvèd dolphin swam.
Above the antique mantel was displayed
As though a window gave upon the sylvan scene
The change of Philomel, by the barbarous king
So rudely forced; yet there the nightingale        100
Filled all the desert with inviolable voice
And still she cried, and still the world pursues,
'Jug Jug' to dirty ears.
And other withered stumps of time
Were told upon the walls; staring forms        105
Leaned out, leaning, hushing the room enclosed.
Footsteps shuffled on the stair.
Under the firelight, under the brush, her hair
Spread out in fiery points
Glowed into words, then would be savagely still.        110

'My nerves are bad to-night. Yes, bad. Stay with me.
'Speak to me. Why do you never speak. Speak.

'What are you thinking of? What thinking? What?
'I never know what you are thinking. Think.'

I think we are in rats' alley                                    115
Where the dead men lost their bones.

"What is that noise?"
                        The wind under the door.
'What is that noise now? What is the wind doing?'
                        Nothing again nothing.                   120
                                        'Do
You know nothing? Do you see nothing? Do you remember
Nothing?'

   I remember
Those are pearls that were his eyes.                             125
'Are you alive, or not? Is there nothing in your head?'
                                                        But

O O O O that Shakespeherian Rag—
It's so elegant
So intelligent                                                  130
'What shall I do now? What shall I do?'
'I shall rush out as I am, and walk the street
With my hair down, so. What shall we do to-morrow?
What shall we ever do?'
                        The hot water at ten.                    135
And if it rains, a closed car at four.
And we shall play a game of chess,
Pressing lidless eyes and waiting for a knock upon the door.

When Lil's husband got demobbed, I said—
I didn't mince my words, I said to her myself,                   140
HURRY UP PLEASE ITS TIME
Now Albert's coming back, make yourself a bit smart.
He'll want to know what you done with that money he gave
   you
To get yourself some teeth. He did, I was there.
You have them all out, Lil, and get a nice set,                 145
He said, I swear, I can't bear to look at you.
And no more can't I, I said, and think of poor Albert,
He's been in the army four years, he wants a good time,
And if you don't give it him, there's others will, I said.
Oh is there, she said. Something o' that, I said.               150
Then I'll know who to thank, she said, and give me a straight
   look.
HURRY UP PLEASE ITS TIME
If you don't like it you can get on with it, I said.

Others can pick and choose if you can't.
But if Albert makes off, it won't be for lack of telling.          155
You ought to be ashamed, I said, to look so antique.
(And her only thirty-one.)
I can't help it, she said, pulling a long face,
It's them pills I took, to bring it off, she said.
(She's had five already, and nearly died of young
    George.)          160
The chemist said it would be all right, but I've never been the
    same.
You *are* a proper fool, I said.
Well, if Albert won't leave you alone, there it is, I said,
What you get married for if you don't want children?
HURRY UP PLEASE ITS TIME          165
Well, that Sunday Albert was home, they had a hot gammon,
And they asked me in to dinner, to get the beauty of it
    hot—
HURRY UP PLEASE ITS TIME
HURRY UP PLEASE ITS TIME
Goonight Bill. Goonight Lou. Goonight May.
    Goonight.          170
Ta ta. Goonight. Goonight.
Good night, ladies, good night, sweet ladies, good night, good
    night.

### III. THE FIRE SERMON

The river's tent is broken: the last fingers of leaf
Clutch and sink into the wet bank. The wind
Crosses the brown land, unheard. The nymphs are
    departed.          175
Sweet Thames, run softly, till I end my song.
The river bears no empty bottles, sandwich papers,
Silk handkerchiefs, cardboard boxes, cigarette ends
Or other testimony of summer nights. The nymphs
    are departed. `
And their friends, the loitering heirs of city directors—          180
Departed, have left no addresses.
By the waters of Leman I sat down and wept . . .
Sweet Thames, run softly till I end my song,
Sweet Thames, run softly, for I speak not loud or long.
But at my back in a cold blast I hear          185
The rattle of the bones, and chuckle spread from ear to ear.
A rat crept softly through the vegetation
Dragging its slimy belly on the bank

While I was fishing in the dull canal
On a winter evening round behind the gashouse                    190
Musing upon the king my brother's wreck
And on the king my father's death before him.
White bodies naked on the low damp ground
And bones cast in a little low dry garret,
Rattled by the rat's foot only, year to year.                    195
But at my back from time to time I hear
The sound of horns and motors, which shall bring
Sweeney to Mrs. Porter in the spring.
O the moon shone bright on Mrs. Porter
And on her daughter                    200
They wash their feet in soda water
*Et O ces voix d'enfants, chantant dans la coupole!*

Twit twit twit
Jug jug jug jug jug jug
So rudely forc'd.                    205

Tereu

Unreal City
Under the brown fog of a winter noon
Mr. Eugenides, the Smyrna merchant
Unshaven, with a pocket full of currants                    210
C.i.f. London: documents at sight,
Asked me in demotic French
To luncheon at the Cannon Street Hotel
Followed by a weekend at the Metropole.

At the violet hour, when the eyes and back                    215
Turn upward from the desk, when the human engine waits
Like a taxi throbbing waiting,
I Tiresias, though blind, throbbing between two lives,
Old man with wrinkled female breasts, can see
At the violet hour, the evening hour that strives                    220
Homeward, and brings the sailor home from sea,
The typist home at teatime, clears her breakfast, lights
Her stove, and lays out food in tins.
Out of the window perilously spread
Her dying combinations touched by the sun's last rays,                    225
On the divan are piled (at night her bed)
Stockings, slippers, camisoles, and stays.
I Tiresias, old man with wrinkled dugs
Perceived the scene, and foretold the rest—
I too awaited the expected guest.                    230
He, the young man carbuncular, arrives,

A small house agent's clerk, with one bold stare,
One of the low on whom assurance sits
As a silk hat on a Bradford millionaire.
The time is now propitious, as he guesses,                    235
The meal is ended, she is bored and tired,
Endeavours to engage her in caresses
Which still are unreproved, if undesired.
Flushed and decided, he assaults at once;
Exploring hands encounter no defence;                         240
His vanity requires no response,
And makes a welcome of indifference.
(And I Tiresias have foresuffered all
Enacted on this same divan or bed;
I who have sat by Thebes below the wall                       245
And walked among the lowest of the dead.)
Bestows one final patronising kiss,
And gropes his way, finding the stairs unlit . . .

    She turns and looks a moment in the glass,
Hardly aware of her departed lover;                           250
Her brain allows one half-formed thought to pass:
"Well now that's done: and I'm glad it's over."
When lovely woman stoops to folly and
Paces about her room again, alone,
She smoothes her hair with automatic hand,                   255
And puts a record on the gramophone.

'This music crept by me upon the waters'
And along the Strand, up Queen Victoria Street.
O City city, I can sometimes hear
Beside a public bar in Lower Thames Street,                   260
The pleasant whining of a mandoline
And a clatter and a chatter from within
Where fishmen lounge at noon: where the walls
Of Magnus Martyr hold
Inexplicable splendour of Ionian white and gold.             265

        The river sweats
        Oil and tar
        The barges drift
        With the turning tide
        Red sails                                            270
        Wide
        To leeward, swing on the heavy spar.
        The barges wash
        Drifting logs
        Down Greenwich reach                                 275

Past the Isle of Dogs.
            Weialala leia
            Wallala leialala

Elizabeth and Leicester
Beating oars                                        280
The stern was formed
A gilded shell
Red and gold
The brisk swell
Rippled both shores                                 285
Southwest wind
Carried down stream
The peal of bells
White towers
            Weialala leia                           290
            Wallala leialala

'Trams and dusty trees.
Highbury bore me. Richmond and Kew
Undid me. By Richmond I raised my knees
Supine on the floor of a narrow canoe.'             295

'My feet are at Moorgate, and my heart
Under my feet. After the event
He wept. He promised 'a new start.'
I made no comment. What should I resent?'

'On Margate Sands.                                  300
I can connect
Nothing with nothing.
The broken fingernails of dirty hands.
My people humble people who expect
Nothing.'                                           305
            la la

To Carthage then I came

Burning burning burning burning
O Lord Thou pluckest me out
O Lord Thou pluckest                                310

burning


IV. DEATH BY WATER

Phlebas the Phoenician, a fortnight dead,
Forgot the cry of gulls, and the deep sea swell
And the profit and loss.
                  A current under sea               315

Picked his bones in whispers. As he rose and fell
He passed the stages of his age and youth
Entering the whirlpool.
                                        Gentile or Jew
O you who turn the wheel and look to windward,                    320
Consider Phlebas, who was once handsome and tall as you.


### V. WHAT THE THUNDER SAID

After the torchlight red on sweaty faces
After the frosty silence in the gardens
After the agony in stony places
The shouting and the crying                                        325
Prison and palace and reverberation
Of thunder of spring over distant mountains
He who was living is now dead
We who were living are now dying
With a little patience                                             330

Here is no water but only rock
Rock and no water and the sandy road
The road winding above among the mountains
Which are mountains of rock without water
If there were water we should stop and drink                       335
Amongst the rock one cannot stop or think
Sweat is dry and feet are in the sand
If there were only water amongst the rock
Dead mountain mouth of carious teeth that cannot spit
Here one can neither stand nor lie nor sit                         340
There is not even silence in the mountains
But dry sterile thunder without rain
There is not even solitude in the mountains
But red sullen faces sneer and snarl
From doors of mudcracked houses                                    345
                                        If there were water

  And no rock
  If there were rock
  And also water
  And water                                                        350
  A spring
  A pool among the rock
  If there were the sound of water only
  Not the cicada
  And dry grass singing                                            355
  But sound of water over a rock

Where the hermit-thrush sings in the pine trees
Drip drop drip drop drop drop drop
But there is no water

Who is the third who walks always beside you?                    360
When I count, there are only you and I together
But when I look ahead up the white road
There is always another one walking beside you
Gliding wrapt in a brown mantle, hooded
I do not know whether a man or a woman                           365
—But who is that on the other side of you?

What is that sound high in the air
Murmur of maternal lamentation
Who are those hooded hordes swarming
Over endless plains, stumbling in cracked earth                  370
Ringed by the flat horizon only
What is the city over the mountains
Cracks and reforms and bursts in the violet air
Falling towers
Jerusalem Athens Alexandria                                      375
Vienna London
Unreal

A woman drew her long black hair out tight
And fiddled whisper music on those strings
And bats with baby faces in the violet light                     380
Whistled, and beat their wings
And crawled head downward down a blackened wall
And upside down in air were towers
Tolling reminiscent bells, that kept the hours
And voices singing out of empty cisterns and exhausted
     wells.                                                       385

In this decayed hole among the mountains
In the faint moonlight, the grass is singing
Over the tumbled graves, about the chapel
There is the empty chapel, only the wind's home.
It has no windows, and the door swings,                          390
Dry bones can harm no one.
Only a cock stood on the rooftree
Co co rico co co rico
In a flash of lightning. Then a damp gust
Bringing rain                                                    395

    Ganga was sunken, and the limp leaves
Waited for rain, while the black clouds
Gathered far distant, over Himavant.

The jungle crouched, humped in silence.
Then spoke the thunder                                              400
DA
*Datta:* what have we given?
My friend, blood shaking my heart
The awful daring of a moment's surrender
Which an age of prudence can never retract                          405
By this, and this only, we have existed
Which is not to be found in our obituaries
Or in memories draped by the beneficent spider
Or under seals broken by the lean solicitor
In our empty rooms                                                  410
DA
*Dayadhvam:* I have heard the key
Turn in the door once and turn once only
We think of the key, each in his prison
Thinking of the key, each confirms a prison                         415
Only at nightfall, aethereal rumours
Revive for a moment a broken Coriolanus
DA
*Damyata:* The boat responded
Gaily, to the hand expert with sail and oar                         420
The sea was calm, your heart would have responded
Gaily, when invited, beating obedient
To controlling hands

                          I sat upon the shore
Fishing, with the arid plain behind me                              425
Shall I at least set my lands in order?
London Bridge is falling down falling down falling down
*Poi s'ascose nel foco che gli affina*
*Quando fiam uti chelidon*—O swallow swallow
*Le Prince d'Aquitaine à la tour abolie*                            430
These fragments I have shored against my ruins
Why then Ile fit you. Hieronymo's mad againe.
Datta. Dayadhvam. Damyata.
            Shantih    shantih    shantih


## NOTES ON THE WASTE LAND

Not only the title, but the plan and a good deal of the incidental
symbolism of the poem were suggested by Miss Jessie L. Weston's
book on the Grail legend: *From Ritual to Romance* (Cambridge).

Indeed, so deeply am I indebted, Miss Weston's book will elucidate the difficulties of the poem much better than my notes can do; and I recommend it (apart from the great interest of the book itself) to any who think such elucidation of the poem worth the trouble. To another work of anthropology I am indebted in general, one which has influenced our generation profoundly; I mean *The Golden Bough;* I have used especially the two volumes *Adonis, Attis, Osiris.* Anyone who is acquainted with these works will immediately recognize in the poem certain references to vegetation ceremonies.

#### I. THE BURIAL OF THE DEAD

Line 20. Cf. *Ezekiel* II, i.

23. Cf. *Ecclesiastes* XII, v.

31. V. *Tristan und Isolde,* I, verses 5-8.

42. Id. III, verse 24.

46. I am not familiar with the exact constitution of the Tarot pack of cards, from which I have obviously departed to suit my own convenience. The Hanged Man, a member of the traditional pack, fits my purpose in two ways: because he is associated in my mind with the Hanged God of Frazer, and because I associate him with the hooded figure in the passage of the disciples to Emmaus in Part V. The Phoenician Sailor and the Merchant appear later; also the 'crowds of people,' and Death by Water is executed in Part IV. The Man with Three Staves (an authentic member of the Tarot pack) I associate, quite arbitrarily, with the Fisher King himself.

60. Cf. Baudelaire:

'Fourmillante cité, cité pleine de rêves,
Où le spectre en plein jour raccroche le passant.'

63. Cf. *Inferno,* III, 55-7:

'si lunga tratta
di gente, ch'io non avrei mai creduto
che morte tanta n'avesse disfatta.'

64. Cf. *Inferno,* IV, 25-7:

'Quivi, secondo che per ascoltare,
non avea pianto, ma' che di sospiri,
che l'aura eterna facevan tremare.'

68. A phenomenon which I have often noticed.

74. Cf. the Dirge in Webster's *White Devil.*

76. V. Baudelaire, Preface to *Fleurs du Mal.*

#### II. A GAME OF CHESS

77. Cf. *Antony and Cleopatra,* II, ii, l. 190.

92. Laquearia. V. *Aeneid,* I, 726:

dependent lychni laquearibus aureis
incensi, et noctem flammis funalia vincunt.

98. Sylvan scene. *Vide* Milton, *Paradise Lost,* IV, 140.

99. V. Ovid, *Metamorphoses*, VI, Philomela.
100. Cf. Part III, l. 204.
115. Cf. Part III, l. 195.
118. Cf. Webster: 'Is the wind in that door still?'
126. Cf. Part I, l. 37, 48.
138. Cf. the game of chess in Middleton's *Women beware Women*.

### III. THE FIRE SERMON

176. V. Spenser, *Prothalamion*.
192. Cf. *The Tempest*, I, ii.
196. Cf. Marvell, *To His Coy Mistress*.
197. Cf. Day, *Parliament of Bees:*
 'When of the sudden, listening, you shall hear,
 'A noise of horns and hunting, which shall bring
 'Actaeon to Diana in the spring,
 'Where all shall see her naked skin . . .'
199. I do not know the origin of the ballad from which these lines are taken: it was reported to me from Sydney, Australia.
202. V. Verlaine, *Parsifal*.
210. The currants were quoted at a price 'carriage and insurance free to London'; and the Bill of Lading, etc., were to be handed to the buyer upon payment of the sight draft.
218. Tiresias, although a mere spectator and not indeed a 'character,' is yet the most important personage in the poem, uniting all the rest. Just as the one-eyed merchant, seller of currants, melts into the Phoenician Sailor, and the latter is not wholly distinct from Ferdinand Prince of Naples, so all the women are one woman, and the two sexes meet in Tiresias. What Tiresias *sees*, in fact, is the substance of the poem. The whole passage from Ovid is of great anthropological interest:

'. . . Cum Iunone iocos et maior vestra profecto est
Quam, quae contingit maribus,' dixisse, 'voluptas.'
Illa negat; placuit quae sit sententia docti
Quaerere Tiresiae: venus huic erat utraque nota.
Nam duo magnorum viridi coeuntia silva
Corpora serpentum baculi violaverat ictu
Deque viro factus, mirabile, femina septem
Egerat autumnos; octavo rursus eosdem
Vidit et 'est vestrae si tanta potentia plagae,'
Dixit 'ut auctoris sortem in contraria mutet,
Nunc quoque vos feriam!' percussis anguibus isdem
Forma prior rediit genetivaque venit imago.
Arbiter hic igitur sumptus de lite iocosa
Dicta Iovis firmat; gravius Saturnia iusto
Nec pro materia fertur doluisse suique
Iudicis aeterna damnavit lumina nocte,

At pater omnipotens (neque enim licet inrita cuiquam
Facta dei fecisse deo) pro lumine adempto
Scire dedit futura poenamque levavit honore.'

221. This may not appear as exact as Sappho's lines, but I had in mind the 'longshore' or 'dory' fisherman, who returns at nightfall.

253. V. Goldsmith, the song in *The Vicar of Wakefield*.

257. V. *The Tempest*, as above.

264. The interior of St. Magnus Martyr is to my mind one of the finest among Wren's interiors. See *The Proposed Demolition of Nineteen City Churches* (P. S. King & Son, Ltd.).

266. The Song of the (three) Thames-daughters begins here. From line 292 to 306 inclusive they speak in turn. V. *Götterdämmerung*, III, i: the Rhine-daughters.

279. V. Froude, *Elizabeth*, Vol. I, ch. iv, letter of De Quadra to Philip of Spain:

'In the afternoon we were in a barge, watching the games on the river. (The queen) was alone with Lord Robert and myself on the poop, when they began to talk nonsense, and went so far that Lord Robert at last said, as I was on the spot there was no reason why they should not be married if the queen pleased.'

293. Cf. *Purgatorio*, V, 133:

'Ricorditi di me, che son la Pia;
Siena mi fe', disfecemi Maremma.'

307. V. St. Augustine's *Confessions:* 'to Carthage then I came, where a cauldron of unholy loves sang all about mine ears.'

308. The complete text of the Buddha's Fire Sermon (which corresponds in importance to the Sermon on the Mount) from which these words are taken, will be found translated in the late Henry Clarke Warren's *Buddhism in Translation* (Harvard Oriental Series). Mr. Warren was one of the great pioneers of Buddhist studies in the Occident.

309. From St. Augustine's *Confessions* again. The collocation of these two representatives of eastern and western asceticism, as the culmination of this part of the poem, is not an accident.

### V. WHAT THE THUNDER SAID

In the first part of Part V three themes are employed: the journey to Emmaus, the approach to the Chapel Perilous (see Miss Weston's book) and the present decay of eastern Europe.

357. This is *Turdus aonalaschkae pallasii*, the hermit-thrush which I have heard in Quebec County. Chapman says (*Handbook of Birds of Eastern North America*) 'it is most at home in secluded woodland and thickety retreats. . . . Its notes are not remarkable for variety or volume, but in purity and sweetness of tone and exquisite modulation they are unequalled.' Its 'water-dripping song' is justly celebrated.

360. The following lines were stimulated by the account of one of the Antarctic expeditions (I forget which, but I think one of Shackleton's): it was related that the party of explorers, at the extremity of their strength, had the constant delusion that there was *one more member* than could actually be counted.

367–77. Cf. Hermann Hesse, *Blick ins Chaos:* 'Schon ist halb Europa, schon ist zumindest der halbe Osten Europas auf dem Wege zum Chaos, fährt betrunken im heiligen Wahn am Abgrund entlang und singt dazu, singt betrunken und hymnisch wie Dmitri Karamasoff sang. Ueber diese Lieder lacht der Bürger beleidigt, der Heilige und Seher hört sie mit Tränen.'

402. Datta, dayadhvam, damyata (give, sympathize, control). The fable of the meaning of the Thunder is found in the *Briha-daranyaka—Upanishad*, 5, 1. A translation is found in Deussen's *Sechzig Upanishads des Veda*, p. 489.

408. Cf. Webster, *The White Devil*, V, vi:

'. . . they'll remarry
Ere the worm pierce your winding-sheet, ere the spider
Make a thin curtain for your epitaphs.'

412. Cf. *Inferno*, XXXIII, 46:

'ed io sentii chiavar l'uscio di sotto
all'orribile torre.'

Also F. H. Bradley, *Appearance and Reality*, p. 346:

'My external sensations are no less private to myself than are my thoughts or my feelings. In either case my experience falls within my own circle, a circle closed on the outside; and, with all its elements alike, every sphere is opaque to the others which surround it. . . . In brief, regarded as an existence which appears in a soul, the whole world for each is peculiar and private to that soul.'

425. V. Weston: *From Ritual to Romance;* chapter on the Fisher King.

428. V. *Purgatorio*, XXVI, 148:

' "Ara vos prec, per aquella valor
"que vos guida al som de l'escalina,
"sovegna vos a temps de ma dolor."
Poi s'ascose nel foco che gli affina.'

429. V. *Pervigilium Veneris*. Cf. Philomela in Parts II and III.

430. V. Gerard de Nerval, Sonnet *El Desdichado*.

432. V. Kyd's *Spanish Tragedy*.

434. Shantih. Repeated as here, a formal ending to an Upanishad. 'The Peace which passeth understanding' is our equivalent to this word.

# Cleanth Brooks

## ELIOT
## THE WASTE LAND

To venture to write anything further on *The Waste Land*, particularly after the work of F.R. Leavis and F.O. Matthiessen, may call for some explanation and even apology. I am obviously indebted to both critics. The justification for such a commentary as this must be made primarily in terms of a difference of intention. Leavis is interested predominantly in Eliot's method of organization. One or two passages in the poem are treated in detail and are highly valuable for a knowledge of the "meaning" of the poem, but the bulk of the poem does not receive this kind of examination. Moreover, I believe, Leavis makes some positive errors. Matthiessen examines more of the poem in detail, and, as far as it goes, his account is excellent. But the plan of his *Achievement of T.S. Eliot* does not allow for a consecutive examination either. He puts his finger on the basic theme, death-in-life, but I do not think that he has given it all the salience it deserves.

I prefer not to raise here the question of how important it is for the reader of the poem to have an explicit intellectual account of the various symbols, and a logical account of their relationships. It may well be that such rationalization is no more than a scaffolding to be got out of the way before we contemplate the poem itself as a poem. But many readers (including myself) find the erection of such a scaffolding valuable—if not absolutely necessary—and if some readers will be tempted to lay more stress on the scaffolding than they properly should, there are perhaps still more readers who will be prevented from getting at the poem at all without the help of such a scaffolding. Furthermore, an interest attaches to Mr. Eliot's own mental processes, and whereas Mr. Matthiessen has quite properly warned us that Eliot's poetry cannot be read as autobiography, many of the symbols and ideas that occur in *The Waste Land* are ideas that are definitely central to Eliot's general intellectual position.

The basic symbol used, that of the waste land, is taken, of course, from Miss Jessie Weston's *From Ritual to Romance*. In the legends she treats there, the land has been blighted by a curse. The crops do not grow, and the animals cannot reproduce. The plight of the land is summed up by, and connected with, the plight of the lord of the land, the Fisher King, who has been rendered impotent by maiming or sickness. The curse can only be removed by the appearance of a knight who will ask the meanings of the various symbols which are displayed to him in the castle. The shift in meaning from physical to spiritual sterility is easily made, and was, as a matter of fact, made in certain of the legends. A knowledge of this symbolism is, as Eliot has already pointed out, essential for an understanding of the poem.

Of hardly less importance to the reader, however, is a knowledge of Eliot's basic method. *The Waste Land* is built on a major contract—a device that is a favorite of Eliot's and to be found in many of his poems, particularly his later poems. The contrast is between two kinds of life and two kinds of death. Life devoid of meaning is death; sacrifice, even the sacrificial death, may be life-giving, an awakening to life. The poem occupies itself to a great extent with this paradox and with a number of variations on it.

Eliot has stated the matter quite explicitly himself in one of his essays. In his "Baudelaire" he says:

> One aphorism which has been especially noticed is the following: *la volupté unique et suprême de l' amour gît dans la certitude de faire le mal.* This means, I think, that Baudelaire has perceived that what distinguishes the relations of man and woman from the copulation of beasts is the knowledge of Good and Evil (of *moral* Good and Evil which are not natural Good and Bad or puritan Right and Wrong). Having an imperfect, vague romantic conception of Good, he was at least able to understand that the sexual act as evil is more dignified, less boring than as the natural, "life-giving," cheery automatism of the modern world. . . . So far as we are human, what we do must be either evil or good; so far as we do evil or good, we are human; and it is better, in a paradoxical way, to do evil than to do nothing: at least, *we exist* [italics mine].

The last statement is highly important for an understanding of *The Waste Land*. The fact that men have lost the knowledge of good and evil keeps them from being alive, and

is the justification for viewing the modern waste land as a
realm in which people do not even exist.

This theme is stated in the quotation that prefaces the
poem. The Sybil says: "I wish to die." Her statement has
several possible interpretations. For one thing, she is saying
what the people who inhabit the waste land are saying. But
she also may be saying what the speaker says in "The
Journey of the Magi": "this Birth was / Hard and bitter
agony for us, like Death, our death. / . . . I should be glad of
another death."

The first section of "The Burial of the Dead" develops the
theme of the attractiveness of death, or of the difficulty in
rousing oneself from the death in life in which the people of
the waste land live. Men are afraid to live in reality. April,
the month of rebirth, is not the most joyful season but the
cruelest. Winter at least kept us warm in forgetful snow.
The idea is one which Eliot has stressed elsewhere. Earlier in
"Gerontion" he had written

> . . . *In the juvescence of the year*
> *Came Christ the tiger*
>
> . . .
>
> *The tiger springs in the new year. Us he devours.*

More lately, in *Murder in the Cathedral*, he has the chorus
say

> *We do not wish anything to happen.*
> *Seven years we have lived quietly,*
> *Succeeded in avoiding notice,*
> *Living and partly living.*

And in another passage: "Now I fear disturbance of the quiet
seasons." Men dislike to be aroused from their death-in-life.

The first part of "The Burial of the Dead" introduces this
theme through a sort of reverie on the part of the protagonist
—a reverie in which speculation on life glides off into
memory of an actual conversation in the Hofgarten and back
into speculation again. The function of the conversation is to
establish to some extent the class and character of the protagonist. The reverie is resumed with line 19:

> *What are the roots that clutch, what branches grow*
> *Out of this stony rubbish?*

The protagonist answers for himself:

> *Son of man,*
> *You cannot say, or guess, for you know only*
> *A heap of broken images, where the sun beats,*
> *And the dead tree gives no shelter, the cricket no relief,*
> *And the dry stone no sound of water*

In this passage there are references to Ezekiel and to Ecclesiastes, and these references indicate what it is that men no longer know: the passage referred to in *Ezekiel* 2:1–3 pictures a world thoroughly secularized:

> 1. And he said unto me, Son of man, stand upon thy feet, and I will speak unto thee. 2. And the spirit entered into me when he spake unto me, and set me upon my feet, that I heard him that spake unto me. 3. And he said unto me, Son of man, I send thee to the children of Israel, to a rebellious nation that hath rebelled against me: they and their fathers have transgressed against me, even unto this very day.

The following passage from *Ecclesiastes* 12:1–9 is not only referred to in this passage; a reference to it also is evidently made in the nightmare vision of section five of the poem:

> 1. Remember now thy Creator in the days of thy youth, while the evil days come not, nor the years draw nigh, when thou shalt say, I have no pleasure in them; 2. While the sun, or the light, or the moon, or the stars, be not darkened, nor the clouds return after the rain: 3. In the day when the keepers of the house shall tremble, and the strong men shall bow themselves, and the grinders cease because they are few, and those that look out of the windows be darkened, 4. And the doors shall be shut in the streets, when the sound of the grinding is low, and he shall rise up at the voice of the bird, and all the daughters of musick shall be brought low; 5. Also when they shall be afraid of that which is high, and fears shall be in the way, and the almond tree shall flourish, and the grasshopper shall be a burden, *and desire shall fail* [italics mine]: because man goeth to his long home, and the mourners go about the streets: 6. Or ever the silver cord be loosed, or the golden bowl be broken, or the pitcher be broken at the fountain, or the wheel broken at the cistern. 7. Then shall the dust return to the earth as it was: and the spirit shall return unto God who gave it. 8. Vanity of vanities, saith the preacher; all is vanity.

The next part, which begins with the scrap of song quoted from Wagner (perhaps another item in the reverie of the protagonist), states the opposite half of the paradox that underlies the poem: namely, that life at its highest moments of meaning and intensity resembles death. The song from Act I of Wagner's *Tristan und Isolde*, "*Frisch weht der Wind*," is sung in the opera by a young sailor aboard the ship that is bringing Isolde to Cornwall. The "*Irisch Kind*" of the song does not properly apply to Isolde at all. The song is merely one of happy and naive love. It brings to the mind of the protagonist an experience of love—the vision of the hyacinth girl as she came back from the hyacinth garden. The poet says

> . . . *my eyes failed, I was neither*
> *Living nor dead, and I knew nothing,*
> *Looking into the heart of light, the silence*

The line that immediately follows this passage, "*Oed' und leer das Meer*," seems at first to be simply an extension of the last figure: that is, "Empty and wide the sea [of silence]." The line, however, as a matter of fact, makes an ironic contrast; for the line as it occurs in Act III of the opera is the reply of the watcher who reports to the wounded Tristan that Isolde's ship is nowhere in sight; the sea is empty. And, though the "*Irisch Kind*" of the first quotation is not Isolde, the reader familiar with the opera will apply it to Isolde when he comes to the line "*Oed' und leer das Meer*." For the question in the song is in essence Tristan's question in Act III: "My Irish child, where dwellest thou?" The two quotations from the opera that frame the ecstasy-of-love passage thus take on a new meaning in the altered context. In the first, love is happy: the boat rushes on with a fair wind behind it. In the second, love is absent; the sea is wide and empty. And the last quotation reminds us that even love cannot exist in the waste land.

The next passage, that in which Madame Sosostris figures, calls for further reference to Miss Weston's book. As Miss Weston has shown, the Tarot cards were originally used to determine the event of the highest importance to the people, the rising of the waters. Madame Sosostris has fallen a long way from the high function of her predecessors. She is engaged merely in vulgar fortunetelling—is merely one item in a generally vulgar civilization. But the symbols of the Tarot pack are unchanged. The various characters are still inscribed on the cards, and she is reading in reality, though she does not know it, the fortune of the protagonist. She finds that his card is that of the drowned Phoenician Sailor, and so she warns him against death by water, not realizing any more than do the other inhabitants of the modern waste land that the way into life may be by death itself. The drowned Phoenician Sailor is a type of the fertility god whose image was thrown into the sea annually as a symbol of the death of summer. As for the other figures in the pack: Belladonna, the Lady of the Rocks, is woman in the waste land. The man with three staves, Eliot says he associates rather arbitrarily with the Fisher King. The term "arbitrarily" indicates that we are not to attempt to find a logical connection here.

The Hanged Man, who represents the hanged god of Frazer (including the Christ), Eliot states in a note, is associated with the hooded figure who appears in "What the Thunder Said." That he is hooded accounts for Madame Sosostris' inability to see him; or rather, here again the palaver of the modern fortuneteller is turned to new and important account by the poet's shifting the matter into a new and serious context. The Wheel and the one-eyed merchant will be discussed later.

After the Madame Sosostris passage, Eliot proceeds to complicate his symbols for the sterility and unreality of the modern waste land by associating it with Baudelaire's *fourmillante cité* and with Dante's Limbo. The passages already quoted from Eliot's essay on Baudelaire will indicate one of the reasons why Baudelaire's lines are evoked here. In Baudelaire's city, dream and reality seem to mix, and it is interesting that Eliot in "The Hollow Men" refers to this same realm of death-in-life as "death's dream kingdom" in contradistinction to "death's other kingdom."

The references to Dante are most important. The line, "I had not thought death had undone so many," is taken from the Third Canto of *The Inferno;* the line, "Sighs, short and infrequent, were exhaled," from the Fourth Canto. Mr. Matthiessen has already pointed out that the Third Canto deals with Dante's Limbo which is occupied by those who on earth had "lived without praise or blame." They share this abode with the angels, "who were not rebels, nor were faithful to God, but were for themselves." They exemplify almost perfectly the secular attitude that dominates the modern world. Their grief, according to Dante, arises from the fact that they "have no hope of death; and their blind life is so debased, that they are envious of every other lot." But though they may not hope for death, Dante calls them "these wretches who never were alive." The people who are treated in the Fourth Canto are those who lived virtuously but who died before the proclamation of the Gospel—they are the unbaptized. This completes the categories of people who inhabit the modern waste land: those who are secularized and those who have no knowledge of the faith. Without a faith their life is in reality a death. To repeat the sentence from Eliot previously quoted: "So far as we do evil or good, we are human; and it is better, in a paradoxical way, to do evil than to do nothing: at least, we exist."

The Dante and Baudelaire references, then, come to the same thing as the allusion to the waste land of the medieval legends; and these various allusions drawn from widely differing sources enrich the comment on the modern city so that it becomes "unreal" on a number of levels: as seen through "the brown fog of a winter dawn"; as the medieval waste land and Dante's Limbo and Baudelaire's Paris are unreal.

The reference to Stetson stresses again the connection between the modern London of the poem and Dante's hell. After the statement, "I could never have believed death had undone so many," follow the words "After I had distinguished some among them, I saw and knew the shade of him who made, through cowardice, the great refusal." The protagonist, like Dante, sees among the inhabitants of the contemporary waste land one whom he recognizes. (The name "Stetson" I take to have no ulterior significance. It is merely an ordinary name such as might be borne by the friend one might see in a crowd in a great city.) Mylae, as Mr. Matthiessen has pointed out to us, is the name of a battle between the Romans and the Carthaginians in the Punic War. The Punic War was a trade war—might be considered a rather close parallel to the war of 1914–18. At any rate, it is plain that Eliot in having the protagonist address the friend in a London street as one who was with him in the Punic War rather than as one who was with him in the World War is making the point that all the wars are one war; all experience, one experience. As Eliot put the idea in *Murder in the Cathedral*:

> *We do not know very much of the future*
> *Except that from generation to generation*
> *The same things happen again and again.*

I am not sure that Leavis and Matthiessen are correct in inferring that the line, "That corpse you planted last year in your garden," refers to the attempt to bury a memory. But whether or not this is true, the line certainly refers also to the buried god of the old fertility rites. It also is to be linked with the earlier passage—"What are the roots that clutch, what branches grow," etc. This allusion to the buried god will account for the ironical, almost taunting tone of the passage. The burial of the dead is now a sterile planting—without hope. But the advice to "keep the Dog far hence," in spite of the tone, is, I believe, well taken and serious. The passage in Webster goes as follows

> *O keep the wolf far hence, that's foe to men,*
> *Or with his nails he'll dig it up again*

Why does Eliot turn the wolf into a dog? And why does he reverse the point of importance from the animal's normal hostility to men to its friendliness? If, as some critics have suggested, he is merely interested in making a reference to Webster's darkest play, why alter the line? I am inclined to take the Dog (the capital letter is Eliot's) as humanitarianism and the related philosophies that in their concern for man extirpate the supernatural—dig up the corpse of the buried god and thus prevent the rebirth of life. For the general idea, see Eliot's essay, *The Humanism of Irving Babbitt.*

The last line of "The Burial of the Dead"—You! hypocrite lecteur!—mon semblable,—mon frère!—the quotation from Baudelaire, completes the universalization of Stetson begun by the reference to Mylae. Stetson is every man, including the reader and Mr. Eliot himself.

If *The Burial of the Dead* gives the general abstract statement on the situation, the second part of *The Waste Land,* "A Game of Chess," gives a more concrete illustration. The easiest contrast in this section—and one that may easily blind the casual reader to a continued emphasis on the contrast betwen the two kinds of life, or the two kinds of death, already commented on—is the contrast between life in a rich and magnificent setting, and life in the low and vulgar setting of a London pub. But both scenes, however antithetical they may appear superficially, are scenes taken from the contemporary waste land. In both of them life has lost its meaning.

I am particularly indebted to Mr. Allen Tate's brilliant comment on the first part of this section. To quote from him, "The woman . . . is, I believe, the symbol of man at the present time. He is surrounded by the grandeurs of the past, but he does not participate in them; they don't sustain him." And to quote from another section of his commentary: "The rich experience of the great tradition depicted in the room receives a violent shock in contrast with a game that symbolizes the inhuman abstraction of the modern mind." Life has no meaning; history has no meaning; there is no answer to the question: "What shall we ever do?" The only thing that has meaning is the abstract game they are to play, a game in which the meaning is assigned and arbitrary, meaning by convention only—in short, a game of chess.

This interpretation will account in part for the pointed reference to Cleopatra in the first lines of the section. But there is, I believe, a further reason for the poet's having compared the lady to Cleopatra. The queen in Shakespeare's drama—"Age cannot wither her, nor custom stale / Her infinite variety"—is perhaps the extreme exponent of love for love's sake—the feminine member of the pair of lovers who threw away an empire for love. But the infinite variety of the life of the woman in "A Game of Chess" *has* been staled. There is indeed no variety at all, and love simply does not exist. The function of the sudden change in the description of the carvings and paintings in the room from the heroic and magnificent to the characterization of the rest of them as "other withered stumps of time" is obvious. But the reference to Philomela is particularly important, for Philomela, it seems to me, is one of the major symbols of the poem.

Miss Weston points out that a section of one of the Grail manuscripts, which is apparently intended as a gloss of the Grail story, tells how the court of the rich Fisher King was withdrawn from the knowledge of men when certain of the maidens who frequented the shrine were raped and had their golden cups taken from them. The curse on the land follows from this act. Miss Weston conjectures that this may be a statement, in the form of parable, of the violation of the older mysteries which were probably once celebrated openly, but were later forced underground into secrecy. Whether or not Mr. Eliot intends a reference to this passage, the violation of a woman makes a very good symbol of the process of secularization. John Crowe Ransom makes the point very neatly for us in his "God Without Thunder." Love is the aesthetic of sex; lust is the science. Love implies a deferring of the satisfaction of the desire; it implies even a certain asceticism and a ritual. Lust drives forward urgently and scientifically to the immediate extirpation of the desire. Our contemporary waste land is in a large part the result of our scientific attitude—of our complete secularization. Needless to say, lust defeats its own ends. The portrayal of "the change of Philomel, by the barbarous king" is a fitting commentary on the scene it ornaments. The waste land of the legend came in this way—the modern waste land has come in this way.

That this view is not mere fine-spun ingenuity is borne out somewhat by the change of tense Eliot employs here, which Mr. Edmund Wilson has commented upon: "And still she cried, and still the world pursues." Apparently the "world" partakes in the barbarous king's action, and still partakes in that action.

To "dirty ears" the nightingale's song is not the one that filled all the desert with inviolable voice—it is "Jug Jug." Edmund Wilson has pointed out that the rendition of the bird's song here represents not merely the Elizabethan neutral notation of the bird's song, but carries associations of the ugly and coarse. The passage is therefore one of many instances of Eliot's device of using something that in one context is innocent, but in another context becomes loaded with a special meaning.

The Philomela passage has another importance, however. If it is a commentary on how the waste land became waste, it also repeats the theme of the death that is the door to life—the theme of the dying god. The raped woman becomes transformed through suffering into the nightingale; through the violation comes the "inviolable voice." The thesis that suffering is action and out of suffering comes poetry, is a favorite one of Eliot's. For example, "Shakespeare, too, was occupied with the struggle—which alone constitutes life for a poet—to transmute his personal and private agonies into something rich and strange, something universal and impersonal." Consider also his statement with reference to Baudelaire: "Indeed, in his way of suffering is already a kind of presence of the supernatural and of the superhuman. He rejects always the purely natural and the purely human; in other words, he is neither 'naturalist' nor 'humanist.'" The theme of the life that is death is stated specifically in the conversation between the man and the woman. She asks the question "Are you alive, or not?" and this time we are sufficiently prepared by the Dante references in "The Burial of the Dead" for the statement here to bear a special meaning. (She also asks "Is there nothing in your head?" He is one of the Hollow Men—"headpiece stuffed with straw.")

These people, as people in the waste land, know nothing, see nothing, do not even live.

But the protagonist, after this reflection that in the waste land of modern life even death is sterile—"I think we are in rats' alley / Where the dead men lost their bones"—remembers a death that was not sterile, remembers a death that was transformed into something rich and strange, the death described in the song from *The Tempest*—"Those are pearls that were his eyes."

The reference to this section of *The Tempest* is, like the Philomela reference, one of Eliot's major symbols. We are to meet it twice more, in later sections of the poem. Some more general comment on it is therefore appropriate here. The song, one remembers, was sung by Ariel in luring Ferdinand, Prince of Naples, on to meet Miranda, and thus to find love, and through this love, to effect the regeneration and deliverance of all the people on the island. Ferdinand says of the song,

> *The ditty doth remember my drowned father.*
> *This is no mortal business, nor no sound*
> *That the earth owes*

The allusion is an extremely interesting example of the device of Eliot's already commented upon, that of taking an item from one context and shifting it into another in which it assumes a new and powerful meaning. This description of a death that is a portal into a realm of the rich and strange—a death that becomes a sort of birth—assumes in the mind of the protagonist an association with that of the drowned god whose effigy was thrown into the water as a symbol of the death of the fruitful powers of nature but which was taken out of the water as a symbol of the revivified god. (See *From Ritual to Romance.*) The passage therefore represents the perfect antithesis to the passage in "The Burial of the Dead": "That corpse you planted last year in your garden," etc. It also, as we have already pointed out, finds its antithesis in the sterile and unfruitful death "in rats' alley" just commented upon. (We shall find that this contrast between the death in rats' alley and the death in *The Tempest* is made again in "The Fire Sermon.")

We have yet to treat the relation of the title of the section, "A Game of Chess," to Middleton's play, *Women Beware Women*, from which the game of chess is taken. In the play, the game is used as a device to keep the widow occupied while her daughter-in-law is being seduced. The seduction amounts almost to a rape, and in a *double entendre* the rape is actually described in terms of the game. We have one more connection with the Philomela symbol therefore. The abstract game is being used in the contemporary waste land, as in the play, to cover up a rape and is a description of the rape itself.

In the second part of "A Game of Chess" we are given a picture of spiritual emptiness, but this time, at the other end of the social scale, as reflected in the talk between two cockney women in a London pub. The account here is straightforward enough and the only matter that calls for comment is the line spoken by Ophelia in *Hamlet* that ends the passage. Ophelia, too, was very much concerned about love, the theme of conversation of the two ladies. As a matter of fact, she was in very much the same position as that of the woman who has been the topic of conversation between the two good ladies we have just heard. She had remarked too once that

> *Young men will do't, if they come to't!*
> *By cock, they are to blame.*

And her poetry (including the line quoted from her here), like Philomela's, had come out of suffering. I think that we are probably to look for the relevance of the allusion to her in some such matter as this rather than in an easy satiric contrast between Elizabethan glories and modern sordidness. After all (in spite of the Marxists) Eliot's objection to the present world is not merely the sentimental one that this happens to be the twentieth century after Christ and not the seventeenth.

"The Fire Sermon" makes much use of several of the symbols already developed. The fire is the sterile burning of lust, and the section is a sermon, although a sermon by example only. This section of the poem also contains some of the most easily apprehended uses of literary allusion. The poem opens on a vision of the modern river. In Spenser's "Prothalamion" the scene described is also a river scene at London, and it is dominated by nymphs and their paramours, and the nymphs are preparing for a bridal. The contrast between Spenser's scene and its twentieth-century equivalent is jarring. The paramours are now "the loitering heirs of city directors," and, as for the bridals of Spenser's Elizabethan maidens, in the stanzas that follow we learn a great deal about those. At the end of the section the speech of the third of the Thames-nymphs summarizes the whole matter for us.

The waters of the Thames are also associated with those of Leman—the poet in the contemporary waste land is in a sort of Babylonian Captivity.

The castle of the Fisher King was always located on the banks of a river or on the sea shore. The title "Fisher King," Miss Weston shows, originates from the use of the fish as a fertility or life symbol. This meaning, however, was often forgotten, and so the title in many of the later Grail romances is accounted for by describing the king as fishing. Eliot uses the reference to fishing for reverse effect. The reference to fishing is part of the realistic detail of the scene—"While I was fishing in the dull canal." But to the reader who knows the Weston references, the reference is to that of the Fisher King of the Grail legends. The protagonist is the maimed and impotent king of the legends.

Eliot proceeds now to tie the waste land symbol to that of *The Tempest,* by quoting one of the lines spoken by Ferdinand, Prince of Naples, that occurs just before Ariel's song, "Full Fathom Five," is heard. But he alters the passage from *The Tempest* somewhat, writing not, "Weeping again the king my father's wreck," but

> *Musing upon the king my brother's wreck*
> *And on the king my father's death before him.*

It is possible that the alteration has been made to bring the account taken from *The Tempest* into accord with the situation in the Percival stories. In Wolfram von Eschenbach's *Parzival,* for instance, Trevrezent, the hermit, is the brother of the Fisher King, Anfortas. He tells Parzival, "His name all men know as Anfortas, and I weep for him evermore." Their father, Frimutel, is, of course, dead.

The protagonist in the poem, then, imagines himself not only in the situation of Ferdinand in *The Tempest* but also in that of one of the characters in the Grail legend; and the wreck, to be applied literally in the first instance, applies metaphorically in the second.

After the lines from *The Tempest* appears again the image of a sterile death from which no life comes, the bones, "rattled by the rat's foot only, year to year." (The collocation of this figure with the vision of the death by water in Ariel's song has already been commented on. The lines quoted from *The Tempest* come just before the song.)

The allusion to Marvell's "To His Coy Mistress" is of course one of the easiest allusions in the poem. Instead of "Time's winged chariot" the poet hears "the sound of horns and motors" of contemporary London. But the passage has been further complicated. The reference has been combined with an allusion to Day's "Parliament of Bees." "Time's winged chariot" of Marvell has not only been changed to the modern automobile; Day's "sound of horns and hunting" has changed to the horns of the motors. And Actaeon will not be brought face to face with Diana, goddess of chastity; Sweeney, type of the vulgar bourgeois, is to be brought to Mrs. Porter, hardly a type of chastity. The reference in the ballad to the feet "washed in soda water" reminds the poet ironically of another sort of foot-washing, the sound of the children singing in the dome heard at the ceremony of the foot-washing that precedes the restoration of the wounded Anfortas (the Fisher King) by Parzival and the taking away of the curse from the waste land. The quotation thus completes the allusion to the Fisher King commenced in line 189—"While I was fishing in the dull canal."

The pure song of the children also reminds the poet of the song of the nightingale, which we have heard in "The Game of Chess." The recapitulation of symbols is continued with a repetition of "Unreal City" and with the reference to the one-eyed merchant.

Mr. Eugenides, the Smyrna merchant, is the one-eyed merchant mentioned by Madame Sosostris. The fact that the merchant is one-eyed apparently means in Madame Sosostris's speech no more than that the merchant's face on the card is shown in profile. But Eliot applies the term to Mr. Eugenides for a totally different effect. The defect corresponds somewhat to Madame Sosostris's bad cold. The Syrian merchants, we learn from Miss Weston's book, were, with slaves and soldiers, the principal carriers of the mysteries that lie at the core of the Grail legends. But in the modern world we find both the representatives of the Tarot divining and the mystery cults in decay. What he carries on his back and what the fortuneteller was forbidden to see is evidently the knowledge of the mysteries (although Mr. Eugenides himself is hardly likely to be more aware of it than Madame Sosostris is aware of the importance of her function). Mr. Eugenides, in terms of his former function, ought to be inviting the protagonist to an initiation into the esoteric cult which holds the secret of life, but on the realistic surface of the poem, in his invitation to "a weekend at the Metropole" he is really inviting him to a homosexual debauch. The homosexuality is "secret" and now a "cult," but a very different cult from that which Mr. Eugenides ought to represent. The end of the new cult is not life but, ironically, sterility.

In the modern waste land, however, even the relation between man and woman is also sterile. The incident between the typist and the carbuncular young man is a picture of "love" so exclusively and practically pursued that it is not love at all. The scene, as Allen Tate puts it, is one of our most terrible insights into Western civilization. The tragic chorus to the scene is Tiresias, into whom perhaps Mr. Eugenides may be said to modulate, Tiresias, the historical "expert" on the relation between the sexes.

The allusions to Sappho's lines and to Goldsmith's made in this passage need little comment. The hour of evening, which in Sappho's poem brings rest to all and brings the sailor home, brings the typist to her travesty of home—"On the divan . . . at night her bed"—and brings the carbuncular young man, the meeting with whom ends not in peace but in sterile burning.

The reminiscence of the lines from Goldsmith's song in the description of the young woman's actions after the departure of her lover gives concretely and ironically the utter breakdown of traditional standards.

It is the music of her gramophone that the protagonist hears "creep by" him "upon the waters." Far from the music that Ferdinand heard bringing him to Miranda and love, it is, one is tempted to think, the music of "O O O O that Shakespeherian Rag" of "A Game of Chess."

But the protagonist says that he *sometimes* hears "The pleasant whining of a mandoline." Significantly enough, it is the music of the fishmen (the fish again as a life symbol) and it comes from beside a church (though—if this is not to rely too much on Eliot's note—the church has been marked for destruction). Life on Lower Thames Street, if not on the Strand, still has meaning as it cannot have meaning for either the typist or the rich woman of "A Game of Chess."

The song of the Thames-daughters brings us back to the opening section of "The Fire Sermon" again, and once more we have to do with the river and the river nymphs. Indeed, the typist incident is framed by the two river nymph scenes. The connection of the river-nymphs with the Rhine-daughters of Wagner's *Götterdämmerung* is easily made.

In the passage in Wagner's opera to which Eliot refers in his note, the opening of Act III, the Rhine-daughters bewail the loss of the beauty of the Rhine occasioned by the theft of the gold, and then beg Siegfried to give them back the Ring made from this gold, finally threatening him with death if he does not give it up. Like the Thames-daughters, they too have been violated; and like the maidens mentioned in the Grail legend, the violation has brought a curse on gods and men. The first of the songs depicts the modern river, soiled with oil and tar. (Compare also with the description of the river in the first part of "The Fire Sermon." The second song depicts the Elizabethan river, also evoked in the first part of "The Fire Sermon." (Leicester and Elizabeth ride upon it in a barge of state. Incidentally, Spenser's "Prothalamion," from which quotation is made in the first part of "The Fire Sermon," mentions Leicester as having formerly lived in the house that forms the setting of that poem.)

In this second song there is also a definite allusion to the passage in *Antony and Cleopatra* already referred to in the opening line of "A Game of Chess":

> *Beating oars*
> *The stern was formed*
> *A gilded shell*

And if we still have any doubt of the allusion, Eliot's note on the passage with its reference to the "barge" and "poop" should settle the matter. We have already commented on the earlier allusion to Cleopatra as the prime example of love for love's sake. The symbol bears something of the same meaning here, and the note Eliot supplies does something to reinforce the "Cleopatra" aspect of Elizabeth. Elizabeth in the presence of the Spaniard De Quadra, though negotiations were going on for a Spanish marriage, "went so far that Lord Robert at last said, as I [De Quadra was a bishop] was on the spot there was no reason why they should not be married if the queen pleased." The passage has a sort of double function. It reinforces the general contrast between Elizabethan magnificence and modern sordidness: in the Elizabethan age love for love's sake had some meaning and therefore some magnificence. But the passage gives something of an opposed effect too: the same sterile love, emptiness of love, obtained in this period too: Elizabeth and the Typist are alike as well as different.

The third Thames-daughter's song depicts another sordid

"love" affair, and unites the themes of the first two songs. It begins with trams and *dusty* trees. With it we are definitely in the waste land again. Pia, whose words she echoes in saying "Highbury bore me. Richmond and Kew / Undid me" was in Purgatory and had hope. The woman speaking here has no hope—she too is in the Inferno: "I can connect / Nothing with nothing." She has just completed, floating down the river in the canoe, what Eliot has described in *Murder in the Cathedral* as

> . . . *the effortless journey, to the empty land*
> . . .
>
> *Where those who were men can no longer turn the mind*
> *To distraction, delusion, escape into dream, pretence,*
> *Where the soul is no longer deceived, for there are no objects, no tones,*
> *No colours, no forms to distract, to divert the soul*
> *From seeing itself, foully united forever, nothing with nothing,*
> *Nor what we call death, but what beyond death is not death*

Now, "on Margate sands," she stands, like the Hollow Men, "on this beach of the tumid river."

The songs of the three Thames-daughters, as a matter of fact, epitomize this whole section of the poem. With reference to the quotations from St. Augustine and Buddha at the end of "The Fire Sermon" Eliot states that "The collocation of these two representatives of eastern and western asceticism, as the culmination of this part of the poem, is not an accident."

It is certainly not an accident. The moral of all the incidents we have been witnessing is that there must be an asceticism—something to check the drive of desire. The wisdom of the East and the West comes to the same thing on this point. Moreover, the image that both St. Augustine and Buddha use for lust is fire. What we have witnessed in the various scenes of "The Fire Sermon" is the sterile burning of lust. Modern man, freed from all restraints, in his cultivation of experience for experience's sake burns, but not with a "hard and gemlike flame." One ought not to pound the point home in this fashion, but to see that the imagery of this section of the poem furnishes illustrations leading up to "The Fire Sermon" is the necessary requirement for feeling the force of the brief allusions here at the end to Buddha and St. Augustine.

Whatever the specific meaning of the symbols, the general function of the section, "Death by Water," is readily apparent. The section forms a contrast with "The Fire Sermon," which precedes it—a contrast between the symbolism of fire and that of water. Also readily apparent is its force as a symbol of surrender and relief through surrender.

Some specific connections can be made, however. The drowned Phoenician Sailor recalls the drowned god of the fertility cults. Miss Weston tells that each year at Alexandria an effigy of the head of the god was thrown into the water as a symbol of the death of the powers of nature, and that this head was carried by the current to Byblos where it was taken out of the water and exhibited as a symbol of the reborn god.

Moreover, the Phoenician Sailor is a merchant—"Forgot . . . the profit and loss." The vision of the drowned sailor gives a statement of the message that the Syrian merchants originally brought to Britain, and which the Smyrna merchant, unconsciously and by ironical negatives, has brought. One of Eliot's notes states that the "merchant . . . melts into the Phoenician Sailor, and the latter is not wholly distinct from Ferdinand Prince of Naples." The death by water would seem to be equated with the death described in Ariel's song in *The Tempest*. There is a definite difference in the tone of the description of this death—"A current under sea / Picked his bones in whispers," as compared with the "other" death—"bones cast in a little low dry garret, / Rattled by the rat's foot only, year to year."

Farther than this it would not be safe to go, but one may point out that whirling (the whirlpool here, the Wheel of Madame Sosostris' palaver) is one of Eliot's symbols frequently used in other poems ("Ash Wednesday," "Gerontion," *Murder in the Cathedral*, and "Burnt Norton") to denote the temporal world. And one may point out the following passage from "Ash Wednesday"

*Although I do not hope to* turn *again*

. . .

*Wavering between the* profit and the loss
*In this brief transit where the dreams cross*
*The dreamcrossed twilight* between birth and dying

(My emphasis.) At least, with a kind of hindsight, one may suggest that section four gives an instance of the conquest of death and time—the "perpetual recurrence of determined seasons," the "world of spring and autumn, birth and dying" —through death itself.

The reference to the "torchlight red on sweaty faces" and to the "frosty silence in the gardens" obviously associates, as we have already pointed out, Christ in Gethsemane with the other hanged gods. The god has now died, and in referring to this, the basic theme finds another strong restatement:

> *He who was living is now dead*
> *We who were living are now dying*
> *With a little patience*

The poet does not say "we who *are* living." It is "we who *were* living." It is the death-in-life of Dante's Limbo. Life in the full sense has been lost.

The passage on the sterility of the waste land and the lack of water, which follows, provides for the introduction later of two highly important passages. The first of these is:

> *There is not even silence in the mountains*
> *But dry sterile thunder without rain*

—lines that look forward to the introduction later of "what the thunder said" when the thunder, no longer sterile, but bringing rain, speaks.

The second of these passages is, "There is not even solitude in the mountains," which looks forward to the reference to the Journey to Emmaus theme a few lines later: "Who is the third who walks always beside you?" The god has returned, has risen, but the travellers cannot tell whether it is really he, or mere illusion induced by their delirium.

The parallelism between the "hooded" figure who walks "always . . . beside you," and the "hooded hordes" is another instance of the sort of parallelism that is really a contrast, one of the type of which Eliot is fond. In the first case, the figure is indistinct because spiritual; in the second, the hooded hordes are indistinct because completely *un-spiritual*—they are the people of the waste land—

> *Shape without form, shade without colour,*
> *Paralysed force, gesture without motion*

—to take two lines from "The Hollow Men," where the people of the waste land once more appear. Or to take another line from the same poem, perhaps their hoods are the "deliberate disguises" that the Hollow Men, the people of the waste land, wear.

Eliot, as his notes tell us, has particularly connected the description here with the "decay of eastern Europe." The hordes represent then the general waste land of the modern world with a special application to the break-up of Eastern Europe, the region with which the fertility cults were especially connected and in which today the traditional values are thoroughly discredited. The cities, Jerusalem, Athens, Alexandria, Vienna, like the London of the first section of the poem, are "unreal," and for the same reason.

The passage that immediately follows develops the unreality into nightmare, but it is a nightmare vision that is not only an extension of the passage beginning, "What is the city over the mountains"—in it appear other figures from earlier in the poem: the lady of "A Game of Chess" who, surrounded by the glory of history and art, sees no meaning in either and threatens to rush out into the street "with my hair down, so," has here let down her hair and fiddles "whisper music on those strings." One remembers in "A Game of Chess" that it was the woman's hair that spoke:

> . . . *her hair*
> *Spread out in fiery points*
> *Glowed into words, then would be savagely still.*

The hair has been immemorially a symbol of fertility, and Miss Weston and Frazer mention sacrifices of hair in order to aid the fertility god.

As we have pointed out earlier in dealing with "The Burial of the Dead," this whole passage is to be connected with the twelfth chapter of *Ecclesiastes*. The "doors of mudcracked houses," and the cisterns in this passage are to be found in *Ecclesiastes*, and the woman fiddling music from her hair is one of "the daughters of music" brought low. The towers and bells from the Elizabeth and Leicester passage of "The Fire Sermon" also appear here, but the towers are upside down, and the bells, far from pealing for an actual occasion or ringing the hours, are "reminiscent." The civilization is breaking up.

The "violet light" also deserves comment. In "The Fire Sermon" it is twice mentioned as the "violet hour," and there it has little more than a physical meaning. It is a description of the hour of twilight. Here it indicates the twilight of the civilization, but it is perhaps something more. Violet is one of the liturgical colors of the church. It symbolizes repentance and it is the color of baptism. The visit to the Perilous Chapel, according to Miss Weston, was an initiation—that is, a baptism. In the nightmare vision, the bats wear baby faces.

The horror built up in this passage is a proper preparation for the passage on the Perilous Chapel which follows it. The journey has not been merely an agonized walk in the desert, though it is that, or merely the journey after the god has died and hope has been lost; it is also the journey to the Perilous Chapel of the Grail story. In Miss Weston's account, the chapel was part of the ritual, and was filled with horrors to test the candidate's courage. In some stories the perilous cemetery is also mentioned. Eliot has used both: "Over the tumbled graves, about the chapel." In many of the Grail stories the chapel was haunted by demons.

The cock in the folklore of many peoples is regarded as the bird whose voice chases away the powers of evil. It is significant that it is after his crow that the flash of lightning comes and the "damp gust / Bringing rain." It is just possible that the cock has a connection also with *The Tempest* symbols. The first song Ariel sings to Ferdinand as he sits "Weeping again the king my father's wreck" ends

> *The strain of strutting chanticleer,*
> *Cry, cock-a-doodle-doo.*

The next stanza is the "Full Fathom Five" song, which Eliot has used as a vision of life gained through death. If this relation holds, here we have an extreme instance of an allusion, in itself innocent, forced into serious meaning through transference to a new context.

As Miss Weston has shown, the fertility cults go back to a very early period and are recorded in Sanskrit legends. In the poem, Eliot has been continually linking up the Christian doctrine with the beliefs of as many peoples as he can. Here he goes back to the very beginnings of Aryan culture, and tells the rest of the story of the rain's coming, not in terms of the setting already developed but in its earliest form. The passage is thus a perfect parallel in method to lines 70–71 in "The Burial of the Dead" (my emphasis):

> *You who were with me in the ships* at Mylae!
> *That corpse you planted* last year *in your garden*

The use of Sanskrit in what the thunder says is thus accounted for. In addition, there is of course a more obvious reason for casting what the thunder said into Sanskrit here: onomatopoeia.

The comments on the three statements of the thunder imply an acceptance of them. The protagonist answers the first question, "what have we given?" with the statement:

> *The awful daring of a moment's surrender*
> *Which an age of prudence can never retract*
> *By this, and this only, we have existed*

Here the larger meaning is stated in terms that imply the sexual meaning. Man cannot be absolutely self-regarding. Even the propagation of the race—even mere "existence"— calls for such a surrender. Living calls for—see the passage already quoted from Eliot's essay on Baudelaire—belief in something more than "life."

The comment on *dayadhvam* (sympathize) is obviously connected with the foregoing passage. The surrender to something outside the self is an attempt (whether on the sexual level or some other) to transcend one's essential isolation. The passage gathers up the symbols previously developed in the poem just as the foregoing passage reflects, though with a different implication, the numerous references to sex made earlier in the poem. For example, the woman in the first part of "A Game of Chess" is recalled to us now by the *dayadhvam* stanza:

> *Speak to me. Why do you never speak. Speak.*
> *What are you thinking of? What thinking? What?*
> *I never know what you are thinking. Think.*

The third statement made by the thunder, *damyata* (control) follows the logical condition for control, sympathy. The figure of the boat catches up the figure of control already given in line 320, "Death by Water"—"O you who turn the wheel and look to windward"—and from "The Burial of the Dead" the figure of happy love in which the ship rushes on with a fair wind behind it: "*Frisch weht der Wind. . . .*"

I cannot accept Mr. Leavis's interpretation of the passage, "I sat upon the shore / Fishing, with the arid plain behind me," as meaning that the poem "exhibits no progression." The comment on what the thunder says would indicate, if other passages did not, that the poem does not "end where it began." It is true that the protagonist does not witness a revival of the waste land; but there are two important relationships involved in his case: a personal one as well as a general one. If secularization has destroyed, or is likely to destroy, modern civilization, the protagonist still has a private obligation to fulfill. Even if the civilization is breaking up— "London Bridge is falling down falling down falling down"— there remains the personal obligation: "Shall I at least set my lands in order?" Consider in this connection the last sentences of Eliot's *Thoughts After Lambeth:* "The World is trying the experiment of attempting to form a civilized but non-Christian mentality. The experiment will fail; but we must be very patient in awaiting its collapse; meanwhile redeeming the time: so that the Faith may be preserved alive through the dark ages before us; to renew and rebuild civilization, and save the World from suicide."

The bundle of quotations with which the poem ends has a very definite relation to the general theme of the poem and to several of the major symbols used in the poem. Before Arnaut leaps back into the refining fire of Purgatory with joy he says: "I am Arnaut who weep and go singing; contrite I see my past folly, and joyful I see before me the day I hope for. Now I pray you by that virtue which guides you to the summit of the stair, at times be mindful of my pain." This note is carried forward by the quotation from "Pervigilium Veneris": "When shall I be like the swallow?" The allusion also connects with the Philomela symbol. (Eliot's note on the passage indicates this clearly.) The sister of Philomela was changed into a swallow as Philomela was changed into a nightingale. The protagonist is asking therefore when shall the spring, the time of love return, but also when will he be reborn out of his sufferings, and—with the special meaning the symbol takes on from the preceding Dante quotation and from the earlier contexts already discussed—he is asking what is asked at the end of one of the minor poems: "When will Time flow away?"

The quotation from "El Desdichado," as Edmund Wilson has pointed out, indicates that the protagonist of the poem has been disinherited, robbed of his tradition. The ruined tower is perhaps also the Perilous Chapel, "only the wind's home," and it is also the whole tradition in decay. The protagonist resolves to claim his tradition and rehabilitate it.

The quotation from *The Spanish Tragedy*—"Why then Ile fit you. Hieronymo's mad againe"—is perhaps the most puzzling of all these quotations. It means, I believe, this: the protagonist's acceptance of what is in reality the deepest truth will seem to the present world mere madness. ("And still she cried, and still the world pursues, / 'Jug Jug' to dirty ears.") Hieronymo in the play, like Hamlet, was "mad" for a purpose. The protagonist is conscious of the interpretation that will be placed on the words that follow—words that will seem to many apparently meaningless babble, but that contain the oldest and most permanent truth of the race:

*Datta. Dayadhvam. Damyata.*

After this statement comes the benediction:

*Shantih shantih shantih*

JOHN CROWE RANSOM

*Alfred A. Knopf*

## Captain Carpenter

Captain Carpenter rose up in his prime
Put on his pistols and went riding out
But had got wellnigh nowhere at that time
Till he fell in with ladies in a rout.

It was a pretty lady and all her train 5
That played with him so sweetly but before
An hour she'd taken a sword with all her main
And twined him of his nose for evermore.

Captain Carpenter mounted up one day
And rode straightway into a stranger rogue 10
That looked unchristian but be that as may
The Captain did not wait upon prologue.

But drew upon him out of his great heart
The other swung against him with a club
And cracked his two legs at the shinny part 15
And let him roll and stick like any tub.

Captain Carpenter rode many a time
From male and female took he sundry harms
He met the wife of Satan crying "I'm
The she-wolf bids you shall bear no more arms." 20

Their strokes and counters whistled in the wind
I wish he had delivered half his blows
But where she should have made off like a hind
The bitch bit off his arms at the elbows.

And Captain Carpenter parted with his ears 25
To a black devil that used him in this wise
O jesus ere his threescore and ten years
Another had plucked out his sweet blue eyes.

Captain Carpenter got up on his roan
And sallied from the gate in hell's despite 30
I heard him asking in the grimmest tone
If any enemy yet there was to fight?

"To any adversary it is fame
If he risk to be wounded by my tongue
Or burnt in two beneath my red heart's flame        35
Such are the perils he is cast among.

"But if he can he has a pretty choice
From an anatomy with little to lose
Whether he cut my tongue and take my voice
Or whether it be my round red heart he choose."        40

It was the neatest knave that ever was seen
Stepping in perfume from his lady's bower
Who at this word put in his merry mien
And fell on Captain Carpenter like a tower.

I would not knock old fellows in the dust        45
But there lay Captain Carpenter on his back
His weapons were the old heart in his bust
And a blade shook between rotten teeth alack.

The rogue in scarlet and grey soon knew his mind
He wished to get his trophy and depart;        50
With gentle apology and touch refined
He pierced him and produced the Captain's heart.

God's mercy rest on Captain Carpenter now
I thought him Sirs an honest gentleman
Citizen husband soldier and scholar enow        55
Let jangling kites eat of him if they can.

But God's deep curses follow after those
That shore him of his goodly nose and ears
His legs and strong arms at the two elbows
And eyes that had not watered seventy years        60

The curse of hell upon the sleek upstart
That got the Captain finally on his back
And took the red red vitals of his heart
And made the kites to whet their beaks clack clack.

# John Berryman

## RANSOM
### CAPTAIN CARPENTER

This is a high-spirited, desolate ballad about a reformer, a redresser of wrongs, primitive in its physical arrangements but so cunning in its moral and symbolic arrangements that what one says when talking about one aspect of the poem one is tempted to contradict when talking about another. Maybe that's not a mistake. I have been told that Mr. Ransom frowns on, or a least is inclined to look askance at, a view which would see the Captain as a Christ figure. I can't care much about this, even if the rumor is true; I used to take more seriously than I do now the denials and asseverations, including my own, of poets about their work. For one thing, one honestly forgets, when considering poems written long before; for a second, a certain sly desire to baffle the onrushing critic is nearly standard in poetic temperament; finally, one gets bored with one's own old work—a condition that extends to the reading of it. More than twenty years ago I heard Mr. Ransom read "Captain Carpenter" at Harvard in a way that proved he couldn't have written it—insensitive and perfunctory; whereas there is at the Library of Congress a reading by him of another early poem, "Philomela," as airy and fresh as if he were making it up as he went along. Maybe not a Christ figure, then, but maybe something of one, given Christ's traditional occupation, his pity, his desire to change the world, his leadership (though the Captain seems to have no followers—a matter we'll come back to), and his failure. None of these items, taken singly, is impressive, but together they are.

More impressive: a figure of chivalry, extremely active, extremely ineffective, a comic and suffering man of war, given to lust (as the Don is in Chapter XVI), continually defeated both in detail and in the end: in short, Don Quixote.

Don Quixote transposed though, of course; and the societies of the composition of the two works need a word or more. The Don was old-fashioned, out of date (his creator was *not:* Cervantes, particularly in part two, was as avant-garde as his only living peer, writing in England), driven mad by romances, but the novelist's attitude towards both him and his ideals is ambivalent, a complex of scorn, nostalgia, and love. In a moment I wish to suggest that precisely this ambivalence characterizes Ransom's feelings for his Captain. But first it must be emphasized that this supreme masterpiece of the Counter Reformation was a product of a Spain in full, rapid, and final decline. Cervantes' loyalty and faith were complete, but his vision was clear and agonized. Long associated with Spanish imperial military power, it was in the wake of the destruction of the Armada that he composed part one of *Don Quixote* (published 1605).

Now it would be uncivil, or grotesque, to attempt to compare with the greatest novel ever written Ransom's vivid little poem, but we are not doing that: we are investigating correspondences in genesis, ambience, intention. Whatever else Christ may have been, he is not a picaresque figure, a man of adventures as the Don and the Captain are. The adventures are almost regularly hopeless, and show forth, indeed, traditions hopelessly defeated. Ransom is the most intransigently Southern of our authors except Faulkner, and neither the slightness of his mode (he has never attempted a long poem, and instead of developing after his early work fell silent) nor the elegance of his irony ought to conceal from us this basic fact. The Civil War may seem a long way back from the 1920s—when Ransom's important work was done—except to a Southerner; and, as the reader will no doubt know, Ransom was a leading figure in the literary-agrarian movement now called the Fugitives, whose chief social manifesto was *I Take My Stand* (1931). The antebellum air of the properties in "Captain Carpenter" gives this purely modern poem a second dimension, and I cannot but remark here that Ransom came slowly (largely under the influence, I believe, of his junior, Allen Tate) to what used to be called modernism: he hated, in print, *The Waste Land* when it appeared. As in *Don Quixote*, then, we attend with the Captain to ambiguous attitudes, failed and even ridiculous ideals, an irretrievable grandeur of senseless aspiration, the persistence into modern life (1605, 1930) of the discredited. Stylistically this double feeling comes clear in the wry, affectionate use of the old-fashioned "well-nigh" and "rout" (old-South for a party, a ball) in a poem from which he deleted the punctuation. It is from one ghostly great mansion of the past to another that the spry, twentieth-century Captain (not a Colonel—that would have been one inch too far) wanders on his doomed quest.

One further, which I will advance as decisive for the view I am here adopting, analogy, and we are done with Cervantes, or almost done. Casual rememberers, I think, among the very few non-Spaniards who have troubled to read *Don Quixote* to the end, feel that the Don has died. But this is not quite so: he has both died and not died; one is shaken with an ambiguity only less mysterious than the corresponding event in *Oedipus at Colonus*. Hesitant in allusion to these unsurpassable works, I suggest all the same that casual rememberers of "Captain Carpenter" see him as totally dismembered. But that is not so, and the meaning of the fact that that is not so will emerge only from some rehearsal of the events of the poem.

Do they need rehearsing? He appears to lose *everything*. Only no: in the brilliant peroration is stealthily concealed the fact that along with his heart is *not* taken his tongue, so presumably he (the tradition, both of Chivalry and Art) talks on, like Faulkner's Man in the Nobel Prize address.

Two points: there may be some anti-Romanism, as in "Lycidas." There may be, in the final line, some assimilation of the feminine-betrayal motif in "The Twa Corbies."

The poem is a fantasia on bruised Southern gentility and the prototype of bruised Christian chivalry, Don Quixote. Just who the female enemy is is not clear. Psychoanalytic suggestions might be in order. Not wanting to bother Mr. Ransom, I once put the matter to our old, close, and intelligent friend Mr. Tate, who said offhand: "Perhaps it's the *World*." I can't do better than that.

As to the "rogue in scarlet and grey," I confess my imbecility. Teasing colors, almost those of my prep school.

ÉDNA ST. VINCENT MILLAY

*The Bettmann Archive*

# EDNA ST. VINCENT MILLAY

## [1892–1950]

*Sonnets*

### I

Oh, think not I am faithful to a vow!
Faithless am I save to love's self alone.
Were you not lovely I would leave you now:
After the feet of beauty fly my own.
Were you not still my hunger's rarest food,   5
And water ever to my wildest thirst,
I would desert you—think not but I would!—
And seek another as I sought you first.
But you are mobile as the veering air,
And all your charms more changeful than the tide,  10
Wherefore to be inconstant is no care:
I have but to continue at your side.
So wanton, light and false, my love, are you.
I am most faithless when I most am true.

### II

And you as well must die, belovèd dust,
And all your beauty stand you in no stead;
This flawless, vital hand, this perfect head,
This body of flame and steel, before the gust
Of Death, or under his autumnal frost,   5
Shall be as any leaf, be no less dead
Than the first leaf that fell,—this wonder fled,
Altered, estranged, disintegrated, lost.
Nor shall my love avail you in your hour.
In spite of all my love, you will arise   10
Upon that day and wander down the air
Obscurely as the unattended flower,
It mattering not how beautiful you were,
Or how belovèd above all else that dies.

### III

What lips my lips have kissed, and where, and why,
I have forgotten, and what arms have lain
Under my head till morning; but the rain
Is full of ghosts tonight, that tap and sigh
Upon the glass and listen for reply,                                    5
And in my heart there stirs a quiet pain
For unremembered lads that not again
Will turn to me at midnight with a cry.
Thus in the winter stands the lonely tree,
Nor knows what birds have vanished one by one,          10
Yet knows its boughs more silent than before:
I cannot say what loves have come and gone,
I only know that summer sang in me
A little while, that in me sings no more.


### IV

#### ON HEARING A SYMPHONY OF BEETHOVEN

Sweet sounds, oh, beautiful music, do not cease!
Reject me not into the world again.
With you alone is excellence and peace,
Mankind made plausible, his purpose plain.
Enchanted in your air benign and shrewd,                       5
With limbs a-sprawl and empty faces pale,
The spiteful and the stingy and the rude
Sleep like the scullions in the fairy-tale.
This moment is the best the world can give:
The tranquil blossom on the tortured stem.                    10
Reject me not, sweet sounds! oh, let me live,
Till Doom espy my towers and scatter them,
A city spell-bound under the aging sun,
Music my rampart, and my only one.


### V

Love is not all: it is not meat nor drink
Nor slumber nor a roof against the rain;
Nor yet a floating spar to men that sink
And rise and sink and rise and sink again;
Love can not fill the thickened lung with breath,          5
Nor clean the blood, nor set the fractured bone;
Yet many a man is making friends with death
Even as I speak, for lack of love alone.
It well may be that in a difficult hour,

Pinned down by pain and moaning for release,                    10
Or nagged by want past resolution's power,
I might be driven to sell your love for peace,
Or trade the memory of this night for food.
It well may be. I do not think I would.

*Robert M. Bender*

---

MILLAY

FIVE SONNETS

In the nineteen-twenties, when American poetry was bursting with life, when T.S. Eliot had already given poetry a new
orientation with the publication of his *Prufrock and Other
Observations* (1917), Edna St. Vincent Millay became
known as the spokesman of her generation. Whether or not
she led, or even helped to shape, the revolt against Victorian-
ism, in life and in literature, is not really at question. She
caught a spirit of her times; her poetry was expressive, to her
ever increasing readers, of a new freedom. Today it is easy to
overlook what was so obvious to her readers in the twenties;
her frankness and her frank sensuality—a frankness that
would have been startling had it come from a man. Here was
a woman invading countless drawing rooms, and a few
garrets it may be hoped, with the most intimate poems about
"unremembered lads" whom she had kissed and shared other
pleasures with, pleasures that an inattentive reader might
miss, but not very likely. Today the shock is gone, and it is
easier to see how well Miss Millay's poetry fits the major
traditions of English poetry.

Her finest work is found in her shorter poems, where she
could startle with an accurately described emotion. And so it
is that of all her poetry, the sonnets endure best. The sonnet
form is ideally suited for the kind of poetry Miss Millay had
to write. It gave her just the medium she needed to display
her craftsmanship and to express the emotions in which she
was most involved.

Sonnets are about love, and Miss Millay's are no exception.
What struck her early readers, and what still makes itself felt,
is that as a woman she is able to play a man's game, and
sometimes even make it seem better. Sonnets are, to be sure,
about love, but usually, at least if we pay heed to the great
period of English sonnet writing, the Renaissance, which
Miss Millay studied very well, that love is inconstant. Great
sequences of sonnets were written just to show how hard-

hearted a lover, always a woman in those days, could be—how obstinate and how fickle. Many sonnets, while celebrating the inconstancy of women, also celebrate the constancy of men. Not so, said Edna St. Vincent Millay, but with a vengeance.

"Oh, think not I am faithful to a vow!" centers on the theme of inconstancy, but what a change from traditional sonnet writing. Here is the woman admitting her own inconstancy, faithful, as she tells us, "to love's self alone." The first eight lines present a clear description of love, put in the most immediate of physical terms so that the loved one (here a man) becomes the object of the poet's (here a woman) most ardent hunger and "wildest thirst." And then, as if to outdo even this description, Miss Millay characterizes the loved one as even more faithless than she is herself.

It has been asserted that not since Shakespeare himself has anyone, man or woman, so succeeded in capturing the movement and the spirit of the Shakespearean sonnet. To be sure, the form is difficult and puts heavy demands upon any poet, calling as it does for three separate quatrains and a concluding couplet. In the hands of mediocre practioneers, even in a few of Shakespeare's own sonnets, the form often breaks down so that instead of a true sonnet, all that is left is a twelve-line poem with the couplet more a final adornment than a necessary conclusion. It is true that in a sonnet such as "Oh, think not I am faithful to a vow!" Miss Millay does capture something of the Shakespearean feeling. The first two quatrains do develop a single theme—the condition of the poet. The third quatrain goes on to present us with a picture of her lover; but then in the couplet, instead of falling for the easy answer, Miss Millay unites all that has gone before with a provoking twist—that the poet's inconstancy stems from her devotion to a love even more inconstant than her own.

There is an immediacy in Miss Millay's early sonnets, which contributes greatly to their emotional impact. It is almost as if she were writing little dramas. In the poem just examined, for example, one gets the sense that, physically, the poet is very close to her lover. She is, in fact, speaking to him with something greater than the intimacy of a love letter. This sense of immediacy is even greater in "And you as well must die, beloved dust." Here the poet is with her lover. As she describes her mood, her sense of physical attachment for the man becomes clear. First she strokes his "flawless, vital hand," then his "perfect head," and then, becoming increasingly sensual, his "body of flame and steel."

This sense of immediacy is nothing new in poetry, though it is perhaps new for a woman poet: Donne's early love lyrics are saturated with this feeling. But it is lacking in the rather polite sonnets written by Victorian ladies, whether Elizabeth Barrett Browning or Christina Rossetti. It is an outstanding quality of Miss Millay's poetry, and in the early years contributed much to her popularity.

In some of her later sonnets Miss Millay lost this quality, but she replaced it with an expanding sense of human concern. The emotions of some of the later sonnets are more generalized. "What lips my lips have kissed, and where, and why," for example, speaks more of the poet's own condition than of any relations she has had with lovers. And even if the emotion is more generalized, the tightness of the poetry is still there. The description of the poet is made quite clear in the first eight lines. We get a sense of reverie and perhaps loneliness, but still of life. And this feeling of life is reinforced, brought as it were fully to the reader's consciousness, by the development of the imagery in the last six lines. The tree standing alone in winter, now vacant, empty of the birds who once sang there, fully captures the spirit of the poet who has known so many lovers. To be sure, the imagery is not very complex and it would be misleading to point to a comparison between this poem and Shakespeare's magnificent sonnet 73, "That time of year thou mayst in me behold." But this image does complete the poem, making the two parts necessary adjuncts to each other.

Even when she turned to more abstract themes—her response to a Beethoven symphony, undoubtedly the Fifth, which she was known to have memorized, or her definition of love ("Love is not all")—Miss Millay was always in control of her form. There is a precise movement to "Love is not all" that is neat and efficient and at the same time not merely mechanical. She achieves this by means of her rhetoric. The catch phrase at the beginning of the sonnet becomes more aggressive as we hear its variation at the beginning of the second quatrain. And then we are brought to consider the definition that has been given when the poet tells us "it may well be," and we know that we are about to have a fresh judgment. The repetition of this phrase, with a variation, "it well may be," is just enough to bring us to the same realization as the poet—that love really is all. In between these two rhetorical turns we are also made to realize that love is so very much in the present, so very much "of this night." Love is abstract, but it becomes very real when given such a sense of immediacy.

In her own day Miss Millay was treated to the most lavish praise, and to some quite violent criticism. From a distance it is easier to see the value of her work. She is not a new Shakespeare, nor has she left the imprint upon modern poetry of her more experimental contemporaries. But in her skill she partakes of the same traditions that Shakespeare did. Using a poetic language of the past, she nevertheless expresses the emotions of her own times. In doing so, she did much to revitalize sonnet writing in the twentieth century.

WILFRED OWEN

(© *Harold Owen*)

# WILFRED OWEN
## [1893–1918]

### Greater Love

Red lips are not so red
  As the stained stones kissed by the English dead.
Kindness of wooed and wooer
Seems shame to their love pure.
O Love, your eyes lose lure                5
  When I behold eyes blinded in my stead!

Your slender attitude
  Trembles not exquisite like limbs knife-skewed,
Rolling and rolling there
Where God seems not to care;             10
Till the fierce Love they bear
  Cramps them in death's extreme decrepitude.

Your voice sings not so soft,—
  Though even as wind murmuring through raftered loft,—
Your dear voice is not dear,           15
Gentle, and evening clear,
As theirs whom none now hear,
  Now earth has stopped their piteous mouths that coughed.

Heart, you were never hot,
  Nor large, nor full like hearts made great with shot;   20
And though your hand be pale,
Paler are all which trail
Your cross through flame and hail:
  Weep, you may weep, for you may touch them not.

# Charles Causley

## OWEN

### GREATER LOVE

In 1915, at the age of twenty-two, Wilfred Owen returned to England after two years as an English tutor in Bordeaux. He was commissioned in the Manchester Regiment, and arrived in France on active service in the last days of 1916, in the midst of a terrible winter and an even more terrible war of attrition.

Owen observed, with an absolutely steady hand and eye, the condition of the soldier at the front: that of a man thrown into a position of frightful isolation through the ignorance of civilians at home about the conditions under which the war was being fought. As the war "progressed," it was an isolation warmed and illumined only by the fellow-feeling of the soldier for the rest of the victims in France and Flanders, whatever language they spoke.

Out of this—one would have thought—unspeakable misery (for poetry, after all, is written not by gods but by men), Owen's voice has slowly emerged. His letters[1] to his family ("I can see no excuse for deceiving you . . .") are the first, resounding intimations of his destiny. Of No Man's Land he wrote, in January 1917:

> It is like the eternal place of gnashing of teeth; the Slough of Despond could be contained in one of its crater-holes; the fires of Sodom and Gomorrah could not light a candle to it—to find the way to Babylon the Fallen. It is pock-marked like a body of foulest disease, and its odour is the breath of cancer. I have not seen any dead. I have done worse. In the dank air I have *perceived* it, and in the darkness, *felt*. . . . No Man's Land under snow is like the face of the moon, chaotic, crater-ridden, uninhabitable, awful, the abode of madness.

[1] Extracts from all letters here quoted from *The Collected Poems of Wilfred Owen*, ed. C. Day Lewis. London, Chatto & Windus, 1963.

By May, Owen found himself for the second time in a casualty-clearing station on the Somme; this time he bore the label of neurasthenia. It was brought on, he wrote, by "living so long by the *disiecta membra* of a friend." In June, he was at the Craiglockhart War Hospital near Edinburgh. Here, a month or so later, arrived one whom Owen venerated as a man and a poet: Siegfried Sassoon. "Though not clearly conscious of it at the time," Sassoon wrote in his autobiography, *Siegfried's Journey*, "I now realize that in a young man of twenty-four his selflessness was extraordinary. The clue to his poetic genius was sympathy, not only in his detached outlook upon humanity but in all his actions and responses towards individuals." Together, Sassoon added, they vowed to "unmask the ugly face of Mars and—in the words of Thomas Hardy—'war's apology wholly stultify.'"

Owen had written poetry since youth, but his greatest period of poetic activity, in every sense of the word, was the twenty-two months that followed his first posting to wartime France. At about the end of August 1918, he returned there. "I'm in hasty retreat towards the Front," he wrote to Sassoon.

Before joining the army, Owen's life had been a somewhat shy and withdrawn one; that of a solitary. Once in uniform he found, as had many before, an unexpected warmth of comradeship, a feeling of solidarity and purpose with his companions, that reduced his sense of personal isolation. His inability to avoid sharing at all times the joys and, more significantly, the sufferings of his fellow men ("even when this seemed useless," wrote a woman friend), was complete.

"Greater love hath no man than this," said Jesus (*John* 15:13), "that a man lay down his life for his friends." In May 1917, Owen had written from hospital in France:

> Already I have comprehended a light which never will filter into the dogma of any national church: namely, that one of Christ's essential commands was: Passivity at any price! Suffer dishonour and disgrace, but never resort to arms. Be bullied, be outraged, be killed; but do not kill. It may be a chimerical and an ignominious principle, but there it is. It can only be ignored . . . And am I not myself a conscientious objector with a very seared conscience? . . . Greater love hath no man than this, that a man lay down his life for a friend. Is it spoken in English only and French? I do not believe so.

As with many of his poems, "Greater Love" contains an echo of Owen's former, formal Christianity. Romantic and sensuous and passionate feeling and imagination, the delicate apprehension of the musical significance of words—qualities he shared with Keats, whom he admired so greatly—are all absorbed effortlessly into a poetic personality that is uniquely Owen's. With a kind of supreme detachment, he takes what originally might seem to be two entirely opposing experiences—that of violent death, and the warm love of one human being for another—and fuses them into a single, homogeneous utterance.

Ideas and images that at first appear antithetical are seen to merge. In "Greater Love," the throbbing ecstasies of dying and death become the raptures and languors of the sexual act between lovers. It is an image that occurs more than once in Owen's verse; as, for example, in "The Last Laugh":

> *"My Love!" one moaned. Love-languid seemed his mood,*
> *Till, slowly lowered, his whole face kissed the mud.*

At the opening of "Greater Love," the red lips of the lover pale in comparison with the soldiers' wasted blood. Not the lover's eyes are seen, but those of one "blinded in my stead." During his first days in the trenches, Owen wrote of a sentry blown down the dug-out stairs and blinded. He refers more specifically to this incident in "The Sentry":

> *Eyeballs, huge-bulged like squids',*
> *Watch my dreams still.*

No Man's Land is a world presided over neither by an anguished Jesus nor a vengeful Jehovah; worse, it is one "where God seems not to care." In the third stanza of "Greater Love," contrasting ideas are again juxtaposed: the voices of the dead, "whom none now hear," speak with a compelling clarity unheard in any living tongue. The human heart, grown, ironically, large and full with white-hot metal, burns with more heat than one filled with the mere love of one human for another. (Owen also wrote, in "Insensibility," of the first effect of terror—that of "constriction"—on the sensibilities). There is, too, the figure of the soldier as Christ, in the dual role of killer and killed. While training troops and awaiting his second posting to France, Owen told Osbert Sitwell that he had been "teaching Christ to lift his cross by numbers, and how to adjust his crown."

In a large number of his poems, Owen sets off haunting reverberations through his skillful use of the half-rhyme. In "Greater Love," the half-rhyme is absent. The structure of the poem has a simple formality: the lines follow a steadily exact pattern. But, as always with Owen, the content of the poem, as well as this particular physical framework, is dictated firmly by the subject. The subject, as Owen wrote in his notes for a Preface to his poems, "is War, and the pity of War. The Poetry is in the pity. . . . All a poet can do today is warn. That is why the true Poets must be truthful."

In October 1918, he was awarded the Military Cross. One week before the Armistice of November 11th, while attempting to get his company over the Sambre Canal in the face of determined machine-gun and artillery fire, Owen was killed. His age was twenty-five. Only four of his poems were published in his lifetime. "Greater Love" first appeared in *Art and Letters* in 1920, and the first edition of Owen's poems was published in the same year.

"Greater Love" is not merely about the death of soldiers. Through the poet's tremendous capacity for self-identification with his subject, his total comprehension of the tragedy of human suffering, the soldiers themselves become the poetry. Owen grasped his theme and rose, with masterly objectivity, above his personal situation. Despite the weight of his physical and imaginative experience, the fearful poignancy of his poetic vision is free from despair.

E. E. CUMMINGS

*Self-portrait*

*The Bettmann Archive*

# E. E. CUMMINGS

[1894–1962]

## What If a Much of a Which of a Wind

what if a much of a which of a wind
gives the truth to summer's lie;
bloodies with dizzying leaves the sun
and yanks immortal stars awry?
Blow king to beggar and queen to seem 5
(blow friend to fiend: blow space to time)
—when skies are hanged and oceans drowned,
the single secret will still be man

what if a keen of a lean wind flays
screaming hills with sleet and snow: 10
strangles valleys by ropes of thing
and stifles forests in white ago?
Blow hope to terror; blow seeing to blind
(blow pity to envy and soul to mind)
—whose hearts are mountains, roots are trees, 15
it's they shall cry hello to the spring

what if a dawn of a doom of a dream
bites this universe in two,
peels forever out of his grave
and sprinkles nowhere with me and you? 20
Blow soon to never and never to twice
(blow life to isn't:blow death to was)
—all nothing's only our hugest home;
the most who die, the more we live

## John Ciardi

### CUMMINGS
### WHAT IF A MUCH OF A WHICH OF A WIND

Most readers of poetry (and all nonreaders who happen into the discussion) find it easy to insist that a poem is made of words, that the dictionary is the final authority in matters of interpretation, that if a poem "means anything at all" it will reveal itself to dictionary definition, and that if it fails to do so it is "meaningless."

It is more perceptive to think of that poem as being made not of words but of word combinations. When these combinations have been established in a good poem, the individual words are substantially released from their duty to the dictionary, taking their force now at least as much from their placement in the poem's combinations as from their dictionary sense. A good poem, that is to say, is written musically, itself calling itself into being in response to itself.

The good reader must allow the words of such a poem to function within their combinations, as elements of the poem's musicality, without being obdurate about forcing them back into subservience to the dictionary. For the dictionary can only try to locate, and not always precisely (some would say never precisely), what the word has meant in the past—an indispensable information, to be sure, but not information enough to tell us how the poet is using it now, in this poem.

Like a piece of music, too, a poem readily becomes involved in its own pattern, pursuing that pattern rather than any essay logic. Pattern is a special sort of formal combination. When two or more elements occur at the same position within a pattern, they take on a special relationship to one another—that relationship suggests what might be called new combinations of meaning but what would better be called combinations of response. For though the dictionary meaning of a given element in a poem may be uncertain, or even ungraspable, the reader's sense of its response to another element in the pattern can be not only certain but inevitable. And once again as in music, it is natural for the elements in any work of art to take on a many-sidedness that may be elusive in itself but firmly fixed in the pattern.

Cummings' poem is obviously tightly patterned. Each line in each stanza is knit to the corresponding line in each of the other two stanzas, and even the parts of the lines correspond. Consequently, no one line is complete in itself. Each has its own unity, but its total function in the poem can be located only as part of a triad.

It is not necessary, once a pattern has been established, for every element within the pattern to be clearly specified in dictionary terms. I have had what I believe to be a firm experience of this poem for many years, but I have never known surely how I should take the phrase "and queen to seem" in stanza one.

There are many things I do know about it. It is, to begin with, part of a parallelism: as *beggar* is to *king*, so *seem* is to *queen*. That being so, it is clearly some sort of opposite to queenliness. Stanza two adds that *seem* is to *queen*, as *terror* is to *hope*, and as *blind* is to *seeing*. And stanza three adds further that it is as *never* to *soon*, and as *twice* to *never* (in which I take *twice* to function as an intensive, signifying "twice-never" rather than "two times").

I am still left with no firm sense of "seem." I am sure of the sort of response that is called for, but I cannot see why Cummings sets that word to call for it. Anyone half-familiar with Cummings' extraordinary rhetoric can, of course, extend "seem" to "mere seeming." And perhaps that is a sufficient guess. And still I cannot hear it as a right tonality in the sequence from *king* – *beggar* to the corresponding elements in the repeated pattern of stanzas two and three. Or perhaps I am being obtuse. Or perhaps Cummings has written slackly. There is precedent enough to support either assumption.

Aside from that confusion (mine or Cummings'), there remain only the first and last lines as moments of possible difficulty, and then only for those who have not read enough Cummings to grasp his personal idiom (as, for example, students are baffled by John Donne only until they grasp his idiom and then discover that he is managing within it a sort of poetic experience that would be unmanageable without it).

So the "most" of the last line will be registered at once by those who speak Cummingsese. But if that is still a new language, the pattern of the poem will readily fix "most" in response to "the single secret" (which is man) and to "they" (who cry a response to the life impulse of spring, as un-man cannot). Accordingly, "most" may be made to answer to various specifications—but all of them must center in the idea of "the most that mankind is at its best." That "most," like all else, must die, but since it must first have been, it gives every man more to live by and toward.

There remains the pun of the first line, which is not part of the pattern (as it would have been had Cummings built a corresponding pun into the first line of each stanza), but which exists as a variation within the pattern.

It is a triple pun. *Which* in English is properly pronounced *hwich*. So pronounced, it is a good onomatopoeia: this is a swishing, hwishing, much of a hwiching wind. In American usage, however, *which* is commonly pronounced *witch*. This wind, therefore, is also much of a witch. But there is also "which" as a muted question: "Which wind?" To which the music answers, "all three." It is a hwiching, witching, much of a whichever wind, a keen of a lean wind, and a dawn of a dream's doom (that dream being, of course, the single secret of the most who die by whom the more we live).

And add that however much the critic may badger the poem in his clumsy trade of taking apart what can exist only in its simultaneity and multiplicity, the poem itself strikes through much as does Blake's "Tyger," a poem that contains elements beyond the reach of any exegesis, and yet one that declares itself to the reader as an instant and compelling experience.

# RICHARD EBERHART

[*b.* 1904]

## *The Groundhog*

In June, amid the golden fields,
I saw a groundhog lying dead.
Dead lay he; my senses shook,
And mind outshot our naked frailty.
There lowly in the vigorous summer                       5
His form began its senseless change,
And made my senses waver dim
Seeing nature ferocious in him.
Inspecting close his maggots' might
And seething cauldron of his being,                      10
Half with loathing, half with a strange love,
I poked him with an angry stick.
The fever rose, became a flame
And Vigour circumscribed the skies,
Immense energy in the sun,                               15
And through my frame a sunless trembling.
My stick had done nor good nor harm.
Then stood I silent in the day
Watching the object, as before;
And kept my reverence for knowledge                      20
Trying for control, to be still,
To quell the passion of the blood;
Until I had bent down on my knees
Praying for joy in the sight of decay.
And so I left; and I returned                            25
In Autumn strict of eye, to see
The sap gone out of the groundhog,
But the bony sodden hulk remained.
But the year had lost its meaning,
And in intellectual chains                               30
I lost both love and loathing,
Mured up in the wall of wisdom.
Another summer took the fields again
Massive and burning, full of life,

But when I chanced upon the spot                    35
There was only a little hair left,
And bones bleaching in the sunlight
Beautiful as architecture;
I watched them like a geometer,
And cut a walking stick from a birch.              40
It has been three years, now.
There is no sign of the groundhog.
I stood there in the whirling summer,
My hand capped a withered heart,
And thought of China and of Greece,                45
Of Alexander in his tent;
Of Montaigne in his tower,
Of Saint Theresa in her wild lament.

RICHARD EBERHART

*Wallace McNamee*
*Staff Photographer of*
*The Washington Post*

EBERHART

THE GROUNDHOG

During more than thirty years of popularity, Richard Eberhart's "The Groundhog" must have led very many to look further among his poems for the qualities of scope, force, and fineness it displays. What influence the poem may have had on readers and writers may be inferred. They will have found a poetry almost as free of explicit argument as of covert reference and complication: a poetry that shapes its meaning typically through inciting the movement of attention among particulars· of an abundant experience precisely rendered at certain points of highest interest. A great fullness—not the overflow of exuberance or the richness of elaboration, but a true abundance of the spirit—distinguishes Eberhart's best work. Being essential in the poetry, rather than a property of its constituents, this virtue may remain undiscovered if the poems are read in haste or in expectation of satisfactions they were not formed to give.

"The Groundhog" is eminently a poem that must be heard. It flows easily and can be read somewhat casually with a loosely controlled beat coming on the more important words three or four or five times to the line. But if it is read with four beats to the line, except where despite allowance for monosyllabic and polysyllabic measures the structure rigorously compels another count, it will be found to order itself more finely. The strait path of the meter is the wide way in which the forces of the poem move.

The poem opens in the first two lines with an exact alternation of light and heavy syllables, which seems to announce the most orderly sort of musical intention; and the effect of this regularity is enhanced by alternation of back and front vowels in the stressed syllables of the first line. The overt meaning is delivered in a statement simple and direct enough for almost any prose. The only hint of complications to come is given by a shock of contrast in the content of the two lines. In June, in the time of the summer solstice, amid the fields of plenty, the dead creature obtrudes. A degree of triteness in the epithet "golden" is almost reassuring. The traditional language and the old image of a color associated with beautiful objects and with splendor and opulence open familiar perspectives, and so too does our recognition in that gold of the ripening glow of change. The animal is seen amid the recurrent fulfillments of the year. Yet the most conclusive of all possible changes has overtaken him.

The following half line affirms this fact, not with a flourish but soberly, with concentrated strength. The opening of the third line, "Dead lay he," though syntactically artificial, is rhetorically natural. By reversal of the usual order of the parts of speech, a significant gradation has been arranged: first the state of deprivation is named; then the action that is sheer inaction, the verb indicating merely passive immobility; and finally, in the noun, subject of the clause but reduced to the objective position, is named the actor deprived of the power of acting. The brief statement, tense with its rhetorical necessity, rings like oratory. The pomp of tone is in part produced by the processional tread of the rhythm, marching a tripled thud without interval of any slack syllable, in the three consecutive accented words *dead. / Dead lay. . . .* In the measure *lay he* we hear neither an iamb nor a spondee (neither *lay hè* nor *lày hè*) but a trochee. Here the metrical strength of the foot emphasizes one syllable of the pair, the first: *lày he.* Yet the importance of the unaccented word gives it a force much greater than the slack syllable commonly possesses. The abruptly repeated word *Dead,* coming at the head of the line and wrenched from its conventional position in the sentence, has metrical strength at least equal to that of *lay,* and it has a considerable rhetorical force besides. Thus the three words opening the third line form a cadence of descending emphasis and pitch: the statement they shape is short and intense, but instead of rising like a cry it descends toward quiet. Within two-and-a-half lines the apparently ultimate fact has been defined.

The rest of the poem is the drama of what is done with that fact. It is a drama of transmutation—of thought, of attitude, and, most of all, of belief. The poem represents in several stages a man's struggle to accept in joy, as he feels he must accept it, that idea of the fundamental process of reality which has predominated in our time. Death manifest in a decaying groundhog has its great power to fascinate and shock mainly because it is seen as an expression of the nature of that process: envisaged as the "senseless change" of the form of the dead beast, death is an image of all sheerly physical process. Insensate force, represented by "Immense energy in the sun," contrasts with the "sunless trembling" of the poet's body as his intelligence grasps the meaning of his position in a universe of senseless change.

The passionate anguish of that first vision of reality is succeeded, at the next stage of the poem, by the poet's passionless contemplation, during the following autumn, of the sunken corpse quieted of its maggots. But this triumph in calm of intellect is a defeat for the heart, because the joy the poet prayed for is absent; and it is a defeat of the mind too, for "the year had lost its meaning." This state of knowledge and of being persists into another summer; the same vision of tremendous energies manifest everywhere in the world returns, exemplified in summer's once more possessing the fields,

*Massive and burning, full of life*

Physical energy, in the movement of masses and in consuming fire, is connoted in the first phrase, and in the second, "full of life," one must recall the groundhog full of a life not his, the energies of "his maggots' might." Charnel hair and bones, stony beauty of severe design in the white remnants and rigor like that of geometrical figures, discipline the imagination but do not stir the passions of the man, whose "withered heart," though freed of fear, remains depleted of the sap of joy.

Shortly, the poem ends—and it may appear to end in romantic suspiration of regret for all the transitory greatness of man, whose highest representatives in action, thought, and ecstasy have vanished like the corpse of the groundhog, of which "no sign" remains. Indeed, with an inconsiderable part of its concluding breath, the poem does so end. It is clear enough that peoples and individuals have vanished in physical death. Yet their spiritual energies, different from the maggots' might and of another process more essential, have continued to act, in a change that is not senseless, through transmission of vital form and quality from culture to culture and from individual life to life. The poet contemplating in joy those three, Alexander, Montaigne, and Saint Theresa, who stood at the peak of vision, and his reader sharing with him the stir and culminant power of the human spirit are assured of the reality of another energy than that of physical process in the universe: the energy of the spiritual process, traditionally imaged as that light of which the physical sun is no more than a sign. The poem comes to an end almost abruptly, as if intensity and immensity suddenly took its breath away.

# W. H. AUDEN

## [b. 1907]

## In Memory of W. B. Yeats

### (d. Jan. 1939)

### I

He disappeared in the dead of winter:
The brooks were frozen, the airports almost deserted,
And snow disfigured the public statues;
The mercury sank in the mouth of the dying day.
O all the instruments agree                                         5
The day of his death was a dark cold day.

Far from his illness
The wolves ran on through the evergreen forests,
The peasant river was untempted by the fashionable quays;
By mourning tongues                                                10
The death of the poet was kept from his poems.

But for him it was his last afternoon as himself,
An afternoon of nurses and rumours;
The provinces of his body revolted,
The squares of his mind were empty,                                15
Silence invaded the suburbs,
The current of his feeling failed: he became his admirers.

Now he is scattered among a hundred cities
And wholly given over to unfamiliar affections;
To find his happiness in another kind of wood                      20
And be punished under a foreign code of conscience.
The words of a dead man
Are modified in the guts of the living.

But in the importance and noise of tomorrow
When the brokers are roaring like beasts on the floor of
     the Bourse,                                                   25
And the poor have the sufferings to which they are
     fairly accustomed,
And each in the cell of himself is almost convinced of
     his freedom;

A few thousand will think of this day
As one thinks of a day when one did something slightly
    unusual.

O all the instruments agree                30
The day of his death was a dark cold day.

II

You were silly like us: your gift survived it all;
The parish of rich women, physical decay,
Yourself; mad Ireland hurt you into poetry.
Now Ireland has her madness and her weather still,    35
For poetry makes nothing happen: it survives
In the valley of its saying where executives
Would never want to tamper; it flows south
From ranches of isolation and the busy griefs,
Raw towns that we believe and die in; it survives,    40
A way of happening, a mouth.

III

Earth, receive an honoured guest;
William Yeats is laid to rest:
Let the Irish vessel lie
Emptied of its poetry.               45

Time that is intolerant
Of the brave and innocent,
And indifferent in a week
To a beautiful physique,

Worships language and forgives         50
Everyone by whom it lives;
Pardons cowardice, conceit,
Lays its honours at their feet.

Time that with this strange excuse
Pardoned Kipling and his views,         55
And will pardon Paul Claudel,
Pardons him for writing well.

In the nightmare of the dark
All the dogs of Europe bark,
And the living nations wait,         60
Each sequestered in its hate;

Intellectual disgrace
Stares from every human face,

W . H . AUDEN

*George Cserna*

And the seas of pity lie
Locked and frozen in each eye.                    65

Follow, poet, follow right
To the bottom of the night,
With your unconstraining voice
Still persuade us to rejoice;

With the farming of a verse                       70
Make a vineyard of the curse,
Sing of human unsuccess
In a rapture of distress;

In the deserts of the heart
Let the healing fountain start,                   75
In the prison of his days
Teach the free man how to praise.

# G. S. Fraser

---

## AUDEN

### IN MEMORY OF W. B. YEATS

This poem is one, and probably the best, of a set of poems grouped together as "occasional poems" at the end of Auden's volume of 1940, *Another Time*. That volume as a whole is centrally important in Auden's development in that it marks the transition in his work between a prospective, prophetic, and popular way of looking at history to what might be called a retrospective, priestly, and in a sense "élitiste" way of doing so. It also marks the crystallization of Auden's sense that conscious and urbane frivolity may be the truest mark, in an age of massive, self-frustrating, and passionately stupid destructiveness, of human seriousness—the concept of poetry as "a serious game."

Yeats had died in France, early in 1939, in his seventy-fourth year, and throughout the 1930s he had been recognized by the poets who are often thought of as Auden's "group"—by Day Lewis, who imitated his style extensively; by Auden himself, who modelled "September 1, 1939" very closely on Yeats's own "Easter, 1916" by MacNeice, who wrote a good, short critical study of Yeats; and by Spender—as the greatest poet, writing in English, of his time. Day Lewis and MacNeice had probably a specially intimate appreciation of Yeats, being themselves born from the Protestant, Anglo-Irish gentry. Yeats had published all these poets in his *Oxford Book of Modern English Verse*, praising them with his usual generosity, but expressing distaste for what he thought of as their fanatical doctrinaire quality, their swallowing of "terrible stone dolls." They themselves were a little embarrassed by having to admire so much a poet who believed in so many things they did not believe in—magic, reincarnation, a cyclical theory of history, romantic love, the good society as consisting of aristocrats and peasants—and who, as a person, had an old-fashioned stagey quality, "Irving with his plume of pride," which was not in the mode in the 1930's in England either.

It is important in reading Auden's poem to conceive clearly the typical attitude of the English intellectual toward Ireland and the Irish tradition. This is partly one of profound historical guilt, and partly an attitude of boredom and irritation: T.S. Eliot perhaps condensed it finally when, speaking not of Ireland but of Scotland, and praising the Scottish poet Hugh McDiarmid, he talked about "small oppressive nationalities." The small nationalities have in fact been *oppressed*. But from the point of view of a nation with a long record of blundering, complacent success behind it, with an instinctive feeling that whatever its present troubles, it will muddle through—like England in the 1930's—the intense national consciousness of the Irish or Scotch *is* oppressive, *is* stuffy. The Irish keep going on about *being* Irish, in a way that the English, in the evening of their power, did not find it necessary to go on about *being* English. The Irish claim a charm from their provenance. Yeats often felt a little of this himself, the stuffiness, the constriction, the envy of exceptional merit:

> *Out of Ireland have I come,*
> *Great hatred, little room*

Auden, therefore, in writing this great commemorative poem, had several problems to solve. He has to state, or imply, that Yeats came out of a rather potty or daft little country, whose main importance, for Auden, is that it "hurt [Yeats] into poetry"; that what Yeats said in poetry is, if translated into prose, mostly silly or dangerous; that Yeats's mode of life, the social and literary success so much promoted by flattered and flattering women, Lady Gregory, Olivia Shakespear, Dorothy Wellesley, is something like the mode of life of a country curate purred at by genteel spinsters. And yet, having said all this, he has to convey a sense of Yeats's superhuman mastery in the handling of words, a mastery that had almost nothing to do with what prose sense, or pragmatic schemes, the words might be translated into. This great, cool poem—cool almost in the American slang sense—is partly, and acutely, about Yeats himself: this is the topic; but more profoundly, and this is the theme, it is about the strange and paradoxical autonomy of poetic utterances. "Do not," one might almost (but too crudely) summarize the drift, "try to judge the things he was saying or the man he was. We all say silly things, and are all silly men. Listen to the magnificent noise he was making."

The first section of the poem deals with the actual day of Yeats's death, a frozen, wintry day (I do not know whether this was historically true, or checked by Auden) in which the fevers and deliriums running through the dying man's nerves and veins, a kind of false *summer*, are contrasted with the blockages, the interrupted communications, the distortions of appearance ("And snow disfigured the public statues") created by *winter*. The poet, a dying emperor, is seen as dissolving into the separate rebellious provinces of his own body. In 1939, when Auden wrote the poem, this same sort of dissolution might be seen coming over a Europe that had once been held together by a concept, such as Christendom, or a diplomatic technique and tradition, such as the Concert of Europe; some large and complex organism was dying, and "dying at the top."

The poem's dead Yeats is "scattered among a hundred cities," divided like the dead Osiris. What remains of him, his poetry, is now divorced from his own history and intention, and exists as what living use can still be made of it: "The words of a dead man / Are modified in the guts of the living."

The metaphor of eating and digesting reinforces the not explicitly stated idea of Yeats as a sacrificed god or king. The idea that in all the noise and obviousness of the future "a few thousand" will remember his death, but remember it only "as one thinks of a day when one did something slightly unusual," suggests a kind of sacramental identification of the reader of Yeats with Yeats, the reader saying, "I, too, in a sort of way died that day," but by its technique of praise through diminishment avoids identifying Yeats with a Christ image or saying that, as a total integral person, he will be resurrected. The emphasis on his weakness and loss of control while dying insists very much that, though grand, though imperial ("The provinces of his body revolted"), he is a man, not a god. But the day of his death is a memorable day, in a minor and analogous way like Christmas or Easter:

> *O all the instruments agree*
> *The day of his death was a dark cold day*

The instruments are the barometer and thermometer; but, with deliberate ambiguity, they are also the instruments of fate or history, which have chosen to remove Yeats from the scene, at the end of one historical era which his voice dominated, and at the beginning of another very "dark" and "cold"—very impenetrable, very uncharitable and uncharismatic—era of history.

The second section is a brief passage of finely controlled blank verse. It is a passage of sharp distinction between "the man who suffers" and "the poet who creates." Yeats was silly (dotty, daft, queer, eccentric) like all poets. He exploited women ("the parish of rich women"), not only in a mood of gallantry or romance. His own personality had its own weakness and absurdities (you survived "yourself"). "Mad Ireland" had hurt him into poetry, but the whole range of "mad" is intended—from the madness of Lear or of Oedipus tearing out his eyes, the madness of an intolerably tormented nation, to the madness of foolish Mad Tom, the madness that can be translated as "daft," "dotty," "potty," "round the bend." Ireland, the irritant, the bit of grit that produced the pearl in Yeats's oyster, is felt as both tragic and farcical. And since Yeats had devoted so much of his poetic and personal time to trying to help into being the kind of ideal Irish republic he dreamt of (aristocratic but liberal, simple peasant Catholics at its base, skeptical Ascendancy gentry at its top), Auden emphasizes almost brutally how little practical effect even the greatest poetry has on history: "poetry makes nothing happen." The landscape and terrain of poetry is an intrapersonal one, "the ranches of isolation and the busy griefs"; all that the river of poetry ever fertilizes is the individual psyche. All that it ever offers is "a way of happening, a mouth"—a style, which we can impose on or select from the historically inevitable: an authentic voice for joy or pain.

The third and last section of the poem is, properly, the most formal. The first section was in iambic lines of unequal length, divided into verse blocks of unequal length; not giving the effect of free verse, however, except in the sense that "Lycidas" is in free verse. There are equivalences of feminine ending, like *forests* and *poems* (where there is also, indeed, an equivalence of successive vowels, *o* and *e*): there are half-rhymes like *rumours* and *admirers:* yet the total effect is, cunningly, at least *apparently* loose and free, a formal and deliberately contrived casualness. One line ends with the carefully chosen, ostentatiously unemotive word "unusual." The blank verse of the second section is very conventional blank verse, its life coming out of its exact conventionality, an impression of formal withdrawal. The seven syllable lines of the quatrains of the last section seem by contrast to move formally, like a funeral march, with a balance in each line between two major and two minor stresses (the rise and fall of the slow-marching soldiers' feet):

> Earth, receive an honoured guest;
> William Yeats is laid to rest:
> Let the Irish vessel lie
> Emptied of its poetry

And with formal movement, the grand last section makes formal statement. The formal statement is that time does not care for what the poets said but for something about the way they said it: time will pardon Kipling for being a jingo, Claudel for being a bully and on the wrong side in the Spanish Civil War. It will pardon Yeats, similarly, for any nonsense he talked. Time "worships language." The time of Yeats's death was a terrible one:

> Intellectual disgrace
> Stares from every human face,
> And the seas of pity lie
> Locked and frozen in each eye

The paradox about the poet, or about the poet's language, is that it can explore every such situation to the depth,

> With the farming of a curse
> Make a vineyard of the curse

start fountains in deserts, teach the essentially free spirit of man to praise, to rejoice that all things are, even in an objective prison. The thematic strength of this splendid poem is in the balancing of the true statements that poetry, in the world of matter, of gross political and social action, can do almost nothing, and yet in the world of spirit, of man's transcendence of his fate, can do almost everything. There can be few finer examples in the English language of irony as celebration.

# September 1, 1939

I sit in one of the dives
On Fifty-second Street
Uncertain and afraid
As the clever hopes expire
Of a low dishonest decade:          5
Waves of anger and fear
Circulate over the bright
And darkened lands of the earth,
Obsessing our private lives;
The unmentionable odour of death          10
Offends the September night.

Accurate scholarship can
Unearth the whole offence
From Luther until now
That has driven a culture mad,          15
Find what occurred at Linz,
What huge imago made
A psychopathic god:
I and the public know
What all schoolchildren learn,          20
Those to whom evil is done
Do evil in return.

Exiled Thucydides knew
All that a speech can say
About Democracy,          25
And what dictators do,
The elderly rubbish they talk
To an apathetic grave;
Analysed all in his book,
The enlightenment driven away,          30
The habit-forming pain,
Mismanagement and grief:
We must suffer them all again.

Into this neutral air
Where blind skyscrapers use          35
Their full height to proclaim

The strength of Collective Man,
Each language pours its vain
Competitive excuse:
But who can live for long                                    40
In an euphoric dream;
Out of the mirror they stare,
Imperialism's face
And the international wrong.

Faces along the bar                                          45
Cling to their average day:
The lights must never go out,
The music must always play,
All the conventions conspire
To make this fort assume                                     50
The furniture of home;
Lest we should see where we are,
Lost in a haunted wood,
Children afraid of the night
Who have never been happy or good.                           55

The windiest militant trash
Important Persons shout
Is not so crude as our wish:
What mad Nijinsky wrote
About Diaghilev                                              60
Is true of the normal heart;
For the error bred in the bone
Of each woman and each man
Craves what it cannot have,
Not universal love                                           65
But to be loved alone.

From the conservative dark
Into the ethical life
The dense commuters come,
Repeating their morning vow;                                 70
"I *will* be true to the wife,
I'll concentrate more on my work,"
And helpless governors wake
To resume their compulsory game:
Who can release them now,                                    75
Who can reach the deaf.
Who can speak for the dumb?

Defenceless under the night
Our world in stupor lies;

Yet, dotted everywhere,       80
Ironic points of light
Flash out wherever the Just
Exchange their messages:
May I, composed like them
Of Eros and of dust,       85
Beleaguered by the same
Negation and despair,
Show an affirming flame.

# Mark Schorer

AUDEN
SEPTEMBER 1, 1939

The first problem presented by this poem is textual. Originally published in *New Republic* of October 18, 1939, "September 1, 1939" was reprinted (with minor changes in punctuation and spelling and with the deletion of the single word "and" at the beginning of the fifth line in the fifth stanza) in the poet's collection of 1940, *Another Time*.

Then, in 1945, in his *Collected Poetry*, and again in his *Collected Shorter Poems* of 1950, Auden himself had deleted the whole of the eighth stanza:

> *All I have is a voice*
> *To undo the folded lie,*
> *The romantic lie in the brain*
> *Of the sensual man-in-the-street*
> *And the lie of Authority*
> *Whose buildings grope the sky:*
> *There is no such thing as the State*
> *And no one exists alone;*
> *Hunger allows no choice*
> *To the citizen or the police;*
> *We must love one another or die*

In 1955, according to the late Oscar Williams, who was then putting together *The New Pocket Anthology of American Verse*, W.H. Auden wrote him to say that the final line of the eighth stanza as he had originally written it read not "We must love one another *or* die" but "We must love one another *and* die." The alteration of the single conjunction considerably alters the meaning not only of the line and stanza but of the entire poem.

Finally, in 1964, in his Introduction to B.C. Bloomfield's *W.H. Auden: A Bibliography*, Auden wrote this:

> Rereading a poem of mine, *1st September, 1939*, after it had been published, I came to the line
> > We must love one another or die.
> and I said to myself: "That's a damned lie! We must

*1025*

die anyway." So, in the next edition, I altered it to
We must love one another and die.
This didn't seem to do either, so I cut the stanza. Still
no good. The whole poem, I realised, was infected
with an incurable dishonesty and must be scrapped.

His admirers may wish to dissent.

Written in the meter of W.B. Yeats's "Easter 1916,"
Auden's poem emulates as well the easy vernacular style of
the earlier poem:

> *I have met them at close of day*
> *Coming with vivid faces*
> *From counter or desk among gray*
> *Eighteenth-century houses—,*

a style capable of quick transformation into heroic rhetorical
statement, or aphoristic generalization, or sudden showers of
images—almost anything one might wish—and yet, whatever
the modulations, maintaining always the integrity of tone. It
is a style that, while taking a highly personal stance and tone,
can utter abstract and public "truths." It is a plain style that,
as Yeats in many other poems showed Auden, can readily
assimilate every kind of reference, from exalted and distantly
historical names (Thucydides, Luther) to the local, the immediate, the special (mad Nijinsky, Diaghilev, "the wife").
Borrowing, too, Yeats's urban setting but making a good deal
more of it, Auden is in some ways writing the same kind of
poem. Both might be called political elegies. But if Yeats's is a
celebration of the martyrdom of Irish revolutionaries whose
death transforms sordid politics into tragic beauty, Auden's
is a bitter and apprehensive comment on the death of a dis-
graceful political era and the birth of terror. In meaning, too,
Auden's poem somehow looks to Yeats, or at least to Auden's
poem "In Memory of W.B. Yeats," for the closing lines of
"September 1, 1939"—

> *May I . . .*
> *Beleaguered by the same*
> *Negation and despair,*
> *Show an affirming flame.*

are really only a compressed version of the last three stanzas
of the great poem to Yeats:

> *Follow, poet, follow right*
> *To the bottom of the night,*
> *With your unconstraining voice*
> *Still persuade us to rejoice;*

*With the farming of a verse*
*Make a vineyard of the curse,*
*Sing of human unsuccess*
*In a rapture of distress;*

*In the deserts of the heart*
*Let the healing fountain start.*
*In the prison of his days*
*Teach the free man how to praise.*

One can hardly imagine a less likely historical moment in which to make affirmations; nor can one well imagine one in which they were more necessary. On September 1, 1939, with the invasion of Poland, a decade of shameful political compromise came to an end and the long waiting war at last broke upon the West. The poet, at once himself, "I," and every ordinary man of good will, "we," sits in the pit of the city and at the nadir of history for democratic man, contemplating some acrid truths. Seventeen months before, Adolf Hitler at Linz, the same town where he was an unwilling and wretched schoolboy, declaring now the Austrian Republic at an end and absorbing it into the German Reich, dramatized the climax of an historical process that began with Luther and the separation of the German states from the Holy Roman Empire. The paradox of that process was that it was at once to create the possibility of the idea of the all-powerful state and of the reality of all-powerful individuals in the form of demented dictators. And these two phenomena of modern history, the badgered, buffetted, and bruised individual now contemplates and tries to comprehend.

The lines of the second stanza pretty well characterize the scope of the poem as a whole, which makes an analytical statement that has simultaneous historical, cultural, political, and psychological significance. It is in the last of these that the poem resolves itself as the poet discovers the "folded" double lie by which modern man attempts to live. He accepts as a reality the abstract notion of the all-powerful state, "the lie of Authority," when in fact "There is no such thing as the State" or as "Collective Man." At the same time he tries to live by the "romantic lie" of self-love, the craving "to be loved alone," when, in fact, "no one exists alone." The first—the monstrous mechanism of destructive Organization—is perhaps an externalization of the death wish, Freud's Thanatos, that "dust" and "despair" of the final stanza. The other—the isolated individual—is the victim of Freud's other drive, that self-regarding "crooked" love, Eros, which mingles with the "dust" in every man. There is another form of love, not named as such, Agape, universal love, and it is that which the Just man, "the freeman" of the Yeats poem, can praise and that can save him. "We must love one another or die."

In that form, the line gives us a way out, implies a *social* rescue. Change the line to read, "We must love one another *and* die," and the meaning of the poem changes as well; for now, with the radical theological implication that, while we must love one another, we will *still* die, the hope for amelioration in this world is extinguished. Drop the entire stanza, however, and one can read the poem in either way, as one wishes.

And perhaps that is what Auden finally wishes us to do. With either the *or* or the *and*, he tells us how to read it, and he may very well have felt that this made the poem excessively didactic, that he

> *Adopted what I would disown*
> *The preacher's loose immodest tone*

as he wrote in another poem. He has written, too, the following:

> Poetry is not concerned with telling people what to do, but with extending our knowledge of good and evil, perhaps making the necessity for action more urgent and its nature more clear, but only leading us to the point where it is possible for us to make a rational and moral choice.

The final version of "September 1, 1939," with the stanza deleted, forces such a choice upon us both as readers and as men, and upon us alone.

# GEORGE BARKER

[*b.* 1913]

## *Three Memorial Sonnets*

*For two young seamen lost overboard in a storm in Mid-Pacific, January, 1940.*

### I

The seagull, spreadeagled, splayed on the wind,
Span backwards shrieking, belly facing upward,
Fled backward with a gimlet in its heart
To see the two youths swimming hand in hand
Through green eternity. O swept overboard     5
Not could the thirty-foot jaws them part,
Or the flouncing skirts that swept them over
Separate what death pronounced was love.

I saw them, the hand flapping like a flag,
And another like a dolphin with a child     10
Supporting him. Was I the shape of Jesus
When to me hopeward their eyeballs swivelled,
Saw I was standing in the stance of vague
Horror; paralysed with mere pity's peace?

### II

From thorax of storms the voices of verbs
Shall call to me without sound, like the silence
Round which cyclones rage, to nurse my nerve
And hang my heart midway, where the balance
Meets. I taste sea swilling in my bowels     5
As I sit shivering in the swing of waves
Like a face in a bubble. As the hull heaves
I and my ghost tread water over hell.

The greedy bitch with sailors in her guts
Green as a dream and formidable as God,     10
Spitting at stars, gnawing at shores, mad randy,
Riots with us on her abdomen and puts

Eternity in our cabins, pitches our pod
To the mouth of the death for which no one is ready.

### III

At midday they looked up and saw their death
Standing up overhead as loud as thunder
As white as angels and as broad as God:
Then, then the shock, the last gasp of breath
As grazing the bulwark they swept over and under,               5
All the green arms around them that load
Their eyes their ears their stomachs with eternals,
Whirled way in a white pool to the stern.

But the most possible of all miracles
Is that the useless tear that did not fall                       10
From the corner of their eyes, was the prize,
The flowers, the gifts, the crystal sepulchre,
The funeral contribution and memorial,
The perfect and nonexistent obsequies.

GEORGE BARKER

*The Estate of Oscar Williams*

## Martha Fodaski

### BARKER
### THREE MEMORIAL SONNETS

George Barker is a poet who wants, as he himself wrote of André Gide, to write his life and have it too. Unlike many of his fellow modern poets, he has dedicated himself wholly and passionately to the vocation of writing poetry. The largely self-educated Anglo-Irish poet, early encouraged by Eliot and appreciated by Yeats, chose, after his first literary successes in England, to become the artist in exile—the itinerate poet-pariah whose life and poetry are the history of his restless wandering. The "Three Memorial Sonnets" record an event that occurred on one of his voyages—a voyage to Japan as visiting professor of English literature at the Imperial Tohuku University in Sendai. In the past two decades he has lived variously in England, the United States, and Italy. He has been recognized in England by grants from his British publisher Faber and Faber, from the King's Bounty, and from the Royal Society of Literature—and in America by invitations to read his poetry at places as various as New York's 92nd Street Y, the University of Texas, and the Library of Congress, where he recorded his verse in 1958.

A controversial figure whose work has been damned for its rhetoric and its sexual and moral exhibitionism—and praised for its brilliant style and its fearless and intense moral vision—Barker has forged a reputation as a powerful lyricist who dares to ask overwhelming questions. More impelled by ideas than Dylan Thomas, to whom he is often compared, Barker is keenly aware of the magic and mystery of language and of the trial and tragedy of human life. In effect renouncing the intellectual self-consciousness that his mentor, Eliot, demands, Barker announced in the title of a 1940 essay that *All Poems are Elegies*—and went on to say that "To be so closely caught up in the teeth of things that they kill you . . . is, truly, to be a poet." Barker's avowal came during the period when he wrote the "Three Memorial Sonnets," which represent both the work of the middle of his career and a perfect amalgam of the verbal and emotional intensity and the elegiac involvement that characterize most of his poems. Always haunted by a dark view of the world, Barker is persistently implicated in the suffering that is often his subject. His poems frequently move, like the sonnets, from an objective event to its subjective significance.

In a poetry extremely sensitive to the artistic and intellectual milieu of the times, Barker persistently seeks to integrate his vast eclectic knowledge into a system of belief that will sustain him personally and poetically. In the work published before 1936, Barker's romantic questor is a visionary. The *tour de force*, "Calamiterror" (1937), witnesses the change from poet-*voyant* to poet-*engagé*. "Lament and Triumph," 1940; "Eros in Dogma," 1944; and "News of the World," 1950 define the poet's involvement in mankind and his tragic response to social, political, and personal crises. The most recent poems, in *A Vision of Beasts and Gods*, 1954; *The View from a Blind I*, 1962; and *The True Confession of George Barker*, 1964, often reveal the guilt-ridden religious rebel who learns that although he cannot affirm a beneficent God, he can affirm life itself or at least the life of the poem. Although sometimes full of cynical self-irony (as in his "mistress-piece," *The True Confession*), the poems finally disclose the Dionysian artist suffering from overfullness of life, a tragic yea sayer. The ethical values of his quondam Catholicism and the claims of biological necessity clash in a poetry of conflict dominated by a visionary Abel and an earth-bound Cain. The warring opposites make poems.

The best poetry achieves its power through a dialectic that is perhaps more honest and is surely more exciting than the sense of detachment that many of his contemporaries communicate. Energy and passion, verbal extravagance and tension go into a Barker poem. The "Three Memorial Sonnets" are masterly examples of his ability to reconcile dissonant elements into a significant organic whole. The seemingly surrealistic imagery and bold orchestration are bound to, and indeed cannot be separated from, values of meaning and feeling in the poems.

The first sonnet begins in an acutely apprehended image of a real event. It concerns, however, the emotional response of the speaker, whose attention is riveted to the horrifying scene. The opening image, with its compelling visual and auditory impact, establishes the scene; the action of the bird parallels, at the same time, the fall of the two sailors, swept backward into the water, and the feelings of the stunned spectator, pierced with dread at the moment of their fall. The violent imagery of the octave is appropriate and essential for picturing the event, for suggesting the stormy sea and the terror of the seamen, and for presenting the speaker's tumultuous feelings. Barker personifies the sea first as a giant with jaws that will swallow the men and then suggests a *femme fatale* whose waves are flouncing skirts. The men themselves look, ironically, like lovers. The speaker, unable to move or to think rationally, is overwhelmed by "pity's peace"—the seeming calm of one dumbstruck by "vague horror."

In the octave the focus on the speaker's visual and emotional response is implicit; in the sestet, the point of view is clearly revealed. Even the disparate similes of the "hand flapping like a flag, / And another like a dolphin with a child / Supporting him" convey the images that the ineffectual gestures of the floundering seamen inspire in the observer. He wonders, "Was I the shape of Jesus," the sailors' hope for mercy or the form of their judgment, to the drowning men in whose rolling eyes he interprets looks of supplication. The automatic gesture of terror-stricken appeal is grimly communicated by "their eyeballs swivelled." The turbulent sea, sailors, and state of the speaker are simultaneously suggested by the startling images.

The second sonnet, equally dazzling, centers on the violent storm and the speaker's feeling of entrapment as he empathizes with the sailors. Because it does not concern his immediate reaction, this sonnet is properly more consistent than the first. Controlled by a series of associations, all of which use the relationship of containers to things contained, it formulates the speaker's fear, no longer "vague horror," but now defined as fear of enclosure—his own fear of drowning. The poem itself comes from inside the storm ("From thorax of storms . . . like the silence / Round which cyclones rage"); so real is the empathy that the speaker tastes the "sea swilling" in his bowels; sitting in the "swing of waves," aware of his insignificance before the elemental fury, he is "like a face in a bubble"; sailors are in the "guts" of the "greedy bitch." The human factors are caught or swallowed by the sea. Deriving from the central pattern, Barker's final image of man's paltry place before the great devourer comes through forcefully: the sea tosses the husk of man, his body, into her mouth, as if it were so much refuse to be eaten by the piggish, female sea—death.

The third sonnet focuses on the sailors. After the first treats the impact on the speaker of the sailors' fall and the second his identification with their doom, the third completes the trilogy from a relatively detached view. After the octave describes the speaker's vivid impression of the drowning itself, the sestet remarks with irony and objectivity that quick death without tears is at least a victory over the hollow conventional observances usually associated with death. The "useless tear that did not fall / . . . was the prize"; the pitiless speed of the drowning marks it as unusual, an event possibly deviating from what man knows about dying. The fact that they had no time for tears is the only substitute the seamen are granted for the customary rites marked by

> *The flowers, the gifts, the crystal sepulchre*
>
> . . .
>
> *The perfect and nonexistent obsequies.*

The catalogue in apposition to "the prize" (that is, the "tear" not shed that paradoxically provides a memorial for the dead men), is of the usual tokens of rites of passage, which, because they are performed with ceremonial correctness, are perfect, but because they are sanctimonious and have little to do with the actual fact of death, are not really obsequies at all. Wilfred Owen's "Anthem for Doomed Youth" and Dylan Thomas' "A Refusal to Mourn" reveal similar attitudes toward the reality of violent death.

Technically, the sonnets reflect the influence of Hopkins. The first lines,

> *The seagull, spreadeagled, splayed . . .*

adapt Hopkins' alliterative technique perfectly to imply the sense of helplessness and the remorseless movement of nature toward death. Carefully wrought consonance, such as the shrieking *s*s that sweep through the first sonnet like a great wind, contributes to a music contrived to transmit urgency and shock. The inversions and daring use of the effusive "O," as well as the sprung rhythm of "Then, then the shock, the last gasp of breath," appropriately express internal stress. The metrical roughness within an otherwise tightly controlled form enforces the central tension between the inescapable fact of death and the equally inescapable fact that witnessing it inspires an awful empathy. Death is as inevitable to man as fourteen lines are to the sonnet, but a man experiencing death vicariously cannot accept it in unquavering iambic pentameter or perfect sonnet rhyme scheme. The off rhyme— *wind-hand, silence-balance, waves-heaves, randy-ready, God-load*—captures the dissonant quality of the experience.

The three poems make up a study in reactions to violent death by water; they become movements of one poem whose dialectical imagery completes the picture of and response to the drowning. The many indications of setting (the sea gull, green water, cabins, bulwark, stern) merge with the archetypal sea imagery of the devouring mother (clearest in the second sonnet, but suggested by jaws and skirts in the first, and in the third by the "green arms around them") in juxtaposition to implications of a conventional Christian reaction that is finally rejected as irrelevant. The sestet of sonnet two reminds us that the elemental amoral female is "formidable as God"; the eternity she brings is green because it means drowning forever in her waters. The octave of sonnet three reiterates the entreaty first suggested in sonnet one; but when the seamen looked up at the noon sun they knew with terrible certainty that they would die. The similes indicate that, for the sailors, it was doomsday, "loud as thunder / As white as angels and as broad as God." The sestet concludes that in spite of their seeming appeal to Jesus, the only miracle is that they did not suffer more. Although the sea is like God and death like His judgment, the spectator accepts with secular courage the fact that death is both inexorable and final.

Even the concluding ironic approval of the way in which the sailors died is appropriate to the emotional development of the trilogy from the shock of the first, to the shudder of the second, to the grim serenity of the third poem. Barker skillfully equates the emotional pattern, the course of the tempest, and the tempestuous action; and all these work together to transmit the initial imprint of the event, the speaker's subsequent fear, and his final resignation. By Barker's own definition of his tragic poetry, this sort of sequence—impact, reaction, resignation—makes for an elegy. The remarkable trilogy here is an eloquently inscribed memorial for the lost seamen. Each time the reader enters its turbulence he finds himself stirred, then purged by its terrible beauty, of his fears of "the death for which no one is ready."

## Allegory of the Adolescent and the Adult

It was when weather was Arabian I went
Over the downs to Alton where winds were wounded
With flowers and swathed me with aroma, I walked
Like Saint Christopher Columbus through a sea's welter
Of gaudy ways looking for a wonder.                    5

Who was I, who knows, no one when I started,
No more than the youth who takes longish strides,
Gay with a girl and obstreperous with strangers,
Fond of some songs, not unusually stupid,
I ascend hills anticipating the strange.               10

Looking for a wonder I went on a Monday,
Meandering over the Alton down and moor;
When was it I went, an hour a year or more,
That Monday back, I cannot remember.
I only remember I went in a gay mood.                  15

Hollyhock here and rock and rose there were,
I wound among them knowing they were no wonder;
And the bird with a worm and the fox in a wood
Went flying and flurrying in front, but I was
Wanting a worse wonder, a rarer one.                   20

So I went on expecting miraculous catastrophe.
What is it, I whispered, shall I capture a creature
A woman for a wife, or find myself a king,
Sleep and awake to find Sleep is my kingdom?
How shall I know my marvel when it comes?              25

Then after long striding and striving I was where
I had so long longed to be, in the world's wind,
At the hill's top, with no more ground to wander
Excepting downward, and I had found no wonder.
Found only the sorrow that I had missed my marvel.     30

Then I remembered, was it the bird or worm,
The hollyhock, the flower or the strong rock,

Was it the mere dream of the man and woman
Made me a marvel? It was not. It was
When on the hilltop I stood in the world's wind.          35

The world is my wonder, where the wind
Wanders like wind, and where the rock is
Rock. And man and woman flesh on a dream.
I look from my hill with the woods behind,
And Time, a sea's chaos, below.          40

# Robin Skelton

BARKER
ALLEGORY OF THE ADOLESCENT AND THE ADULT

If we mean by "allegory" a narrative in which each character and object can be identified as representative of one definite quality, or given a precise denotation, then this poem is no allegory. If we use the word loosely, meaning simply a fable or parable, then the title is meaningful and has been given an appropriate quality of incantatory exuberance by the use of the three chiming *A*s.

The fable itself is straightforward enough. We all go through our adolescence looking for marvels; true maturity begins when we realize that the whole process of our living, and of our questioning it, is a wonder—and all the earth miraculous.

This poem has enhanced its theme with freshness and immediacy in several ways. Local and particular references ("to Alton," "on a Monday") though unimportant thematically, are valuable as gestures that stage the poem's events in our own world of the actual and commonplace. The references to Christopher Columbus and to Arabia operate similarly, the first presenting an aura of the heroic and introducing a suggestion of the far-ranging nature of the journey that is to take place; and the second promoting those notions of the marvelous that are so often connected with Arabia, as Walter de la Mare was clever enough to perceive when he composed his irrational but haunting lyric. These elements of the heroic and the marvelous are also present in the third stanza where the supernormal time-dimension of magical experience is implied, and there are deliberate, though not overserious, references to the romance themes of maiden, king, and fairy kingdom in stanza five. These comparatively unobtrusive allusions do their work well, but the main work of the poem is done by its astonishing alliterative and assonant patterns.

In the first five stanzas all the end words are linked with each other by alliteration, first in *w*, and then in *st*, *m*, *w*, and hard *c* or *k*. These stanzas combine to form one uninterrupted surge of narrative excitement; there is no check to the journey or to the hope for a miracle until the last line of the sixth stanza, where the end word breaks the alliterative pattern, and doubt intrudes upon hope. The seventh stanza also checks the alliterative flow in its second line with the word *rock*, which therefore obtrudes, hard and rocklike, at a point where doubt is intensified. The eighth and final stanza discards the previous alliterative pattern completely and presents a new one, just as the speaker himself substitutes for his earlier unthinking, adolescent hope a more mature and sturdily intellectual acceptance of life's realities. Thus the sound pattern of the poem, as revealed merely in the end words, reflects and intensifies the thematic structure of the poem.

The sound is important in other respects also. The assonance and alliteration in the body of each stanza emphasize the incantatory element in the speaker's reflections and thus intensify our appreciation of the self-intoxicating aspect of the theme. Moreover, by making all the ideas and images appear subordinate to the tune, it suggests that the whole of the speaker's world of perception is both dominated and obscured by his emotional excitement. And poems have to do with history, too, as well as with individual characterization; the alliterative techniques of this particular poem recall what might be called the adolescence of literature as well as the adolescence of the speaker, for they are reminiscent of Anglo-Saxon verse in which the lines were bound together by consonance and assonance rather than by metrical devices. This echoing of the largely heroic verse of the remote past is appropriate in a poem that continually trembles on the verge of epic exuberance.

The use of consonance and assonance is valuable for another reason: it allows the poem a wide freedom of rhythm while preserving the rhetorical advantages of disciplined form. Thus the (usually) four-beat lines include varying numbers of unstressed syllables; and their rhythms, too, vary, as do those of Gerard Manley Hopkins, between the iambic (or trochaic) and the anapaestic (or dactylic) with occasional emphatic spondees. This results in an apparent spontaneity, even recklessness—which is, again, appropriate to the theme and expressive of it.

The poem as a whole makes use of the notion of a wanderer in a particular landscape who, at his journey's end, which is also the end of his meditation, happens on a Truth.

This is a Wordsworthian device, and we may well be re-minded of at least the opening movements of both "Michael" and "Resolution and Independence." The conclusion, how-ever, is not Wordsworthian, but more Bergsonian. We are marvelous because we are part of the impulse of all creation toward immortality, and because man is the highest manifes-tation of the yearning of the spirit of life. As time rose once out of chaos, so we now rise out of time, making it seem a chaos from which we have escaped and climbed as life itself, aeons ago, climbed out of the sea.

In saying this I am not only summing up the poem's final statement but also summarizing its total structure. The fluid and incantatory qualities of its beginning reflect more than the emotionalism of adolescence; they reflect also the flux of life itself in its origins. Moreover, the way in which intuitive excitement is checked by intellectual stirrings, which lead to a harder and more definite attitude, must be regarded as a statement about the evolution of mankind as well as the maturing of an individual. In addition, just as the speaker of the poem must finally recognize the marvel of his own existence, so mankind must realize its possession of divinity, and the poem itself understand the miraculous nature of its own artistry and of the conquest of art over time.

George Barker has written many fine poems—but this is perhaps his most extraordinary lyric achievement, and one of the master poems of our time in its total fusion of message and structure.

DYLAN THOMAS

*The Estate of Oscar Williams*

# DYLAN THOMAS
## [1914–1953]

## *Altarwise by Owl-Light*

### I

Altarwise by owl-light in the half-way house
The gentleman lay graveward with his furies;
Abaddon in the hangnail cracked from Adam,
And, from his fork, a dog among the fairies,
The atlas-eater with a jaw for news,                          5
Bit out the mandrake with to-morrow's scream.
Then, penny-eyed, that gentleman of wounds,
Old cock from nowheres and the heaven's egg,
With bones unbuttoned to the half-way winds,
Hatched from the windy salvage on one leg,                   10
Scraped at my cradle in a walking word
That night of time under the Christward shelter:
I am the long world's gentleman, he said,
And share my bed with Capricorn and Cancer.

### II

Death is all metaphors, shape in one history;              15
The child that sucketh long is shooting up,
The planet-ducted pelican of circles
Weans on an artery the gender's strip;
Child of the short spark in a shapeless country
Soon sets alight a long stick from the cradle;             20
The horizontal cross-bones of Abaddon,
You by the cavern over the black stairs,
Rung bone and blade, the verticals of Adam,
And, manned by midnight, Jacob to the stars.
Hairs of your head, then said the hollow agent,            25
Are but the roots of nettles and of feathers
Over these groundworks thrusting through a pavement
And hemlock-headed in the wood of weathers.

### III

First there was the lamb on knocking knees
And three dead seasons on a climbing grave                    30
That Adam's wether in the flock of horns,
Butt of the tree-tailed worm that mounted Eve,
Horned down with skullfoot and the skull of toes
On thunderous pavements in the garden time;
Rip of the vaults, I took my marrow-ladle                     35
Out of the wrinkled undertaker's van,
And, Rip Van Winkle from a timeless cradle,
Dipped me breast-deep in the descended bone;
The black ram, shuffling of the year, old winter,
Alone alive among his mutton fold,                            40
We rung our weathering changes on the ladder,
Said the antipodes, and twice spring chimed.

### IV

What is the metre of the dictionary?
The size of genesis? the short spark's gender?
Shape without shape? the shape of Pharaoh's echo?            45
(My shape of age nagging the wounded whisper).
Which sixth of wind blew out the burning gentry?
(Questions are hunchbacks to the poker marrow).
What of a bamboo man among your acres?
Corset the boneyards for a crooked boy?                       50
Button your bodice on a hump of splinters,
My camel's eye will needle through the shroud.
Love's reflection of the mushroom features,
Stills snapped by night in the bread-sided field,
Once close-up smiling in the wall of pictures,               55
Arc-lamped thrown back upon the cutting flood.

### V

And from the windy West came two-gunned Gabriel,
From Jesu's sleeve trumped up the king of spots,
The sheath-decked jacks, queen with a shuffled heart;
Said the fake gentleman in suit of spades,                    60
Black-tongued and tipsy from salvation's bottle.
Rose my Byzantine Adam in the night.
For loss of blood I fell on Ishmael's plain,
Under the milky mushrooms slew my hunger,
A climbing sea from Asia had me down                          65
And Jonah's Moby snatched me by the hair,

Cross-stroked salt Adam to the frozen angel
Pin-legged on pole-hills with a black medusa
By waste seas where the white bear quoted Virgil
And sirens singing from our lady's sea-straw.     70

### VI

Cartoon of slashes on the tide-traced crater,
He in a book of water tallow-eyed
By lava's light split through the oyster vowels
And burned sea silence on a wick of words.
Pluck, cock, my sea eye, said medusa's scripture,     75
Lop, love, my fork tongue, said the pin-hilled nettle;
And love plucked out the stinging siren's eye,
Old cock from nowheres lopped the minstrel tongue
Till tallow I blew from the wax's tower
The fats of midnight when the salt was singing;     80
Adam, time's joker, on a witch of cardboard
Spelt out the seven seas, an evil index,
The bagpipe-breasted ladies in the deadweed
Blew out the blood gauze through the wound of manwax.

### VII

Now stamp the Lord's Prayer on a grain of rice,     85
A Bible-leaved of all the written woods
Strip to this tree: a rocking alphabet,
Genesis in the root, the scarecrow word,
And one light's language in the book of trees.
Doom on deniers at the wind-turned statement.     90
Time's tune my ladies with the teats of music,
The scaled sea-sawers, fix in a naked sponge
Who sucks the bell-voiced Adam out of magic,
Time, milk, and magic, from the world beginning.
Time is the tune my ladies lend their heartbreak,     95
From bald pavilions and the house of bread
Time tracks the sound of shape on man and cloud,
On rose and icicle the ringing handprint.

### VIII

This was the crucifixion on the mountain,
Time's nerve in vinegar, the gallow grave     100
As tarred with blood as the bright thorns I wept;
The world's my wound, God's Mary in her grief,
Bent like three trees and bird-papped through her shift,

With pins for teardrops is the long wound's woman.
This was the sky, Jack Christ, each minstrel angle          105
Drove in the heaven-driven of the nails
Till the three-coloured rainbow from my nipples
From pole to pole leapt round the snail-waked world
I by the tree of thieves, all glory's sawbones,
Unsex the skeleton this mountain minute,          110
And by this blowclock witness of the sun
Suffer the heaven's children through my heartbeat.

IX

From the oracular archives and the parchment,
Prophets and fibre kings in oil and letter,
The lamped calligrapher, the queen in splints,          115
Buckle to lint and cloth their natron footsteps,
Draw on the glove of prints, dead Cairo's henna
Pour like a halo on the caps and serpents.
This was the resurrection in the desert,
Death from a bandage, rants the mask of scholars          120
Gold on such features, and the linen spirit
Weds my long gentleman to dusts and furies;
With priest and pharaoh bed my gentle wound,
World in the sand, on the triangle landscape,
With stones of odyssey for ash and garland          125
And rivers of the dead around my neck.

X

Let the tale's sailor from a Christian voyage
Atlaswise hold half-way off the dummy bay
Time's ship-racked gospel on the globe I balance:
So shall winged harbours through the rockbirds' eyes          130
Spot the blown word, and on the seas I image
December's thorn screwed in a brow of holly.
Let the first Peter from a rainbow's quayrail
Ask the tall fish swept from the bible east,
What rhubarb man peeled in her foam-blue channel          135
Has sown a flying garden round that sea-ghost?
Green as beginning, let the garden diving
Soar, with its two bark towers, to that Day
When the worm builds with the gold straws of venom
My nest of mercies in the rude, red tree.          140

# William York Tindall

## THOMAS
### ALTARWISE BY OWL-LIGHT

This sequence of ten sonnets (in which the sestets usually precede the octaves and rhymes are odd) has inspired more comment and caused more disagreement than anything else by Thomas. Some think it his greatest work and some, more moderate, think it the greatest poem of *Twenty-Five Poems*, "nothing short of magnificent," as Dame Edith observed. Others think it a "splendid failure," a good bad poem, a bad good one, or a discouraging muddle. Some, led by Elder Olson, think it about Hercules in the zodiac. Others, thinking it the story of Jesus, hold that it announces new piety. Thomas, in Utah, had this to say: "Those sonnets are only the writings of a boily boy in love with shapes and shadows on his pillow. . . . They would be of interest to another boily boy. Or a boily girl. Boily-girly."

In general agreement with Thomas, I think that the theme is Thomas himself, the constant subject of his verse and prose. Although cheerfully allowing the presence of Jesus, Hercules, the stars, the zodiac, and a generally neglected voyage, I think them analogies, not to be confused with theme. Something like a thing is not the thing itself. Thomas, like Joyce before him, was always comparing himself with Jesus, God, and the devil. As microcosm, Thomas corresponded to the stellar macrocosm. Everything in heaven and on earth was his metaphor for Thomas, who, like Sir Philip Sidney's poet, was always "freely ranging within the zodiac of his own wit." Henry Fielding says: "An author will write the better for having some knowledge of the subject on which he writes." Thomas, who knew a little about the zodiac, knew himself entirely.

He was always complaining that words and analogies, his only way of getting at the object, got between him and it. Here the trouble seems to be that his words and analogies get between the critics and his object. Read in the context of his other poems and his prose, these sonnets seem another portrait of the artist as a young dog—of "a dog among the fairies." Beginning with his begetting, the story proceeds through childhood, and ends with the writing and publication of poems. This is the customary stuff of the novel of the artist's adolescence, here in miniature, however, and in verse.

These ten sonnets, once called "Poems for a Poem," are a fragment of what was to be "a very long poem indeed." In a note to *Twenty-Five Poems* Thomas said: "The last poem in the book contains the first ten sections of a work in progress." As they stand, having progressed no more, these ten sections seem enough—enough for me. As they stand, I find them rich and sea-changed. The moving whole has many fine parts. What more can a man this side of Joyce, Yeats, and Shakespeare do, and what more a man still this side of "Fern Hill," "The Long-Legged Bait," and all the other autobiographies in verse and prose that were to make his later years illustrious?

The narrative—and Thomas said all poems should be narrative—opens with obscure magnificence. The first two lines and the last two of this sonnet are haunting, and in between are many wonders. Puzzling characters are around, doing strange things. A gentleman, a devil, an atlas-eater, a dog, a mandrake, an old cock, and another gentleman (or the same) crowd a landscape by Dali. Tropics and atlas make this unearthly scenery our earth, with stars on their rounds above. As we respond to these marvels, our minds, teased by hints, clamor for fact. Who are these people, we ask, and what are they doing? But we enjoyed the poem before asking this or we should not have asked.

"Altarwise," according to the dictionary, means as an altar is usually placed, and the dictionary definition of "owl-light" is "dusk." But anyone reading the words will see the connection of "owl" with "wise" and "light" with "altar"—a pleasing confusion that may explain the choice of words. An altar is a place of sacrifice and worship. But whether the hero has been made wise by it or is skeptically wise to it is unclear. "The half-way house" is more complex. Thomas was interested in the zodiac, which begins with the Ram in March and, occupying its houses, gets halfway round in autumn. (Thomas, under Libra, was an October man.) But "half-way house," in the context of Thomas' other poems, could mean "womb" or "halfway through life." Since Thomas probably took the phrase from Hopkins' "The Half-Way House," a poem on "the breaking of the bread," Thomas' house could also mean Eucharist or housel. In these holy, dark, vital circumstances and under stellar auspices, a gentleman lies "graveward," which, as any reader of Thomas knows, means womb and tomb. Thomas was fond of "furies." I make this sense of multiple hints: the gentleman is either Thomas' father, daring his fate by begetting a son, or else the gentleman is Thomas himself in the womb, awaiting birth in fated October.

Father and son seem equally involved in the next four lines. Abaddon (from *Revelation* 9:11) is Apollyon, the destroyer, an angel of the bottomless pit. "Hangnail" seems cross or phallus, in both of which Adam and the devil are involved. "Fork" seems the gentleman's crotch, and the "dog among the fairies," Dylan himself among his contemporaries. Consuming the world or its image, he has, as a future reporter for a Swansea paper, "a jaw [nose] for news" and an ear for "tomorrow's [journalistic] scream." Thomas' mandrakes, probably from Donne, can mean children and genitals. The sense of all this excitement and horror seems this: Thomas, the young creative devil-dog-mandrake, is born. Since a son's birth is father's death, the young dog bites out father's mandrake and reports the news.

The emasculated "gentleman of wounds," like crucified Christ, is dead, with pennies on his eyes. Not only father, the gentleman as Christ, is son, a cock begotten by cock, conceived by egg, and hatched. The wonderful "old cock from nowheres" (God, Jesus, father, son, and Lawrence's "Escaped Cock"), on one leg in the "half-way winds," is a weathercock and Christ on the cross. His unbuttoned bones are phallic (to allow cradle scraping) and sepulchral. The "walking word" is Christ as Word and Thomas as poet. As God is one with Jesus, so Thomas with father, whom he killed and replaced. The womb's "night of time" and "Christward shelter" are the graveward half-way house again for the phallic, long gentleman. That the "long world's gentleman" (also long in respect of time maybe, but Mercator's projection in an atlas makes latitude long) is both father and son is suggested by an implied pun on sun, which moves in the last line between the tropics. Sun is God or father and sun is Son or Jesus. Since Father and Son are consubstantial above, so below are father and son. Both Father and Son create by the Word, and down here a poet is born. An "atlas-eater," he has consumed the world he embodies as microcosm and rules like a magus by wizardry.

In the third stanza, the metaphor of sheep, unfolding from

lamb to ram, through wether, mutton, flock, and fold, includes Thomas' present and future conditions, the seasons, and the globe. As a child of one or two years, Thomas is like the lamb of God or Jesus. His "knocking knees," which combine knock-knees with terror and knocking to get out, remind him of his "three dead seasons" (nine months) in the "climbing grave" of the womb. But back to our muttons: "Adam's wether," who "horned" Thomas down in genetic "garden time" must be Father. A wether is generally, but not always, castrated. If emasculate now, like the old gentleman who lost his mandrake, Father must have lost his parts by giving them to a son. The "flock of horns" is the flock he leads: horned sheep or devils perhaps, but hardly cuckolds. *Butt,* combining verb and noun, the butting ram and his object, also combines and divides head and tail. This combination of opposites leads to antipodal skull and foot or death and sex. If "skull" suggests Golgotha, "garden" could also be Gethsemane; for Christ and Adam are both around. Their "thunderous pavements," through which hemlocks thrust, are laid by the "short spark" (line 19). Like Rip Van Winkle, young Thomas wakes from sleep in the "timeless cradle" of the womb, where he has dipped in the "descended bone" of death and sex. There or here, as "Rip of the vaults," he is lord of tomb and womb. In short, as we already know, he is alive and something of a rip. "I took my marrow-ladle / Out of the wrinkled undertaker's van" is one of Thomas' most wonderful pictures, surrealist in all but rational control. Translated, the "undertaker's van" is only the womb, and the "marrow-ladle" is only what serves life and dishes it. But the picture, greater than the translation, is diminished by it.

Starting as white lamb, Thomas will grow to be the black "ram rod" of "Lament," the only one who is not cold mutton in a flock of muttonheads, a ram among the ninnies, and "the black spit of the chapel fold." But *ram* unites this butting future with an innocent present. Spring lamb becomes ram of spring. As a sign of the zodiac, the Ram ushers in the poet's spring as old winter shuffles off. (The sense is clearer than the syntax here.) As unemasculated wether, Thomas the ram, young or old, is a bellwether, leading the flock and boss of the fold. The ladder of the wether's weathers rings because it has rungs. The antipodes, which bring us back to the globe of the first sonnet and the poles of skull and foot, ring spring out twice, like a clock—an ambiguous clock; for ringing twice could mean either that the child is now two years old or one. The sun, moving between Capricorn and

Cancer, brings the world two springs a year. If young Thomas is the whole world, he is one year old. If only a hemisphere, like someone in Plato, Thomas is two.

This merry sonnet, all but metaphysical in tightness and wit, shows the hand and rod of a fairly old ram and a young rip.

A little older in the fourth stanza, young Thomas troubles mother with embarrassing questions about sex and obstetrics. Questions here of "genesis" and the "short spark" are as plain as the questions of shade, shape, and Pharaoh are ghostly. If Pharaoh, as king, is father, Thomas in his pyramid is the "echo." His "shape of age" must be four or five by now. The "wounded whisper" seems mother, wounded by bearing Thomas and by his questions, which are "hunchbacks to the poker marrow." Their shape, that is, is that of the question mark. The poker marrow (spine or penis, bone of life and death) carries the burden of an embryonic hump.

With his question of the "burning gentry" the bad boy gets more embarrassing. These gentry are his parents making love. One sixth of the twelve winds is two winds, those that blew parental fires out. The "bamboo man" is a poker without marrow, is father in mother's "acres."

Peculiar among these sonnets, this one is not inverted. A sestet of a sort follows a sort of octave.

No buttons can conceal the "hump of splinters" (from bone, bamboo, and question marks) in your womb, says this boy, back there by imagination's help; for "My camel's eyes will needle through the shroud," a combination of sewing, hiding, undertaking, and *Matthew* 19:24.

Optics and photography, suggested by those needling eyes, bring the story of this inquisitor to a close. Pictures taken in the darkness of the "bread-sided field," the acres of mother's womb, reveal "love's reflection" in the face of the embryo. Conceived in love, he is love's reflection. The "mushroom features," growing in the dark, are those of Dylan Thomas, who must have studied his reflection in the mirror and reflected on it. His picture is an unfortunate "close-up" on the wall of ancestral pictures. The photographer's arc lamp turns in the amniotic sea to the ark of Noah's flood. Even as a little boy, Thomas was obsessed with wombs, he says. Maybe he is also saying, as he has said before, that his poems of womb and tomb are childish.

In the sestet of stanza five, the boy, a little older still, is playing. With the octave he begins a voyage. This odyssey or

Aeneid, which reappears here and there through the rest of
the sequence, is an analogy for the voyage of life.

The first line is memorable. "Two-gunned Gabriel" from
the "windy West" means that young Dylan, playing in the
park or at the farm, has become Marshal Dylan of Dodge
City. But the sheriff, Gabriel, is also a seraph, angel of the
Annunciation and the Last Trump, in charge, therefore of
birth, death, and rebirth. Though the wild winds of "the
windy West" seem Shelley's "breath of Autumn's being,"
Thomas is enjoying his spring. By a pun, Gabriel's Apocalyptic trump introduces a game of cards, another metaphor for
playing. But cards also mean trickery, here the trickery of
the chapel. Young Thomas, who had a Sunday-school certifi-
cate on his bedroom wall, is "tipsy from salvation's bottle."
The deceiving Sunday school "trumped up" cards from
"Jesu's sleeve": king, queen, and jacks, the royal family, in
fact, and that of Cwmdonkin Drive. "The king of spots"
implies death, father, and, if father and son are one, acne
perhaps; and Thomas, a jack (or every man Jack), is also the
knavish king. The old gentleman as son has become a "fake
gentleman in suit of spades," useful for digging in the park
and for bringing death to mind. What this faker says occupies either the first three lines or the sixth. His "Byzantine
Adam," rising in the night, seems precocious erection. Adam
implies genesis; and Byzantium, between Asia and Europe, is
neither here nor there. The emphatic placing of "Rose" may
bring a further suggestion of Yeats, here, maybe, to hail the
emergence of a younger creator.

Since sailing from Byzantium finds parallel in *Moby
Dick*, the legend of Jonah, and the "Aeneid," two layers of
analogy separate us from the facts of Swansea. Ishmael
Thomas in a city of the "plain" owes as much to the Bible as
to Melville. This outcast was cast out at bloody birth. The
"climbing sea from Asia" that threatens to overwhelm the
outcast Byzantine, is mother, threatening the independence of
her child. But Jonah's Moby or father saves the drowning
lad; for although father and son are one in one sense, in
another, father is still father and son, son. A Freudian contest
between parents for their son continues through the arctic
and marine imagery of the conclusion.

"Cross-stroked" combines swimming and rowing with
weeping Jesus, stricken on the cross of Adam's sin, as salty as
tears, sea, and Lot's wife. "Pin-legged" on a hill is the crucifixion. These images of the boy's paternal savior are fixed in
the Arctic, by "waste seas" on "pole-hills." The "frozen

angel" is both announcing Gabriel, frozen by the crucifixion, and the frozen town of Archangel in Russia, land of the "white bear." This white masculine bear is opposite to the female "black medusa," a petrifying marine creature, swimming in the warm Black Sea. As a dreadful creature of the sea, the black medusa is parallel to the singing "sirens" here and to the "furies" of the first sonnet. "Our lady's sea-straw" makes Mary in the manger another menacing mother on the "deadweed" (line 83), where sirens sing or play the oaten straw. But sirens are the poet's muses. Women, whether marine, vertebrates, or invertebrates, are dangerous and necessary.

But why does the white bear, black siren's opposite, quote Virgil? To tell young Aeneas of the voyage before him? To warn him of sirens along the way or of the Virgin? Or is the Arctic bear hinting the delights of fishing the warm Mediterranean with long-legged bait? A Russian barbarian, is the bear commending the classical and the civilized to a young poet? What songs the white bear sang, though not beyond all conjecture, are a puzzling question.

Those "mushrooms," no longer Thomas' features as in stanza four, are "milky mushrooms"—mother's poisonous breasts, which "slew" the child's hunger and may slay the child. This sonnet celebrates the weaning of those "mushroom features."

With the boys of "Should lanterns shine" and "my world is pyramid," we visit Egypt in stanza nine to inspect mummies, which serve the poet now as images of printing. When set in books, the poems he has written with all the pains of crucifixion are mummies of themselves. They are embalmed; yet publishing them is a kind of resurrection. As the eighth sonnet is "the crucifixion on the mountain," so the ninth is "the resurrection in the desert," that of Egypt's pyramids and of the modern wasteland. Pyramid or tomb is womb again.

In the sestet, "oracular archives" on "parchment" are poems, set in "the caps and serpents" and the "oil and letter" of inky typography, and printed by the "glove of prints," or the "ringing handprint" of the seventh sonnet. Glove has covered hand. The printed playing cards of sonnet five introduced king and queen or father and mother, the poet's creative principles and a subject of his poems. Mummies of prophetical king and queen, buckled like Hopkins' windhover, are inspected by "the lamped calligrapher," Jack Thomas himself, who, having set them down, embalmed them in lint, cloth, henna, and natron (or niter, a word of Egyptian origin). The "halo" of printed poems is their glory.

The octave notices the scholars or critics who rant about these "oracular archives." Unable to see life in mummy cloth ("bandage" and "linen") or in the gold mask on the mummy's face, they see death alone. If, as uncertain syntax allows, the gold masks are on the features ("such features") of critics, these masks are pretentious deceivers. But "the linen spirit"—the spirit of rag paper or of poems on Yeats' mummy cloth—unites "my long gentleman" (Thomas, one with father and love's long tool) with "dust and furies." The poet sees life in the dust of death and in the terrible women—furies, sirens, and the medusa—he has joined. A "gentle wound" connects the poet as priest and king in pyramid with Jesus in the tomb, ripe for resurrection.

"World in the sand" means not only that his world is pyramid but that his enduring poetry is built on the shifting foundation of time. "The triangle landscape" includes pyramid, delta, and, according to Freud, the female principle. On sand maybe, the poet's world or poetic pyramid is built of "stones of odyssey," gathered on his voyage through life, which, Virgilian once (line 69), is now Homeric. "Ash" is a tree of life and a creative wand, as well as dust; and "garland" is what a poet wears. "Ash" and "odyssey," suggesting Joycean auspices for triumph, make the poet one with Stephen and Bloom, and the stones of odyssey, wandering rocks, maybe. "Rivers of the dead" around the poet's neck, which may be the Nile and the Styx, suggest the Book of the Dead, watery poetry of the womb, the weight of poetic tradition, and the albatross of the *Ancient Mariner*.

Imperative mood in the last four lines means hopeful prayer for triumph rather than its announcement. More than pyramidal resting place, a "bed" is that part of a printing press on which the printer's form, filled with type, is laid to begin the printing on paper. As reporter for a Swansea paper, Thomas must have known about "putting the paper to bed."

"Altarwise" and "tree," the first and last words of the sonnets, say all—ambiguously. Devoted to his ceremony, the poet is wise to it. His star-crossed self, nailed to this great, composite tree, finds hope of mercy there and hope of blossoming. The ending, like the beginning, of this sequence is obscure—and magnificent in sound and shape.

## A Refusal to Mourn the Death, by Fire, of a Child in London

Never until the mankind making
Bird beast and flower
Fathering and all humbling darkness
Tells with silence the last light breaking
And the still hour                                                   5
Is come of the sea tumbling in harness

And I must enter again the round
Zion of the water bead
And the synagogue of the ear of corn
Shall I let pray the shadow of a sound             10
Or sow my salt seed
In the least valley of sackcloth to mourn

The majesty and burning of the child's death.
I shall not murder
The mankind of her going with a grave truth          15
Nor blaspheme down the stations of the breath
With any further
Elegy of innocence and youth

Deep with the first dead lies London's daughter,
Robed in the long friends,                                          20
The grains beyond age, the dark veins of her mother
Secret by the unmourning water
Of the riding Thames.
After the first death, there is no other.

# Edwin Honig

## THOMAS
### A REFUSAL TO MOURN THE DEATH, BY FIRE, OF
### A CHILD IN LONDON

This is an elegiac antielegy written in a fierce apocalyptic
light. One cannot read "the round Zion of the water bead,"
"the synagogue of the ear of corn," and the "valley of sackcloth" without thinking of the dire preachments of the Book
of Revelation, which deals with the end of the world and the
life to come. It would be in keeping with the occasion of this
poem to remember such imagery. "A Refusal" was written
against the background of the Blitzkrieg and the terrible
nightly bombardments of the city of London by fire bombs
and rockets during the second World War.

"A Refusal" seeks to tell the truth that lies behind the
ceremonialism and skillful obfuscations of the mourning
poem, to say what is there essentially and barely (this is
similarly the intention in Thomas' longer and homelier poem,
"After the Funeral"). The poet does so dramatically, with
the most impressive kind of magic possible, the kind that
takes place before our eyes. For the whole poem appears to
boil down, in the soothsaying of its composition, to a single
stanza: the last—or, more precisely, to a single line, the last
line of the poem, than which there is none more telling in all
of modern poetry. So that the rest of the poem seems to be
only a stormy, word-excited preamble to this nuggety discovery. But is it simply that?

The poem is an open secret based, first, on the paradox of
mourning without mourning, or of refusing to mourn; then
on the trick of turning four sentences, one upon the other.

The convention of the mourning poem, or elegy, is to
lament the death by singularizing the life that has been lost,
by showing all of creation mourning, then by indicating the
final consolation as one in which the death has been absorbed
by nature. In addition, or as an alternative, if the poet is
Christian, the subject is shown as being more fortunate than
the living because he has reached eternal peace, his heavenly

reward in the bosom of God. From this point of view it is the living—the mourners, those left behind—who either must be pitied or must be made to rejoice in contemplation of the dead person's happier condition.

While stating explicitly that it abjures this view, "A Refusal" condenses and quickly runs through the traditional elegiac formula. All of creation is imagined in "the mankind making / Bird beast and flower / Fathering and all humbling darkness," and the mystery of the resurrection or a last apocalyptic vision is contained in the "still hour . . . of the sea tumbling in harness" and in "the round / Zion of the water bead / and the synagogue of the ear of corn." We suspect that the poet is more devout than pious, more fiercely human than wishfully fatalistic or quietistic. Yet in refusing to go through the empty motions of either the Christian or the elegiac ceremony for mourning, the poet seems to be using religious references to attack empty religious practices, which he calls blasphemous. The child herself becomes identified simply as "London's daughter" buried with "the first dead" and "beyond age," "the dark veins of her mother." In this identification we find a triple association: the first dead are Abel, Adam and Eve; London's daughter is the historical child of the symbolic British motherland; and further, there is the association, through the echoes of Thomas' last stanza, with the personified figures in Edmund Spenser's "Prothalamium":

*A Flocke of Nymphes I chauncèd to espy,*
*All lovely Daughters of the Flood thereby,*

· · ·

*The which on Themmes brode agèd backe doe ryde,*

· · ·

*Sweete Themmes! runne softly, till I end my Song.*

Thomas' last line returns us to the idea of a tragic and irreversible fact: that in Abel's death, the human race first died, so that no death thereafter could be new or different or more grievous. In Abel's (or Adam's or Eve's) death mankind was lost from paradise, to which later, Christ's death, superseding Adam's, restored mankind. When all mankind awakens, after Christ returns, as it is written in the Book of Revelation, then death will have been abolished—and these are the implications of "the round Zion" and "the synagogue of the ear of corn."

Such thematic material is supported by an extraordinary

verbal performance. The first sentence, thirteen lines long and running through more than half the poem, is a virtuoso construction; the syntactical ellipsis is typical of Thomas' mature diction. It snakes along, advancing through parenthetical modifiers and double-facing participles, and projecting itself where it was meant to go, straight, despite delayed subject-verb-object associations, inversions, and multiple piled-up adjectives, to the assertion with which the sentence ends. The strength of the assertion when it comes is almost an imprecation; and this feeling is supported by the second sentence. For the second both sustains and is more direct than the first, serving to announce the refusal of the poet to minimize the child's death by falsifying its mankindness—that is, its common dignity, its human tragedy. At this point we can see that the two sentences of the last stanza have a positive assertive strength which they would lack without the rest. There is not just the balance of these two final sentences with the first two. There is also the sustenance lent the long third sentence by the final short one, and vice versa, catching us up in the brief, unyielding finality, on which note the poem, as well as all mourning from the beginning of time, decisively ends.

## Fern Hill

Now as I was young and easy under the apple boughs
About the lilting house and happy as the grass was green,
   The night above the dingle starry,
     Time let me hail and climb
   Golden in the heydays of his eyes,             5
And honoured among wagons I was prince of the apple towns
And once below a time I lordly had the trees and leaves
     Trail with daisies and barley
   Down the rivers of the windfall light.

And as I was green and carefree, famous among the barns   10
About the happy yard and singing as the farm was home,
   In the sun that is young once only,
     Time let me play and be
   Golden in the mercy of his means,
And green and golden I was huntsman and herdsman,
     the calves                    15
Sang to my horn, the foxes on the hills barked clear and cold,
     And the sabbath rang slowly
   In the pebbles of the holy streams.

All the sun long it was running, it was lovely, the hay-
Fields high as the house, the tunes from the chimneys, it was
       air                     20
   And playing, lovely and watery
     And fire green as grass.
   And nightly under the simple stars
As I rode to sleep the owls were bearing the farm away,
All the moon long I heard, blessed among stables, the night-
     jars                    25
   Flying with the ricks, and the horses
     Flashing into the dark.

And then to awake, and the farm, like a wanderer white
With the dew, come back, the cock on his shoulder: it was all

Shining, it was Adam and maiden, 30
  The sky gathered again
And the sun grew round that very day.
So it must have been after the birth of the simple light
In the first, spinning place, the spellbound horses walking
    warm
  Out of the whinnying green stable 35
   On to the fields of praise.

And honoured among foxes and pheasants by the gay house
Under the new-made clouds and happy as the heart was long
  In the sun born over and over,
   I ran my heedless ways, 40
  My wishes raced through the house-high hay
And nothing I cared, at my sky blue trades, that time allows
In all his tuneful turning so few and such morning songs
  Before the children green and golden
   Follow him out of grace. 45

Nothing I cared, in the lamb white days, that time would
    take me
Up to the swallow-thronged loft by the shadow of my hand,
  In the moon that is always rising,
   Nor that riding to sleep
  I should hear him fly with the high fields 50
And wake to the farm forever fled from the childless land.
Oh as I was young and easy in the mercy of his means,
  Time held me green and dying
  Though I sang in my chains like the sea.

THOMAS
FERN HILL


"Fern Hill," one of Thomas' two chief reminiscent poems, has claims to be considered his finest composition. Its status is that of major poetry.

If one sought to describe this poem within the compass of a single phrase, it might be called "an elegy in praise of lost youth." Lament and celebration sound throughout the work: the latter strongly at the beginning, the former gaining tone as the poem progresses.

But, as with all great threnodies in English—with Milton's "Lycidas," Gray's "Elegy," Shelley's *Adonais*, and Arnold's "Thyrsis"—the particularity of the cause of grief is lost in a sorrow that speaks for all men. Nostalgic recollection of a child's farm holiday is the leaping-off point for the poem; but—once launched—so intense and poignant a memory overtakes the poet that his words convey more than a merely topographical homesickness. The farm becomes Eden before the Fall, and time the angel with a flaming sword.

But no such intrusive personification operates within the poem. The farm is invested with a light as radiant as the unforfeited Garden, and time exercises its function as irrevocably as God's excluding angel. So, though at the end we are faced with nothing worse than a farmstead that cannot be revisited, in actual poetic terms, we have experienced the states of innocence and eternity, and been subjected to corruption, time, and change.

The poem is constructed from six nine-line stanzas, with only an infrequent rhyme. The absence of rhyme suffices to make the lyrically undulating lines more natural. The artifice and architectonic of the poem consist not in the usual technical devices, but in the repetition, in later stanzas, of motifs established in the first. These motifs are not worked out with any mechanical regularity; and their place and precedence in the poem are not formally observed. The motifs I find to be mainly three: the unwitting situation of childhood; the delight in this situation; time's operation, by which the situation becomes a fate.

The first of the three is associated with such phrases as "Now as I was young and easy," "And as I was green and carefree." The second motif is present in "honoured among wagons I was prince of the apple towns," "green and golden I was huntsman and herdsman," "honoured among foxes and pheasants by the gay house." The third motif makes its first appearance, as do the other motifs, in the first stanza,

> *Time let me hail and climb*
> *Golden in the heydays of his eyes*

It is repeated in the second, fifth and sixth stanzas:

> *In the sun that is young once only,*
> *Time let me play and be*
> *Golden in the mercy of his means*
>
> . . .
>
> *And nothing I cared, at my sky blue trades, that time allows*
> *In all his tuneful turning so few and such morning songs*
>
> . . .
>
> *Nothing I cared, in the lamb white days, that time would take me*
> *Up to the swallow-thronged loft by the shadow of my hand*

All three motives come together in the last three lines of the poem:

> *Oh as I was young and easy in the mercy of his means,*
> *Time held me green and dying*
> *Though I sang in my chains like the sea*

They form, as it were, a great resolving chord.

These are but three of the poem's many notes of development. In its six stanzas, we are escorted on a journey from innocence to experience. This direction also marks a journey from grace to corruption, from unity to dissolution. One of the most subtle features of this poem is the manner in which the growing presence of these latter qualities is expressed by a chilling of imagery. The first two stanzas are full of effects of sunlight; and then, in the third, nocturnal objects enter. So far, the images are not sinister; but the first touch of coolness has been conveyed.

# MASTER
# POEMS

## OF THE ENGLISH LANGUAGE

Other books by Oscar Williams

## BOOKS OF POEMS

*The Golden Darkness*
*The Man Coming Toward You*
*That's All That Matters*
*Selected Poems*
*Selected Poems (Revised)*

## ANTHOLOGIES

*The New Poems Series*
*The War Poets*
*A Little Treasury of Modern Poetry*
*A Little Treasury of Great Poetry*
*A Little Treasury of American Poetry*
*A Little Treasury of British Poetry*
*Immortal Poems of the English Language*
*The Pocket Book of Modern Verse*
*The New Pocket Anthology of American Verse*
*Palgrave's The Golden Treasury (Revised)*
*Mentor Book of Major British Poets*
(co-editor, Edwin Honig)
*Mentor Book of Major American Poets*
*The Silver Treasury of Light Verse*

# MASTER
# POEMS

## OF THE ENGLISH LANGUAGE

*Over one hundred poems*
*together with Introductions*
*by leading poets and critics*
*of the English-speaking world*

EDITED BY

## Oscar Williams

TRIDENT PRESS

*New York    1966*

LIBRARY
FEB 25 1966
UNIVERSITY OF THE PACIFIC

146675

*Copyright, ©, 1966, by Trident Press*

*All rights reserved.*
*No part of this book may be reproduced in any form*
*without permission in writing from the publisher,*
*except by a reviewer*
*who may quote brief passages in a review*
*to be printed in a magazine or newspaper.*

*Library of Congress Catalog Card Number: 65-25702*

*Published simultaneously in the United States and Canada*

*Printed in the United States of America*

# ACKNOWLEDGMENTS AND COPYRIGHT NOTICES

The publisher, in the name of the late Oscar Williams, wishes to thank the following persons and firms for permission to reprint the poems and essays listed below.

George Allen & Unwin Ltd., London: Essay on "The Second Coming" by Yeats from *Language as Gesture* by Richard P. Blackmur; by permission of George Allen & Unwin Ltd.

Al Alvarez, London: Essay on the "Holy Sonnets" by Donne © Al Alvarez 1965.

Jonathan Cape Limited, London: Selections from "A Shropshire Lad" from *The Collected Poems of A. E. Housman;* by permission of Jonathan Cape Limited and the Executors of the A. E. Housman Estate.

Chatto & Windus Ltd., London: Essay on "The Rime of the Ancient Mariner" by Coleridge from *Poetry and Its Background* by E. M. W. Tillyard; "The Groundhog" from *Collected Poems* by Richard Eberhart; essay on "The Garden" by Marvell from *Some Versions of Pastoral* by William Empson; "Greater Love" from *Poems* by Wilfred Owen—all these by permission of Chatto & Windus Ltd.

J. M. Dent & Sons Ltd., London: "Altarwise by Owl-Light," "A Refusal to Mourn," "Fern Hill," and "Lament" from *The Collected Poems of Dylan Thomas;* by permission of J. M. Dent & Sons Ltd.

Norma Millay Ellis, Austerlitz, New York: Five sonnets by Millay; by permission of Norma Millay Ellis.

Faber & Faber Ltd., London: "In Memory of W. B. Yeats" and "September 1, 1939" from *Collected Shorter Poems* by W. H. Auden; "Allegory of the Adolescent and the Adult" and "Memorial to Three Young Seamen" from *Collected Poems* by George Barker; "what if a much of a which of a wind" from *Selected Poems* by E. E. Cummings; "The Waste Land" from *Collected Poems* by T. S. Eliot; "Spenser's Ireland" from *Collected Poems of Marianne Moore;* "The Transfiguration" from *Collected Poems* by Edwin Muir; "Sunday Morning" from *The Collected Poems of Wallace Stevens*—all these by permission of Faber & Faber Ltd.

Farrar, Straus & Company, Inc., New York City: Essay on "Altarwise by Owl-Light" from *A Reader's Guide to Dylan Thomas* by William York Tindall, by permission of Farrar, Straus & Company, Inc. Copyright, © 1962, by William York Tindall.

Robert Graves, Mallorca, Spain: Essay on "La Belle Dame Sans Merci" by Keats © 1965 by International Authors N.V.

Grove Press, Inc., New York City: "The Transfiguration" by Muir; by permission of Grove Press, Inc.

Harcourt, Brace & World, Inc., New York City: "what if a much of a which of a wind" by Cummings, copyright, 1944, by E. E. Cummings, reprinted from his volume *Poems 1923–1954;*

"The Waste Land" from *Collected Poems 1909–1962* by T. S. Eliot, copyright, 1936, by Harcourt, Brace & World, Inc.; © 1963, 1964, by T. S. Eliot; essays on "Elegy Written in a Country Church-yard" by Gray and "Tears, Idle Tears" by Tennyson from *The Well Wrought Urn*, copyright, 1947, by Cleanth Brooks; essay on "The Second Coming" by Yeats, copyright, 1940, by Richard P. Blackmur; reprinted from his volume *Language as Gesture*—all these by permission of Harcourt, Brace & World, Inc.

Harvard University Press, Cambridge, Mass.: Sequence of poems by Emily Dickinson; reprinted by permission of the publishers from Thomas H. Johnson, editor, *The Poems of Emily Dickinson*, Cambridge, Mass.: Harvard University Press, Copyright, 1951, 1955, by The President and Fellows of Harvard College.

David Higham Associates Ltd., London: Essay on "Dejection: An Ode" by Coleridge from *The True Voice of Feeling* by Sir Herbert Read.

Holt, Rinehart and Winston, Inc., New York City: Essay on "Song" by Carew from *Introduction to Poetry* by Mark Van Doren, copyright, © 1951, Holt, Rinehart and Winston, Inc.; "Directive," "Stopping by Woods on a Snowy Evening," and "Two Tramps in Mud-Time" from *Complete Poems of Robert Frost;* copyright, 1923, 1947, by Holt, Rinehart and Winston, Inc., copyright, 1936, by Robert Frost, copyright renewed, 1951, by Robert Frost; copyright renewed, © 1964, by Lesley Frost Ballantine; essay on "Ode to a Nightingale" by Keats from *Understanding Poetry*, Revised Edition, by Cleanth Brooks and Robert Penn Warren, copyright, 1938, 1950, © 1960, Holt, Rinehart and Winston, Inc.—all these reprinted by permission of Holt, Rinehart and Winston, Inc.

*University of Kansas City Review*, Kansas City, Mo.: Essay on "Sailing to Byzantium" by Yeats, by permission of Elder Olson and the *University of Kansas City Review*.

Alfred A. Knopf, Inc., New York City: "Captain Carpenter," copyright, 1924, by Alfred A. Knopf, Inc., renewed, 1952, by John Crowe Ransom, reprinted from *Selected Poems*, Revised Edition, by John Crowe Ransom; "Sunday Morning," copyright, 1923, 1952, by Wallace Stevens, copyright, 1923, 1952, by Wallace Stevens, reprinted from *The Collected Poems of Wallace Stevens*—both reprinted by permission of Alfred A. Knopf, Inc.

MacGibbon & Kee Ltd., London: "The Yachts" from *Collected Early Poems* by William Carlos Williams; reprinted by permission of MacGibbon & Kee Ltd.

Macmillan & Co. Ltd., London: "The Darkling Thrush" from *The Collected Poems of Thomas Hardy;* by permission of Macmillan & Co. Ltd. and the Trustees of the Hardy Estate.

The Macmillan Company, New York City: "Spenser's Ireland" from *Collected Poems* by Marianne Moore, copyright, 1941, by Marianne Moore; "Dialogue of Self and Soul" from *Collected Poems* by William Butler Yeats, copyright, 1933, by The Macmillan Company, renewed, 1961, by Bertha Georgie Yeats; "Nineteen Hundred and Nineteen," "Sailing to Byzantium," and "The Tower" from *Collected Poems* by William Butler Yeats, copyright, 1928, by The Macmillan Company, renewed, 1956, by Georgie Yeats; "A Prayer for My Daughter" and "The Second Coming" from *Collected Poems* by William Butler Yeats, copyright, 1924, by The Macmillan Company, renewed, 1952, by Bertha Georgie Yeats—all reprinted by permission of The Macmillan Company.

The Modern Language Association of America, New York City: Essay on "Lycidas" by Milton from Richard Adams' "The Archetypal Pattern of Death and Rebirth in Milton's *Lycidas*," PMLA, LXIV (1949), pages 183–88; reprinted by permission of the Modern Language Association.

The New American Library of World Literature, Inc., for The World Publishing Company, New York City: Essay on "The Rubáiyát of Omar Khayyám of Naishápúr" by FitzGerald from *In General and Particular* by C. M. Bowra, Copyright, © 1964, by C. M. Bowra, published by arrangement with The World Publishing Company, New York.

A. V. Moore, Knebworth, Hertfordshire, England: "Hugh Selwyn Mauberley" by Pound; by permission of Arthur V. Moore for Ezra Pound.

New Directions, Norfolk, Conn.: Essay on "The Garden" by Marvell from *Some Versions of Pastoral* by William Empson, all rights reserved; reprinted by permission of New Directions, Publishers. "Greater Love" from *Collected Poems of Wilfred Owen;* "Hugh Selwyn Mauberley" from *Personae* by Ezra Pound; "Altarwise by Owl-Light," "A Refusal to Mourn," "Fern Hill," and "Lament" from *The Collected Poems of Dylan Thomas;* "The Yachts" from *The Collected Earlier Poems of William Carlos Williams*—all these reprinted by permission of New Directions.

University of North Carolina Press, Chapel Hill, N.C.: Introduction to "The Waste Land" by Eliot from *Modern Poetry and the Tradition* by Cleanth Brooks; by permission of The University of North Carolina Press.

Oxford University Press, London: "The Leaden Echo and the Golden Echo" and "The Wreck of the Deutschland" from *Poems of Gerard Manley Hopkins;* by permission of Oxford University Press (London).

Oxford University Press, Inc., New York City: "The Groundhog" from *Collected Poems 1930–1960* by Richard Eberhart, © 1960, by Richard Eberhart; reprinted by permission of Oxford University Press, Inc.

Laurence Pollinger Limited, London: "Directive," "Stopping by Woods on a Snowy Evening," and "Two Tramps in Mud-Time" from *The Collected Poems* by Robert Frost, by permission of Jonathan Cape Limited and Laurence Pollinger Limited. "The Ship of Death" from *The Complete Poems of D. H. Lawrence*, by permission of William Heinemann Limited, Laurence Pollinger Limited, and the Estate of the late Mrs. Frieda Lawrence; "Captain Carpenter" from *Selected Poems* by John Crowe Ransom; by permission of Eyre & Spottiswoode Limited and Laurence Pollinger Limited.

Prentice-Hall, Inc., Englewood Cliffs, N.J.: Essay on "Ode on a Grecian Urn" by Keats from the book *A Grammar of Motives* by Kenneth Burke, © 1945 by Prentice-Hall, Inc., Englewood Cliffs, New Jersey.

Princeton University Press, Princeton, N.J.: Essay on "The Mental Traveller" by Blake from *Anatomy of Criticism* by Northrup Frye; reprinted by permission of Princeton University Press. Random House, Inc., New York: "In Memory of W. B. Yeats" and "September 1, 1939" by Auden, copyright, 1940, by W. H. Auden; reprinted from *The Collected Poetry of W. H. Auden*, by permission of Random House, Inc.; essay on "Dejection: An Ode" by Coleridge from *The True Voice of Feeling*, by Herbert Read, copyright, 1953, by Herbert Read, reprinted by permission of Pantheon Books, a Division of Random House, Inc.

Rutgers University Press, New Brunswick, N.J.: Essay on "The Tyger" by Blake from *Sex, Symbolism and Psychology in Literature* by Roy P. Basler; permission by Rutgers University Press.

Charles Scribner's Sons, New York City: "Richard Cory," reprinted with the permission of Charles Scribner's Sons from *The Children of the Night* by Edwin Arlington Robinson (Charles Scribner's Sons, 1897).

Martin Secker & Warburg Limited, London: Essay on "Ode: Intimations of Immortality" by Wordsworth from *The Liberal Imagination* by Lionel Trilling; by permission of Martin Secker & Warburg Limited.

Neville Spearman Limited, London: Essay on "Fern Hill" by Thomas from *Dylan Thomas* by Derek Stanford; by permission of Neville Spearman Limited.

Alan Swallow, Publisher, Denver, Colo.: Essay on "To His Coy Mistress" by Marvell, reprinted from *Tradition and Poetic Structure* by J. V. Cunningham, copyright, 1960, by J. V. Cunningham; reprinted by permission of the publisher, Alan Swallow.

Thames and Hudson Ltd., London: Essay on "Altarwise by Owl-Light" from *A Reader's Guide to Dylan Thomas* by William York Tindall; by permission of Thames and Hudson Ltd.

The Viking Press, Inc., New York City: Essay on "Ode: Intimations of Immortality" by Wordsworth from *The Liberal Imagination* by Lionel Trilling, copyright, 1941, by Lionel Trilling; reprinted by permission of The Viking Press, Inc.

A. P. Watt & Son, London: "Dialogue of Self and Soul," "Nineteen Hundred and Nineteen," "Sailing to Byzantium," "A Prayer for My Daughter," and "The Second Coming" from *The Collected Poems of W. B. Yeats;* by permission of Mrs. W. B. Yeats, The Macmillan Company of Canada Ltd., Macmillan & Co. Ltd., and A. P. Watt & Son.

Weidenfield & Nicolson Limited, London: Essay on "The Rubáiyát of Omar Khayyám of Naishápúr" by FitzGerald from *In General and Particular* by C. M. Bowra; by permission of Weidenfield & Nicolson Limited.

Oscar Williams, New York City: "Allegory of the Adolescent and the Adult" and "Memorial for Three Young Seamen" by Barker; by permission of Oscar Williams.

# CONTENTS

PREFACE     *xv*

They Flee from Me by Sir Thomas Wyatt     *1*
   *Essay by Richard Howard*     *3*
The Lie by Sir Walter Raleigh     *7*
   *Essay by Joseph Bennett*     *10*
Epithalamion by Edmund Spenser     *13*
   *Essay by Walter James Miller*     *25*
Loving in Truth by Sir Philip Sidney     *29*
   *Essay by Earle Birney*     *31*
Desire by Sir Philip Sidney     *35*
   *Essay by Walter James Miller*     *36*
The Phœnix and the Turtle by William Shakespeare     *39*
   *Essay by William Empson*     *41*
Sonnets by William Shakespeare     *47*
   *Essay by Robert Gorham Davis*     *57*
   *Essay by William Empson*     *63*
Speeches from the Plays of William Shakespeare     *72*
   *Essay by Walter James Miller*     *76*
To Celia by Ben Jonson     *79*
   *Essay by Earle Birney*     *81*
An Anatomie of the World by John Donne     *85*
   *Essay by Robert M. Bender*     *100*
The Canonization by John Donne     *104*
   *Essay by Edwin Honig*     *106*
A Valediction: Forbidding Mourning by John Donne     *109*
   *Essay by I. A. Richards*     *111*
The Extasie by John Donne     *114*
   *Essay by I. A. Richards*     *116*
Holy Sonnets by John Donne     *123*
   *Essay by A. Alvarez*     *131*
Hymne to God My God, in My Sicknesse by John Donne     *136*
   *Essay by Louis L. Martz*     *137*
To the Virgins, to Make Much of Time by Robert Herrick     *141*
   *Essay by Anthony Ostroff*     *143*
The Collar by George Herbert     *147*
   *Essay by Dudley Fitts*     *149*
Song by Thomas Carew     *153*
   *Essay by Mark Van Doren*     *154*
On the Morning of Christ's Nativity by John Milton     *159*
   *Essay by Jackson Mathews*     *168*
Lycidas by John Milton     *172*
   *Essay by Richard P. Adams*     *177*
L'Allegro by John Milton     *183*

Il Penseroso by John Milton 186
*Essay by Richard Wilbur* 191
The Teare by Richard Crashaw 196
*Essay by Dudley Fitts* 198
To His Coy Mistress by Andrew Marvell 201
*Essay by J. V. Cunningham* 204
The Garden by Andrew Marvell 211
*Essay by William Empson* 213
The World by Henry Vaughan 224
*Essay by R. A. Durr* 226
A Song for St. Cecilia's Day by John Dryden 229
*Essay by David Daiches* 232
A Satire Against Mankind by John Wilmot, Earl of
Rochester 239
*Essay by Robert M. Bender* 245
Verses on the Death of Dr. Swift, D.S.P.D. by Jonathan
Swift 249
*Essay by Jacques Barzun* 262
The Rape of the Lock by Alexander Pope 265
*Essay by A. J. M. Smith* 285
The Vanity of Human Wishes by Samuel Johnson 291
*Essay by Donald Davie* 300
Elegy Written in a Country Churchyard by Thomas Gray 305
*Essay by Cleanth Brooks* 309
Ode to Evening by William Collins 323
*Essay by David Daiches* 326
A Song to David by Christopher Smart 331
*Essay by James Dickey* 339
The Deserted Village by Oliver Goldsmith 341
*Essay by Charles Tomlinson* 353
Auguries of Innocence by William Blake 359
*Essay by Kathleen Raine* 364
The Tyger by William Blake 373
*Essay by Roy P. Basler* 374
The Mental Traveller by William Blake 377
*Essay by Northrop Frye* 380
A Man's a Man for A' That by Robert Burns 383
*Essay by Paul Goodman* 385
Ode: Intimations of Immortality by William Wordsworth 389
*Essay by Lionel Trilling* 395
I Wandered Lonely as a Cloud by William Wordsworth 415
*Essay by Louis Coxe* 416
Lines Composed a Few Miles Above Tintern Abbey by
William Wordsworth 420
*Essay by Richard Eberhart* 424
Resolution and Independence by William Wordsworth 428
*Essay by Geoffrey Grigson* 432
Kubla Khan: Or, a Vision in a Dream by Samuel Taylor
Coleridge 435
*Essay by Kenneth Burke* 439

In the sixth stanza, this chillness grows rapidly. Time takes the child

> *Up to the swallow-thronged loft by the shadow of my hand*

The eeriness of that line, with its suggestion of an evil presence or a mysterious double in the flickering movement of the shadows, and of the ghostly appearance of the swallows in the dim lights of the loft, distills a feeling of sin and death. And now "the sun born over and over," which assured us for a moment in the fifth stanza, is replaced by

> *. . . the moon that is always rising*

which is not sufficient to warm us in the growing cold: the cold of a contracting imagination and heart. By the light of this moon, the happy, daytime vision of the farm vanished, and when the light returns it is to discover "the farm forever fled from the childless land."

## Lament

When I was a windy boy and a bit
And the black spit of the chapel fold,
(Sighed the old ram rod, dying of women),
I tiptoed shy in the gooseberry wood,
The rude owl cried like a telltale tit,                    5
I skipped in a blush as the big girls rolled
Ninepin down on the donkey's common,
And on seesaw sunday nights I wooed
Whoever I would with my wicked eyes,
The whole of the moon I could love and leave              10
All the green leaved little weddings' wives
In the coal black bush and let them grieve.

When I was a gusty man and a half
And the black beast of the beetles' pews,
(Sighed the old ram rod, dying of bitches),               15
Not a boy and a bit in the wick-
Dipping moon and drunk as a new dropped calf,
I whistled all night in the twisted flues,
Midwives grew in the midnight ditches,
And the sizzling beds of the town cried, Quick!—          20
Whenever I dove in a breast high shoal,
Wherever I ramped in the clover quilts,
Whatsoever I did in the coal-
Black night, I left my quivering prints.

When I was a man you could call a man                     25
And the black cross of the holy house,
(Sighed the old ram rod, dying of welcome),
Brandy and ripe in my bright, bass prime,
No springtailed tom in the red hot town
With every simmering woman his mouse                      30
But a hillocky bull in the swelter
Of summer come in his great good time
To the sultry, biding herds, I said,
Oh, time enough when the blood creeps cold,

And I lie down but to sleep in bed,                               35
For my sulking, skulking, coal black soul!

When I was a half of the man I was
And serve me right as the preachers warn,
(Sighed the old ram rod, dying of downfall),
No flailing calf or cat in a flame                               40
Or hickory bull in milky grass
But a black sheep with a crumpled horn,
At last the soul from its foul mousehole
Slunk pouting out when the limp time came;
And I gave my soul a blind, slashed eye,                         45
Gristle and rind, and a roarers' life,
And I shoved it into the coal black sky
To find a woman's soul for a wife.

Now I am a man no more no more
And a black reward for a roaring life,                           50
(Sighed the old ram rod, dying of strangers),
Tidy and cursed in my dove cooed room
I lie down thin and hear the good bells jaw—
For, oh, my soul found a sunday wife
In the coal black sky and she bore angels!                      55
Harpies around me out of her womb!
Chastity prays for me, piety sings,
Innocence sweetens my last black breath,
Modesty hides my thighs in her wings,
And all the deadly virtues plague my death!                     60

# Constantine FitzGibbon

### THOMAS
### LAMENT

Except for "Poem on his Birthday" and the "Author's Preface" to his *Collected Poems*, "Lament" was the last poem that Dylan Thomas completed before his death in 1953. In the last seven years of his short life he wrote only eight poems, including the unfinished "Elegy." However, his output was not so small as this figure might suggest, since most of these were long, some of them very long, poems. Furthermore, he was by then working with an attention to detail—rewriting a single line fifty or more times—that precluded the comparatively easy and abundant flow of his early youth.

These last poems are in some ways foreshadowed by some of the poems in *Deaths and Entrances* (1946), such as the glorious and perfectly achieved "Fern Hill," but they really constitute a corpus of poems on their own, part of a poetic statement left sadly uncompleted by the poet's death. They are far removed from his early poems with their frequent, dense obscurities. When the "Altarwise by Owl-Light" sequence was published, in 1934, a journalist asked Dylan Thomas if he himself always understood the meaning of his poems. He replied, with the arrogance of youth: "No poet ever understood everything he wrote himself." Ten years later he was more modest. I was with him shortly after "Vision and Prayer" was published, in 1945, when a poetess asked him to explain to her precisely what that poem meant. His reply, and it was a genuinely embarrassed reply, was: "Had I known how to make my meaning clearer, I should have done so." By 1950–1951, when he was writing "Lament," he did know how to do so. If his last poems are difficult at times, it is because the emotions and the ideas they express are extremely complex. His means of self-expression, on the other hand, had been purified and clarified. There is not, I think, a single sentence in "Lament" that is not fully and unambiguously comprehensible. This does not mean that the poem can be read as prose, or even that it can be "translated" into prose. No real poem can, without destroying its poetic essence.

Dylan Thomas was an intensely subjective poet. With a very few exceptions all his poems are in some measure autobiographical, or at least are centered about his own being, and none more so than "Lament." They are, too, almost all infused with one unifying idea. In a much quoted line— which Dylan Thomas also admired—W.H. Auden wrote, "We must love one another or die." Dylan Thomas' central concept is far more complex and more tragic. If it were to be put in epigrammatic form, it might be: We must love one another *and* die. For he was, perhaps because of much early sickness, fully convinced that the very act of love, the very deed of conception, is but the first and greatest link in a chain that must lead us to the grave. Though the poet may sing in his chains like the sea, he can never slough them off. Even the windy boy and a bit playing on donkey's common (Cwm-donkin Park) or winking at the girls during the Sunday evening promenade beside the Swansea sea is dying, Dylan, dying. How much more so the gusty man with his roaring life sardined with women and drinks. The three basic facts of our lives are also one, are also a Trinity.

Does God offer us an escape from our predestined tread-mill? Not, according to this poem, the God of the chapel fold, which Dylan Thomas had rejected at an early age and as completely as had his God-hating father from whom he learned so much. But later, when the old ram rod is dying of downfall, when it is time for the poet to build his ship of death (as D.H. Lawrence put it in a poem that Dylan Thomas loved greatly), can the remorseful soul slink from its foul mousehole? In this poem, at least, he rejects this solution, certainly so far as he himself is concerned. Much has been written about the religious nature of Dylan Thomas' poetry, which is certainly dappled with religious images and Christian metaphor. Nevertheless, I am myself convinced that Dylan Thomas, like so many of his contemporaries, did not believe in God but would, at times, have liked to do so; and that he used those images and metaphors because they were known to him from his chapel-going childhood and because of their inherent strength and beauty. Perhaps if he had lived he might have reached a religious conclusion. My own inclination is to guess that he would not, that it would have been hard for him, being the man he was, to go beyond the vague and superstitious pantheism that is evident in the prose introductory note to his *Collected Poems*, the pantheism that gives such a lovely glow, now golden, now ghostly, now triumphant and now tragic, to his nature poems and his poems of country childhood.

What escape remains from the chains of mortality? There is, first, the poet's love for his wife, for a woman's soul, for the Sunday wife whom his own soul found, in its own way. And in this poem, as in his life, his love for Caitlin Thomas is deliberately celebrated as being of an utterly different order from his relationships with other women. And from that love there has come what is the only real hope of escape from inexorable death, his children. We have come full circle, from his own innocence, as he tiptoed shy in the gooseberry wood, to their innocence, which sweetens his last breath, though of course—and this he does not even need to state— they are bound in their chains even as is he in his. The poem is thus complete, the poetic truth resolved, its statement made.

# INDEX OF FIRST LINES

All the world's a stage, 72

Altarwise by owl-light in the half-way house, 1043

And these few precepts in thy memory, 74

And you as well must die, belovèd dust, 989

April is the cruellest month, breeding, 943

As due by my titles I resigne, 123

As Rochefoucault his maxims drew, 249

As virtuous men passe mildly away, 109

Ask me·no more where Jove bestows, 153

At midday they looked up and saw their death, 1030

At the round earths imagin'd corners, blow, 125

Back out of all this now too much for us, 882

Batter my heart, three person'd God; for you, 127

Because I could not stop for Death, 745

Before the beginning of years, 780

The blessèd damozel lean'd out, 729

Captain Carpenter rose up in his prime, 983

Cold in the earth, and the deep snow piled above thee!, 683

Complacencies of the peignoir, and late, 889

contend in a sea which the land partly encloses, 899

The Curfew tolls the knell of parting day, 305

Death be not proud, though some have called thee, 126

Drink to me only with thine eyes, 79

Th' expense of spirit in a waste of shame, 55

Farewell! thou art too dear for my possessing, 53

Father, part of his double interest, 128

Five years have past; five summers, with the length, 420

For Godsake hold your tongue, and let me love, 104

For shame! deny that thou bear'st love to any, 48

For three years, out of key with his time, 911

From fairest creatures we desire increase, 47

From Harmony, from heav'nly Harmony, 229

From thorax of storms the voices of verbs, 1029

Gather ye Rose-buds while ye may, 141

Go, for they call you, Shepherd, from the hill, 716

Go, soul, the body's guest, 7

Grow old along with me!, 665

Had we but World enough, and Time, 201

has not altered;—a place as kind as it is green, 935

He disappeared in the dead of winter, 1013

He jests at scars that never felt a wound, 73

Hence loathed Melancholy, 183

Hence vain deluding joys, 186

How sweet and lovely dost thou make the shame, 54

How to kèep—is there any, is there none such, nowhere, 804

How vainly men themselves amaze, 211

I am a little world made cunningly, 124

I died for beauty, but was scarce, 749

I felt a funeral in my brain, 746

I fled Him, down the nights and down the days, 811

I heard a fly buzz when I died, 746

I leant upon a coppice gate, 787

I Saw Eternity the other night, 224

I sing the body electric, 699

I sit in one of the dives, 1022

I struck the board, and cry'd, "No More; 147

I travel'd thro' a Land of Men, 377

I wandered lonely as a cloud, 415

I weep for Adonais—he is dead!, 527

If aught of oaten stop, or pastoral song, 323

If faithfull soules be alike glorifi'd, 125

If poysonous mineralls, and if that tree, 126

In June, amid the golden fields, 1007

In Xanadu did Kubla Khan, 436

Is it for fear to wet a widow's eye, 48

Is there for honest poverty, 383

It is an ancient Mariner, 465

It was not death, for I stood up, 749

It was when weather was Arabian I went, 1037

"Just the place for a Snark!" the Bellman cried, 757

Let me not to the marriage of true minds, 55

Let observation with extensive view, 291

Let the bird of loudest lay, 39

Look in thy glass, and tell the face thou viewest, 47

Love is not all: it is not meat nor drink, 990

Loveliest of trees, the cherry now, 821

Loving in truth, and fain in verse my love to show, 29

The lunatic, the lover, and the poet, 72

Many ingenious lovely things are gone, 851

My heart aches, and a drowsy numbness pains, 583

My Soul. I summon to the winding ancient stair, 859

Never until the mankind making, 1055

Not from the stars do I my judgement pluck, 49

Not marble nor the gilded monuments, 52

Not mine own fears, nor the prophetic soul, 54

Now as I was young and easy under the apple boughs, 1059

Now it is autumn and the falling fruit, 903
O might those sighes and teares returne againe, 123
O thou, that sit'st upon a throne, 331
"O what can ail thee, knight-at-arms, 593
Oh my blacke Soule! now thou art summoned, 124
Oh, think not I am faithful to a vow!, 989
Oh, to vex me, contraryes meet in one, 129
Once more the storm is howling, and half hid, 839
Out of the mud two strangers came, 869
Poor soul, the centre of my sinful earth, 56
Red lips are not so red, 997
Safe in their alabaster chambers, 748
St. Agnes' Eve—Ah, bitter chill it was!, 600
Saint Peter sat by the celestial gate, 499
The sea is calm to-night, 711
The seagull, spreadeagled, splayed on the wind, 1029
Shall I compare thee to a summer's day?, 50
Show me deare Christ, thy Spouse, so bright and clear, 129
Since brass, nor stone, nor earth, nor boundless sea, 52
Since I am coming to that Holy roome, 136
Since she whom I lov'd hath payd her last debt, 129
So from the ground we felt that virtue branch, 929
So shall I live, supposing thou art true, 53
Spit in my face you Jewes, and pierce my side, 126
A still small voice spake unto me, 641
Sweet Auburn! loveliest village of the plain, 341
Sweet sounds, oh, beautiful music, do not cease!, 990
Swift as a spirit hastening to his task, 547
Tears, idle tears, I know not what they mean, 658
That is no country for old men. The young, 831
That time of year thou mayst in me behold, 52
That's my last Duchess painted on the wall, 677
Then let not winter's ragged hand deface, 48
There was a roaring in the wind all night, 428
There was a time when meadow, grove, and stream, 389
There's a certain slant of light, 745
There's blood between us, love, my love, 737
They fle from me that sometyme did me seke, 1
They that have pow'r to hurt and will do none, 53

This is my playes last scene, here heavens appoint, 125
This is the Month, and this the happy morn, 159
Thou blind man's mark, thou fool's self-chosen snare, 35
Thou hast made me, And shall thy worke decay?, 123
Thou mastering me, 791
Thou still unravish'd bride of quietness, 567
To be, or not to be: that is the question, 74
To see a World in a Grain of Sand, 359
To-morrow, and to-morrow, and to-morrow, 73
Turning and turning in the widening gyre, 846
Tyger! Tyger! burning bright, 373
Wake! For the Sun who scattered into flight, 613
Well! If the Bard was weather-wise, who made, 489
Were I (who to my cost already am, 239
What bright soft thing is this?, 196
What dire Offence from am'rous Causes springs, 265
what if a much of a which of a wind, 1003
What if this present were the worlds last night?, 127
What inn is this, 748
What is your substance, whereof are you made, 51
What lips my lips have kissed, and where, and why, 990
When I consider everything that grows, 49
When I do count the clock that tells the time, 49
When I was a windy boy and a bit, 1064
When, in disgrace with Fortune and men's eyes, 50
When in the chronicle of wasted time, 54
When lilacs last in the dooryard bloom'd, 687
When that rich Soule which to her heaven is gone, 85
When the hounds of spring are on winter's traces, 777
When to the sessions of sweet silent thought, 51
Whenever Richard Cory went down town, 865
Where, like a pillow on a bed, 114
Whose woods these are I think I know, 876
Why are wee by all creatures waited on?, 127
Wilt thou love God, as he thee? then digest, 128
A woman's face with Nature's own hand painted, 50
Ye learnèd sisters, which have oftentimes, 13
Yet once more, O ye Laurels, and once more, 172